AFRICA DEVELOPMENT INDICATORS 2010

THE WORLD BANK

Manufactured in the United States of America
First printing 2010

This volume is a product of the staff of the International Bank for Reconstruction and Development/The World Bank. The findings, interpretations, and conclusions expressed in this volume do not necessarily reflect the views of the Executive Directors of The World Bank or the governments they represent.

The World Bank does not guarantee the accuracy of the data included in this work. The boundaries, colors, denominations, and other information shown on any map in this work do not imply any judgment on the part of The World Bank concerning the legal status of any territory or the endorsement or acceptance of such boundaries.

To order *Africa Development Indicators 2010, The Little Data Book on Africa 2010,* the Africa Development Indicators 2010–Multiple User CD-ROM, please visit www.worldbank.org/publications. To subscribe to Africa Development Indicators Online please visit http://publications.worldbank.org/ADI.

For more information about Africa Development Indicators and its companion products, please visit www.worldbank.org/africa. You can email us at ADI@worldbank.org.

Cover design: Communications Development Incorporated.

Photo credits: front cover, Mark Evans/iStockphoto; back cover, Arne Hoel/World Bank.

The map of Africa is provided by the Map Design Unit/World Bank.

ISBN: 978-0-8213-8202-8
e-ISBN: 978-0-8213-8203-5
DOI: 10.1596/978-0-8213-8202-8
SKU: 18202

Contents

Foreword

"Sunlight is the best disinfectant," Associate Justice of the United States Supreme Court Louis Brandeis said in 1914, referring to the benefits of openness and transparency in tackling corruption in the public sector. Today, thanks to the efforts of Transparency International and other organizations, there is considerable "sunlight" on well known types of corruption—public officials demanding and taking bribes for privileged access to contracts or exemptions from regulations. On average, Africa scores poorly on these indicators, with some exceptions—Botswana, Cape Verde, and Mauritius have consistently done well, and Liberia has made great strides.

This year's *Africa Development Indicators* essay sheds light on a different type of corruption—what the authors call "quiet corruption"—when public servants fail to deliver services or inputs that have been paid for by the government. The most prominent examples are absentee teachers in public schools and absentee doctors in primary clinics. Others include drugs being stolen from public clinics and sold in the private market as well as subsidized fertilizer being diluted before it reaches farmers.

Not only is quiet corruption pervasive in Africa, but—as the essay points out—it hurts the poor disproportionately. Worse still, it can have long-term consequences. Denied an education because of absentee teachers, children suffer in adulthood with low cognitive skills and weak health. The absence of drugs and doctors means unwanted deaths from malaria and other diseases. Receiving diluted fertilizer that fails to produce results, farmers choose not to use any fertilizer, leaving them in low-productivity agriculture.

Quiet corruption does not make the headlines the way bribery scandals do. It has yet to be picked up by Transparency International and other global indexes of corruption. Tackling quiet corruption is at least as difficult as tackling grand corruption. It will require a combination of strong and committed leadership, policies, and institutions at the sectoral level, and—most important—increased accountability and participation by citizens, the demand side of good governance. By highlighting quiet corruption in this year's *Africa Development Indicators*—itself a tool for Africans to hold their governments accountable—we hope that the essay will do for quiet corruption what Justice Brandeis intended with his famous aphorism.

Obiageli K. Ezekwesili
Vice President, Africa Region

Acknowledgments

Africa Development Indicators is a product of the Africa Region of the World Bank.

Jorge Saba Arbache was the director of this book and its companions—Africa Development Indicators Online 2010, Africa Development Indicators 2010—Multiple User CD-ROM, and *The Little Data Book on Africa 2010*. Rose Mungai led the work on data management, consistency checks, and compilation and provided overall data quality assurance. The core team included Mpho Chinyolo, Francoise Genouille, Jane K. Njuguna, and Christophe Rockmore. Jane Njuguna coordinated all stages of production. Richard Crabbe provided useful production support and suggestions. The overall work was carried out under the guidance of Shantayanan Devarajan, Chief Economist of the Africa Region.

Jorge Saba Arbache, James Habyarimana, and Vasco Molini wrote the essay. Balu Bumb, Michael Morris, Giuseppe Iarossi, Gäel Raballand, Stephen Minck, Ian Gregory, David Rohrbach, Aad van Geldermalsen, and Alies van Geldermalsen provided useful inputs to the essay. Jose Luis Irigoyen, Vivien Foster, and Valerie Marie Helene Layrol kindly prepared box 2. Stephen Mink, Nancy Claire Benjamin, Michael Morris, Prasad C. Mohan, Jose Luis Irigoyen, Vivien Foster and Valerie Marie Helene Layrol provided useful comments on an earlier draft of the essay.

Azita Amjadi, Ramgopal Erabelly, Abdolreza Farivari, Richard Fix, Shelley Lai Fu, Malarvizhi Veerappan, Shahin Outadi, William Prince, Abarna Gayathri Manickudi Panchapakesan, and Jomo Tariku collaborated in the data production. Maja Bresslauer, Mahyar Eshragh-Tabary, Victor Gabor, and Soong Sup Lee collaborated in the update of the live database. Mehdi Akhlaghi collaborated in the production of *The Little Data Book on Africa 2010*.

Yohannes Kebede and Michael Mendale prepared the ADI Online data visualization platform.

Jeffrey Lecksell of the World Bank's Map Design Unit coordinated preparation of the map.

The box on measuring the impact of regional integration in the technical notes was prepared by Paul Brenton.

Ann Karasanyi and Ken Omondi provided administrative and logistical support. The team is grateful to the many people who provided useful comments on the publication, especially Inger Andersen, Paul Brenton, Aziz Bouzaher, Cecilia M. Briceno-Garmendia, Donald Bundy, Moulay Driss Zine Eddine El Idrissi, Madhur Gautam, Giuseppe Iarossi, Elizabeth Laura Lule, John F. May, Steven Mink, Emmanuel Mungunasi, Vincent Palmade, Mona Prasad, Karima Saleh, Rachel Sebudde, Giovanni Tanzillo, Christopher Thomas, Franke Toornstra, Marilou Jane D. Uy, Stephen Vincent, and Yi-Kyoung Lee. Their feedback and suggestions helped improve this year's edition.

Staff from External Affairs oversaw printing and dissemination of the book and its companions.

Several institutions provided data to *Africa Development Indicators*. Their contribution is very much appreciated.

Communications Development Incorporated provided design direction, editing, and layout, led by Bruce Ross-Larson and Christopher Trott. Elaine Wilson typeset the book.

Executive summary

Silent and lethal: How quiet corruption undermines Africa's development efforts

The corruption that often captures newspaper headlines and provokes worldwide public disapproval is dominated by loud "big-time corruption," notably administrative and political corruption at the highest government levels. In response to this notoriety, the bulk of anti-corruption measures have been tailored to address this type of corruption. However, recent examinations of the level and quality of service delivery in developing countries, including the *World Development Report 2004*, have highlighted the need to expand the scope of the standard definition of corruption—the abuse of public office for private gain. While acknowledging the importance of big-time corruption in reducing funding for service delivery, recent research has devoted increasing attention to identifying corrupt practices downstream at the frontline of public service provision.

Following this literature, this essay introduces the term "quiet corruption" to indicate various types of malpractice of frontline providers (teachers, doctors, inspectors, and other government representatives) that do not involve monetary exchange. These behaviors include both potentially observable deviations, such as absenteeism, but also hard-to-observe deviations from expected conduct, such as a lower level of effort than expected or the deliberate bending of rules for personal advantage. For example, recent findings indicate that primary school teachers in a number of African countries are not in school 15 to 25 percent of the time (absenteeism), but, in addition, a considerable fraction of those in school are not found teaching (low effort). Frontline provider deviations from expected behavior that meet these requirements broaden the scope of corruption.

With this broader definition in mind, the familiar form of big-time corruption is just the "tip of the iceberg"; the quiet corruption, that is the less frequently observed deviations from expected conduct, is below the surface. In addition to capturing the notion that quiet corruption is not as visible, the iceberg analogy provides two additional insights. First, quiet corruption occurs across a much wider set of transactions directly affecting a large number of beneficiaries. Quiet corruption is present in a large share of health-provider–patient or teacher-pupil interactions, for example. Second, quiet corruption very often has deep long-term consequences on households, farms, and firms. The widespread prevalence of big-time and quiet corruption in Africa significantly undermines the impact of investments to meet the Millennium Development Goals (MDGs). In the parlance of this essay, the iceberg of corruption is sinking considerable efforts to improve the well-being of Africa's citizens, particularly the poor who rely predominantly on publicly provided services.

It is important to raise awareness of the profile of quiet corruption because this malpractice has non-negligible long-term consequences. This essay elaborates both the direct consequences, such as the limitation of the productivity potential of households, firms, and farms, and the indirect consequences, such as distrust of public institutions and the notion that frontline provider malpractice is inevitable and omnipresent. As an example of direct consequences, we might think how poor service delivery caused by absenteeism or low effort on the job might hamper a child's development, with potential permanent effects on adult educational attainment, cognitive skills, and underlying health. As an indirect effect, we might think of the withdrawal of children from school because of beliefs about the low quality of education, which shifts the allocation of time and resources away from human capital formation toward home production or labor market participation.

This essay further shows how quiet corruption manifests itself differently according to the nature of service delivery. It focuses on four key sectors (education, health care, agriculture, and the private sector) whose progress and success are crucial for poverty eradication and more generally achieving the MDGs. In presenting examples and outlining the long-term consequences of quiet corruption in these sectors, this essay contends that one of the main reasons Africa is lagging behind is the poor service delivery that is a consequence of quiet corruption.

The good news is that quiet corruption can be tackled. Whenever a government's determination to deal with quiet corruption has increased, for example, by increasing the availability of information on finances, inputs, and expected outputs, then measurable improvements in service delivery have been possible. Although there is no "one size fits all" recommendation that applies to every sector, this essay advocates the need for strong and highly motivated leadership in the fight against corruption, commitment to and capacity of the national anti-corruption units to pursue operationally effective responses at the ***sector level***, and adequate policies and institutions. An equally important second pillar is increasing transparency in policy formulation and implementation that empowers citizens to raise the accountability of service providers—bolstering the "demand side" for good governance. Finally, successful implementation of anti-corruption reforms also requires that the preferences and interests of all those involved be aligned with achieving the objectives of the reform. This often involves better working conditions.

Given the complexity of the task, the fight against quiet corruption requires tailoring policies to country circumstances, recognizing that priorities and responses may vary depending on different country conditions. This essay outlines a research agenda to identify interventions to address quiet corruption. Experimenting with various ways to empower beneficiaries and continuing the ongoing efforts to tackle big-time corruption will go a long way toward achieving this goal. Indeed, although combating loud and visible forms of corruption is necessary, fighting quiet corruption is critical if governments want to reduce poverty and promote sustainable growth.

Silent and lethal: How quiet corruption undermines Africa's development

Corruption captures newspaper headlines and provokes public disapproval. In addition, the abuse of public office for private gain—the most common definition of corruption—has attracted increasing attention by scholars and policy makers interested in economic development. Specifically, corruption and poor governance help explain why increased funding allocations, such as those aimed at meeting the United Nations Millennium Development Goals (MDGs), have not necessarily translated into improvements in human development indicators, particularly in Africa.[1] Despite considerable funding increases, the region is largely lagging behind in meeting the MDG of reducing child mortality (the number of children dying before age 5 per 1,000 live births). Substantial increases in gross enrollment in primary education in recent years have not been matched by improvements in learning outcomes. Africa's private investment rate is still around 15 percent, much lower than in most developing countries. Agricultural productivity is not increasing fast enough; the yield per hectare is still less than half that in other developing regions. Cutting across all these problems is Africa's fundamental problem, namely weak governance and associated corruption.[2]

Until recently, the debate about corruption and development[3] has been dominated by the identification and measurement of "big-time corruption" (de Sardan 1999), notably administrative and political corruption at the highest levels of government.[4] This focus has produced measures of governance weakness and corruption suitable for cross-country comparisons of political corruption. But these measures are not reliable when it comes to measuring less visible forms of corruption, such as those faced by common citizens as they interact with health and education providers, agriculture extension services, drug inspectors, and the police (see Razafindrakoto and Roubaud 2006).

World Development Report 2004 (World Bank 2003), which examined service delivery, recasts the problem of corruption from a different perspective. While acknowledging the importance of big-time corruption in reducing funding for service delivery, *World Development Report 2004* and subsequent research have devoted increasing attention to analyzing corrupt practices downstream, at the frontline of public service provision (Reinikka and Svensson 2006). This new focus has produced two results. First, it has enabled the identification of malpractice involving small monetary transactions, generally referred to as "petty corruption" (de Sardan 1999), for example, under-the-table payments for services received (Transparency International 2005, 2006) or bribes to tax collectors and low ranking public officials. Second, the concept of corruption has been gradually extended to practices that do not necessarily involve monetary transactions, such as teacher absenteeism (Patrinos and Kagia 2007). Furthermore, new survey tools, such as the Public Expenditure Tracking Survey (PETS) and Quantitative Service Delivery Survey (QSDS), have enabled researchers to track resources and monitor the attendance of frontline providers. These research and survey results have improved the understanding of a broad range of misconduct and contributed to reshaping the policy debate about corruption.

Following the recent findings on frontline provider misconduct, this essay focuses on behaviors that are difficult to observe and quantify, but whose impact on service delivery and regulation has adverse long-term effects on households. We introduce the term "quiet corruption" to indicate various types of malpractice of frontline providers (teachers, doctors, inspectors, and other government officials at the front lines of service provision) that do not involve monetary exchange. These behaviors include not only potentially observable deviations, such as absenteeism, but also hard to observe deviations from expected conduct, such as a lower level of effort than expected or the deliberate bending of rules for personal advantage. For example, education service delivery requires teachers to be present in school as well as to deliver classroom instruction required by the curriculum. Similarly, a building inspector can turn up to inspect the structural integrity of a new shopping mall but choose to exert little effort in executing the task.

Quiet corruption, as opposed to corruption that involves an exchange of money—either political level thefts or small but frequent bribes—is less salient or "noisy," and consequently less likely to attract public attention. Despite its low visibility, quiet corruption is ubiquitous. And it is associated with harmful long-term consequences, particularly for the poor who are more exposed to adverse shocks and more reliant on government services to satisfy their most basic needs.

Two examples illustrate the magnitude of the consequences of quiet corruption. First, among the reasons for low fertilizer usage among African farmers is the poor quality of fertilizers on the market. Despite the capability of manufacturers to produce good fertilizers, poor controls at the producer and wholesaler levels resulted in 43 percent of the analyzed fertilizers sold in West Africa in the 1990s lacking the expected nutrients, meaning that they were basically ineffective (IFDC 1995). It is likely that poor farmers' experiences with low-quality fertilizers discourage fertilizer adoption.

Second, a survey of malaria fatalities in rural Tanzania reported that nearly four out of five children who died of malaria sought medical attention from modern health facilities (de Savigny et al. 2008). A range of manifestations of quiet corruption, including the absence of diagnostic equipment, drug pilfering, provider absenteeism, and very low levels of diagnostic effort, all contributed to this dire statistic (Das and Leonard 2009).

The concept of quiet corruption is captured in Figure 1. The familiar forms of corruption—both big time and petty—are just the "tip of the iceberg"; the less frequently observed deviation from expected conduct is quiet corruption. In addition to capturing the notion that quiet corruption is not very visible, the iceberg analogy provides two additional insights. First, quiet corruption occurs across a much wider set of transactions affecting a large number of beneficiaries directly. Quiet corruption is arguably present in a large share of doctor–patient or teacher-pupil interactions, for example. Second, quiet corruption plausibly has deep long-term consequences on households, farms, and firms. Comparing the long-term consequences of different forms of corruption is a hazardous undertaking. In addition

Figure 1 Big-time and petty corruption are the "tip of the iceberg"

to being affected by the same country level characteristics, all three forms of corruption are related. The quiet corruption of low-level officials may very well have been "justified" in their minds by the misbehavior of their superiors involved in big-time corruption. Likewise, by reducing available resources and compromising the monitoring and enforcement of conduct, big-time corruption encourages low-level civil servants to engage in opportunistic behavior. An instance of teacher absence could be the result of a poor working environment occasioned by big-time corruption or other factors beyond the teacher's and education managers' control. However, it can also be categorized as quiet corruption—the abuse of public office by the teacher. The long-term consequences of this and other instances of absence compound the effects of both big-time and quiet corruption.

Corruption is embedded in the political economy of Africa. A number of studies describe the interaction between various forms of corruption and how it is intrinsically linked to the way power is exercised.[5] In particular, when a social unit is highly diverse ethnically[6]—as is the case in many post-independence African countries—there is likely to be suspicion and division among members, making the process of agreeing to rules for governance extremely difficult. In this context, small groups (elites) that are highly homogeneous are more likely to prevail and impose rules that bias the system in their favor. The enforcement of these biased rules requires either coercion or "additional resources" to ensure the cooperation of members of other groups who will try to avoid such biased rules.

In many African states, the coercion option is not feasible because state power is limited. In contrast, the option to purchase the cooperation of other groups tends to be the most viable. Ruling elites in regimes with limited legitimacy thus regard corruption purely in terms of its political functionality as a source of patronage resources to maintain and strengthen the system of political power.[7] The more these elites are able to privatize state resources, the more they can distribute favors and create a base of consensus for their privileged position. Thus a strategy to control the state creates an environment conducive to misconduct by frontline service providers.

The scheme of insiders profiting from biased rules in the system is mirrored in society. Police exert their influence to extract benefits from the disorganized mass of road users; doctors do not show up in public facilities and instead provide services privately; teachers do not show up in classes since they have a second job and their impunity is guaranteed by their superiors in exchange for other favors, and so forth. It follows that corruption becomes an unavoidable element of daily life for many citizens, and it diffuses throughout the economy; more big-time corruption begets corruption at the frontlines of service delivery, which in turn supports big-time corruption, creating formidable challenges to governance and accountability interventions.

For a number of key public services, the cumulative nature of human development implies that poor service delivery experienced during the early stages of life can have long-term consequences. The direct long-term effects of quiet corruption begin with poor service delivery during early childhood, which is then amplified by subsequent poor service provision throughout childhood. For example, a mother who is a victim of quiet corruption—poor quality antenatal care—might give birth to an underweight child, who will likely suffer a series of health setbacks during childhood that potentially magnify the immediate effects of the poor antenatal care. This amplification process is also driven by families' increasingly negative expectations of service delivery systems, leading to even fewer health service visits and the use of poorer quality alternatives. In the African context, alternative health services are often nonexistent, of low quality, or too costly for the typical household. The family's decision to exit the system leads to a worsening of the public sector and can ultimately result in the collapse of service delivery.[8] For example, as McPake et al. (2000) document, the poor quality of health care services in Uganda created a downward spiral of underutilization of public health facilities. Lower demand for services led to even lower staff attendance and to shorter opening hours of health care facilities.

Considering the pervasiveness of corruption and that the different types are intertwined with the functioning of political and social systems in many developing countries, it is clear that focusing only on the monetary forms of corruption misses the majority of solutions. Hence, this essay attempts to provide a framework to understand the implications of the entire "iceberg" of misconduct that shapes the level and quality of services and regulation in developing countries. The essay outlines evidence of quiet corruption and discusses both direct and indirect long-term consequences on households, businesses, and farms.

The framework in Figure 2 describes the mechanisms through which quiet corruption affects delivery of frontline services, such as medical treatment or in-classroom instruction, and the provision of business regulations, such as trading licenses. The three arrows linking quiet corruption and service delivery represent "pathways of influence." These are denoted as (1) low effort due to absenteeism, (2) low effort on the job, and (3) resource leakage.

Low effort due to absenteeism refers to frontline provider behaviors that restrict the amount of time they are available. Absenteeism implies that providers work less time at the public facility than contracted for, with little or no repercussions on their earnings. The second arrow takes into account the extent to which frontline providers shirk their duties while on the job. Finally, the third arrow refers to providers' involvement in the leakage of key inputs, such as drugs and medicines, in the case of health-care workers, or books and other instructional materials in the case of teachers.

Despite the difficulties in observing attendance and job effort, the lack of transparency and accountability, and the weaknesses of monitoring and enforcement inherent in public service organizations in developing countries, this essay argues that quiet corruption is likely to be equally insidious as big-time corruption. The right-hand portion of Figure 2 illustrates the linkage between poor service delivery today and the direct and indirect long-term consequences of big-time corruption and quiet corruption. Because of its nature, quiet corruption can affect incentives and distort the allocation of resources at the individual, household, firm, and farm levels.

While these long-term consequences are very hard to quantify because of the absence of data that trace out the effects of contemporaneous misconduct on future outcomes and because of the multiplicity of other factors that may contribute to them, combining evidence from both developed and developing countries provides a sense of the magnitude of resulting damage to development. The long-term consequences are divided into direct consequences, such as the limitation of the productivity potential of households, firms, and farms, and indirect consequences, such as distrust of public institutions and the notion that corruption is inevitable and omnipresent. These two components are explained in more detail below.

One direct effect of quiet corruption is the loss of production as a result of the lower quality of inputs. For example, research on corruption in the health-care sector rarely documents how the effect of poor service delivery that might hamper a child's development has permanent effects on adult educational attainment, cognitive skills, and underlying health. The absenteeism of doctors or nurses, for example, might contribute to the non-detection of iron deficiency (Ramakrishnan et al. 1999) or deficiency of other micronutrients in a pregnant mother's diet. The lack of timely intervention affects the development of the fetus and stunts the child's full growth. The consequences of this poor health treatment may manifest during adolescence and adulthood and could affect the individual's productivity (Barker et al. 1995; Smith 2009).

An indirect effect of quiet corruption operates through changing the beliefs and expectations of service beneficiaries. As a result of this transformation, agents may decide to allocate their time in more remunerative activities in the short run at the expense of capital accumulation and investment in activities that produce larger gains only in the long run. A typical case is the non-investment in the human capital of children because of beliefs about the low quality of education, which shifts the allocation of time and resources away from education toward home production or labor market participation. Another example, as mentioned above, is the lack of adoption of fertilizers and other productive inputs by farmers who have had bad prior experiences.

Finally, the notion that corruption is generally ubiquitous and inevitable implies that it is an "accumulating process": the more corrupt the system, the more it produces a downward spiral of malpractice (de Sardan 1999). Within a corrupt environment, people adjust their strategies accordingly and contribute to the general acceptance of the phenomenon, thus making it routine. If professional standards are substituted with a pure "fend for yourself" attitude at every level (Lindelow, Serneels, and Lemma 2005), the system falls into a vicious cycle in which every misconduct is tolerated and the structure of incentives becomes biased against those who adhere to the standards.

Some sectors are more vulnerable to quiet corruption than others; the main determinants are the level of transparency and accountability in the sector, the asymmetry of information, and the discretion and monopoly power of service providers, all of which create incentives for misconduct. The manifestation will also differ from rural to urban areas and will depend on the socioeconomic characteristics and political power of the main clientele. The implication is that reform strategies should differ depending on the nature of service. There will be differences across countries as well, in accord with the levels of accountability and transparency and the systems of monitoring, enforceability of rules and procedures, and punishment of corruption. As a consequence, there is no recipe on how to prevent and fight quiet corruption that is valid for all sectors and countries. The aim of this essay is not to arrive at specific recommendations but rather to stimulate debate around this critical development topic, expecting that it will increase interest and efforts that are much needed to combat quiet corruption.

While quiet corruption is indeed present in all sectors, the next sections present evidence and discuss the consequences of quiet corruption in education, health, the private sector, and agriculture. This selection is based on the importance of these sectors for Africa's development as well as the existing evidence on quiet corruption. For each sector, the presence of quiet corruption in the typology presented in Figure 2

Figure 2 The functioning of quiet corruption and its long-term consequences

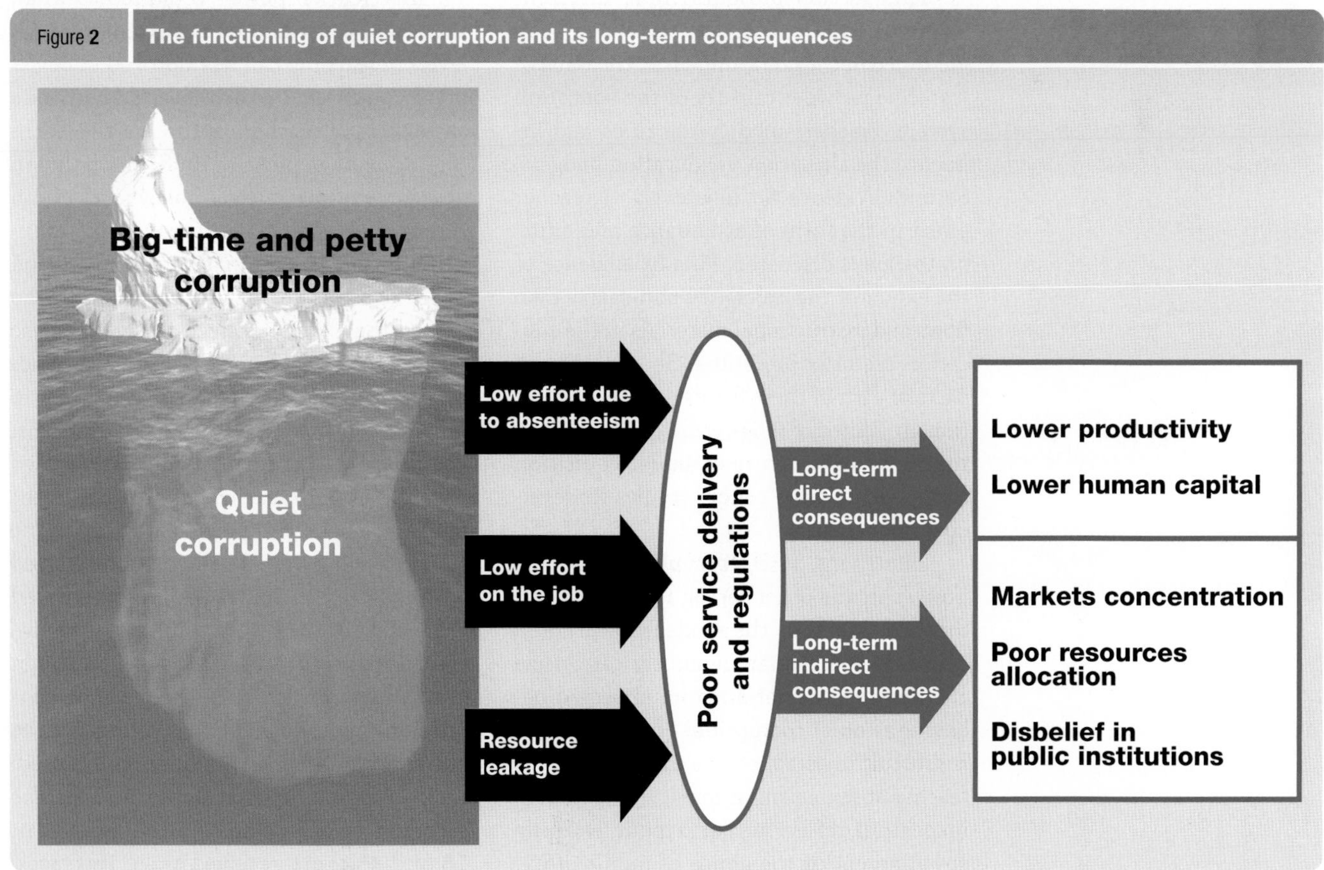

is documented. Furthermore, and to the extent possible, the direct and indirect long-term consequences for economic agents are presented.

Education

The education sector prepares youth for productive engagement in the social, political, and economic realms as adults. In Africa education accounts for a large fraction of government expenditure, with a large share of public resources accruing to teachers. Teacher remuneration accounts for nearly three-quarters of recurrent expenditure in education in developing countries (Bruns, Mingat, and Rakatomalala 2003). Quiet corruption in education, therefore, is not only costly in terms of the direct loss of considerable scarce public resources, but more importantly in terms of its long-term consequences for the human capital base. Given the long term consequences of adults with lower skills and poor attitude, quiet corruption in education undermines the serious efforts being invested in the eradication of poverty and improvement in the competitiveness of African economies (World Bank 2009).

This section presents three different forms of quiet corruption that have been identified in the literature. First, the issue of frontline provider capture of the education system: teachers modify the rules and influence the allocation of education budgets. Second, evidence for low levels of teacher effort in the form of attendance and effort on the job is discussed. Finally, evidence of the extent of the leakage of non-salary cash flows and instructional materials in the education sector is presented. Short-term impacts of each of these forms of quiet corruption are linked to long-term effects through the cumulative nature of skills acquisition and evidence from cohort studies in developed countries.

Identifying quiet corruption in education, as in any other sector, is not straightforward. Much of the evidence presented below does not unambiguously categorize any observed deviation from expected behavior as quiet corruption. For example, it is difficult to establish the extent to which teacher absenteeism or low levels of school inspection reflect either a poor working environment or the abuse of public office. For purposes of this essay, the frequency of documented deviations represents an upper bound of the prevalence of quiet corruption. Following the framework of Figure 2, the long-term consequences are divided into direct and indirect effects.

Teacher capture

A considerable body of evidence documents the capture of service delivery systems by key actors in the service delivery chain (Mizala and Romaguera 2004 and others). "Capture" refers to a situation in which key actors are able to alter the rules, such as the conditions of service or the allocation of expenditure in the sector, to their advantage and to the detriment of service beneficiaries and the society at large. In the case of the education system, teachers are a key group of actors that have exerted considerable influence over both the allocation of resources within the system, but more importantly, the rules that define their conditions of service. Much of this power is exercised as a result of the influence wielded by teacher unions or through the direct involvement of current or retired teachers in local and national politics.

This "teacher power" could represent an important constraint on the extent to which levels of learning can be improved in developing countries. Two examples demonstrate the effects of teacher capture on the learning levels of pupils. In 1998, the Bolivian government introduced a policy to ascertain the quality of teachers through a "teaching sufficiency examination." Participation in the test was voluntary and teachers who passed the exams received a wage increase relative to the traditional wage scale. In addition, head teachers had to pass this test in order to continue in their role as principals. The first round of implementation revealed very low levels of teacher quality: 60 percent of the teachers who participated failed the test and only a very small fraction received a wage increase. The teacher union rejected the results of the test, claiming that the invitation to participate and the assignment of grades were problematic. A series of demonstrations and hunger strikes calling for the elimination of the examinations followed. The government capitulated and in the second year of implementation more than 18,500 teachers received wage increases.

The policy was discontinued and replaced by a range of largely non-performance-based incentives (Mizala and Romaguera 2004).

A 2007 proposal by the ministry of education in Uganda to improve management at the school level through performance contracts with head teachers met a similar fate. In the proposed contracts, head teachers would sign an agreement with the local government outlining a series of goals to be met over a two-year period. Failure to meet these goals could lead to demotions or transfers. Even though the policy explicitly stipulated that head teachers would be the main architects of the performance targets, the teacher union successfully opposed the policy on the basis that the penalties included in the contracts were excessive and unfair.

Other rules that are subverted for teacher benefit include the implicit or explicit sanctioning of additional instruction outside regular school hours. The legitimacy of this practice in a number of countries is particularly pernicious when public teachers selectively cover material during regular school hours and other material during their private tutoring sessions (Jayachandran 2008; Dang and Rogers 2008). The extent to which this extracurricular instruction might be occurring is suggested by the high and increasing prevalence of extra tuition, which is shown in Table 1 using data from the Southern and Eastern Africa Consortium for Monitoring Educational Quality (SACMEQ). While these data are generated from pupil reports that are unreliable for establishing the existence or level of extra tuition fees, they suggest a considerable degree of discrimination: households that cannot afford extra lessons receive less and/or lower quality instruction than is stipulated by the curriculum.

Table 1 Percentage of grade 6 students receiving extra lessons

	Percentage of grade 6 students receiving extra lessons	
Country	**SACMEQ I 1995**	**SACMEQ II 2000**
Mauritius	77.5	86.6
Kenya	68.6	87.7
Zanzibar	46.1	55.9
Zambia	44.8	55.1
Namibia	34.7	44.7
Malawi	22.1	79.7
Total	49.0	68.3

Source: Paviot, Heinsohn, and Korkman (2008).

Low levels of teacher effort

Teacher effort is an important input into learning (Park and Hannum 2002; Hanushek, Kain, and Rivkin 2005). Perhaps the most important form of quiet corruption in education is the low levels of teacher effort that arise from teacher absence and low effort while in school. Evidence on the extent of teacher absence has improved greatly over the last decade. Early evidence comes from head-teacher or teacher self-reports of the duration of absence during a given time period (usually 1–4 weeks). For example, an important UNICEF multi-country survey of 14 developing countries conducted in 1995 and reported in Postlethwaite (1998) reports high levels of head-teacher reported absenteeism. Among the African countries, Tanzania, Uganda, and Zambia were the worst performers. More than half the teachers in Tanzania and Uganda were absent at least one day in the previous week and about a quarter of teachers were absent for two or more days. In Zambia, a quarter of teachers were absent for two or more days. Using a similar methodology, Das et al. (2004) report an average absence duration of two days per month in Zambian primary schools in 2002.

Concerns about the quality of head-teacher or teacher reports of absenteeism have motivated the use of *direct observation* of teacher attendance (Table 2).[9] In this approach, which relies on unannounced visits, a teacher is reported as being absent if he or she cannot be found by the enumeration team at a time that he or she is scheduled to be in school. This methodology has been widely used in western Kenya and a large multi-country study that included Uganda (Chaudhury et al. 2006). Kremer et al. (2004) report that 20 percent of teachers in rural western Kenyan primary schools could not be found during school hours. In Uganda, two waves of surveys using this methodology found teacher absence rates of 27 percent in 2002 and 20 percent in 2007.[10]

The above studies document considerably higher levels of absence among head teachers and other senior teachers.[12] Whether

Table 2	Estimates of teacher absenteeism	
Country	**% teachers absent (direct observation)**	**Days absent per month (teacher self report)**
Uganda (2003)[a]	27	
Uganda (2007)[b]	20	
Kenya (2003)[c]	20	
Zambia (2007)[d]	20	
Burkina Faso (1995–8)[e]		2.2
Cameroon (1995–8)[e]		1.8
Cote d'Ivoire (1995–8)[e]		1.3
Madagascar (1995–8)[e]		2.5
Senegal (1995–8)[e]		4.7
Zambia (2002)[f]		2.0

Sources: a. Chaudhury et al. (2006); b. Habyarimana (2007); c. Glewwe, Kremer, and Moulin (2009)[11]; d. Halsey, Rogers, and Vegas (2009); e. Postlethwaite (1998); f. Das et al. (2004).

this represents low effort is difficult to say because a range of duties may draw principals away from school (to attend meetings or request or collect resources). Taking the example of Uganda, head teachers were twice as likely to be absent as regular teachers (Habyarimana 2007). In addition, assuming that the reported reasons for absence are credible, only half of the absences are officially sanctioned. Perhaps even more consequential is evidence from the multi-country study that documents higher regular teacher absence when the head teacher is absent. Chaudhury et al. (2006) also collected information about the likelihood that teachers were warned or fired for absence. The results from India are indicative of the low levels of sanctions: only one teacher in 3,000 schools had been fired for absence despite high absenteeism rates. The level and quality of instruction provided by teachers is not only a function of their training and attendance patterns, but also of their behavior while in school. Measuring the effort level of teachers in school and the extent to which it qualifies as quiet corruption is challenging. Indeed, a number of studies have tried to quantify this effect with limited success. Some studies rely on adding up the number of class hours using the school's timetable. For example, Postlethwaite (1998) reports that students in his developing country sample received only about 80 percent of the total timetable-derived annual instruction time as those in developed countries. While this measure indicates lower levels of instruction, it assumes that teacher attendance patterns and in-class effort and quality are similar across developed and developing countries. Higher levels of teacher attendance and the use of substitute teachers in developed countries further deepen the instruction time gap between developed and developing countries.

Additional evidence from direct observation studies suggests that in-class behavior of teachers differs from their developed country colleagues. While there are problems of interpretation,[13] direct observation surveys suggest that even among those teachers who are found present in school, in-class effort is low. For instance in western Kenya, Glewwe, Kremer, and Moulin (2009) document that 12 percent of teachers were found to be outside the classroom when they should have been teaching. An even higher fraction is estimated in Uganda where nearly one-third of teachers found were not in the classroom during learning periods (Habyarimana 2007).

Teacher influence and capture could explain much of the low levels of teacher effort documented. For example, the multi-country study finds that teacher absence is not concentrated among a few "ghost" teachers, but rather is driven by the behavior of a large share of teachers. Punishment of poor attendance or tardiness on the job is very rare. In many cases, warning letters or reports of teacher misconduct do not trigger any sanctions.

Leakage of resources

Schools combine instructional materials and teacher and pupil interaction to produce cognitive skills. This essay documents the leakage of two key inputs: instructional materials and school inspection. A teacher with few or no instructional materials will find it harder to impart the necessary skills to her charges. In addition, school inspection ensures that the right pedagogical strategies are being implemented and instructional materials are well deployed.[14]

The clearest example of the extent of leakage of instructional resources comes from two PETS surveys in Uganda in the 1990s. The first study revealed that an average of only 13 percent of the resources intended for schools were reaching them. Poor information flows about the size of the capitation grant and the timing of resource flows provided local education authorities with the cover to divert these resources. These findings motivated a government-led intervention to increase the transparency of grants disbursement. In addition to prosecuting offenders, the newspaper and radio campaign led to large increases in school level funding (Reinnika and Svensson 2005).

In the Zambia PETS of 2002, Das et al. (2004) found that resources meant for renovation were more likely to go to schools in the middle of the wealth distribution, which suggests a degree of collusion between head teachers of middle-tier schools and local education authorities. Other PETS carried out in Africa all point to considerable leakages in non-salary funding (Gauthier 2006).

Finally, the quality of instruction and pace of learning is supposed to be monitored by a variety of standards officials who typically work in the local education authority. Regular inspection provides crucial information about challenges and successes that can be used to generate improvements in service delivery.[15] While low levels of school inspection can be the result of a poor working environment in which willing officials lack the means to conduct their duties, the prima facie evidence is examined as an upper bound of the extent of deviations from norms. It is important to bear in mind that countries have different norms of inspection frequency that determine the extent to which observed rates of inspection differ from stipulated rates. This essay instead presents evidence from a number of sources that simply report the fraction of schools that have been visited by an inspector in the year since the survey. Postlethwaite (1998) suggests that in Madagascar, Togo, Uganda, and Tanzania, more than 70 percent of students were in schools that had not been inspected in the previous year. More recent evidence from a number of surveys (Uganda Unit Cost Study and PETS in Zambia and elsewhere) suggest similarly low levels of inspection.

Long-term consequences for education

While it is difficult to attribute all of the deviations above to misbehavior, establishing the consequences of these deviations is straightforward. The acquisition of skills and competencies is a cumulative process: cognitive achievement today defines how much a child will learn tomorrow. Therefore, quiet corruption today that leads to contemporaneous lower levels of learning has long-term effects. Some of these long-term effects operate through decisions that households make. For example a household might decide that a child who is not learning very much could be better utilized to look after cows. Evidence of this cumulative learning process comes from cohort studies in developed countries that demonstrate the strong correlation between cognitive skills while young and competencies and earnings in adult life (for example, Case and Paxson 2008). For each of the three forms of quiet corruption in education identified above: teacher capture, low effort, and leakage of resources, there is evidence of a negative impact on learning. These short-term impacts translate into long-term consequences through the cumulative nature of skills acquisition and the dynamic decisions of households. In short, quiet corruption has arguably grave consequences for the future competencies of Africa's youth.

Households make dynamic decisions about whether to enroll/continue a child in school and how much to invest in time and resources based on complementary inputs provided by teachers and schools, and particularly, based on perceptions of the child's learning. Each of the three forms of quiet corruption impinges on household decisions and consequently on the competencies and attainment of children. Teacher instruction time is a crucial input in the production of competencies and skills that are crucial in a wide range of market and non-market activities. And the level and quality of teacher instruction time is affected by all three forms of quiet corruption.

The capture of the education system affects attainment and long-run skills acquisition in several ways. First, as the examples above demonstrate, capture supports lower levels of teacher quality and managerial effort at the school level. While evidence of the link between teacher quality and learning outcomes is thin, a study in Israel found that teacher training is associated with learning gains (Angrist and Lavy 2001).

Second, to varying degrees, capture supports deeper levels of quiet corruption: low levels of teacher effort, leakage of instructional materials, and lower levels of inspection.

The effects of teacher absence, leakage of instructional materials, or lower monitoring of learning are well documented. For instance, using data from Zambian primary schools, Das and others (2007) found that an increase in absence duration of one day per month reduces test scores by about 4–8 percent of the average annual gains in English and mathematics. In addition, Kremer, Miguel, and Thornton (2004) found that test score gains in response to a girls' scholarship program in western Kenya are in part the result of increases in teacher attendance of nearly 6 percentage points. Duflo, Hanna, and Ryan (2008) showed test score gains of 0.2 standard deviations that corresponded to a halving of teacher absence in non-formal schools in India.

Several studies document the positive link between more resources and short-term learning gains in Africa. Using the results of a newspaper campaign that increased the amount of funding reaching schools in Uganda, Bjorkman (2006) reported gains in national test scores attributable to the increase in capitation grant flows. In addition, evidence from Zambia suggests that increases in unanticipated funding increase the test scores of grade 6 pupils (Das et al. 2004). Evidence from western Kenya suggests that the randomized provision of textbooks increased learning only for the best students (Glewwe, Kremer, and Moulin 2009). In contrast, a recent study in Brazil showed that higher levels of resource leakage at the municipality level are associated with lower learning gains of pupils (Ferraz, Finan, and Moreira 2009).

While test score outcomes are typically measured for 10- to 14-year-old students, the deleterious effects of quiet corruption extend throughout a child's adolescent and adult life. Two particular channels amplify the long-term consequences. First, low levels of learning occasioned by quiet corruption produce a poor learning environment in the next year that leads to further teacher and student absenteeism. This dynamic is reinforced by the links between student and teacher effort documented by Kremer et al. (2004), leading to even lower learning gains. Second, as mentioned earlier, households make human capital investment decisions on the basis of current and expected learning achievements. A child who is struggling in a school system characterized by quiet corruption is more likely to drop out or be removed from school, leading to permanently low levels of skills and competencies. Evidence from long-term cohort studies (Case, Lubotsky, and Paxson 2002) confirm the long-lasting nature of the adverse effects of learning deficiencies at an early age on productivity in later years and complete the link between quiet corruption and direct long-term consequences.

Health

As in the education sector, quiet corruption in the health care sector is widespread in Africa. However, as in the other sectors discussed in this essay, it is generally very difficult to ascertain the intent and therefore culpability of providers. In laying out the evidence for each of these behaviors in health care and their attendant consequences, we advise the reader to keep this caveat in mind.

Low levels of provider effort

As in the education sector, the quality and level of health services depend on the quality of providers, the frequency of attendance, and effort levels while at work. Evidence on quality and effort levels is only just beginning to emerge and is briefly discussed below. On the other hand, evidence on health provider attendance is considerable and suggests a very discouraging situation. Differences in measurement methodology notwithstanding, reports of health provider absence are very high. PETS in Mozambique and Chad (Gauthier 2006) document a rate of absenteeism in public facilities of around 20 percent. A direct observation survey in Uganda recorded a rate of 37 percent in the first round (2002) that went down 4 percentage points in the second survey in 2003. Bucking this trend is Cameroon, where estimated absence rate is only 5.6 percent.

In another survey based on direct questions to African, Asian, and Latin American physicians who had obtained a master's of public health degree in Europe between 1976 and 1996 (Macq and Van Lerberghe 2000), doctors comprised the category most absent among health care personnel, declaring only 73 percent of their time serving the public, that is, in their official job capacity. The rest of the time was divided between a second job, generally in the private health care sector, or in teaching or other activities often unrelated to the core activity. This is likely a conservative estimate, because respondents have incentives to underreport the effective time spent in other activities.

A study undertaken in Uganda between 1994 and 1997 involving health workers, community members, and the Health Unit Management Committee documents an environment where so-called "coping strategies," activities not directly related to the job position, are predominant (McPake et al. 2000).[16] Health workers, besides openly admitting to extra-legal user fees for services and selling drugs, also declare that their greatest source of income is agriculture, thus implicitly acknowledging a high rate of absenteeism. A comparison of working hours declared with observed working durations over the course of a month reveal a striking gap: effective hours worked are in most cases one-third or less than what is declared. This is consistent with very low utilization of these facilities, which are open for only two to three hours in the morning.

Absenteeism thus gives way to a vicious cycle of low service utilization by the public, which then further reinforces the poor attendance of health workers.[17] For example, Banerjee, Deaton, and Duflo (2004) found that in Rajasthan, India, over the course of 18 months, nurses, who were assigned to staff the clinic on a regular basis, were only to be found in the facilities 12 percent of the time. The record of absences, and therefore closure of facilities, followed no pattern, meaning that patients' likelihood of finding a provider was unpredictable, thereby discouraging patients from using the facilities or keeping appointments.

In addition to high absence rates of health-care workers, a number of studies suggest that quality and effort on the job is very low. Using direct clinic observation and vignettes, Das and Hammer (2005) and Leonard and Masatu (2005) provide a sense of the magnitude of the problems of low quality and effort in health care.[18] Drawing on studies carried out in India, Indonesia, Mexico, Paraguay, and Tanzania, estimates of doctor competence and practice paint a disturbing picture. Restricting the focus to the evidence from Tanzania, Leonard and Masatu (2007) found that health provider competence is considerably poorer in rural areas. However, more appropriate to our definition of quiet corruption, the gap between what providers know and what they do, that is, provider effort, is particularly worse in government facilities.

Leakage of resources

Estimating the degree of resource leakage in health care is very challenging. In many countries, governments do not state how much they have allocated for various health care inputs, depriving the analysts of a benchmark against which to assess receipts.

However, for some resources, leakage can be measured as the difference between stipulated resource flows (typically non-salary budgetary resources) and actual amounts received. Leakage amounts in this category vary from about 38 percent in Kenya to 99 percent in Chad (Table 3). While the differences do not singularly represent leakage close to the frontline of service delivery, the magnitude of the leakage gives a sense of the size and importance of this form of quiet corruption.

In addition to leakage of non-salary cash flows, the leakage of health goods is pervasive. A qualitative survey of 50 health workers in Mozambique and Cape Verde concluded that this practice is widespread, particularly among doctors (Ferrinho et al. 2004). The study also documents an "institutionalization" of this phenomenon: Mozambican health workers report the existence of informal contracts between private clinics

Table 3 Leakage of resources in health care

Country (year)	% of cash/in-kind resources leaked	Resource category
Kenya (2004)	38	Non-salary budget
Tanzania (1999)	41	Non-salary budget
Uganda (2000)	70	Drugs and supplies
Ghana (2000)	80	Non-salary budget
Chad (2004)	99	Non-salary budget

Source: Gauthier (2006).

and public hospitals to ensure a steady supply of certain medicines. Results from a survey of 90 Mozambican health care workers corroborate the findings above (Schwallbach et al. 2000).

Weak regulation of drugs

Quiet corruption in the regulation of pharmaceuticals is rampant and deadly. The efficacy of medication is dependent on the careful regulation of standards in the production, distribution, and prescription of pharmaceuticals. Inadequate or weakly implemented quality controls can lead to distribution of poor quality and often counterfeited drugs, which result in severe health consequences including death of the consumers. Cohen et al. (2007) document the existence of several areas where quiet corruption along the value chain from production to consumption of pharmaceuticals compromises long-term health.

This high vulnerability to corruption derives from the specific features of the health sector. Information between consumer and producer is highly asymmetric. The typical consumer cannot verify in advance the quality of the medication and has to rely on information provided either by the pharmaceutical producer or the health-care provider. Second, the consumer's inability to verify quality necessitates government regulation. The great latitude in regulating pharmaceutical quality is sometimes abused by regulators, either directly as a result of low effort or indirectly through inducements by drug producers or distributors.

For example, pharmaceutical companies should follow specific protocols defined by the World Health Organization in the production and distribution of medication.[19] Failure to comply with mandated procedures for handling raw materials and storing, packaging, and labeling products compromises the quality of the product. Low effort or capture of the regulatory authority implies that these regulations are weakly or selectively enforced, which results in the selling of substandard and sometimes harmful products.

A number of examples highlight the costs of weak regulatory systems. In 1995 in Haiti, 89 people died after using Paracetamol (acetaminophen) cough syrup prepared with diethylene glycol, a toxic chemical used in antifreeze (Cohen et al. 2007). Another study in South Asia (Newton et al. 2001) reported that 38 percent of the anti-malarial, artesunate-based products sold on the market contained a lower-than-standard quantity of active ingredient, drastically reducing their efficacy. Akunyili (2005) found that during the 1990s, Nigeria was flooded with counterfeit drugs that, according to some studies, accounted for more than 50 percent of drugs sold in drugstores. While specific statistics are not available on deaths or serious illnesses caused by fake medicines, anecdotal evidence suggests a connection between drug efficacy and number of fatalities. A further consequence of weak regulation was the total ban of Nigerian-made pharmaceuticals imposed by neighboring countries.

Long-term consequences for health care

Even if drugs are stolen and do not reach facilities, they may be reaching the target population through different channels. Although the distribution may be inequitable due to pricing out particular population segments and could possibly be less effective because medicines are dispensed by non-trained personnel, this outcome does not necessarily imply a dramatic worsening of health conditions in the population. We sidestep this issue by elucidating the link between quiet corruption and contemporaneous and long-term health outcomes and the long-lasting beliefs of health service users.

While there are few micro-level studies that demonstrate a causal link between quiet corruption in health care and poor health outcomes, a number of cross-country regressions suggest a strong relationship. To establish the link between quiet corruption and long-term consequences, a useful starting point is research that has estimated the long-run consequences of malaria eradication (Cutler et al. 2007), famine, and low birth weight on long-term labor market consequences (Almond et al. 2006), and cohort studies in the United Kingdom and United States that examined the effects of low birth weight on cognitive skills and long-term wellbeing—the so-called Barker hypothesis (Barker et al. 1995; Barker 1998).

Cross-country research has demonstrated a negative association between country-level measures of corruption and health care indicators. To the extent that country-level corruption is linked to quiet corruption through the "mirror effect" described in the introduction, these results potentially reflect the effects of quiet corruption. Gupta, Davoodi, and Tiongson (2000) showed that corruption indicators are positively associated with child and infant mortality, the likelihood of an attended birth, immunization coverage, and low birth weight. Closer to one of the forms of quiet corruption defined above, Rajkumar and Swaroop (2008) found that the effectiveness of public health spending in reducing child mortality depends crucially on the perception of higher government integrity. Wagstaff and Claeson (2004), replicating a Filmer, Hammer, and Pritchett (2000) study using more recent data, found that public spending reduces under-five child mortality only where governance is good, as measured by the World Bank's Country Policy and Institutional Assessment (CPIA) score. This study specifically explored the implications of additional spending for reaching the MDGs, and concludes that more spending in medium and low CPIA countries would not reduce child mortality and that per-capita income growth offers a better investment if mortality declines are the objective.

Micro evidence is more specific, enabling a richer description of how quiet corruption in health translates into poor service delivery and documentation of some of the direct and indirect long-term consequences listed in Figure 2. Indirect evidence of the link between service utilization and health outcomes comes from a study in Uganda that estimated the effect of banning user fees on utilization and morbidity (Deininger and Mpuga 2004). In addition to direct effects on service utilization, quiet corruption alters the beliefs of households about the efficacy of treatments obtained in public facilities. Such beliefs reinforce lower service utilization in preference for traditional, sometimes life-threatening, interventions.

Given the importance of physical and cognitive development during a child's gestation and early years, quiet corruption that affects the utilization of key inputs such as prenatal and post-natal care, immunization, and the treatment of infant and child infections is likely to have far-reaching, long-term consequences. Two recent pieces of evidence confirm the link between contemporaneous quiet corruption and birth outcomes. Goldstein et al. (2009) found that absence of a nurse responsible for pre- and post-HIV-test counseling has a great impact on whether prenatal care patients in Kenya are tested for HIV. In addition, they found that women who are not tested and counseled are more likely to give birth without a professional attendant, less likely to receive preventive mother-to-child transmission medication, and less likely to breastfeed their babies.[20] They concluded that reducing absenteeism in public health facilities could reduce vertical transmission of HIV by 0.5–1.5 infections per 1000 live births.

The second piece of evidence comes from an intervention inspired by *World Development Report 2004* (World Bank 2003). Bjorkman and Svensson (2007) document the results of a report card intervention in Uganda in which beneficiaries were provided with information on the performance of their public facility in relation to regional and national standards. The impact of the report card was stunning. It raised both the level of health service utilization and provider attendance and, consequently, reduced infant mortality by one-third, increasing birth weight, and improving other health outcomes.

The link between these two pieces of evidence and long-term consequences is drawn from cohort studies primarily in developed countries that document long-term consequences of low birth weight and short stature during early childhood with long-term cognitive and health outcomes. Height at age three, which is a function of nutrition and health during infancy, affects cognitive skills in adulthood (Case, Lubotsky, and Paxson 2002). Other studies, such as Almond, Chay, and Lee (2005), demonstrate a link between mothers' health during gestation and long-term health and labor market outcomes of the children (for a review of these and other studies, see Smith (2009). Assuming that the same mechanisms operating in these developed countries also apply to developing countries, quiet corruption in health care that particularly affects early childhood outcomes has large and long-lasting effects on the competitiveness of an economy and the well-being of its citizens.

Private Sector and Agriculture

This section describes the long-term consequences of quiet corruption in the private sector and agriculture, areas with a high potential to contribute to economic growth and poverty reduction in Africa. While the prevalence of informal payments for services is widely documented for the private sector, evidence for quiet corruption in both the private sector and agriculture is sparse. Although enterprises are the immediate victims of corruption, our contention is that they do not always bear the ultimate burden because they can often pass on any increased costs to consumers.[21]

A growing body of evidence on the prevalence of quiet corruption in the private sector draws from recent surveys of firms in developing countries. Both the firms' experience of *actual* petty corruption and their *perception* of corruption as an impediment to firm operations were elicited on the survey. While these two sets of questions shed light on the extent and severity of petty corruption, the prevalence of quiet corruption has been difficult to document. However, a careful examination of the survey data is indicative of the contours of quiet corruption.

Table 4 shows results for five corruption indicators for the sub-Saharan African countries surveyed. The first four indicators report the likelihood that firms make any informal payments to obtain licenses, contracts, or other services. The last indicator measures the extent to which corruption is a major or severe constraint to the firms' operations. There is considerable variation in the extent to which firms expect to make informal payments. For example, the share of firms in Cape Verde, Mauritius, and Namibia expected to make informal payments is considerably lower than that of the Organisation for Economic Co-operation and Development (OECD) country average (Investment Climate Assessment 2009). Nevertheless, a large percentage of firms expect that they will make informal payments to obtain government services and contracts. In nearly half the countries (16 of 35), more than 50 percent of firms reported an expectation of having to make informal payments to "get things done." In particular, in Burkina Faso, Cameroon, Democratic Republic of Congo, Guinea, and Kenya, nearly four out of every five firms expected to make informal payments to obtain government services.

While many of these payments tend to be small, their high frequency makes them a considerable cost for firms. For example, Svensson (2003) reported that among Ugandan firms that paid bribes, the average amount of informal payments was equivalent to US $8,280 (a median US $1,820), corresponding to nearly 8 percent of the firms' total costs (1 percent at the median).

In the last column in Table 4, a large fraction of firms report that corruption is a major impediment to firm operations and growth. While it is hard to say how much of the firms' expectations of having to make informal payments are captured by this measure or the extent to which other business environment factors are more important constraints, this category likely incorporates forms of quiet corruption. The last row (Spearman Correlation) reports the results of the comparison between the corruption measures. The Spearman index[22] reveals a positive correlation between incidence measures and the perceived one. Yet, none of the associations is statistically significant, which suggests that the rankings reflect distinct impediments.

The discrepancy between perceived corruption and incidence of corruption has attracted a great deal of attention from scholars and policy makers.[23] Quiet corruption may help explain the divide. As noted by Herrera, Lijane, and Rodriguez (2008), perceived corruption partially captures the invisible element, notably the uncertainty stemming from engaging in corrupt transactions. For firms paying bribes, corruption has an immediate cost in the form of illegal payments—petty corruption—but also an additional cost represented by the capriciousness of interaction with public institutions.

Although corruption can be seen as a "tax" and might still allow companies to operate normally (Shleifer and Vishny 1993), the critical difference between a normal tax and the "corruption tax" is their predictability. In the first case, firms know the level and frequency of payments. In the case of corruption tax, capture by decentralized regulatory officials with considerable discretion engenders uncertainty about the level

Table 4 **Incidence of corruption and perceived corruption in sub-Saharan Africa countries**

	Incidence of corruption				Perceived corruption
	% of firms expected to pay informal payment to public officials (to get things done)	% of firms expected to give gifts to get an operating license	% of firms expected to give gifts in meetings with tax officials	% of firms expected to give gifts to secure a government contract	% of firms identifying corruption as a major constraint
Angola (2006)	46.8	10.08	14.84	38.45	36.06
Benin (2004)	57.65	41.25	21.21	75.43	83.85
Botswana (2006)	27.62	3.29	4.47	22.92	22.58
Burkina Faso (2006)	86.96	0	19.51	80.77	53.96
Burundi (2006)	56.46	40.26	22.63	44.36	19.72
Cameroon (2006)	77.6	50.81	65.43	85.23	52.05
Cape Verde (2006)	5.63	0	10.42	14.08	16.33
Congo, Dem. Rep. (2006)	83.79	66.25	64.42	80.54	20.02
Congo, Rep. (2009)	49.21	42.79	37.1	75.18	65.02
Côte d'Ivoire (2009)	30.64	31.8	13.62	32.34	74.99
Ethiopia (2006)	12.42	2.7	4.35	11.8	23.08
Gabon (2009)	26.09	0	22.81	26.61	41.35
Gambia, the (2006)	52.42	23.42	13.56	50.3	9.78
Ghana (2007)	38.77	22.6	18.08	61.23	9.86
Guinea (2006)	84.75	51.87	57.34	74.58	47.66
Guinea-Bissau (2006)	62.72	15.33	22.7	48.41	44.01
Kenya (2007)	79.22	28.75	32.25	71.2	38.35
Lesotho (2009)	13.96	3.34	9.2	26.37	46.71
Liberia (2009)	55.22	49.63	54.42	51.59	31.19
Madagascar (2009)	19.2	18.6	6.79	14.13	42.71
Malawi (2006)	35.65	4.92	15.33	12.26	46.84
Mali (2007)	28.88	24.04	31.08	80.35	15.7
Mauritania (2006)	82.12	33.23	48.23	76.16	17.1
Mauritius (2009)	1.59	0	0.28	8.81	50.72
Mozambique (2007)	14.84	6.87	9.79	31.65	25.36
Namibia (2006)	11.36	0	2.6	8.08	19.14
Niger (2006)	69.7	8.33	17.05	80	58.54
Nigeria (2007)	40.9	40.29	22.85	44.57	24.7
Rwanda (2006)	19.96	4.58	4.9	14.37	4.35
Senegal (2007)	18.12	21.09	18.66	36.32	23.84
Sierra Leone (2009)	18.8	8.71	8.58	33.85	36.87
South Africa (2007)	15.09	0	3.13	33.2	16.87
Tanzania (2006)	49.47	20.05	14.7	42.69	19.73
Uganda (2006)	51.7	12.86	14.53	46.43	23.57
Zambia (2007)	14.33	2.61	4.89	27.39	12.08
Spearman Correlation Index with perceived corruption	0.28	0.15	0.23	0.18	

Source of raw data: www.enterpisesurveys.org. The higher the percentage, the higher the incidence of and perceived corruption. No Spearman coefficient is statistically significant.

and frequency of informal payments. For example, an uncertain number of interactions with the revenue authority or electricity provider might be required to continue operations. By introducing uncertainty into the cost of regulatory and other publicly provided inputs, the capture of regulatory and other services increases the gap between actual and perceived corruption. The reported gap between perceived and actual corruption could be even larger, given that the existing firms are those that are relatively successful in operating in a corrupt environment. As a result of these selective concerns, Hausmann and Velasco (2005) questioned the reliability of firm-based perceptions of corruption. They note that a more telling indicator is the underlying industrial structure, because responses to quiet corruption in the private sector include a higher degree of informalization and a high market concentration of formal firms.

Weak regulation of agricultural inputs

Another example of the capture of the regulatory function of government that has grave consequences for reducing poverty and increasing economic growth is the market for fertilizers. As with the market for pharmaceuticals, asymmetric information between producers and farmers necessitates public regulation. National standards agencies are supposed to ensure that fertilizer sold on the market meets the required chemical composition consistent with extension recommendations and that packages sold are of the right weight. However, even in developed countries, where strict laws protect consumers from adulteration, the verification of fraud is a serious problem. This is because it is often not easy to trace back at which step of the production or sale the adulteration occurs. To address this problem, a common strategy of the national agencies (such as the U.S. Department of Agriculture) is to require some form of certification of dealers and to conduct spot checks through accredited laboratories.

Unfortunately, for many countries in sub-Saharan Africa, exercising this type of control might be out of reach. Many lack qualified laboratories, skilled staff, and technical tools for conducting even simple surveys. Furthermore, the modalities of product commercialization represent an obstacle for the controls; for example, while in developed countries, fertilizers are sold in bags, in Africa, in part due to the high cost, retail sellers

Box 1 **Quiet corruption in a port authority in Nigeria**

The Lagos port in Nigeria represents an interesting case of a poorly regulated business environment that gives way to quiet corruption episodes. In 2006, the reform of the Lagos port was praised as one of the best in sub-Saharan Africa in the last decade. Within a few months of operation under private ownership, productivity had risen at the container terminals. Chronic delays for berthing space had nearly vanished, leading shipping lines to reduce their congestion surcharge. However, the benefits of this reform did not last long. In February 2009, the Nigerian Ports Authority (NPA) announced a temporary but immediate suspension of ship entry to enable terminals to clear "alarming" backlogs. In addition, for vessels already heading into Lagos, the NPA considered diverting them elsewhere.

How could the situation deteriorate from the post-reform high to this point in less than three years? Raballand and Mjekiqi (2009) attribute it to a customs circular. On June 12, 2008, Customs management issued a circular (Customs Circular No. 026/2008) to disallow the clearance of goods that featured discrepancies such as lack of appropriate import clearance documents and false declaration. This circular, in fact, modified the behavior of some importers/customs brokers; priority clearance in favor of goods that were easily cleared was given, while the others were abandoned in the port. After the publication of this circular, the amount of uncleared and abandoned cargo started to grow and congestion increased.

There are two possible situations that explain cargo abandonment. Importers of prohibited goods or those with other related offences may abandon goods in the port, wait for "their" goods to be auctioned, and then bypass the import regulation to get their goods at a relatively low price. In the second scenario, an importer makes a false declaration including an undervaluation of declared goods and decides when caught to abandon the consignment in order to obtain the goods through auction, which, in any case, is cheaper than full payment of import duties with penalty fees for false declaration and incidental port charges. In both cases, the importer needs to be sure that during the auction process, his cargo will be assigned to him and not to another, which is where collusion with the Port Authority plays an important role. The result of the auction has to be known in advance; otherwise the importer would not abandon the cargo.

These cases present all the characteristics of quiet corruption. In an environment where regulations provide several loopholes, reckless businessmen with the connivance of public authorities manage to avoid clearance costs or to import prohibited goods. However, the mechanism used, abandonment of cargo that is recovered later via a public auction, has consequences, less visible in the short run, that go beyond the direct revenue loss of clearance evasion. As the Nigerian case shows, the long-run effect is the port congestion and delays in clearance that completely eliminated the benefits of the 2006 reform with obvious consequences on the competitiveness of Nigerian producers.

usually open the bags and sell small amounts (about 1–2 kg). This exposes the products to various forms of adulteration, such as addition of sand or substitution of cheaper and unsuitable fertilizer that consumers cannot easily detect. In addition, a particular type of fertilizer adulteration is the addition of heavy metals; varying amounts of arsenic, cadmium, chromium, lead, and nickel have been found in fertilizer materials in sub-Saharan Africa. These contaminants are difficult to detect but can cause serious harm if they get into the food chain.

Although there is little evidence of fertilizer adulteration in sub-Saharan Africa, there is empirical support for nutrient deficiencies in sold fertilizers. A survey of wholesalers by the International Fertilizer Development Center (IFDC 1995) on fertilizer quality in West Africa found that, of the 80 fertilizers analyzed, 43 percent lacked the appropriate nutrients. Of the 685 bags sampled, only 58 percent were within a negligible range of the indicated weight. In addition, 20 percent of the bags sampled did not have information on the type and concentration of nutrients. Furthermore, in only 7 percent of the cases did the labels contain the complete address of the responsible party. To compound the farmers' problem, the IFDC report suggests that frequent cases of deliberate adulteration occur at the retail level where sellers can easily add deleterious or harmful ingredients to increase the weight and sell underweight items or even completely misbranded products.

Episodes of mislabeled fertilizers sold at retail level were documented in Mali during the 1990s, when the country started to import low-cost, but poor quality, stocks from Nigeria (Morris et al. 2007) and more recently in Zimbabwe (Djurfeldt et al. 2005). A recent survey on fertilizers in Kenya (GDS 2005) shows that adulteration and sales of counterfeit products are isolated events. Nonetheless, among the products sold on the market, the survey documents a wide fluctuation in the nitrogen and phosphorus concentration, often not reported on the labels. Furthermore, about 3 to 5 percent of fertilizers are deliberately mislabeled in order to sell inferior quality fertilizers.

On the basis of anecdotal evidence and a more recent analysis conducted by the IFDC (2007) in sub-Saharan Africa, the situation doesn't seem to have improved substantially. A survey conducted in 2007 (IFDC 2007) documents the share of samples of poor-quality fertilizer sold in 10 African countries. Column 3 of Table 5 shows the percentage of fertilizers not satisfying quality standards. As the table illustrates, a considerable share of widely used fertilizers, such as NPK or urea, are of insufficient quality: they either show a high moisture or low nutrient content or simply are wrongly labeled. For typical African farmers, the cost of fertilizer and improved seeds accounts for a large share of their resources. At best, the use of defective inputs does not have any effect on yields, and at worst it degrades the soil. Voortmann (2009) documents that there are even cases of poor application that cause declining yields.

Similar lax regulation has been reported for other key inputs such as improved seeds. In this regard, survey evidence is non-existent and anecdotes from experts and other actors are the only window to misconduct in this area. For example, the lack of control enabled a dishonest company in Zimbabwe to buy sorghum grain from a late maturing variety and sell the same as an early maturing variety. The use the late maturing variety did not provide any grain unless the season was unusually long and completely jeopardized the harvest of many farmers.

While there is no reliable empirical evidence, misconduct that undermines the quality/suitability of agricultural inputs likely has important implications for agricultural productivity. Some recent empirical evidence is suggestive. Initial randomized

Table 5 **The prevalence of substandard fertilizers in West Africa**

Product	Total samples	Deficient samples	Percentage
Urea	50	4	8
Ammonium sulphate	7	2	28.6
Calcium ammonium nitrate (CAN)	9	3	33.3
Triple super phosphate (TSP)	4	0	0
Muriate of potash (MOP)	2	0	0
Diammonium phosphates (DAP)	19	1	5.3
Nitrogen phosphorus potassium (NPK)	54	19	35.2
Total	145	29	20

Note: One sample of ammonium nitrate is excluded.
Source: IFDC (2007).

experiments to measure the impact of fertilizer and improved seeds on yields of maize in Western Kenya found no impact as a result of defective seed or fertilizer. The most recent results of randomized evaluations in the same area, which show that higher than suggested levels of fertilizer use are the most cost-effective, could possibly reflect ineffective enforcement of standards (Duflo, Kremer, and Robinson 2008).

Long-term consequences for the private sector and agriculture

Quiet corruption modifies the structure of incentives for entrepreneurs and farmers to conduct business, which permanently alters their current and future investment decisions. Moreover, as discussed below, the negative effects go beyond the single performance of individual entrepreneurs or farmers. In the case of firms, quiet corruption acts as an additional fixed cost that pushes many companies out of the market or to the informal sector, leaving the most lucrative activities to a few large firms that are well connected with public authorities.[24] A recent paper on Paraguay illustrates the effects of capture of the regulatory function of government by producers. Auriol, Flauchelm, and Straub (2009) showed that, in sectors producing goods for more corrupt public institutions, the formal sector is dominated by a few large firms. These big formal players recoup the additional costs resulting from bribery by marking up prices and passing these costs on to consumers. Furthermore, thanks to their network of relationships with politicians, these big firms are able to obtain favorable access to inputs such as credit (Khwaja and Mian 2005; Li et al. 2008) or obtain a system of regulations biased against new entrants that de facto preserves their dominant position, or both. Hence, the long-run indirect consequences of quiet corruption are a less dynamic economy in which consumers face higher prices.

Evidence for the impact of corruption on increasing the degree of informalization of markets comes from the most recent Investment Climate Assessment data (2006–2009) (World Bank 2009).[25] In the latest round of interviews, entrepreneurs were asked to report the existence of informal competitors in their markets by responding yes or no to the question, "Does this establishment compete against unregistered or informal

Box 2 Quiet corruption in public utilities

In state-owned utilities providing power, telephone, and water services, quiet corruption takes a variety of forms including over-manning, undercollection of bills, and distribution losses. Recent estimates suggest that these forms of quiet corruption cost Africa some US $5.7 billion a year on aggregate, or just short of 1 percent of GDP (Foster and Briceno-Garmendia 2009).

Over-manning takes place when state-owned enterprises retain more employees than is strictly necessary to discharge their functions, often because of political pressure to provide jobs for members of certain interest groups. Over-manning is found to be particularly material in the case of state-owned telephone incumbents, which amount to US $1.5 billion a year, or 0.2 percent of GDP. These enterprises have on average only 94 connections per employee, compared to developing-country benchmarks of 420 connections per employee, an over-employment ratio of 600 percent.

Undercollection of bills is a result of lack of effort on the part of revenue collection officers or their petty corruption in collusion with consumers and is most frequently due to non-payment of bills by government departments. This problem is prevalent in power and water utilities, where non-payment can be found across the income spectrum and carries an overall cost of US $2.4 billion a year, or 0.4 percent of GDP.

Distribution losses take place when utilities fail to adequately maintain distribution networks and, in addition, tolerate clandestine connections, which amount to theft of scarce energy and water resources. African power utilities typically lose 23 percent of their energy in distribution losses. Similarly, African water utilities typically lose 35 percent of their water in distribution losses, nearly twice the 20 percent benchmark. These losses amount to US $1.8 billion a year, or 0.3 percent of GDP.

Table Distribution losses, undercollection, and over-manning costs as a percentage of GDP in sub-Saharan Africa's energy, information and communications technologies (ICT), and water and sanitation services (WSS) sectors

	Energy	ICT	WSS	Total
Distribution losses	0.2	—	0.1	0.3
Undercollection	0.3	—	0.1	0.4
Over-manning	0.0	0.2	0.0	0.2
Total	0.5	0.2	0.2	0.9

Source: Foster and Briceno-Garmendia (2009).

firms?" Table 6 presents the association between the degree of informalization of the market with perceived and experienced corruption. To improve comparisons, the sample is disaggregated by manufacturing and nonmanufacturing status and by the number of regular employees. A negative correlation indicates that as corruption increases, so does the degree of informalization (informalization is a yes/no question; yes= 0 and no=1)).

Table 6 shows that informalization is correlated with both perceived and experienced corruption, suggesting that corruption effectively acts as an entry barrier: many firms unable to afford extra costs are forced to remain in the informal market. This barrier applies in particular to firms with fewer than 35 employees and the retail and services sectors where rates of informality are higher.

While there is evidence of market concentration in Africa, only a few cases document the effect of corruption on market structure.[26] Fafchamps (2004) finds that a small group of well-connected traders captures the most lucrative markets, leaving the remainder to small, inefficient firms that are unable to scale up and challenge these traders' dominant position. In addition, the social network these big firms create plays an important role by limiting competition from outsiders. Ramachandran, Shah, and Tata (2007) are more direct in describing this capture as a "capacity of lobbying"; although generally less efficient, these large, formal firms are better connected, thus protecting their high profit margins by resisting external competition. It follows that, although African markets were broadly liberalized in the 1980s and 1990s, a few enterprises with high market share were able to retain their market power by investing resources in their relationships with the government. Thus quiet corruption acts as a constraint on the competitiveness of African manufacturing and the growth and poverty reduction benefits of private-sector development.

In addition to reinforcing a non-dynamic private sector, quiet corruption in the transport sector further diminishes the prospects of African manufacturing. This is shown by Teravaninthorn and Raballand (2008), who constructed a dataset of transport costs and prices covering 11 routes and 7 countries.[27] Their analysis showed that prices in the main corridors in Africa were higher than in other regions. Furthermore, most of these prices were not supported by the underlying structure of costs, since the transport sector is labor-intensive and wages in Africa are relatively low. For example, in 2007, in China, the average transport price was 5 US cents per ton-kilometer, while in Africa in the Durban-Lusaka corridor it was 6 cents, 8 cents for the Mombasa-Kampala route, and 11 cents for the Douala-Ndjaména corridor. Given that the underlying costs of providing these services are not higher than in China, the only plausible explanation for the price differences is market power. Teravaninthorn and Raballand specifically considered the cost of corruption and found two crucial results. The "corruption tax" in the form of levies that policemen and custom officials charge is significant in West Africa. Such costs account for about 20 to 27 percent of variable operating costs in some corridors, although this "tax" is almost insignificant in Eastern and Southern Africa (1 percent). Yet, this is only the visible part of corruption, the measurable component. Much more important is the untraceable part represented by the extra costs transport companies face when dealing with allocation of freight. It goes without saying that often these "extra costs" are not charged in exchange for any service but are explicitly imposed to create an entry barrier to potential competitors. Insiders, often well connected with the ruling regimes, thus compensate for these costs by imposing very high markups on prices and

Table 6 Correlation between perceived market informalization and incidence of perceived corruption

	% of firms expected to give gifts in meetings with tax officials	% of firms identifying corruption as a major constraint
Total	−0.1011**	−0.1256**
Manufacturing	−0.0955**	−0.0935**
Non-manufacturing	−0.1100**	−0.1319**
No. of employees: 1–6	−0.1368**	−0.0822**
No. of employees: 7–9	−0.0894**	−0.1937**
No. of employees: 10–15	−0.1060**	−0.2136**
No. of employees: 16–35	−0.1354**	−0.1412**
No. of employees: over 35	−0.1079**	−0.0291

**Significant at 5%
Source of raw data: ICA (2009).

enjoy all the benefits of a monopoly. This ultimately enables truckers and freight forwarders to pass on much of these additional costs to final users.

While empirical evidence of the transport case of quiet corruption described above is difficult to find, a striking example of transport market reform in Rwanda after 1994 sheds light on the potential gains that arise from thoroughly addressing the problems quiet corruption can generate. After a radical reform of the transport sector that eliminated entry barriers to the transport market, prices declined by more than 30 percent in nominal terms and almost 75 percent in real terms. This result can be largely attributed to elimination of quiet corruption in the transport sector, since no major investment in infrastructure was carried out during this period in Rwanda.

As with the health care and education sectors, more investment in the transport sector does not necessarily mean that service conditions improve. In fact, the case of transport reform in Rwanda clearly reveals that seriously addressing the effect of quiet corruption, that is the cartelized market structure of the trucking industry, might induce effective gains that eclipse any other potential benefit arising from a pure increase in expenditures. Teravaninthorn and Raballand (2008) noted that, although the condition of African roads is worse than those in other parts of the world, an investment in their improvement is not necessarily bound to succeed in transport price reduction.

Moving on to the long-term effects of quiet corruption on farmers' investment decisions, two main triggers can be identified. In the first case, farmers indirectly pay the cost of the corruption tax that emanates from other sectors. As explained earlier, markets in Africa are generally not competitive and the market of agricultural inputs is not an exception. To the contrary, these products are often imported (Svensson 2003), which leads to even higher informal payments. The high prices of fertilizer force the minority of farmers that purchase fertilizer to use it in rather small doses.

As pointed out earlier, lax regulation of fertilizer quality compounds the affordability problem and often leads to a negligible impact on yields; poor quality fertilizers may even damage crops. Hence, in the long run, farmers that find no increase in yields or find decreases may be driven to reduce or even completely avoid using fertilizers, turning to a low-input type of agriculture. This type of agriculture, as widely documented in literature, is bound to produce low yield and is more exposed to natural shocks.

Final remarks

It is becoming widely accepted that improving service delivery to the poor is both a widespread political demand and central to the realization of the MDGs. Improving governance is integral to achieving these goals. Where transparency and accountability mechanisms are weak or lacking, poor people are often marginalized and development outcomes suffer. This essay attempts to unveil the iceberg that threatens to sink Africa's efforts to improve well being and growth by documenting a broadened scope of corruption beyond the behaviors recently brought to light by innovative survey tools and inspired by *World Development Report 2004*. As discussed, some of these behaviors are not readily observed or are difficult to measure, but their long-term consequences are often severe and cannot be ignored by policy makers, citizens, international institutions, and donor organizations.

This essay outlined a framework to understand the nature and impact of quiet corruption, which captures the implicit and less tangible forms of corruption. The quiet corruption approach embraces the recognition that government spending on social services alone is not sufficient to understand the quantity and quality of public services or the determinants of public service delivery performance. This approach looks at issues that are complementary to the more visible forms of corruption and have broad implications for strategies and policies that focus on results.

Examples of the existence and consequences of quiet corruption—such as the case of low teacher instruction time that leads to poor competencies and ends with the decision of households to disenroll a child—highlighted how quiet corruption can lead to substantial long-term impacts on poverty. The good news is that quiet corruption can be tackled. The report card example from Uganda—in which beneficiaries were provided with information from the second generation of corruption indicators on the performance of their public health facility in relation to regional and national standards and its impacts on the level of health service utilization and provider attendance—confirms this.

Progress in service delivery has been possible because of the increasing determination of governments to deal with corruption, as well as the increasing availability of information on finances, inputs, outputs, pricing, and oversight of public service provision by civil society, which are being used to generate information on performance and to track absenteeism, leakage of funds, and informal user fees. The way forward, however, will require the development of a third generation of indicators—ones that measure quality of services and the performance of service providers. A recent intervention to improve education services in Uttar Pradesh highlights the features that new projects and programs need to incorporate (Banerjee et al. 2008). By teaching households with very little schooling to identify children who are struggling in school, the intervention empowered households to evaluate service quality.

As quiet corruption manifests differently in each economic sector, there is no "one size fits all" recommendation that applies to each and every sector. But vital to fighting quiet corruption at large are strong and highly motivated leadership, commitment of the national anticorruption units to pursue operationally effective responses at the sector level, and good policies and institutions. Equally important is more transparency and increasing accountability and participation by citizens, the "demand side" for good governance. Success will also require the establishment of strategies for addressing weaknesses in existing governance capacity and accountability in the delivery of services. Strengthening enforcement and administrative control, management of public finance, government decentralization, systematic dissemination of information about projects and budgets, and investments in human capital are also essential. Successful implementation of anticorruption reforms will also require that the preferences of all those involved be aligned with achieving the objectives or goals of the reform. This often involves better working conditions.

Of course, given the complexity of the task, the fight against quiet corruption requires tailoring policies to country circumstances, recognizing that priorities and responses may vary depending on the different country conditions. This essay outlines a research agenda to identify interventions to address quiet corruption. Experimenting with various ways to empower beneficiaries and continuing the ongoing efforts to tackle big-time corruption will go a long way toward this goal. Indeed, although combating loud corruption is necessary, fighting quiet corruption is critical if governments want to reduce poverty and promote sustainable growth.

Notes

1. See, for example, Rajkumar and Swaroop (2008) and Amin, Das, and Goldstein (2009).

2. Gupta, Davoodi, and Tiongson (2000) show that corruption is associated with higher levels of infant mortality and school dropout and lower birth weight.

3. Early evidence of negative association between political corruption and development comes from Mauro (1995) and Kaufmann and Wei (1999). For the negative relationship between corruption and the capacity to attract foreign direct investments, see Wei (2000). Tanzi (1998) reviews some of the evidence and finds support that corruption is associated with lower government revenue receipts and also alters the composition of public spending away from productive sectors. Other evidence comes from Baldacci et al. (2004) and Gupta et al. (2000). A recent strand of literature has extended this analysis to examine the extent to which these relationships are affected by institutional quality or the level of corruption (Meon and Sekkat 2005; Mendez and Sepulveda 2006; Aidt 2009).

4. See Scott (1972) for a broad overview of the various forms of political corruption.

5. Harsch (1993); Wunsch (2000).

6. See Olson (1965).

7. See Harsch (1993).

8. See Hirshmann (1970) in this regard.

9. Recent Annual School Censuses use a similar head-teacher reported measure of absence.

10. The 2002 data come from Chaudhury et al. (2006), while the 2007 estimate is from Habyarimana (2007).

11. Two districts in western Kenya.

12. This result suggests that low teacher remuneration is not a major determinant of teacher absence. In fact, the evidence on the relationship between performance pay and teacher absence is quite mixed. Duflo, Hanna, and Ryan (2008) find a positive effect on attendance of a pay-for-inputs performance contract in non-formal schools in India. On the contrary, Glewwe, Kremer, Moulin, and Zitzewitz (2004) and Muralidharan and Sundaraman (2006) do not find evidence of a teacher attendance response to output-based performance pay.

13. Since direct observation requires enumerators to physically establish attendance, the presence of an outsider in a school could be driving some of these "in-school effort" measures and therefore casting some doubt over the validity of these estimates. In addition, they could be affected by the fact that different pedagogical styles entail different levels of direct teacher-pupil interaction.

14. PETS have some important limitations in only being able to define leakage unambiguously for funding flows with clear rules, such as teacher salaries or capitation grants. Given that some important resource flows in some education systems are not rule-based, it is difficult to accurately characterize the extent of leakage.

15. There is evidence of an association between the frequency of inspection and the level of teacher absenteeism (see Chaudhury 2006).

16. The Health Unit Management Committees were established with the objective of overseeing the management of the public health facility. It consists of public health providers together with members of the community.

17. Evidence of the perception of absenteeism in particular in Latin America corroborates these findings. Surveys of hospital nurses' perceptions of the frequency of chronic absenteeism among doctors reported rates of 98 percent in Costa Rica, 30 percent in Nicaragua, 38 percent in Colombia (Giedion, Morales, and Acosta 2001) and 24–31 percent across public and social security hospitals

in Argentina (Schargrodsky, Mera, and Weinschelbaum 2001).

18. Vignettes are hypothetical cases presented to doctors in order to estimate doctor quality. Doctor questions, diagnostics, and prescriptions are compared to expert panels or existing protocols.

19. The so-defined "good manufacturing practice."

20. WHO guidelines on breastfeeding have been relaxed to accommodate the poor availability or suitability of formula.

21. The ability to pass on corruption-related costs to consumers is subject to, among other factors, the demand conditions and market structure.

22. Spearman's rank correlation coefficient is used to analyze the correspondence between the ranking defined by incidence of corruption measures and the ranking obtained by the perceived corruption measure. A positive but insignificant rank correlation suggests that, although higher magnitudes in one indicator occur along with higher magnitudes in the other indicator, the two rankings reflect distinct sources of impediments.

23. In this regard it is worth mentioning the contributions from Kaufmann and Kraay (2007), Gelb et al. (2007), and Gonzalez et al. (2007).

24. The issues of political lobbying and corruption that are focused on obtaining privileged access to rent-seeking activities and the economic and social costs of rent-seeking are broadly treated in the literature. See, for example, Baghawati (1982) and Krusell and Rios-Rull (1996).

25. For an interesting case of high market informalization caused by corruption, see Auriol et al. (2009) on Paraguay.

26. See Biggs and Srivastava (1996) and Van Biesebroeck (2005).

27. Burkina Faso, Cameroon, Chad, Ghana, Kenya, Uganda, and Zambia.

References

Aidt, T. 2009. "Corruption, Institutions, and Economic Development." *Oxford Review of Economic Policy* 25 (2): 271–91.

Akunyili, D. 2005. "Counterfeit and Substandard Drugs, Nigeria's Experience: Implications, Challenges, Actions and Recommendations." Paper presented at World Bank Meeting for Key Interest Groups in Health, Washington, DC, March 11.

Almond, D., K. Chay, and D. Lee. 2005. "The Costs of Low Birth Weight." *Quarterly Journal of Economics* 120 (3): 1031–83.

Almond, D., L. Edlund, H. Li, and J. Zhang. 2006. "Long-Term Effects of the 1959–1961 China Famine: Mainland China and Hong Kong." NBER Working Paper No. 13384. New York: Columbia University.

Amin, S., J. Das, and M. Goldstein. 2009. *Are You Being Served? New Tools for Measuring Service Delivery.* Washington, DC: World Bank.

Angrist, J., and V. Lavy. 2001. "Does Teacher Training Affect Pupil Learning? Evidence from Matched Comparisons in Jerusalem Public Schools." *Journal of Labor Economics* 19 (2): 343–69.

Auriol, E., T. Flochelm, and S. Straub. 2009. "'La Patria Contratista': Public Procurement and Rent-Seeking in Paraguay." Unpublished manuscript.

Baldacci, E., B. Clements, S. Gupta, and C. Mulas-Granados. 2004. "Persistence of Fiscal Adjustments and Expenditure Composition in Low-Income Countries." In S. Gupta, B. Clements, and G. Inchauste (eds.), *Helping Countries Develop: The Role of Fiscal Policy,* 48–66. Washington, DC: International Monetary Fund.

Banerjee, A., A. Deaton, and E. Duflo. 2004. ìWealth, Health and Health Services in Rural Rajasthan.î *American Economic Review* 94 (2): 326ñ30.

Banerjee, A., R. Banerji, E. Duflo, R. Glennerster, and S. Khemani. 2008. "Pitfalls of Participatory Programs: Evidence from a Randomized Evaluation in Education in India," Unpublished manuscript.

Barker, D. J. P. 1998. *Mothers, Babies and Diseases in Later Life.* London: Churchill Livingstone.

Barker, D. J. P., P. D. Gluckman, K. M. Godfrey, J. E. Harding, J. A. Owens, and J. S. Robinson. 1995. "Fetal Nutrition and Cardiovascular Disease in Adult Life." *Lancet* 341: 938–41.

Bhagwati, J. 1982. "Directly Unproductive, Profit Seeking (DUP) Activities." *Journal of Political Economy* 90: 998–1002.

Biggs, T., and P. Srivastava. 1996. "Structural Aspects of Manufacturing in sub-Saharan Africa: Findings from a Seven Country Enterprise Survey." World Bank Discussion Paper No. 346, Africa Technical Department Series. Washington, DC: World Bank.

Björkman, M. 2006. "Does Money Matter for Student Performance? Evidence from a Grant Program in Uganda." Innocenzo Gasparini Institute for Economic Research Working Paper No. 326. Milan: Bocconi University.

Björkman, M., and J. Svensson. 2007. "Power to the People: Evidence from a Randomized Field Experiment of a Community-Based Monitoring Project in Uganda." World Bank Policy Research Working Paper No. 4268. Washington, DC: World Bank.

Bruns, B., A. Mingat, and R. Rakatomalala. 2003. "A Chance for Every Child: Achieving Universal Primary Education by 2015." Washington, DC: World Bank.

Case, A., D. Lubotsky, and C. Paxson. 2002. "Economic Status and Health in Childhood: The Origins of the Gradient." *The American Economic Review* 92 (5): 1308–34.

Case, A., and C. Paxson, 2008. "Stature and Status: Height, Ability, and Labor Market Outcomes." *Journal of Political Economy* 116 (3): 499–532.

Chaudhury, N., J. S. Hammer, M. Kremer, K. Muralidharan, and F. Halsey Rogers. 2006. "Missing in Action: Teacher and Health Worker Absence in Developing Countries." *Journal of Economic Perspectives* 20 (1): 91–116.

Cohen J. C., M. F. Mrazek., L. Hawkins. 2007. "Corruption and Pharmaceuticals: Strengthening Good Governance to Improve Access." In J. E. Campos and S. Pradhan (eds.), *The Many Faces of Corruption.* Washington, DC: World Bank.

Cutler, D., W. Fung, M. Kremer, M. Singhal, and T. Vogl. 2007. "Mosquitoes: The Long-Term Effects of Malaria Eradication in India." National Bureau for Economic Research Working Paper No. 13539. Cambridge, MA: NBER.

Dang, H. A., and H. Rogers. 2008. "The Growing Phenomenon of Private Tutoring: Does It Deepen Human Capital, Widen Inequalities, or Waste Resources?" *World Bank Research Observer* 23 (2): 161–200.

Das, J., S. Dercon, J. Habyarimana, and P. Krishnan. 2004. "When Can School Inputs Improve Test Scores?" Policy Research Working Paper No. 3217. Washington, DC: World Bank.

Das J., S. Dercon, J. Habyarimana, and P. Krishnana. 2007. "Teacher Shocks and Student Learning: Evidence from Zambia." *Journal of Human Resources* 42 (4): 820–62.

Das, J., and J. Hammer. 2005. "Which Doctor? Combining Vignettes and Item Response to Measure Clinical Competence." *Journal of Development Economics* 78 (2): 348–83.

Das, J., and K. Leonard. 2009. "Use of Vignettes to Measure the Quality of Health Care." In S. Amin, J. Das, and M. Goldstein (eds.). *Are You Being Served? New Tools for Measuring Service Delivery*, 299–312. Washington, DC: World Bank.

Deininger, K., and P. Mpuga. 2004. "Economic and Welfare Effects of the Abolition of Health User Fees: Evidence from Uganda." Policy Research Working Paper No. 3276. Washington, DC: World Bank.

Djurfeldt, G., H. Holmen, M. Jirström, and R. Larsson. 2005. *The African Food Crisis: Lessons from the Asian Green Revolution.* Cambridge, MA: CABI Publishing.

Duflo, E., R. Hanna, and S. Ryan. 2008. "Monitoring Works: Getting Teachers to Come to School." Mimeo, Massachusetts Institute of Technology.

Duflo E., M. Kremer, and J. Robinson. 2008. "How High are Rates of Return to Fertilizer? Evidence from Field Experiments in Kenya." Paper presented at the American Economic Association Meeting, New Orleans.

Fafchamps, M. 2004. *Market Institutions in sub-Saharan Africa.* Cambridge, MA: Massachusetts Institute of Technology Press.

Ferraz, C., F. Finan, and D. B. Moreira. 2009. "Corrupting Learning: Evidence from Missing Federal Education Funds in Brazil." Unpublished manuscript.

Ferrinho, P., M. C. Omar, M. de Jesus Fernandes, P. Blaise, M. Bugalho, and W. Van Lerberghe. 2004. "Pilfering for Survival: How Health Workers Use Access to Drugs as a Coping Strategy." *Human Resources for Health* 2 (4): 1–6.

Filmer, D., J. S. Hammer, and L. H. Pritchett. 2000. "Weak Links in the Chain: A Diagnosis of Health Policy in Poor Countries." *World Bank Research Observer* 15 (2): 199–224.

Foster, V., and C. M. Briceno-Garmendia (eds.). 2009. *Africa's Infrastructure: A Time for Transformation.* Washington, DC: World Bank.

Gauthier, B. 2006. "PETS-QSDS in sub-Saharan Africa: A Stocktaking Study." Study commissioned by the World Bank as part of the project Measuring Progress in Public Services Delivery. Washington, DC: World Bank.

Gauthier, B., and W. Wane. 2006. "Leakage of Public Resources in the Health Sector: An Empirical Investigation of Chad." Paper presented at the Center for the Study of African Economies Conference, Oxford, UK.

GDS (Global Development Solutions). 2005. "From Laboratory to the Dining Table: Tracing the Value Chain of Kenyan Maize." Global Development Solutions, LLC. Prepared for World Bank.

Gelb, A., V. Ramachandran , M. Kedia Shah, and G. Turner. 2007. "What Matters to African Firms? The Relevance of Perceptions Data." Policy Research Working Paper No. 4446. Washington, DC: World Bank.

Giedion, U., L. G. Morales, and O. L. Acosta. 2001. "The Impact of Health Reforms on Irregularities in

Bogotá Hospitals." In R. Di Tella and W. D. Savedoff (eds.), *Diagnosis Corruption.* Washington, DC: Inter-American Development Bank.

Glewwe, P., M. Kremer, S. Moulin, and E. Zitzewitz. 2004. "Retrospective vs. Prospective Analyses of School Inputs: The Case of Flip Charts in Kenya." *Journal of Development Economics* 74 (1): 251–68.

Glewwe, P., M. Kremer, and S. Moulin. 2009. "Many Children Left Behind? Textbooks and Test Scores in Kenya." *American Economic Journal: Applied Economics* 1 (1): 112–35.

Goldstein, M., J. Graff-Zivin, J. Habyarimana, C. Pop-Eleches, and H. Thirumurthy. 2009. "Health Worker Absence, HIV Testing and Behavioral Change: Evidence from Western Kenya." Unpublished manuscript.

Gonzalez, A., J. E. Lopez-Cordova, and E. Valladares. 2007. "The Incidence of Graft on Developing Country Firms." Policy Research Working Paper No. 4394. Washington, DC: World Bank.

Gupta, S., H. Davoodi, and E. Tiongson. 2000. "Corruption and the Provision of Health Care and Education Services." IMF Working Paper, WP/00/116. Washington, DC: International Monetary Fund.

Gupta, S., L. de Mello, and R. Sharan. 2000. "Corruption and Military Spending." IMF Working Paper, WP/00/23. Washington, DC: International Monetary Fund.

Habyarimana, J. 2007. "The Determinants of Teacher Absenteeism: Evidence from Panel Data from Uganda." Mimeo, Georgetown University.

Halsey Rogers, F., and E. Vegas. 2009. "No More Cutting Class? Reducing Teacher Absence and Providing Incentives for Performance." Policy Research Working Paper No. 4847. Washington, DC: World Bank.

Hanushek, E., J. Kain, and S. Rivkin. 2005. "Teachers, Schools and Academic Achievement." *Econometrica* 73 (2): 417–58.

Harsch, E. 1993. "Accumulators and Democrats: Challenging State Corruption in Africa." *Journal of Modern African Studies* 31 (1): 31–48.

Hausmann, R., and A. Velasco. 2005. "Slow Growth in Latin America: Common Outcomes, Common Causes." Center for International Development, Harvard University. Unpublished manuscript.

Herrera, A. M., L. Lijane, and P. Rodriguez. 2008. "Bribery and the Nature of Corruption." Unpublished manuscript.

Hirschmann, A. O. 1970. *Exit, Voice and Loyalty: Responses to Decline in Firms, Organizations and States.* Cambridge, MA: Harvard University Press.

IFDC (International Fertilizer Development Center). 1995. "The Quality of Fertilizers in West Africa." Miscellaneous Fertilizer Studies No. 13. Muscle Shoals. AL: IFDC.

IFDC (International Fertilizer Development Center). 2007. "Assessment of Quality and Truth in Labeling of Fertilizers in Africa" Fertilizer Quality and Content Report. Muscle Shoals. AL: IFDC.

Investment Climate Assessment (ICA). 2009. On the website: http://www.enterprisesurveys.org/

Kaufmann, D., and S. Wei. 1999. "Does 'Grease Money' Speed Up the Wheels of Commerce?" National Bureau for Economic Research Working Paper No. 7093. New York: NBER.

Kaufmann, D., and A. Kraay. 2007. "Governance Indicators: Where We Are, Where We Should Be Going." Policy Research Working Paper No. 4370. Washington, DC: World Bank.

Khwaja, A. I., and A. Mian. 2005. "Do Lenders Favor Politically Connected Firms? Rent Provision in an Emerging Financial Market." *Quarterly Journal of Economics* 120 (4): 1371–1411.

Kremer, M., E. Miguel, and R. Thornton. 2004. "Incentives to Learn." NBER Working Paper No. 10971. Cambridge, MA: NBER.

Krusell, P., and J.V. Rios-Rull. 1996. "Vested Interests in a Positive Theory of Stagnation and Growth." *Review of Economic Studies* 63: 301–329.

Jayachandran, S. 2008. "Incentives to Teach Badly? After-School Tutoring in Developing Countries." Unpublished manuscript.

Leive, A., and K. Xu. 2008. "Coping with Out-of-pocket Health Payments: Empirical Evidence from 15 African

Countries." *Bulletin of the World Health Organization* 86 (11): 849–856.

Leonard, K. L., and M. C. Masatu. 2005. "The Use of Direct Clinician Observation and Vignettes for Health Services Quality Evaluation in Developing Countries." *Social Science and Medicine* 61 (9): 1944–51.

Leonard, K. L., and M. C. Masatu. 2007. "Reexamining the Gap between Medical Ability and Practice Using the Hawthorne Effect." University of Maryland. Unpublished manuscript.

Li, H., L. Meng, Q. Wang, and L. A. Zhou. 2008. "Political Connections, Financing and Firm Performance: Evidence from 44 Chinese Private Firms." *Journal of Development Economics* 87 (2): 283–99.

Lindelow, M., P. Serneels, and T. Lemma. 2005. "The Performance of Health Workers in Ethiopia Results from Qualitative Research." Policy Research Working Paper No. 3558. Washington, DC: World Bank.

Macq, J., and W. Van Lerberghe. 2000. "Managing Health Services in Developing Countries: Moonlighting to Serve the Public?" In P. Ferrinho and W.Van Lerberghe (eds.), *Providing Health Care under Adverse Conditions: Health Personnel Performance and Individual Coping Strategies.* Antwerp: ITG Press.

Mauro, P. 1995. "Corruption and Growth." *Quarterly Journal of Economics* 110: 681–712.

McPake, B., E. Asiimwe, F. Mwesigye, M. Ofumb, P. Streefland, and A. Turinde. 2000. "Coping Strategies of Health Workers in Uganda." In P. Ferrinho and W.Van Lerberghe (eds.), *Providing Health Care under Adverse Conditions: Health Personnel Performance and Individual Coping Strategies.* Antwerp: ITG Press.

Mendez, F., and F. Sepulveda. 2006. "Corruption, Growth and Political Regimes: Cross-country Evidence." *European Journal of Political Economy* 22 (1): 82–98.

Meon, P. G., and K. Sekkat. 2005. "Does Corruption Grease or Sand the Wheels of Growth?" *Public Choice* 122: 69–97.

Mizala, A., and P. Romaguera. 2004. "School and Teacher Performance Incentives: The Latin American Experience." Mimeo, University of Chile.

Morris, M., V. A. Kelly, R. J. Kopicki, and D. Byerlee. 2007. "Fertilizer Use in Africa, Lessons Learned and Good Practice Guide." Washington, DC: World Bank.

Muralidharan, K., and V. Sundararman. 2006. "Teacher Incentives in Developing Countries: Experimental Evidence from India." Mimeo, University of California, San Diego.

Newton, P., S. Proux, M. Green, F. Smithuis, J. Rozendaal, and others. 2001. "Fake Artesunate in Southeast Asia" *Lancet* 357 (9272): 1948–50.

Olson, M. 1965. *The Logic of Collective Action.* Cambridge, MA: Harvard University Press.

Park, A., and E. Hannum. 2002. "Do Teachers Affect Learning in Developing Countries? Evidence from Student-Teacher Data from China." Unpublished manuscript.

Patrinos, H. A., and R. Kagia. 2007. "Maximizing the Performance of Education Systems: The Case of Teacher Absenteeism." In J. E. Campos and S. Pradhan (eds.), *The Many Faces of Corruption.* Washington, DC: World Bank.

Paviot, L., N. Heinsohn, and J. Korkman. 2008. "Extra Tuition in Southern and Eastern Africa: Coverage, Growth, and Linkages with Pupil Achievement." *International Journal of Educational Development* 28 (2): 149–60.

Postlethwaite, N. 1998. "The Condition of Primary Schools in Least Developed Countries." *International Review of Education* 44 (4): 289–317.

Raballand, G., and E. Mjekiqi. 2009. "Nigeria's Trade Policy Facilitates Unofficial Trade but not Manufacturing." Unpublished manuscript.

Rajkumar, A. S., and V. Swaroop. 2008. "Public Spending and Outcomes: Does Governance Matter?" *Journal of Development Economics* 86: 96–111.

Ramachandran, V., M. K. Shah, and G. M. Tata. 2007. "How Does Influence-Peddling Impact Industrial Competition? Evidence from Enterprise Surveys in Africa." Working Paper No. 127. Washington, DC: Center for Global Development.

Ramakrishnan, U., R. Manjrekar, J. Rivera, T. Gonzales-Cossio, and R. Martorell. 1999. "Micronutrients and Pregnancy Outcomes: A Review of Literature." *Nutrition Research* 19 (1): 103–59.

Razafindrakoto, M., and F. Roubaud. 2006. "Are International Databases on Corruption Reliable? A Comparison of Expert Opinion Surveys and Household Surveys in sub-Saharan Africa." Manuscript, Institut de Recherche pour le Developpement (IRD/DIAL), Paris, France. Available at http://www.dial.prd.fr/dial_publications/PDF/Doc_travail/2006-17_english.pdf

Reinikka, R., and J. Svensson. 2005. "Fighting Corruption to Improve Schooling: Evidence from a Newspaper Campaign in Uganda." *Journal of the European Economic Association* 3 (2-3): 259–67.

Reinikka, R., and J. Svensson. 2006. "Using Micro-Surveys to Measure and Explain Corruption." *World Development* 34 (2): 359–70.

de Sardan, O. 1999. "A Moral Economy of Corruption in Africa." *Journal of Modern African Studies* 37 (1): 25-52.

de Savigny, D., H. Kasale, C. Mbuya, and G. Reid. 2008. *Fixing Health Systems* (2nd ed.). Ottawa, ON (Canada): International Development Research Centre.

Schargrodsky, E., J. Mera, and F. Weinschelbaum. 2001. "Transparency and Accountability in Argentina's Hospitals." In R. Di Tella and W.D. Savedoff (eds.), *Diagnosis Corruption.* Washington, DC: Inter-American Development Bank.

Scott, J. 1972. *Comparative Political Corruption.* Englewood Cliffs, NJ: Prentice-Hall.

Shleifer, A., and R. Vishny. 1993. "Corruption." *The Quarterly Journal of Economics* 108 (3): 599–617.

Schwalbach, J., M. Abdula, Y. Adam, and Z. Khan. 2000. "Good Samaritan or Exploiter of Illness? Coping Strategies of Mozambican Health Care Providers." In P. Ferrinho and W. Van Lerberghe (eds.), *Providing Health Care under Adverse Conditions: Health Personnel Performance and Individual Coping Strategies.* Antwerp: ITG Press.

Smith, J. 2009. "The Impact of Childhood Health on Adult Labor Market Outcomes." *Review of Economics and Statistics* 91 (3): 478–89.

Svensson, J. 2003. "Who Must Pay Bribes and How Much? Evidence from a Cross-Section of Firms." *Quarterly Journal of Economics* 142: 207–29.

Tanzi, V. 1998. "Corruption Around the World: Causes, Scope and Cures." IMF Working Paper WP/98/63. Washington, DC: International Monetary Fund.

Teravaninthorn, S., and G. Raballand. 2008. "*Transport Process and Costs in Africa, A Review of the Main International Corridors.*" Washington, DC: World Bank.

Transparency International. 2005. *Stealing the Future: Corruption in the Classroom, Ten Real World Experiences.* Berlin: Transparency International.

Transparency International. 2006. "Corruption in Hospitals." Global Corruption Report 2006. Berlin: Transparency International.

Van Biesebroeck, J. 2005. "Firm Size Matters: Growth and Productivity Growth in African Manufacturing." *Economic Development and Cultural Change* 53 (3): 545–83.

Voortman, R. L. 2009. "Explorations into African Land Resource Ecology; On the Chemistry Between Soils, Plants and Fertilizers." (Free University Amsterdam Ph.D. thesis, forthcoming).

Wagstaff, A., and M. Claeson. 2004. *The Millennium Development Goals for Health: Rising to the Challenges.* Washington, DC: World Bank.

Wei, S. 2000. "How Taxing Is Corruption on International Investors?" *Review of Economics and Statistics* 82: 1–11.

World Bank. 2003. *World Development Report 2004: Making Services Work for Poor People.* New York: Oxford University Press.

World Bank. 2009. *African Development Indicators 2008/2009: Youth and Employment in Africa. The Potential, the Problem, the Promise.* Washington, DC: World Bank.

Wunsch, J. S. 2000. "Refunding the African State and Local Self Governance: The Neglected Foundation." *Journal of Modern African Studies* 38 (3): 487–509.

Indicator tables

Users guide

Tables

The tables are numbered by section. Countries are listed alphabetically by subregion (Sub-Saharan Africa and North Africa). Indicators are shown for the most recent year or period for which data are available and, in most tables, for an earlier year or period (usually 1980, 1990, or 1995). Time series data are available on the Africa Development Indicators CD-ROM and ADI Online. The term *country,* used interchangeably with *economy,* does not imply political independence but refers to any territory for which authorities report separate social or economic statistics. Known deviations from standard definitions or breaks in comparability over time or across countries are footnoted in the tables. When available data are deemed too weak to provide reliable measures of levels and trends or do not adequately adhere to international standards, the data are not shown.

Aggregate measure for region and subclassifications

The aggregates are based on the World Bank's regional classification for Sub-Saharan Africa and North Africa, which may differ from common geographic usage. Former Spanish Sahara is not included in any aggregates.

Statistics

Data are shown for economies as they were constituted in 2007, and historical data are revised to reflect current political arrangements. Exceptions are noted in the tables. Consistent time-series data for 1961–2008 are available on the Africa Development Indicators CD-ROM and ADI Online. Data for some indicators, including macroeconomic statistics, Doing Business indicators, investment climate indicators, governance and anticorruption indicators, and Country Policy and Institutional Assessment ratings are provided for later years (usually 2009–10).

Data consistency, reliability, and comparability

Considerable effort has been made to harmonize the data, but full comparability cannot be assured, and care must be taken in interpreting indicators. Many factors affect data availability, comparability, and reliability. Data coverage may be incomplete because of circumstances affecting the collection and reporting of data, such as conflicts. Although drawn from sources thought to be the most authoritative, data should be construed as indicating trends and characterizing differences across economies. Discrepancies in data presented in different editions of *Africa Development Indicators* reflect updates from countries as well as revisions to historical series and changes in methodology. Readers are therefore advised not to compare data series between editions or across World Bank publications.

Classification of economies

For operational and analytical purposes the World Bank's main criterion for classifying economies is gross national income (GNI) per capita (calculated by the *World Bank Atlas* method; box 1). Every economy is classified as low income, middle income (subdivided into lower middle and upper middle), or high income (table 1). Low- and middle-income economies are sometimes referred to as developing economies. The term is used for convenience; it is not intended to imply that all economies in the group are experiencing similar development or that other economies have reached a preferred or final stage of development. Classification by income does not necessarily

Box 1 The *World Bank Atlas* method for converting gross national income to a common denominator

The World Bank uses the *Atlas* conversion factor to calculate gross national income (GNI) and GNI per capita in U.S. dollars for certain operational purposes. It reduces the impact of exchange rate fluctuations in the cross-country comparison of national incomes. The *Atlas* conversion factor for any year is the average of the official exchange rate or alternative conversion factor for that year and the two preceding years, adjusted for differences in relative inflation between the country and Japan, the United Kingdom, the United States, and the euro area averaged together. Inflation is measured by the change in GDP deflator.

The inflation rate for Japan, the United Kingdom, the United States, and the euro area, representing international inflation, is measured by the change in the special drawing rights (SDR, the International Monetary Fund's unit of account) deflator. The SDR deflator is the average of these countries' GDP deflators in SDR terms, weighted by the amount of each country's currency in one SDR unit. Weights vary over time because the SDR's composition and each currency's relative exchange rates change. The SDR deflator is calculated in SDR terms first and then converted to U.S. dollars using the SDR to U.S. dollar *Atlas* conversion factor. The *Atlas* conversion factor is then applied to a country's GNI. The resulting GNI in U.S. dollars is divided by the midyear population for the latest of the three years to derive GNI per capita.

When official exchange rates are deemed unreliable or unrepresentative of the effective exchange rate, an alternative estimate of the exchange rate is used.

The following formulas describe the procedures for computing the conversion factor for year *t:*

$$e_t^* = \frac{1}{3}\left[e_{t-2}\left(\frac{p_t}{p_{t-2}} \Big/ \frac{p_t^{S\$}}{p_{t-2}^{S\$}}\right) + e_{t-1}\left(\frac{p_t}{p_{t-1}} \Big/ \frac{p_t^{S\$}}{p_{t-1}^{S\$}}\right) + e_t\right]$$

and for calculating per capita GNI in U.S. dollars for year *t:*

$$Y_t^{\$} = \left(\frac{Y_t}{N_t}\right) / e_t^*$$

where e_t^* is the *Atlas* conversion factor (national currency to the U.S. dollar), e_t is the average annual exchange rate (national currency to the U.S. dollar), p_t is the GDP deflator, $p_t^{S\$}$ is the SDR deflator in U.S. dollar terms, $Y_t^{\$}$ is current GNI per capita in U.S. dollars, Y_t is current GNI (local currency), and N_t is midyear population.

reflect development status. Because GNI per capita changes over time, the country composition of income groups may change from one edition of *Africa Development Indicators* to the next. Once the classification is fixed for an edition, based on GNI per capita in the most recent year for which data are available (2007 in this edition), all historical data presented are based on the same country grouping.

Low-income economies are those with a GNI per capita of $935 or less in 2007. Middle-income economies are those with a GNI per capita of more than $935 but less than $11,456. Lower middle-income and upper middle-income economies are separated at a GNI per capita of $3,705. High-income economies are those with a GNI per capita of $11,456 or more.

Alternative conversion factors

The World Bank systematically assesses the appropriateness of official exchange rates as conversion factors. An alternative conversion factor is used when the official exchange rate is judged to diverge by an exceptionally large margin from the rate effectively applied to domestic transactions of foreign currencies and traded products. This applies to only a small number of countries. Alternative conversion factors are used in the *Atlas* methodology and elsewhere in *Africa Development Indicators* as single-year conversion factors.

Symbols

..	means that data are not available or that aggregates cannot be calculated because of missing data in the years shown.
$	means current U.S. dollars unless otherwise noted.
0 or 0.0	means zero or small enough that the number would round to zero at the displayed number of decimal places.

Data presentation conventions

A blank means not applicable or, for an aggregate, not analytically meaningful.

A billion is 1,000 million.

Growth rates are in real terms, unless otherwise specified.

The cutoff date for data is September 30, 2009, except for data on official development assistance, for which the cutoff date is December 8, 2009.

Table 1 World Bank classification of economies, 2007

Low income	Lower middle income	Upper middle income	High income
GNI per capita of $935 or less	GNI per capita higher than $935 and less than $3,705	GNI per capita of $3,705 but less than $11,456	GNI per capita of $11,456 and over
Benin	Algeria	Botswana	Equatorial Guinea
Burkina Faso	Angola	Gabon	
Burundi	Cameroon	Libya	
Central African Republic	Cape Verde	Mauritius	
Chad	Congo, Rep.	Seychelles	
Comoros	Djibouti	South Africa	
Congo, Dem. Rep.	Egypt, Arab Rep.		
Côte d'Ivoire	Lesotho		
Eritrea	Morocco		
Ethiopia	Namibia		
Gambia, The	Sudan		
Ghana	Swaziland		
Guinea	Tunisia		
Guinea-Bissau			
Kenya			
Liberia			
Madagascar			
Malawi			
Mali			
Mauritania			
Mozambique			
Niger			
Nigeria			
Rwanda			
São Tomé and Príncipe			
Senegal			
Sierra Leone			
Somalia			
Tanzania			
Togo			
Uganda			
Zambia			
Zimbabwe			

Source: World Bank.

Table 1.1 Basic indicators

	Population (millions)	Land area (thousands of sq km)	GDP per capita Constant 2000 prices: Dollars	GDP per capita Constant 2000 prices: Average annual growth (%)	Life expectancy at birth (years)	Under-five mortality rate (per 1,000)	Gini index	Adult literacy rate (% of ages 15 and older): Male	Adult literacy rate (% of ages 15 and older): Female	Net official development assistance per capita (current $)
	2008	2008	2008[a]	2000–08	2007–08[b]	2007	2000–07[b]	2007	2007	2008
SUB-SAHARAN AFRICA	819.3	23,629	624	2.7	51.5	146	..	..	..	43.6
Excluding South Africa	770.6	22,414	426	3.2	51.6	149	..	..	..	44.9
Excl. S. Africa & Nigeria	619.3	21,504	410	2.9	52.8	139	..	..	..	53.7
Angola	18.0	1,247	1,357	10.4	47.3	158	58.6	..	..	20.5
Benin	8.7	111	359	0.5	61.6	123	38.6	53.1	27.9	74.0
Botswana	1.9	567	4,440	3.2	50.6	40	..	82.8	82.9	376.1
Burkina Faso	15.2	274	263	2.3	52.2	191	39.6	36.7	21.6	65.6
Burundi	8.1	26	111	0.0	50.6	180	33.3	..	..	63.0
Cameroon	18.9	465	710	1.3	50.4	148	44.6	..	..	27.8
Cape Verde	0.5	4	1,632	3.8	71.2	32	50.5	89.4	78.8	438.2
Central African Republic	4.4	623	230	–1.1	44.7	172	43.6	..	..	58.0
Chad	11.1	1,259	251	6.7	50.6	209	39.8	43.0	20.8	37.6
Comoros	0.6	2	370	–0.2	65.1	66	64.3	80.3	69.8	57.9
Congo, Dem. Rep.	64.2	2,267	99	2.4	46.4	161	44.4	..	..	25.1
Congo, Rep.	3.6	342	1,214	1.8	53.7	125	47.3	..	..	139.7
Côte d'Ivoire	20.6	318	530	–1.6	57.8	127	48.4	..	..	29.9
Djibouti	0.8	23	849	1.6	54.8	127	40.0	..	..	142.6
Equatorial Guinea	0.7	28	8,692	15.7	50.5	206	..	..	..	57.1
Eritrea	5.0	101	148	–2.5	57.9	70	..	..	..	28.6
Ethiopia	80.7	1,000	190	5.4	55.4	119	29.8	..	..	41.2
Gabon	1.4	258	4,157	0.1	60.7	91	41.5	90.2	82.2	37.6
Gambia, The	1.7	10	374	2.0	56.1	109	47.3	..	..	56.5
Ghana	23.4	228	327	3.2	56.8	115	42.8	71.7	58.3	55.4
Guinea	9.8	246	417	1.1	58.1	150	43.3	..	..	32.4
Guinea-Bissau	1.6	28	128	–3.3	48.0	198	35.5	..	..	83.5
Kenya	38.5	569	464	1.9	54.1	121	47.7	..	..	35.3
Lesotho	2.0	30	525	3.0	42.6	84	52.5	..	..	71.1
Liberia	3.8	96	148	–4.5	58.4	133	52.6	60.2	50.9	329.6
Madagascar	19.1	582	271	0.9	60.5	112	47.2	..	..	44.0
Malawi	14.3	94	165	1.6	48.3	111	39.0	79.2	64.6	63.9
Mali	12.7	1,220	295	2.1	54.3	196	39.0	..	..	75.8
Mauritania	3.2	1,031	..	2.2	64.1	119	39.0	63.3	48.3	97.1
Mauritius	1.3	2	4,929	3.3	72.4	15	..	90.2	84.7	86.4
Mozambique	21.8	786	365	5.6	42.1	169	47.1	57.2	33.0	91.5
Namibia	2.1	823	2,692	3.9	52.8	68	..	88.6	87.4	97.8
Niger	14.7	1,267	180	0.9	56.9	176	43.9	..	..	41.3
Nigeria	151.3	911	487	4.0	46.8	189	42.9	80.1	64.1	8.5
Rwanda	9.7	25	313	4.3	50.2	181	46.7	..	..	95.7
São Tomé and Príncipe	0.2	1	..	..	65.4	99	..	93.4	82.7	292.2
Senegal	12.2	193	530	1.7	55.7	114	39.2	..	..	86.6
Seychelles	0.1	0	8,267	1.3	73.2	13	..	..	..	139.9
Sierra Leone	5.6	72	262	6.5	47.7	262	42.5	50.0	26.8	66.0
Somalia	9.0	627	..	..	48.1	142	..	..	..	84.7
South Africa	48.7	1,214	3,764	3.1	50.5	59	57.8	88.9	87.2	23.1
Sudan	41.3	2,376	532	5.2	58.3	109	..	..	..	57.6
Swaziland	1.2	17	1,559	1.7	46.4	91	50.7	..	..	57.7
Tanzania	42.5	886	362	3.9	55.9	116	34.6	79.0	65.9	54.9
Togo	6.5	54	245	–0.2	62.7	100	34.4	..	..	51.0
Uganda	31.7	197	348	4.0	53.0	130	42.6	81.8	65.5	52.3
Zambia	12.6	743	387	2.9	45.9	170	50.7	80.8	60.7	86.0
Zimbabwe	12.5	387	..	–5.7	45.1	90	..	94.1	88.3	49.0
NORTH AFRICA	163.7	5,738	2,157	3.0	71.1	35	..	..	..	20.9
Algeria	34.4	2,382	2,191	2.8	72.3	37	..	84.3	66.4	9.2
Egypt, Arab Rep.	81.5	995	1,784	2.8	70.2	36	32.1	..	..	16.5
Libya	6.3	1,760	7,740	2.1	74.2	18	..	94.5	78.4	9.6
Morocco	31.2	446	1,770	3.8	71.1	34	40.9	68.7	43.2	39.0
Tunisia	10.3	155	2,760	4.0	74.3	21	40.8	86.4	69.0	46.4
ALL AFRICA	983.0	29,367	879	2.6	54.8	134	..	..	..	39.8

a. Provisional.
b. Data are for the most recent year available during the period specified.

Table 2.1 Gross domestic product, nominal

	Current prices ($ millions)									Annual average growth (%)		
	1980	1990	2002	2003	2004	2005	2006	2007	2008[a]	1980–89	1990–99	2000–08
SUB-SAHARAN AFRICA	276,250	300,664	364,492	446,761	551,685	648,327	751,217	864,074	1,003,420	0.7	1.5	16.1
Excluding South Africa	197,062	188,777	253,891	280,236	335,765	405,706	494,058	581,182	728,451	–1.1	1.1	17.4
Excl. S. Africa & Nigeria	129,282	160,369	194,665	212,440	247,697	293,138	346,595	414,700	515,586	2.3	0.7	15.7
Angola	..	10,260	11,432	13,956	19,775	30,632	45,163	59,263	83,383	..	–3.8	35.1
Benin	1,405	1,845	2,807	3,558	4,047	4,287	4,623	5,428	6,680	2.3	3.5	14.3
Botswana	1,061	3,792	5,933	8,278	9,827	10,513	11,006	12,324	12,969	12.6	4.4	11.6
Burkina Faso	1,929	3,101	3,290	4,270	5,109	5,427	5,771	6,767	7,948	4.8	0.0	15.1
Burundi	920	1,132	628	595	664	796	919	980	1,163	2.2	–3.3	7.3
Cameroon	6,741	11,152	10,880	13,622	15,775	16,588	17,957	20,692	23,396	7.3	–2.5	12.1
Cape Verde	..	339	616	797	925	1,006	1,202	1,447	1,730	..	6.4	16.6
Central African Republic	797	1,488	1,042	1,139	1,270	1,350	1,477	1,712	1,970	8.1	–4.3	9.5
Chad	1,033	1,739	1,988	2,737	4,415	5,873	6,300	7,006	8,361	5.7	–1.3	27.3
Comoros	124	250	251	324	362	387	403	465	530	8.0	–2.0	12.8
Congo, Dem. Rep.	14,395	9,350	5,548	5,673	6,594	7,239	8,785	9,950	11,588	–6.2	–7.1	13.1
Congo, Rep.	1,706	2,799	3,020	3,564	4,343	6,087	7,731	7,646	10,699	2.3	–2.4	18.6
Côte d'Ivoire	10,175	10,796	11,487	13,737	15,481	16,363	17,367	19,796	23,414	2.0	2.2	10.8
Djibouti	..	452	591	622	666	709	761	818	875	..	1.7	6.1
Equatorial Guinea	..	132	2,147	2,952	5,241	8,217	9,603	12,576	18,525	..	22.5	41.3
Eritrea	..	..	675	598	631	1,161	1,282	1,374	1,654	..	7.2	14.0
Ethiopia	..	12,083	7,790	8,556	10,052	12,305	15,166	19,395	26,487	5.9	–5.7	16.2
Gabon	4,279	5,952	4,932	6,055	7,178	8,666	9,546	11,568	14,435	–0.5	–1.7	15.3
Gambia, The	241	317	370	367	401	461	508	644	782	1.7	3.6	8.0
Ghana	4,445	5,886	6,160	7,624	8,872	10,720	12,715	14,989	16,123	3.2	2.6	17.4
Guinea	6,684	2,667	3,208	3,619	3,938	3,261	3,204	4,564	4,266	–15.6	3.0	4.0
Guinea-Bissau	111	244	204	236	285	302	317	382	430	3.7	–0.6	10.2
Kenya	7,265	8,591	13,149	14,904	16,092	18,769	22,479	26,950	34,507	2.6	7.7	13.3
Lesotho	431	577	670	994	1,290	1,376	1,518	1,670	1,622	0.1	3.8	13.2
Liberia	954	384	559	410	460	530	612	735	870	–0.5	1.8	5.3
Madagascar	4,042	3,081	4,397	5,474	4,364	5,039	5,515	7,347	8,970	–5.2	3.4	9.0
Malawi	1,238	1,881	2,665	2,425	2,625	2,855	3,164	3,586	4,269	1.8	0.2	11.1
Mali	1,787	2,421	3,343	4,362	4,874	5,305	5,866	6,848	8,740	3.4	0.4	16.8
Mauritania	709	1,020	1,150	1,285	1,548	1,837	2,663	2,644	2,858	3.5	1.4	15.2
Mauritius	1,153	2,383	4,549	5,248	6,064	6,290	6,433	6,786	8,651	7.6	6.7	8.2
Mozambique	3,526	2,463	4,201	4,666	5,698	6,579	7,095	8,011	9,735	–4.7	8.3	11.9
Namibia	2,169	2,350	3,361	4,934	6,606	7,262	7,979	8,717	8,564	0.1	4.6	14.2
Niger	2,509	2,481	2,170	2,708	2,897	3,330	3,646	4,246	5,354	–0.2	–1.8	14.2
Nigeria	64,202	28,472	59,117	67,656	87,845	112,249	146,869	165,921	212,080	–12.0	3.2	22.5
Rwanda	1,163	2,584	1,641	1,777	1,971	2,379	2,835	3,412	4,457	8.6	–2.0	12.9
São Tomé and Príncipe	..	..	91	98	107	114	125	145	175	..	..	11.2
Senegal	3,503	5,717	5,334	6,858	8,030	8,688	9,367	11,299	13,209	6.2	–1.8	14.3
Seychelles	147	369	698	706	700	884	968	912	833	9.3	6.0	5.6
Sierra Leone	1,101	650	936	991	1,073	1,215	1,423	1,664	1,953	–4.3	0.6	13.7
Somalia	604	917	..	..	..	..	..	..	..	6.4	..	..
South Africa	80,710	112,014	110,874	166,654	216,012	242,802	257,730	283,743	276,764	4.1	2.1	13.5
Sudan	7,617	12,409	14,976	17,780	21,684	27,386	36,401	46,228	58,443	10.1	0.8	22.4
Swaziland	543	1,115	1,174	1,796	2,282	2,524	2,670	2,894	2,618	1.9	4.4	11.7
Tanzania	..	4,259	9,758	10,283	11,351	14,142	14,331	16,826	20,490	..	8.9	10.7
Togo	1,136	1,628	1,476	1,759	2,061	2,108	2,218	2,499	2,823	4.5	–0.1	10.3
Uganda	1,245	4,304	6,179	6,607	7,924	9,225	9,957	11,892	14,529	20.7	8.8	12.1
Zambia	3,884	3,288	3,716	4,374	5,423	7,157	10,675	11,410	14,314	–3.1	0.2	22.1
Zimbabwe	6,679	8,784	21,897	7,397	4,712	3,418	..	..	..	–0.1	–2.4	–18.8
NORTH AFRICA	111,546	172,192	225,562	249,580	279,434	322,260	370,254	433,252	563,136	4.8	4.2	11.1
Algeria	42,345	62,045	57,053	68,019	85,014	102,339	116,460	134,304	173,882	4.5	–1.2	16.4
Egypt, Arab Rep.	22,912	43,130	87,851	82,924	78,845	89,686	107,484	130,476	162,818	6.8	10.8	5.7
Libya	..	28,905	19,195	23,822	30,498	41,743	49,711	58,333	99,926	..	–0.9	15.6
Morocco	18,821	25,821	40,416	49,823	56,948	59,524	65,637	75,119	86,329	3.7	5.1	11.6
Tunisia	8,743	12,291	21,047	24,992	28,129	28,968	30,962	35,020	40,180	2.3	6.0	9.6
ALL AFRICA	391,472	472,762	589,969	696,175	830,851	970,256	1,121,070	1,296,907	1,566,419	1.9	2.5	14.2

a. Provisional.

Table 2.2 Gross domestic product, real

	Constant prices (2000 $ millions)									Average annual growth (%)		
	1980	1990	2002	2003	2004	2005	2006	2007	2008[a]	1980–89	1990–99	2000–08
SUB-SAHARAN AFRICA	227,428	273,576	367,478	383,138	407,300	430,206	456,824	485,999	510,788	1.8	2.4	5.3
Excluding South Africa	132,111	162,644	226,037	237,297	254,380	269,702	287,820	308,443	327,922	2.1	2.7	5.9
Excl. S. Africa & Nigeria	99,356	127,626	177,831	184,108	195,541	207,687	221,972	238,364	254,170	2.6	2.8	5.6
Angola	..	8,464	10,780	11,137	12,383	14,935	17,707	21,298	24,450	..	1.0	13.6
Benin	1,084	1,412	2,474	2,571	2,650	2,727	2,831	2,961	3,112	2.7	4.7	3.9
Botswana	1,209	3,395	6,715	7,137	7,604	7,960	8,196	8,544	8,458	10.9	5.6	4.4
Burkina Faso	1,101	1,556	2,915	3,150	3,296	3,505	3,698	3,831	4,002	4.0	5.5	5.6
Burundi	559	865	756	747	783	790	830	860	899	4.5	-3.2	2.9
Cameroon	6,339	8,793	10,952	11,393	11,815	12,087	12,476	12,913	13,416	4.5	1.3	3.5
Cape Verde	..	303	577	613	608	648	718	768	814	6.3	5.9	5.5
Central African Republic	735	815	956	884	892	914	950	990	1,018	1.6	1.8	0.6
Chad	665	1,106	1,678	1,925	2,572	2,776	2,780	2,786	2,775	6.7	2.3	10.4
Comoros	136	181	217	223	222	232	234	236	238	2.9	1.2	2.0
Congo, Dem. Rep.	7,016	7,659	4,362	4,614	4,921	5,308	5,605	5,956	6,325	2.1	-5.0	5.5
Congo, Rep.	1,746	2,796	3,503	3,563	3,691	3,975	4,223	4,156	4,388	3.8	0.8	4.0
Côte d'Ivoire	7,727	8,298	10,266	10,106	10,287	10,417	10,488	10,668	10,904	0.7	3.5	0.5
Djibouti	..	660	577	596	619	638	664	693	719	..	-2.3	3.5
Equatorial Guinea	..	207	2,426	2,764	3,815	4,187	4,239	5,148	5,730	..	20.7	18.9
Eritrea	..	..	711	692	702	720	713	722	737	..	7.9	1.3
Ethiopia	..	6,234	8,993	8,798	9,993	11,174	12,387	13,762	15,320	2.1	3.7	8.2
Gabon	3,594	4,298	5,162	5,290	5,361	5,523	5,588	5,899	6,020	0.5	2.9	2.2
Gambia, The	213	305	431	460	493	518	552	587	621	3.5	2.7	5.1
Ghana	2,640	3,267	5,410	5,691	6,010	6,364	6,771	7,184	7,630	2.6	4.3	5.6
Guinea	1,539	2,088	3,372	3,440	3,534	3,651	3,730	3,787	4,105	3.0	4.4	3.1
Guinea-Bissau	115	186	201	186	185	189	196	197	202	3.8	1.4	-0.9
Kenya	7,078	10,544	13,243	13,631	14,325	15,156	16,126	17,248	17,869	4.1	2.2	4.6
Lesotho	380	542	820	852	891	897	970	1,019	1,059	3.3	4.0	3.9
Liberia	1,391	433	599	411	422	444	479	524	561	-3.3	0.2	-1.1
Madagascar	3,099	3,266	3,590	3,941	4,148	4,339	4,557	4,842	5,175	0.8	1.7	3.8
Malawi	1,000	1,243	1,584	1,683	1,779	1,824	1,974	2,143	2,351	2.4	3.8	4.2
Mali	1,536	1,630	2,828	3,039	3,105	3,294	3,469	3,566	3,744	0.5	3.9	5.2
Mauritania	693	816	1,125	1,188	1,249	1,317	1,471	1,499	..	1.9	2.9	5.1
Mauritius	1,518	2,679	4,846	5,000	5,235	5,475	5,672	5,937	6,254	5.9	5.3	4.1
Mozambique	2,462	2,499	5,173	5,485	5,918	6,414	6,971	7,460	7,942	-0.9	6.0	8.0
Namibia	2,292	2,591	4,144	4,320	4,850	4,972	5,328	5,544	5,692	1.1	4.0	5.4
Niger	1,523	1,507	1,984	2,071	2,054	2,206	2,334	2,411	2,640	-0.4	2.4	4.4
Nigeria	31,452	34,978	48,143	53,102	58,731	61,903	65,740	69,981	73,679	0.8	2.4	6.6
Rwanda	1,368	1,673	2,089	2,096	2,207	2,363	2,536	2,737	3,045	2.5	-1.6	6.7
São Tomé and Príncipe	..	..	..	..	..	..	..	..	..	..	..	..
Senegal	2,683	3,463	4,939	5,268	5,579	5,893	6,034	6,315	6,472	2.7	2.8	4.4
Seychelles	292	395	608	572	556	598	647	694	714	3.1	4.5	2.0
Sierra Leone	929	1,014	958	1,047	1,125	1,207	1,296	1,384	1,454	0.5	-5.3	10.3
Somalia	..	..	..	..	..	..	..	..	..	..	..	..
South Africa	95,503	110,945	141,520	145,935	153,034	160,632	169,180	177,804	183,249	1.4	2.0	4.3
Sudan	5,525	7,062	13,832	14,821	15,579	16,564	18,434	20,308	22,002	2.4	5.4	7.4
Swaziland	470	1,033	1,532	1,592	1,632	1,668	1,715	1,776	1,820	7.4	3.1	2.7
Tanzania	..	6,801	10,345	10,931	11,667	12,526	13,370	14,326	15,394	..	2.7	6.8
Togo	964	1,071	1,382	1,419	1,461	1,479	1,537	1,566	1,583	1.5	3.6	2.4
Uganda	..	3,215	6,916	7,363	7,865	8,363	9,265	10,060	11,019	2.3	7.2	7.5
Zambia	2,730	3,028	3,488	3,686	3,886	4,089	4,342	4,611	4,888	1.0	0.2	5.3
Zimbabwe	4,376	6,734	6,883	6,167	5,933	5,618	..	..	..	3.3	2.7	-5.7
NORTH AFRICA	119,695	179,235	263,778	273,960	286,919	300,068	316,723	333,716	353,097	4.2	3.2	4.6
Algeria	35,291	46,367	58,857	62,918	66,190	69,565	70,956	73,085	75,278	2.9	1.7	4.3
Egypt, Arab Rep.	38,506	65,579	105,818	109,211	113,666	118,757	126,890	135,867	145,465	5.5	4.3	4.7
Libya	..	..	37,228	36,204	38,014	40,409	42,511	45,401	48,579	..	..	4.1
Morocco	20,086	29,312	41,137	43,735	45,835	47,201	50,863	52,244	55,275	4.2	2.4	5.0
Tunisia	8,622	12,237	20,738	21,891	23,213	24,136	25,503	27,118	28,501	3.2	4.6	4.9
ALL AFRICA	349,899	454,267	631,251	657,091	694,201	730,249	773,501	819,632	863,827	2.6	2.7	5.0

a. Provisional.

Table 2.3 Gross domestic product growth

	Annual growth (%)											
										Annual average		
	1980	1990	2002	2003	2004	2005	2006	2007	2008[a]	1980–89	1990–99	2000–08
SUB-SAHARAN AFRICA	4.2	1.1	3.3	4.3	6.3	5.6	6.2	6.4	5.1	2.2	2.1	4.9
Excluding South Africa	2.0	2.1	3.1	5.0	7.2	6.0	6.7	7.2	6.3	2.1	2.5	5.4
Excl. S. Africa & Nigeria	1.1	0.6	3.5	3.5	6.2	6.2	6.9	7.4	6.6	2.6	2.4	5.3
Angola	..	–0.3	14.5	3.3	11.2	20.6	18.6	20.3	14.8	4.2	1.0	12.2
Benin	6.8	3.2	4.5	3.9	3.1	2.9	3.8	4.6	5.1	3.1	4.5	4.3
Botswana	12.0	6.8	3.3	6.3	6.5	4.7	3.0	4.2	–1.0	11.5	6.1	4.5
Burkina Faso	0.8	–0.6	4.7	8.0	4.6	6.4	5.5	3.6	4.5	3.7	5.1	5.1
Burundi	1.0	3.5	4.4	–1.2	4.8	0.9	5.1	3.6	4.5	4.3	–1.4	2.6
Cameroon	–2.0	–6.1	4.0	4.0	3.7	2.3	3.2	3.5	3.9	4.0	0.4	3.7
Cape Verde	..	0.7	4.6	6.2	–0.7	6.5	10.8	6.9	6.0	6.4	5.2	5.6
Central African Republic	–4.5	–2.1	–0.6	–7.6	1.0	2.4	4.0	4.2	2.8	0.9	1.3	1.0
Chad	–6.0	–4.2	8.5	14.7	33.6	7.9	0.2	0.2	–0.4	5.4	2.2	8.4
Comoros	..	5.1	4.1	2.5	–0.2	4.2	1.2	0.5	1.0	2.7	1.6	1.9
Congo, Dem. Rep.	2.2	–6.6	3.5	5.8	6.6	7.9	5.6	6.3	6.2	1.8	–5.5	3.6
Congo, Rep.	17.6	1.0	4.8	1.7	3.6	7.7	6.2	–1.6	5.6	6.8	0.8	4.4
Côte d'Ivoire	–11.0	–1.1	–1.4	–1.6	1.8	1.3	0.7	1.7	2.2	–0.2	2.6	0.1
Djibouti	..	..	2.6	3.2	3.8	3.2	4.1	4.3	3.9	..	–2.0	3.1
Equatorial Guinea	..	3.3	19.5	14.0	38.0	9.7	1.3	21.4	11.3	0.9	20.2	21.2
Eritrea	..	..	3.0	–2.7	1.5	2.6	–1.0	1.3	2.0	..	8.1	0.3
Ethiopia	..	2.7	1.5	–2.2	13.6	11.8	10.9	11.1	11.3	2.4	2.7	8.0
Gabon	2.6	5.2	–0.3	2.5	1.3	3.0	1.2	5.6	2.1	1.9	2.5	1.7
Gambia, The	6.3	3.6	–3.3	6.9	7.1	5.1	6.5	6.3	5.9	3.9	3.1	5.1
Ghana	0.5	3.3	4.5	5.2	5.6	5.9	6.4	6.1	6.2	2.0	4.3	5.3
Guinea	2.6	4.3	4.2	2.0	2.7	3.3	2.2	1.5	8.4	2.9	4.3	3.4
Guinea-Bissau	–16.0	6.1	–7.1	–7.1	–0.6	2.2	3.5	0.6	2.7	2.9	2.0	0.2
Kenya	5.6	4.2	0.5	2.9	5.1	5.8	6.4	7.0	3.6	4.2	2.2	4.0
Lesotho	–2.7	6.0	1.6	3.9	4.6	0.7	8.1	5.1	3.9	2.8	3.9	3.9
Liberia	–4.1	–51.0	3.7	–31.3	2.6	5.3	7.8	9.4	7.1	–4.5	1.2	3.7
Madagascar	0.8	3.1	–12.7	9.8	5.3	4.6	5.0	6.2	6.9	0.4	1.6	4.0
Malawi	0.4	5.7	–4.4	6.3	5.7	2.6	8.2	8.6	9.7	1.7	4.1	3.7
Mali	–4.3	–1.9	4.2	7.4	2.2	6.1	5.3	2.8	5.0	0.6	3.6	5.4
Mauritania	3.4	–1.8	1.1	5.6	5.2	5.4	11.7	1.9	..	2.2	2.6	4.5
Mauritius	..	5.8	2.7	3.2	4.7	4.6	3.6	4.7	5.3	5.9	5.4	4.3
Mozambique	..	1.0	8.8	6.0	7.9	8.4	8.7	7.0	6.5	0.4	5.5	7.4
Namibia	..	2.5	4.8	4.2	12.3	2.5	7.1	4.1	2.7	1.1	4.1	4.7
Niger	–2.2	–1.3	3.0	4.4	–0.8	7.4	5.8	3.3	9.5	0.0	1.9	4.3
Nigeria	4.2	8.2	1.5	10.3	10.6	5.4	6.2	6.4	5.3	0.9	3.1	6.0
Rwanda	9.0	–2.4	11.0	0.3	5.3	7.1	7.3	7.9	11.2	3.2	2.1	7.4
São Tomé and Príncipe	..	..	..	..	..	..	..	..	..	..	..	..
Senegal	–3.3	–0.7	0.7	6.7	5.9	5.6	2.4	4.7	2.5	2.4	2.7	4.0
Seychelles	–4.2	7.0	1.2	–5.9	–2.9	7.5	8.3	7.3	2.8	2.1	4.9	2.3
Sierra Leone	4.8	3.4	27.5	9.3	7.5	7.2	7.3	6.8	5.1	1.1	–4.3	10.3
Somalia	..	..	..	..	..	..	..	..	..	..	..	..
South Africa	6.6	–0.3	3.7	3.1	4.9	5.0	5.3	5.1	3.1	2.2	1.4	4.1
Sudan	1.5	–5.5	5.4	7.1	5.1	6.3	11.3	10.2	8.3	3.4	4.4	7.6
Swaziland	12.4	9.8	1.8	3.9	2.5	2.2	2.9	3.5	2.5	8.6	3.7	3.4
Tanzania	..	7.0	7.2	5.7	6.7	7.4	6.7	7.1	7.5	3.8	3.1	6.6
Togo	14.6	–0.2	4.1	2.7	3.0	1.2	3.9	1.9	1.1	2.6	2.6	1.9
Uganda	..	6.5	6.4	6.5	6.8	6.3	10.8	8.6	9.5	3.0	6.9	7.3
Zambia	3.0	–0.5	2.7	5.7	5.4	5.2	6.2	6.2	6.0	1.4	0.4	5.1
Zimbabwe	14.4	7.0	–4.4	–10.4	–3.8	–5.3	..	..	..	5.2	2.6	–5.8
NORTH AFRICA	5.2	4.0	3.1	3.9	4.7	4.6	5.6	5.4	5.8	4.3	3.3	4.5
Algeria	0.8	0.8	4.7	6.9	5.2	5.1	2.0	3.0	3.0	2.8	1.6	3.9
Egypt, Arab Rep.	10.0	5.7	2.4	3.2	4.1	4.5	6.8	7.1	7.1	5.9	4.3	4.9
Libya	..	..	3.3	–2.8	5.0	6.3	5.2	6.8	7.0	..	..	4.1
Morocco	3.6	4.0	3.3	6.3	4.8	3.0	7.8	2.7	5.8	3.9	2.8	4.8
Tunisia	7.4	7.9	1.7	5.6	6.0	4.0	5.7	6.3	5.1	3.6	5.1	4.9
ALL AFRICA	4.5	2.2	3.2	4.1	5.6	5.2	5.9	6.0	5.4	2.9	2.5	4.8

a. Provisional.

Table 2.4 Gross domestic product per capita, real

	Constant prices (2000 $)									Average annual growth (%)		
	1980	1990	2002	2003	2004	2005	2006	2007	2008[a]	1980–89	1990–99	2000–08
SUB-SAHARAN AFRICA	592	533	520	529	548	565	585	608	624	–1.0	–0.6	2.5
Excluding South Africa	371	340	342	350	365	377	393	410	426	–0.9	–0.2	3.0
Excl. S. Africa & Nigeria	348	333	335	338	350	362	377	395	410	–0.2	–0.2	2.9
Angola	..	794	711	712	767	899	1,036	1,213	1,357	..	–2.4	9.4
Benin	305	294	348	349	348	347	348	353	359	–0.4	1.3	0.7
Botswana	1,214	2,483	3,783	3,976	4,189	4,336	4,411	4,541	4,440	7.6	3.3	2.7
Burkina Faso	161	175	230	241	244	252	258	259	263	1.3	2.6	2.3
Burundi	135	152	112	107	109	107	109	110	111	1.2	–3.4	0.2
Cameroon	698	718	659	670	679	679	687	697	710	1.3	–1.6	1.4
Cape Verde	..	854	1,269	1,325	1,294	1,357	1,482	1,562	1,632	..	3.4	3.7
Central African Republic	316	271	239	218	216	218	223	228	230	–1.2	–1.0	–0.9
Chad	144	181	184	203	262	274	266	259	251	3.3	–0.6	5.3
Comoros	405	416	386	387	378	386	382	375	370	0.0	–1.0	–0.1
Congo, Dem. Rep.	250	202	82	84	86	90	92	95	99	–1.2	–8.6	1.9
Congo, Rep.	962	1,143	1,102	1,093	1,105	1,164	1,212	1,170	1,214	2.1	–1.4	1.7
Côte d'Ivoire	918	658	568	548	546	541	533	530	530	–3.2	–0.3	–1.6
Djibouti	..	1,177	757	767	783	794	812	832	849	..	–4.7	1.5
Equatorial Guinea	..	547	4,329	4,796	6,439	6,877	6,779	8,017	8,692	..	15.2	16.2
Eritrea	..	..	178	166	161	159	152	149	148	..	..	–1.9
Ethiopia	..	129	130	124	137	150	162	175	190	..	–0.7	5.2
Gabon	5,274	4,640	4,005	4,020	3,993	4,034	4,004	4,148	4,157	–1.6	–0.9	0.1
Gambia, The	346	340	310	321	333	340	351	363	374	–0.2	–0.8	1.8
Ghana	239	218	264	272	280	290	302	314	327	–1.1	1.6	3.1
Guinea	332	340	387	388	391	396	396	394	417	0.2	1.0	1.5
Guinea-Bissau	137	182	147	133	129	128	130	128	128	2.8	–1.6	–3.2
Kenya	435	450	402	404	413	426	441	460	464	0.3	–0.9	1.7
Lesotho	293	338	425	437	453	453	486	508	525	1.1	2.0	2.9
Liberia	728	200	196	131	131	133	138	144	148	–6.7	–1.9	–3.7
Madagascar	360	290	222	237	242	246	252	260	271	–2.4	–1.7	0.8
Malawi	161	132	129	134	138	138	145	154	165	–2.4	1.6	1.2
Mali	253	213	267	278	276	284	290	289	295	–1.5	1.4	2.4
Mauritania	461	419	413	424	433	445	483	480	..	–0.6	0.2	..
Mauritius	1,572	2,535	4,004	4,089	4,245	4,404	4,527	4,709	4,929	4.8	4.1	3.4
Mozambique	203	185	270	280	295	312	332	349	365	–1.0	2.8	5.6
Namibia	2,309	1,828	2,134	2,194	2,432	2,462	2,603	2,665	2,692	–2.4	1.3	3.2
Niger	263	193	166	168	160	166	170	170	180	–3.0	–1.4	1.3
Nigeria	443	370	367	394	426	438	454	473	487	–2.5	–0.3	3.5
Rwanda	263	234	245	241	250	263	275	290	313	–1.1	–0.9	4.5
São Tomé and Príncipe	..	..	..	..	..	..	..	..	..	..	..	..
Senegal	476	460	473	492	508	522	521	531	530	0.0	0.3	1.4
Seychelles	4,532	5,645	7,267	6,913	6,740	7,209	7,651	8,165	8,267	1.8	2.9	1.1
Sierra Leone	285	248	211	221	229	236	246	255	262	–1.7	–5.7	6.9
Somalia	..	..	..	..	..	..	..	..	..	..	..	..
South Africa	3,463	3,152	3,128	3,186	3,302	3,426	3,570	3,716	3,764	–0.8	–0.7	2.8
Sudan	269	261	380	399	411	428	466	502	532	0.5	2.8	5.1
Swaziland	780	1,196	1,391	1,437	1,463	1,483	1,509	1,542	1,559	4.1	0.7	1.5
Tanzania	..	267	288	296	308	321	333	347	362	..	–0.3	3.9
Togo	346	273	249	249	250	247	250	249	245	–2.3	–0.4	–0.4
Uganda	..	181	266	274	283	291	312	328	348	..	3.5	4.0
Zambia	473	383	318	329	339	348	361	375	387	–2.0	–2.5	2.8
Zimbabwe	601	644	550	493	475	450	..	..	..	0.3	0.1	..
NORTH AFRICA	1,300	1,497	1,772	1,812	1,867	1,922	1,997	2,071	2,157	1.4	1.3	2.9
Algeria	1,876	1,834	1,874	1,973	2,045	2,117	2,128	2,159	2,191	–0.1	–0.3	2.5
Egypt, Arab Rep.	867	1,135	1,452	1,470	1,501	1,539	1,614	1,697	1,784	2.6	2.1	2.8
Libya	..	..	6,686	6,371	6,555	6,828	7,040	7,375	7,740	..	..	2.3
Morocco	1,037	1,213	1,410	1,482	1,536	1,566	1,668	1,693	1,770	1.5	0.7	3.9
Tunisia	1,351	1,501	2,120	2,225	2,337	2,407	2,518	2,652	2,760	0.6	3.0	3.8
ALL AFRICA	735	718	738	750	774	796	824	853	879	–0.2	–0.1	2.5

a. Provisional.

Table 2.5 Gross domestic product per capita growth

	Annual growth (%)									Annual average		
	1980	1990	2002	2003	2004	2005	2006	2007	2008[a]	1980–89	1990–99	2000–08
SUB-SAHARAN AFRICA	1.1	–1.7	0.8	1.7	3.7	3.0	3.6	3.9	2.6	–0.8	–0.7	2.4
Excluding South Africa	–1.0	–0.8	0.5	2.3	4.5	3.3	4.0	4.5	3.7	–0.9	–0.3	2.8
Excl. S. Africa & Nigeria	–1.9	–2.3	0.9	0.9	3.5	3.5	4.1	4.7	3.9	–0.4	–0.4	2.6
Angola	..	–3.1	11.0	0.1	7.8	17.1	15.3	17.1	11.8	1.5	–1.9	9.0
Benin	3.8	–0.1	1.1	0.4	–0.3	–0.5	0.5	1.3	1.8	0.2	1.1	0.9
Botswana	8.0	3.7	2.1	5.1	5.4	3.5	1.7	3.0	–2.2	7.9	3.5	3.2
Burkina Faso	–1.5	–3.4	1.4	4.6	1.3	3.1	2.4	0.7	1.5	1.1	2.1	1.9
Burundi	–1.9	0.9	1.9	–3.9	1.8	–2.1	2.0	0.5	1.4	1.0	–2.8	–0.1
Cameroon	–4.8	–8.9	1.6	1.6	1.4	0.1	1.1	1.5	1.9	0.9	–2.2	1.4
Cape Verde	..	–1.5	2.8	4.4	–2.3	4.9	9.2	5.4	4.5	4.2	3.0	3.9
Central African Republic	–7.0	–4.5	–2.2	–9.0	–0.6	0.7	2.2	2.3	0.9	–1.6	–1.3	–0.7
Chad	–8.1	–7.2	4.5	10.5	28.9	4.4	–2.9	–2.6	–3.1	2.5	–1.0	4.8
Comoros	..	2.4	2.0	0.3	–2.3	2.1	–0.9	–1.9	–1.4	0.1	–0.6	–0.2
Congo, Dem. Rep.	–0.9	–9.7	0.6	2.7	3.4	4.5	2.3	3.3	3.2	–1.2	–8.2	0.7
Congo, Rep.	14.0	–1.8	2.3	–0.8	1.1	5.3	4.1	–3.4	3.7	3.6	–1.4	2.2
Côte d'Ivoire	–15.0	–4.6	–3.5	–3.6	–0.3	–0.9	–1.5	–0.6	–0.1	–4.3	–0.7	–2.1
Djibouti	..	..	0.5	1.3	2.0	1.4	2.3	2.5	2.1	..	–4.5	1.0
Equatorial Guinea	..	–0.1	16.1	10.8	34.2	6.8	–1.4	18.3	8.4	–2.9	16.3	17.8
Eritrea	..	..	–1.3	–6.8	–2.7	–1.4	–4.5	–1.8	–1.2	..	6.5	–3.5
Ethiopia	..	–0.6	–1.1	–4.7	10.7	9.0	8.0	8.3	8.5	–0.8	–0.5	5.3
Gabon	–0.3	1.9	–2.4	0.4	–0.7	1.0	–0.7	3.6	0.2	–1.2	–0.5	–0.3
Gambia, The	2.7	–0.5	–6.4	3.5	3.8	2.0	3.5	3.4	3.0	0.2	–0.7	1.9
Ghana	–1.9	0.5	2.1	2.8	3.2	3.6	4.1	3.9	4.0	–1.0	1.5	2.9
Guinea	–0.3	0.6	2.3	0.2	0.8	1.3	0.1	–0.6	6.0	0.1	1.0	1.3
Guinea-Bissau	–18.5	3.6	–9.4	–9.4	–3.0	–0.2	1.1	–1.6	0.5	0.8	–0.5	–2.1
Kenya	1.7	0.8	–2.0	0.3	2.4	3.1	3.6	4.2	0.9	0.5	–0.7	1.3
Lesotho	–5.2	4.4	0.5	3.0	3.7	–0.1	7.3	4.5	3.4	0.6	2.2	3.0
Liberia	–7.3	–50.0	0.3	–33.1	–0.2	1.8	3.6	4.7	2.4	–6.2	–2.3	–0.5
Madagascar	–1.8	0.1	–15.2	6.7	2.3	1.7	2.2	3.4	4.0	–2.3	–1.4	1.1
Malawi	–2.6	1.8	–6.9	3.6	3.1	0.0	5.5	5.9	6.9	–2.4	1.9	1.0
Mali	–6.4	–4.3	1.1	4.3	–0.9	2.9	2.2	–0.2	1.9	–1.7	0.9	2.3
Mauritania	0.6	–4.3	–1.8	2.6	2.2	2.6	8.7	–0.6	..	–0.4	–0.2	1.6
Mauritius	..	5.0	1.8	2.1	3.8	3.7	2.8	4.0	4.7	4.9	4.2	3.4
Mozambique	..	–0.3	6.1	3.5	5.4	6.0	6.4	5.0	4.5	–0.6	2.6	4.9
Namibia	..	–1.7	3.2	2.8	10.8	1.2	5.7	2.4	1.0	–2.4	1.0	3.1
Niger	–5.2	–4.4	–0.6	0.8	–4.2	3.7	2.2	0.0	6.0	–2.9	–1.6	0.7
Nigeria	1.2	5.1	–1.0	7.6	7.9	2.9	3.7	4.1	3.0	–1.9	0.2	3.5
Rwanda	5.4	–2.0	8.0	–1.4	3.7	5.0	4.7	5.2	8.2	–0.4	1.3	4.3
São Tomé and Príncipe	..	..	9.7	3.6	4.8	3.9	5.0	4.1	3.9	..	..	5.0
Senegal	–6.0	–3.5	–1.9	3.9	3.2	2.9	–0.3	1.9	–0.2	–0.5	–0.1	1.3
Seychelles	–5.4	6.1	–1.8	–4.9	–2.5	7.0	6.1	6.7	1.3	1.2	3.3	1.4
Sierra Leone	2.6	2.1	22.6	4.8	3.3	3.4	4.0	3.9	2.4	–1.2	–4.5	6.7
Somalia	–9.1	–1.5	..	..	..	..	..	..	..	0.8	–1.5	..
South Africa	4.2	–2.3	2.7	1.9	3.6	3.7	4.2	4.1	1.3	–0.3	–0.8	2.7
Sudan	–1.7	–7.7	3.2	5.0	3.0	4.1	8.9	7.7	5.9	0.5	1.8	5.3
Swaziland	9.1	6.0	1.0	3.3	1.9	1.4	1.8	2.2	1.1	4.8	1.2	2.3
Tanzania	..	3.7	4.5	2.9	3.9	4.4	3.8	4.1	4.4	0.6	0.1	3.8
Togo	11.1	–3.0	1.3	0.1	0.4	–1.3	1.3	–0.6	–1.4	–0.9	–0.3	–0.8
Uganda	..	2.7	3.1	3.1	3.4	2.9	7.2	5.1	6.0	–0.5	3.5	3.9
Zambia	–0.3	–3.4	0.4	3.3	3.1	2.8	3.7	3.7	3.4	–1.7	–2.4	2.6
Zimbabwe	10.4	3.9	–4.5	–10.3	–3.7	–5.2	..	..	..	1.4	0.6	–5.9
NORTH AFRICA	2.4	1.6	1.4	2.2	3.1	2.9	3.9	3.7	4.1	1.5	1.3	2.8
Algeria	–2.5	–1.7	3.2	5.3	3.6	3.5	0.5	1.5	1.5	–0.3	–0.4	2.3
Egypt, Arab Rep.	7.4	3.2	0.4	1.3	2.1	2.5	4.9	5.1	5.1	3.2	2.3	2.9
Libya	..	..	1.2	–4.7	2.9	4.2	3.1	4.8	5.0	..	..	2.0
Morocco	1.1	2.0	2.1	5.1	3.7	1.9	6.5	1.5	4.6	1.6	1.1	3.5
Tunisia	4.6	5.4	0.5	4.9	5.1	3.0	4.6	5.3	4.1	1.0	3.3	3.9
ALL AFRICA	1.5	–0.6	0.8	1.7	3.2	2.8	3.5	3.6	3.0	0.0	–0.1	2.3

a. Provisional.

Table

2.6 Gross national income, nominal

	Current prices ($ millions)									Annual average growth (%)		
	1980	1990	2002	2003	2004	2005	2006	2007	2008[a]	1980–89	1990–99	2000–08
SUB-SAHARAN AFRICA	262,202	283,208	345,820	423,700	523,033	612,326	719,137	816,943	943,131	0.8	1.8	16.0
Excluding South Africa	187,659	175,700	238,947	262,139	311,536	375,040	468,354	544,541	679,313	–1.1	1.5	17.3
Excl. S. Africa & Nigeria	121,180	150,392	185,833	201,617	232,519	274,867	324,509	386,366	478,417	2.7	1.1	15.3
Angola	..	8,214	9,791	12,230	17,295	26,601	39,679	50,485	70,958	..	–2.4	35.8
Benin	1,402	1,806	2,781	3,515	4,006	4,259	4,623	5,428	6,652	2.1	3.7	14.4
Botswana	1,028	3,686	5,233	7,559	8,869	9,664	10,230	11,731	12,691	10.8	3.9	11.9
Burkina Faso	1,924	3,094	3,288	4,269	5,102	5,411	5,756	6,752	7,932	4.8	0.0	15.1
Burundi	922	1,117	614	577	646	776	910	974	1,159	1.9	–3.3	7.2
Cameroon	5,618	10,674	10,207	13,097	15,374	16,126	17,706	20,612	23,072	9.0	–2.4	12.9
Cape Verde	..	340	605	781	907	973	1,157	1,420	1,703	..	6.2	16.5
Central African Republic	800	1,465	1,033	1,137	1,268	1,348	1,473	1,702	1,948	7.8	–4.3	9.6
Chad	1,038	1,721	1,928	2,279	3,720	4,847	5,146	5,808	6,693	5.5	–1.2	23.7
Comoros	124	249	250	323	360	385	404	467	531	7.9	–2.0	12.8
Congo, Dem. Rep.	14,102	8,579	5,250	5,485	6,309	6,826	8,316	9,315	10,323	–6.8	–7.0	13.0
Congo, Rep.	1,544	2,324	2,201	2,679	3,247	4,509	5,961	5,548	8,367	1.9	–5.2	19.8
Côte d'Ivoire	9,680	9,209	10,807	13,018	14,763	15,643	16,590	18,913	22,442	1.3	3.3	11.1
Djibouti	..	..	606	673	731	776	834	893	951	..	1.3	7.1
Equatorial Guinea	..	124	1,161	1,392	2,312	4,173	5,163	6,674	11,868	..	16.9	41.0
Eritrea	..	..	669	588	616	1,152	1,273	1,365	1,641	..	7.3	13.9
Ethiopia	..	12,016	7,750	8,490	9,989	12,269	15,127	19,409	26,521	5.8	–5.8	16.3
Gabon	3,856	5,336	4,453	5,342	5,987	7,708	7,902	10,042	12,191	–0.1	–1.9	15.0
Gambia, The	237	291	347	336	366	418	460	597	736	1.6	3.7	7.7
Ghana	4,426	5,774	6,030	7,459	8,674	10,533	12,588	14,851	15,875	2.9	2.6	17.6
Guinea	..	2,518	3,170	3,580	3,879	3,212	3,257	4,497	4,222	..	3.3	4.3
Guinea-Bissau	105	233	195	223	274	290	308	374	422	3.4	–0.7	11.0
Kenya	7,039	8,224	13,028	14,738	15,950	18,763	22,516	27,055	34,288	2.6	8.3	13.5
Lesotho	695	937	834	1,250	1,600	1,680	1,898	2,087	2,043	0.4	1.4	13.0
Liberia	930	..	453	350	373	417	444	560	676	–3.2	..	5.7
Madagascar	4,024	2,958	4,326	5,394	4,285	4,960	5,435	7,288	8,894	–6.0	3.8	9.1
Malawi	1,138	1,837	2,621	2,385	2,582	2,813	3,125	3,563	4,246	2.2	0.2	11.3
Mali	1,768	2,405	3,103	4,203	4,679	5,099	5,524	7,445	8,484	2.8	0.1	17.6
Mauritania	672	1,076	1,276	1,343	1,613	1,901	2,769	2,750	..	4.8	1.8	16.1
Mauritius	1,130	2,363	4,541	5,246	6,028	6,285	6,478	6,853	8,941	7.7	6.6	8.6
Mozambique	3,550	2,320	4,028	4,469	5,358	6,095	6,414	7,274	8,721	–5.6	8.6	11.1
Namibia	1,818	2,388	3,395	5,163	6,689	7,149	7,948	8,610	8,460	0.2	4.5	13.8
Niger	2,476	2,423	2,146	2,718	3,039	3,397	3,647	4,245	5,338	0.1	–1.7	14.3
Nigeria	61,079	25,585	52,716	59,996	78,110	98,881	141,277	155,392	197,319	–12.5	3.7	23.4
Rwanda	1,165	2,572	1,622	1,746	1,936	2,351	2,806	3,395	4,420	8.5	–2.0	13.0
São Tomé and Príncipe	..	..	..	..	..	111	127	151	179	..	..	..
Senegal	..	..	..	..	..	..	9,278	11,203	13,104	..	..	..
Seychelles	142	355	630	663	666	844	924	841	765	8.9	5.9	5.3
Sierra Leone	1,071	580	903	946	1,014	1,166	1,365	1,629	1,914	–4.8	1.5	13.8
Somalia	603	835	..	..	..	..	..	..	..	5.5	..	..
South Africa	77,425	107,918	108,079	162,044	211,700	237,860	252,594	274,723	267,815	4.3	2.2	13.5
Sudan	7,570	11,409	13,697	16,428	19,990	25,397	33,503	41,682	52,386	9.7	1.9	22.2
Swaziland	..	1,174	1,177	1,754	2,284	2,702	2,684	2,957	2,662	..	4.5	11.6
Tanzania	..	4,072	9,579	10,135	11,153	14,002	14,097	16,129	19,876	..	9.3	10.4
Togo	1,096	1,598	1,454	1,736	2,033	2,073	2,180	2,455	2,806	4.6	–0.1	10.5
Uganda	1,237	4,227	6,062	6,484	7,801	8,991	9,712	11,663	14,218	20.7	9.1	12.0
Zambia	3,594	3,008	3,565	4,231	5,026	6,761	9,507	10,026	12,986	–4.1	0.7	20.9
Zimbabwe	6,610	8,494	21,651	7,207	4,503	3,220	..	..	..	–0.2	–2.6	–19.2
NORTH AFRICA	103,183	159,989	234,312	254,999	283,945	326,528	379,219	448,199	580,032	4.9	5.4	11.7
Algeria	41,147	59,955	54,823	65,319	81,414	97,259	111,940	132,594	171,880	4.5	–1.3	16.8
Egypt, Arab Rep.	21,453	42,025	88,763	83,006	78,757	89,474	108,015	131,653	164,215	7.5	11.2	5.6
Libya	..	..	..	24,357	30,253	41,462	50,765	59,730	101,397	..	..	30.7
Morocco	18,402	24,835	39,448	48,783	55,961	58,760	64,703	74,139	85,236	3.3	5.3	11.9
Tunisia	8,450	11,882	20,096	23,957	26,895	27,309	29,553	33,249	35,518	2.0	6.0	9.0
ALL AFRICA	369,535	446,415	581,241	682,334	811,670	944,386	1,104,866	1,272,332	1,530,861	2.1	3.0	14.4

a. Provisional.

Table 2.7 Gross national income, *Atlas* method

	Current prices ($ millions)									Average annual growth (%)		
	1980	1990	2002	2003	2004	2005	2006	2007	2008[a]	1980–89	1990–99	2000–08
SUB-SAHARAN AFRICA	219,358	283,925	333,120	375,065	463,951	577,651	684,310	779,264	893,449	0.9	2.1	14.8
Excluding South Africa	166,400	170,871	214,354	244,444	296,562	352,549	428,428	506,600	613,196	–1.2	1.6	15.7
Excl. S. Africa & Nigeria	114,173	147,023	168,676	188,346	222,319	263,864	306,722	360,905	434,567	2.0	1.2	13.3
Angola	..	7,261	9,134	10,678	14,637	21,941	32,657	45,509	62,113	..	–1.6	35.0
Benin	1,223	1,629	2,523	2,985	3,708	4,316	4,670	5,120	5,951	1.1	3.9	13.1
Botswana	860	3,311	5,475	6,493	7,927	9,811	10,505	11,484	12,328	9.4	5.1	12.0
Burkina Faso	1,726	2,762	3,003	3,684	4,634	5,528	5,989	6,399	7,278	3.5	–0.5	14.3
Burundi	761	1,125	666	623	666	723	843	956	1,092	3.8	–3.5	2.9
Cameroon	4,613	10,553	9,817	11,393	14,183	16,295	17,781	19,489	21,781	8.7	–1.5	11.9
Cape Verde	..	316	571	678	807	972	1,143	1,320	1,561	..	7.0	14.1
Central African Republic	668	1,308	965	1,003	1,187	1,358	1,471	1,608	1,804	7.1	–3.5	7.8
Chad	929	1,504	1,755	1,999	3,254	4,204	4,783	5,463	5,916	4.5	–0.6	23.2
Comoros	..	221	228	271	326	389	411	435	483	8.6	–1.1	12.4
Congo, Dem. Rep.	14,859	7,912	4,555	5,455	6,383	7,000	7,876	8,786	9,843	–8.4	–5.7	12.6
Congo, Rep.	1,248	2,062	2,257	2,440	2,929	3,799	5,021	5,370	7,134	2.4	–5.1	18.2
Côte d'Ivoire	7,929	8,763	9,936	11,191	13,655	15,691	16,519	17,771	20,257	0.9	3.6	9.3
Djibouti	..	..	593	675	754	803	847	895	957	..	1.1	7.9
Equatorial Guinea	..	117	1,180	1,231	1,928	3,170	4,296	6,235	9,875	..	16.3	38.0
Eritrea	..	..	684	647	655	801	983	1,308	1,492	..	4.2	9.4
Ethiopia	..	11,542	8,195	8,167	9,954	12,195	14,298	17,568	22,742	6.4	–4.9	11.5
Gabon	2,811	4,314	4,395	4,727	5,357	7,010	7,397	9,175	10,490	0.5	–0.7	13.4
Gambia, The	207	277	372	369	391	417	457	541	653	0.7	4.2	3.1
Ghana	3,976	5,536	5,502	6,549	8,144	9,966	11,704	13,763	15,744	4.1	2.5	13.7
Guinea	..	2,588	3,171	3,392	3,824	3,862	3,722	3,722	..	..	4.1	2.7
Guinea-Bissau	99	206	185	189	234	283	315	340	386	3.5	–0.4	8.6
Kenya	6,381	8,394	12,878	14,032	16,074	18,604	21,050	24,834	29,541	2.5	6.4	10.1
Lesotho	502	866	902	1,019	1,279	1,603	1,922	2,077	2,179	1.6	3.0	12.6
Liberia	849	..	459	342	364	407	431	531	634	–3.2	..	2.6
Madagascar	3,424	2,632	3,842	4,858	5,184	5,377	5,352	6,357	7,766	–4.1	4.8	7.1
Malawi	1,001	1,625	1,801	2,243	2,822	2,865	3,156	3,547	4,107	2.1	1.4	12.4
Mali	1,492	2,146	2,702	3,476	4,365	5,195	5,546	6,941	7,360	1.5	1.3	16.6
Mauritania	617	1,044	1,246	1,310	1,532	1,792	2,324	2,636	..	4.9	3.8	13.1
Mauritius	..	2,304	4,621	4,997	5,759	6,527	6,846	7,067	8,122	8.7	7.7	7.9
Mozambique	..	2,211	4,332	4,491	5,147	5,986	6,604	7,266	8,119	–3.3	7.2	8.9
Namibia	..	2,300	3,710	4,292	5,537	6,864	7,989	8,536	8,880	0.2	5.4	15.2
Niger	2,083	2,241	2,003	2,381	2,879	3,381	3,646	3,998	4,823	–0.2	–1.8	12.6
Nigeria	47,183	24,151	45,399	55,621	73,419	87,689	119,713	143,293	175,622	–10.6	3.3	23.8
Rwanda	1,119	2,408	1,804	1,759	1,932	2,278	2,627	3,142	3,955	8.3	–2.9	7.0
São Tomé and Príncipe	..	..	..	..	..	117	130	145	164	..	..	..
Senegal	..	..	..	..	..	..	9,304	10,328	11,825	..	..	..
Seychelles	113	332	573	620	680	803	909	940	889	9.7	6.6	7.8
Sierra Leone	1,074	768	928	1,012	1,079	1,198	1,323	1,537	1,785	–6.6	0.6	12.4
Somalia	656	959	..	..	..	..	..	..	..	5.9	..	..
South Africa	58,621	113,320	119,414	131,451	168,226	225,603	256,958	274,323	283,310	4.7	2.9	13.6
Sudan	7,909	12,988	12,905	15,277	18,511	22,946	29,250	36,703	46,520	10.0	0.4	19.3
Swaziland	..	940	1,314	1,417	1,804	2,542	2,684	2,934	2,945	..	7.3	11.0
Tanzania	..	4,607	9,773	10,463	11,564	13,382	14,518	15,934	18,350	..	7.2	9.0
Togo	973	1,433	1,375	1,561	1,877	2,105	2,253	2,361	2,607	3.2	0.4	9.2
Uganda	..	5,396	6,227	6,596	7,642	8,692	10,029	11,397	13,254	21.2	6.1	9.4
Zambia	3,074	3,315	3,454	4,014	4,602	5,849	7,221	9,116	11,986	–6.2	0.5	16.9
Zimbabwe	5,789	8,524	9,973	9,874	7,334	4,467	..	..	..	0.2	–2.1	–2.9
NORTH AFRICA	86,426	152,924	242,799	255,953	280,596	318,146	361,047	417,123	499,568	6.0	4.8	8.5
Algeria	32,949	57,942	54,987	62,068	73,987	89,353	103,878	122,196	146,365	6.6	–1.9	14.6
Egypt, Arab Rep.	18,546	40,173	97,225	93,204	90,725	92,817	101,669	120,049	146,851	8.8	10.2	1.6
Libya	..	..	..	24,288	25,650	34,726	44,645	55,477	72,735	..	..	24.7
Morocco	16,000	23,440	38,743	44,362	53,196	60,348	66,312	70,652	80,544	1.9	5.4	10.6
Tunisia	7,430	11,018	19,533	22,257	26,324	28,754	30,756	32,822	33,998	2.2	6.9	8.7
ALL AFRICA	308,411	440,553	575,774	632,091	746,236	898,214	1,048,300	1,199,655	1,396,577	2.5	3.0	12.4

a. Provisional.

Table

2.8 Gross national income per capita, *Atlas* method

	Current prices ($)									Annual average growth (%)		
	1980	1990	2002	2003	2004	2005	2006	2007	2008[a]	1980–89	1990–99	2000–08
SUB-SAHARAN AFRICA	571	553	471	518	625	759	877	975	1,091	–2.0	–0.6	12.4
Excluding South Africa	467	358	324	360	426	493	584	674	796	–4.1	–1.2	13.5
Excl. S. Africa & Nigeria	400	384	318	346	398	460	521	598	702	–1.0	–1.5	11.3
Angola	..	680	600	680	910	1,320	1,910	2,590	3,450	..	–4.5	32.2
Benin	340	340	350	410	490	550	570	610	690	–1.6	0.4	9.7
Botswana	860	2,420	3,080	3,620	4,370	5,340	5,650	6,100	6,470	6.0	2.6	10.4
Burkina Faso	250	310	240	280	340	400	420	430	480	0.9	–3.3	10.5
Burundi	180	200	100	90	90	100	110	120	140	0.7	–4.7	2.0
Cameroon	510	860	590	670	810	920	980	1,050	1,150	5.4	–4.1	9.5
Cape Verde	..	890	1,260	1,470	1,720	2,040	2,360	2,680	3,130	..	4.7	12.9
Central African Republic	290	430	240	250	290	320	340	370	410	4.4	–5.9	6.5
Chad	200	250	190	210	330	410	460	510	530	1.7	–3.6	17.9
Comoros	..	510	400	470	550	650	670	690	750	5.9	–3.2	9.6
Congo, Dem. Rep.	530	210	90	100	110	120	130	140	150	–11.2	–8.5	8.9
Congo, Rep.	690	840	710	750	880	1,110	1,440	1,510	1,970	–0.6	–7.2	16.6
Côte d'Ivoire	940	690	550	610	720	820	840	880	980	–3.2	0.4	7.3
Djibouti	..	..	780	870	950	1,000	1,030	1,070	1,130	..	–1.6	5.7
Equatorial Guinea	..	310	2,110	2,140	3,250	5,210	6,870	9,710	14,980	..	12.3	36.3
Eritrea	..	..	170	150	150	180	210	270	300	..	1.7	7.4
Ethiopia	..	240	120	120	140	160	190	220	280	3.3	–7.6	10.2
Gabon	4,120	4,660	3,410	3,590	3,990	5,120	5,300	6,450	7,240	–2.5	–3.6	11.7
Gambia, The	340	310	270	260	260	270	290	330	390	–3.1	0.4	1.7
Ghana	360	370	270	310	380	450	520	600	670	0.9	–0.3	11.8
Guinea	..	420	360	380	420	420	400	390	..	..	0.8	0.9
Guinea-Bissau	120	200	140	130	160	190	210	220	250	1.5	–2.7	6.7
Kenya	390	360	390	420	460	520	580	660	770	–1.0	3.3	8.4
Lesotho	390	540	470	520	650	810	960	1,040	1,080	–0.5	1.4	11.5
Liberia	440	..	150	110	110	120	120	150	170	–4.8	..	1.0
Madagascar	400	230	240	290	300	310	300	340	410	–6.6	1.8	5.4
Malawi	160	170	150	180	220	220	230	250	290	–2.1	–0.2	9.5
Mali	250	280	250	320	390	450	460	560	580	–0.8	–1.4	12.7
Mauritania	410	540	460	470	530	600	760	840	..	2.3	1.0	9.9
Mauritius	..	2,180	3,820	4,090	4,670	5,250	5,460	5,610	6,400	7.9	6.5	7.3
Mozambique	..	160	230	230	260	290	310	340	370	–3.7	3.9	6.7
Namibia	..	1,620	1,910	2,180	2,780	3,400	3,900	4,100	4,200	–3.7	2.4	12.7
Niger	360	290	170	190	220	250	270	280	330	–3.0	–5.3	9.3
Nigeria	660	260	350	410	530	620	830	970	1,160	–13.0	0.4	20.9
Rwanda	220	340	210	200	220	250	290	330	410	4.3	–3.0	6.8
São Tomé and Príncipe	..	..	..	..	..	760	840	920	1,020	..	..	..
Senegal	..	..	..	..	..	..	800	870	970	..	..	..
Seychelles	1,760	4,750	6,850	7,490	8,240	9,680	10,740	11,060	10,290	8.8	5.0	6.3
Sierra Leone	330	190	200	210	220	230	250	280	320	–8.8	0.8	8.8
Somalia	100	140	..	..	..	..	..	..	..	6.1	..	..
South Africa	2,130	3,220	2,640	2,870	3,630	4,810	5,420	5,730	5,820	2.1	0.7	11.7
Sudan	390	480	350	410	490	590	740	910	1,130	6.8	–2.2	18.0
Swaziland	..	1,090	1,190	1,280	1,620	2,260	2,360	2,550	2,520	..	4.9	9.7
Tanzania	..	180	270	280	300	340	360	390	430	..	4.2	6.7
Togo	350	370	250	270	320	350	370	370	400	–0.5	–2.4	6.3
Uganda	..	300	240	250	280	300	340	370	420	17.0	2.9	6.8
Zambia	530	420	310	360	400	500	600	740	950	–9.2	–2.3	15.9
Zimbabwe	790	810	800	790	590	360	..	..	..	–3.4	–3.9	–2.9
NORTH AFRICA	939	1,277	1,631	1,693	1,826	2,038	2,276	2,588	3,051	3.2	2.9	8.1
Algeria	1,750	2,290	1,750	1,950	2,290	2,720	3,110	3,610	4,260	3.4	–3.8	13.6
Egypt, Arab Rep.	420	700	1,330	1,250	1,200	1,200	1,290	1,500	1,800	5.9	8.0	1.9
Libya	..	..	..	4,270	4,420	5,870	7,390	9,010	11,590	..	..	23.4
Morocco	830	970	1,330	1,500	1,780	2,000	2,170	2,290	2,580	–0.4	3.6	9.5
Tunisia	1,160	1,350	2,000	2,260	2,650	2,870	3,040	3,210	3,290	–0.3	5.2	7.3
ALL AFRICA	648	696	673	722	832	979	1,116	1,249	1,421	–0.4	0.4	10.6

a. Provisional.

Table 2.9 Gross domestic product deflator (local currency series)

	Index (2000 = 100)											
										Annual average		
	1980	1990	2002	2003	2004	2005	2006	2007	2008[a]	1980–89	1990–99	2000–08
SUB-SAHARAN AFRICA	15	40	111	117	127	139	150	163	183	23	67	133
Excluding South Africa	17	40	111	117	126	139	152	164	186	25	67	133
Excl. S. Africa & Nigeria	20	40	110	117	124	139	149	162	183	26	68	132
Angola	..	..	460	931	1,329	1,780	2,041	2,126	2,548	..	3	1,280
Benin	38	50	111	113	113	116	120	123	135	47	73	115
Botswana	13	41	110	113	119	132	154	174	203	22	62	134
Burkina Faso	52	76	110	111	115	115	115	119	125	67	84	113
Burundi	21	31	107	120	130	151	158	171	213	24	51	139
Cameroon	34	58	105	106	107	110	115	117	119	50	79	109
Cape Verde	..	66	105	106	113	115	123	127	134	60	81	114
Central African Republic	32	70	107	105	106	109	114	116	122	54	83	109
Chad	46	60	116	116	127	157	166	169	190	55	78	139
Comoros	36	70	113	119	121	124	126	133	140	54	82	121
Congo, Dem. Rep.	..	..	639	722	769	937	1,064	1,252	1,495	0	2	829
Congo, Rep.	29	38	84	82	87	113	134	124	153	39	50	107
Côte d'Ivoire	39	50	110	111	112	116	122	125	135	50	75	115
Djibouti	..	69	102	104	108	111	115	118	122	..	85	109
Equatorial Guinea	..	24	87	87	102	145	166	164	203	26	41	127
Eritrea	..	..	138	161	192	260	287	304	359	..	66	213
Ethiopia	..	49	91	102	106	117	130	152	197	42	79	121
Gabon	35	53	94	93	99	116	125	132	151	44	63	112
Gambia, The	15	64	134	170	191	199	202	213	226	31	82	172
Ghana	0	11	166	213	244	280	316	360	424	3	37	249
Guinea	5	48	108	120	145	186	256	300	417	17	77	193
Guinea-Bissau	0	6	99	103	114	118	119	130	143	1	47	114
Kenya	10	24	103	109	117	123	132	138	175	16	57	122
Lesotho	13	40	124	127	135	141	153	167	183	22	67	137
Liberia	2	2	141	145	146	166	181	210	237	2	22	160
Madagascar	4	21	124	127	145	172	192	210	230	10	54	156
Malawi	2	7	217	236	270	311	366	393	428	3	29	272
Mali	35	57	116	117	116	119	124	129	147	50	79	119
Mauritania	20	42	116	119	133	157	203	198	..	29	75	142
Mauritius	21	54	111	117	124	130	135	145	156	33	74	125
Mozambique	0	6	124	131	141	153	167	180	191	1	45	145
Namibia	11	34	123	124	127	134	146	160	179	19	55	134
Niger	49	63	107	107	105	112	115	119	128	63	78	111
Nigeria	2	7	146	162	195	234	280	293	336	3	41	206
Rwanda	20	33	96	117	132	144	158	175	205	25	70	137
São Tomé and Príncipe	..	..	..	..	..	..	..	..	..	..	..	..
Senegal	39	63	106	107	107	110	114	121	129	55	81	111
Seychelles	56	87	110	117	121	142	144	154	193	70	92	132
Sierra Leone	0	5	98	106	123	139	155	171	191	1	41	132
Somalia	..	..	..	..	..	..	..	..	..	..	..	..
South Africa	9	38	119	124	131	139	149	162	180	18	65	135
Sudan	..	..	..	..	..	..	..	..	..	..	..	..
Swaziland	13	40	116	123	130	139	152	165	171	19	69	134
Tanzania	..	15	114	122	132	159	168	183	199	11	49	143
Togo	35	58	105	101	105	106	106	107	112	49	78	105
Uganda	..	28	104	112	129	127	130	139	148	4	69	121
Zambia	0	1	151	181	214	251	285	318	353	0	32	220
Zimbabwe	2	7	394	1,883	9,064	30,632	..	..	..	4	24	7,042
NORTH AFRICA	21	54	105	111	123	133	143	161	181	33	77	129
Algeria	6	16	103	111	123	143	158	169	198	9	50	134
Egypt, Arab Rep.	13	43	105	112	125	133	143	161	181	20	73	129
Libya	..	..	128	166	204	264	300	316	492	..	81	230
Morocco	35	68	102	103	104	105	107	111	114	50	84	105
Tunisia	30	64	105	107	110	114	118	121	127	46	82	112
ALL AFRICA	15	40	110	117	125	139	149	162	182	23	68	132

a. Provisional.

Table 2.10 Gross domestic product deflator (U.S. dollar series)

	Index (2000 = 100)											
										Annual average		
	1980	1990	2002	2003	2004	2005	2006	2007	2008[a]	1980–89	1990–99	2000–08
SUB-SAHARAN AFRICA	121	110	99	117	135	151	164	178	196	108	109	137
Excluding South Africa	149	116	112	118	132	150	172	188	222	123	104	144
Excl. S. Africa & Nigeria	130	126	109	115	127	141	156	174	203	120	113	136
Angola	..	121	106	125	160	205	255	278	341	95	91	185
Benin	130	131	113	138	153	157	163	183	215	103	116	147
Botswana	88	112	88	116	129	132	134	144	153	77	108	121
Burkina Faso	175	199	113	136	155	155	156	177	199	147	135	143
Burundi	164	131	83	80	85	101	111	114	129	153	123	99
Cameroon	106	127	99	120	134	137	144	160	174	102	125	129
Cape Verde	..	112	107	130	152	155	167	188	213	95	117	146
Central African Republic	108	183	109	129	142	148	155	173	194	117	143	139
Chad	155	157	118	142	172	212	227	251	301	121	129	182
Comoros	91	138	116	146	163	167	172	197	223	89	125	154
Congo, Dem. Rep.	205	122	127	123	134	136	157	167	183	133	126	138
Congo, Rep.	98	100	86	100	118	153	183	184	244	84	81	139
Côte d'Ivoire	132	130	112	136	150	157	166	186	215	108	123	147
Djibouti	..	69	102	104	108	111	115	118	122	..	85	109
Equatorial Guinea	..	64	89	107	137	196	227	244	323	54	65	168
Eritrea	..	..	95	86	90	161	180	190	224	..	99	136
Ethiopia	..	194	87	97	101	110	122	141	173	167	151	114
Gabon	119	138	96	114	134	157	171	196	240	96	104	144
Gambia, The	113	104	86	80	81	89	92	110	126	91	109	95
Ghana	168	180	114	134	148	168	188	209	211	177	166	153
Guinea	434	128	95	105	111	89	86	121	104	420	136	101
Guinea-Bissau	97	131	102	127	154	160	162	194	212	105	116	145
Kenya	103	81	99	109	112	124	139	156	193	86	86	126
Lesotho	114	106	82	117	145	153	156	164	153	94	119	129
Liberia	69	89	93	100	109	119	128	140	155	76	101	115
Madagascar	130	94	122	139	105	116	121	152	173	108	101	127
Malawi	124	151	168	144	148	157	160	167	182	118	132	148
Mali	116	149	118	144	157	161	169	192	233	108	132	152
Mauritania	102	125	102	108	124	139	181	176	..	108	140	129
Mauritius	76	89	94	105	116	115	113	114	138	71	104	110
Mozambique	143	99	81	85	96	103	102	107	123	157	93	98
Namibia	95	91	81	114	136	146	150	157	150	79	97	125
Niger	165	165	109	131	141	151	156	176	203	137	127	141
Nigeria	204	81	123	127	150	181	223	237	288	127	76	170
Rwanda	85	154	79	85	89	101	112	125	146	112	123	103
São Tomé and Príncipe	..	..	..	..	..	..	..	..	..	..	..	..
Senegal	131	165	108	130	144	147	155	179	204	120	136	141
Seychelles	50	93	115	123	126	148	150	131	117	65	103	124
Sierra Leone	119	64	98	95	95	101	110	120	134	98	99	107
Somalia	..	..	..	..	..	..	..	..	..	..	..	..
South Africa	85	101	78	114	141	151	152	160	151	88	115	126
Sudan	138	176	108	120	139	165	197	228	266	196	122	158
Swaziland	115	108	77	113	140	151	156	163	144	87	123	125
Tanzania	..	63	94	94	97	113	107	117	133	76	77	106
Togo	118	152	107	124	141	143	144	160	178	106	131	133
Uganda	..	134	89	90	101	110	107	118	132	157	109	104
Zambia	142	109	107	119	140	175	246	247	293	111	111	170
Zimbabwe	153	130	318	120	79	61	..	..	..	136	101	137
NORTH AFRICA	93	96	86	91	97	107	117	130	159	91	92	109
Algeria	120	134	97	108	128	147	164	184	231	128	101	140
Egypt, Arab Rep.	60	66	83	76	69	76	85	96	112	62	76	88
Libya	..	..	52	66	80	103	117	128	206	..	89	104
Morocco	94	88	98	114	124	126	129	144	156	72	99	121
Tunisia	101	100	101	114	121	120	121	129	141	89	111	116
ALL AFRICA	112	104	93	106	120	133	145	158	181	101	102	126

a. Provisional.

Table 2.11 Consumer price index

	Annual growth (%)											
										Annual average		
	1980	1990	2002	2003	2004	2005	2006	2007	2008[a]	1980–89	1990–99	2000–08
SUB-SAHARAN AFRICA												
Angola	..	..	108.9	98.2	43.5	23.0	13.3	12.2	12.5	..	1,122.5	87.7
Benin	..	..	2.5	1.5	0.9	5.4	3.8	1.3	7.9	..	9.7	3.5
Botswana	13.6	11.4	8.0	9.2	6.9	8.6	11.6	7.1	12.7	10.8	10.8	8.8
Burkina Faso	12.2	–0.5	2.2	2.0	–0.4	6.4	2.3	–0.2	10.7	5.0	4.5	3.1
Burundi	2.5	7.0	–1.4	7.9	10.7	13.5	2.8	8.3	24.1	7.2	13.5	11.1
Cameroon	9.6	1.1	2.8	0.6	0.2	2.0	5.1	0.9	5.3	9.1	5.6	2.5
Cape Verde	..	10.7	1.9	1.2	–1.9	0.4	5.4	4.4	6.8	6.7	6.4	2.1
Central African Republic	..	0.0	2.3	4.1	–2.1	2.9	..	..	9.3	3.6	3.9	3.4
Chad	..	–0.7	5.2	–1.8	–5.4	7.9	8.0	–9.0	10.3	3.0	5.5	3.5
Comoros	..	..	..	..	..	..	..	..	..	..	..	..
Congo, Dem. Rep.	46.6	81.3	31.5	12.9	4.0	21.3	13.1	16.9	..	57.0	3,367.2	121.7
Congo, Rep.	..	2.9	4.4	–0.6	2.4	3.1	6.5	2.7	7.3	1.0	8.5	2.8
Côte d'Ivoire	14.7	–0.8	3.1	3.3	1.4	3.9	2.5	1.9	6.3	6.7	6.0	3.2
Djibouti	12.1	..	..	..	..	..	..	..	..	5.3	..	..
Equatorial Guinea	..	0.9	7.6	7.3	4.2	5.6	4.4	2.8	6.6	–5.5	6.6	5.8
Eritrea	..	..	..	..	..	..	..	..	..	..	..	..
Ethiopia	4.5	5.2	1.7	17.8	3.3	11.6	12.3	17.2	44.4	4.6	8.0	11.2
Gabon	12.3	7.7	0.0	2.2	0.4	1.2	–1.4	5.0	5.3	6.5	3.7	1.7
Gambia, The	6.8	12.2	8.6	17.0	14.2	4.8	2.1	5.4	4.5	17.5	5.4	6.9
Ghana	50.1	37.3	14.8	26.7	12.6	15.1	10.9	10.7	16.5	48.3	27.6	18.4
Guinea	..	..	..	..	..	..	..	..	18.4	..	..	18.4
Guinea-Bissau	..	33.0	3.3	–3.5	0.9	3.3	2.0	4.6	10.5	70.5	37.5	3.7
Kenya	13.9	17.8	2.0	9.8	11.6	10.3	14.5	9.8	26.2	11.8	17.4	11.1
Lesotho	16.3	11.6	33.8	6.7	5.0	3.4	6.0	8.0	10.7	13.9	12.4	7.8
Liberia	14.7	..	..	..	..	..	..	..	..	5.6	..	..
Madagascar	18.2	11.8	15.9	–1.2	13.8	18.5	10.8	10.3	9.2	18.6	17.3	10.7
Malawi	..	11.8	14.7	9.6	11.4	15.4	14.0	8.0	8.7	16.8	31.0	14.9
Mali	..	0.6	5.0	–1.3	–3.1	6.4	1.5	1.4	9.2	–0.1	4.2	2.6
Mauritania	..	6.6	3.9	5.2	10.4	12.1	6.2	7.3	7.3	7.5	6.4	6.7
Mauritius	42.0	13.5	6.5	3.9	4.7	4.9	8.9	8.8	9.7	11.2	7.6	6.3
Mozambique	..	47.0	16.8	13.4	12.7	7.2	13.2	8.2	10.3	45.1	34.5	11.5
Namibia	..	..	..	7.2	4.1	2.3	5.1	6.7	10.4	..	..	5.9
Niger	10.3	–0.8	2.6	–1.6	0.3	7.8	0.0	0.1	11.3	3.6	4.3	3.0
Nigeria	10.0	7.4	12.9	14.0	15.0	17.9	8.2	5.4	11.6	20.9	30.6	12.3
Rwanda	7.2	4.2	2.0	7.4	12.3	9.0	8.9	9.1	15.4	4.7	8.6	7.9
São Tomé and Príncipe	..	..	..	..	..	..	..	..	..	..	..	..
Senegal	8.7	0.3	2.2	0.0	0.5	1.7	2.1	5.9	5.8	6.9	4.4	2.4
Seychelles	13.6	3.9	0.2	3.3	3.9	0.9	–0.4	5.3	37.0	4.0	2.0	6.9
Sierra Leone	..	..	..	..	..	..	..	11.5	17.5	..	..	14.5
Somalia	..	..	..	..	..	..	..	..	..	..	..	..
South Africa	13.7	14.3	9.2	5.6	–0.9	2.1	3.2	6.1	9.8	14.6	9.9	5.1
Sudan	25.4	65.2	8.3	7.7	8.4	8.5	7.2	8.0	16.0	36.2	80.4	8.6
Swaziland	18.7	13.1	12.0	7.3	3.4	4.8	5.3	9.5	13.4	15.0	9.5	8.2
Tanzania	30.2	35.8	1.0	5.3	4.7	5.0	7.3	7.0	10.3	30.1	23.1	5.7
Togo	12.3	1.0	3.1	–1.0	0.4	6.8	2.2	1.0	8.7	5.0	7.1	3.0
Uganda	..	33.1	–0.3	8.7	3.7	8.4	7.3	6.1	12.1	111.2	13.0	5.7
Zambia	..	107.0	22.2	21.4	18.0	18.3	9.0	10.7	12.4	69.3	76.2	17.7
Zimbabwe	5.4	17.4	140.1	431.7	282.4	302.1	1,096.7	24,411.0	..	12.8	28.6	3,349.6
NORTH AFRICA												
Algeria	9.5	16.7	1.4	2.6	3.6	1.6	2.5	3.5	4.4	9.0	18.6	2.7
Egypt, Arab Rep.	20.8	16.8	2.7	4.5	11.3	4.9	7.6	9.3	18.3	17.4	10.5	7.1
Libya	9.7	8.5	–9.8	–2.2	–2.2	2.0	3.4	..	..	7.9	6.7	–2.9
Morocco	9.4	6.8	2.8	1.2	1.5	1.0	3.3	2.0	3.8	7.6	4.4	2.0
Tunisia	..	6.5	2.7	2.7	3.6	2.0	4.5	3.1	4.9	7.6	4.9	3.2

a. Provisional.

Table 2.12 Price indexes

	Inflation, GDP deflator (annual %)		Consumer price index (2000 = 100)		Exports of goods and services price index (2000 = 100)		Imports of goods and services price index (2000 = 100)	
	2007	2008[a]	2007	2008[a]	2007	2008[a]	2007	2008[a]
SUB-SAHARAN AFRICA	6.8	10.8	111.8	125.2	..	..	158.0	175.8
Excluding South Africa	6.7	11.2	112.1	126.6	..	..	..	..
Excl. S. Africa & Nigeria	6.8	10.8	111.8	125.2	..	..	158.9	183.1
Angola	4.1	19.9	127.2	143.0	..	..	..	..
Benin	2.9	9.4	105.1	113.5	..	..	..	..
Botswana	13.0	17.2	119.5	134.6	132.9	132.5	181.0	191.3
Burkina Faso	3.7	5.1	102.1	113.0	..	..	..	..
Burundi	8.3	24.5	111.4	138.2	..	..	..	..
Cameroon	2.1	1.7	106.1	111.7	201.7	242.6	163.6	172.5
Cape Verde	3.2	5.4	110.0	117.5	69.3	74.2	118.2	126.5
Central African Republic	2.0	4.6	107.7	117.7	139.1	145.4	184.8	200.6
Chad	1.7	11.9	98.3	108.5	251.5	301.3	251.5	301.3
Comoros	5.2	5.5	..	..	193.3	213.1	193.3	213.1
Congo, Dem. Rep.	17.7	19.5	132.2	..	172.8	162.7	125.1	121.0
Congo, Rep.	–7.9	23.8	109.4	117.4	..	..	..	..
Côte d'Ivoire	2.7	8.1	104.4	111.0	155.3	187.4	183.0	244.0
Djibouti	3.1	3.1	..	..	..	..	..	..
Equatorial Guinea	–1.2	23.7	107.3	114.4	..	..	..	..
Eritrea	5.9	18.0	..	..	111.3	..	113.2	..
Ethiopia	16.8	29.1	131.7	190.1	118.4	141.9	151.5	171.1
Gabon	5.2	14.2	103.6	109.0	246.2	367.4	168.6	197.9
Gambia, The	5.7	6.0	107.5	112.3	116.1	117.2	136.4	164.6
Ghana	13.8	18.0	122.8	143.1	164.3	184.3	164.8	170.9
Guinea	17.4	38.9	100.0	118.4	202.1	131.2	220.0	145.4
Guinea-Bissau	9.6	9.5	106.7	117.8	115.9	..	146.1	..
Kenya	4.7	27.0	125.6	158.6	159.4	203.1	137.1	169.4
Lesotho	9.2	9.6	114.6	126.8	120.6	134.7	89.4	87.2
Liberia	16.0	12.8	..	..	..	..	..	..
Madagascar	9.7	9.6	122.2	133.5	141.7	145.8	140.5	163.7
Malawi	7.4	8.9	123.0	133.8	344.3	429.9	209.7	300.8
Mali	4.1	13.6	103.0	112.4	165.1	..	186.7	..
Mauritania	–2.6	..	113.9	122.3	142.0	..	..	..
Mauritius	7.0	7.6	118.5	130.1	115.4	139.2	132.9	161.8
Mozambique	7.4	6.5	122.5	135.1	141.9	137.5	190.6	197.2
Namibia	9.3	12.0	112.1	123.7	174.4	265.4	142.0	266.3
Niger	3.3	7.6	100.1	111.4	..	..	..	..
Nigeria	4.8	14.4	114.1	127.3	..	..	..	..
Rwanda	10.5	17.4	118.8	137.1	..	..	..	..
São Tomé and Príncipe	19.4	23.7	..	..	..	..	..	..
Senegal	5.6	7.3	108.1	114.3	169.9	183.3	183.5	198.8
Seychelles	6.7	25.3	104.9	143.8	115.6	96.9	115.6	96.9
Sierra Leone	10.3	11.7	111.5	131.0	..	..	..	..
Somalia	..	..	..	..	..	..	..	..
South Africa	9.0	10.8	109.5	120.2	183.9	200.5	157.0	168.1
Sudan	7.0	15.8	115.7	134.3	224.6	261.3	224.7	261.3
Swaziland	8.9	3.4	115.3	130.7	157.4	134.4	117.2	101.1
Tanzania	9.0	8.9	114.8	126.6	..	..	..	..
Togo	1.3	4.4	103.2	112.2	..	..	..	..
Uganda	7.3	6.3	113.9	127.6	131.1	139.5	132.1	137.4
Zambia	11.8	10.8	120.6	135.7	132.3	120.2	106.2	111.2
Zimbabwe	..	..	293,318.0	..	..	..	..	..
NORTH AFRICA	5.4	12.3	107.0	112.0	..	..	136.3	168.1
Algeria	6.8	17.2	106.1	110.9	237.9	367.9	162.5	194.8
Egypt, Arab Rep.	12.6	12.3	117.7	139.2	87.2	106.0	82.9	105.9
Libya	5.4	55.5	..	..	..	..	..	..
Morocco	3.8	3.1	105.4	109.4	152.7	189.6	157.9	191.3
Tunisia	2.4	5.0	107.8	113.1	158.5	202.8	166.6	210.2
ALL AFRICA	6.7	11.3	111.4	123.0	..	..	149.1	172.6

a. Provisional.

Table 2.13 Gross domestic savings

	Share of GDP (%)											
										Annual average		
	1980	1990	2002	2003	2004	2005	2006	2007	2008[a]	1980–89	1990–99	2000–08
SUB-SAHARAN AFRICA	35.4	16.1	22.0	21.5	22.6	24.9	28.6	29.0	33.6	22.2	14.5	24.7
Excluding South Africa	31.4	9.7	20.2	22.1	26.2	29.5	34.1	33.0	36.6	16.1	10.4	26.8
Excl. S. Africa & Nigeria	14.3	12.9	14.7	15.8	18.0	20.1	23.0	23.0	26.6	13.1	12.4	19.1
Angola	..	29.7	23.9	19.2	25.1	37.9	49.5	47.9	62.6	24.0	22.0	35.9
Benin	–6.3	2.2	3.7	6.0	5.5	6.9	..	..	..	–2.4	3.8	5.8
Botswana	26.7	42.6	52.2	50.4	50.7	52.4	52.4	51.2	49.6	35.3	39.7	52.1
Burkina Faso	–7.2	5.4	3.7	4.5	1.8	4.8	2.8	..	..	–1.6	9.0	2.6
Burundi	–0.6	–5.4	–9.7	–8.7	–11.0	–23.1	–19.9	..	..	3.1	–5.2	–12.3
Cameroon	21.7	20.7	19.0	17.8	18.5	18.1	18.9	18.1	19.7	24.2	18.5	18.8
Cape Verde	..	–8.1	–15.7	–15.8	–1.5	4.4	4.6	5.3	8.2	–2.2	–5.6	–4.4
Central African Republic	–8.9	–0.6	4.3	1.6	0.0	0.1	1.4	1.5	1.6	–1.1	3.7	2.2
Chad	..	–7.7	–40.8	18.0	24.5	35.7	43.6	34.6	25.2	–8.1	–0.5	16.9
Comoros	–10.1	–3.2	–4.0	–5.8	–10.6	–12.9	–14.0	–11.4	–8.1	–4.5	–4.5	–8.6
Congo, Dem. Rep.	10.1	9.3	4.0	5.0	4.0	6.4	4.5	8.8	6.9	10.9	8.8	5.3
Congo, Rep.	35.7	23.8	51.0	51.3	51.3	57.6	65.7	57.2	..	31.9	28.8	55.5
Côte d'Ivoire	20.4	11.3	26.7	21.0	20.0	17.2	19.6	14.3	14.8	19.6	17.8	19.0
Djibouti	..	–10.4	4.9	5.3	4.3	8.6	12.2	18.1	..	..	–6.4	5.8
Equatorial Guinea	..	–20.1	79.0	80.1	78.9	83.7	86.1	86.9	72.8	..	13.7	80.3
Eritrea	..	..	–27.4	–40.9	–41.5	–27.2	–17.2	–17.7	..	..	–29.7	–29.2
Ethiopia	..	9.6	9.9	7.7	8.8	2.6	1.5	5.5	3.8	10.5	9.7	6.4
Gabon	60.6	36.9	43.7	48.2	54.6	58.3	57.4	55.0	66.3	44.3	43.6	54.8
Gambia, The	5.8	10.7	12.9	11.1	8.9	4.0	11.2	6.7	6.2	6.5	7.4	9.0
Ghana	4.9	5.5	7.4	7.0	7.3	4.9	5.7	7.6	5.6	4.8	7.5	6.5
Guinea	..	22.2	9.5	7.8	7.4	11.3	10.5	10.4	10.5	15.1	18.3	10.8
Guinea-Bissau	–1.0	2.8	–11.8	–1.6	14.1	11.5	–3.9	7.7	4.9	–0.9	1.5	–0.8
Kenya	18.1	18.5	9.8	10.5	10.8	9.4	8.1	9.0	10.6	18.3	14.6	9.4
Lesotho	–52.0	–42.4	–17.7	–23.0	–17.5	–22.3	–21.4	–23.4	–34.7	–66.3	–34.6	–20.7
Liberia	14.8	..	–3.3	–3.2	–0.7	2.4	–34.6	–30.5	..	2.2	..	–10.5
Madagascar	–1.4	5.5	7.7	8.9	8.5	8.0	14.1	11.1	10.4	2.9	4.2	10.2
Malawi	10.8	13.4	..	–3.4	2.0	–1.1	–1.3	4.9	4.1	12.7	3.4	1.6
Mali	1.1	6.4	11.3	13.3	8.6	11.0	14.8	13.5	..	–0.4	7.6	12.3
Mauritania	–3.5	4.9	–1.9	–5.0	–3.1	–15.0	18.8	18.7	..	3.1	2.4	0.9
Mauritius	14.5	23.5	25.2	24.8	23.4	18.9	17.5	17.5	16.9	20.0	24.1	21.6
Mozambique	–8.9	–5.8	14.9	6.1	10.0	9.3	12.8	11.9	13.0	–6.2	–2.9	10.4
Namibia	38.4	18.2	16.4	10.3	16.8	19.8	26.7	19.1	13.5	10.8	12.7	16.9
Niger	14.6	1.2	5.3	5.1	4.1	13.7	..	..	..	7.3	2.7	6.0
Nigeria[b]	..	..	..	..	..	..	..	..	..	..	..	..
Rwanda	4.2	6.2	–0.5	0.4	4.4	5.1	2.7	2.8	1.3	5.0	–5.5	2.3
São Tomé and Príncipe	..	..	..	..	..	..	..	..	..	..	..	..
Senegal	2.1	2.4	6.8	8.8	7.9	14.1	10.7	8.5	7.7	4.3	5.4	9.4
Seychelles	27.1	20.3	24.4	21.5	14.7	3.1	8.1	–1.9	6.7	24.1	21.7	13.1
Sierra Leone	0.9	8.7	–8.2	–3.7	–0.4	4.2	7.8	6.1	7.5	9.1	2.8	–1.4
Somalia	–12.9	–12.5	..	..	..	..	..	..	..	–6.3	–12.5	..
South Africa	37.9	23.2	19.9	19.2	17.3	17.2	17.1	18.3	18.4	28.5	19.4	18.4
Sudan	2.1	8.2	13.3	15.7	18.7	13.8	13.9	20.5	24.3	4.2	9.6	16.2
Swaziland	1.2	5.3	14.6	18.1	13.5	11.2	11.5	11.6	15.1	3.7	2.0	11.9
Tanzania	..	1.3	11.8	12.0	11.2	9.7	10.7	..	..	..	2.0	10.6
Togo	23.2	14.7	0.6	5.3	4.5	1.5	..	..	..	12.3	6.7	1.8
Uganda	–0.4	0.6	5.9	6.7	9.7	11.3	7.6	8.2	5.8	2.3	4.3	7.7
Zambia	19.3	16.6	7.9	13.0	19.9	21.8	31.5	30.4	24.7	14.0	9.0	17.2
Zimbabwe	13.8	17.5	7.1	6.2	4.1	0.6	..	..	..	16.5	16.9	7.2
NORTH AFRICA	29.5	22.8	24.3	27.6	31.2	35.6	37.2	36.5	45.5	24.9	20.2	31.8
Algeria	43.1	27.1	40.9	44.9	47.7	54.9	56.9	56.5	71.5	31.5	30.1	51.1
Egypt, Arab Rep.	15.2	16.1	13.9	14.3	15.6	15.7	17.1	16.3	17.2	15.5	14.2	15.2
Libya	..	27.2	26.4	..	..	..	..	..	..	..	17.6	27.6
Morocco	14.9	19.9	23.8	24.5	24.2	23.2	24.0	23.4	23.8	16.7	17.8	23.4
Tunisia	24.0	20.0	21.4	21.2	21.2	21.4	21.5	22.4	21.9	22.7	22.3	22.0
ALL AFRICA	34.8	19.2	23.2	24.2	26.0	29.0	31.9	32.0	38.2	24.1	17.2	27.6

a. Provisional.

b. For 1994–2000 Nigeria's values were distorted because the official exchange rate used by the government for oil exports and oil value added was significantly overvalued.

Table 2.14 Gross national savings

	Share of GDP (%)											
										Annual average		
	1980	1990	2002	2003	2004	2005	2006	2007	2008[a]	1980–89	1990–99	2000–08
SUB-SAHARAN AFRICA	13.2	12.9	10.7	11.8	11.6	10.9	10.0	9.8	4.3	13.0	12.3	10.4
Excluding South Africa	4.6	9.1	8.0	9.4	9.8	9.0	7.9	7.8	0.7	7.0	9.2	8.1
Excl. S. Africa & Nigeria	7.0	10.7	10.5	12.4	13.3	12.5	11.2	10.9	0.9	8.7	11.0	10.9
Angola	..	..	9.8	7.6	12.6	24.8	37.1	32.8	47.4	..	4.8	21.6
Benin	..	..	7.3	9.4	8.9	10.6	..	..	..	..	10.8	9.9
Botswana	28.7	43.3	44.1	45.2	46.3	50.9	53.3	55.6	54.8	33.7	41.6	51.0
Burkina Faso	–1.6	13.7	7.5	9.1	5.1	7.9	6.3	..	..	4.7	16.5	6.4
Burundi	..	..	2.9	6.0	5.2	1.1	4.5	..	..	..	1.4	3.2
Cameroon	5.1	16.1	15.1	15.5	16.9	16.6	18.9	19.6	20.2	19.2	13.5	17.2
Cape Verde	..	..	9.4	9.2	21.8	28.8	26.4	26.0	26.8	..	8.1	18.4
Central African Republic	..	..	7.4	3.9	4.4	2.3	6.6	4.5	4.0	..	12.5	5.3
Chad	..	–2.7	–40.2	4.9	13.7	21.3	27.5	20.3	7.8	–3.3	3.5	7.8
Comoros	..	10.1	9.6	7.2	6.5	5.9	5.0	9.1	11.2	..	6.8	8.5
Congo, Dem. Rep.	9.3	0.8	5.3	9.9	6.2	5.6	7.8	8.3	0.2	7.4	0.4	4.7
Congo, Rep.	..	..	24.0	26.7	26.3	31.8	42.9	..	..	..	3.2	28.9
Côte d'Ivoire	..	..	16.8	12.3	12.4	10.0	12.1	7.9	9.6	..	11.9	11.1
Djibouti	..	..	15.6	17.6	16.2	20.1	19.4	..	..	..	11.4	15.1
Equatorial Guinea	..	–22.0	32.5	26.4	22.1	33.6	38.9	38.7	35.7	..	6.0	33.8
Eritrea	..	..	28.6	26.6	20.3	3.9	9.7	..	..	..	15.6	19.6
Ethiopia	..	11.9	19.5	20.6	21.5	16.7	15.1	20.5	16.5	11.8	15.3	18.3
Gabon	..	24.0	32.4	33.8	35.2	45.3	37.3	39.6	48.7	23.5	29.3	39.0
Gambia, The	..	..	18.2	15.2	23.8	11.7	17.0	10.6	10.8	..	16.2	15.1
Ghana	..	..	20.0	20.5	25.7	22.9	21.4	23.6	19.6	..	10.0	21.2
Guinea	..	14.6	9.2	6.8	5.7	9.3	11.8	8.7	9.2	8.8	14.2	9.6
Guinea-Bissau	–6.3	15.3	–1.0	9.8	31.6	24.8	12.8	34.4	22.9	–0.3	5.5	13.0
Kenya	15.4	18.6	13.2	13.5	16.2	16.1	16.2	17.2	17.6	16.2	15.1	15.1
Lesotho	34.5	40.8	24.7	19.5	25.5	21.4	29.1	39.1	24.8	33.0	29.3	27.5
Liberia	..	..	–11.1	–6.4	33.1	39.8	–17.3	–14.7	..	..	..	0.3
Madagascar	..	9.2	8.3	13.0	12.7	11.1	16.2	14.0	12.4	5.0	4.9	12.7
Malawi	..	13.6	..	0.7	4.8	4.2	2.9	9.4	9.1	..	2.3	4.5
Mali	1.9	15.1	9.0	14.4	8.6	11.4	13.0	25.7	..	2.6	14.4	13.8
Mauritania	3.9	17.6	16.8	9.9	8.2	–5.4	28.7	29.2	..	17.1	9.0	12.4
Mauritius	14.0	26.3	26.6	26.3	23.8	19.7	19.1	19.8	22.7	19.7	26.5	23.4
Mozambique	–6.9	2.1	15.0	7.3	10.0	7.7	9.5	9.3	10.4	–3.8	0.1	9.6
Namibia	26.9	34.8	25.6	24.2	28.1	27.9	38.2	29.3	24.8	18.5	27.3	27.7
Niger	13.0	–1.2	4.7	6.4	10.0	17.0	..	..	..	5.5	1.0	7.6
Nigeria[b]	..	..	..	..	..	..	..	..	..	..	..	..
Rwanda	13.3	11.3	10.3	11.3	18.6	20.6	13.1	15.8	13.0	10.9	8.1	14.3
São Tomé and Príncipe	..	..	..	..	..	..	..	..	..	..	..	..
Senegal	..	..	..	..	..	..	18.7	19.1	17.9	..	..	18.6
Seychelles	..	..	16.4	16.7	12.4	2.1	7.5	–3.3	2.7	..	22.0	9.9
Sierra Leone	0.5	2.6	10.6	14.0	9.4	14.7	12.0	9.6	14.1	7.2	0.2	8.0
Somalia	–5.8	..	..	..	..	..	..	..	..	3.2	..	..
South Africa	34.0	19.3	16.9	15.8	14.5	14.0	14.0	14.0	14.0	24.6	16.6	14.9
Sudan	7.9	0.9	9.2	12.2	16.0	12.9	9.7	11.9	15.4	7.4	5.1	11.4
Swaziland	..	19.7	9.8	7.9	6.6	12.3	7.4	18.2	30.5	..	16.4	13.9
Tanzania	..	..	11.1	11.8	10.7	9.7	10.4	..	..	..	2.0	10.4
Togo	..	..	4.1	7.3	6.5	3.2	..	..	..	..	4.5	4.1
Uganda	–0.9	0.6	7.1	7.5	10.8	10.8	12.1	13.8	12.0	2.6	6.5	10.0
Zambia	7.3	6.7	5.9	10.7	13.0	17.7	23.9	22.9	19.8	2.2	0.6	12.4
Zimbabwe	..	15.7	7.0	5.9	4.0	–0.4	..	..	..	17.3	16.0	5.9
NORTH AFRICA	20.7	14.2	14.9	14.5	14.5	13.6	14.2	14.5	..	16.8	11.7	14.2
Algeria	..	..	38.8	43.5	46.3	51.9	54.4	56.8	71.6	..	27.8	49.4
Egypt, Arab Rep.	..	..	..	..	..	..	..	26.3	23.6	..	..	25.0
Libya	..	..	..	..	..	..	..	..	..	..	..	..
Morocco	18.3	24.4	29.4	30.5	30.7	30.6	31.8	32.4	34.4	20.0	21.2	30.5
Tunisia	..	..	22.3	22.1	22.4	20.7	22.7	22.6	16.7	..	21.9	21.8
ALL AFRICA	15.2	13.4	12.3	12.8	12.6	11.8	11.4	11.4	2.8	14.1	12.1	11.2

a. Provisional.

b. For 1994–2000 Nigeria's values were distorted because the official exchange rate used by the government for oil exports and oil value added was significantly overvalued.

Table 2.15 General government final consumption expenditure

	Share of GDP (%)											
										Annual average		
	1980	1990	2002	2003	2004	2005	2006	2007	2008[a]	1980–89	1990–99	2000–08
SUB-SAHARAN AFRICA	12.4	17.2	14.1	15.0	15.0	14.5	13.7	13.4	12.3	15.2	16.7	14.1
Excluding South Africa	11.7	15.3	12.3	12.0	11.6	10.9	10.3	10.0	9.4	13.7	14.0	11.2
Excl. S. Africa & Nigeria	14.6	14.8	13.1	13.0	12.9	12.4	12.0	11.5	10.8	14.2	13.7	12.3
Angola	..	34.5	..	..	..	..	..	..	..	31.5	40.7	..
Benin	8.6	11.0	12.5	13.3	13.6	15.0	..	..	..	12.7	10.5	12.9
Botswana	21.3	24.1	20.9	21.5	21.3	20.6	19.2	19.5	19.2	24.3	26.7	20.6
Burkina Faso	9.2	21.1	25.2	22.2	21.6	22.3	22.0	..	..	15.6	22.5	22.3
Burundi	9.2	10.8	19.1	22.7	26.1	26.5	28.8	..	..	9.3	17.0	22.9
Cameroon	9.7	12.8	10.2	10.0	10.2	10.0	9.6	9.2	12.7	10.0	10.6	10.2
Cape Verde	..	14.7	11.7	14.7	20.6	20.3	20.4	20.6	18.4	13.1	17.0	17.7
Central African Republic	15.1	14.9	12.9	11.0	10.5	13.3	11.1	2.7	3.5	15.6	13.9	10.1
Chad	..	10.0	7.7	7.6	4.9	4.5	5.9	6.1	5.8	11.3	8.1	6.4
Comoros	30.9	24.5	17.4	14.7	14.3	13.5	12.6	12.3	12.1	28.6	20.3	13.9
Congo, Dem. Rep.	8.4	11.5	5.5	6.3	8.2	8.1	7.1	10.4	11.0	9.0	9.9	7.8
Congo, Rep.	17.6	13.8	18.4	17.0	16.0	13.0	13.2	14.1	..	17.7	18.1	14.7
Côte d'Ivoire	16.9	16.8	7.8	8.2	8.3	8.3	8.3	8.4	8.1	16.5	11.9	8.0
Djibouti	..	31.5	28.3	29.5	29.7	27.1	28.3	26.0	..	..	31.8	28.2
Equatorial Guinea	..	39.7	5.1	3.8	2.9	2.7	2.6	2.3	2.6	27.4	25.1	3.3
Eritrea	..	..	41.1	50.3	52.9	37.2	35.9	31.4	..	..	39.7	45.4
Ethiopia	..	13.2	14.8	13.4	13.1	12.3	12.1	10.6	11.3	11.2	9.8	13.3
Gabon	13.2	13.4	11.0	10.1	9.3	8.3	8.4	8.9	7.8	18.3	13.2	9.4
Gambia, The	31.2	13.7	12.9	11.0	16.9	18.4	18.1	16.2	15.8	29.1	13.8	15.3
Ghana	11.2	9.3	9.9	11.5	12.2	11.7	13.4	14.1	13.6	9.0	11.7	11.8
Guinea	..	11.0	7.5	7.8	6.3	5.7	5.6	6.0	4.9	11.8	8.2	6.4
Guinea-Bissau	27.6	10.3	12.8	12.8	13.7	18.1	17.1	15.4	13.9	18.9	8.4	14.5
Kenya	19.8	18.6	17.1	18.1	17.9	17.4	16.6	17.2	10.8	18.3	15.8	16.2
Lesotho	21.8	21.4	28.7	27.6	25.7	26.8	26.8	25.4	26.8	21.8	26.3	27.8
Liberia	19.1	..	13.7	8.5	10.4	11.1	11.5	14.6	..	22.0	..	12.0
Madagascar	12.1	8.0	8.1	9.2	6.9	6.1	4.6	4.7	4.6	9.8	7.9	6.9
Malawi	19.3	15.1	10.7	11.9	12.2	12.1	11.8	11.5	10.9	17.5	16.6	12.4
Mali	11.6	13.8	8.7	8.4	10.0	9.9	9.9	10.7	..	12.3	12.7	9.4
Mauritania	45.3	25.9	22.3	30.1	21.9	22.7	19.9	20.1	..	30.6	14.5	23.3
Mauritius	14.4	12.8	12.8	14.1	14.2	14.4	14.5	13.7	12.9	13.5	13.0	13.6
Mozambique	12.2	13.5	9.4	10.2	10.8	10.4	10.7	11.8	12.3	13.8	9.7	10.4
Namibia	17.4	30.6	21.5	22.2	20.4	19.3	18.4	19.2	18.0	27.9	31.0	20.6
Niger	10.4	15.0	12.2	11.4	13.2	11.7	..	..	..	11.9	14.6	12.3
Nigeria	..	..	..	..	..	..	..	..	..	..	..	..
Rwanda	12.5	10.1	12.5	14.4	12.0	12.0	11.9	10.7	9.1	13.0	11.5	11.7
São Tomé and Príncipe	..	..	..	..	..	..	..	..	..	..	..	..
Senegal	24.8	18.4	13.3	13.3	13.7	9.6	9.7	10.0	10.0	19.3	15.0	11.7
Seychelles	28.7	27.7	22.7	25.5	28.3	21.3	19.8	18.0	14.8	33.1	29.0	22.1
Sierra Leone	8.4	7.8	16.4	15.6	13.5	13.4	13.0	10.5	12.7	7.7	10.6	14.1
Somalia	15.6	..	..	..	..	..	..	..	..	17.6	..	..
South Africa	14.3	19.7	18.4	19.3	19.4	19.4	19.4	19.7	20.2	17.4	19.4	19.1
Sudan	16.0	5.8	10.1	10.8	11.8	17.1	16.7	14.8	16.4	11.1	6.1	12.6
Swaziland	27.0	14.3	16.7	15.3	16.0	15.6	15.3	14.9	23.6	21.5	17.2	17.1
Tanzania	..	17.8	12.4	14.8	15.9	15.2	16.2	..	..	..	14.0	13.8
Togo	22.4	14.2	8.4	9.8	9.7	17.6	18.5	18.6	16.3	16.9	12.8	13.2
Uganda	..	7.5	16.8	15.7	13.9	14.5	14.1	12.9	11.8	9.9	11.1	14.4
Zambia	25.5	19.0	11.8	14.4	18.1	9.7	10.2	10.4	9.0	23.0	17.7	11.5
Zimbabwe	18.5	19.4	17.9	16.6	23.3	27.2	..	..	..	20.1	17.2	19.4
NORTH AFRICA	17.7	16.2	14.9	14.8	14.6	13.4	12.9	12.7	9.5	18.7	16.1	13.6
Algeria	15.2	16.1	15.4	14.8	13.8	11.5	11.3	12.0	6.8	17.2	16.6	12.6
Egypt, Arab Rep.	15.7	11.3	12.5	12.7	12.8	12.7	12.3	11.3	10.8	16.2	10.9	11.9
Libya	..	24.4	16.7	..	..	..	..	..	..	..	24.3	19.6
Morocco	18.3	15.5	18.3	18.1	18.7	19.4	18.5	18.2	15.6	16.6	17.0	18.2
Tunisia	14.5	16.4	15.9	15.7	15.4	15.4	14.7	14.4	13.6	16.5	16.0	15.1
ALL AFRICA	13.6	16.7	14.4	14.9	14.8	14.1	13.3	13.1	11.2	16.0	16.3	13.9

a. Provisional.

Table 2.16 Household final consumption expenditure

	Share of GDP (%)											
										Annual average		
	1980	1990	2002	2003	2004	2005	2006	2007	2008[a]	1980–89	1990–99	2000–08
SUB-SAHARAN AFRICA	58.9	65.3	67.8	67.6	67.9	68.2	67.6	66.6	66.5	63.3	68.1	67.7
Excluding South Africa	..	72.5	73.5	73.1	72.0	72.5	71.6	..	..	72.5	74.2	72.9
Excl. S. Africa & Nigeria	71.4	72.5	73.5	73.1	72.0	72.5	71.6	71.6	72.4	72.4	74.2	72.7
Angola	..	35.8	..	..	..	..	..	..	..	44.5	42.6	..
Benin	97.7	86.8	83.8	80.7	80.9	78.1	..	..	..	89.7	85.7	81.3
Botswana	52.0	33.2	26.9	28.1	28.0	27.0	28.4	29.3	31.2	40.4	33.6	27.3
Burkina Faso	98.0	73.5	71.2	73.3	76.6	72.8	75.2	..	..	86.0	68.5	75.2
Burundi	91.4	94.5	90.6	85.9	84.9	96.6	91.1	..	..	87.5	88.3	89.4
Cameroon	68.6	66.6	70.8	72.2	71.4	72.0	71.5	72.6	67.6	65.8	70.9	71.0
Cape Verde	..	93.4	104.0	101.1	80.9	75.4	75.0	74.1	73.5	89.1	88.6	86.7
Central African Republic	93.7	85.7	82.8	87.4	89.5	86.6	87.5	95.9	94.9	85.5	82.4	87.7
Chad	..	97.6	133.1	74.4	70.6	59.8	50.5	59.3	68.9	96.8	92.5	76.7
Comoros	79.2	78.7	86.6	91.1	96.2	99.5	101.4	99.1	96.0	75.9	84.2	94.8
Congo, Dem. Rep.	81.5	79.1	90.4	88.7	87.9	85.5	88.4	80.8	82.1	80.0	81.3	87.0
Congo, Rep.	46.8	62.4	30.7	31.7	32.7	29.4	21.1	28.7	..	50.3	53.1	29.8
Côte d'Ivoire	62.8	71.9	65.5	70.8	71.7	74.5	72.0	77.3	77.1	63.9	70.3	73.0
Djibouti	..	78.9	66.8	65.2	66.0	64.2	59.5	55.9	..	..	73.8	66.0
Equatorial Guinea	..	80.3	15.9	16.1	18.2	13.6	11.3	10.8	24.5	..	61.2	16.3
Eritrea	..	..	86.3	90.6	88.6	90.0	81.3	86.2	..	..	90.0	83.8
Ethiopia	..	77.2	75.2	78.8	78.2	85.1	86.4	83.9	84.9	78.4	80.5	80.2
Gabon	26.1	49.7	45.3	41.7	36.2	33.3	34.2	36.1	25.8	37.4	43.2	35.7
Gambia, The	63.0	75.6	74.3	78.0	74.2	77.6	70.7	77.1	78.0	64.4	78.8	75.7
Ghana	83.9	85.2	82.7	81.5	80.5	83.5	80.9	78.3	80.8	86.2	80.8	81.7
Guinea	..	66.9	83.0	84.4	86.3	82.9	83.8	83.6	84.6	73.1	73.5	82.8
Guinea-Bissau	73.3	86.9	98.9	88.7	72.2	70.4	86.7	77.0	81.3	82.0	90.1	86.3
Kenya	62.1	62.8	73.2	71.3	71.3	73.2	75.3	73.9	78.6	63.3	69.6	74.4
Lesotho	130.2	121.0	89.0	95.4	91.8	95.5	94.6	98.0	107.9	144.5	108.4	92.9
Liberia	66.1	..	89.7	94.7	90.3	86.4	123.1	115.9	..	75.8	..	98.4
Madagascar	89.3	86.4	84.2	81.9	84.5	85.9	81.3	84.2	85.0	87.2	87.9	82.9
Malawi	69.9	71.5	..	91.6	85.8	88.9	89.6	83.7	85.0	69.8	80.0	85.8
Mali	87.4	79.8	80.0	78.3	81.4	79.1	75.3	75.7	..	88.1	79.7	78.3
Mauritania	58.2	69.2	79.7	74.9	81.2	92.3	61.3	61.2	..	66.3	83.0	75.8
Mauritius	71.0	63.7	62.0	61.1	62.4	66.7	68.0	68.8	70.2	66.5	62.9	64.8
Mozambique	96.7	92.3	75.7	83.7	79.2	80.4	76.5	76.3	74.7	92.3	93.2	79.2
Namibia	44.2	51.2	62.1	67.5	62.8	60.9	54.9	61.8	68.5	61.3	56.3	62.5
Niger	75.1	83.8	82.5	83.6	82.7	74.6	..	..	..	80.8	82.7	81.7
Nigeria	..	..	..	..	..	..	..	..	..	..	..	..
Rwanda	83.3	83.7	88.0	85.3	83.6	82.8	85.4	86.6	89.6	82.0	94.0	86.0
São Tomé and Príncipe	..	..	..	..	..	..	..	..	..	..	..	..
Senegal	73.1	79.2	80.0	77.9	78.4	76.3	79.6	81.5	82.3	76.4	79.6	78.9
Seychelles	44.2	52.0	52.9	52.9	57.0	75.6	72.1	83.9	78.5	42.7	49.3	64.8
Sierra Leone	90.7	83.5	91.8	88.1	86.9	82.3	79.1	83.4	79.8	83.2	86.6	87.3
Somalia	97.3	..	..	..	..	..	..	..	..	100.6	..	..
South Africa	47.8	57.1	61.7	61.5	63.4	63.4	63.5	62.1	61.5	54.2	61.2	62.5
Sudan	81.9	86.1	76.6	73.5	69.5	69.1	69.4	64.8	59.2	84.8	84.3	71.1
Swaziland	71.8	80.4	68.7	66.6	70.5	73.2	73.2	73.5	61.3	74.7	80.8	70.9
Tanzania	..	80.9	75.8	73.1	72.9	75.1	73.1	..	..	..	84.0	75.6
Togo	54.5	71.1	91.0	84.8	85.8	80.9	..	..	..	70.8	80.5	87.3
Uganda	..	91.9	77.3	77.5	76.4	74.2	78.3	78.9	82.4	87.2	84.6	77.8
Zambia	55.2	64.4	80.3	72.6	62.0	68.5	58.3	59.1	66.3	62.9	73.3	71.3
Zimbabwe	67.7	63.1	75.0	77.2	72.6	72.2	..	..	..	63.4	65.9	73.4
NORTH AFRICA	61.3	64.1	61.8	61.4	60.3	59.1	58.2	59.1	57.1	63.1	65.6	60.0
Algeria	41.7	56.8	43.7	40.4	38.5	33.6	31.8	31.5	21.7	51.3	53.3	36.2
Egypt, Arab Rep.	69.2	72.6	73.6	73.0	71.7	71.6	70.6	72.4	72.0	68.3	75.0	72.9
Libya	..	48.4	56.9	..	..	..	..	..	..	..	58.1	52.8
Morocco	66.8	64.6	57.9	57.3	57.1	57.5	57.5	58.4	60.6	66.7	65.3	58.4
Tunisia	61.5	63.6	62.7	63.1	63.4	63.3	63.7	63.2	64.5	60.8	61.7	62.9
ALL AFRICA	60.0	64.7	65.1	65.0	64.7	64.4	63.6	63.3	62.3	63.2	66.9	64.3

a. Provisional.

Table 2.17 Final consumption expenditure plus discrepancy

	Share of GDP (%)											
										Annual average		
	1980	1990	2002	2003	2004	2005	2006	2007	2008[a]	1980–89	1990–99	2000–08
SUB-SAHARAN AFRICA	64.6	83.9	78.0	78.5	77.4	75.1	71.4	71.0	66.4	77.8	85.5	75.3
Excluding South Africa	68.6	90.3	79.8	77.9	73.8	70.5	65.9	67.0	63.4	83.9	89.6	73.2
Excl. S. Africa & Nigeria	85.7	87.1	85.3	84.2	82.0	79.9	77.0	77.0	73.4	86.9	87.6	80.9
Angola	..	70.3	76.1	80.8	74.9	62.1	50.5	52.1	37.4	76.0	78.0	64.1
Benin	106.3	97.8	96.3	94.0	94.5	93.1	..	..	..	102.4	96.2	94.2
Botswana	73.3	57.4	47.8	49.6	49.3	47.6	47.6	48.8	50.4	64.7	60.3	47.9
Burkina Faso	107.2	94.6	96.3	95.5	98.2	95.2	97.2	..	..	101.6	91.0	97.4
Burundi	100.6	105.4	109.7	108.7	111.0	123.1	119.9	..	..	96.9	105.2	112.3
Cameroon	78.3	79.3	81.0	82.2	81.5	81.9	81.1	81.9	80.3	75.8	81.5	81.2
Cape Verde	..	108.1	115.7	115.8	101.5	95.6	95.4	94.7	91.8	102.2	105.6	104.4
Central African Republic	108.9	100.6	95.7	98.4	100.0	99.9	98.6	98.5	98.4	101.1	96.3	97.8
Chad	..	107.7	140.8	82.0	75.5	64.3	56.4	65.4	74.8	108.1	100.5	83.1
Comoros	110.1	103.2	104.0	105.8	110.6	112.9	114.0	111.4	108.1	104.5	104.5	108.6
Congo, Dem. Rep.	89.9	90.7	96.0	95.0	96.0	93.6	95.5	91.2	93.1	89.1	91.2	94.7
Congo, Rep.	64.3	76.2	49.0	48.7	48.7	42.4	34.3	42.8	..	68.1	71.2	44.5
Côte d'Ivoire	79.6	88.7	73.3	79.0	80.0	82.8	80.4	85.7	85.2	80.4	82.2	81.0
Djibouti	..	110.4	95.1	94.7	95.7	91.4	87.8	81.9	..	..	106.4	94.2
Equatorial Guinea	..	120.1	21.0	19.9	21.1	16.3	13.9	13.1	27.2	..	86.3	19.7
Eritrea	..	..	127.4	140.9	141.5	127.2	117.2	117.7	..	..	129.7	129.2
Ethiopia	..	90.4	90.1	92.3	91.2	97.4	98.5	94.5	96.2	89.5	90.3	93.6
Gabon	39.4	63.1	56.3	51.8	45.4	41.7	42.6	45.0	33.7	55.7	56.4	45.2
Gambia, The	94.2	89.3	87.1	88.9	91.1	96.0	88.8	93.3	93.8	93.5	92.6	91.0
Ghana	95.1	94.5	92.6	93.0	92.7	95.1	94.3	92.4	94.4	95.2	92.5	93.5
Guinea	..	77.8	90.5	92.2	92.6	88.7	89.5	89.6	89.5	84.9	81.7	89.2
Guinea-Bissau	101.0	97.2	111.8	101.6	85.9	88.5	103.9	92.3	95.1	100.9	98.5	100.8
Kenya	81.9	81.5	90.2	89.5	89.2	90.6	91.9	91.0	89.4	81.7	85.4	90.6
Lesotho	152.0	142.4	117.7	123.0	117.5	122.3	121.4	123.4	134.7	166.3	134.6	120.7
Liberia	85.2	..	103.3	103.2	100.7	97.6	134.6	130.5	..	97.8	..	110.5
Madagascar	101.4	94.5	92.3	91.1	91.5	92.0	85.9	88.9	89.6	97.1	95.8	89.8
Malawi	89.2	86.6	..	103.4	98.0	101.1	101.3	95.1	95.9	87.3	96.6	98.4
Mali	98.9	93.6	88.7	86.7	91.4	89.0	85.2	86.5	..	100.4	92.4	87.7
Mauritania	103.5	95.1	101.9	105.0	103.1	115.0	81.2	81.3	..	96.9	97.6	99.1
Mauritius	85.5	76.5	74.8	75.2	76.6	81.1	82.5	82.5	83.1	80.0	75.9	78.4
Mozambique	108.9	105.8	85.1	93.9	90.0	90.7	87.2	88.1	87.0	106.2	102.9	89.6
Namibia	61.6	81.8	83.6	89.7	83.2	80.2	73.3	80.9	86.5	89.2	87.3	83.1
Niger	85.4	98.8	94.7	94.9	95.9	86.3	..	..	..	92.7	97.3	94.0
Nigeria	..	..	..	..	..	..	..	..	..	..	..	..
Rwanda	95.8	93.8	100.5	99.6	95.6	94.9	97.3	97.2	98.7	95.0	105.5	97.7
São Tomé and Príncipe	..	..	..	..	..	..	..	..	..	..	..	..
Senegal	97.9	97.6	93.2	91.2	92.1	85.9	89.3	91.5	92.3	95.7	94.6	90.6
Seychelles	72.9	79.7	75.6	78.5	85.3	96.9	91.9	101.9	93.3	75.9	78.3	86.9
Sierra Leone	99.1	91.3	108.2	103.7	100.4	95.8	92.2	93.9	92.5	90.9	97.2	101.4
Somalia	112.9	112.5	..	..	..	..	..	..	..	106.3	112.5	..
South Africa	62.1	76.8	80.1	80.8	82.7	82.8	82.9	81.7	81.6	71.5	80.6	81.6
Sudan	97.9	91.8	86.7	84.3	81.3	86.2	86.1	79.5	75.7	95.8	90.4	83.8
Swaziland	98.8	94.7	85.4	81.9	86.5	88.8	88.5	88.4	84.9	96.3	98.0	88.1
Tanzania	..	98.7	88.2	88.0	88.8	90.3	89.3	..	..	..	98.0	89.4
Togo	76.8	85.3	99.4	94.7	95.5	98.5	..	..	..	87.7	93.3	98.2
Uganda	100.4	99.4	94.1	93.3	90.3	88.7	92.4	91.8	94.2	97.7	95.7	92.3
Zambia	80.7	83.4	92.1	87.0	80.1	78.2	68.5	69.6	75.3	86.0	91.0	82.8
Zimbabwe	86.2	82.5	92.9	93.8	95.9	99.4	..	..	..	83.5	83.1	92.8
NORTH AFRICA	70.5	77.2	75.7	72.4	68.8	64.4	62.8	63.5	54.5	75.1	79.8	68.2
Algeria	56.9	72.9	59.1	55.1	52.3	45.1	43.1	43.5	28.5	68.5	69.9	48.9
Egypt, Arab Rep.	84.8	83.9	86.1	85.7	84.4	84.3	82.9	83.7	82.8	84.5	85.8	84.8
Libya	..	72.8	73.6	..	..	..	..	..	..	..	82.4	72.4
Morocco	85.1	80.1	76.2	75.5	75.8	76.8	76.0	76.6	76.2	83.3	82.2	76.6
Tunisia	76.0	80.0	78.6	78.8	78.8	78.6	78.5	77.6	78.1	77.3	77.7	78.0
ALL AFRICA	65.2	80.8	76.8	75.8	74.0	71.0	68.1	68.0	61.8	75.9	82.8	72.4

a. Provisional.

Table 2.18 Final consumption expenditure plus discrepancy per capita

Current prices ($)

	1980	1990	2002	2003	2004	2005	2006	2007	2008[a]	Annual average 1980–89	Annual average 1990–99	Annual average 2000–08
SUB-SAHARAN AFRICA	465	492	402	484	575	639	688	767	814	464	470	574
Excluding South Africa	379	357	306	322	356	400	444	518	599	351	307	387
Excl. S. Africa & Nigeria	388	365	313	329	364	409	453	529	611	359	314	396
Angola	..	677	574	721	918	1,144	1,334	1,759	1,733	581	469	1,008
Benin	420	376	380	455	503	507	..	..	..	332	343	414
Botswana	781	1,591	1,597	2,287	2,668	2,724	2,817	3,198	3,433	821	1,789	2,432
Burkina Faso	303	331	250	312	371	371	391	..	..	260	235	306
Burundi	224	210	102	93	103	133	145	..	..	215	170	114
Cameroon	581	723	530	658	739	764	802	914	994	663	631	709
Cape Verde	..	1,034	1,568	1,997	1,996	2,016	2,365	2,785	3,185	809	1,201	2,079
Central African Republic	373	497	249	276	308	322	342	389	438	352	341	311
Chad	..	306	307	237	340	372	339	426	565	221	232	325
Comoros	406	593	464	596	682	728	749	824	891	394	507	639
Congo, Dem. Rep.	461	223	99	98	111	115	138	145	168	287	153	116
Congo, Rep.	605	872	466	532	634	755	761	921	..	681	620	618
Côte d'Ivoire	962	760	466	588	657	704	710	843	969	681	630	657
Djibouti	..	891	737	759	806	805	816	804	..	..	833	788
Equatorial Guinea	..	418	806	1,019	1,869	2,204	2,129	2,569	7,637	..	410	2,160
Eritrea	..	..	215	202	205	326	320	334	..	..	239	258
Ethiopia	..	226	102	111	126	161	195	233	316	200	160	163
Gabon	2,472	4,057	2,153	2,383	2,429	2,636	2,917	3,662	3,355	2,570	2,723	2,561
Gambia, The	368	316	232	227	247	290	287	372	442	290	324	296
Ghana	383	372	278	338	384	465	536	606	652	350	358	416
Guinea	..	338	334	376	404	314	305	425	388	1,156	382	352
Guinea-Bissau	134	232	166	171	170	182	219	229	259	171	208	195
Kenya	365	299	361	395	414	478	565	654	801	299	315	490
Lesotho	506	513	408	627	771	850	924	1,027	1,083	460	611	731
Liberia	425	..	189	135	144	155	237	264	..	437	..	188
Madagascar	477	258	251	299	233	263	262	351	420	320	245	284
Malawi	178	172	..	200	200	218	236	245	287	150	180	209
Mali	291	296	280	346	396	407	418	480	..	238	267	345
Mauritania	489	499	431	482	554	713	711	688	..	459	571	556
Mauritius	1,020	1,725	2,813	3,226	3,766	4,103	4,234	4,441	5,666	1,078	2,412	3,768
Mozambique	316	193	187	224	255	291	295	330	389	275	187	265
Namibia	1,346	1,357	1,446	2,249	2,756	2,883	2,859	3,392	3,506	1,459	1,659	2,495
Niger	371	314	172	208	217	217	..	..	..	279	217	189
Nigeria	..	..	..	..	..	..	..	..	..	..	..	..
Rwanda	214	339	193	204	214	251	299	351	453	270	283	264
São Tomé and Príncipe	..	..	..	..	..	..	..	..	..	..	..	..
Senegal	608	741	477	584	673	662	722	869	998	550	580	649
Seychelles	1,667	4,196	6,301	6,688	7,234	10,330	10,510	10,936	9,007	2,170	5,142	8,124
Sierra Leone	335	145	223	217	219	228	249	288	325	248	188	236
Somalia	105	154	..	..	..	..	..	..	..	136	154	..
South Africa	1,818	2,444	1,963	2,941	3,856	4,288	4,511	4,847	4,641	2,094	2,782	3,514
Sudan	364	421	357	404	465	610	793	910	1,070	496	325	583
Swaziland	889	1,222	911	1,328	1,770	1,994	2,078	2,221	1,904	753	1,469	1,624
Tanzania	..	165	239	245	266	327	319	..	..	..	193	269
Togo	314	354	264	292	337	347	..	..	..	271	308	290
Uganda	99	241	223	229	258	285	310	356	432	231	220	283
Zambia	543	347	312	339	379	477	609	645	854	418	340	472
Zimbabwe	791	693	1,625	555	362	272	..	..	..	704	536	676
NORTH AFRICA	854	1,110	1,148	1,196	1,251	1,329	1,467	1,707	1,875	961	1,137	1,390
Algeria	1,281	1,789	1,074	1,176	1,374	1,405	1,504	1,724	1,442	1,697	1,217	1,303
Egypt, Arab Rep.	438	626	1,038	957	879	980	1,133	1,365	1,654	529	809	1,158
Libya	..	4,824	2,537	..	..	..	..	..	..	..	5,113	3,691
Morocco	827	856	1,055	1,274	1,447	1,517	1,637	1,865	2,106	654	1,006	1,438
Tunisia	1,041	1,206	1,691	2,001	2,231	2,271	2,398	2,658	3,038	961	1,467	2,158
ALL AFRICA	536	603	529	603	686	751	813	919	984	554	588	709

a. Provisional.

Table 2.19 Gross fixed capital formation

	Share of GDP (%)											
										Annual average		
	1980	1990	2002	2003	2004	2005	2006	2007	2008[a]	1980–89	1990–99	2000–08
SUB-SAHARAN AFRICA	17.7	18.1	15.5	16.3	16.5	16.6	17.3	18.6	18.5	18.5	17.3	16.8
Excluding South Africa	14.0	17.6	16.3	16.9	16.9	16.8	16.9	18.0	17.8	15.9	18.3	17.1
Excl. S. Africa & Nigeria	17.4	17.0	17.4	18.3	18.8	19.0	19.7	20.7	20.6	16.5	17.9	18.9
Angola	..	11.1	12.6	12.7	9.1	8.1	13.7	14.4	12.3	14.2	23.2	12.4
Benin	..	13.4	18.1	18.1	17.5	18.9	..	..	..	14.8	15.7	18.5
Botswana	34.5	32.4	21.9	21.5	20.2	19.0	17.9	24.4	27.0	29.0	27.2	21.6
Burkina Faso	14.1	17.7	17.1	17.5	19.3	19.4	20.8	..	..	17.4	21.2	18.2
Burundi	13.9	15.2	6.1	10.6	13.0	10.5	16.4	..	..	16.1	9.0	9.9
Cameroon	20.0	17.3	19.8	18.1	18.3	17.7	16.7	16.7	18.7	21.1	14.5	18.0
Cape Verde	..	22.9	20.9	18.7	37.4	37.1	37.5	40.3	42.9	26.9	29.6	30.3
Central African Republic	6.9	11.4	9.0	6.1	6.2	8.9	9.2	8.9	10.3	10.2	11.2	8.5
Chad	..	4.8	59.7	48.6	22.7	19.1	21.2	18.2	14.1	4.4	11.0	29.0
Comoros	28.5	11.9	11.0	10.3	9.4	9.3	9.8	13.8	16.1	24.3	14.6	11.1
Congo, Dem. Rep.	8.8	12.8	9.0	12.2	12.7	..	..	19.6	17.0	11.4	8.0	11.3
Congo, Rep.	35.8	17.2	22.5	25.1	23.6	21.5	22.4	26.7	..	32.5	24.9	23.6
Côte d'Ivoire	24.4	8.5	10.9	9.7	9.8	9.7	9.3	8.6	10.1	15.8	11.4	9.9
Djibouti	..	14.1	10.0	14.4	21.5	19.0	29.9	38.9	..	..	11.1	18.8
Equatorial Guinea	..	17.4	32.4	41.6	40.5	37.6	31.4	33.3	28.2	..	59.5	42.0
Eritrea	..	..	29.8	28.1	22.3	18.5	12.6	10.6	..	..	26.1	22.8
Ethiopia	..	12.9	23.9	21.8	25.5	23.0	24.2	25.0	20.8	15.7	16.5	22.9
Gabon	26.7	21.4	24.5	24.0	24.4	21.3	24.5	26.2	27.3	33.8	25.4	24.4
Gambia, The	..	22.3	21.2	19.2	24.8	..	..	..	..	18.9	20.1	20.0
Ghana	6.1	14.4	18.8	22.9	28.4	29.9	30.4	34.1	32.0	7.9	19.7	27.4
Guinea	..	22.9	13.2	10.1	11.3	14.0	13.3	12.6	12.7	16.4	20.0	13.4
Guinea-Bissau	28.2	29.9	9.6	14.5	23.5	26.5	22.8	25.7	23.8	32.0	25.9	19.2
Kenya	18.3	20.6	17.2	15.8	16.3	18.7	19.1	19.5	24.7	18.8	17.6	18.5
Lesotho	35.6	56.3	46.1	34.0	32.0	28.9	23.8	26.6	28.8	40.7	60.9	35.0
Liberia	..	..	4.7	9.4	13.2	16.4	..	..	..	..	..	9.7
Madagascar	14.4	14.8	14.3	17.9	23.4	22.2	25.3	27.5	35.7	10.8	12.4	22.2
Malawi	22.2	20.1	..	16.2	18.2	21.5	20.7	23.9	30.2	15.8	15.2	19.6
Mali	15.5	23.0	18.6	24.2	21.0	22.6	22.9	23.3	..	17.2	22.5	23.5
Mauritania	..	20.0	21.1	25.9	46.4	44.8	23.3	25.9	..	26.6	13.6	28.6
Mauritius	24.2	28.3	22.3	22.2	22.1	21.3	22.9	24.9	24.2	21.1	27.1	23.2
Mozambique	7.6	22.1	30.0	22.3	18.7	18.7	18.6	18.7	23.0	12.2	20.7	22.3
Namibia	27.2	21.2	19.9	19.1	18.6	18.6	22.1	20.7	22.6	18.6	21.0	19.9
Niger	25.5	11.4	14.0	14.1	16.6	18.9	..	..	..	14.2	9.0	14.5
Nigeria	..	..	..	..	..	..	..	..	..	..	..	..
Rwanda	12.2	14.6	17.7	18.6	20.4	21.6	20.5	20.7	20.8	14.4	14.5	19.7
São Tomé and Príncipe	..	..	..	..	..	..	..	..	..	..	..	..
Senegal	14.6	18.0	24.8	21.2	22.7	29.7	28.2	30.9	30.2	17.4	19.9	25.9
Seychelles	36.5	23.0	25.6	10.4	12.7	24.7	26.1	33.2	28.3	25.6	29.2	25.2
Sierra Leone	14.9	9.6	10.1	13.9	10.7	17.4	15.5	13.4	19.7	11.4	7.2	12.7
Somalia	43.1	14.9	..	..	..	..	..	..	..	26.9	14.9	..
South Africa	25.9	19.1	15.0	15.9	16.2	16.8	18.6	20.5	22.2	23.1	16.3	17.3
Sudan	10.8	10.4	13.2	14.1	17.2	18.9	20.4	20.3	20.2	12.4	10.6	16.4
Swaziland	35.0	14.5	20.1	19.1	16.2	15.4	14.1	13.0	14.9	25.4	16.7	16.9
Tanzania	..	25.8	19.0	18.5	18.2	16.1	16.4	..	..	..	21.0	17.5
Togo	28.2	25.3	18.8	20.9	21.2	22.3	..	..	..	19.0	15.6	20.4
Uganda	..	12.7	20.0	20.7	20.0	22.2	21.0	21.9	23.3	9.3	15.9	20.8
Zambia	18.2	13.5	20.6	24.1	23.1	22.9	23.1	24.2	21.4	12.4	12.4	21.4
Zimbabwe	14.1	18.2	10.2	13.8	17.1	21.0	..	..	..	16.0	20.1	14.3
NORTH AFRICA	26.4	24.1	21.2	20.5	20.8	20.3	20.8	22.9	23.4	26.8	21.4	21.1
Algeria	33.8	27.0	24.4	24.0	24.1	22.3	23.1	25.7	27.9	31.9	26.2	23.9
Egypt, Arab Rep.	24.6	26.9	17.8	16.3	16.4	17.9	18.7	20.9	23.7	27.8	20.4	18.7
Libya	..	13.9	14.4	..	..	..	..	..	..	..	12.7	13.1
Morocco	22.2	24.0	25.2	25.1	26.3	27.5	28.1	31.3	32.0	23.1	22.2	27.4
Tunisia	28.3	24.4	25.4	23.4	22.6	22.2	23.5	23.6	24.1	27.5	25.3	24.1
ALL AFRICA	19.8	20.4	17.8	17.9	18.0	17.9	18.4	20.0	20.4	21.2	18.8	18.4

a. Provisional.

Table 2.20 Gross general government fixed capital formation

	Share of GDP (%)											
										Annual average		
	1980	1990	2002	2003	2004	2005	2006	2007	2008[a]	1980–89	1990–99	2000–08
SUB-SAHARAN AFRICA	..	5.0	4.3	4.4	4.4	4.3	5.1	5.5	5.6	5.4	4.5	4.7
Excluding South Africa	..	5.8	5.4	5.7	5.9	5.7	6.7	7.4	7.2	6.3	6.0	6.2
Excl. S. Africa & Nigeria	..	5.6	5.8	6.2	6.6	6.5	7.9	8.5	8.4	6.0	5.9	6.8
Angola	..	..	6.8	7.6	4.9	5.0	11.3	12.1	10.5	..	7.8	7.8
Benin	..	7.4	6.6	6.1	5.4	6.7	..	..	..	9.1	7.5	6.7
Botswana	0.0	8.6	10.6	10.2	8.7	7.7	8.3	7.7	8.4	9.7	11.7	9.1
Burkina Faso	..	9.7	6.4	6.3	7.2	7.4	8.0	..	..	10.4	10.5	7.0
Burundi	12.8	12.5	4.6	8.3	10.7	8.8	..	..	..	13.8	9.3	6.9
Cameroon	4.4	5.5	2.3	2.3	2.6	2.5	2.4	2.4	4.3	6.9	2.9	2.6
Cape Verde	..	10.3	13.0	9.8	7.7	8.9	8.6	10.1	9.2	19.3	20.3	10.1
Central African Republic	3.7	4.7	4.8	2.2	2.0	4.0	3.7	2.7	3.7	5.5	6.2	3.5
Chad	..	..	10.1	12.5	7.8	7.0	8.0	8.3	7.7	3.8	7.4	9.0
Comoros	23.2	5.2	5.8	5.4	4.4	4.5	5.0	6.8	7.9	18.7	7.0	5.3
Congo, Dem. Rep.	5.1	4.0	1.0	2.7	2.8	..	..	8.8	6.9	4.4	1.7	3.2
Congo, Rep.	..	5.6	8.7	6.5	7.0	5.3	8.6	10.9	..	11.1	6.4	8.0
Côte d'Ivoire	11.4	3.6	3.2	2.7	2.8	2.7	3.1	2.6	3.0	7.1	5.6	2.7
Djibouti	..	9.1	4.5	6.7	7.7	9.3	7.6	12.7	..	..	6.1	6.7
Equatorial Guinea	..	10.5	8.5	9.9	13.1	10.3	15.1	16.9	16.8	..	6.9	11.5
Eritrea	..	..	19.8	20.4	17.0	16.8	11.5	9.4	..	..	17.6	17.5
Ethiopia	..	4.0	14.0	12.8	15.7	14.7	16.7	18.2	14.9	4.9	6.6	14.7
Gabon	5.3	3.9	4.0	3.7	4.2	4.2	4.8	4.5	4.3	6.7	6.5	4.1
Gambia, The	..	7.4	7.9	5.7	10.9	9.0	8.0	3.8	..	10.4	7.8	7.6
Ghana	..	7.5	9.6	8.9	12.4	12.0	12.4	14.3	13.8	6.3	11.1	11.6
Guinea	..	9.7	4.0	4.4	4.0	3.4	3.2	3.3	2.9	7.5	6.1	3.9
Guinea-Bissau	..	27.4	8.9	13.1	18.8	14.5	11.9	13.3	13.2	33.3	20.2	13.0
Kenya	0.0	9.7	4.3	4.2	4.3	3.8	4.9	4.9	4.3	0.8	7.0	4.4
Lesotho	9.9	24.6	11.5	9.1	7.5	7.8	7.1	9.8	10.8	16.1	17.4	9.3
Liberia	..	..	0.0	0.0	0.0	0.0	..	..	..	..	..	0.0
Madagascar	..	7.9	4.8	7.8	10.0	8.7	10.5	7.6	9.8	6.9	6.9	8.2
Malawi	17.5	7.7	..	2.4	2.0	7.0	7.7	13.9	9.5	9.5	9.2	7.9
Mali	..	10.5	7.0	6.9	7.5	7.7	8.6	8.8	..	10.2	10.1	7.8
Mauritania	..	6.2	9.1	12.0	9.1	8.1	5.6	4.7	..	7.6	5.0	8.0
Mauritius	9.1	4.6	7.0	7.9	7.7	6.6	7.1	6.6	4.6	6.0	3.7	6.9
Mozambique	7.6	12.0	12.2	10.5	9.7	8.6	11.8	11.7	16.0	9.5	12.1	11.5
Namibia	15.7	8.2	5.8	6.4	6.3	6.4	6.8	7.0	6.8	10.7	8.2	6.5
Niger	20.4	7.4	8.8	8.4	5.4	6.4	..	..	..	11.2	5.6	7.1
Nigeria	..	..	..	..	..	..	..	..	..	..	..	..
Rwanda	12.2	5.9	5.2	5.4	7.9	9.1	7.6	8.6	10.1	12.1	7.2	7.4
São Tomé and Príncipe	..	..	..	..	..	..	..	..	..	..	..	..
Senegal	4.7	4.1	5.7	6.2	6.7	10.0	9.7	11.2	10.0	3.7	4.5	7.7
Seychelles	..	8.2	7.4	1.7	3.1	4.6	8.1	5.1	3.6	12.0	9.9	7.8
Sierra Leone	5.3	3.9	4.4	4.8	4.6	5.8	5.1	3.5	8.7	4.0	3.8	5.2
Somalia	..	..	..	..	..	..	..	..	..	..	..	..
South Africa	6.4	3.9	2.5	2.6	2.5	2.4	2.7	2.7	2.8	5.7	2.8	2.6
Sudan	6.9	..	3.0	2.9	5.0	5.5	6.4	7.2	7.4	4.3	0.7	4.7
Swaziland	11.9	4.5	12.5	13.0	10.7	9.8	8.7	0.1	0.0	8.0	5.4	7.9
Tanzania	..	10.5	7.6	7.4	7.3	6.4	6.6	..	..	..	5.8	6.7
Togo	20.2	7.3	1.4	3.7	5.3	2.8	3.6	2.0	5.0	11.2	3.7	3.2
Uganda	..	6.2	5.6	5.1	4.9	5.0	4.6	4.9	5.5	4.4	5.6	5.3
Zambia	..	6.2	11.8	11.4	8.7	7.1	4.0	6.2	5.8	..	6.8	8.5
Zimbabwe	1.8	3.4	2.1	2.1	5.1	1.5	..	..	..	2.9	2.9	2.3
NORTH AFRICA	..	9.2	9.2	8.6	8.6	8.9	9.0	9.2	..	11.8	9.5	8.8
Algeria	11.0	8.2	10.0	10.8	10.5	10.8	12.0	12.6	0.0	13.8	7.2	9.2
Egypt, Arab Rep.	..	14.7	9.4	8.3	8.7	9.3	8.0	7.8	6.5	16.9	14.5	8.5
Libya	..	..	..	..	..	..	..	..	..	..	..	..
Morocco	..	4.8	4.0	3.8	3.8	3.7	3.6	4.0	4.5	7.1	4.2	4.1
Tunisia	15.0	8.7	..	..	..	9.8	..	..	..	14.1	11.5	11.1
ALL AFRICA	..	6.5	6.2	5.9	5.9	5.9	6.5	6.8	6.6	7.8	6.3	6.2

a. Provisional.

Table 2.21 Private sector fixed capital formation

	Share of GDP (%)											
										Annual average		
	1980	1990	2002	2003	2004	2005	2006	2007	2008[a]	1980–89	1990–99	2000–08
SUB-SAHARAN AFRICA	11.3	12.5	10.9	11.9	12.0	12.2	12.6	13.5	12.9	12.2	12.6	12.1
Excluding South Africa	..	10.5	10.5	11.1	10.8	10.7	10.9	11.3	10.5	9.5	11.7	10.8
Excl. S. Africa & Nigeria	..	10.1	11.2	12.0	12.0	12.1	12.7	12.9	12.2	9.0	11.4	12.0
Angola	..	1.7	5.8	5.1	4.2	3.0	2.4	2.3	1.8	9.2	16.5	4.5
Benin	..	6.0	11.6	12.0	12.1	12.2	..	..	..	4.5	8.3	11.8
Botswana	34.5	23.8	11.3	11.3	11.5	11.3	9.6	16.7	18.6	19.4	15.5	12.5
Burkina Faso	..	8.0	10.8	11.1	..	..	..	..	..	8.8	10.8	10.4
Burundi	1.1	2.7	1.5	2.3	2.3	1.7	..	..	..	2.3	–0.3	1.9
Cameroon	15.6	11.9	17.5	15.8	15.7	15.2	14.3	14.3	14.3	14.2	11.7	15.5
Cape Verde	..	12.6	7.9	8.9	29.7	28.2	28.9	30.2	33.7	7.6	9.3	20.2
Central African Republic	3.2	6.7	4.2	3.9	4.1	4.9	5.6	6.2	6.6	4.7	5.0	5.0
Chad	..	..	49.6	36.1	14.9	12.0	13.2	9.9	6.4	0.6	4.3	20.0
Comoros	5.3	6.7	5.2	4.9	5.0	4.8	4.9	6.9	8.1	5.5	7.7	5.7
Congo, Dem. Rep.	3.7	8.9	8.0	9.5	10.0	..	..	10.8	10.1	7.1	6.3	8.1
Congo, Rep.	..	11.6	13.8	18.6	16.6	16.2	13.8	15.8	..	11.4	18.5	15.6
Côte d'Ivoire	13.0	4.9	7.7	7.0	7.1	7.0	6.3	6.1	7.1	8.7	6.2	7.2
Djibouti	..	5.1	5.6	7.7	13.8	9.7	22.3	26.2	..	..	5.8	12.1
Equatorial Guinea	..	6.9	23.9	31.7	27.4	27.4	16.2	16.4	11.4	..	52.6	30.6
Eritrea	..	..	10.0	7.7	5.3	1.8	1.1	1.2	..	..	8.6	5.3
Ethiopia	..	8.9	9.9	9.0	9.7	8.3	7.6	6.7	5.9	12.8	9.9	8.2
Gabon	21.4	17.6	20.5	20.2	20.2	17.1	19.7	21.7	23.0	27.2	18.9	20.3
Gambia, The	..	14.9	13.3	13.5	13.9	..	..	..	..	8.6	12.3	11.9
Ghana	..	6.9	9.2	14.0	16.0	17.9	18.0	19.7	18.1	3.8	8.6	15.8
Guinea	..	8.8	9.2	5.7	7.4	10.7	10.2	9.3	9.9	8.9	11.7	9.5
Guinea-Bissau	..	8.4	0.7	1.5	4.7	12.1	11.0	12.4	10.6	10.0	7.7	6.2
Kenya	8.2	10.9	7.7	7.8	7.5	6.7	25.4	24.9	20.4	10.7	9.8	12.8
Lesotho	25.7	31.7	21.2	23.2	17.9	16.8	16.1	14.6	17.5	24.6	43.8	20.5
Liberia	..	..	2.2	4.8	4.2	4.3	..	..	..	..	..	3.5
Madagascar	..	6.9	9.5	10.1	13.4	13.5	14.7	19.8	25.9	3.6	5.5	14.0
Malawi	4.7	12.4	..	13.8	16.2	14.5	13.0	10.0	20.7	6.3	6.0	11.7
Mali	..	12.4	11.6	17.3	13.5	15.0	14.3	14.6	..	9.9	12.4	15.8
Mauritania	..	13.7	11.9	13.9	37.3	36.7	17.7	21.3	..	19.0	13.9	21.9
Mauritius	15.1	23.7	15.3	14.3	14.5	14.8	15.9	18.3	19.5	15.1	23.4	16.3
Mozambique	0.0	10.1	17.7	11.8	8.9	10.1	6.8	6.9	7.1	2.7	8.6	10.8
Namibia	11.4	13.0	13.9	20.1	15.7	16.2	16.4	16.3	15.8	7.8	12.8	15.3
Niger	5.1	4.0	5.2	5.7	11.3	12.5	..	..	..	3.0	3.4	7.4
Nigeria	..	..	..	..	..	..	..	..	..	..	..	..
Rwanda	..	8.7	12.5	13.3	12.5	12.5	13.0	12.1	10.7	7.8	7.2	12.3
São Tomé and Príncipe	..	..	..	..	..	..	..	..	..	..	..	..
Senegal	9.9	13.9	19.2	15.0	16.0	19.7	18.5	19.7	20.2	13.7	15.4	18.2
Seychelles	..	14.8	18.2	8.7	9.7	20.1	18.1	28.1	24.6	10.1	19.3	17.4
Sierra Leone	9.5	5.7	5.7	9.0	6.1	11.6	10.4	9.9	11.0	7.3	3.3	7.5
Somalia	..	..	..	..	..	..	..	..	..	..	..	..
South Africa	19.5	15.3	12.5	13.3	13.6	14.4	15.9	17.9	19.4	17.4	13.5	14.7
Sudan	3.8	..	10.1	11.2	12.2	13.4	14.0	13.0	12.8	8.9	9.9	11.7
Swaziland	23.1	10.1	7.6	6.0	5.5	5.6	5.4	12.9	15.0	17.3	11.3	9.1
Tanzania	..	15.3	11.4	11.1	10.9	9.6	9.8	..	..	..	15.2	10.8
Togo	8.0	18.0	17.4	17.2	15.9	19.5	..	..	..	7.8	11.8	17.3
Uganda	..	6.5	14.4	15.6	15.1	17.3	16.4	16.9	17.9	5.4	10.3	15.5
Zambia	..	7.2	8.8	12.7	14.3	15.8	19.1	18.0	15.5	4.9	5.7	12.9
Zimbabwe	12.3	14.8	8.1	11.7	12.0	19.5	..	..	..	13.1	17.2	12.1
NORTH AFRICA	..	16.0	13.8	13.5	13.9	13.4	14.0	16.3	23.9	13.9	12.8	14.9
Algeria	22.8	18.8	14.5	13.2	13.6	11.5	11.0	13.1	27.9	18.1	19.0	14.7
Egypt, Arab Rep.	..	12.3	8.4	8.1	7.7	8.6	10.7	13.1	20.2	9.3	5.9	10.5
Libya	..	..	..	..	..	..	..	..	..	..	..	..
Morocco	16.7	19.2	21.3	21.3	22.4	23.8	24.5	27.3	27.5	16.1	18.0	23.3
Tunisia	13.3	15.6	..	..	..	12.3	..	..	..	13.5	13.8	13.0
ALL AFRICA	12.7	13.8	12.0	12.5	12.7	12.7	13.2	14.6	16.9	12.9	12.7	13.2

a. Provisional.

Table 2.22 External trade balance (exports minus imports)

	Share of GDP (%)											
										Annual average		
	1980	1990	2002	2003	2004	2005	2006	2007	2008[a]	1980–89	1990–99	2000–08
SUB-SAHARAN AFRICA	2.4	1.8	–1.0	–0.9	0.7	2.1	2.8	1.6	4.1	–0.5	–0.9	1.4
Excluding South Africa	–0.1	–0.7	–3.1	–2.9	1.4	3.9	6.1	3.8	7.3	–3.7	–3.6	2.0
Excl. S. Africa & Nigeria	–5.3	–3.1	–3.9	–4.5	–2.6	–0.5	2.3	1.3	5.1	–4.6	–4.9	–1.1
Angola	..	18.0	11.3	6.6	16.0	29.8	35.8	33.5	50.2	9.1	2.2	23.5
Benin	–21.5	–12.0	–13.9	–12.8	–12.7	–12.6	..	..	..	–17.5	–12.5	–13.0
Botswana	–13.4	5.3	11.5	8.7	9.9	17.2	22.5	10.4	4.6	5.3	9.7	13.3
Burkina Faso	–22.3	–13.5	–12.4	–12.9	–13.5	–15.6	–15.3	..	..	–19.6	–13.5	–14.2
Burundi	–14.5	–19.9	–16.2	–19.3	–24.3	–33.9	–36.2	..	..	–13.5	–14.4	–22.3
Cameroon	0.8	2.9	–0.8	0.3	–0.4	–1.0	2.1	0.8	1.1	0.4	3.7	0.5
Cape Verde	..	–31.0	–36.6	–34.5	–38.9	–32.7	–32.8	–35.0	–34.7	–29.0	–35.2	–34.7
Central African Republic	–15.9	–12.9	–4.6	–4.5	–6.2	–8.8	–7.9	–7.4	–8.7	–12.1	–7.7	–6.3
Chad	–11.9	–14.4	–101.0	–34.1	0.2	15.5	21.3	15.4	10.2	–13.5	–13.6	–13.9
Comoros	–43.2	–22.9	–15.0	–16.1	–19.9	–22.2	–23.8	–25.2	–24.2	–33.3	–22.6	–19.7
Congo, Dem. Rep.	0.1	0.3	–4.9	–7.2	–8.8	–7.6	–11.2	–10.8	–10.1	–0.8	1.2	–6.8
Congo, Rep.	–0.1	7.9	27.6	25.6	27.0	35.6	42.9	30.1	..	–0.5	2.9	31.2
Côte d'Ivoire	–6.2	4.6	16.6	10.9	9.2	7.5	10.3	5.6	4.8	3.2	6.5	8.9
Djibouti	..	–24.6	–5.2	–9.2	–17.2	–10.3	–17.6	–20.8	..	..	–17.5	–13.0
Equatorial Guinea	..	–37.4	47.3	20.4	35.1	43.8	53.7	51.6	46.1	–28.6	–45.8	35.6
Eritrea	..	..	–57.3	–69.0	–63.8	–45.7	–29.7	–28.2	..	..	–55.8	–52.0
Ethiopia	..	–3.3	–14.0	–14.1	–16.7	–20.4	–22.7	–19.4	–17.0	–5.3	–6.8	–16.4
Gabon	33.1	15.2	19.2	24.3	30.2	37.0	32.8	28.8	39.0	9.7	17.7	30.4
Gambia, The	–20.9	–11.7	–8.3	–9.2	–21.1	–22.8	–17.2	–16.5	–18.9	–13.2	–12.6	–14.3
Ghana	–0.7	–9.0	–12.3	–15.9	–21.1	–25.0	–24.7	–26.4	–26.3	–3.1	–12.4	–21.1
Guinea	3.1	–2.4	–4.0	–2.4	–4.0	–2.7	–2.8	–2.2	–2.2	0.8	–3.0	–2.9
Guinea-Bissau	–29.2	–27.1	–21.4	–14.1	–11.3	–13.9	–28.0	–16.6	–20.0	–32.9	–24.5	–20.0
Kenya	–6.4	–5.6	–5.4	–6.0	–6.3	–7.4	–9.9	–11.2	–14.1	–4.9	–3.7	–8.9
Lesotho	–89.1	–98.6	–62.5	–55.6	–48.8	–51.4	–46.3	–49.9	–63.4	–107.4	–95.1	–55.7
Liberia	–0.1	..	–8.1	–12.6	–13.9	–14.0	–54.6	–50.5	..	2.9	–39.6	–20.8
Madagascar	–16.4	–11.4	–6.6	–9.0	–14.8	–14.2	–11.2	–16.4	–25.3	–7.7	–8.2	–12.0
Malawi	–14.0	–9.6	–24.9	–21.8	–18.2	–24.5	–23.9	–21.0	–27.8	–6.7	–14.3	–20.3
Mali	–14.4	–16.6	–7.3	–10.9	–12.4	–11.7	–8.1	–9.8	..	–17.6	–14.9	–11.2
Mauritania	–29.8	–15.1	–23.0	–30.9	–49.4	–59.8	–4.5	–7.2	..	–24.4	–11.2	–27.7
Mauritius	–10.9	–7.2	3.8	2.1	–0.6	–4.4	–7.1	–9.3	–8.2	–3.5	–4.3	–2.5
Mozambique	–16.5	–27.9	–15.1	–16.2	–8.6	–9.4	–5.8	–6.7	–10.0	–18.4	–23.6	–12.0
Namibia	7.8	–15.5	–2.1	–9.1	–2.3	0.1	3.9	–1.9	–9.1	–7.6	–10.0	–3.4
Niger	–13.5	–6.9	–8.9	–9.2	–10.5	–9.4	..	..	..	–8.0	–6.2	–8.9
Nigeria[b]	10.2	14.6	–0.7	2.3	12.9	15.5	15.1	10.5	13.1	1.1	4.1	11.3
Rwanda	–11.9	–8.5	–18.2	–18.3	–15.9	–16.5	–17.8	–17.9	–19.5	–10.3	–19.9	–17.5
São Tomé and Príncipe	..	..	..	..	..	..	..	..	..	..	..	..
Senegal	–14.5	–6.8	–10.4	–12.1	–12.9	–15.6	–17.5	–22.4	–22.5	–12.1	–7.1	–14.6
Seychelles	–11.2	–4.3	–1.2	11.2	2.0	–21.6	–18.0	–35.1	–21.6	–2.3	–8.6	–12.1
Sierra Leone	–15.4	–1.3	–18.3	–17.6	–11.2	–13.2	–7.6	–7.4	–12.2	–3.1	–4.5	–14.1
Somalia	–55.3	–28.0	..	..	..	..	..	..	..	–35.1	–28.0	..
South Africa	8.0	5.5	3.8	2.3	–0.4	–0.8	–3.3	–3.1	–4.0	5.1	2.8	0.2
Sudan	–12.6	–3.0	–6.2	–4.2	–3.8	–9.9	–10.9	–3.8	0.7	–8.3	–6.7	–5.4
Swaziland	–39.4	–9.9	–5.5	–1.0	–2.7	–4.2	–2.6	–1.4	0.1	–23.5	–15.2	–5.0
Tanzania	..	–24.8	–7.4	–6.6	–7.1	–6.5	–5.8	..	..	..	–19.3	–7.0
Togo	–5.3	–11.9	–18.0	–13.6	–13.5	–16.9	–19.5	–20.5	–27.0	–7.2	–9.6	–18.7
Uganda	–6.6	–12.1	–14.3	–14.2	–10.5	–11.1	–13.6	–13.9	–17.7	–6.2	–11.7	–13.3
Zambia	–4.0	–0.7	–14.0	–12.4	–4.4	–2.1	8.4	6.4	2.5	–2.1	–5.6	–5.1
Zimbabwe	–3.2	0.1	–0.9	–5.2	–10.1	–16.2	..	..	..	–0.8	–2.6	–5.2
NORTH AFRICA	–0.6	–3.6	0.9	3.4	4.2	7.7	9.1	6.0	9.5	–4.1	–2.4	5.1
Algeria	4.0	–1.5	9.7	14.4	14.4	23.4	27.3	23.6	34.6	–2.5	1.6	20.2
Egypt, Arab Rep.	–12.4	–12.7	–4.4	–2.6	–1.4	–2.3	–1.6	–4.6	–6.6	–13.2	–6.7	–3.9
Libya	..	8.6	11.4	..	..	..	..	..	..	..	3.6	14.1
Morocco	–9.4	–5.4	–2.1	–2.8	–5.0	–5.6	–5.5	–9.1	–9.4	–7.4	–4.9	–5.3
Tunisia	–5.4	–7.0	–4.3	–3.9	–2.9	–0.4	–2.3	–2.4	–3.1	–6.1	–4.3	–3.1
ALL AFRICA	1.6	–0.2	–0.3	0.6	1.9	3.9	4.9	3.0	6.0	–1.9	–1.4	2.7

a. Provisional.

b. For 1994–2000 Nigeria's values were distorted because the official exchange rate used by the government for oil exports and oil value added was significantly overvalued.

Table 2.23 Exports of goods and services, nominal

	Current prices ($ millions)									Annual average		
	1980	1990	2002	2003	2004	2005	2006	2007	2008[a]	1980–89	1990–99	2000–08
SUB-SAHARAN AFRICA	83,549	79,598	113,518	145,066	184,997	231,923	277,748	318,957	413,690	66,396	87,532	212,485
Excluding South Africa	54,740	52,169	76,939	98,305	127,300	165,412	201,670	229,410	314,556	39,889	55,783	151,925
Excl. S. Africa & Nigeria	34,967	40,236	58,121	69,425	88,700	113,180	138,282	163,152	222,731	32,451	43,553	106,876
Angola	..	3,992	8,406	9,716	13,780	24,286	33,317	43,809	74,618	2,613	4,265	24,774
Benin	222	264	380	487	539	577	..	..	..	214	327	448
Botswana	563	2,087	2,811	3,697	4,357	5,120	5,581	5,797	5,928	999	2,350	4,386
Burkina Faso	173	340	290	376	549	542	665	..	..	189	286	417
Burundi	81	89	39	50	64	91	99	..	..	111	89	63
Cameroon	1,880	2,251	2,169	2,757	3,061	3,393	4,131	4,563	6,837	2,240	2,198	3,484
Cape Verde	..	43	194	253	138	171	229	285	345	41	79	214
Central African Republic	201	220	162	154	168	170	207	254	284	181	185	194
Chad	175	234	252	674	2,252	3,234	3,852	3,476	3,677	153	254	1,989
Comoros	11	36	40	51	46	48	47	57	68	22	40	47
Congo, Dem. Rep.	2,372	2,759	1,174	1,483	1,994	2,242	2,517	2,705	2,693	2,016	1,595	1,850
Congo, Rep.	1,024	1,502	2,462	2,825	3,662	5,160	6,717	5,582	..	1,092	1,393	3,895
Côte d'Ivoire	3,561	3,421	5,747	6,297	7,517	8,354	9,144	9,222	11,953	3,142	4,129	7,429
Djibouti	..	244	228	248	246	288	307	484	..	..	210	276
Equatorial Guinea	..	42	2,139	2,859	4,724	7,183	8,332	10,299	14,498	32	160	5,892
Eritrea	..	..	86	43	43	67	84	86	..	..	132	73
Ethiopia	..	672	982	1,139	1,498	1,858	2,105	2,488	3,074	608	715	1,679
Gabon	2,770	2,740	2,642	3,350	4,465	5,610	6,203	7,487	11,151	1,964	2,728	5,243
Gambia, The	103	190	157	158	184	185	203	214	235	108	195	188
Ghana	376	993	2,625	3,101	3,487	3,475	4,581	5,057	5,940	554	1,684	3,677
Guinea	2,084	829	785	806	829	925	1,073	1,700	1,187	2,021	798	983
Guinea-Bissau	14	24	61	71	92	94	59	107	128	15	32	82
Kenya	2,144	2,207	3,274	3,590	4,283	5,342	5,977	7,042	8,599	1,805	2,594	4,869
Lesotho	91	98	390	520	721	703	759	880	767	67	187	591
Liberia	613	..	111	133	171	201	175	245	..	519	43	160
Madagascar	539	512	704	1,264	1,424	1,356	1,649	2,233	2,363	414	673	1,500
Malawi	307	447	907	723	655	559	595	845	998	295	465	690
Mali	263	415	1,066	1,153	1,237	1,359	1,884	1,871	..	255	514	1,262
Mauritania	261	465	382	356	473	659	1,453	1,524	..	387	465	716
Mauritius	539	1,529	2,757	3,099	3,350	3,556	3,868	4,194	5,331	764	2,191	3,548
Mozambique	383	201	1,188	1,353	1,828	2,164	2,831	3,010	3,114	215	373	1,915
Namibia	1,712	1,220	1,546	2,141	2,630	2,937	3,628	4,173	3,335	1,139	1,543	2,605
Niger	617	372	330	438	491	512	..	..	..	420	325	403
Nigeria	18,859	12,366	18,839	28,891	38,609	52,238	63,404	66,617	92,201	7,725	12,563	45,140
Rwanda	168	145	133	139	200	245	275	332	360	173	107	221
São Tomé and Príncipe	..	..	..	..	..	..	..	..	..	..	..	..
Senegal	837	1,453	1,523	1,826	2,123	2,340	2,401	2,875	3,294	989	1,347	2,121
Seychelles	100	230	586	671	684	717	860	993	1,091	123	298	732
Sierra Leone	252	146	164	230	247	292	355	349	487	187	155	263
Somalia	200	90	..	..	..	..	..	..	..	119	90	..
South Africa	28,555	27,149	36,578	46,760	57,700	66,527	76,171	89,567	100,562	26,088	31,523	60,733
Sudan	806	499	1,996	2,613	3,822	4,992	6,015	9,287	13,292	841	579	5,069
Swaziland	405	658	1,172	1,872	2,056	2,250	2,259	2,311	2,101	394	886	1,812
Tanzania	..	538	1,631	2,022	2,538	2,964	3,106	..	..	..	962	2,185
Togo	580	545	498	595	691	850	938	1,048	1,142	464	441	732
Uganda	242	312	693	752	1,008	1,310	1,524	1,990	2,272	371	500	1,209
Zambia	1,608	1,180	1,030	1,256	2,079	2,482	4,120	4,802	5,267	1,060	1,099	2,548
Zimbabwe	1,561	2,009	2,019	1,854	2,002	1,941	..	..	..	1,530	2,469	2,141
NORTH AFRICA	37,505	46,844	66,974	80,326	99,923	126,988	147,357	172,176	261,135	34,399	48,912	121,273
Algeria	14,541	14,546	20,012	26,028	34,067	48,761	56,953	63,297	102,773	12,221	12,420	43,828
Egypt, Arab Rep.	6,992	8,647	16,091	18,074	22,258	27,214	32,191	39,469	61,354	6,654	12,435	27,766
Libya	..	11,468	9,164	..	..	..	..	..	..	..	8,527	10,099
Morocco	3,273	6,830	12,186	14,282	16,726	19,234	22,449	26,892	35,089	3,790	8,363	18,701
Tunisia	3,518	5,353	9,520	10,950	13,199	14,402	15,600	18,958	26,186	3,312	7,168	14,112
ALL AFRICA	122,545	126,555	180,495	225,868	285,752	359,801	426,557	492,585	674,727	101,527	136,479	334,315

a. Provisional.

Table

2.24 Imports of goods and services, nominal

	Current prices ($ millions)											
										Annual average		
	1980	1990	2002	2003	2004	2005	2006	2007	2008[a]	1980–89	1990–99	2000–08
SUB-SAHARAN AFRICA	76,874	74,318	117,172	149,237	181,048	218,168	256,486	305,310	372,119	67,736	90,366	201,602
Excluding South Africa	54,910	53,452	84,902	106,320	122,534	149,665	171,702	207,051	261,529	46,219	62,474	139,405
Excl. S. Africa & Nigeria	41,883	45,176	65,628	78,904	95,211	114,757	130,295	157,764	196,532	38,640	51,177	106,642
Angola	..	2,147	7,110	8,801	10,621	15,144	17,129	23,941	32,731	1,895	4,032	14,212
Benin	524	486	772	944	1,055	1,119	..	..	..	447	579	864
Botswana	705	1,888	2,130	2,979	3,380	3,308	3,109	4,512	5,333	842	1,896	3,199
Burkina Faso	603	758	697	928	1,240	1,390	1,547	..	..	567	640	1,016
Burundi	214	314	140	165	225	360	432	..	..	254	234	229
Cameroon	1,829	1,931	2,254	2,712	3,128	3,562	3,763	4,395	6,587	2,219	1,816	3,401
Cape Verde	..	148	419	529	497	500	624	791	945	118	237	554
Central African Republic	327	411	210	205	246	289	324	381	455	292	282	283
Chad	298	485	2,259	1,608	2,241	2,324	2,509	2,400	2,823	305	469	1,944
Comoros	64	93	77	103	118	134	143	174	196	67	93	120
Congo, Dem. Rep.	2,354	2,731	1,447	1,892	2,573	2,792	3,499	3,778	3,863	2,107	1,537	2,415
Congo, Rep.	1,026	1,282	1,629	1,913	2,488	2,994	3,398	3,281	..	1,093	1,309	2,325
Côte d'Ivoire	4,190	2,927	3,837	4,796	6,093	7,132	7,356	8,106	10,838	2,906	3,406	6,129
Djibouti	..	355	259	305	361	361	441	654	..	..	295	365
Equatorial Guinea	..	92	1,124	2,256	2,882	3,583	3,179	3,809	5,953	61	270	2,828
Eritrea	..	..	473	456	446	598	465	474	..	..	482	486
Ethiopia	..	1,069	2,072	2,346	3,174	4,366	5,547	6,255	7,577	1,093	1,330	3,915
Gabon	1,354	1,837	1,694	1,882	2,299	2,400	3,068	4,154	5,517	1,586	1,823	2,692
Gambia, The	153	227	188	192	269	290	290	320	383	137	242	260
Ghana	407	1,522	3,380	4,316	5,356	6,160	7,723	9,020	10,188	709	2,509	5,881
Guinea	1,878	892	912	892	986	1,013	1,163	1,802	1,281	1,953	905	1,085
Guinea-Bissau	46	90	104	104	124	137	148	170	214	67	91	138
Kenya	2,608	2,691	3,981	4,478	5,290	6,740	8,200	10,064	13,456	2,154	3,071	6,725
Lesotho	475	666	808	1,072	1,350	1,411	1,462	1,713	1,796	496	926	1,234
Liberia	614	..	156	184	235	275	509	616	..	491	180	287
Madagascar	1,202	864	993	1,756	2,072	2,070	2,269	3,438	4,630	668	942	2,240
Malawi	480	629	1,570	1,251	1,134	1,259	1,353	1,597	2,186	384	716	1,293
Mali	520	817	1,311	1,630	1,841	1,979	2,360	2,542	..	536	882	1,742
Mauritania	473	619	647	753	1,239	1,758	1,573	1,715	..	576	607	1,135
Mauritius	665	1,701	2,584	2,988	3,389	3,830	4,325	4,823	6,044	809	2,334	3,747
Mozambique	965	888	1,821	2,108	2,320	2,783	3,245	3,550	4,091	773	1,001	2,573
Namibia	1,542	1,584	1,616	2,589	2,780	2,927	3,317	4,337	4,117	1,284	1,844	2,790
Niger	957	545	523	688	795	825	..	..	..	583	448	629
Nigeria	12,324	8,203	19,245	27,360	27,282	34,849	41,280	49,192	64,469	7,362	11,214	32,656
Rwanda	307	364	430	464	513	638	781	944	1,228	354	405	652
São Tomé and Príncipe	..	..	..	..	..	..	..	..	..	..	..	..
Senegal	1,344	1,840	2,078	2,657	3,162	3,694	4,037	5,407	6,262	1,408	1,719	3,432
Seychelles	117	246	594	593	671	908	1,034	1,313	1,271	123	344	836
Sierra Leone	421	154	336	404	367	452	464	471	724	225	191	416
Somalia	534	346	..	..	..	..	..	..	..	403	346	..
South Africa	22,073	21,016	32,316	42,967	58,544	68,549	84,692	98,333	111,723	21,441	27,961	62,348
Sudan	1,763	877	2,924	3,367	4,650	7,701	9,995	11,041	12,883	1,744	1,289	6,390
Swaziland	619	768	1,237	1,889	2,117	2,357	2,329	2,350	2,098	515	1,109	1,894
Tanzania	..	1,595	2,353	2,703	3,344	3,881	3,941	..	..	..	2,000	2,958
Togo	640	738	763	833	969	1,206	1,371	1,561	1,905	542	586	1,107
Uganda	324	834	1,575	1,693	1,838	2,332	2,878	3,638	4,846	619	1,039	2,401
Zambia	1,764	1,203	1,552	1,796	2,319	2,631	3,221	4,068	4,909	1,148	1,283	2,606
Zimbabwe	1,771	2,002	2,218	2,238	2,477	2,495	..	..	..	1,598	2,661	2,390
NORTH AFRICA	38,163	53,024	64,846	71,794	88,203	102,168	113,750	146,378	207,611	40,285	53,422	102,010
Algeria	12,847	15,472	14,491	16,239	21,808	24,838	25,211	31,633	42,597	13,875	11,636	22,271
Egypt, Arab Rep.	9,822	14,109	19,917	20,219	23,330	29,246	33,931	45,443	72,031	10,787	16,572	32,078
Libya	..	8,996	6,979	..	..	..	..	..	..	..	7,464	5,968
Morocco	5,033	8,227	13,038	15,691	19,547	22,569	26,044	33,750	43,188	4,955	9,907	22,025
Tunisia	3,987	6,220	10,421	11,918	14,026	14,521	16,322	19,799	27,451	3,834	7,842	14,919
ALL AFRICA	116,318	127,628	182,015	221,784	270,088	321,633	372,122	453,488	581,372	108,793	143,884	304,525

a. Provisional.

Table 2.25 Exports of goods and services as a share of GDP

	Share of GDP (%)											
										Annual average		
	1980	1990	2002	2003	2004	2005	2006	2007	2008[a]	1980–89	1990–99	2000–08
SUB-SAHARAN AFRICA	30.2	26.4	31.3	32.6	33.8	36.2	37.4	37.4	41.9	25.2	27.3	35.3
Excluding South Africa	27.8	27.6	30.3	35.1	37.9	40.8	40.8	39.5	43.2	23.2	30.1	37.7
Excl. S. Africa & Nigeria	27.0	25.1	29.9	32.7	35.8	38.6	39.9	39.3	43.2	24.1	28.1	36.0
Angola	..	38.9	73.5	69.6	69.7	79.3	73.8	73.9	89.5	34.8	63.4	77.3
Benin	15.8	14.3	13.5	13.7	13.3	13.5	..	..	..	16.6	16.4	14.1
Botswana	53.1	55.1	47.4	44.7	44.3	48.7	50.7	47.0	45.7	62.0	51.2	47.7
Burkina Faso	9.0	11.0	8.8	8.8	10.7	10.0	11.5	..	..	9.5	11.1	9.7
Burundi	8.8	7.9	6.2	8.4	9.6	11.4	10.7	..	..	10.4	9.0	8.7
Cameroon	27.9	20.2	19.9	20.2	19.4	20.5	23.0	22.1	29.2	25.7	20.9	22.2
Cape Verde	..	12.7	31.5	31.7	14.9	17.0	19.1	19.7	19.9	15.5	16.9	23.5
Central African Republic	25.2	14.8	15.5	13.5	13.2	12.6	14.0	14.8	14.4	20.5	16.2	14.9
Chad	16.9	13.5	12.7	24.6	51.0	55.1	61.1	49.6	44.0	14.3	16.1	36.6
Comoros	8.7	14.3	15.7	15.8	12.7	12.5	11.7	12.2	12.8	14.7	17.4	13.9
Congo, Dem. Rep.	16.5	29.5	21.2	26.1	30.2	31.0	28.6	27.2	23.2	21.4	23.1	25.4
Congo, Rep.	60.0	53.7	81.5	79.3	84.3	84.8	86.9	73.0	..	52.0	60.2	80.9
Côte d'Ivoire	35.0	31.7	50.0	45.8	48.6	51.1	52.7	46.6	51.1	37.1	36.8	47.6
Djibouti	..	53.8	38.6	39.9	37.0	40.6	40.3	59.2	..	..	43.2	41.0
Equatorial Guinea	..	32.2	99.6	96.8	90.1	87.4	86.8	81.9	78.3	35.9	52.9	91.2
Eritrea	..	..	12.7	7.3	6.8	5.8	6.5	6.3	..	..	22.0	9.0
Ethiopia	..	5.6	12.6	13.3	14.9	15.1	13.9	12.8	11.6	6.6	8.1	13.1
Gabon	64.7	46.0	53.6	55.3	62.2	64.7	65.0	64.7	77.2	53.3	54.0	63.4
Gambia, The	42.7	59.9	42.5	43.1	46.0	40.0	39.9	33.3	30.1	47.8	52.6	39.9
Ghana	8.5	16.9	42.6	40.7	39.3	32.4	36.0	33.7	36.8	11.2	25.2	39.5
Guinea	31.2	31.1	24.5	22.3	21.0	28.4	33.5	37.2	27.8	29.6	23.8	27.2
Guinea-Bissau	12.7	9.9	29.8	30.0	32.1	31.3	18.7	28.0	29.8	9.9	13.3	28.9
Kenya	29.5	25.7	24.9	24.1	26.6	28.5	26.6	26.1	24.9	25.7	27.6	25.1
Lesotho	21.0	17.0	58.2	52.3	55.9	51.1	50.0	52.7	47.3	16.5	23.4	49.4
Liberia	64.3	..	19.9	32.4	37.3	37.9	28.6	33.3	..	55.3	11.4	29.2
Madagascar	13.3	16.6	16.0	23.1	32.6	26.9	29.9	30.4	26.3	13.6	20.1	27.2
Malawi	24.8	23.8	34.0	29.8	25.0	19.6	18.8	23.6	23.4	23.7	25.1	25.3
Mali	14.7	17.1	31.9	26.4	25.4	25.6	32.1	27.3	..	15.8	20.8	28.6
Mauritania	36.8	45.6	33.3	27.7	30.6	35.9	54.6	57.7	..	47.9	36.7	40.0
Mauritius	46.8	64.2	60.6	59.1	55.2	56.5	60.1	61.8	61.6	53.1	61.5	60.4
Mozambique	10.9	8.2	28.3	29.0	32.1	32.9	39.9	37.6	32.0	6.8	12.8	30.4
Namibia	78.9	51.9	46.0	43.4	39.8	40.5	45.5	47.9	38.9	61.2	49.7	42.7
Niger	24.6	15.0	15.2	16.2	16.9	15.4	..	..	..	21.0	16.2	16.4
Nigeria	29.4	43.4	31.9	42.7	44.0	46.5	43.2	40.1	43.5	21.4	42.0	43.2
Rwanda	14.4	5.6	8.1	7.9	10.1	10.3	9.7	9.7	8.1	10.4	6.0	9.1
São Tomé and Príncipe	..	..	..	..	..	..	..	..	..	..	..	..
Senegal	23.9	25.4	28.5	26.6	26.4	26.9	25.6	25.4	24.9	27.4	26.4	26.8
Seychelles	68.0	62.5	84.0	95.1	97.8	81.1	88.8	108.8	130.9	62.1	59.9	94.0
Sierra Leone	22.9	22.4	17.6	23.2	23.0	24.1	24.9	20.9	24.9	19.5	19.8	21.4
Somalia	33.2	9.8	..	..	..	..	..	..	..	15.5	9.8	..
South Africa	35.4	24.2	33.0	28.1	26.7	27.4	29.6	31.6	36.3	28.8	23.5	30.1
Sudan	10.6	4.0	13.3	14.7	17.6	18.2	16.5	20.1	22.7	7.4	5.4	16.8
Swaziland	74.6	59.0	99.8	104.2	90.1	89.1	84.6	79.9	80.2	70.2	61.1	88.1
Tanzania	..	12.6	16.7	19.7	22.4	21.0	21.7	..	..	..	16.4	19.2
Togo	51.1	33.5	33.8	33.8	33.5	40.3	42.3	41.9	40.4	46.1	30.2	36.5
Uganda	19.4	7.2	11.2	11.4	12.7	14.2	15.3	16.7	15.6	11.6	9.8	13.3
Zambia	41.4	35.9	27.7	28.7	38.3	34.7	38.6	42.1	36.8	34.4	32.8	33.6
Zimbabwe	23.4	22.9	9.2	25.1	42.5	56.8	..	..	..	21.4	34.1	32.1
NORTH AFRICA	33.6	27.2	29.7	32.2	35.8	39.4	39.8	39.7	46.4	26.5	26.4	35.5
Algeria	34.3	23.4	35.1	38.3	40.1	47.6	48.9	47.1	59.1	23.8	25.8	43.7
Egypt, Arab Rep.	30.5	20.0	18.3	21.8	28.2	30.3	29.9	30.3	37.7	22.2	21.8	25.6
Libya	..	39.7	47.7	..	..	..	..	..	..	..	28.7	37.6
Morocco	17.4	26.5	30.2	28.7	29.4	32.3	34.2	35.8	40.6	22.2	25.9	32.1
Tunisia	40.2	43.6	45.2	43.8	46.9	49.7	50.4	54.1	65.2	36.9	42.5	49.7
ALL AFRICA	31.3	26.8	30.6	32.4	34.4	37.1	38.0	38.0	43.1	25.6	26.9	35.1

a. Provisional.

Table 2.26 Imports of goods and services as a share of GDP

	Share of GDP (%)											
										Annual average		
	1980	1990	2002	2003	2004	2005	2006	2007	2008[a]	1980–89	1990–99	2000–08
SUB-SAHARAN AFRICA	27.8	24.7	32.3	33.6	33.1	34.0	34.5	35.8	37.7	25.8	28.2	33.8
Excluding South Africa	27.9	28.3	33.4	37.9	36.5	36.9	34.8	35.6	35.9	26.8	33.8	35.7
Excl. S. Africa & Nigeria	32.4	28.2	33.7	37.1	38.4	39.1	37.6	38.0	38.1	28.7	33.0	37.2
Angola	..	20.9	62.2	63.1	53.7	49.4	37.9	40.4	39.3	25.6	61.3	53.8
Benin	37.3	26.3	27.5	26.5	26.1	26.1	..	..	..	34.1	28.9	27.0
Botswana	66.4	49.8	35.9	36.0	34.4	31.5	28.2	36.6	41.1	56.7	41.5	34.4
Burkina Faso	31.3	24.5	21.2	21.7	24.3	25.6	26.8	..	..	29.2	24.6	24.0
Burundi	23.3	27.8	22.3	27.7	33.9	45.3	47.0	..	..	23.8	23.4	31.0
Cameroon	27.1	17.3	20.7	19.9	19.8	21.5	21.0	21.2	28.2	25.3	17.2	21.7
Cape Verde	..	43.7	68.1	66.3	53.8	49.7	51.9	54.7	54.7	44.6	52.1	58.2
Central African Republic	41.1	27.6	20.1	18.0	19.4	21.4	21.9	22.3	23.1	32.5	24.0	21.3
Chad	28.9	27.9	113.7	58.7	50.8	39.6	39.8	34.3	33.8	27.7	29.7	50.5
Comoros	51.9	37.1	30.8	31.8	32.6	34.7	35.5	37.3	36.9	47.9	40.0	33.7
Congo, Dem. Rep.	16.4	29.2	26.1	33.3	39.0	38.6	39.8	38.0	33.3	22.2	21.9	32.2
Congo, Rep.	60.1	45.8	53.9	53.7	57.3	49.2	43.9	42.9	..	52.6	57.3	49.7
Côte d'Ivoire	41.2	27.1	33.4	34.9	39.4	43.6	42.4	40.9	46.3	33.9	30.3	38.6
Djibouti	..	78.4	43.7	49.1	54.2	50.9	57.9	80.0	..	..	60.7	54.0
Equatorial Guinea	..	69.6	52.3	76.4	55.0	43.6	33.1	30.3	32.1	64.5	98.6	55.6
Eritrea	..	..	70.0	76.3	70.7	51.5	36.3	34.5	..	..	77.8	61.0
Ethiopia	..	8.8	26.6	27.4	31.6	35.5	36.6	32.2	28.6	11.9	14.9	29.6
Gabon	31.6	30.9	34.3	31.1	32.0	27.7	32.1	35.9	38.2	43.6	36.3	33.0
Gambia, The	63.6	71.6	50.8	52.3	67.1	62.8	57.1	49.8	49.0	61.0	65.3	54.1
Ghana	9.2	25.9	54.9	56.6	60.4	57.5	60.7	60.2	63.2	14.3	37.6	60.6
Guinea	28.1	33.4	28.4	24.6	25.0	31.1	36.3	39.5	30.0	28.8	26.9	30.1
Guinea-Bissau	41.8	37.0	51.2	44.1	43.4	45.2	46.7	44.6	49.8	42.8	37.7	48.8
Kenya	35.9	31.3	30.3	30.0	32.9	35.9	36.5	37.3	39.0	30.6	31.3	34.1
Lesotho	110.1	115.6	120.7	107.9	104.7	102.5	96.3	102.6	110.8	123.9	118.5	105.1
Liberia	64.4	..	27.9	44.9	51.2	51.9	83.2	83.8	..	52.4	51.0	50.1
Madagascar	29.7	28.0	22.6	32.1	47.5	41.1	41.1	46.8	51.6	21.3	28.3	39.2
Malawi	38.8	33.4	58.9	51.6	43.2	44.1	42.8	44.5	51.2	30.4	39.4	45.6
Mali	29.1	33.7	39.2	37.4	37.8	37.3	40.2	37.1	..	33.4	35.7	39.8
Mauritania	66.7	60.7	56.2	58.6	80.0	95.7	59.1	64.9	..	72.2	47.9	67.7
Mauritius	57.6	71.4	56.8	56.9	55.9	60.9	67.2	71.1	69.9	56.6	65.8	62.9
Mozambique	27.4	36.1	43.4	45.2	40.7	42.3	45.7	44.3	42.0	25.1	36.4	42.4
Namibia	71.1	67.4	48.1	52.5	42.1	40.3	41.6	49.7	48.1	68.7	59.7	46.1
Niger	38.1	22.0	24.1	25.4	27.4	24.8	..	..	..	29.0	22.4	25.3
Nigeria	19.2	28.8	32.6	40.4	31.1	31.0	28.1	29.6	30.4	20.3	37.8	32.0
Rwanda	26.4	14.1	26.2	26.1	26.0	26.8	27.5	27.7	27.5	20.7	26.0	26.6
São Tomé and Príncipe	..	..	..	..	..	..	..	..	..	..	..	..
Senegal	38.4	32.2	39.0	38.7	39.4	42.5	43.1	47.9	47.4	39.6	33.5	41.4
Seychelles	79.1	66.7	85.2	84.0	95.8	102.7	106.9	143.9	152.5	64.4	68.4	106.2
Sierra Leone	38.2	23.8	35.9	40.8	34.2	37.2	32.6	28.3	37.1	22.5	24.2	35.5
Somalia	88.5	37.7	..	..	..	..	..	..	..	50.6	37.7	..
South Africa	27.3	18.8	29.1	25.8	27.1	28.2	32.9	34.7	40.4	23.8	20.7	29.9
Sudan	23.1	7.1	19.5	18.9	21.4	28.1	27.5	23.9	22.0	15.7	12.1	22.2
Swaziland	114.0	68.9	105.3	105.2	92.8	93.4	87.2	81.2	80.1	93.7	76.3	93.1
Tanzania	..	37.5	24.1	26.3	29.5	27.4	27.5	..	..	..	35.6	26.2
Togo	56.4	45.3	51.7	47.4	47.0	57.2	61.8	62.5	67.5	53.3	39.8	55.2
Uganda	26.0	19.4	25.5	25.6	23.2	25.3	28.9	30.6	33.4	17.8	21.5	26.6
Zambia	45.4	36.6	41.8	41.1	42.8	36.8	30.2	35.6	34.3	36.5	38.4	38.7
Zimbabwe	26.5	22.8	10.1	30.3	52.6	73.0	..	..	..	22.2	36.7	37.3
NORTH AFRICA	34.2	30.8	28.7	28.8	31.6	31.7	30.7	33.8	36.9	30.6	28.8	30.3
Algeria	30.3	24.9	25.4	23.9	25.7	24.3	21.6	23.6	24.5	26.3	24.2	23.5
Egypt, Arab Rep.	42.9	32.7	22.7	24.4	29.6	32.6	31.6	34.8	44.2	35.4	28.5	29.4
Libya	..	31.1	36.4	..	..	..	..	..	..	..	25.1	23.5
Morocco	26.7	31.9	32.3	31.5	34.3	37.9	39.7	44.9	50.0	29.6	30.9	37.3
Tunisia	45.6	50.6	49.5	47.7	49.9	50.1	52.7	56.5	68.3	43.0	46.8	52.8
ALL AFRICA	29.7	27.0	30.9	31.9	32.5	33.1	33.2	35.0	37.1	27.5	28.4	32.4

a. Provisional.

Table 2.27 Balance of payments and current account

	Exports of goods and services		Imports of goods and services		Total trade (exports and imports)	
	Current prices ($ millions) 2008[a]	Share of GDP (%) 2008[a]	Current prices ($ millions) 2008[a]	Share of GDP (%) 2008[a]	Current prices ($ millions) 2008[a]	Share of GDP (%) 2008[a]
SUB-SAHARAN AFRICA	413,690	41.9	372,119	37.7	785,809	76.9
Excluding South Africa	314,556	43.2	261,529	35.9	576,086	..
Excl. S. Africa & Nigeria	222,731	43.2	196,532	38.1	419,264	..
Angola	74,618	89.5	32,731	39.3	107,349	128.7
Benin	..	..	..	..	..	..
Botswana	5,928	45.7	5,333	41.1	11,261	86.8
Burkina Faso	..	..	..	..	..	..
Burundi	..	..	..	..	..	..
Cameroon	6,837	29.2	6,587	28.2	13,424	57.4
Cape Verde	345	19.9	945	54.7	1,290	74.6
Central African Republic	284	14.4	455	23.1	739	37.5
Chad	3,677	44.0	2,823	33.8	6,500	77.7
Comoros	68	12.8	196	36.9	264	49.7
Congo, Dem. Rep.	2,693	23.2	3,863	33.3	6,556	56.6
Congo, Rep.	..	..	..	..	..	..
Côte d'Ivoire	11,953	51.1	10,838	46.3	22,791	97.3
Djibouti	..	..	..	..	..	..
Equatorial Guinea	14,498	78.3	5,953	32.1	20,451	110.4
Eritrea	..	..	..	..	..	..
Ethiopia	3,074	11.6	7,577	28.6	10,650	40.2
Gabon	11,151	77.2	5,517	38.2	16,668	115.5
Gambia, The	235	30.1	383	49.0	619	79.1
Ghana	5,940	36.8	10,188	63.2	16,128	100.0
Guinea	1,187	27.8	1,281	30.0	2,468	57.9
Guinea-Bissau	128	29.8	214	49.8	342	79.6
Kenya	8,599	24.9	13,456	39.0	22,055	63.9
Lesotho	767	47.3	1,796	110.8	2,564	158.1
Liberia	..	..	..	..	..	..
Madagascar	2,363	26.3	4,630	51.6	6,993	78.0
Malawi	998	23.4	2,186	51.2	3,184	74.6
Mali	..	..	..	..	..	..
Mauritania	..	..	..	..	..	..
Mauritius	5,331	61.6	6,044	69.9	11,376	131.5
Mozambique	3,114	32.0	4,091	42.0	7,205	74.0
Namibia	3,335	38.9	4,117	48.1	7,452	87.0
Niger	..	..	..	..	..	..
Nigeria	92,201	43.5	64,469	30.4	156,670	73.9
Rwanda	360	8.1	1,228	27.5	1,587	35.6
São Tomé and Príncipe	..	..	..	..	..	..
Senegal	3,294	24.9	6,262	47.4	9,557	72.4
Seychelles	1,091	130.9	1,271	152.5	2,361	283.4
Sierra Leone	487	24.9	724	37.1	1,211	62.0
Somalia	..	..	..	..	..	..
South Africa	100,562	36.3	111,723	40.4	212,285	76.7
Sudan	13,292	22.7	12,883	22.0	26,174	44.8
Swaziland	2,101	80.2	2,098	80.1	4,198	160.4
Tanzania	..	..	..	..	..	..
Togo	1,142	40.4	1,905	67.5	3,047	107.9
Uganda	2,272	15.6	4,846	33.4	7,118	49.0
Zambia	5,267	36.8	4,909	34.3	10,176	71.1
Zimbabwe	..	..	..	..	..	..
NORTH AFRICA	261,135	46.4	207,611	36.9	468,746	..
Algeria	102,773	59.1	42,597	24.5	145,370	83.6
Egypt, Arab Rep.	61,354	37.7	72,031	44.2	133,385	81.9
Libya	..	..	..	..	..	..
Morocco	35,089	40.6	43,188	50.0	78,277	90.7
Tunisia	26,186	65.2	27,451	68.3	53,637	133.5
ALL AFRICA	674,727	43.1	581,372	37.1	1,256,099	..

a. Provisional.

Net income		Net current transfers		Current account balance		Total reserves including gold	
Current prices ($ millions)	Share of GDP (%)	Current prices ($ millions)	Share of GDP (%)	Current prices ($ millions)	Share of GDP (%)	Current prices ($ millions)	Share of GDP (%)
2007	2007	2007	2007	2007	2007	2008[a]	2008[a]
..	..	..	..	–4,164	..	156,071	15.6
..	..	..	..	16,615	..	122,001	16.7
..	..	..	..	–5,356	..	68,402	13.3
–8,778	–14.8	–222	–0.4	9,402	15.9	18,359	22.0
..	..	..	..	..	..	1,260	18.9
–346	–2.8	1,105	9.0	2,434	19.8	9,119	70.3
..	..	..	..	..	..	926	11.7
–6	–0.6	241	24.6	–116	–11.8	267	22.9
–385	–1.9	416	2.0	–547	–2.6	3,112	13.3
–31	–2.1	301	20.8	–197	–13.6	258	14.9
..	..	..	..	..	..	131	6.7
..	..	..	..	..	..	1,355	16.2
..	..	..	..	..	..	113	21.3
..	..	..	..	..	..	..	..
–1,885	–24.7	–38	–0.5	–2,181	–28.5	3,881	36.3
–810	–4.1	–379	–1.9	–146	–0.7	2,252	9.6
24	2.9	79	9.7	–171	–21.0	..	..
..	..	..	..	..	..	4,431	23.9
..	..	..	..	..	..	..	..
40	0.2	3,387	17.5	–828	–4.3	871	3.3
..	..	..	..	..	..	1,935	13.4
–40	–6.2	76	11.9	–53	–8.2	..	..
–139	–0.9	2,043	13.6	–2,151	–14.4	..	..
–63	–1.4	–131	–2.9	–456	–10.0	..	..
..	..	..	..	..	..	124	29.0
–192	–0.7	2,108	7.8	–1,102	–4.1	2,879	8.3
420	25.2	625	37.4	212	12.7	..	..
–150	–20.4	1,139	155.0	–211	–28.7	..	..
..	..	..	..	..	..	982	11.0
..	..	..	..	..	..	..	..
–291	–4.3	400	5.8	–581	–8.5	1,071	12.3
..	..	..	..	..	..	..	..
223	3.3	125	1.8	–434	–6.4	1,796	20.8
–592	–7.4	602	7.5	–785	–9.8	..	..
–158	–1.8	1,000	11.5	747	8.6	1,293	15.1
..	..	..	..	..	..	702	13.1
–16,746	–10.1	18,016	10.9	21,972	13.2	53,599	25.3
–15	–0.4	413	12.1	–147	–4.3	596	13.4
4	3.1	1	0.8	–67	–46.1	..	..
–74	–0.7	1,290	11.4	–1,311	–11.6	1,601	12.1
–71	–7.8	50	5.5	–264	–28.9	64	7.7
–104	–6.3	78	4.7	–181	–10.9	..	..
..	..	..	..	..	..	..	..
–9,085	–3.2	–2,953	–1.0	–20,780	–7.3	34,070	12.3
–2,253	–4.9	382	0.8	–3,268	–7.1	1,399	2.4
64	2.2	194	6.7	–66	–2.3	752	28.7
–79	–0.5	617	3.7	–1,856	–11.0	2,893	14.1
..	..	..	..	..	..	580	20.5
–246	–2.1	1,108	9.3	–528	–4.4	2,301	15.8
–1,383	–12.1	530	4.6	–505	–4.4	1,096	7.7
..	..	..	..	..	..	..	..
..	..	..	..	27,839	..	310,523	55.1
..	..	..	..	..	..	148,099	85.2
1,388	1.1	8,322	6.4	412	0.3	34,331	21.1
1,971	3.4	–219	–0.4	28,454	48.8	96,335	96.4
–405	–0.5	7,703	10.3	–122	–0.2	22,720	26.3
–1,754	–5.0	1,619	4.6	–904	–2.6	9,039	22.5
..	..	..	..	23,675	..	466,594	29.8

Table 2.28 Exchange rates and purchasing power parity

	Official exchange rate (local currency units to $)			Purchasing power parity (PPP) conversion factor (local currency units to international $)			Ratio of PPP conversion factor to market exchange rate		
	2006	2007	2008	2006	2007	2008	2006	2007	2008
SUB-SAHARAN AFRICA									
Excluding South Africa									
Excl. S. Africa & Nigeria									
Angola	49.5	50.2	58.9	80.4	76.7	75.0	0.6	0.7	0.8
Benin	219.2	219.7	235.3	522.9	479.3	447.8	0.4	0.5	0.5
Botswana	2.7	3.0	3.4	5.8	6.1	6.8	0.5	0.5	0.5
Burkina Faso	193.9	196.0	201.5	522.9	479.3	447.8	0.4	0.4	0.5
Burundi	347.2	366.2	446.2	1,028.7	1,081.9	1,185.7	0.3	0.3	0.4
Cameroon	252.9	251.5	250.3	522.9	479.3	447.8	0.5	0.5	0.6
Cape Verde	71.8	72.2	74.5	87.9	80.6	75.3	0.8	0.9	1.0
Central African Republic	266.6	264.8	271.1	522.9	479.3	447.8	0.5	0.6	0.6
Chad	214.1	212.2	232.5	522.9	479.3	447.8	0.4	0.4	0.5
Comoros	223.7	229.2	236.6	392.2	359.5	335.9	0.6	0.6	0.7
Congo, Dem. Rep.	235.9	270.4	316.2	468.3	516.7	559.3	0.5	0.5	0.6
Congo, Rep.	308.8	277.1	335.9	522.9	479.3	447.8	0.6	0.6	0.8
Côte d'Ivoire	291.2	291.4	308.4	522.9	479.3	447.8	0.6	0.6	0.7
Djibouti	84.6	85.0	85.8	177.7	177.7	177.9	0.5	0.5	0.5
Equatorial Guinea	318.8	306.9	371.5	522.9	479.3	447.8	0.6	0.6	0.8
Eritrea	6.8	7.0	8.1	15.4	15.4	15.4	0.4	0.5	0.5
Ethiopia	2.4	2.8	3.5	8.7	9.0	9.6	0.3	0.3	0.4
Gabon	268.1	274.8	307.3	522.9	479.3	447.8	0.5	0.6	0.7
Gambia, The	7.4	7.7	7.9	28.1	24.9	..	0.3	0.3	0.3
Ghana	0.4	0.5	0.5	0.9	0.9	..	0.4	0.5	0.5
Guinea	1,624.1	1,857.1	2,524.2	..	..	..	0.3	0.4	0.4
Guinea-Bissau	212.1	226.4	242.7	522.9	479.3	447.8	0.4	0.5	0.5
Kenya	30.7	31.3	39.0	72.1	67.3	69.2	0.4	0.5	0.6
Lesotho	3.7	3.9	4.2	6.8	7.0	8.3	0.5	0.6	0.5
Liberia	29.7	33.5	37.0	58.0	61.3	63.2	0.5	0.5	0.6
Madagascar	702.0	750.0	804.7	2,142.3	1,873.9	1,708.4	0.3	0.4	0.4
Malawi	45.0	47.1	50.2	136.0	140.0	..	0.3	0.3	0.4
Mali	242.3	245.7	273.1	522.9	479.3	447.8	0.5	0.5	0.6
Mauritania	124.4	118.0	..	268.6	258.6	..	0.5	0.4	..
Mauritius	14.8	15.4	16.2	31.7	31.3	28.5	0.5	0.5	0.6
Mozambique	11.6	12.1	12.6	25.4	25.8	..	0.5	0.5	0.5
Namibia	4.5	4.8	5.3	6.8	7.0	8.3	0.7	0.7	0.6
Niger	225.4	226.9	239.0	522.9	479.3	447.8	0.4	0.5	0.5
Nigeria	69.8	71.3	79.8	128.7	125.8	118.5	0.5	0.6	0.7
Rwanda	198.2	213.5	245.3	551.7	547.0	546.8	0.4	0.4	0.4
São Tomé and Príncipe	6,516.4	7,578.5	9,176.0	12,448.6	13,536.8	14,695.2	0.5	0.6	0.6
Senegal	254.4	261.8	275.0	522.9	479.3	447.8	0.5	0.5	0.6
Seychelles	3.3	3.5	4.2	5.5	6.7	9.5	0.6	0.5	0.4
Sierra Leone	1,164.5	1,251.2	1,367.5	2,961.9	2,985.2	2,980.7	0.4	0.4	0.5
Somalia	..	..	..	..	..	..	..	..	..
South Africa	4.0	4.3	4.6	6.8	7.0	8.3	0.6	0.6	0.6
Sudan	1.1	1.2	1.3	2.2	2.0	2.1	0.5	0.6	0.7
Swaziland	3.5	3.7	3.8	6.8	7.0	8.3	0.5	0.5	0.5
Tanzania	403.8	428.6	456.9	1,251.9	1,245.0	1,196.3	0.3	0.3	0.4
Togo	233.9	230.9	236.0	522.9	479.3	447.8	0.4	0.5	0.5
Uganda	614.8	642.5	668.5	1,831.5	1,723.5	1,720.7	0.3	0.4	0.4
Zambia	2,654.2	2,890.7	3,133.5	3,603.1	4,002.5	3,745.7	0.7	0.7	0.8
Zimbabwe	..	..	..	164.4	9,675.8	..	..	..	..
NORTH AFRICA									
Algeria	34.1	35.5	40.7	72.6	69.3	64.6	0.5	0.5	0.6
Egypt, Arab Rep.	1.7	1.8	2.0	5.7	..	..	0.3	0.3	0.4
Libya	0.8	0.8	1.3	1.3	1.3	1.2	0.6	0.7	1.0
Morocco	4.8	4.9	4.9	8.8	8.2	7.8	0.5	0.6	0.6
Tunisia	0.6	0.6	0.6	1.3	1.3	1.2	0.4	0.5	0.5
ALL AFRICA									

Real effective exchange rate (index, 2000 = 100)			Gross domestic product					
			PPP $ billions			Per capita PPP $		
2006	2007	2008	2006	2007	2008	2006	2007	2008
			1,466.2	1,606.6	1,731.8	1,878.5	2,009.7	2,113.9
			1,039.9	1,147.0	1,248.6	1,418.3	1,526.1	1,620.3
			768.0	850.1	929.3	1,305.2	1,408.3	1,500.7
..	..	..	73.4	90.6	106.3	4,295.0	5,162.6	5,898.5
..	..	..	11.0	11.8	12.7	1,356.7	1,410.8	1,467.9
..	..	..	23.6	25.2	25.5	12,683.8	13,405.6	13,391.8
..	..	..	15.6	16.5	17.7	1,083.7	1,119.8	1,161.3
76.9	71.4	73.7	2.7	2.9	3.1	358.0	369.3	382.8
113.4	114.7	119.1	37.1	39.4	41.9	2,042.1	2,127.8	2,215.1
..	..	..	1.5	1.6	1.7	3,034.0	3,283.0	3,504.3
114.4	115.1	123.8	2.9	3.1	3.3	679.2	713.3	735.7
126.7	..	..	15.4	15.8	16.1	1,469.9	1,470.4	1,455.3
..	..	..	0.7	0.7	0.8	1,152.1	1,160.5	1,169.0
32.8	31.9	31.6	17.4	19.0	20.6	287.5	304.8	321.4
..	..	..	13.1	13.2	14.3	3,755.3	3,724.3	3,945.9
116.0	118.0	123.3	31.2	32.6	34.0	1,584.9	1,618.0	1,651.2
..	..	..	1.6	1.7	1.8	1,951.7	2,052.6	2,140.2
150.8	158.7	170.9	15.8	19.6	22.3	25,186.2	30,577.1	33,872.9
..	..	..	2.9	3.0	3.2	620.9	625.9	632.1
99.6	..	..	54.0	61.6	70.1	704.9	783.3	868.1
100.5	105.6	109.8	18.6	20.2	21.0	13,340.8	14,188.7	14,526.5
54.2	59.4	68.3	1.9	2.1	2.3	1,219.9	1,294.5	1,362.8
116.4	115.7	109.2	28.7	31.2	33.9	1,281.2	1,366.3	1,452.1
..	..	..	10.3	10.7	11.8	1,089.9	1,111.7	1,204.0
..	..	..	0.8	0.8	0.8	518.9	524.0	537.8
..	..	..	52.7	57.9	61.3	1,442.1	1,542.3	1,589.9
129.4	128.8	117.0	2.8	3.0	3.2	1,401.4	1,503.3	1,587.8
..	..	..	1.2	1.3	1.5	344.8	370.6	387.8
..	..	..	16.8	18.4	20.0	929.6	986.7	1,048.9
74.8	66.0	51.0	9.6	10.7	11.9	704.6	765.8	836.8
..	..	..	12.7	13.4	14.3	1,057.8	1,083.2	1,127.6
..	..	..	5.8	6.0	..	1,889.4	1,927.5	..
..	..	..	13.3	14.2	15.3	10,577.2	11,296.4	12,079.3
..	..	..	15.6	17.1	18.6	743.4	801.4	855.4
..	..	..	12.0	12.8	13.4	5,847.2	6,145.5	6,342.7
..	..	..	8.5	9.0	10.0	615.7	631.8	684.0
133.3	130.7	144.7	268.0	292.9	315.0	1,851.8	1,979.0	2,081.9
..	..	..	7.9	8.7	9.9	856.5	924.6	1,021.9
..	..	..	0.2	0.3	0.3	1,533.5	1,638.2	1,738.5
..	..	..	19.2	20.7	21.6	1,660.3	1,737.3	1,772.0
..	..	..	1.6	1.8	1.9	18,995.3	20,810.2	21,529.6
73.6	73.9	79.8	3.6	4.0	4.3	686.5	732.2	766.3
..	..	..	..	..	..	..	..	..
99.5	90.9	76.9	433.2	467.4	492.2	9,141.2	9,767.7	10,108.6
..	..	..	71.1	80.4	89.0	1,798.5	1,989.3	2,153.3
..	..	..	5.2	5.5	5.8	4,549.9	4,773.1	4,928.2
..	..	..	44.4	48.9	53.7	1,107.5	1,184.0	1,262.9
112.4	113.5	121.8	5.0	5.2	5.4	806.8	823.2	829.5
88.1	90.3	92.7	29.6	32.9	36.9	996.8	1,075.4	1,164.7
180.0	153.9	145.7	14.5	15.8	17.1	1,205.7	1,283.0	1,355.8
..	..	..	..	..	..	..	..	..
			886.7	958.1	1,033.9	5,590.0	5,945.1	6,315.0
83.2	82.3	85.0	248.1	262.3	276.0	7,437.7	7,747.9	8,032.7
..	..	..	367.3	403.7	441.6	4,672.4	5,042.3	5,416.4
..	..	..	80.7	88.4	96.7	13,357.2	14,364.2	15,402.4
92.9	92.6	93.7	120.2	126.8	137.0	3,942.7	4,108.3	4,388.5
84.6	82.3	81.6	70.4	76.9	82.6	6,955.5	7,520.2	7,996.1
			2,350.7	2,562.1	2,763.0	2,503.0	2,667.2	2,810.8

Table 2.29 Agriculture value added

	Share of GDP (%)											
										Annual average		
	1980	1990	2002	2003	2004	2005	2006	2007	2008[a]	1980–89	1990–99	2000–08
SUB-SAHARAN AFRICA	18.5	21.8	18.0	15.8	13.9	13.7	14.1	14.4	14.6	20.9	19.9	15.5
Excluding South Africa	23.4	32.1	24.2	23.4	21.0	20.4	20.2	20.0	19.3	29.2	31.5	22.3
Excl. S. Africa & Nigeria	27.9	29.5	24.6	24.9	23.4	22.5	22.1	21.6	20.3	28.7	29.3	23.5
Angola	..	17.9	7.9	8.3	8.6	7.7	8.9	9.7	10.1	15.2	11.3	8.3
Benin	35.4	36.1	33.8	32.1	32.1	32.2	..	..	..	33.8	36.1	33.7
Botswana	12.7	4.5	2.2	2.2	2.0	1.8	1.7	1.7	1.6	7.8	3.9	2.0
Burkina Faso	28.4	28.0	32.6	33.4	30.6	33.0	32.8	..	..	28.9	32.0	32.1
Burundi	57.6	51.1	36.5	36.1	36.1	31.6	..	..	..	53.1	46.0	35.3
Cameroon	28.7	24.0	20.4	20.1	19.0	19.0	19.3	19.0	19.1	24.4	22.9	19.7
Cape Verde	..	14.4	7.1	6.8	9.7	9.2	8.7	8.5	8.1	16.6	12.9	8.6
Central African Republic	37.6	43.8	51.0	56.9	52.6	51.7	52.0	50.9	50.3	41.4	45.6	51.9
Chad	45.7	27.9	37.9	32.3	22.9	20.9	20.9	20.8	19.0	36.3	35.4	28.4
Comoros	34.0	41.4	50.2	50.5	50.9	51.0	45.2	45.3	45.8	36.3	40.2	48.6
Congo, Dem. Rep.	25.3	30.1	50.1	50.1	46.1	43.8	42.1	38.9	..	29.0	46.5	47.4
Congo, Rep.	11.7	12.9	6.3	6.4	5.9	4.6	4.0	5.0	..	10.0	10.5	5.4
Côte d'Ivoire	25.9	32.5	25.7	25.6	23.2	22.8	22.9	23.9	23.7	27.1	27.2	24.1
Djibouti	..	2.7	3.1	3.1	3.1	3.1	3.2	3.5	..	2.8	3.0	3.2
Equatorial Guinea	..	58.9	6.3	5.4	4.0	2.6	2.7	2.7	2.0	62.4	40.3	4.7
Eritrea	..	..	14.7	13.4	12.6	21.2	23.3	23.3	..	..	20.6	17.4
Ethiopia	..	51.7	40.4	38.9	40.4	43.0	44.4	43.0	39.8	53.3	55.4	42.3
Gabon	6.8	7.3	6.1	6.1	5.6	4.9	4.9	4.8	4.6	7.7	7.7	5.5
Gambia, The	27.0	24.3	24.9	28.2	29.1	28.3	26.3	24.8	24.7	29.2	24.6	27.8
Ghana	57.9	44.8	35.1	36.5	38.0	37.5	35.6	34.0	32.2	51.9	39.5	35.5
Guinea	..	24.7	18.7	21.5	15.0	19.0	12.7	15.8	7.5	24.2	19.5	16.5
Guinea-Bissau	42.2	56.9	56.4	56.8	51.9	50.0	50.1	48.8	51.5	47.0	53.7	52.0
Kenya	27.8	25.3	25.9	25.8	24.9	24.2	23.8	23.0	18.9	28.0	26.7	24.8
Lesotho	22.4	20.9	9.2	8.7	8.6	7.2	7.8	6.7	6.5	21.2	16.6	8.6
Liberia	32.2	54.4	75.5	71.6	68.2	65.8	55.5	54.0	..	33.5	67.2	67.0
Madagascar	26.7	26.1	29.8	26.8	26.2	25.7	25.1	24.3	23.4	30.5	26.4	25.9
Malawi	39.2	38.5	34.6	33.8	32.8	29.3	30.5	30.1	28.5	39.2	33.5	32.3
Mali	43.6	44.1	32.3	35.8	33.4	33.7	34.1	33.4	..	41.1	42.9	34.5
Mauritania	28.5	26.6	23.6	25.1	23.1	21.4	12.1	11.3	..	27.5	31.0	20.8
Mauritius	14.0	11.0	6.3	5.4	5.4	5.3	4.9	4.7	4.0	12.9	9.1	5.2
Mozambique	33.9	34.1	25.4	25.4	24.8	24.5	24.7	24.4	25.4	37.8	32.3	23.9
Namibia	10.5	10.6	10.0	10.2	8.9	10.4	9.7	9.5	7.5	10.4	10.1	9.6
Niger	43.1	35.3	39.6	40.0	..	..	..	..	..	38.6	39.4	39.4
Nigeria	..	..	47.1	41.5	33.4	32.4	31.7	32.2	31.9	..	..	35.8
Rwanda	45.8	32.5	35.5	38.5	38.8	38.9	41.9	38.9	34.6	40.2	40.6	38.0
São Tomé and Príncipe	..	..	19.9	21.1	22.6	16.8	..	..	..	..	..	20.0
Senegal	17.9	17.9	13.6	15.4	13.9	14.5	13.2	12.2	13.6	19.6	17.7	14.4
Seychelles	6.8	4.8	3.0	3.0	3.0	2.5	2.4	2.4	2.3	6.1	3.9	2.7
Sierra Leone	30.4	44.0	44.9	44.2	43.5	43.5	45.0	42.5	41.0	37.4	45.6	44.8
Somalia	64.4	62.7	..	..	..	..	..	..	..	62.7	62.7	..
South Africa	5.8	4.2	3.8	3.2	2.8	2.4	2.5	2.8	2.3	5.0	3.8	2.9
Sudan	29.9	39.0	40.2	36.9	33.1	30.2	28.5	26.9	24.4	33.2	40.5	33.5
Swaziland	19.5	8.9	8.9	7.9	7.4	7.1	6.4	6.3	6.7	16.4	10.2	7.8
Tanzania	..	42.0	41.2	41.4	42.3	37.7	37.5	..	..	..	43.0	40.4
Togo	27.5	33.8	38.1	40.8	41.2	43.7	..	..	..	31.8	37.4	39.3
Uganda	71.8	53.3	23.4	24.5	21.7	25.1	24.0	22.3	20.8	54.8	44.3	24.1
Zambia	14.0	18.2	19.9	20.5	21.5	21.0	20.3	19.7	18.1	14.3	18.8	20.1
Zimbabwe	15.1	14.8	12.7	15.0	14.1	13.4	..	..	..	14.8	15.0	14.5
NORTH AFRICA	11.4	12.8	12.6	12.7	11.8	10.3	10.4	9.9	10.4	11.7	12.6	11.4
Algeria	7.9	10.4	9.2	9.7	9.4	7.7	7.6	7.8	9.2	9.1	10.3	8.7
Egypt, Arab Rep.	17.4	18.4	15.4	15.3	14.3	14.0	13.2	13.4	14.3	18.9	16.2	14.5
Libya	..	..	..	..	..	..	..	..	..	..	..	..
Morocco	18.4	17.7	14.7	15.5	14.7	13.2	15.2	12.2	14.2	16.2	16.9	14.2
Tunisia	14.1	15.7	10.3	12.1	12.7	11.2	10.8	10.3	10.0	13.8	14.0	11.3
ALL AFRICA	15.9	18.2	15.8	14.6	13.1	12.6	12.9	12.9	13.1	17.3	17.1	13.9

a. Provisional.

Table

2.30 Industry value added

	Share of GDP (%)											
										Annual average		
	1980	1990	2002	2003	2004	2005	2006	2007	2008[a]	1980–89	1990–99	2000–08
SUB-SAHARAN AFRICA	30.4	32.6	28.5	29.7	31.4	33.4	34.3	34.1	36.9	31.4	30.7	31.9
Excluding South Africa	22.7	29.5	28.9	31.4	35.1	38.4	39.4	38.8	43.2	25.4	28.5	35.0
Excl. S. Africa & Nigeria	24.1	24.2	26.3	27.4	29.8	33.2	34.8	35.4	39.5	22.4	23.7	31.1
Angola	..	40.8	68.2	67.4	66.1	72.6	69.7	72.4	86.3	39.4	56.9	71.1
Benin	12.3	13.2	13.7	13.7	13.3	13.4	..	..	..	14.0	13.7	13.7
Botswana	43.9	56.9	50.7	47.6	48.2	49.3	50.9	45.5	43.3	52.4	50.5	49.5
Burkina Faso	19.8	20.4	19.8	20.3	21.6	21.9	22.0	..	..	20.4	20.0	21.0
Burundi	11.7	17.3	16.7	17.0	17.0	18.2	..	..	..	13.7	16.9	17.1
Cameroon	23.5	28.8	29.6	28.4	28.4	29.6	30.6	29.9	31.9	30.2	28.6	30.2
Cape Verde	..	21.4	16.1	19.7	15.2	16.7	16.1	16.4	16.7	19.0	19.7	16.6
Central African Republic	18.9	18.1	14.3	14.9	13.3	13.4	13.4	13.4	13.5	15.2	19.1	14.0
Chad	9.0	16.9	14.3	23.4	46.0	52.8	55.7	39.1	34.9	13.2	13.3	32.2
Comoros	13.2	8.3	11.6	12.7	12.2	11.0	11.8	11.9	12.0	12.5	11.4	11.8
Congo, Dem. Rep.	33.1	28.2	21.1	21.1	23.9	25.9	25.6	26.0	..	28.7	20.4	22.9
Congo, Rep.	46.6	40.6	63.3	61.5	63.6	68.6	70.2	59.8	..	45.1	45.4	65.6
Côte d'Ivoire	19.7	23.2	22.9	21.6	23.1	25.9	25.9	25.3	25.3	20.8	22.2	24.3
Djibouti	..	19.2	14.0	14.0	14.5	14.8	14.8	15.4	..	17.6	14.6	14.3
Equatorial Guinea	..	10.2	87.3	87.6	91.1	93.8	93.6	93.8	95.0	8.5	37.9	90.4
Eritrea	..	..	20.7	22.2	23.2	19.2	17.2	18.4	..	..	16.5	20.3
Ethiopia	..	10.6	12.9	13.1	12.8	11.9	11.7	12.4	11.7	11.0	9.6	12.2
Gabon	60.4	43.0	51.7	52.0	55.3	61.4	61.2	60.2	73.7	53.7	48.2	58.1
Gambia, The	13.0	11.0	13.1	12.7	11.4	11.7	12.4	12.8	13.0	11.8	11.7	12.2
Ghana	11.9	16.8	25.3	25.2	24.7	25.1	26.0	26.1	26.1	12.8	22.5	25.5
Guinea	..	34.6	30.4	28.9	29.5	33.1	36.7	42.6	33.0	33.8	29.2	32.8
Guinea-Bissau	18.7	17.4	12.9	12.8	12.4	13.0	12.8	12.0	12.0	15.2	12.0	12.5
Kenya	17.8	16.3	15.5	15.6	16.2	17.0	16.5	15.8	12.0	16.8	15.4	15.4
Lesotho	24.2	28.8	28.6	27.4	28.3	28.8	30.8	32.7	31.4	23.8	36.5	29.1
Liberia	25.2	16.8	8.0	10.6	13.4	15.7	16.7	18.6	..	25.8	11.0	13.0
Madagascar	14.3	11.7	13.6	14.1	14.5	14.3	14.8	16.2	16.1	12.3	11.2	14.4
Malawi	20.2	24.7	15.6	16.8	16.7	18.2	17.6	17.9	17.1	20.2	20.4	16.8
Mali	11.9	15.4	25.4	21.8	21.9	22.3	22.2	22.1	..	13.7	15.6	22.4
Mauritania	24.4	25.8	25.0	21.5	25.4	26.4	44.0	42.1	..	24.4	24.3	29.5
Mauritius	22.3	27.7	27.5	26.6	25.7	24.5	23.5	24.7	24.5	24.1	28.0	25.7
Mozambique	31.5	16.9	21.2	23.6	24.8	23.0	23.8	22.8	23.0	23.4	15.8	22.9
Namibia	52.7	34.3	29.5	26.4	27.0	26.7	32.2	33.2	20.3	41.4	27.4	27.7
Niger	22.9	16.2	17.0	17.3	..	..	..	..	..	19.8	17.4	17.3
Nigeria	..	..	29.6	35.7	41.1	43.0	41.6	38.9	43.1	..	..	39.0
Rwanda	21.5	24.6	13.9	12.8	13.7	14.0	13.5	13.9	12.3	21.0	19.5	13.5
São Tomé and Príncipe	..	..	17.1	17.8	21.0	20.5	..	..	..	..	..	18.7
Senegal	17.9	19.9	22.3	21.3	21.8	20.7	20.6	21.7	20.9	18.4	21.1	21.3
Seychelles	15.6	16.3	30.3	27.4	28.2	21.9	20.5	22.7	22.4	16.5	21.5	25.6
Sierra Leone	20.2	18.0	23.2	23.3	23.5	23.5	24.3	23.2	22.8	14.8	30.8	23.8
Somalia	7.5	..	..	..	..	..	..	..	..	7.5	..	..
South Africa	45.5	36.4	30.1	28.6	27.7	27.4	27.6	27.6	26.1	40.4	31.9	28.2
Sudan	12.9	14.7	19.7	20.9	24.2	26.7	27.6	29.2	32.3	14.2	13.0	24.4
Swaziland	25.9	36.8	38.5	39.6	38.4	38.0	41.0	42.1	43.3	27.2	36.9	39.7
Tanzania	..	16.1	14.9	15.2	15.2	13.8	14.4	..	..	..	14.3	14.7
Togo	24.8	22.5	18.5	22.2	22.8	24.0	..	..	..	22.0	21.0	20.4
Uganda	4.5	10.4	22.8	22.5	20.7	23.4	22.7	24.0	23.7	8.9	13.8	22.5
Zambia	39.1	45.3	23.4	24.1	26.0	28.5	31.9	34.8	39.5	40.9	34.8	28.2
Zimbabwe	27.9	29.8	18.8	19.2	18.0	16.8	..	..	..	27.6	27.1	19.1
NORTH AFRICA	42.1	35.4	38.3	39.1	40.3	41.9	42.7	41.8	45.2	38.7	34.8	40.3
Algeria	53.8	44.0	48.7	50.6	52.3	57.6	58.9	57.9	72.2	47.9	45.5	55.9
Egypt, Arab Rep.	35.1	27.3	32.6	33.4	34.7	34.1	36.2	34.7	37.0	29.2	29.9	33.8
Libya	..	..	..	..	..	..	..	..	..	..	..	..
Morocco	30.9	32.4	24.3	25.0	25.7	25.3	24.4	24.2	18.4	32.9	30.5	24.2
Tunisia	31.1	29.8	29.6	28.3	28.2	28.9	29.2	29.6	28.4	31.5	28.8	28.8
ALL AFRICA	33.1	33.5	32.2	33.1	34.7	36.6	37.5	37.1	40.2	33.5	32.1	35.1

a. Provisional.

Table 2.31 Services plus discrepancy value added

	Share of GDP (%)											
										Annual average		
	1980	1990	2002	2003	2004	2005	2006	2007	2008[a]	1980–89	1990–99	2000–08
SUB-SAHARAN AFRICA	32.9	44.0	43.6	44.8	45.1	43.6	42.8	42.5	38.8	39.4	47.1	43.5
Excluding South Africa	29.8	41.3	38.8	37.6	37.1	35.3	35.6	36.1	34.4	36.6	40.9	36.7
Excl. S. Africa & Nigeria	38.6	41.4	43.1	41.9	40.7	38.6	38.3	37.9	35.0	39.3	41.6	39.8
Angola	..	41.2	24.0	24.3	25.3	19.8	21.4	17.9	3.7	45.4	31.8	20.6
Benin	52.3	50.7	52.6	54.2	54.6	54.4	..	..	..	52.2	50.2	52.6
Botswana	29.9	31.8	39.9	41.8	41.2	40.5	39.6	45.1	47.3	30.6	37.5	40.9
Burkina Faso	48.5	48.8	41.1	40.2	41.0	41.8	43.7	..	..	47.8	42.8	41.9
Burundi	23.2	23.0	36.8	36.9	36.9	41.0	..	..	..	24.5	27.7	37.6
Cameroon	39.6	44.9	42.4	44.1	45.3	48.8	47.5	48.6	46.4	40.4	42.9	44.8
Cape Verde	..	64.3	76.9	73.4	75.1	74.1	75.3	75.2	..	64.4	67.4	74.7
Central African Republic	37.6	30.2	28.6	23.5	29.2	29.8	29.0	30.2	30.3	37.0	29.6	28.7
Chad	46.7	50.5	43.9	40.4	28.7	24.4	25.1	28.8	28.6	48.6	47.9	34.2
Comoros	52.8	50.3	38.3	36.7	36.9	38.0	..	..	..	51.2	48.4	38.0
Congo, Dem. Rep.	36.1	39.0	27.0	27.0	28.0	28.4	27.3	29.8	..	37.8	32.0	27.1
Congo, Rep.	41.7	46.5	30.4	32.0	30.5	26.8	25.8	35.1	..	44.9	44.1	29.0
Côte d'Ivoire	54.4	44.3	51.4	52.8	53.7	51.3	51.2	50.9	51.0	52.0	50.6	51.6
Djibouti	..	65.4	70.4	69.5	69.4	71.0	72.2	72.4	..	65.1	70.1	70.9
Equatorial Guinea	..	26.6	4.8	5.2	3.8	2.9	2.8	2.7	2.3	23.9	19.4	3.7
Eritrea	..	..	54.2	55.3	54.7	53.4	54.1	54.1	..	..	52.7	54.9
Ethiopia	..	32.8	39.5	40.9	38.2	37.1	36.5	37.5	41.7	30.1	29.7	38.1
Gabon	32.8	49.7	42.2	41.9	39.1	33.8	33.9	34.9	21.7	38.6	44.0	36.4
Gambia, The	47.6	48.6	52.2	49.8	45.9	48.0	48.2	48.9	48.8	45.1	49.1	48.0
Ghana	30.2	38.4	39.6	38.2	37.3	37.4	38.4	40.0	41.7	35.3	38.0	39.1
Guinea	..	44.5	43.9	43.0	49.4	41.8	45.0	36.0	54.9	42.7	48.4	44.7
Guinea-Bissau	34.4	19.3	29.1	28.6	29.7	28.1	28.7	31.0	29.3	34.8	29.7	29.7
Kenya	39.7	44.1	47.4	47.5	47.7	47.8	48.6	49.5	58.1	41.7	44.7	48.6
Lesotho	44.5	40.4	55.8	55.9	53.4	54.5	52.4	51.3	52.3	43.1	39.7	54.1
Liberia	32.3	28.8	16.4	17.7	18.4	18.4	27.9	27.5	..	34.0	21.8	20.0
Madagascar	47.8	53.5	50.8	50.8	50.2	50.8	51.5	52.4	53.4	46.2	54.9	51.6
Malawi	30.3	22.3	41.4	39.2	39.7	41.4	41.2	39.7	37.5	29.5	36.1	39.9
Mali	34.7	37.4	34.5	34.7	36.5	36.2	36.0	..	..	37.6	33.5	35.2
Mauritania	41.0	37.3	42.9	44.5	41.8	42.5	35.9	36.7	..	38.5	36.0	40.8
Mauritius	48.5	45.0	55.2	55.6	56.0	57.2	59.1	59.3	60.1	47.2	49.7	56.9
Mozambique	26.0	40.9	44.8	41.5	40.8	43.3	41.0	41.4	41.3	34.0	44.9	42.8
Namibia	31.2	45.3	51.9	56.6	55.9	54.5	50.5	49.7	65.4	41.7	51.9	54.8
Niger	34.0	48.6	43.4	42.7	..	..	..	..	..	41.6	43.2	43.4
Nigeria	..	..	20.3	19.9	23.2	23.5	25.9	27.8	29.0	..	..	24.2
Rwanda	32.6	42.8	50.6	48.8	47.5	47.2	44.7	47.1	53.1	38.8	39.9	48.5
São Tomé and Príncipe	..	..	63.0	61.2	56.4	62.7	..	..	..	..	..	61.3
Senegal	53.3	52.0	51.8	51.1	51.9	51.7	54.9	55.7	56.9	51.0	50.9	52.8
Seychelles	77.5	78.9	66.7	69.6	68.8	75.6	77.1	74.9	75.3	77.4	74.6	71.7
Sierra Leone	41.4	31.8	25.8	27.0	27.8	28.0	25.9	29.4	31.9	41.3	18.7	26.0
Somalia	22.2	..	..	..	..	..	..	..	..	23.5	..	..
South Africa	42.7	50.2	57.1	58.8	59.2	59.2	58.6	58.2	54.8	46.8	55.6	58.2
Sudan	48.3	42.5	35.7	37.4	36.5	37.4	38.6	38.9	38.0	46.3	42.8	37.2
Swaziland	40.5	39.6	34.8	35.1	36.5	38.2	37.1	36.9	33.6	40.4	37.7	35.7
Tanzania	..	33.3	36.1	35.3	34.1	30.3	30.9	..	..	..	34.8	34.2
Togo	47.7	43.7	43.3	37.1	36.0	32.4	..	..	..	46.2	41.7	40.3
Uganda	23.4	30.5	47.2	46.0	42.7	44.8	46.6	46.3	47.3	31.2	34.3	45.5
Zambia	39.7	24.8	46.8	46.2	45.8	45.8	44.7	36.6	27.8	34.8	35.2	43.0
Zimbabwe	53.1	45.4	58.1	55.0	52.2	40.0	..	..	..	49.0	46.3	51.4
NORTH AFRICA	38.4	41.9	46.8	45.1	43.7	41.8	40.9	42.6	40.3	40.4	43.3	43.3
Algeria	31.6	37.0	33.8	32.0	31.0	28.1	28.1	29.1	23.7	34.9	35.8	30.0
Egypt, Arab Rep.	42.9	49.5	45.6	44.9	45.1	45.9	44.7	47.3	50.4	47.5	47.8	46.3
Libya	..	..	..	..	..	..	..	..	..	..	..	..
Morocco	50.3	46.8	49.9	49.1	49.6	51.3	50.2	52.3	58.5	49.9	47.8	51.1
Tunisia	54.8	54.5	60.2	59.7	59.1	59.9	60.1	60.0	61.6	54.8	57.3	59.9
ALL AFRICA	34.2	43.4	44.8	45.2	45.1	43.5	42.6	42.9	39.7	39.6	45.9	43.7

a. Provisional.

Table 2.32 Central government finances, expense, and revenue

	Finances Share of GDP (%)								
	Revenue, excluding grants			Expense			Cash surplus or deficit		
	1990	2000	2007	1990	2000	2007	1990	2000	2007
SUB-SAHARAN AFRICA	..	..	..	..	..	..	..	..	..
Excluding South Africa	..	..	..	..	..	..	..	..	..
Excl. S. Africa & Nigeria	..	..	..	..	..	..	..	..	..
Angola	..	..	..	..	..	..	..	..	..
Benin[a]	..	..	..	..	..	..	..	..	..
Botswana[a]	50.8	..	..	26.7	..	..	19.1	..	..
Burkina Faso	..	..	..	..	..	..	..	..	..
Burundi[a]	..	..	..	..	..	..	..	..	..
Cameroon[a]	14.3	..	..	14.6	..	..	−5.6	..	..
Cape Verde	..	..	..	..	..	..	..	..	..
Central African Republic	..	..	..	..	..	..	..	..	..
Chad	..	..	..	..	..	..	..	..	..
Comoros	..	..	..	..	..	..	..	..	..
Congo, Dem. Rep.[a]	1.0	0.0	..	1.7	0.0	..	−0.7	0.0	..
Congo, Rep.	..	..	..	..	..	..	..	..	..
Côte d'Ivoire[a]	..	16.7	19.2	..	..	20.5	..	..	−0.8
Djibouti	..	..	..	..	..	..	..	..	..
Equatorial Guinea	..	..	..	..	..	..	..	..	..
Eritrea	..	..	..	..	..	..	..	..	..
Ethiopia[a]	..	..	..	..	..	..	..	..	..
Gabon	..	..	..	..	..	..	..	..	..
Gambia, The[a]	19.4	..	..	15.5	..	..	0.1	..	..
Ghana[a]	12.5	..	25.7	..	..	29.4	..	..	−7.7
Guinea[a]	..	..	..	..	..	..	..	..	..
Guinea-Bissau	..	..	..	..	..	..	..	..	..
Kenya	..	19.7	18.9	..	16.8	19.7	..	2.0	−3.0
Lesotho	42.1	48.3	60.3	31.5	..	45.4	−0.5	..	8.8
Liberia	..	..	..	..	..	..	..	..	..
Madagascar	..	11.7	11.9	..	10.6	11.2	..	−2.0	−2.7
Malawi	..	..	..	..	..	..	..	..	..
Mali	..	13.4	16.2	..	11.6	15.2	..	−3.4	−5.6
Mauritania	..	..	..	..	..	..	..	..	..
Mauritius	24.3	22.0	20.9	20.4	21.6	21.3	0.3	−1.1	−2.3
Mozambique	..	..	..	..	..	..	..	..	..
Namibia	31.3	28.6	..	..	27.6	..	..	−2.6	..
Niger	..	..	13.6	..	..	11.8	..	..	−0.9
Nigeria	..	..	..	..	..	..	..	..	..
Rwanda[a]	10.8	..	..	12.7	..	..	−5.4	..	..
São Tomé and Príncipe	..	..	..	..	..	..	..	..	..
Senegal	..	16.9	..	..	12.8	..	..	−0.9	..
Seychelles	..	38.7	40.4	..	43.1	41.2	..	−13.9	−6.0
Sierra Leone[a]	5.6	11.4	..	..	28.7	..	..	−9.3	..
Somalia	..	..	..	..	..	..	..	..	..
South Africa	..	26.3	31.9	..	27.9	30.0	..	−2.0	1.6
Sudan[a]	..	..	..	..	..	..	..	..	..
Swaziland[a]	..	..	..	..	..	..	..	..	..
Tanzania	..	..	..	..	..	..	..	..	..
Togo[a]	..	..	17.0	..	..	17.5	..	..	−0.8
Uganda[a]	..	10.8	..	..	15.5	..	..	−1.9	..
Zambia[a]	20.4	..	17.6	..	..	22.9	..	..	−0.8
Zimbabwe[a]	24.1	..	..	24.5	..	..	−2.6	..	..
NORTH AFRICA	..	..	..	..	..	..	..	..	..
Algeria[a]	..	38.3	40.4	..	20.8	18.7	..	9.7	6.2
Egypt, Arab Rep.[a]	23.0	..	27.1	24.0	..	29.3	−2.0	..	−4.6
Libya	..	..	..	..	..	..	..	..	..
Morocco	..	..	34.8	..	..	29.2	..	..	2.5
Tunisia[a]	30.7	29.2	30.0	30.4	27.6	29.0	−3.2	−2.7	−2.2
ALL AFRICA	..	..	..	..	..	..	..	..	..

(continued)

Table 2.32 Central government finances, expense, and revenue (continued)

	Finances Share of GDP (%)								
	Net incurrance of liabilities						Total debt		
	Domestic			Foreign					
	1990	2000	2007	1990	2000	2007	1990	2000	2007
SUB-SAHARAN AFRICA	..	..	..	..	..	..	..	..	..
Excluding South Africa	..	..	..	..	..	..	..	..	..
Excl. S. Africa & Nigeria	..	..	..	..	..	..	..	..	..
Angola	..	..	..	..	..	..	3.1	18.7	7.6
Benin[a]	..	..	..	..	..	..	..	..	..
Botswana[a]	−0.8	..	..	0.0	..	..	..	..	..
Burkina Faso	..	..	..	..	..	..	..	..	..
Burundi[a]	..	..	..	..	..	..	..	2.4	5.1
Cameroon[a]	..	..	..	5.2	..	..	..	..	..
Cape Verde	..	..	..	..	..	..	1.7	3.0	..
Central African Republic	..	..	..	..	..	..	..	..	..
Chad	..	..	..	..	..	..	..	2.9	..
Comoros	..	..	..	..	..	..	0.4	1.6	4.1
Congo, Dem. Rep.[a]	0.6	..	..	..	..	..	..	..	..
Congo, Rep.	..	..	..	..	..	..	8.2	9.0	3.0
Côte d'Ivoire[a]	..	−0.9	..	..	1.7	..	11.7	8.3	3.1
Djibouti	..	..	..	..	..	..	..	2.4	..
Equatorial Guinea	..	..	..	..	..	..	..	..	..
Eritrea	..	..	..	..	..	..	..	0.5	1.5
Ethiopia[a]	..	..	..	..	..	..	2.0	1.7	0.9
Gabon	..	..	..	..	..	..	..	..	..
Gambia, The[a]	..	..	..	..	..	..	..	..	..
Ghana[a]	..	..	5.1	..	..	2.3	..	7.1	2.7
Guinea[a]	..	..	..	..	..	..	6.3	3.9	1.6
Guinea-Bissau	..	..	..	..	..	..	..	6.1	8.9
Kenya	..	..	2.1	..	..	..	9.2	4.7	1.5
Lesotho	−7.4	..	..	8.5	..	..	..	..	6.4
Liberia	..	..	..	..	..	..	..	..	..
Madagascar	..	1.3	0.7	..	1.7	2.2	..	..	..
Malawi	..	..	..	..	..	..	..	..	..
Mali	..	−1.0	..	..	3.0	3.5	..	..	..
Mauritania	..	..	..	..	..	..	12.7	7.1	3.5
Mauritius	4.4	3.1	−0.6	−0.5	−0.4	2.1	6.5	10.8	3.8
Mozambique	..	..	..	..	..	..	2.3	2.4	13.1
Namibia	..	..	..	..	..	..	..	..	..
Niger	..	..	−1.9	..	..	2.4	..	..	..
Nigeria	..	..	..	..	..	..	..	..	..
Rwanda[a]	3.3	..	..	..	..	..	..	..	..
São Tomé and Príncipe	..	..	..	..	..	..	..	..	121.6
Senegal	..	0.3	..	..	0.5	..	5.6	..	..
Seychelles	..	0.7	−5.4	..	13.1	11.9	..	2.1	..
Sierra Leone[a]	..	..	..	..	..	..	3.3	7.3	3.5
Somalia	..	..	..	..	..	..	..	..	..
South Africa	..	1.6	0.3	..	0.3	−0.2	..	2.9	1.6
Sudan[a]	..	..	..	..	..	..	..	..	..
Swaziland[a]	..	..	..	..	..	..	..	..	..
Tanzania	..	..	..	..	..	..	4.2	0.7	0.3
Togo[a]	..	..	−0.5	..	..	0.7	..	..	..
Uganda[a]	..	0.6	..	..	2.0	..	3.6	2.6	0.5
Zambia[a]	6.8	..	..	1.0	..	..	..	..	..
Zimbabwe[a]	..	..	..	..	..	..	5.1	..	..
NORTH AFRICA	..	..	..	..	..	..	..	..	..
Algeria[a]	..	0.4	−3.6	..	−2.4	−1.2	..	..	2.2
Egypt, Arab Rep.[a]	..	..	7.3	..	..	0.5	..	..	..
Libya	..	..	..	..	..	..	..	..	..
Morocco	..	..	−2.9	..	..	0.1	..	7.3	5.3
Tunisia[a]	3.6	0.6	0.3	1.8	−0.2	−1.0	10.7	9.6	7.7
ALL AFRICA	..	..	..	..	..	..	..	..	..

Goods and services			Compensation of employees			Interest payments			Subsidies and other transfers			Other expenses		
Expense Share of expense (%)														
1990	2000	2007	1990	2000	2007	1990	2000	2007	1990	2000	2007	1990	2000	2007
..	..	..	..	..	..	..	..	..	..	..	..	..	..	..
..	..	..	..	..	..	..	..	..	..	..	..	..	..	..
..	..	..	..	..	..	..	..	..	..	..	..	..	..	..
..	..	..	..	..	..	..	..	..	..	..	..	..	..	..
..	..	..	..	..	..	..	..	..	..	..	..	..	..	..
35.2	..	..	29.1	..	..	2.8	..	..	31.8	..	..	1.1	..	..
..	..	..	..	..	..	..	..	..	..	..	..	..	..	..
..	..	..	..	..	..	..	..	..	..	..	..	..	..	..
16.7	..	..	55.6	..	..	7.8	..	..	13.3	..	..	..	..	..
..	..	..	..	..	..	..	..	..	..	..	..	..	..	..
..	..	..	..	..	..	..	..	..	..	..	..	..	..	..
..	..	..	..	..	..	..	..	..	..	..	..	..	..	..
..	..	..	..	..	..	..	..	..	..	..	..	..	..	..
56.3	59.4	..	25.4	27.4	..	7.4	..	..	..	13.2	..	..	..	..
..	..	..	..	..	..	..	..	..	..	..	..	..	..	..
..	..	34.2	..	..	32.9	..	..	8.5	..	..	17.7	..	..	6.7
..	..	..	..	..	..	..	..	..	..	..	..	..	..	..
..	..	..	..	..	..	..	..	..	..	..	..	..	..	..
..	..	..	..	..	..	..	..	..	..	..	..	..	..	..
..	..	..	..	..	..	..	..	..	..	..	..	..	..	..
..	..	..	..	..	..	..	..	..	..	..	..	..	..	..
31.3	..	..	31.7	..	..	23.6	..	..	13.4	..	..	..	..	..
..	..	14.9	..	..	37.5	..	..	10.6	..	..	37.0	..	..	..
..	..	..	..	..	..	..	..	..	..	..	..	..	..	..
..	..	..	..	..	..	..	..	..	..	..	..	..	..	..
..	21.3	15.5	..	55.2	43.5	..	17.8	10.9	..	3.4	..	..	2.2	..
30.8	..	36.7	38.6	..	32.9	18.7	..	5.5	8.9	..	10.7	2.9	..	6.3
..	..	..	..	..	..	..	..	..	..	..	..	..	..	..
..	17.7	13.9	..	40.7	46.0	..	13.4	10.1	..	9.7	14.0	..	18.6	16.0
..	..	..	..	..	..	..	..	..	..	..	..	..	..	..
..	37.6	37.8	..	36.5	32.6	..	8.0	2.4	..	0.4	15.8	..	17.5	11.4
..	..	..	..	..	..	..	..	..	..	..	..	..	..	..
10.5	11.6	11.9	44.8	38.2	35.4	17.9	12.3	14.6	25.7	32.8	33.4	1.2	5.2	4.7
..	..	..	..	..	..	..	..	..	..	..	..	..	..	..
..	21.6	..	..	51.2	..	..	7.3	..	..	..	..	..	..	..
..	..	29.6	..	..	30.2	..	..	3.0	..	..	9.3	..	..	28.0
..	..	..	..	..	..	..	..	..	..	..	..	..	..	..
35.3	..	..	43.5	..	..	7.9	..	..	15.5	..	..	..	..	..
..	..	..	..	..	..	..	..	..	..	..	..	..	..	..
..	26.0	..	..	41.4	..	..	10.7	..	..	18.7	..	..	..	..
..	24.6	24.3	..	36.3	32.0	..	17.3	16.5	..	21.6	26.9	..	..	0.3
..	14.9	..	..	23.4	..	..	21.9	..	..	5.5	..	..	34.3	..
..	..	..	..	..	..	..	..	..	..	..	..	..	..	..
..	11.3	10.5	..	15.6	14.2	..	18.1	8.8	..	52.9	59.1	..	2.2	8.2
..	..	..	..	..	..	..	..	..	..	..	..	..	..	..
..	..	..	..	..	..	..	..	..	..	..	..	..	..	..
..	..	..	..	..	..	..	..	..	..	..	..	..	..	..
..	..	25.1	..	..	30.7	..	..	5.9	..	..	26.6	..	..	11.7
..	55.1	..	..	12.3	..	..	5.2	..	..	27.4	..	..	..	..
..	..	31.9	..	..	30.3	..	..	6.9	..	..	24.1	..	..	6.8
21.7	..	..	40.9	..	..	17.8	..	..	..	..	..	..	..	..
..	..	..	..	..	..	..	..	..	..	..	..	..	..	..
..	6.4	5.4	..	33.8	28.2	..	19.0	4.6	..	40.8	32.4	..	..	29.4
22.4	..	7.8	26.6	..	24.1	16.3	..	17.6	..	..	39.4	..	..	11.0
..	..	..	..	..	..	..	..	..	..	..	..	..	..	..
..	..	8.7	..	..	45.7	..	..	6.7	..	..	29.4	..	..	9.5
7.0	8.6	6.3	31.4	39.8	37.9	10.9	12.1	9.1	44.9	..	37.0	5.8	..	9.7
..	..	..	..	..	..	..	..	..	..	..	..	..	..	..

(continued)

Table 2.32 Central government finances, expense, and revenue (continued)

	Revenue																				
	Share of revenue (%)																				
	Interest payments			Taxes on income, profits, and capital gains			Taxes on goods and services			Taxes on international trade			Other taxes			Social contributions			Grants and other revenue		
	1990	2000	2007	1990	2000	2007	1990	2000	2007	1990	2000	2007	1990	2000	2007	1990	2000	2007	1990	2000	2007
SUB-SAHARAN AFRICA	..	..	..	..	..	..	..	..	..	..	..	..	..	..	..	..	..	..	..	..	..
Excluding South Africa	..	..	..	..	..	..	..	..	..	..	..	..	..	..	..	..	..	..	..	..	..
Excl. S. Africa & Nigeria	..	..	..	..	..	..	..	..	..	..	..	..	..	..	..	..	..	..	..	..	..
Angola	..	..	..	..	..	..	..	..	..	..	..	..	..	..	..	..	..	..	..	..	..
Benin	..	..	..	..	..	..	..	..	..	..	..	..	..	..	..	..	..	..	..	..	..
Botswana	1.4	..	..	37.6	..	..	1.8	..	..	12.9	..	..	0.1	..	..	..	..	..	47.6	..	..
Burkina Faso	..	..	..	..	..	..	..	..	..	..	..	..	..	..	..	..	..	..	..	..	..
Burundi	..	..	..	..	..	..	..	..	..	..	..	..	..	..	..	..	..	..	..	..	..
Cameroon	8.0	..	..	18.9	..	..	22.2	..	..	15.5	..	..	4.6	..	..	1.8	..	..	27.5	..	..
Cape Verde	..	..	..	..	..	..	..	..	..	..	..	..	..	..	..	..	..	..	..	..	..
Central African Republic	..	..	..	..	..	..	..	..	..	..	..	..	..	..	..	..	..	..	..	..	..
Chad	..	..	..	..	..	..	..	..	..	..	..	..	..	..	..	..	..	..	..	..	..
Comoros	..	..	..	..	..	..	..	..	..	..	..	..	..	..	..	..	..	..	..	..	..
Congo, Dem. Rep.	10.1	..	..	2.2	0.0	..	1.5	0.0	..	3.8	0.0	..	0.1	0.0	..	1.0	..	..	2.3	0.0	..
Congo, Rep.	..	..	..	..	..	..	..	..	..	..	..	..	..	..	..	..	..	..	..	..	..
Côte d'Ivoire	..	23.2	8.9	..	23.0	..	..	19.9	..	..	38.8	..	..	3.7	..	..	8.1	6.9	..	6.4	..
Djibouti	..	..	..	..	..	..	..	..	..	..	..	..	..	..	..	..	..	..	..	..	..
Equatorial Guinea	..	..	..	..	..	..	..	..	..	..	..	..	..	..	..	..	..	..	..	..	..
Eritrea	..	..	..	..	..	..	..	..	..	..	..	..	..	..	..	..	..	..	..	..	..
Ethiopia	..	..	..	..	..	..	..	..	..	..	..	..	..	..	..	..	..	..	..	..	..
Gabon	..	..	..	..	..	..	..	..	..	..	..	..	..	..	..	..	..	..	..	..	..
Gambia, The	16.6	..	..	11.3	..	..	32.9	..	..	37.7	..	..	0.5	..	..	0.3	..	..	17.3	..	..
Ghana	10.2	..	9.6	0.0	..	..	0.0	..	..	0.0	..	..	..	..	..	..	..	..	0.0	..	..
Guinea	..	..	..	..	..	..	..	..	..	..	..	..	..	..	..	..	..	..	..	..	..
Guinea-Bissau	..	..	..	..	..	..	..	..	..	..	..	..	..	..	..	..	..	..	..	..	..
Kenya	..	15.2	10.9	..	28.5	..	..	41.4	..	..	15.0	..	..	0.5	..	..	0.0	..	..	14.7	..
Lesotho	10.8	10.0	4.0	8.7	17.2	..	16.0	12.5	..	43.6	41.4	..	0.1	..	..	..	..	..	31.6	28.9	..
Liberia	..	..	..	..	..	..	..	..	..	..	..	..	..	..	..	..	..	..	..	..	..
Madagascar	..	9.3	7.0	..	11.6	..	..	21.5	..	..	39.6	..	..	1.2	..	..	..	..	..	26.0	..
Malawi	..	..	..	..	..	..	..	..	..	..	..	..	..	..	..	..	..	..	..	..	..
Mali	..	5.0	1.7	..	12.5	..	..	41.6	..	..	11.3	..	..	5.0	..	..	..	..	..	29.5	..
Mauritania	..	..	..	..	..	..	..	..	..	..	..	..	..	..	..	..	..	..	..	..	..
Mauritius	14.9	11.9	14.8	13.7	11.4	..	20.6	37.9	..	45.7	27.5	..	6.1	5.4	..	4.5	5.3	5.0	9.4	12.5	..
Mozambique	..	..	..	..	..	..	..	..	..	..	..	..	..	..	..	..	..	..	..	..	..
Namibia	1.3	6.9	..	32.6	31.8	..	23.9	20.8	..	25.3	36.4	..	0.9	1.1	..	..	..	..	17.2	9.9	..
Niger	..	..	1.8	..	..	..	..	..	..	..	..	..	..	..	..	..	..	..	..	..	..
Nigeria	..	..	..	..	..	..	..	..	..	..	..	..	..	..	..	..	..	..	..	..	..
Rwanda	7.3	..	..	14.0	..	..	27.1	..	..	20.5	..	..	3.1	..	..	5.4	..	..	30.0	..	..
São Tomé and Príncipe	..	..	..	..	..	..	..	..	..	..	..	..	..	..	..	..	..	..	..	..	..
Senegal	..	7.4	..	..	21.3	..	..	33.7	..	..	29.5	..	..	3.3	..	..	..	..	..	12.2	..
Seychelles	..	18.6	16.7	..	17.3	..	..	5.1	..	..	41.0	..	..	1.6	..	..	13.8	18.1	..	21.3	..
Sierra Leone	25.7	32.5	..	29.7	15.4	..	22.1	7.6	..	38.1	29.4	..	0.2	..	..	..	..	..	9.9	47.7	..
Somalia	..	..	..	..	..	..	..	..	..	..	..	..	..	..	..	..	..	..	..	..	..
South Africa	..	19.1	8.3	..	51.7	..	..	33.1	..	..	3.0	..	..	2.8	..	..	2.1	1.9	..	7.4	..
Sudan	..	..	..	..	..	..	..	..	..	..	..	..	..	..	..	..	..	..	..	..	..
Swaziland	..	..	..	..	..	..	..	..	..	..	..	..	..	..	..	..	..	..	..	..	..
Tanzania	..	..	..	..	..	..	..	..	..	..	..	..	..	..	..	..	..	..	..	..	..
Togo	..	..	5.6	..	..	..	..	..	..	..	..	..	..	..	..	..	..	..	..	..	..
Uganda	..	4.7	..	..	9.9	..	..	29.4	..	..	21.8	..	..	0.1	..	..	..	..	..	38.7	..
Zambia	7.1	..	7.2	39.5	..	33.1	37.4	..	35.8	17.2	..	8.1	0.2	..	0.2	0.0	..	..	5.8	..	22.7
Zimbabwe	17.7	..	..	43.7	..	..	25.6	..	..	17.1	..	..	1.1	..	..	3.3	..	..	9.2	..	..
NORTH AFRICA																					
Algeria	..	10.3	2.1	..	79.5	..	..	7.0	..	..	8.9	..	..	1.0	..	..	..	..	..	3.5	..
Egypt, Arab Rep.	16.0	..	18.7	23.1	..	33.2	16.3	..	22.4	16.5	..	5.9	13.0	..	3.4	14.5	..	..	40.3	..	51.8
Libya	..	..	..	..	..	..	..	..	..	..	..	..	..	..	..	..	..	..	..	..	..
Morocco	..	..	5.6	..	..	..	..	..	..	..	..	..	..	..	..	..	..	13.2	..	..	..
Tunisia	10.6	11.3	8.8	12.3	20.4	29.1	19.1	37.1	34.4	27.5	10.7	6.5	4.8	4.4	4.8	13.0	17.0	18.1	23.4	10.5	12.0
ALL AFRICA	..	..	..	..	..	..	..	..	..	..	..	..	..	..	..	..	..	..	..	..	..

a. Data were reported on a cash basis and have been adjusted to the accrual framework.

Table 2.33 Structure of demand

	Share of GDP (%)																	
	Household final consumption expenditure			General government final consumption expenditure			Gross fixed capital formation			Exports of goods and services			Imports of goods and services			Gross national savings		
	1990	2000	2008[a]	1990	2000	2008[a]	1990	2000	2008[a]	1990	2000	2008[a]	1990	2000	2008[a]	1990	2000	2008[a]
SUB-SAHARAN AFRICA	65.3	68.7	66.5	17.2	14.6	12.3	18.1	15.9	18.5	26.4	34.1	41.9	24.7	31.1	37.7	12.9	12.9	4.3
Excluding South Africa	72.5	73.8	..	15.3	11.9	9.4	17.6	16.7	17.8	27.6	38.0	43.2	28.3	35.0	35.9	9.1	11.0	0.7
Excl. S. Africa & Nigeria	72.5	73.8	72.4	14.8	12.5	10.8	17.0	17.5	20.6	25.1	33.5	43.2	28.2	35.8	38.1	10.7	14.1	0.9
Angola	35.8	..	..	34.5	..	..	11.1	15.1	12.3	38.9	89.6	89.5	20.9	62.8	39.3	..	23.8	47.4
Benin	86.8	82.4	..	11.0	11.6	..	13.4	18.9	..	14.3	15.2	..	26.3	28.1	..	..	10.9	..
Botswana	33.2	23.2	31.2	24.1	22.9	19.2	32.4	21.7	27.0	55.1	52.6	45.7	49.8	33.7	41.1	43.3	51.7	54.8
Burkina Faso	73.5	78.5	..	21.1	20.8	..	17.7	18.7	..	11.0	9.1	..	24.5	25.2	..	13.7	5.1	..
Burundi	94.5	88.5	..	10.8	17.5	..	15.2	6.1	..	7.9	7.8	..	27.8	19.9	..	..	1.2	..
Cameroon	66.6	70.2	67.6	12.8	9.5	12.7	17.3	16.0	18.7	20.2	23.3	29.2	17.3	19.7	28.2	16.1	16.0	20.2
Cape Verde	93.4	92.9	73.5	14.7	21.3	18.4	22.9	19.7	42.9	12.7	27.5	19.9	43.7	61.4	54.7	..	9.1	26.8
Central African Republic	85.7	80.8	94.9	14.9	14.0	3.5	11.4	9.5	10.3	14.8	19.8	14.4	27.6	24.1	23.1	..	8.2	4.0
Chad	97.6	86.8	68.9	10.0	7.7	5.8	4.8	20.9	14.1	13.5	16.9	44.0	27.9	34.7	33.8	–2.7	7.9	7.8
Comoros	78.7	94.0	96.0	24.5	11.7	12.1	11.9	10.1	16.1	14.3	16.7	12.8	37.1	32.5	36.9	10.1	9.9	11.2
Congo, Dem. Rep.	79.1	88.0	82.1	11.5	7.5	11.0	12.8	3.5	17.0	29.5	22.4	23.2	29.2	21.4	33.3	0.8	–1.3	0.2
Congo, Rep.	62.4	29.1	..	13.8	11.6	..	17.2	20.9	..	53.7	80.3	..	45.8	43.6	..	..	30.1	..
Côte d'Ivoire	71.9	74.9	77.1	16.8	7.2	8.1	8.5	11.2	10.1	31.7	40.4	51.1	27.1	33.3	46.3	..	8.0	9.6
Djibouti	78.9	76.8	..	31.5	29.7	..	14.1	8.8	..	53.8	35.1	..	78.4	50.4	..	..	5.4	..
Equatorial Guinea	80.3	20.9	24.5	39.7	4.6	2.6	17.4	61.3	28.2	32.2	98.6	78.3	69.6	85.4	32.1	–22.0	45.7	35.7
Eritrea	..	79.1	..	..	63.8	..	..	23.8	..	..	15.1	..	..	81.8	..	..	12.2	..
Ethiopia	77.2	73.8	84.9	13.2	17.9	11.3	12.9	20.3	20.8	5.6	12.0	11.6	8.8	24.0	28.6	11.9	16.2	16.5
Gabon	49.7	32.2	25.8	13.4	9.6	7.8	21.4	21.9	27.3	46.0	69.0	77.2	30.9	32.7	38.2	24.0	42.2	48.7
Gambia, The	75.6	77.8	78.0	13.7	13.7	15.8	22.3	17.4	..	59.9	48.0	30.1	71.6	56.8	49.0	..	13.6	10.8
Ghana	85.2	84.3	80.8	9.3	10.2	13.6	14.4	23.1	32.0	16.9	48.8	36.8	25.9	67.2	63.2	..	15.7	19.6
Guinea	66.9	77.7	84.6	11.0	6.8	4.9	22.9	18.9	12.7	31.1	23.6	27.8	33.4	27.9	30.0	14.6	13.3	9.2
Guinea-Bissau	86.9	94.6	81.3	10.3	14.0	13.9	29.9	11.3	23.8	9.9	31.8	29.8	37.0	51.6	49.8	15.3	–2.7	22.9
Kenya	62.8	77.7	78.6	18.6	15.1	10.8	20.6	16.7	24.7	25.7	21.6	24.9	31.3	31.7	39.0	18.6	13.0	17.6
Lesotho	121.0	81.5	107.9	21.4	33.8	26.8	56.3	48.9	28.8	17.0	32.6	47.3	115.6	98.5	110.8	40.8	30.8	24.8
Liberia	..	..	..	..	..	..	..	..	..	..	21.5	..	..	26.0	..	..	..	..
Madagascar	86.4	83.2	85.0	8.0	9.0	4.6	14.8	15.0	35.7	16.6	30.7	26.3	28.0	38.0	51.6	9.2	9.4	12.4
Malawi	71.5	81.6	85.0	15.1	14.6	10.9	20.1	12.3	30.2	23.8	25.6	23.4	33.4	35.3	51.2	13.6	2.2	9.1
Mali	79.8	79.4	..	13.8	8.6	..	23.0	24.6	..	17.1	26.8	..	33.7	39.4	..	15.1	16.0	..
Mauritania	69.2	82.8	..	25.9	25.8	..	20.0	19.4	..	45.6	46.2	..	60.7	74.2	..	17.6	0.8	..
Mauritius	63.7	63.0	70.2	12.8	13.1	12.9	28.3	25.3	24.2	64.2	62.7	61.6	71.4	64.6	69.9	26.3	25.3	22.7
Mozambique	92.3	79.5	74.7	13.5	9.0	12.3	22.1	31.0	23.0	8.2	17.5	32.0	36.1	37.0	42.0	2.1	14.8	10.4
Namibia	51.2	63.1	68.5	30.6	23.5	18.0	21.2	16.6	22.6	51.9	40.9	38.9	67.4	44.5	48.1	34.8	25.4	24.8
Niger	83.8	83.4	..	15.0	13.0	..	11.4	11.2	..	15.0	17.8	..	22.0	25.7	..	–1.2	2.8	..
Nigeria	..	..	..	..	..	..	..	..	..	43.4	54.0	43.5	28.8	32.0	30.4	..	..	..
Rwanda	83.7	87.7	89.6	10.1	11.0	9.1	14.6	18.3	20.8	5.6	8.7	8.1	14.1	25.7	27.5	11.3	12.9	13.0
São Tomé and Príncipe	..	..	..	..	..	..	..	..	..	..	..	..	..	..	..	..	..	..
Senegal	79.2	76.0	82.3	18.4	12.8	10.0	18.0	22.4	30.2	25.4	27.9	24.9	32.2	37.2	47.4	..	..	17.9
Seychelles	52.0	53.9	78.5	27.7	24.2	14.8	23.0	25.2	28.3	62.5	78.2	130.9	66.7	81.4	152.5	..	17.2	2.7
Sierra Leone	83.5	100.0	79.8	7.8	14.3	12.7	9.6	6.9	19.7	22.4	18.1	24.9	23.8	39.3	37.1	2.6	–9.0	14.1
Somalia	..	..	..	..	..	..	14.9	..	..	9.8	..	..	37.7	..	..	..	..	..
South Africa	57.1	63.0	61.5	19.7	18.1	20.2	19.1	15.1	22.2	24.2	27.9	36.3	18.8	24.9	40.4	19.3	15.8	14.0
Sudan	86.1	76.5	59.2	5.8	7.6	16.4	10.4	12.1	20.2	4.0	15.3	22.7	7.1	17.7	22.0	0.9	10.1	15.4
Swaziland	80.4	78.0	61.3	14.3	18.7	23.6	14.5	17.4	14.9	59.0	76.1	80.2	68.9	90.1	80.1	19.7	12.8	30.5
Tanzania	80.9	79.2	..	17.8	10.6	..	25.8	17.4	..	12.6	16.8	..	37.5	24.2	..	..	10.1	..
Togo	71.1	92.0	..	14.2	10.2	16.3	25.3	17.8	..	33.5	30.7	40.4	45.3	50.7	67.5	..	0.4	..
Uganda	91.9	77.8	82.4	7.5	14.5	11.8	12.7	19.2	23.3	7.2	10.6	15.6	19.4	22.5	33.4	0.6	8.6	12.0
Zambia	64.4	87.4	66.3	19.0	9.5	9.0	13.5	16.0	21.4	35.9	27.1	36.8	36.6	41.5	34.3	6.7	–1.3	19.8
Zimbabwe	63.1	72.8	..	19.4	13.9	..	18.2	11.8	..	22.9	35.9	..	22.8	36.2	..	15.7	9.6	..
NORTH AFRICA	64.1	61.3	57.1	16.2	14.5	9.5	24.1	20.1	23.4	27.2	28.4	46.4	30.8	25.0	36.9	14.2	12.9	..
Algeria	56.8	41.6	21.7	16.1	13.6	6.8	27.0	20.7	27.9	23.4	41.2	59.1	24.9	21.4	24.5	..	41.3	71.6
Egypt, Arab Rep.	72.6	75.9	72.0	11.3	11.2	10.8	26.9	18.9	23.7	20.0	16.2	37.7	32.7	22.8	44.2	..	..	23.6
Libya	48.4	46.6	..	24.4	20.5	..	13.9	12.9	..	39.7	35.0	..	31.1	15.2	..	..	..	..
Morocco	64.6	61.4	60.6	15.5	18.4	15.6	24.0	26.0	32.0	26.5	28.0	40.6	31.9	33.4	50.0	24.4	24.0	34.4
Tunisia	63.6	60.7	64.5	16.4	15.6	13.6	24.4	26.0	24.1	43.6	44.5	65.2	50.6	48.2	68.3	..	23.2	16.7
ALL AFRICA	64.7	65.3	62.3	16.7	14.5	11.2	20.4	17.8	20.4	26.8	31.7	43.1	27.0	28.5	37.1	13.4	12.9	2.8

a. Provisional.

Table 3.1 Millennium Development Goal 1: eradicate extreme poverty and hunger

	International poverty line															
	Share of population below PPP $1.25 a day				Poverty gap ratio at PPP $1.25 a day (incidence × depth of poverty)				Share of population below PPP $2 a day				Poverty gap ratio at PPP $2 a day (incidence × depth of poverty)			
	Surveys 1990–99[b]		Surveys 2000–07[b]		Surveys 1990–99[b]		Surveys 2000–07[b]		Surveys 1990–99[b]		Surveys 2000–07[b]		Surveys 1990–99[b]		Surveys 2000–07[b]	
	Year	Percent	Year	Percent	Year	Percent	Year	Percent	Year	Percent	Year	Percent	Year	Percent	Year	Percent
SUB-SAHARAN AFRICA																
Angola		..	2000	54.3		..	2000	29.9		..	2000	70.2		..	2000	42.3
Benin		..	2003	47.3		..	2003	15.7		..	2003	75.3		..	2003	33.5
Botswana	1994	31.2		..	1994	11.0		..	1994	49.4		..	1994	22.3		..
Burkina Faso	1998	70.0	2003	56.5	1998	30.2	2003	20.3	1998	87.6	2003	81.2	1998	49.1	2003	39.2
Burundi	1998	86.4	2006	81.3	1998	47.3	2006	36.4	1998	95.4	2006	93.4	1998	64.1	2006	56.0
Cameroon	1996	51.5	2001	32.8	1996	18.9	2001	10.2	1996	74.4	2001	57.7	1996	36.0	2001	23.6
Cape Verde		..	2001	20.6		..	2001	5.9		..	2001	40.2		..	2001	14.9
Central African Republic	1993	82.8	2003	62.4	1993	57.0	2003	28.3	1993	90.7	2003	81.9	1993	68.4	2003	45.3
Chad		..	2003	61.9		..	2003	25.6		..	2003	83.3		..	2003	43.9
Comoros		..	2004	46.1		..	2004	20.8		..	2004	65.0		..	2004	34.2
Congo, Dem. Rep.		..	2006	59.2		..	2006	25.3		..	2006	79.5		..	2006	42.4
Congo, Rep.		..	2005	54.1		..	2005	22.8		..	2005	74.4		..	2005	38.8
Côte d'Ivoire	1998	24.1	2002	23.3	1998	6.7	2002	6.8	1998	49.1	2002	46.8	1998	18.1	2002	17.6
Djibouti	1996	4.8	2002	18.8	1996	1.6	2002	5.3	1996	15.1	2002	41.2	1996	4.5	2002	14.6
Equatorial Guinea		..		..		..		..		..		..		..		..
Eritrea		..		..		..		..		..		..		..		..
Ethiopia	1995	60.5	2005	39.0	1995	21.2	2005	9.6	1995	84.6	2005	77.5	1995	41.2	2005	28.8
Gabon		..	2005	4.8		..	2005	0.9		..	2005	19.6		..	2005	5.0
Gambia, The	1998	66.7	2003	34.3	1998	34.7	2003	12.1	1998	82.0	2003	56.7	1998	50.0	2003	24.9
Ghana	1998	39.1	2006	30.0	1998	14.4	2006	10.5	1998	63.3	2006	53.6	1998	28.5	2006	22.3
Guinea	1994	36.8	2003	70.1	1994	11.5	2003	32.2	1994	63.8	2003	87.2	1994	26.4	2003	50.2
Guinea-Bissau	1993	52.1	2002	48.8	1993	20.6	2002	16.5	1993	75.7	2002	77.9	1993	37.4	2002	34.8
Kenya	1997	19.6	2005	19.7	1997	4.6	2005	6.1	1997	42.7	2005	39.9	1997	14.7	2005	15.1
Lesotho	1995	47.6	2003	43.4	1995	26.7	2003	20.8	1995	61.1	2003	62.2	1995	37.3	2003	33.0
Liberia		..	2007	83.7		..	2007	40.8		..	2007	94.8		..	2007	59.5
Madagascar	1999	82.3	2005	67.8	1999	44.3	2005	26.5	1999	93.1	2005	89.6	1999	61.0	2005	46.9
Malawi	1998	83.1	2004	73.9	1998	46.0	2004	32.3	1998	93.5	2004	90.4	1998	62.3	2004	51.8
Mali	1994	86.1	2006	51.4	1994	53.1	2006	18.8	1994	93.9	2006	77.1	1994	67.2	2006	36.5
Mauritania	1996	23.4	2000	21.2	1996	7.1	2000	5.7	1996	48.3	2000	44.1	1996	17.8	2000	15.9
Mauritius		..		..		..		..		..		..		..		..
Mozambique	1997	81.3	2003	74.7	1997	42.0	2003	35.4	1997	92.9	2003	90.0	1997	59.4	2003	53.5
Namibia	1993	49.1		..	1993	24.6		..	1993	62.2		..	1993	36.5		..
Niger	1994	78.2	2005	65.9	1994	38.6	2005	28.1	1994	91.5	2005	85.6	1994	56.5	2005	46.6
Nigeria	1996	68.5	2004	64.4	1996	32.1	2004	29.6	1996	86.4	2004	83.9	1996	49.7	2004	46.9
Rwanda		..	2000	76.6		..	2000	38.2		..	2000	90.3		..	2000	55.7
São Tomé and Príncipe		..		..		..		..		..		..		..		..
Senegal	1995	54.1	2005	33.5	1995	19.5	2005	10.8	1995	79.4	2005	60.3	1995	37.9	2005	24.6
Seychelles		..		..		..		..		..		..		..		..
Sierra Leone	1990	62.8	2003	53.4	1990	44.8	2003	20.3	1990	75.0	2003	76.1	1990	54.0	2003	37.5
Somalia		..		..		..		..		..		..		..		..
South Africa	1995	21.4	2000	26.2	1995	5.2	2000	8.2	1995	39.9	2000	42.9	1995	15.0	2000	18.3
Sudan		..		..		..		..		..		..		..		..
Swaziland	1995	78.6	2001	62.9	1995	47.7	2001	29.4	1995	89.3	2001	81.0	1995	61.6	2001	45.8
Tanzania	1992	72.6	2000	88.5	1992	29.7	2000	46.8	1992	91.3	2000	96.6	1992	50.1	2000	64.4
Togo		..	2006	38.7		..	2006	11.4		..	2006	69.3		..	2006	27.9
Uganda	1999	60.5	2005	51.5	1999	24.5	2005	19.1	1999	82.7	2005	75.6	1999	42.9	2005	36.4
Zambia	1998	55.4	2004	64.3	1998	26.9	2004	32.8	1998	74.8	2004	81.5	1998	41.7	2004	48.3
Zimbabwe		..		..		..		..		..		..		..		..
NORTH AFRICA																
Algeria	1995	6.8		..	1995	1.4		..	1995	23.6		..	1995	6.4		..
Egypt, Arab Rep.	1996	2.5	2005	2.0	1996	0.5	2005	0.5	1996	26.3	2005	18.4	1996	5.0	2005	3.5
Libya		..		..		..		..		..		..		..		..
Morocco	1999	6.8	2007	2.5	1999	1.2	2007	0.5	1999	24.4	2007	14.0	1999	6.5	2007	3.1
Tunisia	1995	6.5	2000	2.6	1995	1.3	2000	0.5	1995	20.4	2000	12.8	1995	5.8	2000	3.0

Share of population below national poverty line[a] (poverty headcount ratio)				Share of urban population below national poverty line[a] (poverty headcount ratio)				Share of rural population below national poverty line[a] (poverty headcount ratio)			
Surveys 1990–99[b]		Surveys 2000–07[b]		Surveys 1990–99[b]		Surveys 2000–07[b]		Surveys 1990–99[b]		Surveys 2000–07[b]	
Year	Percent	Year	Percent	Year	Percent	Year	Percent	Year	Percent	Year	Percent
	..		..		..		..		..		..
1999	29.0	2003	39.0	1999	23.3	2003	29.0	1999	33.0	2003	46.0
	..		..		..		..		..		..
1998	54.6	2003	46.4	1998	22.4	2003	19.2	1998	61.1	2003	52.4
1998	68.0		..	1998	66.5		..	1998	64.6		..
1996	53.3	2007	39.9	1996	41.4	2007	12.2	1996	59.6	2007	55.0
	..		..		..		..		..		..
	..		..		..		..		..		..
1996	64.0		..	1996	63.0		..	1996	67.0		..
	..		..		..		..		..		..
	..	2004	71.3		..	2004	61.5		..	2004	75.7
	..	2005	42.3		..		..		..	2005	49.2
	..		..		..		..		..		..
	..		..		..		..		..		..
	..		..		..		..		..		..
1994	53.0		..		..		..		..		..
1996	45.5	2000	44.2	1996	33.3	2000	37.0	1996	47.0	2000	45.0
	..		..		..		..		..		..
1998	57.6	2003	61.3	1998	48.0	2003	57.0	1998	61.0	2003	63.0
1997	39.5	2005	28.5	1997	19.4	2005	10.8	1997	49.6	2005	39.2
1994	40.0		..		..		..		..		..
	..	2002	65.7		..	2002	52.6		..		..
1997	52.3	2005	45.9	1997	49.2	2005	33.7	1997	52.9	2005	49.1
1994	66.6	2002	56.3	1994	36.7	2002	41.5	1994	68.9	2002	60.5
	..	2007	63.8		..	2007	55.1		..	2007	67.7
1999	71.3	2005	68.7	1999	52.1	2005	52.0	1999	76.7	2005	68.7
1998	65.3	2004	52.4	1998	54.9	2004	25.4	1998	66.5	2004	55.9
1998	63.8		..	1998	30.1		..	1998	75.9		..
1996	50.0	2000	46.3	1996	30.1	2000	25.4	1996	65.5	2000	61.2
1992	10.6		..		..		..		..		..
1996	69.4	2002	54.1	1996	62.0	2002	51.5	1996	71.3	2002	55.3
	..		..		..		..		..		..
1993	63.0		..	1993	52.0		..	1993	66.0		..
1992	34.1	2003	54.7	1992	30.4	2003	43.1	1992	36.4	2003	63.8
1993	51.2	2005	56.9		..	2005	13.0[e]		..	2005	62.5
	..		..		..		..		..		..
1992	33.4		..	1992	23.7		..	1992	40.4		..
	..		..		..		..		..		..
	..	2003	65.9		..	2003	56.4		..	2003	78.5
	..		..		..		..		..		..
1995	31.0	2008	22.0		..		..		..		..
	..		..		..		..		..		..
	..	2001	69.2		..	2001	49.0		..	2001	75.0
1991	38.6	2007	33.6	1991	28.1[f]	2007	16.4[f]	1991	40.8	2007	37.6
	..		..		..		..		..		..
1999	33.8	2005	31.1	1999	9.6	2005	13.4	1999	37.4	2005	34.2
1998	72.9	2006	59.3	1998	56.0	2006	26.7	1998	83.1	2006	76.8
1996	34.9		..	1996	7.9		..	1996	48.0		..
1995	22.6		..	1995	14.7		..	1995	30.3		..
1996	22.9	2000	16.7	1996	22.5		..	1996	23.3		..
	..		..		..		..		..		..
1999	19.0		..	1999	12.0		..	1999	27.2		..
1995	7.6		..	1995	3.6		..	1995	13.9		..

(continued)

Table 3.1 Millennium Development Goal 1: eradicate extreme poverty and hunger (continued)

	Share of poorest quintile in national consumption or income[a]				Prevalence of child malnutrition, underweight (% of children under age 5)				Population below minimum dietary energy consumption	
	Surveys 1990–99[b]		Surveys 2000–07[b]		Surveys 1990–99[b]		Surveys 2000–08[b]		Share (%)	Total (millions)
	Year	Percent	Year	Percent	Year	Percent	Year	Percent	2004–06[c]	2004–06[c]
SUB-SAHARAN AFRICA										
Angola		..	2000	2.0	1996	37.0	2001	27.5	44	7.1
Benin		..	2003	6.9		..	2001	21.5	19	1.6
Botswana	1995	3.1		..		..	2000	10.7	26	0.5
Burkina Faso	1998	6.1	2003	7.0	1999	33.7	2003	35.2	9	1.3
Burundi	1998	5.1	2006	9.0		..	2000	38.9	63	4.9
Cameroon	1996	5.7	2001	5.6	1998	17.8	2004	15.1	23	4.0
Cape Verde		..	2001	4.5		..		..	14	0.1
Central African Republic	1993	2.0	2003	5.2	1995	23.3	2000	21.8	41	1.7
Chad		..	2003	6.3	1997	34.3	2004	33.9	38	3.9
Comoros		..	2004	2.6	1996	22.3	2000	25.0	51	0.4
Congo, Dem. Rep.		..	2006	5.5		..	2001	33.6	75	43.9
Congo, Rep.		..	2005	5.0		..	2005	11.8	21	0.8
Côte d'Ivoire	1998	5.8	2002	5.0	1999	18.2	2006	16.7	14	2.5
Djibouti	1996	6.4	2002	6.0		..		..	31	0.2
Equatorial Guinea		..		..		..	2004	10.6	..	..
Eritrea		..		..	1996	38.3	2002	34.5	66	3.0
Ethiopia	1995	7.2	2005	9.3		..	2005	34.6	44	34.6
Gabon		..	2005	6.1		..	2001	8.8	[d]	..
Gambia, The	1998	4.0	2003	4.8		..	2006	15.8	29	0.5
Ghana	1998	5.6	2006	5.2	1999	20.3	2008	13.9	8	1.7
Guinea	1994	6.4	2003	5.8	1999	21.2	2005	22.5	16	1.5
Guinea-Bissau	1993	5.2	2002	7.2		..	2000	21.9	31	0.5
Kenya	1997	6.0	2005	4.7	1998	17.6	2003	16.5	30	10.8
Lesotho	1995	1.5	2003	3.0		..	2005	16.6	15	0.3
Liberia		..	2007	6.4		..	2007	20.4	38	1.3
Madagascar	1999	5.9	2005	6.2	1997	35.5	2004	36.8	35	6.6
Malawi	1998	4.8	2004	7.0	1992	24.4	2005	18.4	29	3.8
Mali	1994	4.6	2006	6.5	1996	38.2	2006	27.9	10	1.2
Mauritania	1996	6.4	2000	6.2		..	2001	30.4	8	0.2
Mauritius		..		..		..		..	6	0.1
Mozambique	1997	5.6	2003	5.4	1997	28.1	2003	21.2	37	7.5
Namibia	1993	1.5		..	1992	21.5	2007	17.5	19	0.4
Niger	1994	6.0	2005	5.9	1998	45.0	2006	39.9	28	3.8
Nigeria	1996	5.1	2004	5.1	1990	35.1	2003	27.2	8	11.3
Rwanda		..	2000	5.3	1992	24.3	2005	18.0	40	3.7
São Tomé and Príncipe		..		..		..	2000	10.1	5	0.0
Senegal	1995	6.5	2005	6.2	1993	21.9	2005	14.5	25	2.9
Seychelles		..		..		..		..	8	0.0
Sierra Leone	1990	1.1	2003	6.1		..	2005	28.3	46	2.5
Somalia		..		..		..	2006	32.8	..	..
South Africa	1995	3.6	2000	3.1		..		..	[d]	..
Sudan		..		..		..	2000	38.4	20	7.5
Swaziland	1995	2.7	2001	4.5		..	2000	9.1	18	0.2
Tanzania	1992	7.4	2000	7.3	1999	25.3	2005	16.7	35	13.6
Togo		..	2006	7.6	1998	23.2		..	37	2.3
Uganda	1999	6.0	2005	6.1	1995	21.5	2001	19.0	15	4.4
Zambia	1998	3.4	2004	3.6	1997	19.6	2002	23.3	45	5.2
Zimbabwe	1995	4.6		..	1999	11.5	2006	14.0	39	5.1
NORTH AFRICA										
Algeria	1995	6.9		..	1995	11.3	2002	10.2	[d]	..
Egypt, Arab Rep.	1996	9.5	2005	9.0	1996	10.8	2005	5.4	[d]	..
Libya		..		..	1995	4.3		..	[d]	..
Morocco	1999	6.4	2007	6.5	1992	8.1	2004	9.9	[d]	..
Tunisia	1995	5.6	2000	5.9		..		..	[d]	..

a. Data are based on expenditure shares, except for Namibia, for which data are based on income shares.
b. Data are for the most recent year available during the period specified.
c. Average over the period.
d. Less than 5 percent.
e. Refers to Kigali only.
f. Refers to Dar es Salaam only.

Table 3.2 Millennium Development Goal 2: achieve universal primary education

	Net primary enrollment ratio (% of relevant age group)			Primary completion rate (% of relevant age group)			Share of cohort reaching grade 5 (% of grade 1 students)			Youth literacy rate (% of ages 15–24)		
	1991	2000	2007–08[a]	1991	2000	2007–08[a]	1991	2000	2001–07[a]	1991	2000	2007
SUB-SAHARAN AFRICA												
Angola	50.3	..	..	34.7	..	..	..	..	..	..	..	..
Benin	41.1	51.8	..	20.7	34.9	..	54.8	84.0	71.5	..	..	52.4
Botswana	88.3	81.6	..	89.5	89.9	..	84.0	89.5	82.5	89.3	..	94.1
Burkina Faso	27.0	35.4	58.1	19.5	25.0	37.1	69.7	69.1	79.6	20.2	..	39.3
Burundi	53.0	42.6	81.2	45.9	24.9	39.2	61.7	56.1	66.2	..	73.3	..
Cameroon	69.4	..	..	53.0	49.9	55.5	..	..	84.3	..	..	..
Cape Verde	91.1	97.7	84.5	..	101.8	86.2	..	..	92.2	..	..	97.3
Central African Republic	51.8	..	56.2	26.7	..	30.5	23.0	..	59.5	..	58.5	..
Chad	33.9	53.1	..	17.9	22.3	30.4	50.5	53.9	37.7	..	37.6	44.4
Comoros	56.7	55.1	..	..	..	..	..	..	80.3	..	..	89.5
Congo, Dem. Rep.	53.9	..	..	45.9	..	50.7	54.7	..	..	..	..	..
Congo, Rep.	81.9	..	53.8	54.3	..	72.3	60.1	..	66.3	..	..	..
Côte d'Ivoire	44.6	52.2	..	43.4	39.1	44.7	72.5	87.6	78.3	..	60.7	..
Djibouti	28.5	26.9	45.3	26.9	28.0	..	87.3	..	89.9	..	..	..
Equatorial Guinea	96.2	90.7	67.1	..	..	66.7	..	..	32.6	..	94.9	..
Eritrea	14.7	37.8	41.2	..	36.4	46.4	..	60.5	59.9	..	..	..
Ethiopia	21.9	38.4	71.4	..	21.6	46.3	18.3	64.6	64.4	..	..	..
Gabon	93.9	..	..	..	..	..	..	..	69.3	..	..	97.0
Gambia, The	46.4	68.5	66.5	..	73.9	69.0	..	98.7	73.0	..	..	..
Ghana	53.6	60.2	72.9	61.2	..	77.7	80.5	66.2	88.6	..	70.7	77.8
Guinea	27.4	47.9	73.6	17.4	32.8	64.2	58.6	..	82.8	..	..	..
Guinea-Bissau	37.9	45.2	..	..	26.9	..	..	..	..	..	..	..
Kenya	..	66.2	86.3	..	..	..	..	..	82.9	..	80.3	..
Lesotho	72.0	77.7	..	58.9	60.1	..	65.9	66.7	73.7	..	..	..
Liberia	..	66.2	30.9	..	..	54.7	..	..	..	..	..	71.8
Madagascar	64.3	64.6	98.5	33.3	35.5	61.5	21.1	..	42.3	..	70.2	..
Malawi	48.5	..	87.0	28.7	65.7	55.4	64.4	51.9	43.4	..	..	83.0
Mali	24.6	..	63.0	12.6	32.8	52.2	69.7	91.7	81.2	..	..	..
Mauritania	36.4	64.5	80.4	34.1	52.6	59.4	75.3	59.6	63.7	..	61.3	66.4
Mauritius	91.3	92.9	95.4	106.6	104.6	93.5	97.4	99.3	99.0	..	94.5	96.2
Mozambique	42.1	56.1	..	26.4	16.1	46.3	34.2	51.9	64.0	..	..	52.9
Namibia	85.9	81.2	86.5	..	84.9	77.1	62.3	94.2	97.8	88.1	..	92.7
Niger	24.1	27.2	44.9	17.6	18.4	39.6	62.4	74.0	72.0	..	..	..
Nigeria	55.2	60.8	..	..	..	..	89.1	..	82.9	71.2	..	86.7
Rwanda	66.9	..	93.6	35.4	20.7	..	59.9	39.1	45.8	74.9	77.6	..
São Tomé and Príncipe	95.6	..	97.1	..	..	75.6	..	..	78.7	93.8	..	95.2
Senegal	45.3	56.5	71.9	..	37.7	50.1	84.5	72.3	65.0	..	..	..
Seychelles	..	..	..	..	112.9	113.9	..	91.0	98.7	..	..	..
Sierra Leone	43.1	..	..	..	..	80.8	..	..	..	..	..	54.1
Somalia	..	..	..	..	..	..	..	..	..	..	..	..
South Africa	90.2	91.7	85.8	75.8	90.1	84.5	..	..	82.4	..	..	95.4
Sudan	..	41.2	..	42.0	37.5	50.0	93.8	..	70.5	..	77.2	..
Swaziland	74.8	75.4	87.0	59.9	64.3	74.6	77.0	73.9	82.1	..	88.4	..
Tanzania	50.5	53.4	..	62.4	..	111.7	81.3	81.4	87.2	..	..	77.5
Togo	64.0	76.5	77.2	34.9	61.0	57.4	48.0	73.8	54.3	..	74.4	..
Uganda	51.1	..	94.6	..	..	..	36.0	56.7	48.7	69.8	..	86.3
Zambia	78.0	67.2	94.0	..	60.1	88.1	..	..	89.0	..	..	75.1
Zimbabwe	84.1	83.5	..	97.2	..	..	76.1	..	69.7	..	..	91.2
NORTH AFRICA												
Algeria	88.9	91.6	95.4	79.5	82.6	95.1	94.5	97.2	96.0	..	..	92.5
Egypt, Arab Rep.	86.2	93.4	95.7	..	98.1	98.5	..	99.0	96.8	..	..	..
Libya	..	..	..	..	..	..	..	..	..	..	..	98.9
Morocco	56.1	75.8	88.8	48.1	56.7	83.4	75.1	80.1	83.9	..	..	75.1
Tunisia	93.5	93.8	95.0	74.2	86.7	99.9	86.4	93.1	96.4	..	..	95.7

a. Data are for the most recent year available during the period specified.

Table 3.3 Millennium Development Goal 3: promote gender equity and empower women

	Ratio of girls to boys in primary and secondary school (%)			Ratio of literate young women to men (% of ages 15–24)			Women in national parliament (% of total seats)			Share of women employed in the nonagricultural sector (%)		
	1991	2000	2007–08[a]	1990	2000	2007	1990	2000	2008	1990	2000	2000–08[a]
SUB-SAHARAN AFRICA												
Angola	..	..	..	..	..	..	15.0	16.0	37.3	..	..	..
Benin	49.5	64.2	..	..	..	64.9	3.0	6.0	10.8	..	..	24.3
Botswana	108.7	101.6	..	107.4	..	102.6	5.0	..	11.1	33.5	39.4	42.4
Burkina Faso	62.3	70.0	84.0	52.9	..	70.9	..	8.0	15.3	12.5	..	..
Burundi	81.8	..	90.0	..	91.6	..	..	6.0	30.5	14.3	..	..
Cameroon	83.0	..	84.5	..	..	..	14.0	6.0	13.9	..	..	..
Cape Verde	..	..	103.8	..	..	101.4	12.0	11.0	18.1	..	38.9	38.9
Central African Republic	59.8	..	..	..	66.6	..	4.0	7.0	10.5	..	..	46.8
Chad	41.6	55.9	64.3	..	41.7	66.4	..	2.0	5.2	3.8	..	..
Comoros	71.1	84.1	..	..	..	94.2	0.0	..	3.0	..	..	..
Congo, Dem. Rep.	..	..	73.4	..	..	..	5.0	..	8.4	25.9	..	..
Congo, Rep.	85.1	84.5	..	..	..	..	14.0	12.0	7.3	26.1	..	..
Côte d'Ivoire	65.3	69.1	..	..	73.6	..	6.0	..	8.9	..	..	..
Djibouti	70.5	71.0	80.0	..	..	..	0.0	0.0	13.8	..	..	26.7
Equatorial Guinea	..	86.3	..	..	100.2	..	13.0	5.0	6.0	10.5	..	..
Eritrea	..	77.4	77.8	..	..	..	..	15.0	22.0	..	..	..
Ethiopia	68.4	65.1	82.6	..	..	..	..	2.0	21.9	..	..	47.3
Gabon	..	95.8	..	..	..	97.9	13.0	8.0	16.7	..	..	..
Gambia, The	65.6	83.0	103.4	..	..	..	8.0	2.0	9.4	20.9	..	..
Ghana	78.5	89.4	95.4	..	86.2	95.1	..	9.0	10.9	..	31.7	31.7
Guinea	44.9	61.3	76.1	..	..	..	..	9.0	19.3	..	..	..
Guinea-Bissau	..	65.0	..	..	..	..	20.0	..	14.0	10.8	..	..
Kenya	93.6	97.6	95.2	..	101.1	..	1.0	4.0	8.9	21.4	..	..
Lesotho	123.5	107.2	..	..	..	..	..	4.0	25.0	..	..	..
Liberia	..	72.7	..	..	..	111.6	..	..	12.5	..	..	11.4
Madagascar	97.5	..	96.5	..	93.9	..	7.0	8.0	7.9	..	35.6	37.7
Malawi	81.3	92.6	99.8	..	..	98.3	10.0	8.0	13.0	10.5	..	..
Mali	57.1	68.5	76.0	..	..	..	..	12.0	10.2	..	..	34.6
Mauritania	71.3	95.0	102.6	..	81.9	89.3	..	4.0	22.1	..	35.8	35.8
Mauritius	101.6	98.2	..	..	101.7	102.0	7.0	8.0	17.1	36.7	38.6	37.5
Mozambique	71.5	74.9	85.4	..	..	81.2	16.0	..	34.8	11.4	..	..
Namibia	106.4	103.2	103.8	105.5	..	103.8	7.0	22.0	26.9	..	48.8	46.8
Niger	53.3	65.8	71.5	..	..	..	5.0	1.0	12.4	11.0	..	..
Nigeria	77.2	80.1	..	76.8	..	95.7	..	..	7.0	..	18.6	21.1
Rwanda	92.1	96.1	100.2	..	97.9	..	17.0	17.0	56.3	..	33.0	33.0
São Tomé and Príncipe	..	..	100.0	95.9	..	100.5	12.0	9.0	1.8	..	34.8	37.7
Senegal	68.8	82.0	93.6	..	..	..	13.0	12.0	22.0	..	..	10.6
Seychelles	..	101.4	105.6	..	..	..	16.0	24.0	23.5	..	..	..
Sierra Leone	66.8	..	86.4	..	..	68.1	..	9.0	13.2	..	..	23.2
Somalia	..	..	..	..	..	..	4.0	..	8.2	21.7	..	..
South Africa	103.9	100.4	99.8	..	..	101.8	3.0	30.0	33.0	..	..	43.1
Sudan	77.5	..	87.6	..	84.4	..	..	..	18.1	22.2	..	..
Swaziland	97.7	95.4	91.7	..	103.2	..	4.0	3.0	..	..	..	..
Tanzania	96.7	..	..	..	..	96.5	..	16.0	30.4	..	..	29.3
Togo	58.9	69.1	75.2	..	76.0	..	5.0	..	11.1	41.0	..	..
Uganda	81.7	92.8	98.5	81.7	..	95.4	12.0	18.0	30.7	..	..	39.0
Zambia	..	91.3	95.6	..	..	82.3	7.0	10.0	15.2	..	33.7	33.7
Zimbabwe	92.1	94.5	..	..	..	93.9	11.0	14.0	15.2	15.4	20.4	21.9
NORTH AFRICA												
Algeria	82.9	..	..	..	..	96.2	2.0	3.0	7.7	..	13.0	17.0
Egypt, Arab Rep.	81.4	92.4	..	..	..	..	4.0	2.0	1.8	20.5	18.6	20.7
Libya	..	..	..	..	..	98.3	..	..	7.7	..	..	15.8
Morocco	69.6	82.4	88.1	..	..	79.3	0.0	1.0	10.5	28.7	26.2	28.2
Tunisia	86.1	100.0	..	..	..	97.2	4.0	12.0	22.8	..	24.6	25.3

a. Data are for the most recent year available during the period specified.

Table 3.4 Millennium Development Goal 4: reduce child mortality

	Under-five mortality rate (per 1,000)			Infant mortality rate (per 1,000 live births)			Child immunization rate, measles (% of children ages 12–23 months)		
	1990	2000	2007	1990	2000	2007	1990	2000	2007
SUB-SAHARAN AFRICA									
Angola	258	158	158	150	116	116	38	88	88
Benin	184	123	123	111	78	78	79	61	61
Botswana	57	40	40	45	33	33	87	90	90
Burkina Faso	206	191	191	112	104	104	79	94	94
Burundi	189	180	180	113	108	108	74	75	75
Cameroon	139	148	148	85	87	87	56	74	74
Cape Verde	60	32	32	45	24	24	79	74	74
Central African Republic	171	172	172	113	113	113	82	62	62
Chad	201	209	209	120	124	124	32	23	23
Comoros	120	66	66	88	49	49	87	65	65
Congo, Dem. Rep.	200	161	161	127	108	108	38	79	79
Congo, Rep.	104	125	125	67	79	79	75	67	67
Côte d'Ivoire	151	127	127	104	89	89	56	67	67
Djibouti	175	127	127	116	84	84	85	74	74
Equatorial Guinea	170	206	206	103	124	124	88	51	51
Eritrea	147	70	70	88	46	46	..	95	95
Ethiopia	204	119	119	122	75	75	38	65	65
Gabon	92	91	91	60	60	60	76	55	55
Gambia, The	153	109	109	104	82	82	86	85	85
Ghana	120	115	115	76	73	73	61	95	95
Guinea	231	150	150	137	93	93	35	71	71
Guinea-Bissau	240	198	198	142	118	118	53	76	76
Kenya	97	121	121	64	80	80	78	80	80
Lesotho	102	84	84	81	68	68	80	85	85
Liberia	205	133	133	138	93	93	..	95	95
Madagascar	168	112	112	103	70	70	47	81	81
Malawi	209	111	111	124	71	71	81	83	83
Mali	250	196	196	148	117	117	43	68	68
Mauritania	130	119	119	81	75	75	38	67	67
Mauritius	24	15	15	20	13	13	76	98	98
Mozambique	201	168	168	135	115	115	59	77	77
Namibia	87	68	68	57	47	47	..	69	69
Niger	304	176	176	143	83	83	25	47	47
Nigeria	230	189	189	120	97	97	54	62	62
Rwanda	195	181	181	117	109	109	83	99	99
São Tomé and Príncipe	101	99	99	65	64	64	71	86	86
Senegal	149	114	114	72	59	59	51	84	84
Seychelles	19	13	13	17	12	12	86	99	99
Sierra Leone	290	262	262	169	155	155	..	67	67
Somalia	203	142	142	121	88	88	30	34	34
South Africa	64	59	59	49	46	46	79	83	83
Sudan	125	109	109	79	69	69	57	79	79
Swaziland	96	91	91	70	66	66	85	91	91
Tanzania	157	116	116	96	73	73	80	90	90
Togo	150	100	100	89	65	65	73	80	80
Uganda	175	130	130	106	82	82	52	68	68
Zambia	163	170	170	99	103	103	90	85	85
Zimbabwe	95	90	90	62	59	59	87	66	66
NORTH AFRICA									
Algeria	69	37	37	54	33	33	83	92	92
Egypt, Arab Rep.	93	36	36	68	30	30	86	97	97
Libya	41	18	18	35	17	17	89	98	98
Morocco	89	34	34	69	32	32	79	95	95
Tunisia	52	21	21	41	18	18	93	98	98

Table 3.5 Millennium Development Goal 5: improve maternal health

	Maternal mortality ratio (per 100,000 live births)		Births attended by skilled health staff (% of total)			
	Modeled estimate	National estimate	Surveys 1990–99[a]		Surveys 2000–08[a]	
	2005	2000–07[a]	Year	Percent	Year	Percent
SUB-SAHARAN AFRICA						
Angola	1,400	..	1996	22.5	2007	47.3
Benin	840	397	1996	59.8	2006	77.7
Botswana	380	..	1996	87.0	2000	94.2
Burkina Faso	700	..	1999	30.9	2006	53.5
Burundi	1,100	615		..	2005	33.6
Cameroon	1,000	669	1998	58.2	2006	63.0
Cape Verde	210	15	1998	88.5	2005	77.5
Central African Republic	980	543	1995	45.9	2006	53.4
Chad	1,500	1,099	1997	15.0	2004	14.4
Comoros	400	380	1996	51.6	2000	61.8
Congo, Dem. Rep.	1,100	1,289		..	2007	74.0
Congo, Rep.	740	781		..	2005	83.4
Côte d'Ivoire	810	543	1999	47.1	2006	56.8
Djibouti	650	..		..	2003	60.6
Equatorial Guinea	680	..	1994	5.0	2000	64.6
Eritrea	450	..	1995	20.6	2002	28.3
Ethiopia	720	673		..	2005	5.7
Gabon	520	519		..	2000	85.5
Gambia, The	690	730	1990	44.1	2006	56.8
Ghana	560	..	1998	44.3	2006	49.7
Guinea	910	980	1999	34.8	2005	38.0
Guinea-Bissau	1,100	405	1993	25.0	2006	38.8
Kenya	560	414	1998	44.3	2003	41.6
Lesotho	960	762	1993	60.9	2004	55.4
Liberia	1,200	..		..	2007	46.4
Madagascar	510	469	1997	47.3	2004	51.3
Malawi	1,100	807	1992	54.8	2006	53.6
Mali	970	464	1996	40.0	2006	49.0
Mauritania	820	747	1991	40.0	2007	60.9
Mauritius	15	22	1999	98.5	2003	98.4
Mozambique	520	408	1997	44.2	2003	47.7
Namibia	210	271	1992	68.2	2006	81.4
Niger	1,800	648	1998	17.6	2006	32.9
Nigeria	1,100	..	1999	41.6	2003	35.2
Rwanda	1,300	750	1992	25.8	2008	52.1
São Tomé and Príncipe	..	148		..	2006	80.7
Senegal	980	401	1999	48.3	2005	51.9
Seychelles	..	57		..		..
Sierra Leone	2,100	1,800		..	2005	43.2
Somalia	1,400	1,044	1999	34.2	2006	33.0
South Africa	400	166	1998	84.4	2003	92.0
Sudan	450	..	1991	86.3	2006	49.2
Swaziland	390	589	1994	56.0	2007	69.0
Tanzania	950	578	1999	35.8	2005	43.4
Togo	510	..	1998	50.5	2006	62.0
Uganda	550	435	1995	37.8	2006	42.1
Zambia	830	729	1999	47.1	2007	46.5
Zimbabwe	880	555	1999	72.5	2006	68.5
NORTH AFRICA						
Algeria	180	..	1992	77.0	2006	95.2
Egypt, Arab Rep.	130	84	1998	55.2	2008	78.9
Libya	97	..	1995	94.4		..
Morocco	240	227	1995	39.6	2004	62.6
Tunisia	100	..	1995	80.5	2000	89.9

a. Data are for the most recent year available during the period specified.

Table 3.6 Millennium Development Goal 6: combat HIV/AIDS, malaria, and other diseases

	Prevalence of HIV (% of ages 15–49)		Contraceptive use, any method (% of married women ages 15–49)				Children sleeping under insecticide-treated nets (% of children under age 5)	
			Surveys 1990–99[a]		Surveys 2000–08[a]		Surveys 2000–08[a]	
	1990	2007	Year	Percent	Year	Percent	Year	Percent
SUB-SAHARAN AFRICA								
Angola	0.3	2.1	1996	8.1	2001	6.2	2006	17.7
Benin	0.1	1.2	1996	16.4	2006	17.0	2006	20.2
Botswana	4.7	23.9	1996	47.6	2000	44.4		..
Burkina Faso	1.9	1.6	1999	11.9	2006	17.4	2006	9.6
Burundi	1.7	2.0		..	2002	19.7	2005	8.3
Cameroon	0.8	5.1	1998	19.3	2006	29.2	2006	13.1
Cape Verde	..	..	1998	52.9	2005	61.3		..
Central African Republic	1.8	6.3	1995	14.8	2006	19.0	2006	15.1
Chad	0.7	3.5	1997	4.1	2004	2.8		..
Comoros	<0.1	<0.1	1996	21.0	2000	25.7	2000	9.3
Congo, Dem. Rep.	..	..	1991	7.7	2007	20.6	2007	5.8
Congo, Rep.	5.1	3.5		..	2005	44.3	2005	6.1
Côte d'Ivoire	2.2	3.9	1999	15.0	2006	12.9	2006	5.9
Djibouti	0.2	3.1		..	2006	17.8	2006	1.3
Equatorial Guinea	1.0	3.4		..	2000	10.1	2000	0.7
Eritrea	0.1	1.3	1995	8.0	2002	8.0	2002	4.2
Ethiopia	0.7	2.1	1997	3.3	2005	14.7	2007	33.1
Gabon	0.9	5.9		..	2000	32.7		..
Gambia, The	..	0.9	1990	11.8	2001	17.5	2006	49.0
Ghana	0.1	1.9	1999	22.0	2008	23.5	2008	28.2
Guinea	0.2	1.6	1999	6.2	2005	9.1	2005	0.3
Guinea-Bissau	0.2	1.8		..	2006	10.3	2006	39.0
Kenya	..	..	1998	39.0	2003	39.3	2003	6.0
Lesotho	0.8	23.2	1992	23.2	2004	37.3		..
Liberia	0.4	1.7		..	2007	11.4	2005	3.0
Madagascar	..	0.1	1999	25.0	2004	27.1	2000	0.2
Malawi	2.1	11.9	1996	21.9	2006	41.0	2006	23.0
Mali	0.2	1.5	1996	6.7	2006	8.2	2006	27.1
Mauritania	<0.1	0.8	1992	4.1	2007	9.3	2003	2.1
Mauritius	<0.1	1.7	1991	74.6	2002	75.8		..
Mozambique	1.4	12.5	1997	5.6	2004	16.5	2008	22.8
Namibia	1.2	15.3	1992	28.9	2007	55.1		..
Niger	0.1	0.8	1998	8.2	2006	11.2	2006	7.4
Nigeria	0.7	3.1	1999	15.3	2007	14.7	2003	1.2
Rwanda	9.2	2.8	1996	13.7	2008	36.4	2008	24.0
São Tomé and Príncipe	..	..		..	2000	29.3	2007	54.0
Senegal	0.1	1.0	1999	10.5	2005	11.8	2008	31.0
Seychelles	..	..		..		..		..
Sierra Leone	0.2	1.7	1992	2.6	2008	8.2	2008	25.9
Somalia	<0.1	0.5	1999	7.9	2006	14.6	2006	9.2
South Africa	0.8	18.1	1998	56.3	2003	60.3		..
Sudan	0.8	1.4	1999	7.0	2006	7.6	2006	27.6
Swaziland	0.9	26.1		..	2007	50.6	2006	0.6
Tanzania	4.8	6.2	1999	25.4	2005	26.4	2007	25.7
Togo	0.7	3.3	1998	23.5	2006	16.8	2006	38.4
Uganda	13.7	5.4	1995	14.8	2006	23.7	2006	9.7
Zambia	8.9	15.2	1999	22.0	2007	40.8	2008	41.1
Zimbabwe	14.2	15.3	1999	53.5	2006	60.2	2005	2.9
NORTH AFRICA								
Algeria	..	0.1	1995	56.9	2006	61.4		..
Egypt, Arab Rep.	..	..	1998	51.7	2008	60.3		..
Libya	..	..	1995	45.2		..		..
Morocco	..	0.1	1997	58.4	2004	63.0		..
Tunisia	..	0.1	1995	60.0	2006	60.2		..

(continued)

Table 3.6 Millennium Development Goal 6: combat HIV/AIDS, malaria, and other diseases (continued)

	Incidence of tuberculosis (per 100,000 people)		Tuberculosis cases detected under DOTS (% of estimated cases)			
			Surveys 1990–99[a]		Surveys 2000–07[a]	
	1999	2007	Year	Percent	Year	Percent
SUB-SAHARAN AFRICA						
Angola	245.0	286.5	1999	50.7	2007	101.8
Benin	83.8	90.9	1999	85.8	2006	86.0
Botswana	587.7	731.4	1999	71.9	2007	57.2
Burkina Faso	181.7	226.2	1999	16.0	2007	18.4
Burundi	294.9	367.0	1999	36.3	2007	26.8
Cameroon	154.0	191.7	1999	20.8	2007	91.4
Cape Verde	161.8	150.5		..	2007	44.0
Central African Republic	277.3	345.1	1996	61.5	2006	70.8
Chad	240.0	298.7	1999	34.9	2007	18.5
Comoros	58.7	42.0	1998	54.4	2006	41.6
Congo, Dem. Rep.	314.7	391.7	1999	50.4	2007	60.7
Congo, Rep.	323.9	403.1	1998	54.6	2007	55.7
Côte d'Ivoire	337.9	420.5	1999	44.4	2007	42.2
Djibouti	694.7	812.5	1999	74.5	2007	42.3
Equatorial Guinea	205.6	255.9	1998	86.2	2004	74.9
Eritrea	83.6	95.4	1999	40.7	2007	34.5
Ethiopia	303.9	378.2	1999	24.6	2007	28.1
Gabon	210.1	406.4		..	2007	66.2
Gambia, The	220.9	258.4	1998	72.8	2007	63.9
Ghana	212.0	202.9	1999	31.0	2007	35.9
Guinea	190.0	287.4	1999	53.2	2007	53.5
Guinea-Bissau	188.0	219.9		..	2006	67.6
Kenya	381.9	352.6	1999	60.0	2007	72.1
Lesotho	519.1	636.6	1998	78.2	2007	16.5
Liberia	236.9	277.1	1998	43.8	2006	69.3
Madagascar	213.0	250.8	1998	67.4	2007	69.5
Malawi	417.3	345.7	1999	45.4	2007	41.4
Mali	297.4	318.9	1999	18.8	2007	22.9
Mauritania	271.6	317.7		..	2007	39.3
Mauritius	24.7	22.4	1999	93.4	2007	68.7
Mozambique	346.6	431.3	1999	50.5	2007	49.0
Namibia	616.2	766.8	1999	85.0	2007	83.6
Niger	149.1	174.3	1999	37.2	2007	52.8
Nigeria	249.7	310.7	1999	12.3	2007	22.6
Rwanda	319.0	397.0	1999	44.0	2007	25.4
São Tomé and Príncipe	115.9	101.1		..		..
Senegal	232.2	271.5	1999	48.1	2007	48.3
Seychelles	37.1	32.4	1998	67.1	2005	62.1
Sierra Leone	355.0	573.9	1998	36.2	2007	36.9
Somalia	248.7	248.7	1999	45.6	2007	63.9
South Africa	478.8	948.2	1999	66.1	2007	78.1
Sudan	208.0	243.3	1999	27.3	2007	30.6
Swaziland	690.5	1,198.0		..	2007	54.7
Tanzania	326.5	297.4	1999	56.0	2007	50.5
Togo	366.9	429.2	1999	11.2	2007	15.1
Uganda	324.1	329.6	1999	59.6	2007	50.9
Zambia	603.3	506.1		..	2007	58.3
Zimbabwe	628.4	782.1	1999	49.4	2007	26.6
NORTH AFRICA						
Algeria	46.6	56.6	1997	132.5	2007	98.4
Egypt, Arab Rep.	28.1	21.0	1999	37.7	2007	72.2
Libya	23.0	17.2	1999	148.0	2007	161.8
Morocco	115.2	91.6	1999	91.0	2007	92.8
Tunisia	26.8	26.0	1999	93.6	2007	78.2

a. Data are for the most recent year available during the period specified.

Table 3.7 Millennium Development Goal 7: ensure environmental sustainability

	Forest area (% of total land area)			Nationally protected areas (% of total land area)	GDP per unit of energy use (2000 PPP $ per kg of oil equivalent)		
	1990	2000	2007	2006	1990	2000	2006
SUB-SAHARAN AFRICA							
Angola	48.9	47.9	47.2	10.1	5.4	4.6	6.9
Benin	30.0	24.2	20.1	23.6	3.2	4.2	3.8
Botswana	24.2	22.1	20.7	30.8	7.4	9.3	11.7
Burkina Faso	26.1	25.3	24.7	14.0	..	..	..
Burundi	11.3	7.7	5.2	6.0	..	..	..
Cameroon	52.7	48.0	44.7	8.6	5.0	4.6	5.1
Cape Verde	14.3	20.4	21.0	..	..	..	..
Central African Republic	37.2	36.8	36.4	15.2	..	..	..
Chad	10.4	9.8	9.3	9.1	..	..	..
Comoros	6.4	4.3	2.4	..	..	..	..
Congo, Dem. Rep.	62.0	59.6	58.7	8.6	1.9	0.9	1.0
Congo, Rep.	66.5	66.1	65.7	14.3	10.5	11.4	10.5
Côte d'Ivoire	32.1	32.5	32.8	12.2	5.4	4.4	4.1
Djibouti	0.2	0.2	0.2	..	..	..	..
Equatorial Guinea	66.3	60.9	57.1	16.2	..	..	..
Eritrea	..	15.6	15.3	5.0	..	3.5	4.0
Ethiopia	16.7	13.7	12.7	18.6	1.8	1.8	2.3
Gabon	85.1	84.7	84.4	13.5	11.2	10.6	9.9
Gambia, The	44.2	46.1	47.5	..	..	..	..
Ghana	32.7	26.8	23.2	15.9	2.5	2.6	2.9
Guinea	30.1	28.1	27.1	6.1	..	..	..
Guinea-Bissau	78.8	75.4	73.0	10.2	..	..	..
Kenya	6.5	6.3	6.1	12.1	3.0	2.7	2.8
Lesotho	0.2	0.2	0.3	0.2	..	..	..
Liberia	42.1	35.9	31.5	15.8	..	..	..
Madagascar	23.5	22.4	21.9	2.6	..	..	..
Malawi	41.4	37.9	35.5	19.5	..	..	..
Mali	11.5	10.7	10.1	2.1	..	..	..
Mauritania	0.4	0.3	0.2	..	..	..	..
Mauritius	19.2	18.7	18.0	3.3	..	..	..
Mozambique	25.4	24.8	24.4	5.8	0.9	1.3	1.7
Namibia	10.6	9.8	9.1	5.2	..	8.3	7.9
Niger	1.5	1.0	1.0	6.6	..	..	..
Nigeria	18.9	14.4	11.3	6.2	1.9	2.0	2.5
Rwanda	12.9	13.9	21.7	8.1	..	..	..
São Tomé and Príncipe	28.5	28.5	28.5	..	..	..	..
Senegal	48.6	46.2	44.6	11.2	5.8	5.5	6.2
Seychelles	87.0	87.0	87.0	8.3	..	..	..
Sierra Leone	42.5	39.8	37.9	4.1	..	..	..
Somalia	13.2	12.0	11.1	0.3	..	..	..
South Africa	7.6	7.6	7.6	6.1	3.0	3.0	3.2
Sudan	32.1	29.7	27.9	4.8	2.5	3.4	3.9
Swaziland	27.4	30.1	32.0	3.1	..	..	..
Tanzania	46.8	42.1	38.9	38.7	2.2	2.2	2.1
Togo	12.6	8.9	6.4	11.1	2.6	2.0	2.0
Uganda	25.0	20.6	17.5	31.9	..	..	..
Zambia	66.1	60.1	55.9	40.4	1.8	1.7	1.9
Zimbabwe	57.5	49.4	43.7	14.8	..	..	..
NORTH AFRICA							
Algeria	0.8	0.9	1.0	5.0	6.6	6.3	6.6
Egypt, Arab Rep.	0.0	0.1	0.1	5.3	5.8	6.1	5.7
Libya	0.1	0.1	0.1	0.1	..	3.7	4.4
Morocco	9.6	9.7	9.8	1.1	9.3	8.0	8.3
Tunisia	4.1	6.2	7.0	1.5	6.4	6.9	7.8

(continued)

Table 3.7 Millennium Development Goal 7: ensure environmental sustainability (continued)

	Carbon dioxide emissions per capita (metric tons)			Population with sustainable access to an improved water source (%)			Population with sustainable access to improved sanitation (%)		
	1990	2000	2006	1990	2000	2006	1990	2000	2006
SUB-SAHARAN AFRICA									
Angola	0.4	0.7	0.6	39	44	51	26	40	50
Benin	0.1	0.2	0.4	63	64	65	12	24	30
Botswana	1.6	2.5	2.6	93	95	96	38	45	47
Burkina Faso	0.1	0.1	0.1	34	56	72	5	9	13
Burundi	0.1	0.0	0.0	70	71	71	44	42	41
Cameroon	0.1	0.2	0.2	49	63	70	39	47	51
Cape Verde	0.2	0.4	0.6	..	80	..	..	41	..
Central African Republic	0.1	0.1	0.1	58	63	66	11	22	31
Chad	0.0	0.0	0.0	..	34	48	5	7	9
Comoros	0.2	0.2	0.1	93	88	85	18	29	35
Congo, Dem. Rep.	0.1	0.0	0.0	43	45	46	15	25	31
Congo, Rep.	0.5	0.3	0.4	..	70	71	..	20	20
Côte d'Ivoire	0.5	0.4	0.3	67	75	81	20	22	24
Djibouti	0.7	0.6	0.6	76	83	92	..	65	67
Equatorial Guinea	0.3	0.5	7.0	43	43	43	51	51	51
Eritrea	0.0	0.2	0.1	43	54	60	3	4	5
Ethiopia	0.1	0.1	0.1	13	29	42	4	7	11
Gabon	6.6	1.0	1.5	..	85	87	..	36	36
Gambia, The	0.2	0.2	0.2	..	86	86	..	49	52
Ghana	0.3	0.3	0.4	56	72	80	6	9	10
Guinea	0.2	0.2	0.1	45	61	70	13	16	19
Guinea-Bissau	0.2	0.2	0.2	..	58	57	..	30	33
Kenya	0.2	0.3	0.3	41	51	57	39	41	42
Lesotho	..	..	..	..	77	78	..	34	36
Liberia	0.2	0.2	0.2	57	63	64	40	32	32
Madagascar	0.1	0.1	0.2	39	45	47	8	11	12
Malawi	0.1	0.1	0.1	41	63	76	46	55	60
Mali	0.1	0.1	0.0	33	51	60	35	42	45
Mauritania	1.4	0.5	0.5	37	50	60	20	22	24
Mauritius	1.4	2.3	3.1	100	100	100	94	94	94
Mozambique	0.1	0.1	0.1	36	41	42	20	27	31
Namibia	0.0	0.9	1.4	57	81	93	26	32	35
Niger	0.1	0.1	0.1	41	41	42	3	5	7
Nigeria	0.5	0.6	0.7	50	49	47	26	28	30
Rwanda	0.1	0.1	0.1	65	65	65	29	25	23
São Tomé and Príncipe	0.6	0.6	0.7	..	82	86	..	22	24
Senegal	0.4	0.4	0.4	67	72	77	26	27	28
Seychelles	1.6	7.0	8.8	..	87	..	..	..	..
Sierra Leone	0.1	0.1	0.2	..	57	53	..	12	11
Somalia	0.0	0.1	0.0	..	23	29	..	21	23
South Africa	9.5	8.4	8.7	81	89	93	55	57	59
Sudan	0.2	0.2	0.3	64	69	70	33	34	35
Swaziland	0.5	1.1	0.9	..	59	60	..	50	50
Tanzania	0.1	0.1	0.1	49	53	55	35	34	33
Togo	0.2	0.3	0.2	49	55	59	13	12	12
Uganda	0.0	0.1	0.1	43	56	64	29	32	33
Zambia	0.3	0.2	0.2	50	54	58	42	49	52
Zimbabwe	1.6	1.2	0.9	78	80	81	44	45	46
NORTH AFRICA									
Algeria	3.1	3.8	4.0	94	89	85	88	92	94
Egypt, Arab Rep.	1.3	2.0	2.1	94	97	98	50	61	66
Libya	9.2	9.3	9.2	71	71	..	97	97	97
Morocco	1.0	1.2	1.5	75	80	83	52	65	72
Tunisia	1.6	2.1	2.3	82	90	94	74	81	85

Table 3.8 Millennium Development Goal 8: develop a global partnership for development

	Debt sustainability					
	Heavily Indebted Poor Countries (HIPC) Debt Initiative		Debt service relief committed ($ millions)[a]	Public and publicly guaranteed debt service (% of exports)		
	Decision point[a]	Completion point[a]		1990	2000	2005–07[b]
SUB-SAHARAN AFRICA						
Angola				7.1	20.4	10.0
Benin	Jul. 2000	Mar. 2003	460	8.6	10.9	8.1
Botswana				4.3	2.0	0.9
Burkina Faso	Jul. 2000	Apr. 2002	930	7.7	15.1	10.1
Burundi	Aug. 2005	Jan. 2009	1,472	40.7	25.1	42.1
Cameroon	Oct. 2000	Apr. 2006	4,917	12.4	13.9	5.6
Cape Verde				8.9	10.5	4.8
Central African Republic	Sep. 2007	Jun. 2009		7.5	..	..
Chad	May 2001		260	2.3	..	..
Comoros				2.5	..	..
Congo, Dem. Rep.	Jul. 2003	Floating	10,389	..	..	..
Congo, Rep.	Mar. 2006	Floating	2,881	30.8	0.5	1.2
Côte d'Ivoire	Mar. 1998/Mar. 2009			14.7	14.9	1.6
Djibouti				..	4.8	12.0
Equatorial Guinea				..	..	..
Eritrea				..	2.8	2.8
Ethiopia	Nov. 2001	Apr. 2004	3,275	33.1	12.2	4.6
Gabon				3.8	8.8	1.4
Gambia, The	Dec. 2000	Dec. 2007	90	17.9	..	12.8
Ghana	Feb. 2002	Jul. 2004	3,500	19.9	12.0	2.6
Guinea	Dec. 2000	Floating	800	17.7	17.3	11.6
Guinea-Bissau	Dec. 2000	Floating	790	22.0	..	46.4
Kenya				22.7	15.7	6.0
Lesotho				4.1	10.3	6.9
Liberia	Mar. 2008			..	..	111.5
Madagascar	Dec. 2000	Oct. 2004	1,900	31.9	8.4	4.9
Malawi	Dec. 2000	Aug. 2006	1,000	22.4	10.8	5.8
Mali	Sep. 2000	Mar. 2003	895	9.7	10.2	3.2
Mauritania	Feb. 2000	Jun. 2002	1,100	24.8	..	..
Mauritius				4.5	16.3	2.5
Mozambique	Apr. 2000	Sep. 2001	4,300	17.2	7.0	1.2
Namibia				..	..	..
Niger	Dec. 2000	Apr. 2004	1,190	3.2	6.0	9.4
Nigeria				22.3	8.2	1.4
Rwanda	Dec. 2000	Apr. 2005	1,316	9.4	14.8	3.3
São Tomé and Príncipe	Dec. 2000	Mar. 2007	200	28.6	21.0	37.7
Senegal	Jun. 2000	Apr. 2004	850	13.7	13.2	3.3
Seychelles				7.6	3.3	8.2
Sierra Leone	Mar. 2002	Dec. 2006	950	7.7	29.6	3.5
Somalia				..	..	..
South Africa				..	5.5	3.3
Sudan				4.5	10.1	3.2
Swaziland				5.3	2.1	1.9
Tanzania	Apr. 2000	Nov. 2001	3,000	25.1	10.8	2.1
Togo	Nov. 2008			8.6	3.2	2.1
Uganda	Feb. 2000	May 2000	1,950	47.1	6.5	2.4
Zambia	Dec. 2000	Apr. 2005	3,900	12.6	17.4	0.9
Zimbabwe				18.2	..	..
NORTH AFRICA						
Algeria				63.3	..	..
Egypt, Arab Rep.				23.2	8.5	4.7
Libya				..	..	..
Morocco				23.1	23.0	8.5
Tunisia				23.9	20.5	11.3

(continued)

Table 3.8 Millennium Development Goal 8: develop a global partnership for development (continued)

	Youth unemployment rate (ages 15–24)						Information and communications								
	Total (share of total labor force)		Male (share of male labor force)		Female (share of female labor force)		Fixed-line and mobile telephone subscribers (per 100 people)			Personal computers (per 100 people)			Internet users (per 100 people)		
	Year	Percent	Year	Percent	Year	Percent	1990	2000	2008	1990	2000	2005–07[a]	1995	2000	2008
SUB-SAHARAN AFRICA															
Angola	..	..	..	..	..	..	0.7	0.6	38.2	..	0.1	0.6	..	0.1	3.1
Benin	2002	0.8	2002	1.1	2002	0.6	0.3	1.6	..	0.1	0.2	0.7	..	0.2	1.8
Botswana	2001	39.7	2001	33.9	2001	46.1	1.9	20.7	85.5	1.0	3.5	4.8	0.1	2.9	4.2
Burkina Faso	..	..	..	..	..	..	0.2	0.7	..	0.0	0.1	0.6	..	0.1	0.9
Burundi	..	..	..	..	..	..	0.1	0.6	6.3	..	0.1	0.9	0.0	0.1	0.8
Cameroon	..	..	..	..	..	..	0.3	1.3	33.7	0.1	0.3	1.1	..	0.3	..
Cape Verde	..	..	..	..	..	..	2.3	16.9	70.1	..	5.7	14.0	..	1.8	20.6
Central African Republic	..	..	..	..	..	..	0.2	0.4	..	..	0.2	0.3	..	0.1	0.4
Chad	..	..	..	..	..	..	0.1	0.2	..	..	0.1	0.2	..	0.0	1.2
Comoros	..	..	..	..	..	..	0.8	1.3	..	0.0	0.6	0.9	..	0.3	..
Congo, Dem. Rep.	..	..	..	..	..	..	0.1	0.0	14.5	..	..	0.0	..	0.0	0.5
Congo, Rep.	..	..	..	..	..	..	0.6	3.0	..	..	0.4	0.6	..	0.0	4.3
Côte d'Ivoire	..	..	..	..	..	..	0.6	4.3	52.5	..	0.5	1.7	0.0	0.2	3.2
Djibouti	..	..	..	..	..	..	1.0	1.4	..	0.6	0.9	2.4	0.0	0.2	..
Equatorial Guinea	..	..	..	..	..	..	0.3	2.1	..	..	0.4	1.5	..	0.1	1.8
Eritrea	..	..	..	..	..	..	..	0.8	3.0	..	0.2	0.8	0.0	0.1	3.0
Ethiopia	2006	24.9	2006	19.5	2006	29.4	0.3	0.4	5.1	..	0.1	0.7	0.0	0.0	0.4
Gabon	..	..	..	..	..	..	2.2	12.9	..	0.6	1.0	3.4	..	1.2	6.2
Gambia, The	..	..	..	..	..	..	0.7	3.0	73.2	0.1	1.2	3.5	0.0	0.9	6.9
Ghana	2000	16.6	2000	16.4	2000	16.7	0.3	1.8	50.2	0.1	0.3	0.6	0.0	0.2	4.3
Guinea	..	..	..	..	..	..	0.2	0.8	..	0.1	0.3	0.5	0.0	0.1	0.9
Guinea-Bissau	..	..	..	..	..	..	0.6	0.9	32.0	..	..	0.2	..	0.2	2.4
Kenya	..	..	..	..	..	..	0.7	1.3	42.8	0.1	0.5	1.4	0.0	0.3	8.7
Lesotho	..	..	..	..	..	..	0.8	2.3	..	..	..	0.3	..	0.2	3.6
Liberia	2007	4.7	2007	5.7	2007	3.7	0.4	0.3	..	..	..	..	..	0.0	..
Madagascar	2005	2.3	2005	1.7	2005	2.8	0.3	0.8	26.2	..	0.2	0.6	..	0.2	1.7
Malawi	..	..	..	..	..	..	0.3	0.8	..	..	0.1	0.2	..	0.1	2.2
Mali	..	..	..	..	..	..	0.1	0.5	26.4	0.0	0.1	0.8	..	0.1	1.0
Mauritania	..	..	..	..	..	..	0.3	1.3	67.8	..	1.0	4.6	..	0.2	..
Mauritius	2007	24.6	2007	20.0	2007	31.3	5.5	38.8	110.2	3.2	10.1	17.6	..	7.3	29.9
Mozambique	..	..	..	..	..	..	0.4	0.8	20.6	..	0.3	1.4	..	0.1	1.6
Namibia	2001	44.8	2001	40.4	2001	49.3	3.7	10.2	..	..	4.0	24.0	0.0	1.6	5.4
Niger	2001	3.2	2001	4.0	2001	1.7	0.1	0.2	..	..	0.0	0.1	..	0.0	0.5
Nigeria	..	..	..	..	..	..	0.3	0.5	42.5	0.5	0.6	0.8	..	0.1	7.3
Rwanda	..	..	..	..	..	..	0.1	0.7	13.8	..	..	0.3	..	0.1	3.1
São Tomé and Príncipe	..	..	..	..	..	..	1.9	3.3	..	..	..	3.9	..	4.6	15.4
Senegal	..	..	..	..	..	..	0.6	4.6	46.1	0.7	1.6	2.2	0.0	0.4	8.4
Seychelles	2002	20.3	..	..	..	..	12.4	57.4	125.7	..	13.6	21.2	..	7.4	37.1
Sierra Leone	2004	5.2	2004	7.3	2004	3.5	0.3	0.7	..	..	..	..	0.0	0.1	0.3
Somalia	..	..	..	..	..	..	0.2	1.5	..	..	..	0.9	0.0	0.2	..
South Africa	2007	46.9	2007	43.0	2007	52.0	9.4	30.2	..	2.8	6.6	8.5	0.7	5.5	8.6
Sudan	..	..	..	..	..	..	0.2	1.2	27.9	0.0	0.3	10.7	0.0	0.0	9.2
Swaziland	..	..	..	..	..	..	1.6	6.0	..	..	1.1	3.7	0.0	0.9	4.1
Tanzania	2001	8.9	..	..	..	..	0.3	0.8	30.9	..	0.3	0.9	..	0.1	1.2
Togo	..	..	..	..	..	..	0.3	1.8	26.1	0.3	1.9	3.1	0.0	1.9	5.4
Uganda	..	..	..	..	..	..	0.2	0.8	27.6	0.0	0.2	1.7	0.0	0.2	7.9
Zambia	2000	21.4	2000	23.1	2000	19.5	0.8	1.7	28.8	..	0.7	1.1	0.0	0.2	5.5
Zimbabwe	2002	24.9	2002	28.2	2002	21.4	1.2	4.1	..	0.3	1.6	6.9	0.0	0.4	11.4
NORTH AFRICA															
Algeria	2006	24.3	2004	42.8	2004	46.3	3.2	6.1	..	0.3	0.7	1.1	0.0	0.5	..
Egypt, Arab Rep.	2005	34.1	2005	23.3	2005	62.2	2.8	9.8	65.4	0.4	1.1	4.6	0.0	0.6	15.4
Libya	..	..	..	..	..	..	5.0	12.1	..	..	..	2.2	..	0.2	..
Morocco	2007	17.6	2007	18.2	2007	16.1	1.7	13.2	82.6	0.3	1.2	3.6	0.0	0.7	33.0
Tunisia	2005	30.7	2005	31.4	2005	29.3	3.7	11.2	95.0	..	2.2	7.5	0.0	2.7	27.1

Note: 0.0 indicates less than 1.
a. As of 2009.
b. Data are for the most recent year available during the period specified.

Table 4.1 Doing Business indicators

	Overall ranking		Starting a business: Number of procedures		Starting a business: Time required for each procedure (days)		Starting a business: Cost (% of GNI per capita)		Starting a business: Minimum capital (% of GNI per capita)		Registering property: Number of procedures		Registering property: Time required (days)		Registering property: Cost (% of property value)	
	2009	2010	2009	2010	2009	2010	2009	2010	2009	2010	2009	2010	2009	2010	2009	2010
SUB-SAHARAN AFRICA	..	..	10	9	48	45	118.6	197.5	180.5	152.2	7	7	91	80	10.3	10.0
Angola	170	169	8	8	68	68	196.8	151.1	39.1	29.0	7	7	334	184	11.6	11.4
Benin	172	172	7	7	31	31	196.0	155.5	347.0	290.8	4	4	120	120	11.9	11.8
Botswana	39	45	10	10	78	61	2.3	2.1	0.0	0.0	4	5	11	16	4.9	5.0
Burkina Faso	155	147	5	4	16	14	62.3	50.3	458.8	428.2	6	4	136	59	13.4	13.2
Burundi	177	176	11	11	32	32	215.0	151.6	0.0	0.0	5	5	94	94	7.7	6.3
Cameroon	167	171	13	12	37	34	137.1	121.1	188.0	182.9	5	5	93	93	17.8	17.8
Cape Verde	147	146	12	9	52	24	35.7	17.0	47.5	38.9	6	6	73	73	7.7	7.6
Central African Republic	183	183	11	8	22	22	237.6	244.9	513.9	507.1	5	5	75	75	18.6	18.6
Chad	176	178	19	19	75	75	175.0	176.7	365.1	369.3	6	6	44	44	22.7	22.7
Comoros	153	162	11	11	23	24	188.6	182.1	280.8	261.8	5	5	24	24	20.8	20.8
Congo, Dem. Rep.	182	182	13	13	155	149	435.4	391.0	0.0	0.0	8	8	57	57	9.2	9.8
Congo, Rep.	179	179	10	10	37	37	106.4	86.5	131.2	96.5	7	7	116	116	10.8	10.3
Côte d'Ivoire	163	168	10	10	40	40	135.1	133.3	215.9	204.9	6	6	62	62	13.9	13.9
Djibouti	157	163	11	11	37	37	200.2	195.1	514.0	500.5	7	7	40	40	13.2	13.2
Equatorial Guinea	169	170	20	20	136	136	101.7	100.4	15.4	12.4	6	6	23	23	6.2	6.2
Eritrea	175	175	13	13	84	84	102.2	76.5	396.7	297.0	12	12	101	101	5.2	5.2
Ethiopia	111	107	7	5	16	9	29.8	18.9	693.6	492.4	12	10	43	41	3.1	2.2
Gabon	151	158	9	9	58	58	20.3	17.8	30.2	26.5	7	7	39	39	10.5	10.5
Gambia, The	135	140	8	8	27	27	254.9	215.1	0.0	0.0	5	5	371	371	4.6	4.6
Ghana	87	92	9	8	34	33	32.7	26.4	16.6	13.4	5	5	34	34	1.2	1.1
Guinea	171	173	13	13	41	41	135.7	139.2	476.9	489.7	6	6	104	104	13.9	13.9
Guinea-Bissau	181	181	16	16	233	213	460.7	323.0	1,015.0	779.9	9	9	211	211	5.4	7.6
Kenya	84	95	12	12	30	34	39.7	36.5	0.0	0.0	8	8	64	64	4.1	4.2
Lesotho	128	130	7	7	40	40	37.8	27.0	14.5	11.9	6	6	101	101	8.2	8.0
Liberia	159	149	6	5	31	20	61.6	52.9	0.0	0.0	10	10	50	50	13.3	13.2
Madagascar	144	134	5	2	7	7	11.0	7.1	289.8	0.0	7	7	74	74	7.5	9.7
Malawi	131	132	10	10	39	39	125.9	108.0	0.0	0.0	6	6	88	88	3.3	3.2
Mali	162	156	10	7	25	15	121.5	89.2	390.4	334.6	5	5	29	29	20.3	20.0
Mauritania	161	166	9	9	19	19	33.9	34.7	422.6	450.4	4	4	49	49	5.2	5.2
Mauritius	24	17	5	5	6	6	5.0	4.1	0.0	0.0	4	4	210	26	10.7	10.7
Mozambique	140	135	10	10	26	26	22.9	19.3	122.5	0.0	8	8	42	42	12.9	11.3
Namibia	54	66	10	10	66	66	22.1	20.4	0.0	0.0	9	9	23	23	9.9	9.6
Niger	174	174	11	9	19	17	170.1	118.7	702.1	613.7	4	4	35	35	11.1	11.0
Nigeria	121	125	8	8	31	31	90.1	76.7	0.0	0.0	13	13	82	82	20.9	20.9
Rwanda	143	67	8	2	14	3	108.9	10.1	0.0	0.0	4	4	315	60	0.6	0.5
São Tomé and Príncipe	180	180	10	10	144	144	88.9	81.7	0.0	0.0	7	7	62	62	10.9	10.9
Senegal	152	157	4	4	8	8	72.7	63.7	236.2	206.9	6	6	124	124	20.6	20.6
Seychelles	105	111	9	9	38	38	8.3	7.3	0.0	0.0	4	4	33	33	7.0	7.0
Sierra Leone	156	148	6	6	17	12	145.8	118.8	0.0	0.0	7	7	86	236	12.9	12.4
Somalia	..	..	..	..	..	..	..	..	..	..	..	..	..	..	..	..
South Africa	32	34	6	6	22	22	6.0	5.9	0.0	0.0	6	6	24	24	8.8	8.7
Sudan	149	154	10	10	39	36	50.8	36.0	0.0	0.0	6	6	9	9	3.1	3.0
Swaziland	114	115	13	13	61	61	35.1	33.9	0.6	0.5	11	11	46	46	7.1	7.1
Tanzania	126	131	12	12	29	29	41.5	36.8	0.0	0.0	9	9	73	73	4.4	4.4
Togo	166	165	13	7	53	75	251.3	205.0	559.9	514.0	5	5	295	295	13.4	13.1
Uganda	106	112	18	18	25	25	100.7	84.4	0.0	0.0	13	13	77	77	4.1	3.5
Zambia	999	90	6	6	18	18	28.6	28.4	1.5	1.3	6	6	39	39	6.6	6.6
Zimbabwe	160	159	10	10	96	96	432.7	4,999.5	0.0	0.0	4	5	30	31	25.1	10.1
NORTH AFRICA	..	..	9	9	14	14	14.3	12.5	12.9	10.7	8	8	52	51	4.9	4.8
Algeria	134	136	14	14	24	24	10.8	12.1	36.6	31.0	14	11	51	47	7.5	7.1
Egypt, Arab Rep.	116	106	6	6	7	7	18.3	16.1	2.0	0.0	7	7	72	72	0.9	0.9
Libya	..	..	..	..	..	..	..	..	..	..	..	..	..	..	..	..
Morocco	130	128	6	6	12	12	20.0	16.1	13.1	11.8	8	8	47	47	4.9	4.9
Tunisia	73	69	10	10	11	11	7.9	5.7	0.0	0.0	4	4	39	39	6.1	6.1

(continued)

Table 4.1 Doing Business indicators (continued)

	Enforcing contracts						Dealing with construction permits						Protecting investors (0 least protection to 10 most protection)			
	Number of procedures		Time required (days)		Cost (% of debt)		Number of procedures		Time required (days)		Cost (% of GNI per capita)		Disclosure index		Director liability index	
	2009	2010	2009	2010	2009	2010	2009	2010	2009	2010	2009	2010	2009	2010	2009	2010
SUB-SAHARAN AFRICA	**39**	**39**	**669**	**656**	**48.7**	**48.9**	**17**	**17**	**266**	**259**	**2,603.9**	**2,148.9**	**5**	**5**	**3**	**3**
Angola	46	46	1,011	1,011	44.4	44.4	12	12	328	328	831.1	597.7	5	5	6	6
Benin	42	42	825	825	64.7	64.7	15	15	410	410	303.6	254.4	6	6	1	1
Botswana	29	29	987	687	28.0	28.0	24	24	167	167	311.9	246.2	7	7	8	8
Burkina Faso	37	37	446	446	85.6	83.0	15	15	214	132	931.1	721.2	6	6	1	1
Burundi	44	44	832	832	38.6	38.6	22	22	212	212	11,303.8	7,968.2	4	4	1	1
Cameroon	43	43	800	800	46.6	46.6	15	15	426	426	1,277.2	1,242.5	6	6	1	1
Cape Verde	37	37	425	425	21.8	21.8	18	18	120	120	639.1	523.3	1	1	5	5
Central African Republic	43	43	660	660	82.0	82.0	21	21	239	239	278.9	275.2	6	6	1	1
Chad	41	41	743	743	77.4	77.4	9	9	181	181	974.7	985.9	6	6	1	1
Comoros	43	43	506	506	89.4	89.4	18	18	164	164	77.9	72.6	6	6	1	1
Congo, Dem. Rep.	43	43	645	625	151.8	151.8	14	14	322	322	1,725.8	1,485.1	3	3	3	3
Congo, Rep.	44	44	560	560	53.2	53.2	14	14	169	169	345.6	265.6	6	6	1	1
Côte d'Ivoire	33	33	770	770	41.7	41.7	21	22	628	629	243.3	230.9	6	6	1	1
Djibouti	40	40	1,225	1,225	34.0	34.0	14	14	195	195	982.8	948.3	5	5	2	2
Equatorial Guinea	40	40	553	553	18.5	18.5	18	18	201	201	159.4	128.4	6	6	1	1
Eritrea	39	39	405	405	22.6	22.6	..	..	..	..	..	..	4	4	5	5
Ethiopia	38	37	690	620	15.2	15.2	12	12	128	128	790.7	561.3	4	4	4	4
Gabon	38	38	1,070	1,070	34.3	34.3	16	16	210	210	39.4	34.5	6	6	1	1
Gambia, The	32	32	434	434	37.9	37.9	17	17	146	146	394.0	336.4	2	2	1	1
Ghana	36	36	487	487	23.0	23.0	18	18	220	220	1,281.6	10,999.0	7	7	5	5
Guinea	50	50	276	276	45.0	45.0	32	32	255	255	243.0	249.6	6	6	1	1
Guinea-Bissau	41	41	1,140	1,140	25.0	25.0	15	15	167	167	2,628.8	2,020.0	6	6	1	1
Kenya	40	40	465	465	34.2	47.2	10	11	125	120	46.3	161.7	3	3	2	2
Lesotho	41	41	695	695	19.5	19.5	15	15	601	601	817.1	670.4	2	2	1	1
Liberia	41	41	1,280	1,280	35.0	35.0	25	24	321	77	60,988.7	28,295.9	4	4	1	1
Madagascar	38	38	871	871	42.4	42.4	16	16	178	178	764.8	630.7	5	5	6	6
Malawi	42	42	432	432	142.4	142.4	21	21	213	213	1,289.2	1,094.8	4	4	7	7
Mali	39	36	710	626	52.0	52.0	14	14	215	185	955.1	818.5	6	6	1	1
Mauritania	46	46	370	370	23.2	23.2	25	25	201	201	475.0	506.3	5	5	3	3
Mauritius	37	36	750	720	17.4	17.4	18	18	107	107	41.0	35.5	6	6	8	8
Mozambique	30	30	730	730	142.5	142.5	17	17	381	381	747.9	632.0	5	5	4	4
Namibia	33	33	270	270	35.8	35.8	12	12	139	139	181.8	124.7	5	5	5	5
Niger	39	39	545	545	59.6	59.6	17	17	265	265	2,694.0	2,355.0	6	6	1	1
Nigeria	39	39	457	457	32.0	32.0	18	18	350	350	693.4	573.4	5	5	7	7
Rwanda	24	24	310	260	78.7	78.7	14	14	210	210	607.1	456.1	2	7	5	9
São Tomé and Príncipe	43	43	1,185	1,185	50.5	50.5	13	13	255	255	740.5	631.4	3	3	1	1
Senegal	44	44	780	780	26.5	26.5	16	16	220	220	528.7	463.1	6	6	1	1
Seychelles	38	38	720	720	14.3	14.3	19	19	144	144	47.0	30.3	4	4	8	8
Sierra Leone	40	40	515	515	149.5	149.5	25	25	283	283	452.2	368.5	3	6	6	7
Somalia	..	..	..	..	..	..	..	..	..	..	..	..	..	..	..	..
South Africa	30	30	600	600	33.2	33.2	17	17	174	174	27.5	24.5	8	8	8	8
Sudan	53	53	810	810	19.8	19.8	19	19	271	271	240.3	206.4	0	0	6	6
Swaziland	40	40	972	972	23.1	23.1	13	13	93	93	94.9	91.8	0	0	1	1
Tanzania	38	38	462	462	14.3	14.3	21	22	308	328	2,087.0	3,281.3	3	3	4	4
Togo	41	41	588	588	47.5	47.5	15	15	277	277	1,400.1	1,285.3	6	6	1	1
Uganda	38	38	535	510	44.9	44.9	16	16	143	143	703.5	584.0	2	2	5	5
Zambia	35	35	471	471	38.7	38.7	17	17	254	254	1,023.1	912.7	3	3	6	6
Zimbabwe	38	38	410	410	32.0	32.0	19	19	1,426	1,426	16,368.8	24,468.3	8	8	1	1
NORTH AFRICA	**42**	**42**	**705**	**705**	**23.8**	**23.8**	**22**	**22**	**184**	**176**	**433.5**	**2,658.3**	**5**	**6**	**4**	**4**
Algeria	47	46	630	630	21.9	21.9	22	22	240	240	46.8	39.6	6	6	6	6
Egypt, Arab Rep.	42	41	1,010	1,010	26.2	26.2	28	25	249	218	376.7	331.6	8	8	3	3
Libya	..	..	..	..	..	..	..	..	..	..	..	..	..	..	..	..
Morocco	40	40	615	615	25.2	25.2	19	19	163	163	292.5	263.7	6	6	2	2
Tunisia	39	39	565	565	21.8	21.8	20	20	84	84	1,017.8	998.3	0	5	5	5

a. Average of the disclosure, director liability, and shareholder suits indexes.

b. Average of the rigidity of hours, difficulty of hiring, and difficulty of firing indexes.

Protecting investors (0 least protection to 10 most protection)				Employing workers (0 least rigid or difficult to 100 most rigid or difficult)									
Shareholder suits index		Investor protection index[a]		Rigidity of hours index		Difficulty of hiring index		Difficulty of firing index		Firing cost (weeks of wages)		Rigidity of employment index[b]	
2009	2010	2009	2010	2009	2010	2009	2010	2009	2010	2009	2010	2009	2010
5	5	4.3	4.4	30	30	38	38	40	40	68	67	36	36
6	6	5.7	5.7	60	60	67	67	70	70	58	58	66	66
3	3	3.3	3.3	40	40	39	39	40	40	36	36	40	40
3	3	6.0	6.0	0	0	0	0	40	40	90	90	13	13
4	4	3.7	3.7	20	20	33	33	10	10	34	34	21	21
5	5	3.3	3.3	53	53	0	0	30	30	26	26	28	28
6	6	4.3	4.3	20	20	28	28	70	70	33	33	39	39
6	6	4.0	4.0	33	33	33	33	70	70	93	93	46	46
5	5	4.0	4.0	40	40	61	61	50	50	22	22	50	50
5	5	4.0	4.0	20	20	39	39	40	40	36	36	33	33
5	5	4.0	4.0	40	40	39	39	40	40	100	100	40	40
4	4	3.3	3.3	47	47	50	72	70	70	31	31	56	63
3	3	3.3	3.3	40	40	78	78	70	70	33	33	63	63
3	3	3.3	3.3	47	47	33	33	20	20	49	49	33	33
0	0	2.3	2.3	40	40	67	67	30	30	56	56	46	46
4	4	3.7	3.7	60	60	67	67	70	70	133	133	66	66
5	5	4.7	4.7	40	40	0	0	20	20	69	69	20	20
5	5	4.3	4.3	20	20	33	33	30	30	40	40	28	28
3	3	3.3	3.3	60	60	17	17	80	80	43	43	52	52
5	5	2.7	2.7	40	40	0	0	40	40	26	26	27	27
6	6	6.0	6.0	20	20	11	11	50	50	178	178	27	27
1	1	2.7	2.7	20	20	33	33	20	20	26	26	24	24
5	5	4.0	4.0	27	27	67	67	70	70	87	87	54	54
10	10	5.0	5.0	0	0	22	22	30	30	47	47	17	17
8	8	3.7	3.7	20	20	22	22	0	0	44	44	14	14
6	6	3.7	3.7	20	20	22	22	40	40	84	84	27	27
6	6	5.7	5.7	40	40	89	89	40	40	30	30	56	56
5	5	5.3	5.3	0	0	44	44	20	20	84	84	21	21
3	4	3.3	3.7	20	20	33	33	40	40	31	31	31	31
3	3	3.7	3.7	20	20	56	56	40	40	31	31	39	39
9	9	7.7	7.7	13	33	0	0	40	20	35	4	18	18
9	9	6.0	6.0	33	33	67	67	20	20	134	134	40	40
6	6	5.3	5.3	20	20	0	0	20	20	24	24	13	13
3	3	3.3	3.3	53	53	100	100	50	50	35	35	68	68
5	5	5.7	5.7	0	0	0	0	20	20	50	50	7	7
1	3	2.7	6.3	40	0	44	11	30	10	26	26	38	7
6	6	3.3	3.3	67	67	50	50	60	60	91	91	59	59
2	2	3.0	3.0	53	53	72	72	50	50	38	38	59	59
5	5	5.7	5.7	13	13	44	44	50	50	39	39	36	36
8	6	5.7	6.3	40	40	33	33	50	50	189	189	41	41
..	..	..	..	..	..	..	..	..	..	..	..	..	..
8	8	8.0	8.0	20	20	56	56	30	30	24	24	35	35
4	4	3.3	3.3	20	20	39	39	50	50	118	118	36	36
5	5	2.0	2.0	0	0	11	11	20	20	53	53	10	10
8	8	5.0	5.0	13	13	100	100	50	50	18	18	54	54
4	4	3.7	3.7	40	40	61	83	40	40	36	36	47	54
5	5	4.0	4.0	0	0	0	0	0	0	13	13	0	0
7	7	5.3	5.3	33	33	22	11	20	20	178	178	25	21
4	4	4.3	4.3	40	40	0	0	60	60	446	446	33	33
4	4	4.3	4.7	28	28	43	40	58	58	63	63	43	42
4	4	5.3	5.3	40	40	44	44	40	40	17	17	41	41
5	5	5.3	5.3	20	20	0	0	60	60	132	132	27	27
..	..	..	..	..	..	..	..	..	..	..	..	..	..
1	1	3.0	3.0	40	40	100	89	50	50	85	85	63	60
6	6	3.7	5.3	13	13	28	28	80	80	17	17	40	40

Table 4.2 Investment climate

	Private sector fixed capital formation (% of GDP)	Net foreign direct investment ($ millions)	Domestic credit to private sector (% of GDP)	Enterprise Surveys: Firms that believe the court system is fair, impartial, and uncorrupt (%)	Viewed by firms as a major constraint (% of firms): Corruption	Crime, theft, and discord	Tax rates	Finance	Electricity	Labor regulations	Labor skills	Transportation	Customs and trade regulations
	2008[a]	2007–08[b]	2008[a]	2007–09[b]	2007–09[b]	2007–09[b]	2007–09[b]	2007–09[b]	2007–09[b]	2007–09[b]	2007–09[b]	2007–09[b]	2007–09[b]
SUB-SAHARAN AFRICA	12.9		39.4										
Angola	1.8	–1,805.1	12.7	..	..	..	..	..	..	..	..	..	..
Benin	..	..	20.9	..	..	..	..	..	..	..	..	..	..
Botswana	18.6	–32.3	22.0	..	..	..	..	..	..	..	..	..	..
Burkina Faso	..	..	18.6	..	..	..	..	..	..	..	..	..	..
Burundi	..	0.5	21.5	..	..	..	..	..	..	..	..	..	..
Cameroon	14.3	589.2	10.4	..	..	..	..	..	..	..	..	..	..
Cape Verde	33.7	191.5	54.1	..	..	..	..	..	..	..	..	..	..
Central African Republic	6.6	..	7.0	..	..	..	..	..	..	..	..	..	..
Chad	6.4	..	3.7	..	..	..	..	..	..	..	..	..	..
Comoros	8.1	..	11.5	..	..	..	..	..	..	..	..	..	..
Congo, Dem. Rep.	10.1	..	..	..	..	..	..	..	..	..	..	..	..
Congo, Rep.	..	2,638.4	3.5	32.3	65.0	44.1	40.9	44.8	71.1	24.5	51.5	48.4	45.9
Côte d'Ivoire	7.1	426.9	16.3	35.3	75.0	53.8	30.5	66.6	39.8	6.1	26.7	38.2	19.4
Djibouti	..	195.4	27.8	..	..	..	..	..	..	..	..	..	..
Equatorial Guinea	11.4	..	4.4	..	..	..	..	..	..	..	..	..	..
Eritrea	..	..	..	..	..	..	..	..	..	..	..	..	..
Ethiopia	5.9	222.0	..	..	..	..	..	..	..	..	..	..	..
Gabon	23.0	..	8.6	41.3	41.4	34.1	30.9	30.4	58.0	16.4	42.7	48.8	35.1
Gambia, The	..	68.5	..	..	..	..	..	..	..	..	..	..	..
Ghana	18.1	970.4	..	59.8	38.8	0.9	30.6	66.2	86.2	1.7	4.6	17.6	9.8
Guinea	9.9	385.9	..	..	..	..	..	..	..	..	..	..	..
Guinea-Bissau	10.6	..	9.1	..	..	..	..	..	..	..	..	..	..
Kenya	20.4	691.7	26.4	22.3	79.2	3.9	58.2	41.8	27.6	4.3	3.3	30.6	23.6
Lesotho	17.5	130.3	10.9	33.2	46.7	33.5	47.1	28.6	44.3	11.3	16.5	19.8	21.7
Liberia	..	131.6	..	44.3	31.2	26.8	19.0	35.0	59.1	2.6	5.1	39.3	15.6
Madagascar	25.9	..	11.1	28.8	42.7	48.1	40.8	39.4	54.6	2.2	17.0	26.6	18.7
Malawi	20.7	..	..	..	..	..	..	..	..	..	..	..	..
Mali	..	65.5	17.1	49.6	28.9	0.6	54.0	60.4	55.7	1.9	8.0	20.1	8.2
Mauritania	..	..	..	..	..	..	..	..	..	..	..	..	..
Mauritius	19.5	325.3	93.6	63.6	50.7	41.5	25.1	46.3	42.9	8.8	45.7	45.8	17.7
Mozambique	7.1	587.0	18.7	16.6	14.8	1.8	30.8	50.1	24.8	6.0	18.8	23.0	12.2
Namibia	15.8	718.5	47.1	..	..	..	..	..	..	..	..	..	..
Niger	..	..	11.0	..	..	..	..	..	..	..	..	..	..
Nigeria	..	5,618.7	33.1	53.5	40.9	4.1	20.9	53.1	75.9	4.0	6.3	28.1	5.0
Rwanda	10.7	80.1	..	..	..	..	..	..	..	..	..	..	..
São Tomé and Príncipe	..	32.2	28.3	..	..	..	..	..	..	..	..	..	..
Senegal	20.2	272.7	24.2	55.4	18.1	0.5	40.5	49.2	57.7	4.8	9.5	27.4	15.1
Seychelles	24.6	240.8	38.3	..	..	..	..	..	..	..	..	..	..
Sierra Leone	11.0	94.5	7.1	29.7	36.9	14.2	42.5	34.6	53.4	11.4	16.0	29.9	26.9
Somalia	..	..	..	..	..	..	..	..	..	..	..	..	..
South Africa	19.4	11,936.5	79.6	59.6	15.1	1.0	4.6	15.5	20.8	5.9	8.7	3.9	1.9
Sudan	12.8	2,425.6	10.9	..	..	..	..	..	..	..	..	..	..
Swaziland	15.0	14.3	25.6	..	..	..	..	..	..	..	..	..	..
Tanzania	..	647.0	16.3	..	..	..	..	..	..	..	..	..	..
Togo	..	..	19.2	..	..	..	..	..	..	..	..	..	..
Uganda	17.9	787.4	14.1	..	..	..	..	..	..	..	..	..	..
Zambia	15.5	983.9	15.3	55.0	14.8	1.0	25.5	20.1	11.9	5.9	8.0	10.6	9.8
Zimbabwe	..	..	..	..	..	..	..	..	..	..	..	..	..
NORTH AFRICA	23.9	18,544.3	34.4										
Algeria	27.9	..	12.9	..	64.7	0.9	46.7	50.1	48.1	13.8	36.8	24.7	36.1
Egypt, Arab Rep.	20.2	10,913.3	42.8	..	7.3	0.0	49.5	25.0	19.8	27.1	30.6	5.2	23.5
Libya	..	3,921.8	6.3	..	..	..	..	..	..	..	..	..	..
Morocco	27.5	2,193.8	79.5	43.5	13.4	0.0	55.7	31.6	37.0	15.8	31.0	8.2	14.3
Tunisia	..	1,515.3	66.6	..	..	..	..	..	..	..	..	..	..

a. Provisional.
b. Data are for the most recent year available during the period specified.

Enterprise Surveys										
Regulation and tax administration					Average time to clear customs (days)					
Number of tax payments 2010	Time to prepare, file, and pay taxes (hours) 2010	Total tax rate (% of profit) 2010	Highest marginal tax rate, corporate (%) 2007–09[b]	Time dealing with officials (% of management time) 2007–09[b]	Direct exports 2007–09[b]	Imports 2007–09[b]	Interest rate spread (lending rate minus deposit rate) 2008[a]	Listed domestic companies 2008	Market capitalization of listed companies (% of GDP) 2008[a]	Turnover ratio for traded stocks (%) 2008[a]
38	**302**	**66.8**			**10.1**	**15.9**				
31	272	53.2	..	..	..	..	6.1	..	..	..
55	270	73.3	..	..	..	..	..	..	..	..
19	140	17.1	15.0	..	..	..	7.9	19	27.4	3.1
46	270	44.9	..	..	..	..	..	..	..	..
32	140	278.6	..	..	..	..	..	..	..	..
41	1,400	50.5	..	..	..	..	..	..	..	..
56	100	49.7	..	..	..	..	6.2	..	..	..
54	504	203.8	..	..	..	..	..	..	..	..
54	122	60.9	..	..	..	..	..	..	..	..
20	100	41.1	..	..	..	..	4.5	..	..	..
32	308	322.0	..	..	..	..	..	..	..	..
61	606	65.5	..	6.0	..	31.4	..	..	..	..
66	270	44.7	35.0	1.8	16.6	31.2	..	38	30.2	4.1
35	114	38.7	..	..	..	..	..	..	..	..
46	296	59.5	..	..	..	..	..	..	..	..
18	216	84.5	..	..	..	..	..	..	..	..
19	198	31.1	30.0	..	..	..	..	..	..	..
26	272	44.7	..	2.8	3.8	10.3	..	..	..	..
50	376	292.4	..	..	..	..	..	..	..	..
33	224	32.7	22.0	4.0	6.8	6.8	..	35	21.1	5.2
56	416	49.9	..	..	..	..	..	..	..	..
46	208	45.9	..	..	..	..	..	..	..	..
41	417	49.7	..	5.1	12.0	12.0	8.7	53	31.6	11.8
21	324	18.5	..	5.6	5.4	4.4	8.5	..	..	..
32	158	43.7	..	7.5	..	6.7	..	..	..	..
23	201	39.2	..	17.1	14.2	19.3	33.5	..	..	..
19	157	25.8	..	..	..	..	..	14	41.5	3.9
58	270	52.1	..	2.4	9.1	9.1	..	..	..	..
38	696	86.1	..	..	..	..	..	..	..	..
7	161	22.9	15.0	9.4	10.3	11.7	11.4	41	39.8	8.9
37	230	34.3	32.0	3.3	10.4	10.4	7.3	..	..	..
37	375	9.6	..	..	..	..	5.4	7	7.2	2.8
41	270	46.5	..	..	..	..	..	..	..	..
35	938	32.2	..	6.1	12.8	12.8	3.5	213	23.5	29.3
34	160	31.3	..	..	..	..	..	..	..	..
42	424	47.2	..	..	..	..	19.7	..	..	..
59	666	46.0	..	2.9	8.9	8.9	..	..	..	..
16	76	44.1	..	..	..	..	7.8	..	..	..
29	357	235.6	..	7.4	..	12.2	14.8	..	..	..
..	..	..	..	..	..	..	..	..	..	..
9	200	30.2	28.0	6.0	5.9	5.9	3.5	425	177.5	60.6
42	180	36.1	..	..	..	..	..	..	..	..
33	104	36.6	..	..	..	..	6.7	7	..	..
48	172	45.2	30.0	..	..	..	6.9	7	6.3	..
53	270	52.7	..	..	..	..	..	..	..	..
32	161	35.7	30.0	..	..	..	..	6	..	..
37	132	16.1	..	4.6	6.6	6.6	12.5	..	..	..
51	270	39.4	..	..	..	..	..	81	..	..
28	**379**	**54.9**			**9.8**	**9.8**	**5.7**			
34	451	72.0	..	..	16.8	16.8	6.3	..	..	..
29	480	43.0	20.0	0.0	8.7	8.7	5.7	373	52.7	61.9
..	..	..	..	..	..	..	3.5	..	..	..
28	358	41.7	..	11.4	3.8	3.8	..	77	76.2	31.1
22	228	62.8	..	..	..	..	..	49	15.9	25.5

Table 4.3 Financial sector infrastructure

	Macroeconomy							
	Foreign currency sovereign ratings		Gross national savings (% of GDP)		Money and quasi money (M2) (% of GDP)		Real interest rate (%)	
	Long-term 2009	Short-term 2009	2007	2008[b]	2007	2008[b]	2007	2008[b]
SUB-SAHARAN AFRICA			9.8	4.3	37.4	37.8		
Angola	..	..	32.8	47.4	16.2	18.1	13.0	-6.3
Benin	B	B	..	..	30.7	32.9	..	..
Botswana	..	..	55.6	54.8	37.5	40.6	2.9	-0.5
Burkina Faso	..	..	..	..	21.3	22.8	..	..
Burundi	..	..	..	..	34.7	34.4	7.9	-6.4
Cameroon	B	B	19.6	20.2	18.1	19.6	12.7	..
Cape Verde	B+	B	26.0	26.8	77.2	75.4	7.1	4.3
Central African Republic	..	..	4.5	4.0	14.7	14.5	12.8	..
Chad	..	..	20.3	7.8	11.8	11.8	13.0	..
Comoros	..	..	9.1	11.2	25.6	26.7	5.1	1.4
Congo, Dem. Rep.	..	..	8.3	0.2	10.4	..	..	..
Congo, Rep.	..	..	..	..	18.9	17.7	24.9	..
Côte d'Ivoire	..	..	7.9	9.6	27.0	27.8	..	..
Djibouti	..	..	..	..	78.0	83.7	7.9	..
Equatorial Guinea	..	..	38.7	35.7	6.4	6.2	16.4	..
Eritrea	..	..	..	..	115.8	..	..	..
Ethiopia	..	..	20.5	16.5	25.3	..	..	..
Gabon	BB-	B	39.6	48.7	18.2	16.9	9.3	..
Gambia, The	..	..	10.6	10.8	50.1	..	21.0	..
Ghana	B+	B	23.6	19.6	..	..	..	..
Guinea	..	..	8.7	9.2	..	..	..	..
Guinea-Bissau	..	..	34.4	22.9	33.9	38.4	..	..
Kenya	B+	B	17.2	17.6	39.1	35.0	8.3	-10.2
Lesotho	..	..	39.1	24.8	32.2	33.4	4.6	6.0
Liberia	..	..	-14.7	..	23.1	..	-0.8	..
Madagascar	..	..	14.0	12.4	20.6	20.5	32.2	32.3
Malawi	..	..	9.4	9.1	14.8	..	18.9	..
Mali	..	..	25.7	..	29.1	25.7	..	..
Mauritania	..	..	29.2	..	..	..	26.7	..
Mauritius	..	..	19.8	22.7	101.3	102.8	13.9	12.9
Mozambique	..	..	9.3	10.4	28.1	31.0	11.3	11.0
Namibia	..	..	29.3	24.8	38.5	38.2	3.2	1.6
Niger	..	..	..	..	15.7	15.7	..	..
Nigeria	BB-	B	..	..	22.5	29.4	11.6	0.9
Rwanda	B-	B	15.8	13.0	..	..	4.8	..
São Tomé and Príncipe	..	..	..	..	38.6	34.2	10.9	7.0
Senegal	..	..	19.1	17.9	34.3	33.4	..	..
Seychelles	..	..	-3.3	2.7	79.2	66.6	3.9	-10.8
Sierra Leone	..	..	9.6	14.1	19.7	20.6	13.3	11.5
Somalia	..	..	..	..	..	..	..	..
South Africa	BBB+	F2	14.0	14.0	62.5	64.3	3.8	3.9
Sudan	..	..	11.9	15.4	20.2	18.2	..	..
Swaziland	..	..	18.2	30.5	23.6	26.3	3.9	11.1
Tanzania	..	..	..	..	27.2	27.9	6.5	5.6
Togo	..	..	..	..	34.8	38.8	..	..
Uganda	B	B	13.8	12.0	19.0	20.7	11.0	..
Zambia	..	..	22.9	19.8	20.5	21.6	6.3	7.5
Zimbabwe	..	..	..	..	..	..	..	..
NORTH AFRICA			14.5	..	69.4	65.6		
Algeria	..	..	56.8	71.6	54.7	53.9	1.1	-7.8
Egypt, Arab Rep.	..	..	26.3	23.6	88.5	84.2	-0.1	0.0
Libya	BBB+	F2	..	..	30.4	26.4	0.6	-31.8
Morocco	BBB-	F3	32.4	34.4	97.5	101.3	..	..
Tunisia	..	..	22.6	16.7	59.2	61.0	..	..

a. Data are consolidated for regional security markets where they exist.
b. Provisional.

Intermediation						Capital markets[a]					
Domestic credit to private sector (% of GDP)		Interest rate spread (lending rate minus deposit rate)		Ratio of bank non-performing loans to total gross loans (%)		Listed domestic companies		Market capitalization of listed companies (% of GDP)		Turnover ratio for traded stocks (%)	
2007	2008[b]	2007	2008[b]	2007	2008[b]	2007	2008	2007	2008[b]	2007	2008[b]
69.6	39.4										
10.5	12.7	10.9	6.1	..	..	..	..	..	..	..	..
20.0	20.9	..	..	..	..	..	..	..	..	..	..
20.1	22.0	7.6	7.9	..	..	18	19	47.8	27.4	2.2	3.1
16.8	18.6	..	..	..	..	..	..	..	..	..	..
23.4	21.5	..	..	..	..	..	..	..	..	..	..
9.2	10.4	10.8	..	..	..	..	..	..	..	..	..
47.7	54.1	7.3	6.2	..	..	..	..	..	..	..	..
6.7	7.0	10.8	..	..	..	..	..	..	..	..	..
2.9	3.7	10.8	..	..	..	..	..	..	..	..	..
9.7	11.5	8.0	4.5	..	..	..	..	..	..	..	..
3.7	..	..	..	..	..	..	..	..	..	..	..
2.5	3.5	10.8	..	..	..	..	..	..	..	..	..
16.1	16.3	..	..	..	..	38	38	42.2	30.2	2.5	4.1
23.4	27.8	8.1	..	..	..	..	..	..	..	..	..
2.9	4.4	10.8	..	..	..	..	..	..	..	..	..
25.6	..	..	..	..	..	..	..	..	..	..	..
..	..	..	..	..	..	..	..	..	..	..	..
12.0	8.6	10.8	..	7.6	..	..	..	..	..	..	..
16.2	..	15.0	..	..	..	..	..	..	..	..	..
..	..	..	..	6.4	..	32	35	15.9	21.1	3.9	5.2
..	..	..	..	..	..	..	..	..	..	..	..
5.7	9.1	..	..	..	..	..	..	..	..	..	..
27.2	26.4	8.2	8.7	22.7	..	51	53	49.7	31.6	10.6	11.8
10.1	10.9	7.7	8.5	3.0	..	..	..	..	..	..	..
10.0	..	11.3	..	..	..	..	..	..	..	..	..
10.2	11.1	28.5	33.5	..	..	..	..	..	..	..	..
10.5	..	21.7	..	..	..	9	14	..	41.5	..	3.9
18.9	17.1	..	..	..	..	..	..	..	..	..	..
..	..	15.5	..	..	..	..	..	..	..	..	..
83.5	93.6	10.1	11.4	..	..	90	41	83.5	39.8	8.0	8.9
13.5	18.7	7.7	7.3	2.6	..	..	..	..	..	..	..
50.4	47.1	5.3	5.4	2.8	..	9	7	8.1	7.2	3.7	2.8
9.4	11.0	..	..	..	..	..	..	..	..	..	..
25.3	33.1	6.7	3.5	8.4	..	212	213	52.0	23.5	28.2	29.3
..	..	9.1	..	..	..	..	..	..	..	..	..
31.6	28.3	19.7	19.7	..	..	..	..	..	..	..	..
22.7	24.2	..	..	18.6	..	..	..	..	..	..	..
32.5	38.3	7.8	7.8	..	..	..	..	..	..	..	..
5.3	7.1	15.0	14.8	31.7	..	..	..	..	..	..	..
..	..	..	..	..	..	..	..	..	..	..	..
163.9	79.6	4.0	3.5	1.4	..	422	425	293.8	177.5	55.0	60.6
12.6	10.9	..	..	..	..	..	..	..	..	..	..
25.4	25.6	6.1	6.7	4.0	..	6	7	7.0	..	..	..
14.9	16.3	7.4	6.9	..	..	7	7	..	6.3	..	..
21.3	19.2	..	..	..	..	..	..	..	..	..	..
10.5	14.1	9.8	..	4.1	..	..	6	..	..	..	..
11.9	15.3	9.7	12.5	..	..	15	..	20.6	..	4.1	..
..	..	457.5	..	..	..	82	81	..	..	5.1	..
37.7	34.4										
13.4	12.9	6.3	6.3	..	..	..	..	..	..	..	..
50.6	42.8	6.4	5.7	..	..	435	373	106.8	52.7	45.6	61.9
7.2	6.3	3.5	3.5	..	..	..	..	..	..	..	..
69.9	79.5	..	..	7.9	..	74	77	100.5	76.2	42.1	31.1
64.3	66.6	..	..	17.3	..	50	49	15.3	15.9	13.3	25.5

Table 5.1 International trade and tariff barriers

	Trade											
								Average (% of GDP)		Annual growth (%)		
	Total (% of GDP) 2008[a]	Merchandise (% of GDP) 2008[a]	Services (% of GDP) 2007–08[a]	Exports of goods and services ($ millions) 2008[a]	Imports of goods and services ($ millions) 2008[a]	Exports of goods and services (% of GDP) 2008[a]	Imports of goods and services (% of GDP) 2008[a]	Exports of goods and services 2007–08[a]	Imports of goods and services 2007–08[a]	Exports of goods and services 2008[a]	Imports of goods and services 2008[a]	Terms of trade index (2000=100) 2008[a]
SUB-SAHARAN AFRICA	76.9	65.4	13.6	413,690	372,119	41.9	37.7	35.3	33.8	..	6.5	
Angola	128.7	104.8	21.9	74,618	32,731	89.5	39.3	77.3	53.8	..	..	..
Benin	..	45.5	..	..	..	..	..	14.1	27	..	..	..
Botswana	86.8	78.8	15.5	5,928	5,333	45.7	41.1	47.7	34.4	2.5	1.1	69.3
Burkina Faso	..	30.4	..	..	..	..	..	9.7	24	..	..	..
Burundi	..	39.5	21.2	..	..	..	..	8.7	31	..	..	..
Cameroon	57.4	37.2	10.1	6,837	6,587	29.2	28.2	22.2	21.7	24.6	1.4	140.6
Cape Verde	74.6	49.6	54.3	345	945	19.9	54.7	23.5	58.2	13.0	1.1	58.7
Central African Republic	37.5	25.1	..	284	455	14.4	23.1	14.9	21.3	6.9	1.1	72.5
Chad	77.7	77.7	..	3,677	2,823	44	33.8	36.6	50.5	–11.7	1.0	100.0
Comoros	49.7	38.7	..	68	196	12.8	36.9	13.9	33.7	8.5	1.0	100.0
Congo, Dem. Rep.	56.6	69.5	..	2,693	3,863	23.2	33.3	25.4	32.2	5.7	1.1	134.5
Congo, Rep.	..	111.2	50.3	..	..	..	..	80.9	49.7	..	..	..
Côte d'Ivoire	97.3	73.7	17.1	11,953	10,838	51.1	46.3	47.6	38.6	7.4	1.0	76.8
Djibouti	..	74.2	43.6	..	..	..	..	41	54	..	..	..
Equatorial Guinea	110.4	118.7	..	14,498	5,953	78.3	32.1	91.2	55.6	..	..	..
Eritrea	..	33.3	..	..	..	..	..	9	61	..	..	..
Ethiopia	40.2	34.4	16.1	3,074	7,577	11.6	28.6	13.1	29.6	3.1	1.1	82.9
Gabon	115.5	75.5	..	11,151	5,517	77.2	38.2	63.4	33	–0.2	1.1	185.7
Gambia, The	79.1	43.9	29.7	235	383	30.1	49	39.9	54.1	8.8	1.0	71.2
Ghana	100	99.5	25.5	5,940	10,188	36.8	63.2	39.5	60.6	4.7	1.1	107.9
Guinea	57.9	68.0	7.5	1,187	1,281	27.8	30	27.2	30.1	7.7	1.1	90.2
Guinea-Bissau	79.6	60.1	..	128	214	29.8	49.8	28.9	48.8	..	..	..
Kenya	63.9	46.5	15.4	8,599	13,456	24.9	39	25.1	34.1	–4.2	1.1	119.9
Lesotho	158.1	180.6	11.2	767	1,796	47.3	110.8	49.4	105.1	–22.0	1.1	154.5
Liberia	..	129.5	216.4	..	..	..	..	29.2	50.1	..	..	..
Madagascar	78	60.0	..	2,363	4,630	26.3	51.6	27.2	39.2	2.9	1.2	89.1
Malawi	74.6	58.3	..	998	2,186	23.4	51.2	25.3	45.6	–5.4	1.0	142.9
Mali	..	48.1	16.8	..	..	..	..	28.6	39.8	..	..	..
Mauritania	..	122.5	..	..	..	..	..	40	67.7	..	..	..
Mauritius	131.5	80.9	51.6	5,331	6,044	61.6	69.9	60.4	62.9	5.4	1.0	86.0
Mozambique	74	68.8	15.4	3,114	4,091	32	42	30.4	42.4	6.8	1.1	69.7
Namibia	87	87.3	12.8	3,335	4,117	38.9	48.1	42.7	46.1	–47.5	0.5	99.7
Niger	..	42.4	..	..	..	..	..	16.4	25.3	..	..	..
Nigeria	73.9	58.3	9.5	92,201	64,469	43.5	30.4	43.2	32	..	..	..
Rwanda	35.6	30.5	13.2	360	1,228	8.1	27.5	9.1	26.6	..	..	..
São Tomé and Príncipe	..	60.4	15.8	..	..	..	..	..	..	..	..	..
Senegal	72.4	61.3	21.6	3,294	6,262	24.9	47.4	26.8	41.4	6.2	1.1	92.2
Seychelles	283.4	163.3	84.9	1,091	1,271	130.9	152.5	94	106.2	31.0	1.2	100.0
Sierra Leone	62	39.9	8.2	487	724	24.9	37.1	21.4	35.5	..	..	..
Somalia	..	..	..	..	..	..	..	..	..	..	..	..
South Africa	76.7	65.1	10.7	100,562	111,723	36.3	40.4	30.1	29.9	3.0	1.1	119.3
Sudan	44.8	37.0	7.2	13,292	12,883	22.7	22	16.8	22.2	23.0	1.0	100.0
Swaziland	160.4	152.4	33.2	2,101	2,098	80.2	80.1	88.1	93.1	6.4	1.0	133.0
Tanzania	..	47.9	18.9	..	..	..	..	19.2	26.2	..	..	..
Togo	107.9	82.5	..	1,142	1,905	40.4	67.5	36.5	55.2	..	..	..
Uganda	49	48.0	12.3	2,272	4,846	15.6	33.4	13.3	26.6	7.3	1.3	101.5
Zambia	71.1	71.0	10.5	5,267	4,909	36.8	34.3	33.6	38.7	20.7	1.2	108.1
Zimbabwe	..	..	..	..	..	..	..	32.1	37.3	..	..	..
NORTH AFRICA	..	66.0	20.9	261,135	207,611	46.4	36.9	35.5	30.3	..	16.7	
Algeria	83.6	67.5	..	102,773	42,597	59.1	24.5	43.7	23.5	5.0	1.1	188.8
Egypt, Arab Rep.	81.9	45.4	26.3	61,354	72,031	37.7	44.2	25.6	29.4	27.8	1.2	100.1
Libya	..	74.6	4.7	..	..	..	..	37.6	23.5	..	..	..
Morocco	90.7	71.5	23.4	35,089	43,188	40.6	50	32.1	37.3	5.1	1.1	99.1
Tunisia	133.5	109.3	22	26,186	27,451	65.2	68.3	49.7	52.8	8.0	1.1	96.5

Structure of merchandise exports (% of total)					Structure of merchandise imports (% of total)				
Food 2007	Agricultural raw materials 2007	Fuel 2007	Ores and metals 2007	Manufactures 2007	Food 2007	Agricultural raw materials 2007	Fuel 2007	Ores and metals 2007	Manufactures 2007
..	**..**	**..**	**..**	**..**	**9.9**	**1.1**	**17.8**	**2.5**	**64.2**
..	..	..	..	..	..	..	..	..	..
..	..	..	..	..	..	..	..	..	..
2.8	0.2	0.2	23.2	73.1	13.1	0.9	15.6	2.3	67.4
..	..	..	..	..	..	..	..	..	..
35.0	4.2	3.8	2.1	20.7	12.4	0.9	28.0	0.9	57.6
..	..	..	..	..	..	..	..	..	..
40.8	0.0	0.0	..	58.8	25.7	1.4	11.1	0.9	59.9
..	..	..	..	..	..	..	..	..	..
..	..	..	..	..	..	..	..	..	..
13.8	..	..	..	6.3	19.5	0.2	0.8	0.2	53.4
..	..	..	..	..	..	..	..	..	..
..	..	..	..	..	..	..	..	..	..
39.5	8.8	32.6	0.4	18.1	17.4	0.6	30.2	1.4	48.8
..	..	..	..	..	..	..	..	..	..
..	..	..	..	..	..	..	..	..	..
..	..	..	..	..	..	..	..	..	..
61.1	19.9	0.0	2.9	13.4	7.0	0.9	13.3	1.4	77.3
..	..	..	..	..	..	..	..	..	..
81.6	6.2	..	0.5	11.7	31.1	1.9	16.9	1.0	49.1
46.6	4.9	0.6	2.4	10.5	14.5	1.1	1.6	1.6	81.1
..	..	..	..	..	..	..	..	..	..
..	..	..	..	..	..	..	..	..	..
42.8	11.9	4.3	2.8	36.8	11.0	1.9	21.3	2.2	62.4
..	..	..	..	..	..	..	..	..	..
..	..	..	..	..	..	..	..	..	..
31.5	3.4	4.7	3.3	56.8	14.6	1.0	16.6	0.3	67.0
85.6	3.8	0.0	0.0	10.6	10.6	1.0	13.8	0.7	73.9
7.0	13.8	0.5	0.2	3.2	14.8	0.5	22.2	0.5	61.8
..	..	..	..	..	..	..	..	..	..
31.1	0.6	0.1	0.8	67.1	18.8	2.5	18.3	1.1	57.6
11.1	2.8	15.5	64.0	5.8	17.8	0.9	16.2	0.3	46.8
23.6	0.5	0.4	34.5	39.1	15.4	0.6	10.3	0.8	72.5
14.3	2.6	1.5	63.3	5.6	23.6	4.7	17.0	1.4	52.9
..	..	..	..	..	..	..	..	..	..
44.5	4.6	0.0	46.3	4.6	13.7	1.8	8.6	2.8	73.1
..	..	..	..	..	..	..	..	..	..
36.8	2.9	19.3	4.1	36.1	25.1	1.5	26.6	1.3	45.5
97.8	0.0	0.0	0.0	2.2	22.1	1.2	25.3	0.4	48.3
..	..	..	..	..	..	..	..	..	..
..	..	..	..	..	..	..	..	..	..
6.6	2.1	10.6	29.3	50.7	5.2	1.0	18.6	3.3	64.7
..	..	..	..	..	5.3	0.3	0.3	0.3	93.2
21.1	7.2	1.2	0.5	69.8	21.2	1.0	15.6	1.0	60.9
35.0	6.8	0.6	12.6	16.6	11.7	0.8	29.9	1.3	55.4
15.7	9.3	0.0	12.8	62.2	14.6	1.1	27.0	2.3	54.9
62.2	7.6	1.3	2.2	20.8	12.5	1.0	18.7	1.2	62.9
7.5	1.2	0.5	77.7	12.5	5.2	0.4	12.3	4.8	76.1
16.3	11.4	0.6	19.2	48.3	10.6	3.8	18.0	6.2	54.4
6.0	**0.5**	**63.4**	**2.7**	**25.0**	**15.7**	**2.8**	**12.9**	**3.1**	**59.9**
0.2	0.0	98.4	0.5	0.9	19.8	2.3	1.1	1.9	74.9
7.9	1.6	52.2	2.8	18.6	19.5	3.7	14.7	3.5	42.4
..	..	..	..	..	..	..	..	..	..
19.1	1.5	3.8	10.3	65.1	12.3	2.6	20.0	3.5	61.4
9.5	0.5	16.2	1.4	69.8	9.8	2.2	12.8	3.4	70.7

(continued)

Table 5.1 International trade and tariff barriers (continued)

	Export indexes (0 low to 100 high)			Competitiveness indicator (%)		Tariff barriers, all products (%)								
	Diversification 2007	Concentration 2006	Destination 2006	Sectoral effect 2003–07	Global effect 2003–07	Binding coverage 2007	Simple mean bound rate 2007	Simple mean tariff 2007–08[a]	Dispersion around the mean 2007–08[a]	Weighted mean tariff 2007–08[a]	Share of lines with international peaks 2007–08[a]	Share of lines with domestic peaks 2007–08[a]	Share of lines that are bound 2007	Share of lines with specific rates 2007–08[a]
SUB-SAHARAN AFRICA	..	52.7	43.2			54.3	38.9	11.3	0.9	7.4	37.2	3.1	50.6	0.0
Angola	1.1	95.5	..	17.0	44.5	..	..	7.4	0.9	7.4	23.6	2.9	100.0	0.0
Benin	6.4	62.3	41.6	2.2	–22.0	..	..	13.7	0.6	16.6	52.7	0.0	39.3	0.0
Botswana	2.8	72.5	74.0	–9.9	–6.4	..	..	8.2	1.5	8.7	31.4	7.6	96.6	0.0
Burkina Faso	1.9	58.0	63.3	–9.7	11.1	..	..	12.4	0.6	9.2	44.6	0.0	39.2	0.0
Burundi	2.6	60.7	45.9	3.7	12.7	..	..	12.8	0.8	10.7	34.1	0.0	21.8	0.0
Cameroon	3.3	51.2	38.1	3.9	–4.1	..	..	18.6	0.6	12.5	52.6	0.0	13.3	0.0
Cape Verde	9.0	47.5	54.4	–8.2	21.4	..	..	13.8	1.2	12.2	45.6	14.7	..	0.0
Central African Republic	5.5	46.9	40.1	–7.4	–11.7	..	..	17.5	0.6	13.6	47.4	0.0	62.5	0.0
Chad	1.1	..	..	–4.8	589.7	..	..	17.0	0.6	13.6	44.8	0.0	13.5	0.0
Comoros	4.9	47.5	50.4	–31.4	14.8	..	..	8.1	0.6	6.6	45.2	0.0	..	0.0
Congo, Dem. Rep.	7.6	38.4	..	15.1	14.0	..	..	12.9	0.5	11.6	42.6	0.0	100.0	0.0
Congo, Rep.	1.4	86.9	..	–2.7	5.7	..	..	18.6	0.6	14.7	52.6	0.0	16.1	0.0
Côte d'Ivoire	7.7	..	..	–8.0	–4.9	..	..	12.7	..	10.3	45.2	0.0	..	0.0
Djibouti	5.9	19.1	..	–0.8	31.6	..	..	..	..	..	..	..	100.0	..
Equatorial Guinea	1.3	90.4	..	14.1	23.8	..	..	18.3	0.6	15.6	52.3	0.0	..	0.0
Eritrea	2.1	18.0	31.2	–5.7	190.3	..	..	..	..	..	..	..	..	..
Ethiopia	4.7	43.2	25.3	1.4	12.7	..	..	16.7	0.7	11.9	50.2	0.0	..	0.0
Gabon	1.9	83.7	60.3	13.2	–14.8	100.0	21.5	18.5	0.6	14.0	52.5	0.0	100.0	0.0
Gambia, The	6.6	50.6	58.3	–7.3	–5.8	..	..	18.7	0.2	14.7	90.9	0.0	13.7	0.0
Ghana	4.5	44.2	28.8	–5.1	0.0	..	..	13.0	0.5	9.8	40.8	0.0	14.3	0.0
Guinea	3.2	65.7	30.7	16.0	–19.9	..	..	13.9	0.6	12.5	57.7	0.0	38.9	0.0
Guinea-Bissau	1.2	74.9	..	–13.0	–6.1	..	..	14.0	0.6	14.0	55.0	0.0	97.8	0.0
Kenya	21.9	18.8	24.5	–3.7	–4.1	..	..	12.0	1.0	8.8	36.7	0.5	14.6	0.0
Lesotho	6.6	46.6	61.9	–14.6	5.5	..	..	8.8	1.5	13.7	35.2	5.4	100.0	0.0
Liberia	3.5	..	..	0.6	–18.9	..	..	..	..	..	..	..	..	..
Madagascar	21.2	19.6	45.3	–14.4	–2.3	30.5	27.3	12.1	0.6	8.3	41.1	0.0	29.7	0.0
Malawi	3.8	59.9	30.9	–9.2	4.8	..	..	10.5	0.8	8.1	39.9	0.0	31.2	0.0
Mali	2.0	73.9	24.1	–9.9	–8.9	..	..	12.6	0.6	10.1	44.5	0.0	40.6	0.0
Mauritania	3.9	74.0	36.0	17.8	10.3	..	..	12.6	0.6	10.1	49.0	0.0	39.3	0.0
Mauritius	13.4	28.3	39.4	–6.9	–8.5	17.7	98.3	3.4	2.6	2.3	14.0	14.7	17.8	0.0
Mozambique	3.5	57.4	61.9	–1.1	32.1	..	..	11.0	0.7	7.7	36.7	0.0	13.6	0.0
Namibia	9.1	30.0	37.6	6.8	24.8	..	..	6.5	1.5	1.1	25.8	7.2	96.6	0.0
Niger	1.4	47.2	46.1	21.5	2.1	96.6	44.8	12.8	0.6	7.1	47.0	0.0	96.8	0.0
Nigeria	1.3	85.2	41.9	16.4	8.5	..	..	10.7	0.7	8.9	33.5	3.4	19.2	0.0
Rwanda	4.1	54.4	50.2	14.9	–36.2	..	..	19.3	0.6	11.6	55.2	0.0	100.0	0.0
São Tomé and Príncipe	3.9	86.9	47.1	–9.8	–15.9	..	..	..	..	..	..	..	..	..
Senegal	22.3	24.7	29.9	–4.2	–2.9	..	..	13.0	0.6	10.1	47.7	0.0	100.0	0.0
Seychelles	3.9	62.8	53.2	–1.7	–18.4	..	..	6.5	4.3	28.3	12.8	12.8	..	0.0
Sierra Leone	7.3	53.9	97.4	–6.6	10.8	..	..	..	..	..	..	..	100.0	..
Somalia	6.6	..	..	–5.4	–2.1	..	..	..	..	..	..	..	..	..
South Africa	45.6	15.6	23.1	6.0	–1.9	96.1	19.4	7.9	1.6	4.7	25.8	7.3	96.6	0.0
Sudan	1.2	87.2	82.4	12.4	23.7	..	..	14.2	..	11.4	34.7	0.0	..	0.0
Swaziland	20.0	41.5	75.9	–5.8	1.1	..	..	9.7	1.5	7.9	36.4	8.8	96.6	0.0
Tanzania	30.1	35.3	24.9	–1.1	2.6	..	..	12.5	0.9	10.3	38.1	0.6	13.4	0.0
Togo	9.3	28.9	32.2	3.1	–32.3	..	..	13.6	0.6	13.6	50.9	0.0	14.0	0.0
Uganda	10.4	25.1	23.6	–3.8	5.5	..	..	12.6	1.0	10.6	38.8	0.5	15.8	0.0
Zambia	2.5	68.4	43.5	27.9	51.1	17.1	106.9	10.6	0.7	4.9	48.7	0.0	16.7	0.0
Zimbabwe	10.8	22.3	35.8	9.8	–22.5	22.2	93.4	..	1.8	..	..	..	21.0	..
NORTH AFRICA	..	..	..			..	..	..	..	..	..	..	..	..
Algeria	2.4	60.6	36.8	–0.4	15.8	..	..	16.3	0.6	9.5	60.7	0.0	..	0.0
Egypt, Arab Rep.	17.2	35.6	24.8	4.8	26.2	..	..	12.5	4.4	8.3	18.0	0.3	99.3	0.0
Libya	1.3	79.9	..	17.5	14.6	..	..	..	..	..	..	..	..	..
Morocco	67.3	15.9	37.1	–4.2	2.1	..	..	11.7	1.2	9.4	41.1	0.3	100.0	0.0
Tunisia	35.8	18.7	42.7	–4.2	5.3	..	..	..	..	..	..	..	57.6	..

a. Provisional.

b. Data are for the most recent year available during the period specified.

Tariff barriers, primary products (%)			Tariff barriers, manufactured products (%)			GATS commitments index (0 least liberal to 100 most liberal)	Average cost to ship 20 ft container from port to final destination ($)		Average time to clear customs (days)	
Simple mean tariff 2007–08[a]	Dispersion around the mean 2007–08[a]	Weighted mean tariff 2007–08[a]	Simple mean tariff 2007–08[a]	Dispersion around the mean 2007–08[a]	Weighted mean tariff 2007–08[a]	2008	Direct export 2010	Import 2010	Direct exports 2007–09[b]	Imports 2007–09[b]
12.4	0.9	5.9	11.1	0.9	7.9	11.1	1,918	2,909	10.1	15.9
11.9	0.9	14.4	6.7	1.0	5.8	4.4	2,250	3,240	..	..
16.5	0.6	13.2	13.3	0.6	17.6	6.2	1,251	1,400	..	..
3.2	1.7	0.7	8.5	1.6	9.2	4.4	2,810	3,264	..	..
14.8	0.6	12.8	12.2	0.6	8.3	3.2	2,262	3,830	..	..
11.7	0.8	7.9	12.9	0.8	11.3	35.4	2,747	4,285	..	..
21.9	0.6	10.8	18.2	0.6	14.4	3.1	1,250	2,002	..	..
16.2	1.2	13.0	13.2	1.3	11.7	..	1,325	1,129	..	..
18.9	0.6	13.9	17.3	0.6	13.2	2.5	5,491	5,554	..	..
20.6	0.6	18.3	16.5	0.6	12.7	2.7	5,497	6,150	..	..
4.0	0.5	3.0	9.1	0.5	9.5	..	1,073	1,057	..	..
14.1	0.5	12.1	12.7	0.5	11.4	11.2	2,607	2,483	..	..
21.9	0.6	18.6	18.2	0.6	14.1	2.2	2,490	2,959	..	31.4
15.2	..	10.7	12.3	..	10.1	..	1,969	2,577	16.6	31.2
..	..	..	..	..	..	4.8	836	911	..	..
21.5	0.6	21.4	17.8	0.6	14.3	..	1,411	1,411	..	..
..	..	..	..	..	..	..	1,431	1,581	..	..
19.7	0.6	11.8	16.4	0.7	11.9	..	1,940	29,993	..	..
21.1	0.6	15.2	18.1	0.6	13.7	6.3	1,945	1,955	3.8	10.3
17.0	0.2	12.2	19.2	0.2	17.4	51.7	831	922	..	..
16.8	0.4	14.4	12.5	0.6	8.8	13.9	1,013	1,203	6.8	6.8
15.4	0.6	14.0	13.7	0.6	11.2	4.8	855	1,391	..	..
16.5	0.6	16.9	13.5	0.6	12.5	2.4	1,545	2,349	..	..
16.9	1.1	8.4	11.5	1.0	9.0	3.2	2,055	2,190	12.0	12.0
6.0	1.7	4.9	9.0	1.5	14.1	47.3	1,549	1,715	5.4	4.4
..	..	..	..	..	..	..	1,232	1,212	..	6.7
13.9	0.7	4.2	11.9	0.6	10.4	0.4	1,279	1,660	14.2	19.3
13.8	0.8	10.3	10.0	0.8	7.5	14.7	1,713	2,570	..	..
15.2	0.6	11.2	12.2	0.6	9.9	3.0	2,075	2,955	9.1	9.1
11.2	0.7	9.2	12.8	0.6	11.0	3.3	1,520	1,523	..	..
5.4	3.4	3.4	3.0	2.9	1.9	9.2	737	689	10.3	11.7
13.9	0.8	8.0	10.5	0.7	7.5	5.0	1,100	1,475	10.4	10.4
3.6	1.7	0.6	6.9	1.6	1.3	3.9	1,686	1,813	..	..
15.2	0.6	5.8	12.4	0.6	9.7	2.3	3,545	3,545	..	..
12.3	0.7	9.6	10.5	0.8	8.1	10.8	1,263	1,440	12.8	12.8
17.1	0.6	8.8	19.5	0.6	12.6	5.6	3,275	5,070	..	..
..	..	..	..	..	..	..	690	577	..	..
14.9	0.6	9.3	12.8	0.6	11.0	19.8	1,098	1,940	8.9	8.9
14.0	8.6	50.5	4.8	4.0	6.4	..	1,839	1,839	..	..
..	..	..	..	..	..	27.5	1,573	1,639	..	12.2
..	..	..	..	..	..	..	..	..	..	..
5.2	1.8	1.7	8.2	1.7	6.1	53.4	1,531	1,807	5.9	5.9
18.0	..	11.6	13.7	..	11.3	..	2,050	2,900	..	..
9.8	1.7	3.1	9.7	1.5	8.7	8.2	2,184	2,249	..	..
18.5	1.1	12.0	11.9	1.0	9.8	1.0	1,262	1,475	..	..
16.0	0.6	9.3	13.3	0.6	17.3	4.0	940	963	..	..
19.3	1.1	20.4	11.9	1.0	9.4	3.2	3,190	3,390	..	..
8.0	0.6	5.7	10.8	0.8	4.4	14.2	2,664	3,335	6.6	6.6
..	1.0	..	..	1.9	..	6.9	3,280	5,101	..	..
..	..	..	..	..	..	..	867	1,027	9.8	9.8
17.0	0.6	8.8	16.2	0.6	9.8	..	1,248	1,428	16.8	16.8
36.2	11.6	6.3	9.5	1.3	9.8	10.9	737	823	8.7	8.7
..	..	..	..	..	..	..	..	..	..	..
19.3	2.3	11.4	10.9	1.1	8.2	15.4	700	1,000	3.8	3.8
..	..	..	..	..	..	5.5	783	858	..	..

Table 5.2 Top three exports and share in total exports, 2007

	First		Second	
	Product	Share of total exports (%)	Product	Share of total exports (%)
SUB-SAHARAN AFRICA				
Angola	Petroleum oils and oils from bituminous minerals, crude	96.7		
Benin	Cotton, not carded, combed	29.8	Petroleum oils and oils from bituminous minerals, noncrude	20.8
Botswana	Diamonds, not mounted or set	56.0	Nickel mattes	21.2
Burkina Faso	Cotton, not carded, combed	71.6	Sesamum seeds	4.3
Burundi	Coffee, not roasted, not decaffeinated	62.1	Black tea (fermented) and partly fermented tea in packages exceeding 3 kg	4.3
Cameroon	Petroleum oils and oils from bituminous minerals, crude	52.7	Wood sawn or chipped lengthwise, sliced or peeled, more than 6mm thick	9.1
Cape Verde	Fish, frozen, excluding fish fillets and other fish meat	25.4	Cotton, not carded, combed	12.9
Central African Republic	Wood in the rough or roughly squared	30.3	Diamonds, not mounted or set, unsorted	21.4
Chad	Petroleum oils and oils from bituminous minerals, crude	95.3	Cotton, not carded, combed	2.3
Comoros	Vessels and other floating structures for breaking up	31.0	Cloves (whole fruit, cloves and stems)	19.8
Congo, Dem. Rep.	Petroleum oils and oils from bituminous minerals, crude	83.2		
Congo, Rep.	Diamonds, not mounted or set	24.6	Petroleum oils and oils from bituminous minerals, crude	14.9
Côte d'Ivoire	Cocoa beans, whole or broken, raw or roasted	29.4	Petroleum oils and oils from bituminous minerals, crude	17.0
Djibouti	Sheep	26.9	Goats	24.0
Equatorial Guinea	Petroleum oils and oils from bituminous minerals, crude	87.9	Methanol (methyl alcohol)	3.9
Eritrea	Natural uranium and its compounds	69.1	Nuclear reactors, boilers, machinery & mechanical appliance	6.4
Ethiopia	Coffee, not roasted, not decaffeinated	42.1	Sesamum seeds	16.3
Gabon	Petroleum oils and oils from bituminous minerals, crude	71.8	Manganese ores and concentrates	9.6
Gambia, The	Cashew nuts, in shells	36.0	Titanium ores and concentrates	8.5
Ghana	Cocoa beans, whole or broken, raw or roasted	45.6	Manganese ores and concentrates	8.4
Guinea	Aluminium ores and concentrates	52.4	Aluminium oxide other than artificial	15.3
Guinea-Bissau	Cashew nuts, in shells	91.3		
Kenya	Cut flowers and flower buds, fresh	13.7	Other black tea (fermented) and other partly fermented tea	11.8
Lesotho	Diamonds, not mounted or set	28.9	Articles, knitted or crocheted of cotton	18.5
Liberia	Tankers	46.1	Other vessels for transport of goods and/or persons	21.9
Madagascar	Articles, knitted or crocheted of wool or fine animal hair	12.4	Shrimps and prawns	10.1
Malawi	Tobacco, partly or wholly stemmed	49.5	Raw sugar not containing added flavor	8.8
Mali	Cotton, not carded, combed	70.8	Guavas, mangoes, and mangosteens	4.4
Mauritania	Iron ores and concentrates, including roasted iron pyrites	45.3	Petroleum oils and oils from bituminous minerals, noncrude	19.0
Mauritius	T-shirts, singlets, and other vests, knitted or crocheted of cotton	17.5	Cane sugar and chemically pure sucrose, solid	15.9
Mozambique	Aluminium, not alloyed	51.3	Petroleum oils and oils from bituminous minerals, noncrude	9.9
Namibia	Diamonds, not mounted or set	20.2	Unwrought zinc, containing by weight 99.99 percent or more of zinc	18.7
Niger	Natural uranium and its compounds	83.7	Paintings, drawings, and pastels	2.2
Nigeria	Petroleum oils and oils from bituminous minerals, crude	87.5	Liquefied natural gas	6.6
Rwanda	Coffee, not roasted, not decaffeinated	43.2	Tin ores and concentrates	15.6
São Tomé and Príncipe	Cocoa beans, whole or broken, raw or roasted	49.5	Prefabricated buildings	4.6
Senegal	Petroleum oils and oils from bituminous minerals, noncrude	14.3	Phosphoric acid and polyphosphoric acids	9.5
Seychelles	Tunas, skipjack, and bonito (*Sarda spp.*)	47.8	Yellowfin tunas (*Thunnus albacares*)	11.0
Sierra Leone	Diamonds, not mounted or set	31.1	Aluminium ores and concentrates	11.7
Somalia	Goats	33.7	Live bovine animals other than purebred breeding animals	10.5
South Africa	Platinum, unwrought or in powder form	7.6	Diamonds, not mounted or set	6.1
Sudan	Petroleum oils and oils from bituminous minerals, crude	92.3		
Swaziland	Raw sugar not containing added flavor	12.7	Food preparations not elsewhere specified or included	10.2
Tanzania	Tobacco, partly or wholly stemmed	8.5	Coffee, not roasted, not decaffeinated	7.5
Togo	Cocoa beans, whole or broken, raw or roasted	25.3	Petroleum oils and oils from bituminous minerals, noncrude	13.0
Uganda	Coffee, not roasted, not decaffeinated	25.6	Fish fillets and other fish meat, fresh or chilled	12.8
Zambia	Refined copper, cathodes and sections of cathodes	62.1	Copper ores and concentrates	6.3
Zimbabwe	Nickel, not alloyed	22.7	Tobacco, partly or wholly stemmed	11.1
NORTH AFRICA				
Algeria	Petroleum oils and oils from bituminous minerals, crude	63.1	Petroleum oils and oils from bituminous minerals, noncrude	10.5
Egypt, Arab Rep.	Liquefied natural gas	18.2	Petroleum oils and oils from bituminous minerals, crude	11.6
Libya	Petroleum oils and oils from bituminous minerals, crude	86.2	Petroleum oils and oils from bituminous minerals, noncrude	8.9
Morocco	Phosphoric acid and polyphosphoric acids	5.2	Elec. int. circuits & microassemblies, other monolithic integrated circuits	3.8
Tunisia	Petroleum oils and oils from bituminous minerals, crude	3.8	Trousers, bib and brace overalls, breeches, and shorts, cotton	5.6
AFRICA[a]	**Petroleum oils and oils from bituminous minerals, crude**	**48.6 (19.5)**	**Petroleum oils and oils from bituminous minerals, noncrude**	**4.3 (4.0)**

Note: Products are reported when accounting for more than 2 percent of total exports.
a. Values in parentheses are Africa's share of total world exports.
b. As reported.

Third		Number of exports accounting for 75 percent of total exports
Product	Share of total exports (%)	
Copper waste and scrap	10.9	5
Copper mattes	3.7	2
Guavas, mangoes, and mangosteens	2.6	2
Other black tea (fermented) and other partly fermented tea	3.4	6
Cocoa beans, whole or broken, raw or roasted	6.1	5
Cocoa paste, not deflated	10.2	9
Cotton, not carded or combed	16.8	4
		1
Essential oils, including concretes and absolutes resinoids extracted oleoresins	19.0	4
		1
Cobalt ores and concentrates	14.7	6
Cocoa paste, not deflated	6.3	9
Petroleum oils and oils from bituminous minerals, crude	14.0	4
Liquefied natural gas	3.2	1
Sesamum seeds	3.3	2
Cut flowers and flower buds, fresh	6.5	7
Wood in the rough or roughly squared	0.0[b]	2[b]
Ground nut oil and its fractions, crude	8.5	11
Petroleum oils and oils from bituminous minerals, noncrude	4.1	10
Copper ores and concentrates	7.9	3
		1
Petroleum oils and oils from bituminous minerals, noncrude	5.9	51
Men's or boys' suits, ensembles, jackets, blazers, trousers, bib and brace overalls, breeches and shorts (other than swimwear), cotton	14.5	6
Natural rubber latex	11.6	3
Women's or girls' suits, ensembles, jackets, blazers, dresses, skirts, divided skirts, trousers, bib and brace overalls, breeches and shorts (other than swimwear)	8.0	26
Other black tea (fermented) and other partly fermented tea	5.7	6
Sesamum seeds	2.0	2
Molluscs or aquatic invertebrates other than crustaceans, other than live, fresh or chilled	9.7	4
Prepared of preserved fish, tunas, skipjack, and bonito (*Sarda spp.*)	9.5	24
Electrical energy (optional heading)	5.1	5
Natural uranium and its compounds alloys, dispersions (including cermets), ceramic products, and mixtures containing natural uranium	12.1	7
		1
Petroleum oils and oils from bituminous minerals, noncrude	2.0	1
Other black tea (fermented) and other partly fermented tea	13.7	4
Parts and accessories (other than covers, carrying cases and the like) suitable for use solely or principally with machines of headings 84.69–84.72	4.6	12
Ground nut oil and its fractions, crude	7.1	34
Other fish, frozen, excluding fillets and other meat, skipjack or stripe bellied bonito	7.9	5
Titanium ores and concentrates	11.2	8
Pure-bred breeding animals	10.4	7
Gold (including gold plated with platinum) unwrought form	5.1	102
		3
Mixtures of odoriferous substances of a kind used in the food or drink	9.9	25
Fish fillets and other fish meat, fresh or chilled	7.4	36
Portland cement, aluminous cement, slag cement, supersulphate cement, and similar hydraulic cements, in the form of clinkers	8.3	9
Tobacco, partly or wholly stemmed	7.3	16
Cobalt mattes and other intermediate products of cobalt	5.3	4
Nickel ores and concentrates	9.4	13
Liquefied natural gas	9.7	3
Petroleum oils and oils from bituminous minerals, noncrude	8.7	68
		1
Natural calcium phosphates, natural aluminium calcium phosphates, and phosphatic chalk unground	3.2	72
Ignition wiring sets and other wiring sets of a kind used in vehicles, aircraft, or ships	4.6	82
Liquefied natural gas	**3.4 (22.4)**	**37**

Table 5.3 Regional integration, trade blocs

	Year established	Year of entry into force of most recent agreement	Type of most recent agreement[a]	Merchandise exports within bloc ($ millions) 1990	1995	2000	2004	2005	2006	2007
Economic and Monetary Community of Central African States (CEMAC)	1994	1999	CU	114	120	96	174	198	245	304
Common Market for Eastern and Southern Africa (COMESA)	1994	1994	FTA	830	1,367	1,443	2,420	2,866	3,468	4,582
East African Community (EAC)	1996	2000	CU	132	628	689	930	1043	1,279	1,587
Economic Community of Central African States (ECCAS)	1983	2004[b]	NNA	133	157	181	221	251	310	385
Economic Community of West African States (ECOWAS)	1975	1993	PS	1,384	1,875	2,715	4,366	2,497	5,957	7,341
Indian Ocean Commission (IOC)	1984	2005[b]	NNA	75	113	106	155	159	172	204
Southern African Development Community (SADC)	1992	2000	FTA	1,720	3,615	4,427	6,655	7,798	8,694	11,952
West African Economic and Monetary Union (WAEMU/UEMOA)	1994	2000	CU	499	560	741	1,233	1,390	1,545	1,917

	Year established	Year of entry into force of most recent agreement	Type of most recent agreement[a]	Merchandise exports within bloc (% of total bloc exports) 1990	1995	2000	2004	2005	2006	2007
Economic and Monetary Community of Central African States (CEMAC)	1994	1999	CU	2.0	2.1	1.0	1.2	0.9	0.9	1.1
Common Market for Eastern and Southern Africa (COMESA)	1994	1994	FTA	3.6	6.1	4.6	5.0	4.5	4.2	4.7
East African Community (EAC)	1996	2000	CU	7.4	19.5	22.6	18.9	17.6	19.3	20.4
Economic Community of Central African States (ECCAS)	1983	2004[b]	NNA	1.3	1.5	1.0	0.8	0.6	0.5	0.6
Economic Community of West African States (ECOWAS)	1975	1993	PS	9.7	9.0	7.6	9.3	9.3	8.4	9.4
Indian Ocean Commission (IOC)	1984	2005[b]	NNA	4.8	5.9	4.4	4.3	4.6	4.8	5.7
Southern African Development Community (SADC)	1992	2000	FTA	17.9	32.8	9.5	9.7	9.3	9.1	10.1
West African Economic and Monetary Union (WAEMU/UEMOA)	1994	2000	CU	11.3	10.3	13.1	12.9	13.4	13.1	15.2

	Year established	Year of entry into force of most recent agreement	Type of most recent agreement[a]	Merchandise exports by bloc (% of world exports)						
				1990	1995	2000	2004	2005	2006	2007
Economic and Monetary Community of Central African States (CEMAC)	1994	1999	CU	0.2	0.1	0.1	0.1	0.2	0.2	0.2
Common Market for Eastern and Southern Africa (COMESA)	1994	1994	FTA	0.7	0.4	0.5	0.5	0.6	0.7	0.7
East African Community (EAC)	1996	2000	CU	0.1	0.1	0.0	0.1	0.1	0.1	0.1
Economic Community of Central African States (ECCAS)	1983	2004[b]	NNA	0.3	0.2	0.3	0.3	0.4	0.5	0.5
Economic Community of West African States (ECOWAS)	1975	1993	PS	0.4	0.4	0.6	0.5	0.6	0.6	0.6
Indian Ocean Commission (IOC)	1984	2005[b]	NNA	0.0	0.0	0.0	0.0	0.0	0.0	0.0
Southern African Development Community (SADC)	1992	2000	FTA	0.3	0.2	0.7	0.7	0.8	0.8	0.9
West African Economic and Monetary Union (WAEMU/UEMOA)	1994	2000	CU	0.1	0.1	0.1	0.1	0.1	0.1	0.1

Note: **Economic and Monetary Community of Central Africa (CEMAC; formerly Central African Customs and Economic Union [UDEAC]),** Cameroon, the Central African Republic, Chad, the Republic of Congo, Equatorial Guinea, and Gabon; **Common Market for Eastern and Southern Africa (COMESA),** Burundi, Comoros, the Democratic Republic of Congo, Djibouti, the Arab Republic of Egypt, Eritrea, Ethiopia, Kenya, Libyan Arab Republic, Madagascar, Malawi, Mauritius, Rwanda, Seychelles, Sudan, Swaziland, Uganda, Zambia, and Zimbabwe; **East African Community (EAC),** Burundi, Kenya, Rwanda, Tanzania, and Uganda; **Economic Community of Central African States (ECCAS),** Angola, Burundi, Cameroon, the Central African Republic, Chad, the Democratic Republic of Congo, the Republic of Congo, Equatorial Guinea, Gabon, and São Tomé and Príncipe; **Economic Community of West African States (ECOWAS),** Benin, Burkina Faso, Cape Verde, Côte d'Ivoire, the Gambia, Ghana, Guinea, Guinea-Bissau, Liberia, Mali, Niger, Nigeria, Senegal, Sierra Leone, and Togo; **Indian Ocean Commission (IOC),** Comoros, Madagascar, Mauritius, Réunion, and Seychelles; **Southern African Development Community (SADC; formerly Southern African Development Coordination Conference),** Angola, Botswana, the Democratic Republic of Congo, Lesotho, Madagascar, Malawi, Mauritius, Mozambique, Namibia, Seychelles, South Africa, Swaziland, Tanzania, Zambia, and Zimbabwe; **West African Economic and Monetary Union (UEMOA),** Benin, Burkina Faso, Côte d'Ivoire, Guinea-Bissau, Mali, Niger, Senegal, and Togo.

a. CU is customs union; FTA is free trade agreement; NNA is not notified agreement, which refers to preferential trade agreements established among member countries that are not notified to the World Trade Organization (these agreements may be functionally equivalent to any of the other agreements); and PS is partial scope agreement.

b. Years of the most recent agreement are collected from the official website of the trade bloc.

Table 6.1 Water and sanitation

	Access, supply side	Access, demand side						Quality of supply	Financing		
	Internal fresh water resources per capita (cubic meters)	Population with sustainable access to an improved water source			Population with sustainable access to improved sanitation			Water supply failure for firms receiving water (average days per year)	Committed nominal investment in water projects with private participation ($ millions)	ODA gross disbursements for water supply and sanitation sector ($ millions)	
		(% of total population)	(% of urban population)	(% of rural population)	(% of total population)	(% of urban population)	(% of rural population)				
	2007	2006	2006	2006	2006	2006	2006	2006	2000–08[a]	2007	2008
SUB-SAHARAN AFRICA	**4,859**	**58**	**81**	**46**	**31**	**43**	**24**			**1,381.9**	**1,668.1**
Angola	8,431	51	62	39	50	79	16	83.5	..	41.8	22.3
Benin	1,227	65	78	57	30	59	11	..	..	51.1	63.5
Botswana	1,276	96	100	90	47	60	30	0.0	..	1.3	2.2
Burkina Faso	846	72	97	66	13	41	6	11.8	..	79.5	60.5
Burundi	1,284	71	84	70	41	44	41	94.1	..	12.4	15.7
Cameroon	14,731	70	88	47	51	58	42	6.8	0.0	4.2	18.5
Cape Verde	610	..	..	..	..	..	..	12.8	..	3.7	6.4
Central African Republic	32,463	66	90	51	31	40	25	..	..	1.6	1.9
Chad	1,394	48	71	40	9	23	4	..	..	18.9	25.5
Comoros	1,910	85	91	81	35	49	26	..	..	1.6	1.3
Congo, Dem. Rep.	14,423	46	82	29	31	42	25	81.8	..	39.4	61.9
Congo, Rep.	62,516	71	95	35	20	19	21	..	0.0	1.3	1.8
Côte d'Ivoire	3,819	81	98	66	24	38	12	..	..	4.5	7.9
Djibouti	360	92	98	54	67	76	11	..	..	1.7	3.2
Equatorial Guinea	40,485	43	45	42	51	60	46	..	..	0.7	0.0
Eritrea	578	60	74	57	5	14	3	..	..	3.4	8.2
Ethiopia	1,551	42	96	31	11	27	8	..	..	75.6	106.5
Gabon	115,340	87	95	47	36	37	30	..	..	0.0	18.6
Gambia, The	1,857	86	91	81	52	50	55	..	..	15.8	9.1
Ghana	1,325	80	90	71	10	15	6	..	0.0	118.8	124.4
Guinea	23,505	70	91	59	19	33	12	..	..	14.5	14.7
Guinea-Bissau	10,383	57	82	47	33	48	26	43.2	..	3.3	3.0
Kenya	552	57	85	49	42	19	48	..	..	50.8	100.3
Lesotho	2,607	78	93	74	36	43	34	..	..	7.9	18.8
Liberia	55,138	64	72	52	32	49	7	..	..	3.1	7.1
Madagascar	18,114	47	76	36	12	18	10	..	..	12.7	17.4
Malawi	1,160	76	96	72	60	51	62	..	..	15.4	13.9
Mali	4,865	60	86	48	45	59	39	..	..	38.0	47.1
Mauritania	128	60	70	54	24	44	10	92.5	..	12.1	21.9
Mauritius	2,182	100	100	100	94	95	94	..	..	13.1	11.9
Mozambique	4,693	42	71	26	31	53	19	..	..	72.6	81.6
Namibia	2,961	93	99	90	35	66	18	10.2	0.0	5.9	11.8
Niger	247	42	91	32	7	27	3	..	3.4	21.8	38.1
Nigeria	1,493	47	65	30	30	35	25	..	..	87.4	108.7
Rwanda	1,005	65	82	61	23	34	20	..	..	38.3	37.7
São Tomé and Príncipe	13,796	86	88	83	24	29	18	..	..	0.8	0.9
Senegal	2,169	77	93	65	28	54	9	..	0.0	75.5	76.1
Seychelles	..	..	100	..	..	..	100	..	..	0.0	0.2
Sierra Leone	29,518	53	83	32	11	20	5	..	..	15.1	13.3
Somalia	690	29	63	10	23	51	7	..	..	2.5	1.9
South Africa	936	93	100	82	59	66	49	..	0.0	12.1	52.7
Sudan	742	70	78	64	35	50	24	..	120.7	20.9	21.8
Swaziland	2,293	60	87	51	50	64	46	18.1	..	0.0	1.0
Tanzania	2,035	55	81	46	33	31	34	..	8.5	127.5	148.8
Togo	1,825	59	86	40	12	24	3	..	..	1.4	3.0
Uganda	1,273	64	90	60	33	29	34	..	0.0	92.3	64.2
Zambia	6,513	58	90	41	52	55	51	..	0.0	52.0	39.5
Zimbabwe	985	81	98	72	46	63	37	..	..	0.2	12.1
NORTH AFRICA	**291**	**92**	**96**	**87**	**75**	**90**	**59**	**..**		**376.3**	**462.8**
Algeria	332	85	87	81	94	98	87	..	874.0	5.7	4.6
Egypt, Arab Rep.	23	98	99	98	66	85	52	..	..	76.5	55.7
Libya	98	..	..	..	97	97	96	..	..	0.0	0.0
Morocco	940	83	100	58	72	85	54	..	..	188.5	301.0
Tunisia	410	94	99	84	85	96	64	..	..	95.3	98.5

a. Data are for the most recent year available during the period specified.

Table 6.2 Transportation

	Access, supply side				Access, demand side		
			Road density			Vehicle fleet (per 1,000 people)	
	Road network (km)	Rail lines (km)	Ratio to arable land (road km/1,000 sq km arable land)	Ratio to total land (road km/100 sq km of land area)	Rural access (% of rural population within 2 km of an all-season road)	Commercial vehicles	Passenger vehicles
	2000–07[a]	2000–07[a]	2000–07[a]	2000–07[a]	2000–07[a]	2000–06[a]	2000–06[a]
SUB-SAHARAN AFRICA	..	..	..	6.9	..	..	..
Angola	51,429	..	17.1	4.1	..	..	8
Benin	19,000	..	6.9	17.2	32	..	13
Botswana	25,798	..	107.5	4.6	..	113	47
Burkina Faso	92,495	..	19.1	33.8	25	7	5
Burundi	12,322	..	12.5	48.0	..	..	1
Cameroon	51,346	974	8.6	11.0	22	11	11
Cape Verde	1,350	..	27.0	33.5	..	..	..
Central African Republic	24,307	..	12.6	3.9	..	..	1
Chad	40,000	..	9.3	3.2	..	6	..
Comoros	880	..	11.0	47.3	..	1	1
Congo, Dem. Rep.	153,497	3,641	22.9	6.8	26	..	..
Congo, Rep.	17,289	795	34.9	5.1	..	..	8
Côte d'Ivoire	80,000	639	28.6	25.2	..	..	7
Djibouti	3,065	..	3,065.0	13.2	..	..	..
Equatorial Guinea	2,880	..	22.2	10.3	..	..	..
Eritrea	4,010	..	7.1	4.0	..	..	..
Ethiopia	42,429	..	3.0	4.2	33	2	1
Gabon	9,170	810	28.2	3.6	..	..	..
Gambia, The	3,742	..	11.2	37.4	..	7	5
Ghana	57,614	977	14.4	25.3	..	18	12
Guinea	44,348	..	27.7	18.1	37	14	8
Guinea-Bissau	3,455	..	11.5	12.3	..	1	..
Kenya	63,265	1,917	12.0	11.1	..	18	9
Lesotho	5,940	..	18.0	19.6	..	..	..
Liberia	10,600	..	27.9	11.0	..	..	6
Madagascar	49,827	..	16.9	8.6	22	..	..
Malawi	15,451	710	5.4	16.4	..	..	..
Mali	18,709	733	4.4	1.5	..	..	..
Mauritania	11,066	..	23.1	1.1	..	..	..
Mauritius	2,021	..	22.0	99.6	..	138	104
Mozambique	30,400	..	7.6	3.9	12	..	..
Namibia	42,237	..	51.8	5.1	..	85	42
Niger	18,550	..	1.3	1.5	33	5	4
Nigeria	193,200	3,528	5.9	21.2	..	..	17
Rwanda	14,008	..	12.2	56.8	..	3	1
São Tomé and Príncipe	320	..	53.3	33.3	..	..	..
Senegal	13,576	906	4.6	7.1	..	14	10
Seychelles	458	..	458.0	99.6	..	121	74
Sierra Leone	11,300	..	21.1	15.8	22	4	2
Somalia	22,100	..	21.2	3.5	..	..	..
South Africa	364,131	24,487	24.7	30.0	..	151	103
Sudan	11,900	5,478	0.7	0.5	..	..	..
Swaziland	3,594	..	20.2	20.9	..	84	40
Tanzania	78,891	4,460	8.3	8.9	16	..	1
Togo	7,520	..	3.0	13.8	..	..	10
Uganda	70,746	259	13.6	35.9	..	5	2
Zambia	91,440	1,273	17.4	12.3	51	..	..
Zimbabwe	97,267	..	30.1	25.1	..	..	45
NORTH AFRICA	57,626	12,892	..	7.0	..	..	47
Algeria	108,302	3,572	14.5	4.6	..	91	58
Egypt, Arab Rep.	92,370	5,195	31.2	9.3	..	..	29
Libya	83,200	..	45.8	4.7	..	257	232
Morocco	57,625	1,907	7.2	12.9	..	59	46
Tunisia	19,232	2,218	6.9	12.4	..	95	83

(continued)

Table 6.2 Transportation (continued)

	Quality		Pricing		Financing		
	Roads						
	Road network in good or fair condition (%)	Ratio of paved to total roads (%)	Price of diesel fuel ($ per liter)	Price of gasoline ($ per liter)	Committed nominal investment in transport projects with private participation ($ millions)	ODA gross disbursements for transportation and storage ($ millions)	
	2000–08[a]	2000–07[a]	2008	2008	2000–07[a]	2007	2008
SUB-SAHARAN AFRICA	..	12.1	1.06	1.14	187.0	2,047.3	2,460.1
Angola	..	10.4	0.39	0.53	53.0	0.8	1.8
Benin	67.7	9.5	1.03	1.03	..	52.9	99.4
Botswana	..	32.6	1.02	0.88	..	0.1	0.1
Burkina Faso	91.3	4.2	1.33	1.38	..	115.8	38.2
Burundi	24.0	10.4	1.23	1.39	..	23.8	34.3
Cameroon	62.7	8.4	1.04	1.14	0.0	66.6	92.1
Cape Verde	..	69.0	1.43	1.84	..	42.7	76.1
Central African Republic	..	..	1.44	1.44	..	2.6	5.1
Chad	63.3	0.8	1.32	1.30	..	15.8	58.2
Comoros	..	76.5	..	..	0.5	3.4	0.6
Congo, Dem. Rep.	23.2	1.8	1.21	1.23	..	101.4	159.4
Congo, Rep.	..	5.0	0.57	0.81	..	30.6	28.2
Côte d'Ivoire	74.1	8.1	1.20	1.33	0.0	0.0	6.7
Djibouti	..	45.0	..	..	300.0	5.6	3.6
Equatorial Guinea	..	..	..	..	72.0	..	..
Eritrea	..	21.8	1.07	2.53	..	2.3	1.8
Ethiopia	73.0	12.8	0.89	0.92	..	218.9	313.8
Gabon	25.0	10.2	0.90	1.14	91.8	7.3	7.0
Gambia, The	94.6	19.3	0.75	0.79	..	6.5	6.4
Ghana	83.4	14.9	0.90	0.90	0.0	112.3	119.3
Guinea	44.2	9.8	1.02	1.02	..	10.8	35.5
Guinea-Bissau	..	27.9	..	..	..	32.5	16.8
Kenya	66.0	14.1	1.14	1.20	0.0	110.9	97.5
Lesotho	56.5	18.3	0.93	0.79	..	8.3	16.1
Liberia	..	6.2	1.03	0.74	..	13.8	31.2
Madagascar	33.7	11.6	1.43	1.55	0.0	159.5	117.8
Malawi	88.5	45.0	1.67	1.78	..	14.2	33.0
Mali	62.0	18.0	1.10	1.30	55.4	121.5	81.0
Mauritania	..	26.8	1.06	1.49	..	50.1	41.6
Mauritius	..	100.0	..	..	..	2.6	1.5
Mozambique	61.3	18.7	1.37	1.71	186.9	140.8	100.5
Namibia	68.3	12.8	0.88	0.78	..	26.9	25.8
Niger	66.8	20.5	0.97	0.99	..	44.1	60.7
Nigeria	64.2	15.0	1.13	0.59	262.1	42.8	44.3
Rwanda	31.0	19.0	1.37	1.37	..	20.6	50.7
São Tomé and Príncipe	..	68.1	..	..	..	4.9	3.7
Senegal	41.8	29.3	1.26	1.35	55.4	62.6	82.9
Seychelles	..	96.0	..	..	..	..	..
Sierra Leone	..	8.0	0.91	0.91	..	10.2	22.6
Somalia	..	11.8	1.15	1.12	..	1.5	0.1
South Africa	65.0	17.3	0.95	0.87	3,483.0	0.6	0.4
Sudan	..	36.3	0.45	0.65	30.0	0.5	29.3
Swaziland	..	30.0	0.93	0.86	..	11.3	0.0
Tanzania	71.4	8.6	1.30	1.11	134.0	156.3	162.8
Togo	..	31.6	0.88	0.89	..	0.0	0.0
Uganda	29.3	23.0	1.22	1.30	0.0	112.7	178.5
Zambia	51.6	22.0	1.61	1.70	15.6	27.0	77.0
Zimbabwe	60.0	19.0	1.05	1.30	..	0.0	0.0
NORTH AFRICA	..	68.0	0.20	0.49	1,731.0	637.9	617.9
Algeria	..	70.2	0.20	0.34	161.0	72.0	90.4
Egypt, Arab Rep.	..	81.0	0.20	0.49	730.0	142.2	110.2
Libya	..	57.2	0.12	0.14	..	..	..
Morocco	..	61.9	0.83	1.29	140.0	290.4	265.7
Tunisia	..	65.8	0.84	0.96	840.0	123.2	144.7

a. Data are for the most recent year available during the period specified.

Table 6.3 Information and communication technology

	Access, supply side: Telephone subscribers (per 100 people)			Access, demand side				Quality: Telephone faults	
	Total 2008	Mainline telephone 2008	Mobile telephone 2008	Unmet demand (% of mainline telephones) 2006	Households with own telephone (% of households) 2007–09[a]	Average delay for firm in obtaining a mainline phone connection (days) 2007–09[a]	Internet users (per 100 people) 2008	Total (per 100 mainlines) 2006	Cleared by next working day (%) 2006
SUB-SAHARAN AFRICA	**30.3**	**0.9**	**32.0**				**4.5**		
Angola	38.2	0.6	37.6	..	..	..	3.1	..	..
Benin	..	..	39.7	70.2	2.8	..	1.8	7.0	14.8
Botswana	85.5	7.5	78.0	..	..	..	4.2	..	..
Burkina Faso	..	..	16.8	..	..	..	0.9	..	..
Burundi	6.3	0.4	6.0	..	..	..	0.8	..	..
Cameroon	33.7	1.1	32.6	..	..	..	..	..	..
Cape Verde	70.1	14.4	55.7	0.6	..	..	20.6	3.0	91.5
Central African Republic	..	..	3.5	..	..	..	0.4	..	..
Chad	..	..	16.4	..	..	..	1.2	..	..
Comoros	..	..	..	..	..	..	..	..	..
Congo, Dem. Rep.	14.5	0.1	14.4	..	..	..	0.5	..	..
Congo, Rep.	..	..	50.0	..	..	25.5	4.3	..	..
Côte d'Ivoire	52.5	1.7	50.7	..	17.4	5.8	3.2	..	..
Djibouti	..	..	..	..	..	..	..	..	..
Equatorial Guinea	..	..	52.5	..	..	..	1.8	..	..
Eritrea	3.0	0.8	2.2	22.7	..	..	3.0	63.8	41.6
Ethiopia	5.1	1.1	3.9	7.7	..	..	0.4	..	47.0
Gabon	..	..	89.8	4.7	12.8	8.6	6.2	..	..
Gambia, The	73.2	2.9	70.2	..	..	..	6.9	..	..
Ghana	50.2	0.6	49.6	0.7	6.9	184.3	4.3	3.2	76.5
Guinea	..	..	26.4	..	..	..	0.9	..	..
Guinea-Bissau	32.0	0.3	31.8	..	..	..	2.4	..	..
Kenya	42.8	0.7	42.1	21.1	..	27.1	8.7	70.1	63.7
Lesotho	..	..	28.8	..	5.6	53.7	3.6	..	..
Liberia	..	..	19.3	..	..	..	..	..	..
Madagascar	26.2	0.9	25.3	..	2.0	29.9	1.7	36.0	54.8
Malawi	..	..	12.5	..	..	..	2.2	..	..
Mali	26.4	0.7	25.7	..	2.4	43.4	1.0	..	..
Mauritania	67.8	2.4	65.4	..	2.9	..	..	..	..
Mauritius	110.2	28.7	81.4	..	76.3	38.6	29.9	..	..
Mozambique	20.6	0.4	20.2	4.2	..	10.7	1.6	46.0	87.0
Namibia	..	..	49.8	..	17.0	..	5.4	..	..
Niger	..	..	11.4	..	0.6	..	0.5	..	..
Nigeria	42.5	0.9	41.6	..	..	7.6	7.3	..	..
Rwanda	13.8	0.2	13.6	..	..	..	3.1	..	76.0
São Tomé and Príncipe	..	..	30.4	3.6	..	..	15.4	14.0	98.0
Senegal	46.1	2.0	44.1	0.0	17.0	8.9	8.4	2.0	85.0
Seychelles	125.7	26.9	98.8	10.6	64.0	..	37.1	6.0	90.0
Sierra Leone	..	..	18.1	..	..	21.4	0.3	..	..
Somalia	..	..	..	..	..	..	..	..	..
South Africa	..	..	92.4	..	54.6	23.5	8.6	..	..
Sudan	27.9	0.9	27.1	0.0	10.0	..	9.2	5.0	90.0
Swaziland	..	..	39.1	..	..	..	4.1	0.7	70.0
Tanzania	30.9	0.3	30.6	0.7	9.3	..	1.2	..	93.0
Togo	26.1	2.2	24.0	11.3	7.0	..	5.4	..	..
Uganda	27.6	0.5	27.0	..	2.7	..	7.9	..	..
Zambia	28.8	0.7	28.0	..	5.1	17.3	5.5	..	..
Zimbabwe	..	..	13.3	47.0	..	..	11.4	57.0	44.0
NORTH AFRICA	**72.2**	**13.2**	**59.0**				**20.9**		
Algeria	..	..	..	0.0	38.0	40.8	..	..	..
Egypt, Arab Rep.	65.4	14.7	50.6	0.4	67.7	85.5	15.4	0.1	88.0
Libya	..	..	..	..	..	..	..	..	..
Morocco	82.6	9.6	73.1	..	18.1	6.4	33.0	..	..
Tunisia	95.0	12.0	83.0	1.1	..	..	27.1	20.0	68.5

(continued)

Table 6.3 Information and communication technology (continued)

	Pricing							Financing				
	Price basket for Internet ($ per month)	Cost of 3-minute call during peak hours ($)			Connection charge ($)			Annual investment ($ millions)			Committed nominal investment in telecommunication projects with private participation ($ millions)	ODA gross disbursements for communication ($ millions)
		Fixed telephone local	Cellular local	To U.S.	Residential telephone	Business telephone	Mobile cellular	Fixed telephone service	Mobile communication	Telecommunications		
	2007	2007	2006	2007	2007	2006	2006	2006	2006	2006	2007	2008
SUB-SAHARAN AFRICA	42.3	0.19	0.72	0.19	46.3	52.2	9.6				9,509.9	191.7
Angola	63.1	0.30	0.90	0.30	58.7	58.7	..	..	..	..	198.0	11.4
Benin	43.1	0.03	0.96	0.03	201.6	366.6	9.6	..	..	3.9	205.0	0.8
Botswana	29.7	0.17	0.20	0.17	37.5	55.0	3.4	268.5	135.5	404.0	28.0	0.3
Burkina Faso	67.8	0.21	1.03	0.21	52.2	52.2	114.8	134.2	66.6	202.6	88.8	5.0
Burundi	86.0	..	0.58	..	..	..	2.9	..	..	..	0.0	1.6
Cameroon	48.3	0.31	1.32	0.31	83.5	208.7	9.6	..	125.2	211.4	149.4	8.7
Cape Verde	48.3	..	1.22	..	..	..	46.0	8.7	5.0	15.9	0.0	0.2
Central African Republic	130.4	0.21	0.57	0.21	73.9	73.9	38.3	..	..	..	12.0	0.1
Chad	105.0	..	1.05	..	..	..	7.7	..	..	..	53.5	0.1
Comoros	20.8	0.14	0.70	0.14	112.7	112.7	63.8	..	..	..	..	..
Congo, Dem. Rep.	..	..	..	..	..	..	..	..	..	..	320.0	3.9
Congo, Rep.	..	..	..	..	..	..	..	..	..	..	90.0	0.2
Côte d'Ivoire	20.3	0.38	2.26	0.38	20.9	20.9	19.1	20.3	266.2	382.5	253.7	1.2
Djibouti	41.5	..	0.51	..	..	..	56.3	..	..	..	..	0.3
Equatorial Guinea	..	..	..	..	..	..	..	..	..	..	9.3	0.0
Eritrea	..	..	0.33	..	..	..	91.1	4.4	9.2	16.5	0.0	0.1
Ethiopia	14.6	..	0.29	..	..	..	42.3	37.5	..	60.3	..	4.0
Gabon	..	..	1.03	..	..	..	3.8	..	..	..	131.4	0.0
Gambia, The	..	..	..	..	..	..	..	..	..	..	0.0	0.3
Ghana	9.4	0.16	0.45	0.16	85.5	0.7	7.0	..	..	..	420.0	0.9
Guinea	..	..	..	..	..	..	..	..	..	..	18.0	0.1
Guinea-Bissau	..	..	..	..	..	..	..	..	..	..	39.5	0.2
Kenya	63.9	0.08	1.17	0.08	34.2	50.4	34.7	174.3	618.6	792.9	877.0	6.0
Lesotho	77.5	0.24	..	0.24	43.0	44.7	7.4	..	..	..	4.8	0.0
Liberia	..	..	..	..	..	..	..	..	..	..	17.0	0.0
Madagascar	28.9	0.19	0.45	0.19	31.5	31.5	4.7	14.9	34.3	50.8	119.6	0.4
Malawi	52.7	0.09	0.60	0.09	..	..	3.1	..	..	..	37.0	0.6
Mali	43.2	0.15	0.85	0.15	80.6	41.8	57.4	..	..	93.9	87.0	0.5
Mauritania	37.3	0.22	0.50	0.22	18.5	18.5	11.1	4.6	25.6	30.2	30.1	0.2
Mauritius	16.4	0.07	0.11	0.07	31.9	63.9	..	..	..	..	26.1	1.4
Mozambique	34.4	0.35	0.40	0.35	18.8	18.8	0.2	..	..	21.4	65.6	7.9
Namibia	55.8	0.19	1.23	0.19	37.8	37.8	7.2	..	..	..	8.5	8.0
Niger	84.5	0.16	0.92	0.16	49.7	74.5	..	..	..	..	110.0	0.5
Nigeria	40.8	0.14	0.61	0.14	71.5	71.5	3.9	..	..	..	2,761.0	4.7
Rwanda	79.7	..	0.80	..	..	..	22.7	..	9.8	..	114.4	6.5
São Tomé and Príncipe	39.4	0.11	0.61	0.11	29.6	..	..	..	..	1.1	..	1.6
Senegal	40.4	0.21	0.57	0.21	20.9	20.9	40.2	57.4	126.3	183.8	567.0	2.0
Seychelles	59.5	0.13	1.63	0.13	78.2	78.2	9.1	..	..	12.8	0.0	..
Sierra Leone	..	..	1.03	..	..	..	..	..	..	..	26.3	0.0
Somalia	..	..	..	..	..	..	..	..	..	..	0.0	..
South Africa	28.2	0.19	1.42	0.19	54.4	54.4	22.0	..	..	..	1,217.0	4.5
Sudan	28.9	..	0.31	..	..	..	..	..	..	..	478.0	0.3
Swaziland	39.1	0.08	1.33	0.08	30.2	50.5	5.8	..	..	..	3.8	0.0
Tanzania	19.7	0.24	0.74	0.24	16.1	16.1	5.8	..	..	..	301.5	3.3
Togo	37.0	0.19	0.72	0.19	104.3	104.3	17.2	26.4	41.1	67.4	0.0	0.0
Uganda	51.7	0.26	0.62	0.26	68.7	68.7	5.5	..	..	..	500.6	10.8
Zambia	78.6	0.15	..	0.15	12.5	37.5	..	..	..	..	141.0	1.2
Zimbabwe	..	..	..	..	..	..	..	1.3	2.2	3.5	0.0	0.3
NORTH AFRICA	13.6	0.02	0.33	0.02	44.4	25.7	3.8				4,111.0	10.9
Algeria	23.1	0.00	0.22	0.00	0.0	0.0	16.5	..	..	..	561.0	2.3
Egypt, Arab Rep.	4.2	0.02	0.16	0.02	108.5	35.9	17.4	1,018.2	1,451.2	2,669.8	2,758.0	1.2
Libya	..	..	0.34	..	..	..	3.8	374.2	212.5	..	..	0.0
Morocco	15.6	0.24	1.14	0.24	73.2	146.5	3.4	..	..	..	716.0	0.9
Tunisia	11.6	0.02	0.33	0.02	15.6	15.6	3.8	86.4	216.4	311.8	76.0	2.4

a. Data are for the most recent year available during the period specified.

Table 6.4 Energy

	Access, demand side								
	Energy production						Electric power consumption (kWh per capita)	GDP per unit of energy use (2000 PPP $ per kg of oil equivalent)	Solid fuels use (% of population)
	Total (billion kWh)	Source[a] (% of total)							
		Hydroelectric	Coal	Natural gas	Nuclear	Oil			
	2006	2006	2006	2006	2006	2006	2006	2006	2007
SUB-SAHARAN AFRICA									
Angola	3.0	90.1	0.0	0.0	0.0	9.9	148.0	6.9	47.7
Benin	0.1	0.0	0.0	0.0	0.0	100.0	74.1	3.8	94.3
Botswana	1.0	0.0	99.4	0.0	0.0	0.6	1,419.1	11.7	42.5
Burkina Faso	..	..	..	..	..	..	..	..	95.0
Burundi	..	..	..	..	..	..	..	..	95.0
Cameroon	4.0	94.1	0.0	0.0	0.0	5.9	185.6	5.1	80.6
Cape Verde	..	..	..	..	..	..	..	..	36.2
Central African Republic	..	..	..	..	..	..	..	..	95.0
Chad	..	..	..	..	..	..	..	..	93.6
Comoros	..	..	..	..	..	..	..	..	76.0
Congo, Dem. Rep.	7.9	99.7	0.0	0.0	0.0	0.3	95.7	1.0	95.0
Congo, Rep.	0.5	82.1	0.0	17.9	0.0	0.0	164.4	10.5	83.9
Côte d'Ivoire	5.5	27.3	0.0	72.7	0.0	0.0	174.5	4.1	77.2
Djibouti	..	..	..	..	..	..	..	..	13.3
Equatorial Guinea	..	..	..	..	..	..	..	..	..
Eritrea	0.3	0.0	0.0	0.0	0.0	99.3	..	4.0	62.7
Ethiopia	3.3	99.7	0.0	0.0	0.0	0.3	38.4	2.3	95.0
Gabon	1.7	54.8	0.0	15.3	0.0	29.5	1,017.5	9.9	27.5
Gambia, The	..	..	..	..	..	..	..	..	94.7
Ghana	8.4	66.7	0.0	0.0	0.0	33.3	311.9	2.9	85.9
Guinea	..	..	..	..	..	..	..	..	95.0
Guinea-Bissau	..	..	..	..	..	..	..	..	95.0
Kenya	6.5	50.6	0.0	0.0	0.0	30.5	145.3	2.8	68.7
Lesotho	..	..	..	..	..	..	..	..	72.1
Liberia	..	..	..	..	..	..	..	..	..
Madagascar	..	..	..	..	..	..	..	..	95.0
Malawi	..	..	..	..	..	..	..	..	95.0
Mali	..	..	..	..	..	..	..	..	95.0
Mauritania	..	..	..	..	..	..	..	..	60.6
Mauritius	..	..	..	..	..	..	..	..	5.0
Mozambique	14.7	99.9	0.0	0.1	0.0	0.1	461.4	1.7	95.0
Namibia	1.6	94.1	5.2	0.0	0.0	0.6	1,545.5	7.9	58.5
Niger	..	..	..	..	..	..	..	..	95.0
Nigeria	23.1	33.4	0.0	57.8	0.0	8.8	116.4	2.5	78.8
Rwanda	..	..	..	..	..	..	..	..	95.0
São Tomé and Príncipe	..	..	..	..	..	..	..	..	..
Senegal	2.4	9.6	0.0	1.9	0.0	85.1	156.8	6.2	55.7
Seychelles	..	..	..	..	..	..	..	..	5.0
Sierra Leone	..	..	..	..	..	..	..	..	95.0
Somalia	..	..	..	..	..	..	..	..	95.0
South Africa	251.9	1.5	93.5	0.0	4.7	0.0	4,809.9	3.2	17.3
Sudan	4.2	32.5	0.0	0.0	0.0	67.5	90.3	3.9	89.9
Swaziland	..	..	..	..	..	..	..	..	60.8
Tanzania	2.8	51.7	3.8	43.8	0.0	0.6	57.8	2.1	95.0
Togo	0.2	41.2	0.0	0.0	0.0	57.5	101.7	2.0	95.0
Uganda	..	..	..	..	..	..	..	..	95.0
Zambia	9.4	99.4	0.2	0.0	0.0	0.4	710.0	1.9	85.7
Zimbabwe	9.8	56.8	43.0	0.0	0.0	0.2	955.3	..	71.2
NORTH AFRICA									
Algeria	35.2	0.6	0.0	97.2	0.0	2.2	869.9	6.6	5.0
Egypt, Arab Rep.	115.4	11.2	0.0	72.1	0.0	16.1	1,303.7	5.7	5.0
Libya	24.0	0.0	0.0	40.9	0.0	59.1	3,688.4	4.4	5.0
Morocco	23.2	6.9	58.1	12.8	0.0	21.4	685.1	8.3	6.8
Tunisia	14.1	0.7	0.0	84.9	0.0	14.2	1,220.7	7.8	5.0

(continued)

Table 6.4 Energy (continued)

	Quality						Financing	
	Firms identifying electricity as major or very severe obstacle to business operation and growth (%)	Average delay for firm in obtaining electrical connection (days)	Electric power transmission and distribution losses (% of output)	Electrical outages of firms (average number of days per year)	Firms that share or own their own generator (%)	Firms using electricity from generator (%)	Committed nominal investment in energy projects with private participation ($ millions)	ODA gross disbursements for energy ($ millions)
	2007–09[b]	2007–09[b]	2006	2006–09[b]	2007–09[b]	2007–09[b]	2007	2008
SUB-SAHARAN AFRICA								**1,044.2**
Angola	..	..	14.5	..	..	..	..	3.0
Benin	..	..	..	..	..	..	..	29.6
Botswana	..	..	14.9	..	..	..	28.0	0.4
Burkina Faso	..	..	..	..	..	..	..	39.5
Burundi	..	..	..	..	..	..	0.0	1.1
Cameroon	..	..	14.7	..	..	..	0.0	5.6
Cape Verde	..	..	..	..	..	..	..	1.8
Central African Republic	..	..	..	..	..	..	12.0	..
Chad	..	..	..	..	..	..	..	2.5
Comoros	..	..	..	..	..	..	..	..
Congo, Dem. Rep.	..	..	3.7	..	..	..	320.0	36.0
Congo, Rep.	71.1	8.5	64.2	25.3	81.8	56.3	..	0.0
Côte d'Ivoire	39.8	20.9	18.6	4.5	6.5	15.1	..	81.9
Djibouti	..	..	..	..	..	..	..	7.3
Equatorial Guinea	..	..	..	..	..	..	9.3	0.0
Eritrea	..	..	..	..	..	..	0.0	12.3
Ethiopia	..	..	10.0	..	..	..	..	54.5
Gabon	58.0	34.5	17.7	7.8	22.9	9.7	0.0	..
Gambia, The	..	..	..	..	..	..	..	0.0
Ghana	86.2	24.4	15.6	9.7	26.6	29.5	100.0	34.3
Guinea	..	..	..	..	..	..	..	6.7
Guinea-Bissau	..	..	..	..	..	..	..	3.9
Kenya	27.6	40.5	17.0	7.3	65.7	14.7	0.0	57.0
Lesotho	44.3	13.9	..	7.2	30.9	..	..	-0.1
Liberia	59.1	..	..	5.6	66.5	97.1	17.0	16.5
Madagascar	54.6	92.1	..	13.7	29.3	18.6	..	21.4
Malawi	..	..	..	..	..	..	..	2.1
Mali	55.7	48.4	..	4.4	23.8	16.0	..	11.8
Mauritania	..	..	..	..	..	..	30.1	26.4
Mauritius	42.9	19.2	..	3.6	24.5	3.4	..	..
Mozambique	24.8	12.7	14.1	3.1	12.6	10.8	..	54.6
Namibia	..	..	22.1	..	..	..	..	0.8
Niger	..	..	..	..	..	..	110.0	1.7
Nigeria	75.9	7.7	27.1	26.8	85.7	60.9	280.0	66.9
Rwanda	..	..	..	..	..	..	..	26.4
São Tomé and Príncipe	..	..	..	..	..	..	..	0.0
Senegal	57.7	9.4	25.5	11.8	55.4	24.7	..	90.2
Seychelles	..	..	..	..	..	..	0.0	..
Sierra Leone	53.4	14.8	..	15.9	81.8	44.8	1.2	18.2
Somalia	..	..	..	..	..	..	0.0	..
South Africa	20.8	15.8	8.7	2.2	18.4	10.9	..	5.2
Sudan	..	..	15.2	..	..	..	478.0	2.0
Swaziland	..	..	..	..	..	..	3.8	..
Tanzania	..	..	20.9	..	..	..	..	61.4
Togo	..	..	45.7	..	..	..	..	21.6
Uganda	..	..	..	..	..	..	810.8	158.0
Zambia	11.9	97.0	6.4	4.2	13.7	19.5	..	1.5
Zimbabwe	..	..	7.2	..	..	..	..	0.2
NORTH AFRICA								**667.2**
Algeria	48.1	49.1	17.9	5.1	39.5	7.4	..	0.4
Egypt, Arab Rep.	19.8	142.7	10.9	8.7	29.9	14.3	469.0	330.9
Libya	..	..	7.3	..	..	..	..	3.0
Morocco	37.0	18.8	18.5	2.5	18.0	6.5	..	244.1
Tunisia	..	..	12.5	..	..	..	..	67.4

a. Shares may not sum to 100 percent because other sources of generated electricity (such as geothermal, solar, and wind) are not shown.
b. Data are for the most recent year available during the period specified.

Table 7.1 Education

	Literacy rate (%)						Primary education						
	Youth (ages 15–24)			Adult (ages 15 and older)			Gross enrollment ratio (% of relevant age group)			Net enrollment ratio (% of relevant age group)			Student-teacher ratio
	Total 2007	Male 2007	Female 2007	Total 2007	Male 2007	Female 2007	Total 2007-08[a]	Male 2007-08[a]	Female 2007-08[a]	Total 2007-08[a]	Male 2007-08[a]	Female 2007-08[a]	2007-08[a]
SUB-SAHARAN AFRICA													
Angola	..	..	..	..	..	..	..	..	..	..	..	..	..
Benin	52.4	63.4	41.1	40.5	53.1	27.9	..	..	..	..	..	..	..
Botswana	94.1	92.9	95.3	82.9	82.8	82.9	..	..	..	..	..	..	..
Burkina Faso	39.3	46.7	33.1	28.7	36.7	21.6	71.0	76.0	65.9	58.1	62.3	53.9	48.9
Burundi	..	..	..	..	..	..	114.5	118.7	110.3	81.2	82.2	80.3	52.0
Cameroon	..	..	..	..	..	..	109.6	117.9	101.3	..	..	..	44.4
Cape Verde	97.3	96.6	97.9	83.8	89.4	78.8	101.5	104.6	98.3	84.5	85.3	83.7	24.9
Central African Republic	..	..	..	..	..	..	73.6	86.2	61.2	56.2	64.7	47.9	89.6
Chad	44.4	53.4	35.4	31.8	43.0	20.8	74.0	87.1	60.8	..	..	..	60.4
Comoros	89.5	92.1	86.8	75.1	80.3	69.8	..	..	..	..	..	..	..
Congo, Dem. Rep.	..	..	..	..	..	..	85.1	94.1	76.2	..	..	..	38.3
Congo, Rep.	..	..	..	..	..	..	105.9	110.0	101.8	53.8	56.0	51.6	58.5
Côte d'Ivoire	..	..	..	..	..	..	72.1	80.6	63.7	..	..	..	41.0
Djibouti	..	..	..	..	..	..	55.5	58.9	52.1	45.3	47.9	42.7	34.0
Equatorial Guinea	..	..	..	..	..	..	124.2	127.5	121.0	67.1	68.0	66.2	27.6
Eritrea	..	..	..	..	..	..	54.9	59.9	49.9	41.2	43.9	38.5	47.9
Ethiopia	..	..	..	..	..	..	90.8	96.7	84.8	71.4	74.3	68.5	..
Gabon	97.0	98.0	95.9	86.2	90.2	82.2	..	..	..	..	..	..	..
Gambia, The	..	..	..	..	..	..	83.4	80.4	86.4	66.5	63.8	69.3	40.9
Ghana	77.8	79.7	75.8	65.0	71.7	58.3	103.7	104.4	103.1	72.9	72.5	73.3	32.2
Guinea	..	..	..	..	..	..	90.8	97.8	83.6	73.6	78.6	68.5	45.4
Guinea-Bissau	..	..	..	..	..	..	..	..	..	..	..	..	..
Kenya	..	..	..	..	..	..	112.6	113.5	111.8	86.3	86.3	86.3	45.6
Lesotho	..	..	..	..	..	..	..	..	..	..	..	..	..
Liberia	71.8	67.9	75.7	55.5	60.2	50.9	83.4	88.2	78.5	30.9	31.9	29.8	23.8
Madagascar	..	..	..	..	..	..	141.4	143.7	139.1	98.5	98.0	98.9	48.7
Malawi	83.0	83.7	82.3	71.8	79.2	64.6	116.5	114.4	118.6	87.0	84.0	90.1	66.8
Mali	..	..	..	..	..	..	83.1	92.3	74.0	63.0	69.8	56.2	51.7
Mauritania	66.4	70.0	62.5	55.8	63.3	48.3	103.2	100.4	106.3	80.4	78.1	82.9	42.5
Mauritius	96.2	95.3	97.2	87.4	90.2	84.7	101.4	101.4	101.4	95.4	94.7	96.1	21.5
Mozambique	52.9	58.4	47.5	44.4	57.2	33.0	111.0	118.8	103.3	..	..	..	64.8
Namibia	92.7	90.9	94.4	88.0	88.6	87.4	109.2	109.7	108.8	86.5	84.1	89.0	29.9
Niger	..	..	..	..	..	..	53.3	60.8	45.5	44.9	51.1	38.3	39.7
Nigeria	86.7	88.6	84.7	72.0	80.1	64.1	..	..	..	..	..	..	..
Rwanda	..	..	..	..	..	..	147.4	146.1	148.6	93.6	92.3	94.9	69.3
São Tomé and Príncipe	95.2	95.0	95.5	87.9	93.4	82.7	130.2	131.4	129.0	97.1	97.8	96.5	..
Senegal	..	..	..	..	..	..	83.5	83.6	83.5	71.9	72.0	71.9	34.2
Seychelles	..	..	..	..	..	..	125.3	126.1	124.6	..	..	..	12.5
Sierra Leone	54.1	64.4	43.9	38.1	50.0	26.8	147.1	154.9	139.3	..	..	..	43.7
Somalia	..	..	..	..	..	..	..	..	..	..	..	..	..
South Africa	95.4	94.6	96.3	88.0	88.9	87.2	102.5	104.3	100.7	85.8	85.6	86.0	31.0
Sudan	..	..	..	..	..	..	66.4	71.3	61.2	..	..	..	36.7
Swaziland	..	..	..	..	..	..	113.4	117.8	109.0	87.0	86.2	87.8	32.4
Tanzania	77.5	78.9	76.2	72.3	79.0	65.9	112.4	112.2	112.6	..	..	..	52.6
Togo	..	..	..	..	..	..	97.1	104.2	90.0	77.2	82.3	72.2	39.1
Uganda	86.3	88.3	84.2	73.6	81.8	65.5	116.2	115.7	116.7	94.6	93.2	96.1	57.0
Zambia	75.1	82.4	67.8	70.6	80.8	60.7	119.0	120.7	117.2	94.0	93.7	94.4	49.3
Zimbabwe	91.2	94.1	88.3	91.2	94.1	88.3	..	..	..	..	..	..	..
NORTH AFRICA													
Algeria	92.5	94.2	90.6	75.4	84.3	66.4	109.7	113.2	106.0	95.4	96.1	94.5	24.0
Egypt, Arab Rep.	..	..	..	..	..	..	104.7	107.5	101.7	95.7	97.9	93.5	27.1
Libya	98.9	99.7	98.0	86.8	94.5	78.4	..	..	..	..	..	..	..
Morocco	75.1	83.8	66.5	55.6	68.7	43.2	107.2	113.0	101.3	88.8	91.2	86.4	27.4
Tunisia	95.7	97.0	94.3	77.7	86.4	69.0	104.7	106.0	103.2	95.0	94.6	95.5	18.2

(continued)

Table 7.1 Education (continued)

	Secondary education							Tertiary education			Public spending on education (%)	
	Gross enrollment ratio (% of relevant age group)			Net enrollment ratio (% of relevant age group)			Student-teacher ratio	Gross enrollment ratio (% of relevant age group)			Share of government expenditure	Share of GDP
	Total 2007-08[a]	Male 2007-08[a]	Female 2007-08[a]	Total 2007-08[a]	Male 2007-08[a]	Female 2007-08[a]	2007-08[a]	Total 2007-08[a]	Male 2007-08[a]	Female 2007-08[a]	2007	2007
SUB-SAHARAN AFRICA												
Angola	..	..	..	..	..	..	..	..	..	..	..	..
Benin	..	..	..	..	..	..	..	..	..	..	..	..
Botswana	..	..	..	..	..	..	..	..	..	..	21.0	8.1
Burkina Faso	18.1	20.7	15.3	14.1	16.2	11.9	30.3	3.0	4.0	2.0	..	..
Burundi	15.2	17.7	12.8	..	..	..	28.0	1.9	2.6	1.2	..	..
Cameroon	25.2	28.0	22.2	..	..	..	..	7.2	8.0	6.3	17.0	3.9
Cape Verde	79.3	72.7	86.0	60.7	56.8	64.6	19.0	8.9	8.1	9.8	16.4	5.7
Central African Republic	..	..	..	..	..	..	..	..	..	..	..	..
Chad	18.8	26.0	11.6	..	..	..	32.9	..	..	..	..	..
Comoros	..	..	..	..	..	..	..	..	..	..	..	..
Congo, Dem. Rep.	33.4	43.6	23.1	..	..	..	15.7	4.1	6.0	2.1	..	..
Congo, Rep.	..	..	..	..	..	..	..	..	..	..	..	..
Côte d'Ivoire	..	..	..	..	..	..	..	7.9	10.5	5.3	..	..
Djibouti	29.5	34.7	24.2	24.4	28.4	20.4	34.3	2.6	3.1	2.1	22.8	8.6
Equatorial Guinea	..	..	..	..	..	..	..	..	..	..	..	..
Eritrea	29.2	34.3	24.2	25.1	29.3	21.0	49.3	..	..	..	..	..
Ethiopia	30.5	36.5	24.4	..	..	..	..	2.7	4.1	1.4	23.3	5.5
Gabon	..	..	..	..	..	..	..	..	..	..	..	..
Gambia, The	48.6	49.7	47.5	40.1	40.1	40.0	22.7	..	..	..	..	..
Ghana	53.3	56.5	50.1	44.9	47.1	42.7	17.5	5.8	7.5	4.1	..	..
Guinea	37.6	47.8	27.0	30.1	37.4	22.4	38.2	..	..	..	..	..
Guinea-Bissau	..	..	..	..	..	..	..	..	..	..	..	..
Kenya	52.8	56.3	49.3	44.8	47.0	42.6	26.6	3.5	4.4	2.5	..	..
Lesotho	..	..	..	..	..	..	..	..	..	..	..	..
Liberia	..	..	..	..	..	..	..	..	..	..	..	..
Madagascar	26.4	27.0	25.7	21.2	21.1	21.3	24.3	3.2	3.4	3.0	16.4	3.4
Malawi	28.3	30.8	25.7	23.9	25.0	22.8	..	0.5	0.7	0.3	..	..
Mali	31.6	38.6	24.7	..	..	..	35.6	4.4	..	..	..	..
Mauritania	25.2	26.7	23.6	16.8	17.8	15.7	26.6	4.0	..	..	..	..
Mauritius	..	..	..	..	..	..	..	14.0	12.9	15.0	..	..
Mozambique	18.3	21.2	15.5	2.6	2.8	2.3	36.9	..	..	..	..	..
Namibia	59.0	54.4	63.6	49.6	44.4	54.8	24.6	..	..	..	..	..
Niger	10.6	13.2	8.1	9.0	11.1	6.9	27.3	1.0	1.7	0.5	..	..
Nigeria	..	..	..	..	..	..	..	..	..	..	..	..
Rwanda	18.1	19.1	17.1	..	..	..	22.0	..	..	..	19.0	4.9
São Tomé and Príncipe	46.3	44.7	47.9	38.1	36.1	40.2	..	..	..	..	..	..
Senegal	26.3	29.8	22.7	22.2	25.0	19.4	25.2	7.7	10.0	5.5	..	..
Seychelles	111.8	105.3	119.1	94.3	..	..	13.3	..	..	..	..	..
Sierra Leone	31.6	37.5	25.8	22.8	26.7	19.0	23.9	..	..	..	..	..
Somalia	..	..	..	..	..	..	..	..	..	..	..	..
South Africa	97.1	94.8	99.4	73.4	71.1	75.7	29.0	..	..	..	17.4	5.4
Sudan	33.4	34.6	32.1	..	..	..	18.5	..	..	..	..	..
Swaziland	54.4	57.5	51.3	29.2	31.6	26.8	19.1	..	..	..	..	..
Tanzania	..	..	..	25.8	27.6	24.0	..	1.5	2.0	1.0	..	..
Togo	39.3	51.6	27.2	..	..	..	35.5	5.2	..	..	17.2	3.7
Uganda	22.5	24.6	20.4	18.9	19.9	17.9	18.4	..	..	..	..	..
Zambia	43.1	45.7	40.6	40.9	43.7	38.1	42.6	..	..	..	..	1.5
Zimbabwe	..	..	..	..	..	..	..	..	..	..	..	..
NORTH AFRICA												
Algeria	..	..	..	..	..	..	..	24.0	20.1	28.1	..	..
Egypt, Arab Rep.	..	..	..	..	..	..	..	..	..	..	12.6	3.8
Libya	..	..	..	..	..	..	..	..	..	..	..	..
Morocco	55.8	60.1	51.4	..	..	..	..	11.3	12.0	10.7	..	..
Tunisia	88.0	..	..	..	..	..	15.9	30.8	24.7	37.2	..	..

a. Data are for the most recent year available during the period specified.

Table 7.2 Health

	Mortality						Diseases			
	Life expectancy at birth (years)			Under-five mortality rate (per 1,000)	Infant mortality rate (per 1,000 live births)	Maternal mortality ratio, modeled estimate (per 100,000 live births)	Prevalence of HIV (% of ages 15–49)	Incidence of tuberculosis (per 100,000 people)	Malaria	
	Total	Male	Female						Clinical cases reported	Reported deaths
	2007–08[a]	2007–08[a]	2007–08[a]	2007	2007	2005	2007	2007	2008	2008
SUB-SAHARAN AFRICA	**51.5**	**50.5**	**52.6**	**146**	**88**	**899**	**5.0**	**369**	**25,729,664**	**91,244**
Angola	47.3	45.3	49.3	158	116	1,400	2.1	287	1,377,992	9,465
Benin	61.6	60.5	62.8	123	78	840	1.2	91	..	..
Botswana	50.6	50.5	50.7	40	33	380	23.9	731	1,201	12
Burkina Faso	52.2	50.7	53.8	191	104	700	1.6	226	36,514	7,834
Burundi	50.6	49.2	52.2	180	108	1,100	2.0	367	876,741	226
Cameroon	50.4	50.0	50.8	148	87	1,000	5.1	192	1,650,749	7,673
Cape Verde	71.2	68.6	73.9	32	24	210	..	151	35	2
Central African Republic	44.7	43.3	46.1	172	113	980	6.3	345	152,260	456
Chad	50.6	49.3	52.0	209	124	1,500	3.5	299	57,644	1,018
Comoros	65.1	63.0	67.4	66	49	400	<0.1	42	..	47
Congo, Dem. Rep.	46.4	45.2	47.7	161	108	1,100	..	392	1,462,300	18,928
Congo, Rep.	53.7	52.8	54.7	125	79	740	3.5	403	..	..
Côte d'Ivoire	57.8	56.5	59.1	127	89	810	3.9	421	1,343,654	1,249
Djibouti	54.8	53.6	56.0	127	84	650	3.1	813	119	..
Equatorial Guinea	50.5	49.3	51.7	206	124	680	3.4	256	50,758	..
Eritrea	57.9	55.6	60.3	70	46	450	1.3	95	4,702	19
Ethiopia	55.4	54.0	56.9	119	75	720	2.1	378	458,561	1,169
Gabon	60.7	59.5	62.1	91	60	520	5.9	406	40,701	156
Gambia, The	56.1	54.5	57.8	109	82	690	0.9	258	10,910	403
Ghana	56.8	55.9	57.7	115	73	560	1.9	203	827,438	3,889
Guinea	58.1	56.1	60.1	150	93	910	1.6	287	33,405	441
Guinea-Bissau	48.0	46.5	49.6	198	118	1,100	1.8	220	11,299	487
Kenya	54.1	53.0	55.2	121	80	560	..	353	839,904	..
Lesotho	42.6	42.9	42.3	84	68	960	23.2	637	..	..
Liberia	58.4	57.1	59.8	133	93	1,200	1.7	277	606,952	345
Madagascar	60.5	58.9	62.2	112	70	510	0.1	251	89,138	276
Malawi	48.3	48.1	48.4	111	71	1,100	11.9	346	4,986,779	7,748
Mali	54.3	52.1	56.6	196	117	970	1.5	319	..	1,227
Mauritania	64.1	62.4	66.0	119	75	820	0.8	318	302	..
Mauritius	72.4	69.1	75.9	15	13	15	1.7	22	..	..
Mozambique	42.1	41.7	42.4	169	115	520	12.5	431	4,831,491	4,424
Namibia	52.8	52.5	53.1	68	47	210	15.3	767	4,907	171
Niger	56.9	57.8	56.0	176	83	1,800	0.8	174	413,252	2,691
Nigeria	46.8	46.4	47.3	189	97	1,100	3.1	311	143,079	8,677
Rwanda	50.2	48.5	52.1	181	109	1,300	2.8	397	228,015	563
São Tomé and Príncipe	65.4	63.6	67.4	99	64	..	..	101	1,572	16
Senegal	55.7	54.2	57.3	114	59	980	1.0	272	202,466	722
Seychelles	73.2	68.9	77.7	13	12	..	..	32	..	..
Sierra Leone	47.7	46.4	49.0	262	155	2,100	1.7	574	154,459	871
Somalia	48.1	46.9	49.4	142	88	1,400	0.5	249	23,905	21
South Africa	50.5	49.0	52.0	59	46	400	18.1	948	7,796	43
Sudan	58.3	56.8	59.9	109	70	450	1.4	243	457,362[c]	1,125[c]
Swaziland	46.4	47.0	45.7	91	66	390	26.1	1,198	58	5
Tanzania	55.9	55.1	56.8	116	73	950	6.2	297	67	29
Togo	62.7	61.0	64.5	100	65	510	3.3	429	273,471	2,663
Uganda	53.0	52.4	53.6	130	82	550	5.4	330	894,505	2,372
Zambia	45.9	45.4	46.5	170	103	830	15.2	506	3,080,301	3,781
Zimbabwe	45.1	44.8	45.4	90	59	880	15.3	782	92,900	..
NORTH AFRICA	**71.1**	**69.4**	**73.0**	**35**	**30**	**156**		**42**	**418**	**..**
Algeria	72.3	70.9	73.7	37	33	180	0.1	57	196	..
Egypt, Arab Rep.	70.2	68.5	72.0	36	30	130	..	21	80	..
Libya	74.2	71.7	76.9	18	17	97	..	17	..	..
Morocco	71.1	69.0	73.4	34	32	240	0.1	92	142	..
Tunisia	74.3	72.4	76.3	21	18	100	0.1	26	..	..

(continued)

Table 7.2 Health (continued)

	Prevention and treatment										
	Child immunization rate (% of children ages 12–23 months)		Malnutrition (% of children under age 5)		Births attended by skilled health staff (% of total)	Contraceptive use (% of married women ages 15–49)		Children sleeping under insecticide-treated nets (% of under age 5)	Tuberculosis cases detected under DOTS (% of estimated cases)	Tuberculosis treatment success rate (% of registered cases)	Children with fever receiving any antimalarial treatment same or next day (% of under age 5)
	Measles	DPT[b]	Stunting	Underweight		Any method	Modern method				
	2007	2007	2000–08[a]	2000–08[a]	2000–08[a]	2000–08[a]	2000–08[a]	2000–08[a]	2007	2006	2000–08[a]
SUB-SAHARAN AFRICA	73	73	..	..	..	..	..	..	47.1	75.5	..
Angola	88	83	50.8	27.5	47.3	6.2	4.5	17.7	101.8	17.7	28.0
Benin	61	67	39.1	21.5	77.7	17.0	5.9	20.2	..	..	54.0
Botswana	90	97	29.1	10.7	94.2	44.4	42.1	..	57.2	72.5	..
Burkina Faso	94	99	43.1	35.2	53.5	17.4	13.3	9.6	18.4	72.8	48.0
Burundi	75	74	63.1	38.9	33.6	19.7	8.5	8.3	26.8	82.6	30.0
Cameroon	74	82	35.4	15.1	63.0	29.2	12.0	13.1	91.4	74.2	58.0
Cape Verde	74	81	..	..	77.5	61.3	..	..	44.0	78.6	..
Central African Republic	62	54	44.6	21.8	53.4	19.0	8.6	15.1	..	..	57.0
Chad	23	20	44.8	33.9	14.4	2.8	1.7	..	18.5	54.2	53.0
Comoros	65	75	46.9	25.0	61.8	25.7	19.3	9.3	..	..	62.7
Congo, Dem. Rep.	79	87	44.4	33.6	74.0	20.6	5.8	5.8	60.7	86.2	29.8
Congo, Rep.	67	80	31.2	11.8	83.4	44.3	12.7	6.1	55.7	52.5	48.0
Côte d'Ivoire	67	76	40.1	16.7	56.8	12.9	8.0	5.9	42.2	73.2	36.0
Djibouti	74	88	..	..	60.6	17.8	17.1	1.3	42.3	77.5	9.5
Equatorial Guinea	51	33	35.0	10.6	64.6	10.1	6.1	0.7	..	..	48.6
Eritrea	95	97	43.7	34.5	28.3	8.0	5.1	4.2	34.5	89.7	3.6
Ethiopia	65	73	50.7	34.6	5.7	14.7	13.7	33.1	28.1	84.1	9.5
Gabon	55	38	26.3	8.8	85.5	32.7	11.8	..	66.2	46.5	..
Gambia, The	85	90	27.6	15.8	56.8	17.5	12.7	49.0	63.9	57.7	62.6
Ghana	95	94	28.0	13.9	49.7	23.5	16.6	28.2	35.9	76.4	24.0
Guinea	71	75	39.3	22.5	38.0	9.1	4.0	0.3	53.5	75.4	43.5
Guinea-Bissau	76	63	36.1	21.9	38.8	10.3	6.1	39.0	..	..	45.7
Kenya	80	81	35.8	16.5	41.6	39.3	31.5	6.0	72.1	85.1	24.0
Lesotho	85	83	45.2	16.6	55.4	37.3	35.2	..	16.5	66.5	..
Liberia	95	88	39.4	20.4	46.4	11.4	10.3	3.0	..	..	58.8
Madagascar	81	82	52.8	36.8	51.3	27.1	16.7	0.2	69.5	78.0	34.2
Malawi	83	87	52.5	18.4	53.6	41.0	38.4	23.0	41.4	78.0	23.9
Mali	68	68	38.5	27.9	49.0	8.2	6.3	27.1	22.9	76.0	31.7
Mauritania	67	75	39.5	30.4	60.9	9.3	8.0	2.1	39.3	40.6	20.7
Mauritius	98	97	..	..	98.4	75.8	39.3	..	68.7	91.7	..
Mozambique	77	72	47.0	21.2	47.7	16.5	11.7	22.8	49.0	82.7	23.0
Namibia	69	86	29.6	17.5	81.4	55.1	53.5	..	83.6	76.4	9.8
Niger	47	39	54.8	39.9	32.9	11.2	5.0	7.4	52.8	76.5	33.0
Nigeria	62	54	43.0	27.2	35.2	14.7	9.1	1.2	22.6	76.4	33.3
Rwanda	99	97	51.7	18.0	52.1	36.4	26.1	24.0	25.4	86.4	5.6
São Tomé and Príncipe	86	97	35.2	10.1	80.7	29.3	27.4	54.0	..	..	24.7
Senegal	84	94	20.1	14.5	51.9	11.8	10.0	31.0	48.3	76.0	22.0
Seychelles	99	99	..	..	..	..	..	..	..	..	..
Sierra Leone	67	64	46.9	28.3	43.2	8.2	6.0	25.9	36.9	87.1	30.1
Somalia	34	39	42.1	32.8	33.0	14.6	1.2	9.2	63.9	89.0	7.9
South Africa	83	97	..	..	92.0	60.3	60.3	..	78.1	73.8	..
Sudan	79	84	47.6	38.4	49.2	7.6	5.7	27.6	30.6	81.7	..
Swaziland	91	95	36.6	9.1	69.0	50.6	46.8	0.6	54.7	42.5	0.6
Tanzania	90	83	44.4	16.7	43.4	26.4	19.5	25.7	50.5	84.7	56.7
Togo	80	88	..	..	62.0	16.8	11.1	38.4	15.1	67.3	47.7
Uganda	68	64	44.8	19.0	42.1	23.7	17.9	9.7	50.9	69.6	61.8
Zambia	85	80	52.5	23.3	46.5	40.8	26.5	41.1	58.3	84.9	43.3
Zimbabwe	66	62	35.8	14.0	68.5	60.2	57.9	2.9	26.6	60.0	4.7
NORTH AFRICA	96	97	24.3	4.6	70.4	59.3	53.1	..	..	..	..
Algeria	92	95	21.6	10.2	95.2	61.4	52.0	..	98.4	90.8	..
Egypt, Arab Rep.	97	98	23.8	5.4	78.9	60.3	57.6	..	72.2	86.9	..
Libya	98	98	..	..	..	..	..	..	161.8	76.5	..
Morocco	95	95	23.1	9.9	62.6	63.0	52.0	..	92.8	86.6	..
Tunisia	98	98	..	..	89.9	60.2	51.5	..	78.2	90.6	..

Water and sanitation						Human resources		
Population with sustainable access to an improved water source			Population with sustainable access to improved sanitation			Health workers (per 1,000 people)		
(% of total population) 2006	(% of urban population) 2006	(% of rural population) 2006	(% of total population) 2006	(% of urban population) 2006	(% of rural population) 2006	Physicians 2005	Nurses and midwives 2005	Community workers 2005
58	**81**	**46**	**31**	**43**	**24**	**..**	**..**	**..**
51	62	39	50	79	16	0.1	1.4	..
65	78	57	30	59	11	0.0	0.8	0.0
96	100	90	47	60	30	0.4	2.7	..
72	97	66	13	41	6	0.1	0.5	0.1
71	84	70	41	44	41	0.0	0.2	0.1
70	88	47	51	58	42	0.2	1.6	..
..	..	..	..	..	..	0.5	0.9	0.1
66	90	51	31	40	25	0.1	0.4	0.0
48	71	40	9	23	4	0.0	0.3	0.0
85	91	81	35	49	26	0.2	0.7	0.1
46	82	29	31	42	25	0.1	0.5	..
71	95	35	20	19	21	0.2	1.0	0.0
81	98	66	24	38	12	0.1	0.6	..
92	98	54	67	76	11	0.2	0.4	0.0
43	45	42	51	60	46	0.3	0.5	0.6
60	74	57	5	14	3	0.1	0.6	..
42	96	31	11	27	8	0.0	0.2	0.2
87	95	47	36	37	30	0.3	5.0	..
86	91	81	52	50	55	0.1	1.3	0.3
80	90	71	10	15	6	0.2	0.9	..
70	91	59	19	33	12	0.1	0.5	0.0
57	82	47	33	48	26	0.1	0.7	1.5
57	85	49	42	19	48	0.1	1.2	..
78	93	74	36	43	34	0.1	0.6	..
64	72	52	32	49	7	0.0	0.3	0.0
47	76	36	12	18	10	0.3	0.3	0.0
76	96	72	60	51	62	0.0	0.6	..
60	86	48	45	59	39	0.1	0.6	0.0
60	70	54	24	44	10	0.1	0.6	0.1
100	100	100	94	95	94	1.1	3.7	0.2
42	71	26	31	53	19	0.0	0.3	..
93	99	90	35	66	18	0.3	3.1	..
42	91	32	7	27	3	0.0	0.2	..
47	65	30	30	35	25	0.3	1.7	0.9
65	82	61	23	34	20	0.1	0.4	1.4
86	88	83	24	29	18	0.5	1.9	0.9
77	93	65	28	54	9	0.1	0.3	..
..	100	..	..	..	100	1.5	7.9	..
53	83	32	11	20	5	0.0	0.5	0.1
29	63	10	23	51	7	..	..	..
93	100	82	59	66	49	0.8	4.1	0.2
70	78	64	35	50	24	0.3	0.9	0.1
60	87	51	50	64	46	0.2	6.3	3.7
55	81	46	33	31	34	0.0	0.4	..
59	86	40	12	24	3	0.0	0.4	0.1
64	90	60	33	29	34	0.1	0.7	..
58	90	41	52	55	51	0.1	2.0	..
81	98	72	46	63	37	0.2	0.7	0.0
92	**96**	**87**	**75**	**90**	**59**	**..**	**..**	**..**
85	87	81	94	98	87	1.1	2.2	0.0
98	99	98	66	85	52	2.4	3.4	..
..	..	..	97	97	96	1.3	4.8	..
83	100	58	72	85	54	0.5	0.8	..
94	99	84	85	96	64	1.3	2.9	..

(continued)

Table 7.2 Health (continued)

	Health expenditure								
	Share of GDP (%)			Share of total health expenditure (%)			Out-of-pocket (% of private expenditure on health)	Private prepaid plans (% of private expenditure on health)	Health expenditure per capita ($)
	Total 2006	Public 2006	Private 2006	Public 2006	Private 2006	External resources for health 2006	2006	2006	2006
SUB-SAHARAN AFRICA	**5.7**	**2.4**	**3.3**	**41.5**	**58.5**	**..**	**46.9**	**..**	**54**
Angola	2.6	2.3	0.3	86.8	13.2	7.0	100.0	0.0	71
Benin	4.7	2.4	2.3	50.2	49.8	21.0	94.9	5.1	26
Botswana	7.1	5.4	1.7	76.5	23.5	5.8	27.5	5.2	379
Burkina Faso	6.3	3.6	2.7	56.9	43.1	32.9	91.5	2.1	27
Burundi	8.7	0.7	8.0	8.6	91.4	47.5	57.4	..	10
Cameroon	4.6	1.0	3.6	21.2	78.8	8.0	94.8	..	45
Cape Verde	4.9	3.8	1.1	78.3	21.7	17.5	99.7	0.3	112
Central African Republic	4.0	1.5	2.5	38.3	61.7	21.2	95.0	..	14
Chad	4.9	2.6	2.3	53.9	46.1	17.7	96.2	0.4	29
Comoros	3.2	1.8	1.4	55.1	44.9	31.9	100.0	0.0	16
Congo, Dem. Rep.	6.8	1.3	5.5	18.7	81.3	51.9	48.9	..	10
Congo, Rep.	2.1	1.5	0.6	71.7	28.3	3.4	100.0	..	44
Côte d'Ivoire	3.8	0.9	2.9	23.6	76.4	8.3	87.8	12.2	35
Djibouti	6.8	5.0	1.8	74.1	25.9	30.1	98.6	1.4	63
Equatorial Guinea	2.1	1.7	0.4	80.4	19.6	3.5	75.6	0.0	440
Eritrea	3.6	1.7	1.9	45.9	54.1	37.6	100.0	0.0	8
Ethiopia	3.9	2.3	1.6	59.3	40.7	42.7	80.6	3.0	7
Gabon	4.5	3.3	1.2	73.0	27.0	1.8	100.0	..	351
Gambia, The	5.0	2.8	2.2	56.8	43.2	34.7	71.2	4.6	15
Ghana	5.1	1.7	3.4	34.2	65.8	22.6	77.8	6.0	33
Guinea	5.8	0.8	5.0	14.1	85.9	11.8	99.5	0.0	20
Guinea-Bissau	5.8	1.5	4.3	26.3	73.7	33.4	55.8	0.0	12
Kenya	4.6	2.2	2.4	47.8	52.2	14.9	80.0	6.9	29
Lesotho	6.8	4.0	2.8	58.9	41.1	14.3	68.9	..	51
Liberia	4.8	1.2	3.6	25.8	74.2	50.7	65.7	0.0	7
Madagascar	3.2	2.0	1.2	62.8	37.2	49.4	52.5	10.7	9
Malawi	12.9	8.9	4.0	69.0	31.0	59.6	28.4	15.7	21
Mali	5.8	2.9	2.9	49.6	50.4	17.6	99.5	0.5	31
Mauritania	2.2	1.5	0.7	69.5	30.5	18.0	100.0	0.0	19
Mauritius	3.9	2.0	1.9	51.1	48.9	1.0	80.6	10.0	230
Mozambique	5.0	3.5	1.5	70.8	29.2	60.3	40.6	0.6	16
Namibia	8.7	3.8	4.9	43.5	56.5	22.4	5.7	64.0	281
Niger	5.9	3.2	2.7	54.7	45.3	32.8	96.5	3.0	16
Nigeria	3.8	1.1	2.7	29.7	70.3	5.9	90.4	6.7	33
Rwanda	10.9	4.6	6.3	42.5	57.5	52.4	38.6	9.2	33
São Tomé and Príncipe	6.3	5.4	0.9	85.0	15.0	50.5	100.0	0.0	49
Senegal	5.8	3.3	2.5	56.9	43.1	12.3	77.0	19.5	44
Seychelles	6.3	4.7	1.6	75.1	24.9	3.4	62.5	0.0	565
Sierra Leone	4.0	1.5	2.5	36.4	63.6	33.5	56.4	3.7	12
Somalia	..	..	..	..	..	..	..	..	..
South Africa	8.0	3.0	5.0	37.7	62.3	0.9	17.5	77.7	425
Sudan	3.8	1.4	2.4	36.8	63.2	6.5	100.0	..	37
Swaziland	6.3	4.1	2.2	65.8	34.2	12.3	41.4	18.5	155
Tanzania	6.4	3.7	2.7	57.8	42.2	43.9	54.3	7.7	23
Togo	6.0	1.3	4.7	21.2	78.8	12.3	84.2	4.3	21
Uganda	7.0	1.8	5.2	25.4	74.6	31.2	51.0	0.2	24
Zambia	6.2	3.8	2.4	60.7	39.3	38.1	67.2	3.7	58
Zimbabwe	9.3	4.5	4.8	48.7	51.3	17.3	50.3	28.8	38
NORTH AFRICA	**4.8**	**2.5**	**2.4**	**51.2**	**48.8**	**..**	**88.6**	**..**	**117**
Algeria	4.2	3.4	0.8	81.1	18.9	0.1	94.6	5.2	148
Egypt, Arab Rep.	6.3	2.6	3.7	41.4	58.6	0.8	94.9	0.2	92
Libya	2.4	1.6	0.8	66.3	33.7	0.0	100.0	0.0	219
Morocco	5.3	1.4	3.9	26.2	73.8	2.5	77.3	22.7	113
Tunisia	5.1	2.3	2.8	44.2	55.8	0.9	81.7	16.6	156

a. Data are for the most recent year available during the period specified.
b. Diphtheria, pertussis, and tetanus toxoid.
c. Data are for 15 northern states only.

Table 8.1 Rural development

	Rural population (%)				Rural population density (rural population per sq. km of arable land)	Share of rural population below the national poverty line				Rural population poverty gap (%)			
	Share of total population		Annual growth			Surveys 1990–99[a]		Surveys 2000–07[a]		Surveys 1990–99[a]		Surveys 2000–07[a]	
	2007	2008	2007	2008	2007	Year	Percent	Year	Percent	Year	Percent	Year	Percent
SUB-SAHARAN AFRICA	**64.0**	**63.5**	**1.7**	**1.7**	**..**		**..**		**..**		**..**		**..**
Angola	44.2	43.3	0.7	0.6	235.1		..		..		..		..
Benin	59.2	58.8	2.5	2.5	184.0	1999	33.0	2003	46.0	1999	9.4	2003	14.0
Botswana	41.2	40.4	−0.6	−0.6	309.9		..		..		..		..
Burkina Faso	80.9	80.4	2.4	2.4	229.8	1998	61.1	2003	52.4		..	2003	17.6
Burundi	89.9	89.6	2.7	2.6	708.2	1998	64.6		..		..		..
Cameroon	44.1	43.2	0.1	0.1	137.0	1996	59.6	2007	55.0		..	2007	17.5
Cape Verde	41.1	40.4	−0.3	−0.4	404.4		..		..		..		..
Central African Republic	61.6	61.4	1.6	1.6	138.9		..		..		..		..
Chad	73.8	73.3	2.2	2.2	184.7	1996	67.0		..	1996	26.3		..
Comoros	72.0	71.9	2.3	2.3	565.4		..		..		..		..
Congo, Dem. Rep.	66.7	66.0	1.9	1.9	620.8		..	2004	75.7		..	2004	34.9
Congo, Rep.	39.0	38.7	0.9	0.8	280.1		..	2005	49.2		..		..
Côte d'Ivoire	51.9	51.2	1.0	1.0	372.8		..		..		..		..
Djibouti	13.1	12.7	−1.3	−1.3	8,394.0		..		..		..		..
Equatorial Guinea	60.8	60.6	2.4	2.3	300.3		..		..		..		..
Eritrea	79.7	79.3	2.6	2.6	603.1		..		..		..		..
Ethiopia	83.3	83.0	2.2	2.2	466.7	1996	47.0	2000	45.0		..	2000	12.0
Gabon	15.4	15.0	−1.2	−1.3	67.6		..		..		..		..
Gambia, The	44.4	43.6	0.9	0.8	206.2	1998	61.0	2003	63.0		..		..
Ghana	50.7	50.0	0.7	0.6	282.9	1997	49.6	2005	39.2		..	2005	13.5
Guinea	66.0	65.6	1.4	1.5	288.6		..		..		..		..
Guinea-Bissau	70.2	70.2	2.1	2.1	360.8		..		..		..		..
Kenya	78.7	78.4	2.3	2.3	568.0	1997	52.9	2005	49.1	1997	19.3	2005	17.5
Lesotho	75.3	74.5	−0.4	−0.4	503.2	1994	68.9	2002	60.5		..		..
Liberia	40.5	39.9	2.7	2.8	381.9		..	2007	67.7		..	2007	26.3
Madagascar	70.8	70.5	2.2	2.2	446.6	1999	76.7	2005	68.7	1999	36.1		..
Malawi	81.7	81.2	1.9	1.9	379.1	1998	66.5	2004	55.9		..	2004	8.6
Mali	68.4	67.8	2.2	2.2	173.9	1998	75.9		..		..		..
Mauritania	59.2	59.0	2.2	2.2	410.6	1996	65.5	2000	61.2		..		..
Mauritius	57.6	57.5	0.5	0.5	806.6		..		..		..		..
Mozambique	63.9	63.2	0.7	0.7	307.1	1996	71.3	2002	55.3	1996	29.9	2002	20.9
Namibia	63.7	63.2	0.7	0.7	165.7		..		..		..		..
Niger	83.5	83.5	3.2	3.2	80.6	1993	66.0		..		..		..
Nigeria	52.4	51.6	0.9	0.8	212.3	1992	36.4	2003	63.8		..	2003	26.6
Rwanda	81.9	81.7	2.3	2.4	645.6		..	2005	62.5		..		..
São Tomé and Príncipe	40.3	39.4	−0.2	−0.2	706.8		..		..		..		..
Senegal	57.9	57.6	2.2	2.2	230.6	1992	40.4		..	1992	16.4		..
Seychelles	46.1	45.7	−0.5	0.5	3,923.4		..		..		..		..
Sierra Leone	62.6	62.2	2.3	2.0	376.8		..	2003	78.5		..	2003	34.6
Somalia	63.9	63.5	2.2	2.2	555.8		..		..		..		..
South Africa	39.7	39.3	−0.2	0.5	131.1		..		..		..		..
Sudan	57.4	56.6	0.7	0.7	120.2		..		..		..		..
Swaziland	75.3	75.1	0.9	1.0	487.3		..	2001	75.0		..		..
Tanzania	74.9	74.5	2.3	2.3	343.6	1991	40.8	2007	37.6		..		..
Togo	58.7	58.0	1.3	1.3	150.3		..		..		..		..
Uganda	87.2	87.0	3.1	3.1	485.6	1999	37.4	2005	34.2	1999	11.2	2005	9.7
Zambia	64.7	64.6	2.2	2.2	151.5	1998	83.1	2006	76.8		..	2006	38.8
Zimbabwe	63.1	62.7	−0.8	−0.7	243.4	1996	48.0		..		..		..
NORTH AFRICA	**47.4**	**47.2**	**1.1**	**1.1**	**..**		**..**		**..**		**..**		**..**
Algeria	35.4	34.8	−0.3	−0.3	160.5	1995	30.3		..	1995	4.5		..
Egypt, Arab Rep.	57.3	57.3	1.8	1.7	1,520.6	1996	23.3		..		..		..
Libya	22.6	22.5	1.1	1.1	79.6		..		..		..		..
Morocco	44.3	44.0	0.4	0.4	169.6	1999	27.2		..	1999	6.7		..
Tunisia	33.9	33.5	−0.2	−0.2	125.7	1995	13.9		..	1990	3.3		..

(continued)

Table 8.1 Rural development (continued)

	Share of rural population with sustainable access (%)		
	To an improved water source	To improved sanitation facilities	To transportation (within 2 km of an all-season road)
	2006	2006	2000–07[a]
SUB-SAHARAN AFRICA	46	24	..
Angola	39	16	..
Benin	57	11	32
Botswana	90	30	..
Burkina Faso	66	6	25
Burundi	70	41	..
Cameroon	47	42	22
Cape Verde	73	19	..
Central African Republic	51	25	..
Chad	40	4	..
Comoros	81	26	..
Congo, Dem. Rep.	29	25	26
Congo, Rep.	35	21	..
Côte d'Ivoire	66	12	..
Djibouti	54	11	..
Equatorial Guinea	42	46	..
Eritrea	57	3	..
Ethiopia	31	8	33
Gabon	47	30	..
Gambia, The	81	55	..
Ghana	71	6	..
Guinea	59	12	37
Guinea-Bissau	47	26	..
Kenya	49	48	..
Lesotho	74	34	..
Liberia	52	7	..
Madagascar	36	10	22
Malawi	72	62	..
Mali	48	39	..
Mauritania	54	10	..
Mauritius	100	94	..
Mozambique	26	19	12
Namibia	90	18	..
Niger	32	3	33
Nigeria	30	25	..
Rwanda	61	20	..
São Tomé and Príncipe	83	18	..
Senegal	65	9	..
Seychelles	75	100	..
Sierra Leone	32	5	22
Somalia	10	7	..
South Africa	82	49	..
Sudan	64	24	..
Swaziland	51	46	..
Tanzania	46	34	16
Togo	40	3	..
Uganda	60	34	..
Zambia	41	51	51
Zimbabwe	72	37	..
NORTH AFRICA	87	59	..
Algeria	81	87	..
Egypt, Arab Rep.	98	52	..
Libya	68	96	..
Morocco	58	54	..
Tunisia	84	64	..

a. Data are for the most recent year available during the period specified.

Table 8.2 Agriculture

	Agriculture value added (% of GDP)	Gross production index (1999–2001=100)					Cereal (thousands of metric tons)			Trade			
										Agricultural		Food	
		Agriculture total	Crop	Livestock	Food	Cereal	Production	Exports	Imports	Exports ($ millions)	Imports ($ millions)	Exports ($ millions)	Imports ($ millions)
	2008[a]	2007	2007	2007	2007	2007	2007	2007	2007	2007	2007	2007	2007
SUB-SAHARAN AFRICA	14.6	..	..	..	..	..	..	2,983	24,224	20,746	25,711	12,052	20,894
Angola	10.1	151	179	99	153	133	731	1,519	616	7	1,556	6	1,155
Benin	..	104	102	124	109	120	1,221	1	983	217	908	69	846
Botswana	1.6	111	110	111	111	170	48	18	145	151	518	133	398
Burkina Faso	..	123	120	129	122	136	3,736	5	111	319	247	70	177
Burundi	..	100	102	79	101	113	279	17	87	56	87	1	78
Cameroon	19.1	109	111	103	113	119	1,567	0	558	802	510	511	433
Cape Verde	8.1	117	102	132	117	11	12	0	86	1	193	0	160
Central African Republic	50.3	100	101	99	104	133	201	0	44	43	38	16	31
Chad	19	105	100	114	110	166	3,083	0	151	110	93	55	88
Comoros	45.8	105	106	98	105	100	21	0	50	8	45	8	41
Congo, Dem. Rep.	..	96	96	96	96	96	1,522	0	429	42	542	5	491
Congo, Rep.	..	122	114	156	122	181	10	5	227	65	376	28	329
Côte d'Ivoire	23.7	107	107	110	115	97	1,396	0	1,200	3,476	949	2,594	804
Djibouti	..	153	101	167	153	90	0	25	123	58	368	57	274
Equatorial Guinea	2	95	95	102	95	..	..	12	21	4	84	4	39
Eritrea	..	102	104	100	102	86	177	0	214	3	78	3	77
Ethiopia	39.8	135	134	137	135	138	13,666	3	694	1,028	526	353	462
Gabon	4.6	103	103	102	103	126	34	3	113	57	318	3	259
Gambia, The	24.7	69	64	108	69	81	281	0	153	34	142	32	114
Ghana	32.2	124	125	107	124	109	1,852	0	836	1,482	1,044	1,439	968
Guinea	7.5	127	125	142	129	145	2,601	0	463	98	368	43	309
Guinea-Bissau	51.5	114	114	118	114	123	203	2	47	65	75	65	61
Kenya	18.9	134	123	150	136	126	3,755	0	1,032	2,164	1,043	641	885
Lesotho	6.5	88	77	98	88	62	73	55	41	4	55	1	51
Liberia	..	114	113	124	119	132	155	0	209	95	161	3	141
Madagascar	23.4	119	124	109	121	145	4,109	1	347	185	284	146	227
Malawi	28.5	137	137	136	138	144	3,637	4	123	773	151	256	109
Mali	..	127	122	138	145	147	3,510	410	267	312	326	113	268
Mauritania	..	112	103	114	112	105	155	6	394	19	462	18	375
Mauritius	4	101	88	146	101	252	0	0	295	358	553	323	432
Mozambique	25.4	114	112	133	99	83	2,173	26	811	334	482	150	426
Namibia	7.5	100	128	93	100	115	114	22	69	231	581	163	377
Niger	..	145	151	137	146	138	3,840	5	294	84	232	79	185
Nigeria	31.9	119	118	119	119	126	30,850	17	3,582	564	2,712	419	2,384
Rwanda	34.6	120	120	122	120	167	341	16	117	76	101	5	87
São Tomé and Príncipe	..	114	113	126	114	144	3	3	13	4	23	4	18
Senegal	13.6	75	65	117	74	70	885	0	1,594	297	1,270	196	1,140
Seychelles	2.3	97	97	98	98	..	..	95	20	4	101	2	84
Sierra Leone	41	182	188	141	185	323	739	0	155	25	150	20	130
Somalia	..	103	96	104	103	55	196	0	352	79	381	77	265
South Africa	2.3	107	93	126	109	80	9,547	0	3,379	4,109	4,333	2,676	2,922
Sudan	24.4	124	116	130	124	194	6,572	145	1,476	315	1,186	256	1,002
Swaziland	6.7	107	104	116	109	25	69	1,374	186	231	245	219	200
Tanzania	..	134	146	104	134	167	5,895	1,359	873	677	701	288	631
Togo	..	107	105	123	121	113	820	119	151	206	116	161	89
Uganda	20.8	105	104	111	105	121	2,631	2	500	674	477	160	418
Zambia	18.1	117	124	106	115	143	1,537	324	61	266	158	74	127
Zimbabwe	..	71	61	97	82	57	1,251	17	531	531	362	106	328
NORTH AFRICA	10.4	..	..	..	..	..	..	104	29,423	4,426	18,330	3,799	15,745
Algeria	9.2	136	150	120	137	208	4,133	56	7,283	87	5,244	75	4,671
Egypt, Arab Rep.	14.3	115	114	117	116	113	22,059	1	10,509	1,503	5,440	1,245	4,732
Libya	..	102	103	101	102	94	209	1,464	2,357	10	1,734	1	1,587
Morocco	14.2	117	121	110	118	71	2,541	1	6,150	1,538	4,010	1,349	3,190
Tunisia	10	119	126	105	119	136	2,020	1,250	3,125	1,288	1,903	1,129	1,564

(continued)

Table 8.2 Agriculture (continued)

	Share of land area (%)							
	Permanent cropland 2007	Cereal cropland 2007	Irrigated land (% of cropland) 2002–05[b]	Fertilizer consumption (100 grams per hectare of arable land) 2001–06[b]	Agricultural machinery (tractors per 100 sq km of arable land) 2006	Agricultural employment (% of total employment) 2000–07[b]	Agriculture value added per worker (2000 $) 2005–06[b]	Cereal yield (kilograms per hectare) 2007
SUB-SAHARAN AFRICA	1.0	3.9	3.5	111.9	13.1	..	291	1,251
Angola	0.2	1.2	2.2	36.6	31.2	..	208	490
Benin	2.4	8.8	0.4	–	0.7	..	532	1,258
Botswana	0.0	0.2	0.3	230.0	250.0	29.9	333	555
Burkina Faso	0.2	11.9	0.5	73.7	4.0	..	167	1,148
Burundi	13.6	8.4	1.5	–	1.7	..	62	1,289
Cameroon	2.6	2.5	0.4	90.2	0.8	60.6	631	1,338
Cape Verde	0.7	3.7	6.1	48.6	11.6	..	1,566	800
Central African Republic	0.1	0.3	0.1	3.1	0.2	..	377	1,092
Chad	0.0	2.0	0.8	48.6	0.4	..	215	1,211
Comoros	29.6	8.6	..	37.5	0.8	..	382	1,313
Congo, Dem. Rep.	0.4	0.9	0.1	2.9	3.6	..	146	773
Congo, Rep.	0.1	0.0	0.4	94.4	14.1	..	..	798
Côte d'Ivoire	13.2	2.6	1.1	227.7	33.4	..	808	1,710
Djibouti	..	0.0	..	–	61.5	..	63	1,667
Equatorial Guinea	3.2	..	..	–	18.5	..	1,084	..
Eritrea	0.0	3.9	3.5	0.2	7.1	..	96	454
Ethiopia	1.0	7.9	2.5	139.5	2.2	8.6	188	1,720
Gabon	0.7	0.1	1.4	84.6	29.2	..	1,734	1,663
Gambia, The	0.6	21.6	0.6	5.0	3.2	..	230	1,300
Ghana	10.5	6.1	0.5	126.5	8.8	..	322	1,328
Guinea	2.7	7.4	5.4	13.3	26.5	..	206	1,437
Guinea-Bissau	8.9	4.9	4.5	80.0	0.7	..	252	1,472
Kenya	0.9	3.6	1.8	367.2	26.3	..	338	1,857
Lesotho	0.1	5.2	0.9	343.7	66.7	..	240	463
Liberia	2.2	1.2	0.5	–	8.4	..	..	1,290
Madagascar	1.0	2.8	30.6	25.5	1.9	82.0	173	2,511
Malawi	1.3	19.8	2.2	182.9	4.8	..	116	1,953
Mali	0.1	2.6	4.9	91.0	5.5	41.5	295	1,114
Mauritania	0.0	0.2	9.8	64.4	7.9	..	384	844
Mauritius	2.0	0.0	20.8	2,581.2	59.8	9.1	5,226	7,667
Mozambique	0.4	2.9	2.6	49.5	14.2	..	163	942
Namibia	0.0	0.3	1.0	28.7	38.7	29.9	1,484	412
Niger	0.0	7.1	0.5	–	0.1	..	163	424
Nigeria	3.3	23.3	0.8	–	8.3	..	..	1,453
Rwanda	11.1	13.2	0.6	3.0	0.5	..	197	1,049
São Tomé and Príncipe	49.0	1.4	18.2	..	138.9	27.9	..	2,308
Senegal	0.3	5.6	4.8	73.3	2.3	33.7	203	823
Seychelles	10.9	..	..	200.0	400.0	..	556	..
Sierra Leone	1.1	10.2	4.7	6.0	1.1	68.5	..	1,014
Somalia	0.0	0.7	15.7	4.8	12.1	..	..	417
South Africa	0.8	2.8	9.5	475.6	43.4	8.8	2,470	2,796
Sudan	0.1	3.9	10.2	24.9	9.6	..	684	708
Swaziland	0.8	3.5	26.0	393.3	223.3	..	1,199	1,146
Tanzania	1.4	5.6	1.8	68.1	22.6	76.5	320	1,193
Togo	3.1	12.7	0.3	–	0.3	..	346	1,187
Uganda	11.2	8.8	0.1	14.2	8.7	68.7	171	1,525
Zambia	0.0	1.3	2.9	138.9	11.4	71.6	208	1,542
Zimbabwe	0.3	5.0	5.2	410.7	74.3	..	200	649
NORTH AFRICA	0.8	2.2	..	893.4	142.5	35.00	2,211	2,483.8
Algeria	0.4	1.2	6.9	116.4	135.5	20.7	2,266	1,391
Egypt, Arab Rep.	0.5	2.9	100.0	4,455.3	329.6	31.2	2,213	7,663
Libya	0.2	0.2	21.9	421.4	227.1	..	..	637
Morocco	2.0	10.9	15.4	559.3	61.5	43.3	2,047	521
Tunisia	14.0	9.1	7.4	387.9	140.4	..	2,704	1,434

a. Provisional.

b. Data are for the most recent year available during the period specified.

Table 8.3 Environment

	Forest area (% of land area)		Renewable internal fresh water resources		Annual fresh water withdrawals (billions of cubic meters)	Water productivity (2000 $ per cubic meter of fresh water withdrawal)		
			Total (billions of cubic meters)	Per capita (cubic meters)		Total	Agriculture	Industry
	1990	2007	2007	2007	2000–04[a]	2001–04[a]	2001–04[a]	2001–04[a]
SUB-SAHARAN AFRICA	29.4	26.2	3,884	4,859	0.6	1.2		
Angola	48.9	47.2	148	8,431	0.4	26.1	2.5	109.7
Benin	30.0	20.1	10	1,227	0.1	18.2	14.4	11.4
Botswana	24.2	20.7	2	1,276	0.2	31.8	1.7	97.3
Burkina Faso	26.1	24.7	13	846	0.8	3.3	1.0	100.6
Burundi	11.3	5.2	10	1,284	0.3	2.5	1.2	7.0
Cameroon	52.7	44.7	273	14,731	1.0	10.2	2.8	41.9
Cape Verde	14.3	21.0	0	610	..	..	..	..
Central African Republic	37.2	36.4	141	32,463	0.0	38.4	479.5	35.7
Chad	10.4	9.3	15	1,394	0.2	6.0	3.0	..
Comoros	6.4	2.4	1	1,910	..	..	..	..
Congo, Dem. Rep.	62.0	58.7	900	14,423	0.4	12.0	19.3	14.4
Congo, Rep.	66.5	65.7	222	62,516	0.0	76.1	..	..
Côte d'Ivoire	32.1	32.8	77	3,819	0.9	11.2	4.2	23.5
Djibouti	0.2	0.2	0	360	0.0	29.0	5.7	..
Equatorial Guinea	66.3	57.1	26	40,485	0.1	11.6	120.5	62.1
Eritrea	..	15.3	3	578	0.6	1.2	0.2	160.5
Ethiopia	16.7	12.7	122	1,551	5.6	1.6	0.8	51.2
Gabon	85.1	84.4	164	115,340	0.1	42.2	6.3	285.1
Gambia, The	44.2	47.5	3	1,857	0.0	13.8	6.6	13.5
Ghana	32.7	23.2	30	1,325	1.0	5.1	2.7	13.3
Guinea	30.1	27.1	226	23,505	1.5	2.1	0.4	31.7
Guinea-Bissau	78.8	73.0	16	10,383	0.2	1.2	0.8	3.2
Kenya	6.5	6.1	21	552	2.7	5.0	1.9	21.8
Lesotho	0.2	0.3	5	2,607	0.1	15.7	8.6	10.5
Liberia	42.1	31.5	200	55,138	0.1	5.1	..	..
Madagascar	23.5	21.9	337	18,114	15.0	0.3	0.1	2.2
Malawi	41.4	35.5	16	1,160	1.0	1.7	0.8	5.6
Mali	11.5	10.1	60	4,865	6.5	0.4	0.2	8.3
Mauritania	0.4	0.2	0	128	1.7	0.6	0.2	6.0
Mauritius	19.2	18.0	3	2,182	0.7	6.9	0.5	66.7
Mozambique	25.4	24.4	100	4,693	0.6	6.7	1.6	90.6
Namibia	10.6	9.1	6	2,961	0.3	13.0	2.0	71.1
Niger	1.5	1.0	4	247	2.2	0.8	0.3	31.9
Nigeria	18.9	11.3	221	1,493	8.0	5.7	..	..
Rwanda	12.9	21.7	10	1,005	0.2	11.6	6.3	19.6
São Tomé and Príncipe	28.5	28.5	2	13,796	..	..	..	..
Senegal	48.6	44.6	26	2,169	2.2	2.2	0.3	18.4
Seychelles	87.0	87.0	..	..	0.0	46.5	19.1	48.6
Sierra Leone	42.5	37.9	160	29,518	0.4	1.7	..	..
Somalia	13.2	11.1	6	690	3.3	..	..	..
South Africa	7.6	7.6	45	936	12.5	10.6	0.5	50.8
Sudan	32.1	27.9	30	742	37.3	0.3	0.1	9.8
Swaziland	27.4	32.0	3	2,293	1.0	1.4	0.2	46.0
Tanzania	46.8	38.9	84	2,035	5.2	2.0	0.9	61.7
Togo	12.6	6.4	12	1,825	0.2	8.2	6.5	63.8
Uganda	25.0	17.5	39	1,273	..	..	..	..
Zambia	66.1	55.9	80	6,513	1.7	1.9	0.5	5.6
Zimbabwe	57.5	43.7	12	985	4.2	1.6	0.3	4.3
NORTH AFRICA	1.2	1.4	47	291	93.9	2.6		
Algeria	0.8	1.0	11	332	6.1	9.0	1.2	38.0
Egypt, Arab Rep.	0.0	0.1	2	23	68.3	1.5	0.3	7.7
Libya	0.1	0.1	1	98	4.3	8.0	..	..
Morocco	9.6	9.8	29	940	12.6	2.9	0.4	26.6
Tunisia	4.1	7.0	4	410	2.6	7.4	1.1	50.5

(continued)

Table 8.3 Environment (continued)

	Water pollution: Emissions of organic water pollutants (kilograms per day)	Energy: Energy production (kilotons of oil equivalent)		Energy use (kilotons of oil equivalent)		Combustible renewables and waste (% of total energy use)	
	2000–05[a]	1990	2006	1990	2006	1990	2006
SUB-SAHARAN AFRICA							
Angola	..	28,652	79,158	6,285	10,264	68.8	63.9
Benin	..	1,774	1,720	1,678	2,815	93.2	61.1
Botswana	3,440	910	1,075	1,273	1,959	33.1	23.2
Burkina Faso	..	..	..	..	..	..	..
Burundi	..	..	..	..	..	..	..
Cameroon	..	10,976	10,314	5,032	7,083	75.9	79.2
Cape Verde	..	..	..	..	..	..	..
Central African Republic	..	..	..	..	..	..	..
Chad	..	..	..	..	..	..	..
Comoros	..	..	..	..	..	..	..
Congo, Dem. Rep.	..	12,019	17,822	11,907	17,513	84.0	92.4
Congo, Rep.	..	8,746	15,421	797	1,205	59.5	57.6
Côte d'Ivoire	..	3,382	9,338	4,413	7,287	72.0	63.8
Djibouti	..	..	..	..	..	..	..
Equatorial Guinea	..	..	..	..	..	..	..
Eritrea	2,871	..	515	..	704	..	73.0
Ethiopia	24,137	14,052	20,357	15,045	22,319	92.8	90.0
Gabon	..	14,630	12,144	1,243	1,823	59.8	56.3
Gambia, The	..	..	..	..	..	..	..
Ghana	15,419	4,392	6,504	5,338	9,503	73.1	63.3
Guinea	..	..	..	..	..	..	..
Guinea-Bissau	..	..	..	..	..	..	..
Kenya	..	9,013	14,258	11,220	17,948	75.9	73.6
Lesotho	13,153	..	..	..	..	..	..
Liberia	..	..	..	..	..	..	..
Madagascar	88,887	..	..	..	..	..	..
Malawi	32,672	..	..	..	..	..	..
Mali	..	..	..	..	..	..	..
Mauritania	..	..	..	..	..	..	..
Mauritius	351	..	..	..	..	..	..
Mozambique	..	5,608	10,698	5,966	8,804	93.2	81.6
Namibia	..	..	317	..	1,476	..	12.7
Niger	..	..	..	..	..	..	..
Nigeria	..	150,452	235,340	70,904	105,075	79.8	79.6
Rwanda	..	..	..	..	..	..	..
São Tomé and Príncipe	..	..	..	..	..	..	..
Senegal	6,621	964	1,231	1,840	3,016	52.0	39.6
Seychelles	..	..	..	..	..	..	..
Sierra Leone	..	..	..	..	..	..	..
Somalia	..	..	..	..	..	..	..
South Africa	183,841	114,535	158,676	91,230	129,815	11.4	10.5
Sudan	38,567	8,775	30,701	10,661	17,713	81.5	77.5
Swaziland	..	..	..	..	..	..	..
Tanzania	..	9,064	19,427	9,808	20,805	91.0	91.0
Togo	..	1,054	2,039	1,298	2,404	80.6	84.5
Uganda	2,105	..	..	..	..	..	..
Zambia	..	4,918	6,663	5,464	7,309	73.4	78.2
Zimbabwe	..	8,550	8,759	9,381	9,578	50.4	63.3
NORTH AFRICA		238,982	360,309	79,782	139,688	2.7	2.4
Algeria	..	104,439	173,207	23,919	36,700	0.1	0.2
Egypt, Arab Rep.	..	54,869	77,830	31,974	62,501	3.3	2.3
Libya	..	73,173	101,970	11,543	17,769	1.1	0.9
Morocco	72,779	773	670	7,206	13,977	4.4	3.2
Tunisia	..	5,728	6,632	5,140	8,741	12.4	13.3

a. Data are for the most recent year available during the period specified.
b. Hydrofluorocarbons, perfluorocarbons, and sulphur hexafluoride.

Greenhouse gas emissions																	
		Methane						Nitrous oxide						Other greenhouse gases[b] (thousands of metric tons of carbon dioxide equivalent)		ODA gross disbursements for forestry ($ millions)	ODA gross disbursements for general environment protection ($ millions)
Carbon dioxide (thousands of metric tons)		Total (kilotons of carbon dioxide equivalent)		Agricultural (% of total)		Industrial (% of total)		Total (metric tons of carbon dioxide equivalent)		Agricultural (% of total)		Industrial (% of total)					
1990	2006	1990	2005	1990	2005	1990	2005	1990	2005	1990	2005	1990	2005	1990	2005	2008	2008
																98.4	329.1
4,429	10,582	13,630	37,020	65.7	39.1	21.6	11.6	5,110	28,350	80.4	35.9	0.0	0.0	0	0	0.1	0.9
715	3,109	2,730	4,840	60.1	47.5	16.1	8.9	2,120	4,660	90.6	68.0	0.0	0.0	0	0	1.7	2.5
2,171	4,770	130	4,480	84.6	71.9	7.7	17.9	0	2,460	..	96.3	..	0.0	0	0	0.2	9.6
587	788	..	..	..	..	..	..	..	..	..	..	..	..	..	..	2.4	6.0
304	198	..	..	..	..	..	..	..	..	..	..	..	..	..	..	0.0	1.6
1,738	3,645	10,500	15,110	57.0	56.0	20.2	17.9	8,290	14,540	85.5	85.0	0.0	0.0	810	890	9.5	7.9
88	308	..	..	..	..	..	..	..	..	..	..	..	..	..	..	0.5	7.7
198	249	..	..	..	..	..	..	..	..	..	..	..	..	..	..	5.6	0.4
147	396	..	..	..	..	..	..	..	..	..	..	..	..	..	..	0.6	2.5
77	88	..	..	..	..	..	..	..	..	..	..	..	..	..	..	..	0.0
4,070	2,200	2,670	5,750	20.2	11.8	47.9	49.6	820	2,250	23.2	15.6	0.0	0.0	0	0	4.0	12.4
1,188	1,463	27,720	50,320	42.9	26.3	10.4	7.7	19,390	38,680	43.7	23.2	0.0	0.0	0	0	0.6	2.3
5,797	6,882	5,410	15,320	49.9	20.6	18.9	11.2	2,460	12,350	82.1	25.0	0.0	0.0	0	0	0.0	2.7
400	488	..	..	..	..	..	..	..	..	..	..	..	..	..	..	0.0	0.3
121	4,356	..	..	..	..	..	..	..	..	..	..	..	..	..	..	0.0	0.0
..	554	2,090	2,410	75.6	77.6	11.0	7.5	1,340	2,350	97.0	99.1	0.0	0.0	0	0	0.0	0.6
3,018	6,006	39,110	47,740	78.4	77.2	9.3	10.0	50,730	63,130	97.9	98.6	0.0	0.0	0	0	5.0	8.8
6,087	2,057	3,120	2,040	6.7	4.4	46.5	79.9	1,850	420	13.0	57.1	0.0	0.0	0	0	2.1	4.6
191	334	..	..	..	..	..	..	..	..	..	..	..	..	..	..	0.1	0.0
3,931	9,240	5,310	8,630	42.7	49.6	13.7	10.7	4,540	10,520	84.1	88.6	0.0	0.0	190	170	10.8	4.9
1,056	1,360	..	..	..	..	..	..	..	..	..	..	..	..	..	..	1.5	3.3
253	279	..	..	..	..	..	..	..	..	..	..	..	..	..	..	..	2.0
5,823	12,151	19,410	20,310	71.4	65.0	15.7	18.0	21,830	19,060	97.6	96.4	0.0	0.0	0	0	2.0	28.3
..	..	..	..	..	..	..	..	..	..	..	..	..	..	..	..	0.1	0.2
484	785	..	..	..	..	..	..	..	..	..	..	..	..	..	..	0.7	0.7
986	2,834	..	..	..	..	..	..	..	..	..	..	..	..	..	..	0.5	17.5
612	1,049	..	..	..	..	..	..	..	..	..	..	..	..	..	..	4.4	2.9
422	568	..	..	..	..	..	..	..	..	..	..	..	..	..	..	0.4	7.4
2,666	1,665	..	..	..	..	..	..	..	..	..	..	..	..	..	..	0.0	10.9
1,463	3,850	..	..	..	..	..	..	..	..	..	..	..	..	..	..	..	0.1
1,001	2,039	9,430	11,680	61.9	64.3	17.5	16.9	2,950	9,930	72.5	99.7	0.0	0.0	0	0	1.1	14.3
7	2,831	4,320	4,260	90.7	89.9	3.7	4.7	4,240	4,620	97.2	99.1	0.0	0.0	0	0	1.7	2.4
1,052	935	..	..	..	..	..	..	..	..	..	..	..	..	..	..	0.3	3.9
45,371	97,262	59,690	78,290	33.9	33.7	47.3	45.5	28,050	39,030	87.9	87.1	0.0	0.0	120	80	0.1	8.1
682	796	..	..	..	..	..	..	..	..	..	..	..	..	..	..	2.1	3.3
66	103	..	..	..	..	..	..	..	..	..	..	..	..	..	..	0.0	0.3
3,183	4,261	5,550	6,340	76.2	75.9	4.5	4.7	6,220	10,250	95.8	99.0	0.0	0.0	0	10	2.9	24.7
114	744	..	..	..	..	..	..	..	..	..	..	..	..	..	..	..	0.2
389	994	..	..	..	..	..	..	..	..	..	..	..	..	..	..	0.0	1.2
18	172	..	..	..	..	..	..	..	..	..	..	..	..	..	..	..	0.1
333,531	414,649	52,260	59,200	31.2	23.8	52.4	54.3	26,460	29,250	88.0	82.7	3.6	7.3	1,450	2,600	0.2	16.2
5,559	10,813	39,760	67,310	69.1	73.3	21.4	21.5	39,400	59,750	94.1	96.2	0.0	0.0	0	0	2.5	2.1
425	1,016	..	..	..	..	..	..	..	..	..	..	..	..	..	..	0.0	0.0
2,372	5,372	26,860	39,460	66.4	63.5	21.3	20.3	23,300	31,690	91.3	84.3	0.0	0.0	0	0	6.0	15.2
774	1,221	1,790	2,840	56.4	48.6	18.4	14.8	1,990	5,470	93.5	88.8	0.0	0.0	0	0	0.1	0.0
818	2,706	..	..	..	..	..	..	..	..	..	..	..	..	..	..	2.4	3.1
2,446	2,471	9,820	16,770	72.5	68.6	8.1	5.7	4,800	11,410	72.5	65.1	0.0	3.7	0	0	0.5	9.4
16,658	11,081	10,850	10,400	65.4	60.4	22.2	24.8	8,970	10,160	89.4	97.1	5.9	0.0	0	20	0.1	0.7
231,949	423,452	63,380	83,440	32.3	31.2	43.5	41.7	47,260	62,930	92.4	84.8	4.7	6.7	2,580	2,250	8.0	153.6
78,888	132,715	18,570	24,310	19.3	15.3	61.2	66.3	8,780	10,330	90.9	89.1	4.4	7.2	230	110	0.3	5.7
75,940	166,800	23,250	32,960	39.0	44.2	33.4	31.2	16,980	27,810	88.6	85.6	8.2	11.5	2,250	1,820	0.0	92.1
40,315	55,495	8,750	8,540	11.8	8.9	79.1	77.6	2,860	2,050	96.5	91.7	0.0	0.0	100	290	..	0.0
23,540	45,316	9,070	13,240	57.6	41.6	6.2	2.6	14,380	15,510	98.5	75.2	0.0	0.0	0	0	2.3	8.2
13,266	23,126	3,740	4,390	42.2	34.2	26.2	32.1	4,260	7,230	87.1	94.2	10.6	4.1	0	30	5.4	38.2

Table 8.4 Fossil fuel emissions

	Carbon dioxide emissions						Carbon dioxide emissions from fossil fuel (thousands of metric tons)					
	Total (thousands of metric tons)			Per capita (metric tons)			Total			Solid fuel consumption		
	1990	2005	2006	1990	2005	2006	1990	2005	2006	1990	2005	2006
SUB-SAHARAN AFRICA	463,488	649,627	641,720	0.9	0.9	0.8	130,131	181,797	179,591	111,351	143,525	144,853
Angola	4,429	9,856	10,582	0.4	0.6	0.6	1,208	2,688	2,886	0	0	0
Benin	715	2,567	3,109	0.1	0.3	0.4	195	700	848	0	0	0
Botswana	2,171	4,525	4,770	1.6	2.5	2.6	592	1,234	1,301	592	702	748
Burkina Faso	587	788	788	0.1	0.1	0.1	160	215	215	0	0	0
Burundi	304	169	198	0.1	0.0	0.0	83	46	54	4	2	2
Cameroon	1,738	3,718	3,645	0.1	0.2	0.2	..	..	..	..	..	..
Cape Verde	88	297	308	0.2	0.6	0.6	24	81	84	0	0	0
Central African Republic	198	235	249	0.1	0.1	0.1	54	64	68	0	0	0
Chad	147	392	396	0.0	0.0	0.0	40	107	108	0	0	0
Comoros	77	88	88	0.2	0.1	0.1	21	24	24	0	0	0
Congo, Dem. Rep.	4,070	2,145	2,200	0.1	0.0	0.0	1,110	585	600	209	273	287
Congo, Rep.	1,188	1,606	1,463	0.5	0.5	0.4	324	438	399	0	0	0
Côte d'Ivoire	5,797	8,166	6,882	0.5	0.4	0.3	1,581	2,227	1,877	0	0	0
Djibouti	400	473	488	0.7	0.6	0.6	109	129	133	0	0	0
Equatorial Guinea	121	4,341	4,356	0.3	7.1	7.0	33	1,184	1,188	0	0	0
Eritrea	..	752	554	..	0.2	0.1	..	205	151	..	0	0
Ethiopia	3,018	5,489	6,006	0.1	0.1	0.1	823	1,497	1,638	0	0	0
Gabon	6,087	1,870	2,057	6.6	1.4	1.5	1,660	510	561	0	0	0
Gambia, The	191	319	334	0.2	0.2	0.2	52	87	91	0	0	0
Ghana	3,931	7,473	9,240	0.3	0.3	0.4	1,072	2,038	2,520	2	0	0
Guinea	1,056	1,360	1,360	0.2	0.1	0.1	288	371	371	0	0	0
Guinea-Bissau	253	271	279	0.2	0.2	0.2	69	74	76	0	0	0
Kenya	5,823	10,952	12,151	0.2	0.3	0.3	1,588	2,987	3,314	110	78	87
Lesotho	..	..	..	..	..	..	..	..	..	..	..	..
Liberia	484	737	785	0.2	0.2	0.2	132	201	214	0	0	0
Madagascar	986	2,798	2,834	0.1	0.2	0.2	269	763	773	9	7	7
Malawi	612	1,049	1,049	0.1	0.1	0.1	167	286	286	13	43	36
Mali	422	568	568	0.1	0.0	0.0	115	155	155	0	0	0
Mauritania	2,666	1,650	1,665	1.4	0.6	0.5	727	450	454	4	0	0
Mauritius	1,463	3,410	3,850	1.4	2.7	3.1	399	930	1,050	54	264	350
Mozambique	1,001	1,855	2,039	0.1	0.1	0.1	273	506	556	42	0	0
Namibia	7	2,724	2,831	0.0	1.3	1.4	2	743	772	0	40	38
Niger	1,052	928	935	0.1	0.1	0.1	287	253	255	125	132	133
Nigeria	45,371	113,868	97,262	0.5	0.8	0.7	12,374	31,055	26,526	35	8	8
Rwanda	682	766	796	0.1	0.1	0.1	186	209	217	0	0	0
São Tomé and Príncipe	66	103	103	0.6	0.7	0.7	18	28	28	0	0	0
Senegal	3,183	5,577	4,261	0.4	0.5	0.4	868	1,521	1,162	0	110	121
Seychelles	114	697	744	1.6	8.4	8.8	31	190	203	0	0	0
Sierra Leone	389	1,005	994	0.1	0.2	0.2	106	274	271	0	0	0
Somalia	18	253	172	0.0	0.0	0.0	5	69	47	0	0	0
South Africa	333,531	409,090	414,649	9.5	8.7	8.7	90,963	111,570	113,086	72,365	96,006	96,887
Sudan	5,559	11,000	10,813	0.2	0.3	0.3	1,516	3,000	2,949	0	0	0
Swaziland	425	1,019	1,016	0.5	0.9	0.9	116	278	277	116	104	105
Tanzania	2,372	5,086	5,372	0.1	0.1	0.1	647	1,387	1,465	3	54	58
Togo	774	1,338	1,221	0.2	0.2	0.2	211	365	333	0	0	0
Uganda	818	2,339	2,706	0.0	0.1	0.1	223	638	738	0	0	0
Zambia	2,446	2,365	2,471	0.3	0.2	0.2	667	645	674	227	98	104
Zimbabwe	16,658	11,550	11,081	1.6	0.9	0.9	4,543	3,150	3,022	3,976	2,526	2,405
NORTH AFRICA	231,949	436,883	423,452	1.9	2.8	2.7	63,259	119,150	115,487	3,567	7,179	6,461
Algeria	78,888	138,178	132,715	3.1	4.2	4.0	21,515	37,685	36,195	825	666	759
Egypt, Arab Rep.	75,940	173,481	166,800	1.3	2.2	2.1	20,711	47,313	45,491	917	924	807
Libya	40,315	54,894	55,495	9.2	9.3	9.2	10,995	14,971	15,135	4	0	0
Morocco	23,540	47,531	45,316	1.0	1.6	1.5	6,420	12,963	12,359	1,278	4,610	4,014
Tunisia	13,266	22,799	23,126	1.6	2.3	2.3	3,618	6,218	6,307	72	0	0

Carbon dioxide emissions from fossil fuel (thousands of metric tons)											
Liquid fuel consumption			Gas fuel consumption			Gas flaring			Cement production		
1990	2005	2006	1990	2005	2006	1990	2005	2006	1990	2005	2006
42,650	49,717	46,722	..	..	..	..	..	..	2,906	5,050	5,284
489	1,717	1,882	276	383	408	409	409	409	35	179	187
154	666	814	0	0	0	0	0	0	41	34	34
0	532	553	0	0	0	0	0	0	0	0	0
160	211	211	0	0	0	0	0	0	0	4	4
79	44	52	0	0	0	0	0	0	0	0	0
..	..	..	..	..	..	..	..	..	..	..	..
24	81	84	0	0	0	0	0	0	0	0	0
54	64	68	0	0	0	0	0	0	0	0	0
40	107	108	0	0	0	0	0	0	0	0	0
21	24	24	0	0	0	0	0	0	0	0	0
838	312	312	0	0	0	0	0	0	63	0	0
265	358	315	1	12	12	46	0	0	12	69	72
1,513	1,228	934	0	910	855	0	0	0	68	88	88
109	129	133	0	0	0	0	0	0	0	0	0
33	41	44	0	251	251	0	892	892	0	0	0
..	199	145	..	0	0	..	0	0	..	6	6
777	1,284	1,407	0	0	0	0	0	0	46	213	231
583	409	460	138	66	66	924	0	0	16	35	35
52	87	91	0	0	0	0	0	0	0	0	0
978	1,780	2,262	0	0	0	0	0	0	92	258	258
288	322	322	0	0	0	0	0	0	0	49	49
69	74	76	0	0	0	0	0	0	0	0	0
1,273	2,620	2,928	0	0	0	0	0	0	205	289	299
..	..	..	..	..	..	..	..	..	..	..	..
125	181	193	0	0	0	0	0	0	7	20	21
252	736	746	0	0	0	0	0	0	8	20	20
141	221	223	0	0	0	0	0	0	13	22	27
112	155	155	0	0	0	0	0	0	3	0	0
709	409	403	0	0	0	0	0	0	14	41	51
345	666	699	0	0	0	0	0	0	0	0	0
220	392	414	0	38	44	0	0	0	11	76	98
2	703	733	0	0	0	0	0	0	0	0	0
159	115	116	0	0	0	0	0	0	3	7	7
9,823	13,074	8,939	2,041	5,048	5,621	0	12,600	11,549	476	326	408
177	195	203	0	0	0	0	0	0	8	14	14
18	28	28	0	0	0	0	0	0	0	0	0
801	1,047	643	3	7	6	0	0	0	64	357	392
31	190	203	0	0	0	0	0	0	0	0	0
106	251	239	0	0	0	0	0	0	0	23	32
0	69	47	0	0	0	0	0	0	5	0	0
16,596	11,526	12,046	940	2,269	2,384	0	0	0	1,062	1,768	1,768
1,493	2,955	2,922	0	0	0	0	0	0	23	45	27
0	173	172	0	0	0	0	0	0	0	0	0
571	962	1,018	0	185	196	0	0	0	73	186	193
157	256	224	0	0	0	0	0	0	54	109	109
219	552	652	0	0	0	0	0	0	4	86	86
381	488	508	0	0	0	0	0	0	59	59	61
471	542	522	0	0	0	0	0	0	95	82	95
34,171	62,318	59,847	17,482	39,130	37,748	..	..	..	4,167	8,378	8,913
6,835	17,089	16,688	10,619	16,706	14,955	2,373	1,688	1,753	862	1,536	2,040
14,323	25,099	23,388	3,552	17,346	17,352	0	0	0	1,918	3,944	3,944
6,058	10,112	9,820	2,599	3,010	3,260	1,969	1,357	1,564	367	492	490
4,541	6,620	6,550	30	237	299	0	0	0	571	1,496	1,496
2,414	3,398	3,401	682	1,831	1,882	1	79	81	449	910	943

Table 9.1 Labor force participation

	Labor force ages 15 and older					
	Total (thousands)		Male (% of total labor force)		Female (% of total labor force)	
	2000	2007	2000	2007	2000	2007
SUB-SAHARAN AFRICA	261,534	318,017	57.3	56.6	42.7	43.4
Angola	6,176	7,798	54.3	53.4	45.7	46.6
Benin	2,677	3,427	59.3	59.4	40.7	40.6
Botswana	631	690	57.3	56.4	42.7	43.6
Burkina Faso	5,259	6,648	52.4	52.9	47.6	47.1
Burundi	3,180	4,249	47.6	48.4	52.4	51.6
Cameroon	5,885	6,943	59.1	58.7	40.9	41.3
Cape Verde	150	184	60.5	58.4	39.5	41.6
Central African Republic	1,734	1,963	54.4	55.0	45.6	45.0
Chad	3,311	4,316	54.3	51.4	45.7	48.6
Comoros	237	284	56.9	56.6	43.1	43.4
Congo, Dem. Rep.	18,817	23,579	60.9	61.3	39.1	38.7
Congo, Rep.	1,202	1,452	58.8	59.3	41.2	40.7
Côte d'Ivoire	6,465	7,414	70.0	69.7	30.0	30.3
Djibouti	297	352	57.0	56.8	43.0	43.2
Equatorial Guinea	199	250	66.4	67.5	33.6	32.5
Eritrea	1,436	1,981	58.5	59.0	41.5	41.0
Ethiopia	29,025	37,435	54.6	52.6	45.4	47.4
Gabon	527	631	55.7	55.8	44.3	44.2
Gambia, The	575	713	54.2	53.6	45.8	46.4
Ghana	8,520	10,111	51.6	51.0	48.4	49.0
Guinea	3,968	4,601	53.0	52.9	47.0	47.1
Guinea-Bissau	542	631	60.6	61.8	39.4	38.2
Kenya	14,183	17,373	53.5	53.7	46.5	46.3
Lesotho	800	861	47.7	47.5	52.3	52.5
Liberia	1,095	1,442	60.0	59.7	40.0	40.3
Madagascar	6,904	8,934	51.8	51.4	48.2	48.6
Malawi	4,866	5,781	49.7	49.9	50.3	50.1
Mali	2,743	3,441	64.6	62.5	35.4	37.5
Mauritania	1,043	1,312	57.6	57.2	42.4	42.8
Mauritius	527	572	65.8	63.8	34.2	36.2
Mozambique	8,569	9,905	44.1	43.9	55.9	56.1
Namibia	620	695	55.0	53.4	45.0	46.6
Niger	3,632	4,558	68.5	68.5	31.5	31.5
Nigeria	38,597	46,114	66.0	64.2	34.0	35.8
Rwanda	3,632	4,374	47.1	46.9	52.9	53.1
São Tomé and Príncipe	44	52	63.7	61.3	36.3	38.7
Senegal	4,014	4,909	58.5	57.4	41.5	42.6
Seychelles	..	..	..	..	..	..
Sierra Leone	1,654	2,039	51.0	48.8	49.0	51.2
Somalia	2,777	3,413	61.6	61.1	38.4	38.9
South Africa	15,543	17,620	56.1	54.9	43.9	45.1
Sudan	10,413	12,504	71.3	69.6	28.7	30.4
Swaziland	413	445	50.2	50.2	49.8	49.8
Tanzania	16,805	20,250	50.2	50.3	49.8	49.7
Togo	2,081	2,579	61.6	61.7	38.4	38.3
Uganda	10,636	13,388	52.2	52.2	47.8	47.8
Zambia	3,996	4,643	57.1	56.9	42.9	43.1
Zimbabwe	5,139	5,161	53.4	54.6	46.6	45.4
NORTH AFRICA	46,740	56,636	75.2	73.2	24.8	26.8
Algeria	11,061	13,907	71.7	67.9	28.3	32.1
Egypt, Arab Rep.	20,592	25,499	77.3	74.8	22.7	25.2
Libya	1,846	2,265	78.7	76.4	21.3	23.6
Morocco	10,011	11,225	74.4	75.2	25.6	24.8
Tunisia	3,230	3,740	75.0	73.3	25.0	26.7

Participation rate, ages 15 and older (%)						Participation rate, ages 15–64 (%)					
Total		Male		Female		Total		Male		Female	
2000	2007	2000	2007	2000	2007	2000	2007	2000	2007	2000	2007
69.5	69.7	81.1	79.9	69.5	69.7	70.7	70.9	82.0	80.8	59.7	61.2
81.7	81.7	90.8	89.2	73.0	74.5	83.0	83.0	91.6	89.9	74.7	76.4
72.7	72.1	87.6	85.7	58.1	58.5	73.5	72.9	87.8	86.0	59.2	59.6
58.9	55.7	69.0	63.4	49.3	48.2	60.1	57.5	69.6	64.4	50.9	50.6
83.2	83.3	90.3	89.8	76.5	77.1	85.2	85.3	91.4	90.7	79.4	79.9
91.4	89.9	92.1	90.4	90.7	89.5	92.1	90.5	92.6	90.9	91.7	90.2
65.0	63.8	77.7	75.4	52.5	52.4	65.3	64.6	78.3	76.1	52.5	53.0
60.1	60.1	79.8	75.4	43.5	46.5	62.8	62.7	81.7	76.9	46.5	49.8
77.3	76.8	87.1	87.1	68.4	67.3	77.7	77.1	87.4	87.5	68.6	67.3
72.5	74.1	80.2	77.3	65.0	71.0	72.7	74.5	79.9	76.8	65.6	72.3
72.7	73.1	83.1	83.0	62.4	63.2	73.5	74.0	83.4	83.4	63.7	64.5
71.5	71.6	89.3	89.7	54.6	54.3	72.8	72.9	90.4	90.8	55.8	55.4
68.8	69.1	82.3	82.8	56.0	55.8	69.2	69.4	83.1	83.7	55.7	55.4
63.9	62.5	85.8	84.7	40.3	39.2	64.8	63.4	86.6	85.7	41.2	39.9
69.1	67.3	79.5	77.0	59.0	57.8	72.0	70.4	82.0	79.8	62.0	61.0
67.4	66.6	91.5	91.5	44.4	42.6	69.6	68.7	93.9	93.8	46.2	44.2
70.5	70.0	86.2	85.8	56.1	55.4	71.7	71.2	87.1	86.9	57.4	56.5
81.8	85.3	90.9	91.0	73.1	79.7	83.7	86.9	92.0	91.8	75.6	82.1
72.3	70.9	82.0	79.8	63.0	62.1	74.7	72.8	83.9	81.5	65.6	64.1
77.4	76.9	85.2	83.8	69.6	70.1	77.6	77.2	85.0	83.7	70.1	70.8
74.3	72.5	76.3	73.3	72.3	71.6	75.3	73.8	76.9	74.0	73.6	73.6
84.7	84.1	89.7	88.9	79.7	79.4	86.7	86.1	90.5	89.6	82.8	82.6
71.5	71.4	88.6	89.9	55.3	53.6	73.1	72.7	89.9	91.3	56.9	54.8
81.3	80.8	88.1	87.3	74.7	74.4	82.6	82.1	88.9	88.1	76.5	76.1
73.1	70.9	78.9	75.0	68.6	67.6	74.3	72.1	79.7	75.8	70.1	69.1
69.5	69.9	84.7	84.5	54.5	55.4	70.4	70.8	85.0	84.7	55.8	56.7
82.4	85.2	85.8	88.4	79.0	82.1	83.0	86.6	86.1	89.2	80.1	84.1
77.4	77.8	78.9	79.5	76.1	76.3	76.8	77.2	78.1	78.6	75.6	75.7
50.3	50.1	67.8	65.1	34.6	36.5	52.3	52.1	70.2	67.0	36.3	38.4
70.3	70.1	81.4	79.9	59.3	60.2	72.2	72.0	82.7	81.3	61.6	62.6
60.0	59.5	79.9	77.2	40.6	42.4	64.6	64.7	84.6	82.5	44.4	46.8
83.6	82.9	79.4	77.2	87.3	88.1	83.9	83.2	79.1	76.8	88.0	89.1
55.9	53.8	63.9	59.0	48.5	48.8	57.4	55.2	65.3	60.3	49.9	50.3
63.5	63.5	87.7	87.5	39.1	39.3	64.1	64.1	88.6	88.3	39.7	39.9
55.1	54.5	73.7	70.6	37.0	38.7	56.0	55.4	75.0	71.6	37.5	39.4
84.2	80.0	85.0	79.2	83.6	80.8	85.7	81.3	86.1	80.2	85.3	82.2
53.9	56.5	70.3	70.8	38.2	42.7	56.6	59.3	73.1	73.5	40.7	45.6
74.4	73.7	88.2	86.2	60.8	61.5	76.1	75.5	90.4	88.4	62.0	62.9
..	..	..	..	..	..	..	..	..	..	..	..
67.4	66.1	71.6	67.4	63.4	64.9	69.2	67.9	72.7	68.1	65.9	67.7
70.5	71.1	88.6	88.5	53.1	54.3	71.7	72.4	90.0	89.8	54.0	55.4
53.2	53.4	61.5	60.2	45.4	47.0	55.8	55.7	63.7	61.8	48.2	49.8
51.6	51.5	73.7	71.6	29.6	31.3	52.4	52.3	73.8	71.7	30.9	32.8
68.9	65.1	74.3	68.5	64.2	62.0	70.5	66.8	74.8	69.2	66.8	64.7
89.1	88.6	91.2	90.3	87.1	87.0	90.3	90.2	91.5	91.2	89.0	89.3
69.5	68.9	87.3	86.7	52.4	51.8	70.5	69.8	88.0	87.4	53.4	52.7
86.1	85.9	90.9	90.3	81.3	81.6	87.5	87.2	91.5	90.8	83.5	83.6
69.7	70.1	80.9	80.5	58.9	59.8	70.0	70.5	81.2	80.8	59.2	60.3
71.4	69.7	79.1	79.7	64.0	59.9	72.0	71.1	79.6	80.9	64.6	61.4
49.9	50.5	75.5	74.4	49.9	50.5	52.3	53.2	78.5	77.8	26.2	28.8
55.0	57.3	78.8	77.5	31.2	36.9	57.2	59.7	81.9	80.7	32.1	38.1
46.5	47.3	72.1	71.2	21.1	23.8	49.0	50.2	75.2	74.8	22.7	25.7
50.9	52.7	76.0	77.5	22.9	25.9	52.4	54.8	78.0	80.0	23.9	27.3
53.0	51.4	80.9	79.8	26.5	24.7	55.4	53.9	83.7	82.8	28.3	26.6
48.3	48.3	72.5	70.9	24.2	25.7	51.1	51.2	76.0	74.3	26.1	27.9

Table 9.2 Labor force composition

	Sector[a]					
	Agriculture		Industry		Services	
	Male (% of male employment) 2000–07[b]	Female (% of female employment) 2000–07[b]	Male (% of male employment) 2000–07[b]	Female (% of female employment) 2000–07[b]	Male (% of male employment) 2000–07[b]	Female (% of female employment) 2000–07[b]
SUB-SAHARAN AFRICA						
Angola	..	..	..	..	..	..
Benin	..	..	..	..	..	..
Botswana	35.1	24.3	19.2	10.8	45.5	64.8
Burkina Faso	..	..	..	..	..	..
Burundi	..	..	..	..	..	..
Cameroon	53.1	68.4	14.1	3.9	25.5	22.5
Cape Verde	..	..	..	..	..	..
Central African Republic	..	..	..	..	..	..
Chad	..	..	..	..	..	..
Comoros	..	..	..	..	..	..
Congo, Dem. Rep.	..	..	..	..	..	..
Congo, Rep.	..	..	..	..	..	..
Côte d'Ivoire	..	..	..	..	..	..
Djibouti	..	..	..	..	..	..
Equatorial Guinea	..	..	..	..	..	..
Eritrea	..	..	..	..	..	..
Ethiopia	11.7	5.5	26.8	17.4	60.6	76.6
Gabon	..	..	..	..	..	..
Gambia, The	..	..	..	..	..	..
Ghana	..	..	..	..	..	..
Guinea	..	..	..	..	..	..
Guinea-Bissau	..	..	..	..	..	..
Kenya	..	..	..	..	..	..
Lesotho	..	..	..	..	..	..
Liberia	..	..	..	..	..	..
Madagascar	81.5	82.5	5.1	1.6	13.4	15.9
Malawi	..	..	..	..	..	..
Mali	49.8	29.9	17.8	14.7	32.4	55.3
Mauritania	..	..	..	..	..	..
Mauritius	9.9	7.6	35.5	25.8	53.9	66.1
Mozambique	..	..	..	..	..	..
Namibia	33.7	25.2	19.1	9.3	47.1	65.4
Niger	..	..	..	..	..	..
Nigeria	..	..	..	..	..	..
Rwanda	..	..	..	..	..	..
São Tomé and Príncipe	30.6	22.8	26.3	5.9	42.6	70.7
Senegal	34.1	33.0	20.2	4.9	32.5	42.0
Seychelles	..	..	..	..	..	..
Sierra Leone	66	71.1	10.3	2.5	23.4	26.3
Somalia	..	..	..	..	..	..
South Africa	10.6	6.5	35.3	13.5	53.8	79.7
Sudan	..	..	..	..	..	..
Swaziland	..	..	..	..	..	..
Tanzania	72.7	80.0	6.6	2.1	20.7	17.9
Togo	..	..	..	..	..	..
Uganda	61.8	75.7	10.3	5.3	27.6	19.2
Zambia	65.2	78.6	8.8	2.0	26.0	18.4
Zimbabwe	..	..	..	..	..	..
NORTH AFRICA						
Algeria	20.4	22.3	25.6	28.2	53.8	49.4
Egypt, Arab Rep.	28.3	43.3	25.8	6.0	45.6	50.6
Libya	..	..	..	..	..	..
Morocco	36.7	61.3	22.4	14.5	40.8	24.1
Tunisia	..	..	..	..	..	..

a. Components may not sum to 100 percent because of unclassified data.
b. Data are for the most recent year available during the period specified.

Status[a]								
Wage and salaried workers			Self-employed workers			Contributing family workers		
Total (% of total employed) 2000–07[b]	Male (% of males employed) 2000–07[b]	Female (% of females employed) 2000–07[b]	Total (% of total employed) 2000–07[b]	Male (% of males employed) 2000–07[b]	Female (% of females employed) 2000–07[b]	Total (% of total employed) 2000–07[b]	Male (% of males employed) 2000–07[b]	Female (% of females employed) 2000–07[b]
..	..	..	..	..	..	..	..	..
..	..	..	..	..	..	..	..	..
73.2	74.4	71.9	12.2	8.1	16.8	2.2	2.2	2.2
..	..	..	..	..	..	..	..	..
..	..	..	..	..	..	..	..	..
19.2	29.3	8.7	59.3	57.0	61.7	18.2	9.5	27.2
38.9	43.8	33.0	31.8	32.6	30.9	10.3	6.5	14.8
..	..	..	..	..	..	..	..	..
..	..	..	..	..	..	..	..	..
..	..	..	..	..	..	..	..	..
..	..	..	..	..	..	..	..	..
..	..	..	..	..	..	..	..	..
..	..	..	..	..	..	..	..	..
..	..	..	..	..	..	..	..	..
..	..	..	..	..	..	..	..	..
..	..	..	..	..	..	..	..	..
46.3	49.3	42.7	42.8	41.8	44.0	10.0	7.8	12.7
..	..	..	..	..	..	..	..	..
..	..	..	..	..	..	..	..	..
..	..	..	..	..	..	..	..	..
..	..	..	..	..	..	..	..	..
..	..	..	..	..	..	..	..	..
..	..	..	..	..	..	..	..	..
..	..	..	..	..	..	..	..	..
..	..	..	..	..	..	..	..	..
13.4	16.0	10.8	43.7	51.6	35.4	52.3	32.1	73.0
..	..	..	..	..	..	..	..	..
13.6	15.2	11.4	71.4	66.4	78.4	15.0	18.4	10.2
..	..	..	..	..	..	..	..	..
79.2	77.2	83.2	18.0	21.2	11.6	2.2	0.9	4.7
..	..	..	..	..	..	..	..	..
72.8	76.0	68.8	22.3	20.4	26.6	4.4	3.2	5.8
..	..	..	..	..	..	..	..	..
..	..	..	..	..	..	..	..	..
..	..	..	..	..	..	..	..	..
..	..	..	..	..	..	..	..	..
..	..	..	..	..	..	..	..	..
..	..	..	..	..	..	..	..	..
7.6	11.3	3.7	..	..	..	18.1	14.8	21.6
..	..	..	..	..	..	..	..	..
82.4	83.5	80.8	17.0	16.0	18.3	0.4	0.3	0.6
..	..	..	..	..	..	..	..	..
..	..	..	..	..	..	..	..	..
10.5	15.3	6.1	78.1	75.0	80.9	11.4	9.7	13.0
..	..	..	..	..	..	..	..	..
14.5	22.2	7.5	59.4	67.5	52.1	26.1	10.3	40.5
18.7	25.7	9.0	59.7	49.0	29.2	19.6	25.4	61.8
37.7	51.0	23.1	50.4	38.6	63.2	11.9	10.4	13.6
59.8	61.9	49.8	31.7	30.7	36.6	8.2	7.1	13.6
61.8	63.7	53.7	25.1	27.7	13.7	13.1	8.6	32.6
..	..	..	..	..	..	..	..	..
43.2	46.8	33.4	29.3	36.1	11.1	27.4	17.0	55.3
64.3	..	..	26.8	..	..	8.7	..	..

Table 9.3 Unemployment

	Unemployment (% ages 15 and older)			Youth unemployment (% ages 15–24)		
	Total 2000–07[b]	Male 2000–07[b]	Female 2000–07[b]	Total 2000–07[b]	Male 2000–07[b]	Female 2000–07[b]
SUB-SAHARAN AFRICA						
Angola	..	..	..	..	..	..
Benin	0.7	0.9	0.4	0.8	1.1	0.6
Botswana	17.6	15.3	19.9	39.7	33.9	46.1
Burkina Faso	..	..	..	..	..	..
Burundi	..	..	..	..	..	..
Cameroon	7.5	8.2	6.7	..	..	..
Cape Verde	..	..	..	..	..	..
Central African Republic	..	..	..	..	..	..
Chad	..	..	..	..	..	..
Comoros	..	..	..	..	..	..
Congo, Dem. Rep.	..	..	..	..	..	..
Congo, Rep.	..	..	..	..	..	..
Côte d'Ivoire	..	..	..	..	..	..
Djibouti	..	..	..	..	..	..
Equatorial Guinea	..	..	..	..	..	..
Eritrea	..	..	..	..	..	..
Ethiopia	5.4	2.7	8.2	24.9	19.5	29.4
Gabon	..	..	..	..	..	..
Gambia, The	..	..	..	..	..	..
Ghana	..	..	..	16.6	16.4	16.7
Guinea	..	..	..	..	..	..
Guinea-Bissau	..	..	..	..	..	..
Kenya	..	..	..	..	..	..
Lesotho	..	..	..	..	..	..
Liberia	5.6	6.8	4.2	4.7	5.7	3.7
Madagascar	2.6	1.7	3.5	2.3	1.7	2.8
Malawi	7.8	5.4	10.0	..	..	..
Mali	8.8	7.2	10.9	..	..	..
Mauritania	33.0	25.2	41.2	..	..	..
Mauritius	8.5	5.3	14.4	24.6	20.0	31.3
Mozambique	..	..	..	..	..	..
Namibia	21.9	19.4	25.0	44.8	40.4	49.3
Niger	1.5	1.7	0.9	3.2	4.0	1.7
Nigeria	..	..	..	..	..	..
Rwanda	..	..	..	..	..	..
São Tomé and Príncipe	16.7	11.0	24.5	..	..	..
Senegal	..	..	..	..	..	..
Seychelles	5.5	6.1	4.9	20.3	..	..
Sierra Leone	3.4	4.5	2.3	5.2	7.3	3.5
Somalia	..	..	..	..	..	..
South Africa	23.0	20.0	26.6	46.9	43.0	52.0
Sudan	..	..	..	..	..	..
Swaziland	..	..	..	..	..	..
Tanzania	4.7	4.4	5.8	8.9	..	..
Togo	..	..	..	..	..	..
Uganda	3.2	2.5	3.9	..	..	..
Zambia	12.9	14.1	11.3	21.4	23.1	19.5
Zimbabwe	4.2	4.2	4.1	24.9	28.2	21.4
NORTH AFRICA						
Algeria	12.3	17.5	18.1	24.3	42.8	46.3
Egypt, Arab Rep.	11.2	7.1	25.1	34.1	23.3	62.2
Libya	..	..	..	..	..	..
Morocco	10.0	10.1	10.0	17.6	18.2	16.1
Tunisia	14.2	13.1	17.3	30.7	31.4	29.3

a. Components may not sum to 100 percent because of unclassified data.
b. Data are for the most recent year available during the period specified.

Unemployment by education level[a]
(% of total unemployed)

Primary			Secondary			Tertiary		
Total 2000–07[b]	Male 2000–07[b]	Female 2000–07[b]	Total 2000–07[b]	Male 2000–07[b]	Female 2000–07[b]	Total 2000–07[b]	Male 2000–07[b]	Female 2000–07[b]
..	..	..	..	..	..	..	..	..
..	..	..	..	..	..	..	..	..
65.5	64.4	66.3	27.3	23.9	30.2	..	..	..
47.0	44.4	58.3	19.7	16.7	33.3	6.1	5.6	8.3
..	..	..	..	..	..	..	..	..
..	..	..	..	..	..	..	..	..
..	..	..	..	..	..	..	..	..
..	..	..	..	..	..	..	..	..
..	..	..	..	..	..	..	..	..
..	..	..	..	..	..	..	..	..
..	..	..	..	..	..	..	..	..
..	..	..	..	..	..	..	..	..
..	..	..	..	..	..	..	..	..
..	..	..	..	..	..	..	..	..
..	..	..	..	..	..	..	..	..
..	..	..	..	..	..	..	..	..
35.9	50.6	30.8	13.3	19.0	11.3	3.2	5.7	2.3
..	..	..	..	..	..	..	..	..
..	..	..	..	..	..	..	..	..
..	..	..	..	..	..	..	..	..
..	..	..	..	..	..	..	..	..
..	..	..	..	..	..	..	..	..
..	..	..	..	..	..	..	..	..
..	..	..	..	..	..	..	..	..
..	..	..	..	..	..	..	..	..
67.7	68.7	67.1	..	..	..	9.3	14.0	6.6
..	..	..	..	..	..	..	..	..
..	..	..	..	..	..	..	..	..
..	..	..	..	..	..	..	..	..
44.2	49.5	39.7	48.5	41.4	53.2	6.4	8.1	3.5
..	..	..	..	..	..	..	..	..
..	..	..	..	..	..	..	..	..
..	..	..	..	..	..	..	..	..
..	..	..	..	..	..	..	..	..
60.7	62.8	59.4	24.1	23.0	24.9	5.9	0.5	9.4
..	..	..	..	..	..	..	..	..
40.2	42.2	37.9	6.9	7.5	6.2	2.5	2.8	2.1
..	..	..	..	..	..	..	..	..
..	..	..	..	..	..	..	..	..
..	..	..	..	..	..	..	..	..
36.2	39.8	32.9	56.3	52.7	59.7	4.5	4.0	5.0
..	..	..	..	..	..	..	..	..
..	..	..	..	..	..	..	..	..
..	..	..	..	..	..	..	..	..
..	..	..	..	..	..	..	..	..
..	..	..	..	..	..	..	..	..
..	..	..	..	..	..	..	..	..
..	..	..	..	..	..	..	..	..
59.3	65.2	32.5	23.0	21.4	30.4	11.4	6.6	33.0
..	..	..	..	..	..	..	..	..
..	..	..	..	..	..	..	..	..
51.1	57.7	36.6	22.4	21.7	23.9	21.6	16.2	33.5
79.1	83.3	70.4	..	..	..	13.6	9.0	23.3

Table 9.4 Migration and population

	International migration							Population				
								Population dynamics				
	Migrant stock			Workers remittances, received		Migrant remittance inflows						
	Share of population (%) 2005	Total 2005	Net migration 2005	Total ($ millions) 2007	Share of GDP (%) 2007	Total ($ millions) 2007	Share of GDP (%) 2007	Total (millions) 2008	Male (% of total) 2008	Female (% of total) 2008	Annual growth rate (%) 2008	Fertility rate (births per woman) 2007
SUB-SAHARAN AFRICA	2.15	16,338,433	–1,599,939			18,615.4	2.2	819.3	49.8	50.2	2.5	5.1
Angola	0.34	56,055	175,000	..	..	..	..	18.0	49.3	50.7	2.7	5.8
Benin	2.38	187,584	98,831	..	..	224.0	4.1	8.7	50.4	49.6	3.2	5.5
Botswana	4.37	80,148	20,000	80.0	0.7	141.2	1.2	1.9	49.9	50.1	1.3	2.9
Burkina Faso	5.55	772,814	100,000	..	..	50.0	0.7	15.2	49.9	50.1	2.9	6.0
Burundi	1.11	81,566	191,600	0.2	0.0	0.2	0.0	8.1	49.0	51.0	3.0	4.7
Cameroon	1.19	211,880	–12,121	154.0	0.7	167.4	0.8	18.9	50.0	50.0	2.0	4.3
Cape Verde	2.34	11,183	–12,500	138.5	9.6	138.9	9.6	0.5	47.8	52.2	1.4	2.8
Central African Republic	1.8	75,623	–45,000	..	..	..	..	4.4	49.1	50.9	1.8	4.6
Chad	3.53	358,446	218,966	..	..	..	..	11.1	49.7	50.3	2.8	6.2
Comoros	2.27	13,661	–10,000	..	..	12.0	2.6	0.6	50.2	49.8	2.4	4.3
Congo, Dem. Rep.	0.82	480,105	–236,676	..	..	..	..	64.2	49.6	50.5	2.9	6.3
Congo, Rep.	3.77	128,838	3,527	..	..	14.8	0.2	3.6	49.9	50.1	1.8	4.4
Côte d'Ivoire	12.32	2,371,277	–338,732	..	..	179.4	0.9	20.6	51.0	49.0	2.3	4.7
Djibouti	13.72	110,333	0	3.5	0.4	28.6	3.5	0.8	50.0	50.0	1.8	4.0
Equatorial Guinea	0.95	5,800	15,000	..	..	..	..	0.7	49.6	50.4	2.7	5.4
Eritrea	0.32	14,612	229,376	..	..	..	..	5.0	49.2	50.9	3.2	5.1
Ethiopia	0.74	554,021	–340,460	355.9	1.8	357.8	1.8	80.7	49.7	50.3	2.6	5.4
Gabon	17.86	244,550	9,566	..	..	11.0	0.1	1.4	49.9	50.1	1.9	3.4
Gambia, The	15.18	231,739	31,127	45.7	7.1	47.3	7.4	1.7	49.6	50.4	2.8	5.1
Ghana	7.62	1,669,267	11,690	117.4	0.8	117.4	0.8	23.4	50.7	49.3	2.1	4.3
Guinea	4.35	401,217	–425,000	15.1	0.3	150.7	3.3	9.8	50.5	49.5	2.3	5.5
Guinea-Bissau	1.31	19,219	1,181	..	..	29.0	7.6	1.6	49.5	50.5	2.2	5.7
Kenya	2.22	790,071	25,144	645.2	2.4	1,588.0	5.9	38.5	50.0	50.0	2.7	5.0
Lesotho	0.32	6,247	–36,000	12.9	0.8	443.3	26.6	2.0	47.1	52.9	0.6	3.4
Liberia	2.9	96,793	62,452	..	..	64.6	8.8	3.8	49.7	50.3	4.6	5.2
Madagascar	0.23	39,699	–5,000	..	..	11.0	0.2	19.1	49.8	50.2	2.7	4.8
Malawi	2.11	278,806	–30,000	..	..	1.0	0.0	14.3	49.7	50.3	2.6	5.6
Mali	1.42	165,448	–134,204	323.1	4.7	343.9	5.0	12.7	49.4	50.6	3.1	6.5
Mauritania	2.23	66,053	30,000	..	..	2.0	0.1	3.2	50.7	49.3	2.5	4.4
Mauritius	3.28	40,824	0	..	..	215.0	3.2	1.3	49.6	50.4	0.7	1.7
Mozambique	1.98	406,075	–20,000	30.9	0.4	99.4	1.2	21.8	48.6	51.4	1.9	5.1
Namibia	6.52	131,630	–1,000	6.2	0.1	16.2	0.2	2.1	49.3	50.7	1.6	3.6
Niger	1.38	182,960	–28,497	..	..	78.1	1.8	14.7	50.1	49.9	3.3	7.0
Nigeria	0.69	972,126	–170,000	17,945.9	10.8	9,221.0	5.6	151.3	50.1	49.9	2.3	5.3
Rwanda	4.85	435,749	5,931	28.3	0.8	51.3	1.5	9.7	48.4	51.6	2.8	5.4
São Tomé and Príncipe	3.53	5,387	–7,000	2.0	1.4	2.0	1.4	0.2	49.5	50.5	1.9	3.9
Senegal	1.95	220,208	–100,000	1,106.7	9.8	1,191.8	10.6	12.2	49.6	50.4	2.7	5.0
Seychelles	10.18	8,441	..	10.9	1.2	11.2	1.2	0.1	..	..	1.5	..
Sierra Leone	2.98	152,101	336,000	146.3	8.8	148.4	8.9	5.6	48.7	51.3	2.6	5.2
Somalia	0.26	21,271	–200,000	..	..	..	..	9.0	49.6	50.4	3.0	6.0
South Africa	2.66	1,248,732	700,001	..	..	833.7	0.3	48.7	49.3	50.7	1.8	2.7
Sudan	1.65	639,686	–531,781	1,766.7	3.8	1,769.2	3.8	41.3	50.4	49.7	2.3	4.2
Swaziland	3.43	38,574	–46,077	1.5	0.1	100.5	3.5	1.2	48.8	51.2	1.4	3.6
Tanzania	2.05	797,701	–345,000	8.3	0.1	14.3	0.1	42.5	49.8	50.2	2.9	5.6
Togo	3.05	182,823	–3,570	..	..	229.0	9.2	6.5	49.5	50.5	2.5	4.3
Uganda	2.27	652,408	–5,000	451.6	3.8	451.6	3.8	31.7	50.1	49.9	3.3	6.4
Zambia	2.45	287,337	–81,713	59.3	0.5	59.3	0.5	12.6	49.9	50.1	2.5	5.9
Zimbabwe	3.14	391,345	–700,000	..	..	..	..	12.5	48.4	51.7	0.1	3.5
NORTH AFRICA	0.76	1,192,628	–1,048,004			18,238.0	4.2	163.7	50.2	49.8	1.6	2.6
Algeria	0.74	242,446	–140,000	..	..	2,120.0	1.6	34.4	50.5	49.5	1.5	2.4
Egypt, Arab Rep.	0.32	246,745	–291,405	7,655.8	5.9	7,655.8	5.9	81.5	50.3	49.7	1.8	2.9
Libya	10.43	617,536	14,000	..	..	16.0	0.0	6.3	51.7	48.3	2.0	2.7
Morocco	0.17	51,020	–550,000	6,730.5	9.0	6,730.5	9.0	31.2	49.1	50.9	1.2	2.4
Tunisia	0.35	34,881	–80,599	1,446.3	4.1	1,715.8	4.9	10.3	50.3	49.7	1.0	2.0

Population													
Age composition (% of total)									Dependency ratio (% of working-age population)	Geographic distribution (%)			
Ages 0–14			Ages 15–64			Ages 65 and older				Share of total population		Annual growth	
Total 2008	Male 2008	Female 2008	Total 2008	Male 2008	Female 2008	Total 2008	Male 2008	Female 2008	2008	Rural population 2008	Urban population 2008	Rural population 2008	Urban population 2008
42.7	21.5	21.2	54.2	26.9	27.3	3.1	1.4	1.7	85	63.5	36.5	1.7	3.9
45.3	22.6	22.7	52.3	25.7	26.6	2.5	1.1	1.4	91	43.3	56.7	0.6	4.2
43.2	22.0	21.2	53.6	27.1	26.4	3.2	1.3	1.9	87	58.8	41.2	2.5	4.1
33.7	17.0	16.7	62.6	31.4	31.2	3.7	1.5	2.2	60	40.4	59.6	–0.6	2.5
46.2	23.5	22.7	51.8	25.6	26.2	2.0	0.8	1.2	93	80.4	19.6	2.4	5.1
39.0	19.5	19.5	58.2	28.4	29.9	2.8	1.1	1.7	72	89.6	10.4	2.6	5.9
41.1	20.7	20.4	55.4	27.7	27.7	3.6	1.6	1.9	81	43.2	56.8	0.1	3.4
36.9	18.6	18.4	58.7	27.7	31.0	4.3	1.5	2.9	70	40.4	59.6	–0.4	2.7
40.9	20.4	20.5	55.2	27.0	28.2	3.9	1.7	2.2	81	61.4	38.6	1.6	2.2
45.8	23.0	22.8	51.3	25.4	25.9	2.9	1.3	1.6	95	73.3	26.7	2.2	4.5
38.2	19.4	18.8	58.7	29.4	29.3	3.1	1.4	1.7	70	71.9	28.1	2.3	2.6
47.0	23.5	23.4	50.4	24.9	25.5	2.7	1.2	1.5	98	66.0	34.0	1.9	4.7
40.7	20.5	20.2	55.5	27.7	27.8	3.8	1.7	2.1	80	38.7	61.3	0.8	2.4
40.9	20.5	20.4	55.3	28.5	26.9	3.8	2.0	1.8	81	51.2	48.8	1.0	3.7
36.6	18.5	18.2	60.2	30.1	30.1	3.2	1.4	1.8	66	12.7	87.3	–1.4	2.2
41.2	20.7	20.5	55.8	27.6	28.3	3.0	1.3	1.6	79	60.6	39.4	2.4	3.0
41.5	20.9	20.6	56.0	27.3	28.8	2.4	0.9	1.5	78	79.3	20.7	2.6	5.3
43.9	22.1	21.8	53.0	26.3	26.7	3.2	1.4	1.7	89	83.0	17.0	2.2	4.4
36.8	18.6	18.2	58.9	29.4	29.5	4.3	2.0	2.4	70	15.0	85.0	–1.3	2.4
42.5	21.4	21.1	54.7	26.9	27.8	2.8	1.3	1.5	83	43.6	56.4	0.8	4.2
38.7	19.8	18.9	57.7	29.2	28.5	3.6	1.7	1.9	73	50.0	50.0	0.6	3.6
43.0	21.9	21.1	53.9	27.2	26.6	3.2	1.4	1.8	86	65.6	34.4	1.5	3.7
42.7	21.4	21.3	53.9	26.6	27.3	3.4	1.6	1.9	86	70.2	29.8	2.1	2.5
42.8	21.5	21.3	54.6	27.2	27.4	2.7	1.2	1.4	83	78.4	21.6	2.3	4.0
39.2	19.7	19.5	56.1	25.4	30.7	4.8	2.0	2.7	78	74.5	25.5	–0.4	3.4
42.9	21.6	21.3	54.0	26.7	27.3	3.1	1.4	1.7	85	39.9	60.1	2.8	5.6
43.3	21.7	21.6	53.7	26.7	27.0	3.1	1.4	1.6	86	70.5	29.5	2.2	3.8
46.4	23.4	23.0	50.5	24.8	25.7	3.1	1.4	1.7	98	81.2	18.8	1.9	5.2
44.2	22.3	21.9	53.4	25.9	27.5	2.3	1.1	1.2	87	67.8	32.2	2.2	4.8
39.8	20.5	19.3	57.6	29.1	28.5	2.7	1.1	1.6	74	59.0	41.0	2.2	3.0
23.2	11.8	11.4	69.8	35.0	34.8	7.0	2.8	4.2	43	57.5	42.5	0.5	0.8
44.1	22.1	22.0	52.7	25.1	27.6	3.3	1.4	1.9	90	63.2	36.8	0.7	4.0
37.4	18.8	18.6	59.0	29.0	30.1	3.6	1.5	2.1	69	63.2	36.8	0.7	3.2
49.7	25.4	24.3	48.3	23.8	24.6	2.0	0.9	1.1	107	83.5	16.5	3.2	3.8
42.7	21.6	21.1	54.2	27.0	27.2	3.1	1.4	1.7	84	51.6	48.4	0.9	3.7
42.2	20.9	21.3	55.3	26.5	28.8	2.5	1.0	1.5	81	81.7	18.3	2.4	4.3
41.0	20.7	20.3	55.0	27.0	27.9	4.1	1.8	2.3	82	39.4	60.6	–0.2	3.2
43.8	22.1	21.7	53.8	26.4	27.4	2.4	1.1	1.3	86	57.6	42.4	2.2	3.3
..	..	..	..	..	..	..	..	..	..	45.7	54.3	0.5	2.4
43.3	21.5	21.7	54.9	26.3	28.6	1.9	0.9	1.0	82	62.2	37.8	2.0	3.4
44.9	22.5	22.4	52.4	25.8	26.6	2.7	1.2	1.5	91	63.5	36.5	2.2	4.1
30.8	15.5	15.3	64.9	32.1	32.8	4.4	1.7	2.7	54	39.3	60.7	0.5	2.5
39.5	20.1	19.4	56.9	28.6	28.3	3.6	1.6	1.9	76	56.6	43.4	0.7	4.3
40.0	20.1	19.9	56.7	27.4	29.4	3.3	1.4	1.9	76	75.1	24.9	1.0	2.6
44.7	22.5	22.2	52.3	26.0	26.3	3.1	1.4	1.7	91	74.5	25.5	2.3	4.6
40.3	20.1	20.1	56.3	27.8	28.4	3.5	1.5	2.0	78	58.0	42.0	1.3	4.2
49.0	24.7	24.3	48.4	24.2	24.2	2.6	1.2	1.4	106	87.0	13.0	3.1	4.5
46.3	23.3	23.0	50.7	25.2	25.5	3.0	1.4	1.6	97	64.6	35.4	2.2	2.9
40.2	20.2	20.1	55.7	26.4	29.3	4.0	1.8	2.3	79	62.7	37.3	–0.7	1.4
30.1	15.4	14.7	65.1	32.6	32.5	4.8	2.2	2.6	54	47.2	52.8	1.1	2.0
27.8	14.2	13.6	67.6	34.2	33.4	4.6	2.1	2.5	48	34.8	65.2	–0.3	2.5
32.5	16.6	15.9	63.0	31.6	31.4	4.5	2.1	2.5	59	57.3	42.7	1.8	1.9
30.2	15.4	14.7	65.7	34.3	31.5	4.1	2.1	2.1	52	22.5	77.5	1.1	2.2
28.8	14.6	14.2	65.9	32.1	33.8	5.3	2.4	2.9	52	44.0	56.0	0.4	1.8
23.7	12.2	11.5	69.6	34.9	34.7	6.7	3.2	3.6	44	33.5	66.5	–0.2	1.6

Table 10.1 HIV/AIDS

	Estimated number of people living with HIV/AIDS (thousands)			Estimated HIV prevalence rate (%) Adults (ages 15–49)								
				Point estimate			Low estimate			High estimate		
	1990	2005	2007	1990	2005	2007	1990	2005	2007	1990	2005	2007
SUB-SAHARAN AFRICA	22,000.0	20,300.0	22,000.0	2.1	5.1	5.0	..	5.4	4.6	..	6.8	5.4
Angola	15.0	170.0	190.0	0.3	2.0	2.1	<0.1	1.6	1.7	4.3	2.8	2.5
Benin	3.5	61.0	64.0	0.1	1.3	1.2	<0.1	1.1	1.1	0.7	1.5	1.4
Botswana	33.0	290.0	300.0	4.7	24.9	23.9	3.8	23.9	22.5	5.4	25.9	24.9
Burkina Faso	84.0	130.0	130.0	1.9	1.7	1.6	0.1	1.5	1.4	3.3	2.0	1.9
Burundi	51.0	120.0	110.0	1.7	2.4	2.0	1.4	1.7	1.3	2.3	3.0	2.5
Cameroon	49.0	540.0	540.0	0.8	5.4	5.1	0.6	4.7	3.9	1.4	6.1	6.2
Cape Verde	..	..	..	..	..	..	..	..	..	..	..	..
Central African Republic	26.0	150.0	160.0	1.8	6.4	6.3	1.4	6.0	5.9	3.4	6.8	6.7
Chad	19.0	190.0	200.0	0.7	3.5	3.5	0.1	3.0	2.4	6.0	4.1	4.3
Comoros	..	<0.2	<0.2	<0.1	<0.1	<0.1	..	..	..	<0.1	<0.1	<0.1
Congo, Dem. Rep.	..	1,000.0	..	..	3.2	..	..	1.8	1.2	..	4.9	1.5
Congo, Rep.	62.0	80.0	79.0	5.1	3.7	3.5	3.0	3.2	2.8	7.0	4.3	4.2
Côte d'Ivoire	130.0	520.0	480.0	2.2	4.6	3.9	0.2	4.1	3.2	6.0	5.0	4.5
Djibouti	<1	15.0	16.0	0.2	3.1	3.1	0.1	2.4	2.3	0.7	3.8	3.8
Equatorial Guinea	1.8	10.0	11.0	1.0	3.6	3.4	0.1	2.8	2.6	1.3	4.9	4.6
Eritrea	2.1	34.0	38.0	0.1	1.2	1.3	<0.1	0.9	0.8	1.0	1.7	2.0
Ethiopia	190.0	900.0	980.0	0.7	2.1	2.1	0.5	1.9	1.8	1.1	2.3	2.2
Gabon	4.0	46.0	49.0	0.9	6.0	5.9	0.5	4.6	4.4	1.4	8.2	8.3
Gambia, The	<0.2	7.6	8.2	..	0.9	0.9	..	0.4	0.4	<0.1	1.3	1.3
Ghana	4.1	260.0	260.0	0.1	2.0	1.9	0.1	1.8	1.7	0.2	2.2	2.2
Guinea	6.3	78.0	87.0	0.2	1.5	1.6	0.1	1.3	1.3	0.8	1.9	2.2
Guinea-Bissau	<1	16.0	16.0	0.2	1.9	1.8	0.1	1.3	1.3	0.3	2.6	2.6
Kenya	..	..	..	..	..	..	2.7	6.1	7.1	3.6	8.1	8.5
Lesotho	5.9	270.0	270.0	0.8	23.4	23.2	0.6	22.2	21.9	1.1	24.6	24.5
Liberia	4.2	29.0	35.0	0.4	1.5	1.7	0.1	1.2	1.4	5.3	1.9	2.0
Madagascar	<0.1	12.0	14.0	..	0.1	0.1	..	<0.1	<0.1	..	0.2	0.2
Malawi	90.0	900.0	930.0	2.1	12.3	11.9	0.9	11.4	11.0	7.4	13.3	12.9
Mali	6.9	97.0	100.0	0.2	1.5	1.5	<0.1	1.3	1.2	0.3	1.8	1.8
Mauritania	<0.1	13.0	14.0	<0.1	0.8	0.8	..	0.5	0.5	0.1	1.5	1.5
Mauritius	<0.1	9.4	13.0	<0.1	1.2	1.7	..	0.8	1.0	0.1	2.2	3.6
Mozambique	94.0	1,300.0	1,500.0	1.4	12.2	12.5	0.4	10.7	10.9	5.4	14.1	14.7
Namibia	8.1	180.0	200.0	1.2	15.3	15.3	0.7	12.7	12.4	1.9	17.9	18.1
Niger	3.1	55.0	60.0	0.1	0.8	0.8	<0.1	0.6	0.6	0.2	1.0	1.1
Nigeria	340.0	2,500.0	2,600.0	0.7	3.2	3.1	0.1	2.7	2.3	8.7	3.7	3.8
Rwanda	260.0	160.0	150.0	9.2	3.1	2.8	8.0	2.8	2.4	10.5	3.5	3.2
São Tomé and Príncipe	..	..	..	..	..	..	..	..	..	..	..	..
Senegal	2.4	49.0	67.0	0.1	0.8	1.0	<0.1	0.6	0.7	0.2	0.9	1.4
Seychelles	..	..	..	..	..	..	..	..	..	..	..	..
Sierra Leone	3.4	50.0	55.0	0.2	1.6	1.7	<0.1	1.3	1.3	0.5	2.0	2.4
Somalia	<1	23.0	24.0	<0.1	0.5	0.5	..	0.3	0.3	0.2	1.0	1.0
South Africa	160.0	5,600.0	5,700.0	0.8	18.2	18.1	0.5	15.4	15.4	1.2	21.1	20.9
Sudan	100.0	300.0	320.0	0.8	1.4	1.4	0.1	1.0	1.0	1.8	1.9	2.0
Swaziland	3.9	180.0	190.0	0.9	26.4	26.1	0.7	25.3	25.1	1.3	27.4	27.1
Tanzania	610.0	1,400.0	1,400.0	4.8	6.4	6.2	4.3	6.0	5.8	5.0	6.7	6.6
Togo	14.0	120.0	130.0	0.7	3.4	3.3	0.3	2.9	2.7	1.7	4.1	4.1
Uganda	1,200.0	980.0	940.0	13.7	6.1	5.4	12.4	5.8	5.0	16.1	6.7	6.1
Zambia	360.0	1,000.0	1,100.0	8.9	15.0	15.2	5.1	14.1	14.3	13.1	16.3	16.4
Zimbabwe	710.0	1,500.0	1,300.0	14.2	19.0	15.3	13.1	18.3	14.6	15.0	19.9	16.1
NORTH AFRICA												
Algeria	..	19.0	21.0	..	0.1	0.1	..	<0.1	<0.1	..	0.2	0.2
Egypt, Arab Rep.	<1	8.1	9.2	..	..	..	..	..	<0.1	0.1	0.1	0.1
Libya	..	..	..	..	..	..	..	..	<0.2	..	..	0.2
Morocco	1.9	18.0	21.0	..	0.1	0.1	..	<0.1	<0.1	0.1	0.2	0.2
Tunisia	<0.5	3.2	3.7	..	0.1	0.1	..	<0.1	<0.1	0.1	0.2	0.2

Estimated HIV prevalence rate (%)											
Young men (ages 15–24)						Young women (ages 15–24)					
Point estimate		Low estimate		High estimate		Point estimate		Low estimate		High estimate	
2005	2007	2005	2007	2005	2007	2005	2007	2005	2007	2005	2007
..	1.1	1.3	0.8	1.7	1.4	..	3.2	3.7	2.6	5.1	3.8
0.9	0.2	0.4	0.1	1.4	0.4	2.5	0.3	1.2	0.1	4.2	0.5
0.4	0.3	0.2	0.1	0.6	0.5	1.1	0.9	0.6	0.6	1.8	1.2
5.7	5.1	5.6	2.1	7.5	7.9	15.3	15.3	15.2	10.0	20.3	20.8
0.5	0.5	0.3	0.2	0.6	0.8	1.4	0.9	0.8	0.5	2.0	1.3
0.8	0.4	0.7	0.2	0.9	0.7	2.3	1.3	2.0	0.6	2.7	2.0
4.1	1.2	1.3	0.5	1.6	2.2	6.8	4.3	4.4	1.0	5.3	5.9
..	..	..	..	..	..	..	..	..	..	..	..
2.5	1.1	0.9	0.5	4.5	1.5	7.4	5.5	2.7	4.1	13.1	7.0
0.9	2.0	0.4	0.9	1.6	2.9	2.2	2.8	0.9	1.3	3.9	4.1
<0.1	0.1	0.2	<0.1	0.2	0.2	<0.1	<0.1	0.2	0.1	0.2	0.1
0.8	..	0.3	0.1	1.3	0.4	2.2	..	1.0	0.7	3.8	1.2
1.2	0.8	0.6	0.3	1.9	1.1	3.7	2.3	1.9	1.3	5.7	3.3
1.7	0.8	0.9	0.3	2.7	1.3	5.1	2.4	2.6	1.0	7.9	3.4
0.7	0.7	0.2	0.3	1.6	1.1	2.1	2.1	0.5	1.4	4.6	3.0
0.7	0.8	0.6	0.4	0.9	1.4	2.3	2.5	1.8	1.7	2.7	3.7
0.6	0.3	0.3	0.1	1.0	0.6	1.6	0.9	0.7	0.4	2.7	1.6
..	0.5	0.2	0.2	0.8	0.7	..	1.5	0.5	1.1	2.3	1.9
1.8	1.3	0.9	0.6	3.0	2.4	5.4	3.9	2.7	2.0	8.7	6.3
0.6	0.2	0.2	0.1	1.0	0.4	1.7	0.6	0.7	0.3	2.9	1.0
0.2	0.4	0.2	0.2	0.3	0.6	1.3	1.3	1.1	0.9	1.5	1.7
0.5	0.4	0.4	0.2	0.5	0.6	1.4	1.2	1.1	0.9	1.6	1.8
0.9	0.4	0.4	0.2	1.5	0.8	2.5	1.2	1.1	0.3	4.3	2.5
1.0	..	0.9	0.8	1.2	2.5	5.2	..	4.5	4.6	6.0	8.4
5.9	5.9	5.5	2.5	6.2	9.6	14.1	14.9	13.3	10.6	15.0	18.4
..	0.4	..	0.2	..	0.6	..	1.3	..	0.8	..	1.7
0.6	0.2	0.2	0.1	1.3	0.3	0.3	0.1	0.1	<0.1	0.6	0.2
3.4	2.4	1.4	0.9	5.9	3.8	9.7	8.4	3.9	6.7	16.8	10.4
0.4	0.4	0.3	0.2	0.5	0.5	1.2	1.1	0.9	0.7	1.5	1.5
0.2	0.9	0.1	0.4	0.3	1.9	0.5	0.5	0.2	0.2	1.0	1.0
..	1.8	..	0.8	..	4.5	..	1.0	..	0.5	..	2.2
3.6	2.9	2.0	1.2	5.3	4.2	10.7	8.5	6.0	5.9	15.8	11.1
4.4	3.4	1.7	1.4	8.1	5.3	13.4	10.3	5.2	6.2	24.7	14.5
0.2	0.9	0.1	0.4	0.4	1.5	0.8	0.5	0.3	0.3	1.4	0.8
0.9	0.8	0.4	0.3	1.5	1.2	2.7	2.3	1.3	1.2	4.4	3.3
0.8	0.5	0.7	0.3	0.8	0.7	2.0	1.4	1.9	0.9	2.0	1.9
..	..	..	..	..	..	..	..	..	..	..	..
0.2	0.3	0.1	0.1	0.4	0.5	0.6	0.8	0.2	0.5	1.1	1.2
..	..	..	..	..	..	..	..	..	..	..	..
0.4	0.4	0.2	0.2	0.6	0.7	1.1	1.3	0.6	0.7	1.7	1.9
0.2	0.6	0.1	0.3	0.4	1.4	0.6	0.3	0.3	0.1	1.1	0.6
4.5	4.0	4.0	1.7	4.9	6.0	14.8	12.7	13.2	9.1	16.3	17.0
..	0.3	..	0.2	..	0.5	..	1.0	..	0.6	..	1.5
7.7	5.8	3.9	2.2	12.1	9.3	22.7	22.6	11.5	17.7	35.9	27.2
2.8	0.5	2.5	0.4	3.1	0.7	3.8	0.9	3.4	0.5	4.2	1.3
0.8	0.8	0.4	0.4	1.2	1.2	2.2	2.4	1.0	1.4	3.6	3.3
2.3	1.3	1.9	0.6	2.6	1.9	5.0	3.9	4.2	2.7	5.7	5.2
3.8	3.6	3.6	1.6	4.0	5.2	12.7	11.3	11.9	8.5	13.6	14.2
4.4	2.9	2.3	1.2	6.9	4.4	14.7	7.7	7.7	3.8	23.2	11.7
..	0.1	..	<0.1	..	0.3	..	0.1	..	<0.1	..	0.2
..	..	..	<0.1	..	<0.1	..	..	..	<0.1	..	<0.1
..	..	..	..	..	..	..	..	..	..	..	..
..	0.1	..	<0.1	..	0.2	..	0.1	..	<0.1	..	0.2
..	0.1	..	<0.1	..	0.2	..	<0.1	..	0.1	..	0.1

(continued)

Table 10.1 HIV/AIDS (continued)

	Deaths of adults and children due to HIV/AIDS (thousands)									AIDS orphans (ages 0–17, thousands)					
	Point estimate			Low estimate			High estimate			Point estimate		Low estimate		High estimate	
	1990	2005	2007	1990	2005	2007	1990	2005	2007	2005	2007	2005	2007	2005	2007
SUB-SAHARAN AFRICA	..	2,000.0	1,500.0	..	..	1,300.0	..	..	1,700.0	12,000.0	11,600.0	..	10,600.0	..	15,300.0
Angola	<1.0	9.9	11.0	<0.1	6.0	7.1	8.5	33.0	28.0	160.0	50.0	95.0	20.0	230.0	260.0
Benin	<0.1	3.7	3.3	..	3.0	2.7	1.7	4.6	4.4	62.0	29.0	38.0	22.0	89.0	40.0
Botswana	<1.0	12.0	11.0	<0.5	9.4	6.6	<1.0	15.0	17.0	120.0	95.0	110.0	81.0	150.0	110.0
Burkina Faso	3.7	9.6	9.2	<0.1	7.2	7.4	7.3	12.0	11.0	120.0	100.0	89.0	62.0	150.0	130.0
Burundi	2.2	13.0	11.0	1.7	11.0	8.6	3.5	16.0	14.0	120.0	120.0	94.0	100.0	170.0	150.0
Cameroon	1.0	43.0	39.0	<1.0	34.0	33.0	1.9	52.0	45.0	122.7	300.0	200.0	230.0	290.0	390.0
Cape Verde	..	..	..	..	..	..	..	..	..	..	..	..	..	..	..
Central African Republic	<1.0	12.0	11.0	..	10.0	9.5	1.0	13.0	12.0	140.0	72.0	62.0	58.0	200.0	86.0
Chad	<1.0	12.0	14.0	<0.1	7.7	11.0	11.0	24.0	20.0	57.0	85.0	28.0	42.0	97.0	270.0
Comoros	..	..	..	..	..	..	..	<0.1	<0.1	..	<0.1	..	0.2	..	0.2
Congo, Dem. Rep.	..	90.0	..	..	47.0	24.0	..	150.0	34.0	680.0	..	380.0	270.0	1,000.0	380.0
Congo, Rep.	1.6	7.3	6.4	1.0	6.2	3.0	3.0	8.9	10.0	110.0	69.0	70.0	57.0	150.0	84.0
Côte d'Ivoire	3.3	48.0	38.0	<0.5	41.0	33.0	20.0	56.0	43.0	450.0	420.0	280.0	320.0	630.0	530.0
Djibouti	..	1.0	1.1	..	<1.0	<1.0	<0.1	1.3	1.3	5.7	5.2	1.9	1.9	12.0	9.6
Equatorial Guinea	<0.1	..	..	..	..	..	<0.2	<1.0	<1.0	4.6	4.8	3.5	3.8	5.9	6.1
Eritrea	<0.1	2.4	2.6	..	1.6	1.8	<1	3.9	3.9	36.0	18.0	20.0	12.0	56.0	32.0
Ethiopia	3.7	80.0	67.0	2.3	69.0	57.0	6.7	91.0	77.0	..	650.0	280.0	540.0	870.0	780.0
Gabon	<0.1	2.1	2.3	..	1.2	1.4	<0.2	3.3	3.7	20.0	18.0	13.0	11.0	29.0	28.0
Gambia, The	..	<0.5	..	..	..	..	<0.1	<1.0	<1.0	3.8	2.7	2.2	1.3	6.0	4.7
Ghana	..	22.0	21.0	..	19.0	18.0	<0.1	25.0	24.0	139.6	160.0	..	130.0	139.6	200.0
Guinea	<0.5	4.1	4.5	<0.2	2.8	3.3	2.1	5.6	5.9	28.0	25.0	18.0	15.0	43.0	39.0
Guinea-Bissau	..	1.1	1.1	..	<1.0	<1.0	<0.1	1.5	1.5	11.0	5.9	6.0	4.2	16.0	8.3
Kenya	..	..	..	5.6	110.0	85.0	8.5	160.0	130.0	1,100.0	..	890.0	990.0	1,300.0	1,400.0
Lesotho	..	20.0	18.0	..	17.0	16.0	<0.1	22.0	20.0	97.0	110.0	88.0	93.0	110.0	120.0
Liberia	<0.1	2.1	2.3	..	1.5	1.7	1.5	6.1	4.7	..	15.0	..	10.0	..	87.0
Madagascar	..	..	<1.0	..	..	..	<0.1	1.0	1.3	13.0	3.4	5.0	2.1	24.0	6.0
Malawi	1.5	71.0	68.0	<1.0	64.0	59.0	5.5	80.0	77.0	550.0	550.0	310.0	470.0	780.0	640.0
Mali	<0.2	5.5	5.8	..	4.0	46.0	<1.0	7.0	7.3	94.0	44.0	70.0	27.0	120.0	56.0
Mauritania	..	1.0	1.0	..	0.5	0.5	0.1	1.0	1.3	6.9	3.0	3.9	1.5	10.0	5.9
Mauritius	..	<0.2	<1.0	..	<0.5	<0.5	<0.1	<0.5	<0.5	..	<0.5	..	1.0	..	1.0
Mozambique	2.7	78.0	81.0	<1.0	62.0	67.0	36.0	98.0	98.0	510.0	400.0	390.0	280.0	670.0	590.0
Namibia	<0.2	9.2	5.1	..	7.0	3.1	0.5	12.0	7.1	85.0	66.0	42.0	50.0	120.0	85.0
Niger	<0.1	3.4	4.0	..	2.5	3.0	0.2	5.1	5.6	46.0	25.0	20.0	18.0	85.0	39.0
Nigeria	9.6	180.0	170.0	<1.0	130.0	130.0	280.0	390.0	270.0	930.0	1,200.0	510.0	640.0	1,300.0	4,100.0
Rwanda	12.0	14.0	7.8	7.1	12.0	5.7	22.0	16.0	10.0	210.0	220.0	170.0	190.0	260.0	250.0
São Tomé and Principe	..	..	..	..	..	..	..	..	..	..	..	..	..	..	..
Senegal	<0.2	1.1	1.8	..	1.0	1.2	<0.5	1.8	2.6	25.0	8.4	14.0	4.6	39.0	14.0
Seychelles	..	..	..	..	..	..	..	..	..	..	..	..	..	..	..
Sierra Leone	<0.1	3.2	3.3	..	1.7	2.3	<0.2	5.1	4.7	31.0	16.0	19.0	6.4	49.0	26.0
Somalia	<0.1	1.4	1.6	..	<1.0	<1.0	<0.2	2.5	3.0	23.0	8.8	11.0	4.9	45.0	16.0
South Africa	2.6	330.0	350.0	1.5	260.0	270.0	4.7	420.0	420.0	1,200.0	1,400.0	970.0	1,100.0	1,400.0	1,800.0
Sudan	1.3	24.0	25.0	<0.1	16.0	17.0	3.2	33.0	32.0	..	..	..	..	..	..
Swaziland	<0.1	10.0	10.0	..	8.9	8.6	<0.2	12.0	12.0	63.0	56.0	45.0	48.0	77.0	65.0
Tanzania	18.0	120.0	96.0	14.0	110.0	86.0	23.0	130.0	110.0	1,100.0	970.0	910.0	850.0	1,200.0	1,100.0
Togo	<0.5	8.6	9.1	<0.1	6.7	6.9	2.0	11.0	12.0	88.0	68.0	51.0	50.0	130.0	91.0
Uganda	57.0	89.0	77.0	39.0	77.0	68.0	150.0	110.0	89.0	1,000.0	1,200.0	870.0	1,100.0	1,300.0	1,400.0
Zambia	6.9	75.0	56.0	<1.0	67.0	47.0	12.0	86.0	66.0	710.0	600.0	630.0	530.0	830.0	660.0
Zimbabwe	19.0	160.0	140.0	15.0	150.0	130.0	24.0	180.0	150.0	1,100.0	1,000.0	780.0	920.0	1,300.0	1,100.0
NORTH AFRICA															
Algeria	..	<1.0	<1.0	..	<0.5	<0.5	..	1.4	1.6	..	..	..	..	..	..
Egypt, Arab Rep.	..	<0.5	<0.5	..	..	..	<0.1	<1.0	<1.0	..	..	..	..	..	..
Libya	..	..	..	..	..	..	..	..	..	..	..	..	..	..	..
Morocco	..	<1.0	<1.0	..	<0.5	..	<0.1	1.3	1.5	..	..	..	..	..	..
Tunisia	..	<0.2	<0.2	..	..	..	<0.1	<0.5	<0.5	..	..	..	..	..	..

HIV-positive pregnant women receiving antiretrovirals to reduce the risk of mother-to-child transmission								ODA gross disbursements ($ millions)			
		Share of total (WHO/UNAIDS methodology, %)									
Total		Point estimate		Low estimate		High estimate		For social mitigation of HIV/AIDS		For STD control, including HIV/AIDS	
2005	2006	2005	2007	2005	2007	2005	2007	2005	2007	2005	2007
								35.5	76.7	1,731.3	2,683.1
..	1,645	2	9	2	7	3	13	0.7	1.8	24.9	19.2
1,214	1,830	27	40	23	35	31	47	..	0.0	27.3	8.9
7,543	12,419	64	>95	59	>95	70	>95	0.1	2.3	17.8	43.1
937	1,480	11	18	9	15	13	22	0.4	1.0	24.7	18.7
..	..	..	..	..	..	..	..	0.3	0.7	25.3	8.4
3,592	7,516	10	22	9	18	12	34	0.0	0.0	7.7	30.8
12	51	..	..	..	..	..	..	..	..	6.3	0.0
803	3,714	7	34	7	30	8	38	..	0.0	6.0	1.4
193	..	1	1	<1	1	2	2	..	0.0	19.4	3.5
..	–	..	0	..	..	..	..	..	..	0.1	0.3
1,725	3,435	5	9	4	8	6	10	..	1.2	31.0	34.8
1,093	240	23	5	20	4	28	7	..	..	0.5	2.7
2,543	3,240	8	12	7	9	9	16	0.1	0.2	25.2	46.1
16	..	2	..	2	..	3	..	0.0	..	10.7	4.8
..	..	..	..	..	..	..	..	..	..	2.2	0.4
88	168	4	7	3	4	5	11	..	0.0	8.3	7.8
2,341	4,888	4	7	3	7	4	8	0.3	1.4	152.3	245.0
90	494	4	21	3	14	5	32	..	0.0	0.7	3.2
87	133	..	..	11	17	37	58	..	0.0	15.2	3.3
1,078	2,896	7	21	7	18	8	24	0.0	0.6	21.3	40.5
77	679	1	11	1	8	2	14	0.0	0.0	20.4	4.5
..	349	20	24	..	17	..	34	..	0.0	0.4	1.3
19,403	52,858	24	69	21	61	28	80	0.5	4.7	84.4	222.1
1,811	3,966	14	32	13	29	16	36	..	2.7	8.1	18.5
130	224	5	7	4	6	6	9	..	..	4.7	7.7
8	25	..	..	1	3	3	9	0.0	0.0	16.9	10.5
5,076	23,158	7	32	6	28	8	36	1.0	3.8	64.7	147.3
415	1,018	..	..	4	10	6	15	0.1	0.0	11.2	20.0
10	45	..	..	1	6	4	20	..	0.0	0.4	0.9
..	19	..	..	..	6	..	23	..	..	0.0	1.3
8,490	44,975	9	46	8	39	11	56	1.2	6.2	81.3	149.1
4,055	..	43	64	36	53	52	80	0.2	0.0	29.0	83.9
57	1,006	..	..	1	20	3	47	..	0.0	12.1	5.7
532	12,278	<1	7	<1	5	<1	10	0.9	1.0	132.7	213.7
5,785	6,485	51	60	45	51	58	71	1.0	1.6	63.3	97.9
8	22	..	..	..	..	..	..	..	..	0.1	0.3
57	264	..	..	1	4	2	9	0.0	..	24.4	16.5
..	..	>95	..	..	..	..	..	..	..	..	0.0
57	919	1	21	1	15	2	29	..	0.0	12.8	5.9
..	11	3	..	..	1	..	2	..	0.0	6.0	7.9
75,077	127,164	34	57	29	49	40	69	4.7	9.9	131.9	284.2
..	..	..	..	..	..	..	..	..	0.2	11.0	14.4
4,780	8,772	36	67	33	60	40	74	0.1	0.2	22.7	20.1
..	..	..	..	..	..	..	..	1.8	6.1	135.1	194.1
720	705	9	9	7	7	11	11	..	0.0	6.6	11.6
12,073	26,484	15	34	13	29	17	39	0.8	5.4	141.1	241.3
14,071	35,314	19	47	17	41	22	52	0.8	1.6	121.0	141.1
8,461	15,381	13	29	12	27	14	32	0.1	2.4	64.1	97.5
								0.5	0.0	5.6	15.5
..	19	..	..	..	3	..	12	..	0.0	1.1	1.7
..	5	..	..	..	2	..	2	..	0.0	0.6	1.4
..	..	..	..	..	..	..	..	..	0.0	..	1.5
..	42	..	..	..	8	..	18	..	0.0	3.9	5.8
..	1	..	..	..	1	..	3	..	0.0	0.0	5.1

Table 11.1 Malaria

	Population (millions)		Clinical cases of malaria reported		Reported deaths due to malaria		Under-five mortality rate (per 1,000)	Children sleeping under insecticide-treated nets (% of children under age 5)	Children with fever receiving any antimalarial treatment (% of children under age 5 with fever)		Pregnant women receiving two doses of intermittent preventive treatment (%)
									Same or next day	Any time	
	2007	2008	2007	2008	2007	2008	2007	2000–08[a]	2000–08[a]	2000–08[a]	2000–08[a]
SUB-SAHARAN AFRICA	799.5	819.3	38,610,206	25,729,664	104,199	91,244	146				
Angola	17.6	18.0	1,295,535	1,377,992	9,812	9,465	158	17.7	18	28	3
Benin	8.4	8.7	..	..	1,195	..	123	20.2	42	54	3
Botswana	1.9	1.9	464	1,201	6	12	40	..	..	..	..
Burkina Faso	14.8	15.2	44,246	36,514	6,472	7,834	191	9.6	41	48	1
Burundi	7.8	8.1	860,606	876,741	167	226	180	8.3	19	30	..
Cameroon	18.5	18.9	313,083	1,650,749	1,811	7,673	148	13.1	38	58	6
Cape Verde	0.5	0.5	18	35	2	2	32	..	..	..	..
Central African Republic	4.3	4.4	119,477	152,260	578	456	172	15.1	42	57	9
Chad	10.8	11.1	58,288	57,644	617	1,018	209	..	..	53	..
Comoros	0.6	0.6	..	..	..	47	66	9.3	..	63	..
Congo, Dem. Rep.	62.4	64.2	759,059	1,462,300	14,637	18,928	161	5.8	..	30	5
Congo, Rep.	3.6	3.6	..	..	..	..	125	6.1	22	48	..
Côte d'Ivoire	20.1	20.6	1,277,670	1,343,654	797	1,249	127	5.9	26	36	8
Djibouti	0.8	0.8	210	119	1	..	127	1.3	3	10	..
Equatorial Guinea	0.6	0.7	..	50,758	..	..	206	0.7	..	49	..
Eritrea	4.8	5.0	9,195	4,702	42	19	70	4.2	2	4	..
Ethiopia	78.6	80.7	451,816	458,561	991	1,169	119	33.1	4	10	..
Gabon	1.4	1.4	45,186	40,701	216	156	91	..	..	..	..
Gambia, The	1.6	1.7	439,798	10,910	424	403	109	49.0	52	63	33
Ghana	22.9	23.4	476,484	827,438	4,622	3,889	115	28.2	48	24	27
Guinea	9.6	9.8	28,646	33,405	..	441	150	0.3	..	44	..
Guinea-Bissau	1.5	1.6	14,284	11,299	370	487	198	39.0	27	46	7
Kenya	37.5	38.5	9,610,691	839,904	..	..	121	6.0	15	24	13
Lesotho	2.0	2.0	..	..	..	..	84	..	..	..	..
Liberia	3.6	3.8	492,272	606,952	310	345	133	3.0	26	59	12
Madagascar	18.6	19.1	43,674	89,138	428	276	112	0.2	..	34	..
Malawi	13.9	14.3	4,442,197	4,986,779	8,541	7,748	111	23.0	20	24	45
Mali	12.3	12.7	1,291,853	..	1,782	1,227	196	27.1	15	32	4
Mauritania	3.1	3.2	..	302	..	..	119	2.1	10	21	..
Mauritius	1.3	1.3	..	..	..	..	15	..	..	..	..
Mozambique	21.4	21.8	6,155,082	4,831,491	5,816	4,424	169	22.8	8	23	16
Namibia	2.1	2.1	4,242	4,907	181	171	68	..	..	10	0
Niger	14.2	14.7	138,902	413,252	1,420	2,691	176	7.4	25	33	..
Nigeria	148.0	151.3	2,969,950	143,079	10,289	8,677	189	1.2	15	33	..
Rwanda	9.5	9.7	382,686	228,015	1,772	563	181	24.0	8	6	17
São Tomé and Príncipe	0.2	0.2	2,080	1,572	3	16	99	54.0	17	25	..
Senegal	11.9	12.2	95,169	202,466	1,935	722	114	31.0	9	22	49
Seychelles	0.1	0.1	..	..	..	..	13	..	..	..	..
Sierra Leone	5.4	5.6	653,987	154,459	324	871	262	25.9	45	30	2
Somalia	8.7	9.0	16,058	23,905	33	21	142	9.2	3	8	1
South Africa	47.9	48.7	6,327	7,796	37	43	59	..	..	..	..
Sudan	40.4	41.3	560,428[b]	457,362[b]	1,254[b]	1,125[b]	109	27.6	..	..	..
Swaziland	1.2	1.2	84	58	14	5	91	0.6	..	1	..
Tanzania	41.3	42.5	293	67	12,593	29	116	25.7	51	57	22
Togo	6.3	6.5	221,110	273,471	1,236	2,663	100	38.4	38	48	18
Uganda	30.6	31.7	1,050,240	894,505	7,003	2,372	130	9.7	29	62	16
Zambia	12.3	12.6	4,248,295	3,080,301	6,183	3,781	170	41.1	29	43	63
Zimbabwe	12.4	12.5	30,521	92,900	285	..	90	2.9	3	5	6
NORTH AFRICA	161.2	163.7	393	418	..	..	35				
Algeria	33.9	34.4	288	196	..	..	37	..	..	..	..
Egypt, Arab Rep.	80.1	81.5	30	80	..	..	36	..	..	..	..
Libya	6.2	6.3	..	..	..	..	18	..	..	..	..
Morocco	30.9	31.2	75	142	..	..	34	..	..	..	..
Tunisia	10.2	10.3	..	..	..	..	21	..	..	..	..

a. Data are for the most recent year available during the period specified.
b. Data are for 15 northern states only.

Table 12.1 Aid and debt relief

	Net official development assistance ($ millions)									
	From all donors		From DAC donors		From non-DAC donors		From multilateral donors		From other donors	
	2007	2008	2007	2008	2007	2008	2007	2008	2007	2008
SUB-SAHARAN AFRICA	32,332	35,689	19,668	21,254	316	406	12,349	14,029	39	41
Angola	246	369	86	184	18	34	142	151	0	0
Benin	474	641	238	303	3	7	233	331	0	0
Botswana	108	716	64	683	–1	–1	45	35	..	0
Burkina Faso	951	998	412	475	15	7	524	515	1	0
Burundi	473	509	200	255	0	0	273	253	0	0
Cameroon	1,908	525	1,697	298	9	11	203	216	0	0
Cape Verde	165	219	114	163	1	0	50	55	0	..
Central African Republic	177	256	118	129	0	0	59	128	0	..
Chad	354	416	223	277	0	0	130	138	0	0
Comoros	44	37	20	21	0	1	25	15	..	..
Congo, Dem. Rep.	1,241	1,610	788	944	1	8	452	657	..	0
Congo, Rep.	119	505	48	421	1	1	70	84	..	0
Côte d'Ivoire	171	617	112	193	1	4	59	419	0	1
Djibouti	112	121	75	66	0	10	37	45	0	..
Equatorial Guinea	31	38	26	24	0	0	6	13	0	0
Eritrea	157	143	45	53	3	7	109	84	2	7
Ethiopia	2,563	3,327	1,242	1,839	34	35	1,287	1,453	24	20
Gabon	51	55	34	38	1	1	16	16	0	0
Gambia, The	73	94	33	28	3	4	37	62	0	0
Ghana	1,154	1,293	708	723	2	6	443	564	0	0
Guinea	228	319	122	209	10	2	96	109	0	0
Guinea-Bissau	122	132	44	53	0	1	78	78	..	0
Kenya	1,323	1,360	824	951	3	4	496	405	0	1
Lesotho	129	143	62	66	–1	0	67	78	0	0
Liberia	698	1,250	226	809	1	37	471	404	0	0
Madagascar	895	841	387	274	6	4	502	563	0	0
Malawi	742	913	401	432	11	9	330	471	0	0
Mali	1,020	964	558	531	4	0	458	432	1	0
Mauritania	342	311	133	139	1	24	208	147	1	0
Mauritius	69	110	44	16	–2	–2	28	95	0	0
Mozambique	1,778	1,994	1,073	1,340	22	4	682	650	2	0
Namibia	217	207	144	150	1	2	73	54	0	0
Niger	542	605	233	269	2	2	307	335	0	0
Nigeria	1,956	1,290	1,385	636	1	3	570	651	0	1
Rwanda	722	931	374	450	2	3	347	477	0	0
São Tomé and Príncipe	36	47	31	26	0	0	5	21	..	..
Senegal	872	1,058	451	544	32	48	390	465	1	0
Seychelles	9	12	1	5	–1	0	8	7	0	0
Sierra Leone	545	367	381	175	0	–1	164	193	0	0
Somalia	384	758	257	565	4	8	124	185	0	0
South Africa	810	1,125	597	881	1	2	213	242	1	1
Sudan	2,112	2,384	1,664	1,818	114	106	334	459	3	6
Swaziland	51	67	12	18	0	–1	39	50	..	0
Tanzania	2,820	2,331	1,831	1,366	8	5	981	960	0	0
Togo	121	330	65	176	–1	–1	58	154	0	0
Uganda	1,737	1,657	1,002	1,005	4	5	731	647	0	0
Zambia	998	1,086	713	703	1	1	284	382	1	0
Zimbabwe	479	611	371	530	1	2	106	79	1	0
NORTH AFRICA	2,911	3,420	1,913	2,113	199	168	798	1,139	2	1
Algeria	390	316	289	241	8	–23	93	98	..	0
Egypt, Arab Rep.	1,107	1,348	787	960	82	114	238	274	1	1
Libya	19	60	15	52	2	2	3	6	..	0
Morocco	1,073	1,217	628	612	118	81	327	524	0	0
Tunisia	321	479	194	248	–10	–7	137	237	0	0

(continued)

Table 12.1 Aid and debt relief (continued)

	Net private official development assistance ($ millions)						Net official development assistance					
	From all donors		From DAC donors		From non-DAC donors		Share of GDP (%)		Per capita ($)		Share of gross capital formation (%)	
	2007	2008	2007	2008	2007	2008	2007	2008	2007	2008	2007	2008
SUB-SAHARAN AFRICA	31,203	5,606	30,994	5,337	209	269	3.7	3.5	40.4	43.6	19.2	18.7
Angola	293	2,151	292	2,145	0	6	0.4	0.4	14.0	20.5	2.9	3.6
Benin	35	4	35	4	..	..	8.7	9.6	56.5	74.0	..	..
Botswana	30	−89	30	−89	..	..	0.9	5.5	57.2	376.1	2.1	12.3
Burkina Faso	−60	17	−60	17	..	..	14.1	12.6	64.4	65.6	..	..
Burundi	11	−38	11	−38	..	..	48.3	43.7	60.4	63.0	..	..
Cameroon	−173	90	−173	90	..	0	9.2	2.2	103.0	27.8	53.3	12.0
Cape Verde	−10	45	−10	45	..	..	11.4	12.6	335.9	438.2	28.3	29.5
Central African Republic	15	−22	15	−22	..	0	10.3	13	40.7	58.0	116.3	126.1
Chad	52	43	52	43	..	..	5	5	32.8	37.6	26.2	33.1
Comoros	−76	1	−76	1	..	..	9.6	7	70.8	57.9	69.5	43.8
Congo, Dem. Rep.	−26	0	−28	0	3	0	12.5	13.9	19.9	25.1	63.8	81.7
Congo, Rep.	777	124	776	123	0	1	1.6	4.7	33.4	139.7	5.7	..
Côte d'Ivoire	100	49	99	47	2	2	0.9	2.6	8.5	29.9	10.0	26.2
Djibouti	21	33	21	33	..	..	13.7	13.8	135.0	142.6	35.4	..
Equatorial Guinea	−265	−1,014	−265	−1,014	..	..	0.2	0.2	48.8	57.1	0.7	0.8
Eritrea	2	−6	2	−6	..	..	11.4	8.7	32.4	28.6	108.2	..
Ethiopia	−53	−140	−59	−145	6	5	13.2	12.6	32.6	41.2	53.0	60.3
Gabon	638	−241	638	−241	..	..	0.4	0.4	36.0	37.6	1.7	1.4
Gambia, The	32	3	32	3	..	..	11.4	12	45.3	56.5	49.0	47.8
Ghana	571	206	570	190	2	15	7.7	8	50.5	55.4	22.6	25.1
Guinea	12	−61	12	−61	1	0	5	7.5	23.7	32.4	39.6	58.7
Guinea-Bissau	−20	−15	−20	−15	..	..	32	30.6	79.4	83.5	131.7	123.3
Kenya	1,113	−25	1,113	−25	0	..	4.9	3.9	35.2	35.3	24.3	16.0
Lesotho	−9	−5	−9	−5	..	..	7.7	8.8	64.2	71.1	29.1	30.7
Liberia	1,427	829	1,427	828	0	0	95	143.7	192.5	329.6	475.1	..
Madagascar	278	206	144	96	134	110	12.2	9.4	48.1	44.0	44.3	26.3
Malawi	−18	−5	−18	−5	..	..	20.7	21.4	53.3	63.9	80.1	66.9
Mali	28	−25	28	−25	..	..	14.9	11	82.7	75.8	63.9	..
Mauritania	−140	−9	−140	−9	..	..	12.9	10.9	109.5	97.1	49.9	..
Mauritius	11,684	1,237	11,684	1,140	..	97	1	1.3	54.6	86.4	3.8	5.0
Mozambique	272	−10	272	−10	..	..	22.2	20.5	83.2	91.5	119.0	88.9
Namibia	−37	317	−37	317	..	..	2.5	2.4	104.5	97.8	11.9	10.7
Niger	−221	−26	−221	−26	..	..	12.8	11.3	38.2	41.3	..	..
Nigeria	−544	1,845	−569	1,835	26	10	1.2	0.6	13.2	8.5	..	..
Rwanda	47	10	47	10	..	0	21.2	20.9	76.4	95.7	102.2	100.6
São Tomé and Príncipe	−17	−5	−17	−5	..	..	24.8	26.9	227.7	292.2	..	..
Senegal	127	163	127	163	0	1	7.7	8	73.3	86.6	25.0	26.5
Seychelles	128	35	128	35	..	..	1	1.5	102.7	139.9	2.9	5.1
Sierra Leone	−96	2	−96	2	..	..	32.8	18.8	100.6	66.0	243.9	95.6
Somalia	7	4	7	4	..	..	..	..	44.2	84.7	..	..
South Africa	11,415	5,735	11,385	5,718	30	17	0.3	0.4	16.9	23.1	1.3	1.8
Sudan	19	−14	16	−17	4	3	4.6	4.1	52.2	57.6	18.8	17.3
Swaziland	−5	2	−5	2	..	..	1.8	2.6	44.0	57.7	13.5	17.2
Tanzania	−447	123	−449	122	2	1	16.8	11.4	68.3	54.9	..	..
Togo	82	32	82	32	..	..	4.9	11.7	19.3	51.0	..	..
Uganda	38	112	38	112	..	..	14.6	11.4	56.7	52.3	66.1	48.4
Zambia	169	399	169	399	0	0	8.8	7.6	81.1	86.0	36.5	34.1
Zimbabwe	46	19	46	19	..	..	..	..	38.4	49.0	..	..
NORTH AFRICA	11,907	20,309	11,782	20,076	125	232	0.7	0.6	18.1	20.9	2.6	2.3
Algeria	1,874	222	1,874	218	1	4	0.3	0.2	11.5	9.2	0.9	0.5
Egypt, Arab Rep.	5,348	15,203	5,312	15,183	36	20	0.8	0.8	13.8	16.5	4.1	3.5
Libya	1,879	1,488	1,840	1,447	39	42	0	0.1	3.2	9.6	..	..
Morocco	1,495	1,584	1,495	1,579	0	5	1.4	1.4	34.8	39.0	4.4	4.2
Tunisia	931	1,367	881	1,206	50	161	0.9	1.2	31.4	46.4	3.7	4.8

a. As of 2009.

Net official development assistance								
Share of imports of goods and services (%)		Share of central government expenditures (%)		Cereal food aid shipments (thousands of metric tons)		Heavily Indebted Poor Countries (HIPC) Debt Initiative		Debt service relief committed ($ millions)[a]
2007	2008	2007	2008	2005	2006	Decision point[a]	Completion point[a]	
4.4	3.5	25.4	24.9	3,035	2,204			52,315
0.4	0.3	..	..	38	7			
..	..	..	..	9	6	Jul. 2000	Mar. 2003	460
1.0	6.4	4.5	28.7	..	..			
..	..	..	..	28	24	Jul. 2000	Apr. 2002	930
..	..	..	..	67	38	Aug. 2005	Jan. 2009	1,472
21.3	3.9	100.0	17.7	15	5	Oct. 2000	Apr. 2006	4,917
15.4	16.9	55.5	68.8	25	16			
27.8	34.7	389.6	375.0	7	8	Sep. 2007	Jun. 2009	
6.0	6.4	82.8	85.7	63	61	May 2001		260
19.3	14.1	77.6	58.2	..	..			
19.1	24.6	120.2	126.1	68	80	Jul. 2003	Floating	10,389
1.3	..	11.0	..	4	5	Mar. 2006	Floating	2,881
1.0	2.7	10.3	32.4	21	13	Mar. 1998/Mar. 2009		
9.9	..	52.8	..	16	8			
0.2	0.2	10.9	7.7	..	..			
28.1	..	36.4	..	91	10			
29.3	31.2	124.6	110.9	699	504	Nov. 2001	Apr. 2004	3,275
0.4	0.3	5.0	4.8	..	..			
13.7	15.2	70.4	76.0	10	6	Dec. 2000	Dec. 2007	90
8.2	8.0	54.7	59.0	66	21	Feb. 2002	Jul. 2004	3,500
6.5	12.9	82.8	153.7	29	19	Dec. 2000	Floating	800
44.1	38.5	208.6	221.0	4	7	Dec. 2000	Floating	790
7.7	6.2	28.6	36.5	143	245			
5.0	5.6	30.4	33.0	15	7			
81.2	..	652.4	..	48	42	Mar. 2008		
15.8	12.0	257.2	204.5	36	37	Dec. 2000	Oct. 2004	1,900
30.4	28.7	180.4	195.6	95	52	Dec. 2000	Aug. 2006	1,000
23.1	..	138.8	..	28	49	Sep. 2000	Mar. 2003	895
10.6	..	64.4	..	63	38	Feb. 2000	Jun. 2002	1,100
0.8	1.0	7.4	9.8	..	..			
27.1	27.7	188.2	166.8	119	81	Apr. 2000	Sep. 2001	4,300
2.6	2.8	13.0	13.4	1	0			
..	..	..	..	101	93	Dec. 2000	Apr. 2004	1,190
1.7	0.8	..	..	..	..			
56.6	58.6	198.6	228.6	29	19	Dec. 2000	Apr. 2005	1,316
..	..	..	..	1	0	Dec. 2000	Mar. 2007	200
10.5	11.1	77.2	80.1	15	12	Jun. 2000	Apr. 2004	850
0.4	0.5	5.3	9.8	..	..			
66.5	30.3	312.3	147.7	27	19	Mar. 2002	Dec. 2006	950
..	..	..	..	102	115			
0.4	0.5	1.5	2.0	..	..			
10.4	9.1	30.9	24.8	541	425			
1.1	1.6	11.7	10.9	15	4			
..	..	..	..	62	7	Apr. 2000	Nov. 2001	3,000
4.7	10.8	26.1	71.7	0	0	Nov. 2008		
30.9	23.3	113.2	97.0	142	36	Feb. 2000	May 2000	1,950
11.3	10.7	83.9	84.0	74	19	Dec. 2000	Apr. 2005	3,900
..	..	..	..	115	68			
1.0	0.8	5.8	7.0	34	35			
0.4	0.2	2.4	2.7	29	10			
1.3	1.0	7.5	7.7	5	24			
..	..	..	..	..	..			
1.8	1.6	7.8	9.1	..	..			
0.8	0.9	6.4	8.8	..	..			

Table 12.2 Status of Paris Declaration indicators

	PDI-1		PDI-2			PDI-3		PDI-4		PDI-5			
	Operational national development strategies[a]		Reliable public financial management[b]		Reliable country procurement systems[c]	Government budget estimates comprehensive and realistic (%)		Technical assistance aligned and coordinated with country programs (%)		Aid for government sectors uses country public financial management systems (%)		Aid for government sectors uses of country procurement systems (%)	
	2005	2007	2005	2007	2007	2005	2007	2005	2007	2005	2007	2005	2007
SUB-SAHARAN AFRICA													
Angola[d]													
Benin	C	C	4.0	3.5	..	46.7	28.5	56.3	53.9	51.8	47.5	64.1	63.3
Botswana[d]													
Burkina Faso	C	B	4.0	4.0	..	67.5	92.2	3.4	56.4	44.5	43.2	60.4	53.8
Burundi	D	C	2.5	3.0	..	39.3	53.9	42.6	41.0	24.5	32.7	19.4	34.6
Cameroon	C	C	3.5	3.5	B	..	85.7	..	29.9	..	53.1	..	63.1
Cape Verde	C	C	3.5	4.0	..	85.1	90.2	92.7	39.3	64.1	22.5	53.5	22.1
Central African Republic	D	D	2.0	2.0	..	..	36.4	..	36.5	..	23.8	..	10.2
Chad	C	C	3.0	9.0	..	..	87.9	..	64.4	..	1.0	..	10.6
Comoros[d]													
Congo, Dem. Rep.	D	D	2.5	2.5	..	81.0	58.3	10.7	38.1	12.9	0.0	30.8	0.8
Congo, Rep.													
Côte d'Ivoire	D	E	2.5	2.0	..	..	64.4	..	30.9	..	0.0	..	9.3
Djibouti[d]													
Equatorial Guinea[d]													
Eritrea[d]													
Ethiopia	C	B	3.5	4.0	..	74.4	61.7	27.3	66.8	45.2	46.7	42.8	41.4
Gabon	..	..	9.0	9.0	..	..	22.4	..	70.4	..	4.7	..	32.3
Gambia, The[d]													
Ghana	C	B	3.5	4.0	C	96.1	94.5	40.4	73.8	62.1	50.8	51.9	56.1
Guinea[d]													
Guinea-Bissau[d]													
Kenya	D	C	3.5	3.5	..	90.9	64.2	60.2	63.8	47.3	53.6	44.7	36.8
Lesotho[d]													
Liberia	D	D	9.0	9.0	..	..	0.0	..	35.3	..	32.0	..	0.0
Madagascar	C	C	3.0	3.5	..	..	87.0	..	70.9	..	21.5	..	25.9
Malawi	C	C	3.0	3.0	C	53.6	63.7	46.6	52.3	54.7	49.9	35.0	35.4
Mali	C	C	4.0	3.5	..	60.0	72.6	15.1	75.4	29.5	34.4	44.6	34.8
Mauritania	B	C	2.0	2.5	..	65.4	57.4	19.5	53.4	4.4	8.3	19.7	22.2
Mauritius[d]													
Mozambique	C	C	3.5	3.5	..	83.3	82.5	38.1	26.9	35.8	43.5	38.0	53.8
Namibia[d]													
Niger	C	C	3.5	3.5	B	99.5	90.7	15.3	50.2	27.1	25.5	48.7	36.5
Nigeria	..	C	3.0	3.0	..	..	6.3	..	70.6	..	0.0	..	0.0
Rwanda	B	B	3.5	4.0	B	49.0	51.0	57.8	83.6	39.2	42.0	46.0	42.9
São Tomé and Príncipe[d]													
Senegal	C	C	3.5	3.5	B	88.9	87.7	18.1	54.1	22.7	19.0	28.9	41.3
Seychelles[d]													
Sierra Leone	D	C	3.5	3.5	B	..	53.6	..	22.5	..	20.1	..	38.3
Somalia[d]													
South Africa	..	..	..	..	..	70.8	..	95.1	..	38.1	..	43.7	..
Sudan	D	D	2.5	2.0	..	..	84.6	..	53.2	..	3.1	..	0.4
Swaziland[d]													
Tanzania	B	B	4.5	4.0	B	89.5	83.6	49.5	60.5	65.9	71.5	61.2	68.5
Togo	..	..	2.0	2.0	..	..	68.9	..	28.9	..	4.4	..	15.5
Uganda	B	B	4.0	4.0	B	79.1	98.4	41.6	58.1	60.2	57.0	54.2	36.9
Zambia	C	B	3.0	3.5	C	51.9	73.5	32.4	34.5	34.1	59.4	43.5	71.0
Zimbabwe[d]													
NORTH AFRICA													
Algeria[d]													
Egypt, Arab Rep.	..	..	9.0	9.0	..	58.2	57.4	76.3	86.2	28.2	12.0	24.9	22.7
Libya	..	..	..	..	..	..	..	..	..	..	..	..	..
Morocco	..	..	9.0	9.0	..	..	79.8	..	82.2	..	78.9	..	81.1
Tunisia[d]													

Note: See *Technical notes* for further details. PDI is Paris Declaration Indicator.

a. Ratings range from A to E, where A means the development strategy substantially achieves good practices; B means it is largely developed toward achieving good practices; C means it reflects action taken toward achieving good practices; D means it incorporates some elements of good practice; and E means it reflects little action toward achieving good practices.

b. Ratings range from 1 (low) to 6 (high).

c. Ratings range from A (high) to D (low). Indicator was not collected in 2005.

d. Did not take part in the Survey on Monitoring the Paris Declaration.

PDI-6 Project implementation units parallel to country structures (number)		PDI-7 Aid disbursements on schedule and recorded by government (%)		PDI-8 Bilateral aid that is untied (%)		PDI-9 Aid provided in the framework of program-based approaches (%)		PDI-10 Donor missions coordinated (%)		PDI-10 Country analysis coordinated (%)		PDI-11 Existence of a monitorable performance assessment framework[a]		PDI-12 Existence of a mutual accountability review[a]	
2005	2007	2005	2007	2005	2007	2005	2007	2005	2007	2005	2007	2005	2007	2005	2007
29.0	58.0	53.0	31.6	79.3	98.8	60.8	49.0	14.5	25.1	37.5	44.0	C	C	B	B
131.0	102.0	91.7	91.6	92.4	91.8	45.3	57.2	16.8	12.8	45.2	39.0	C	C	B	B
37.0	29.0	52.5	44.4	59.8	90.6	53.6	35.5	24.3	13.5	55.0	73.8	D	D	B	A
..	38.0	..	50.8	..	98.5	..	39.6	..	25.8	..	49.2	D	D	..	B
10.0	18.0	92.2	96.4	22.3	60.3	36.7	30.9	10.5	43.4	34.1	64.5	D	C	A	B
..	11.0	..	45.2	..	86.7	..	34.3	..	9.8	..	23.2	D	D	..	B
..	17.0	..	0.0	..	81.2	..	1.5	..	18.1	..	35.0	D	D	..	..
34.0	146.0	82.9	19.5	88.1	93.9	53.8	20.8	38.4	21.3	35.2	22.9	D	D	B	B
..	29.0	..	67.0	..	91.7	..	2.6	..	65.0	..	75.0	D	E	..	B
103.0	56.0	95.9	73.4	38.8	82.2	52.6	65.6	26.7	29.4	49.5	69.5	C	C	A	A
..	5.0	..	16.8	..	99.7	..	0.0	..	4.7	..	36.8	..	..	..	B
45.0	16.0	91.6	82.3	89.9	91.8	52.7	68.8	19.7	39.0	39.9	59.8	C	C	A	A
17.0	21.0	44.0	46.5	78.3	84.5	44.6	30.5	9.2	48.4	32.3	78.0	C	C	B	B
..	16.0	..	0.0	..	82.4	..	21.3	..	11.0	..	65.6	D	D	..	B
..	48.0	..	79.5	..	83.9	..	43.5	..	23.8	..	41.6	C	C	..	B
69.0	51.0	57.7	58.1	96.9	90.5	31.8	42.0	23.8	22.3	60.0	60.8	C	C	A	A
65.0	60.0	70.7	68.2	95.0	93.4	48.1	40.6	7.4	15.2	30.0	39.3	D	D	B	B
23.0	27.0	39.4	52.1	72.9	67.0	36.7	35.1	13.8	11.4	58.9	25.4	C	C	B	B
40.0	26.0	70.1	73.7	89.0	90.8	46.3	46.4	46.5	16.8	63.2	31.7	C	B	A	A
52.0	47.0	73.2	77.5	83.8	84.3	31.2	49.0	20.9	15.4	39.9	31.8	D	D	B	B
..	23.0	..	7.1	..	99.2	..	3.9	..	19.1	..	32.8	..	C	..	B
48.0	41.0	65.6	66.8	81.6	95.1	41.5	38.4	8.5	20.8	36.4	42.0	C	C	B	B
23.0	55.0	69.3	60.8	90.8	93.0	57.3	38.9	15.1	16.6	40.5	28.1	C	C	B	B
..	2.0	..	29.7	..	91.6	..	26.9	..	27.1	..	56.3	D	D	..	B
15.0	..	44.2	..	97.2	97.4	26.5	..	18.8	..	75.0	..	..	..	A	..
..	105.0	..	51.6	..	79.9	..	19.2	..	14.9	..	44.7	D	D	..	B
56.0	28.0	70.2	60.8	94.6	98.9	55.5	60.8	17.3	15.8	38.3	64.9	B	B	A	A
..	13.0	..	14.3	..	56.1	..	38.9	..	15.1	..	20.7	..	..	..	B
54.0	55.0	84.0	74.4	81.0	85.4	49.9	65.7	17.2	21.0	40.1	54.0	B	B	B	B
24.0	34.0	50.1	85.1	99.1	99.6	47.1	46.8	14.7	15.9	45.8	46.4	D	C	A	B
100.0	32.0	29.2	78.9	46.7	75.0	61.2	48.9	18.1	21.6	40.0	56.1	..	..	A	B
..	..	..	..	..	..	..	..	..	..	..	..	..	..	..	..
..	47.0	..	68.3	..	90.1	..	70.3	..	11.7	..	25.0	..	..	..	B

Table 12.3 Capable states

	Investment climate			Enforcing contracts		
	Firms that believe the court system is fair, impartial, and uncorrupt (%)	Viewed by firms as major or very severe constraints (% of firms)				
		Corruption	Crime, theft, and disorder	Number of procedures	Time required (days)	Cost (% of debt)
	2007–09[b]	2007–09[b]	2007–09[b]	2010	2010	2010
SUB-SAHARAN AFRICA	..	..	..	39	656	48.9
Angola	..	..	..	46	1,011	44.4
Benin	..	..	..	42	825	64.7
Botswana	..	..	..	29	687	28.0
Burkina Faso	..	..	..	37	446	83.0
Burundi	..	..	..	44	832	38.6
Cameroon	..	..	..	43	800	46.6
Cape Verde	..	..	..	37	425	21.8
Central African Republic	..	..	..	43	660	82.0
Chad	..	..	..	41	743	77.4
Comoros	..	..	..	43	506	89.4
Congo, Dem. Rep.	..	..	..	43	625	151.8
Congo, Rep.	32.3	65.0	44.1	44	560	53.2
Côte d'Ivoire	35.3	75.0	53.8	33	770	41.7
Djibouti	..	..	..	40	1,225	34.0
Equatorial Guinea	..	..	..	40	553	18.5
Eritrea	..	..	..	39	405	22.6
Ethiopia	..	..	..	37	620	15.2
Gabon	41.3	41.4	34.1	38	1,070	34.3
Gambia, The	..	..	..	32	434	37.9
Ghana	59.8	9.9	0.9	36	487	23.0
Guinea	..	..	..	50	276	45.0
Guinea-Bissau	..	..	..	41	1,140	25.0
Kenya	22.3	38.4	3.9	40	465	47.2
Lesotho	33.2	46.7	33.5	41	695	19.5
Liberia	44.3	31.2	26.8	41	1,280	35.0
Madagascar	28.8	42.7	48.1	38	871	42.4
Malawi	..	..	..	42	432	142.4
Mali	49.6	15.7	0.6	36	626	52.0
Mauritania	..	..	..	46	370	23.2
Mauritius	63.6	50.7	41.5	36	720	17.4
Mozambique	16.6	25.4	1.8	30	730	142.5
Namibia	..	..	..	33	270	35.8
Niger	..	..	..	39	545	59.6
Nigeria	53.5	24.7	4.1	39	457	32.0
Rwanda	..	..	..	24	260	78.7
São Tomé and Príncipe	..	..	..	43	1,185	50.5
Senegal	55.4	23.8	0.5	44	780	26.5
Seychelles	..	..	..	38	720	14.3
Sierra Leone	29.7	36.9	14.2	40	515	149.5
Somalia	..	..	..	..	..	..
South Africa	59.6	16.9	1.0	30	600	33.2
Sudan	..	..	..	53	810	19.8
Swaziland	..	..	..	40	972	23.1
Tanzania	..	..	..	38	462	14.3
Togo	..	..	..	41	588	47.5
Uganda	..	..	..	38	510	44.9
Zambia	55.0	12.1	1.0	35	471	38.7
Zimbabwe	..	..	..	38	410	32.0
NORTH AFRICA	..	..	..	42	705	23.8
Algeria	..	64.3	0.9	46	630	21.9
Egypt, Arab Rep.	..	59.3	0.0	41	1,010	26.2
Libya	..	..	..	..	..	..
Morocco	43.5	27.3	0.0	40	615	25.2
Tunisia	..	..	..	39	565	21.8

a. Average of the disclosure, director liability, and shareholder suits indexes.
b. Data are for the most recent year available during the period specified.

	Protecting investors (0 least desirable to 10 most desirable)			Regulation and tax administration			
Disclosure index 2010	Director liability index 2010	Shareholder suits index 2010	Investor protection index[a] 2010	Number of tax payments 2010	Time required to prepare, file, and pay taxes (hours) 2010	Total tax rate (% of profit) 2010	Extractive Industries Transparency Initiative status 2009
5	3	5	4.4	38	302	66.8	
5	6	6	5.7	31	272	53.2	
6	1	3	3.3	55	270	73.3	
7	8	3	6.0	19	140	17.1	
6	1	4	3.7	46	270	44.9	
4	1	5	3.3	32	140	278.6	Candidate
6	1	6	4.3	41	1400	50.5	
1	5	6	4.0	56	100	49.7	Candidate
6	1	5	4.0	54	504	203.8	
6	1	5	4.0	54	122	60.9	Candidate
6	1	5	4.0	20	100	41.1	
3	3	4	3.3	32	308	322.0	
6	1	3	3.3	61	606	65.5	Candidate
6	1	3	3.3	66	270	44.7	Candidate
5	2	0	2.3	35	114	38.7	Candidate
6	1	4	3.7	46	296	59.5	
4	5	5	4.7	18	216	84.5	Candidate
4	4	5	4.3	19	198	31.1	
6	1	3	3.3	26	272	44.7	Intent to implement
2	1	5	2.7	50	376	292.4	Candidate
7	5	6	6.0	33	224	32.7	
6	1	1	2.7	56	416	49.9	Candidate
6	1	5	4.0	46	208	45.9	Candidate
3	2	10	5.0	41	417	49.7	
2	1	8	3.7	21	324	18.5	
4	1	6	3.7	32	158	43.7	
5	6	6	5.7	23	201	39.2	Compliant
4	7	5	5.3	19	157	25.8	Candidate
6	1	4	3.7	58	270	52.1	
5	3	3	3.7	38	696	86.1	Candidate
6	8	9	7.7	7	161	22.9	Candidate
5	4	9	6.0	37	230	34.3	
5	5	6	5.3	37	375	9.6	Candidate
6	1	3	3.3	41	270	46.5	
5	7	5	5.7	35	938	32.2	Candidate
7	9	3	6.3	34	160	31.3	Candidate
3	1	6	3.3	42	424	47.2	
6	1	2	3.0	59	666	46.0	Candidate
4	8	5	5.7	16	76	44.1	
6	7	6	6.3	29	357	235.6	
..	..	..	..	..	..	..	Candidate
8	8	8	8.0	9	200	30.2	
0	6	4	3.3	42	180	36.1	
0	1	5	2.0	33	104	36.6	
3	4	8	5.0	48	172	45.2	
6	1	4	3.7	53	270	52.7	Candidate
2	5	5	4.0	32	161	35.7	
3	6	7	5.3	37	132	16.1	
8	1	4	4.3	51	270	39.4	Candidate
6	4	4	4.7	28	379	54.9	
6	6	4	5.3	34	451	72.0	
8	3	5	5.3	29	480	43.0	
..	..	..	..	..	..	..	
6	2	1	3.0	28	358	41.7	
5	5	6	5.3	22	228	62.8	

..

Table 12.4 Governance and anticorruption indicators

	Governance indicators[a]											
	Voice and accountability		Political stability and absence of violence		Government effectiveness		Regulatory quality		Rule of law		Control of corruption	
	1996	2008	1996	2008	1996	2008	1996	2008	1996	2008	1996	2008
SUB-SAHARAN AFRICA												
Angola	−1.5	−1.1	−2.3	−0.4	−1.3	−1.0	−1.4	−0.9	−1.5	−1.3	−1.0	−1.2
Benin	0.7	0.3	1.0	0.4	0.0	−0.5	0.2	−0.5	−0.3	−0.5	..	−0.4
Botswana	0.8	0.6	0.8	1.0	0.2	0.7	0.7	0.5	0.6	0.6	0.4	1.0
Burkina Faso	−0.3	−0.3	0.1	−0.1	−0.7	−0.7	−0.1	−0.3	−0.3	−0.4	−0.3	−0.4
Burundi	−1.5	−0.7	−2.0	−1.4	−1.0	−1.2	−1.6	−1.2	−0.9	−1.1	..	−1.0
Cameroon	−1.2	−1.0	−1.4	−0.5	−1.1	−0.8	−0.8	−0.7	−1.4	−1.0	−1.2	−0.9
Cape Verde	0.8	1.0	1.0	0.9	−0.1	0.1	−0.8	0.0	0.5	0.5	..	0.8
Central African Republic	−0.5	−1.0	−0.2	−1.8	−0.9	−1.5	−0.3	−1.3	−0.3	−1.4	..	−0.9
Chad	−0.9	−1.5	−0.6	−1.9	−0.7	−1.5	−0.9	−1.3	−0.9	−1.6	..	−1.5
Comoros	0.0	−0.4	1.0	−1.0	−0.7	−1.9	−0.8	−1.5	..	−1.0	..	−0.8
Congo, Dem. Rep.	−1.6	−1.5	−2.1	−2.3	−1.8	−1.9	−2.6	−1.4	−2.0	−1.7	−2.2	−1.3
Congo, Rep.	−0.5	−1.2	−1.4	−0.6	−1.4	−1.3	−0.9	−1.2	−1.4	−1.2	−0.7	−1.2
Côte d'Ivoire	−0.8	−1.2	−0.2	−1.9	0.0	−1.4	0.0	−0.9	−0.7	−1.5	0.4	−1.2
Djibouti	−0.7	−1.1	0.2	−0.1	−1.0	−1.0	0.2	−0.8	−0.3	−0.5	..	−0.3
Equatorial Guinea	−1.7	−1.9	−0.7	−0.1	−1.5	−1.4	−1.0	−1.4	−1.2	−1.3	−1.1	−1.6
Eritrea	−1.1	−2.2	0.3	−0.8	−0.4	−1.4	0.0	−2.1	−0.3	−1.2	..	−0.4
Ethiopia	−0.8	−1.3	−1.0	−1.8	−0.9	−0.4	−1.8	−0.9	−0.9	−0.6	−1.1	−0.7
Gabon	−0.4	−0.8	−0.6	0.2	−0.8	−0.7	0.0	−0.7	−1.0	−0.6	−1.4	−1.1
Gambia, The	−1.3	−1.0	0.1	0.1	−0.4	−0.8	−1.8	−0.4	0.4	−0.3	0.4	−0.8
Ghana	−0.3	0.5	−0.2	0.1	−0.4	−0.1	0.1	0.1	−0.4	−0.1	−0.5	−0.1
Guinea	−1.1	−1.3	−1.5	−1.9	−1.1	−1.4	0.2	−1.2	−1.4	−1.6	0.4	−1.4
Guinea-Bissau	−0.3	−0.8	−0.7	−0.4	−0.7	−1.3	0.1	−1.2	−1.7	−1.4	−1.1	−1.2
Kenya	−0.8	−0.2	−0.8	−1.3	−0.4	−0.6	−0.4	−0.1	−1.0	−1.0	−1.1	−1.0
Lesotho	−0.2	0.0	0.5	0.0	0.1	−0.3	−0.6	−0.6	−0.3	−0.3	..	0.0
Liberia	−1.4	−0.3	−2.6	−1.0	−1.8	−1.4	−3.1	−1.3	−2.3	−1.2	−1.8	−0.6
Madagascar	0.4	−0.2	0.0	−0.4	−1.0	−0.6	−0.5	−0.3	−1.0	−0.5	0.4	−0.1
Malawi	0.0	−0.2	−0.3	0.1	−0.6	−0.7	−0.2	−0.4	−0.6	−0.3	−0.5	−0.6
Mali	0.7	0.3	0.4	−0.2	−0.8	−0.8	0.0	−0.3	−0.6	−0.4	−0.3	−0.5
Mauritania	−1.0	−0.9	0.5	−0.9	0.2	−1.0	−0.9	−0.6	−0.9	−1.0	..	−0.8
Mauritius	0.8	0.9	0.7	0.8	0.3	0.6	0.1	1.0	0.7	0.9	0.5	0.5
Mozambique	0.0	0.0	−0.6	0.3	−0.4	−0.4	−1.0	−0.5	−1.0	−0.7	−0.4	−0.6
Namibia	0.6	0.6	0.4	1.0	0.5	0.3	0.1	0.1	0.4	0.4	0.7	0.6
Niger	−1.0	−0.4	−0.1	−0.8	−1.1	−0.8	−1.2	−0.5	−0.9	−0.8	−0.3	−0.8
Nigeria	−1.8	−0.6	−1.6	−2.0	−1.4	−1.0	−1.1	−0.6	−1.4	−1.1	−1.3	−0.9
Rwanda	−1.3	−1.2	−2.0	−0.1	−1.2	−0.2	−1.8	−0.5	−1.5	−0.5	..	0.0
São Tomé and Príncipe	0.5	0.2	1.0	0.3	−0.7	−0.7	−0.3	−0.7	..	−0.5	..	−0.4
Senegal	−0.1	−0.2	−0.6	−0.2	−0.2	−0.1	−0.4	−0.3	−0.5	−0.3	−0.5	−0.5
Seychelles	0.0	0.0	1.0	0.9	−0.6	0.0	−1.4	−0.7	..	0.2	..	0.2
Sierra Leone	−0.9	−0.3	−2.4	−0.2	−0.7	−1.1	−0.9	−0.9	−1.3	−1.0	−1.8	−1.1
Somalia	−1.9	−1.9	−2.4	−3.3	−1.8	−2.5	−2.9	−2.8	−2.1	−2.7	−1.8	−1.9
South Africa	0.9	0.7	−1.1	0.0	0.6	0.8	0.0	0.6	0.2	0.1	0.6	0.3
Sudan	−2.0	−1.8	−2.6	−2.4	−1.5	−1.4	−1.9	−1.4	−1.6	−1.5	−1.1	−1.5
Swaziland	−1.1	−1.2	0.0	0.2	−0.3	−0.7	0.1	−0.6	0.8	−0.5	..	−0.4
Tanzania	−0.7	−0.1	−0.3	0.0	−1.0	−0.5	−0.1	−0.4	−0.4	−0.3	−1.1	−0.5
Togo	−1.0	−1.1	−0.6	−0.1	−0.7	−1.4	0.6	−1.1	−1.4	−0.8	−1.1	−1.0
Uganda	−0.5	−0.5	−1.3	−0.9	−0.6	−0.5	0.3	−0.1	−0.7	−0.5	−0.6	−0.8
Zambia	−0.5	−0.1	−0.6	0.3	−0.7	−0.7	0.3	−0.3	−0.6	−0.5	−1.1	−0.5
Zimbabwe	−0.6	−1.5	−0.7	−1.6	−0.3	−1.6	−0.8	−2.2	−0.7	−1.8	−0.2	−1.4
NORTH AFRICA												
Algeria	−1.3	−1.1	−2.4	−1.2	−0.7	−0.5	−0.9	−0.8	−1.2	−0.7	−0.4	−0.4
Egypt, Arab Rep.	−1.0	−1.2	−0.9	−0.7	−0.1	−0.4	0.2	−0.2	0.1	−0.1	0.1	−0.7
Libya	−1.8	−1.9	−1.6	0.5	−0.7	−0.8	−2.1	−0.9	−1.3	−0.7	−1.0	−0.8
Morocco	−0.6	−0.7	−0.7	−0.5	−0.2	−0.1	0.2	0.0	0.2	−0.1	0.3	−0.3
Tunisia	−0.9	−1.3	0.3	0.3	0.3	0.4	0.6	0.1	−0.2	0.2	−0.1	0.0

a. The rating scale for each criterion ranges from −2.5 (weak performance) to 2.5 (very high performance).

b. 0–20 indicates that budget documents provide scant or no information, 21–40 indicates minimal information, 41–60 indicates some information, 61–80 indicates significant information, and 81–100 indicates extensive information. In 2008 the International Budget Partnership made three changes in the methodology applied to its Open Budget Survey, which is the basis for the open budget index.

c. Data are for the most recent year available during the period specified.

Share of firms (%)							
Expected to pay informal payment to public officials to get things done	Expected to give gifts to obtain an operating license	Expected to give gifts in meetings with tax officials	Expected to give gifts to secure a government contract	Identifying corruption as a major constraint	Mean corruption perceptions index score (0 low to 10 high)		Open budget index overall score[b]
2007–09[c]	2007–09[c]	2007–09[c]	2007–09[c]	2007–09[c]	2007	2008–09[c]	2008
..	..	..	..	..	2.2	1.9	3.0
..	..	..	..	..	2.7	3.1	..
..	..	..	..	..	5.4	5.8	62.0
..	..	..	..	..	2.9	3.5	14.0
..	..	..	..	..	2.5	1.9	..
..	..	..	..	..	2.4	4.0	5.0
..	..	..	..	..	4.9	5.1	..
..	..	..	..	..	2.0	2.0	..
..	..	..	..	..	1.8	1.6	7.0
..	..	..	..	..	2.6	2.5	..
..	..	..	..	..	1.9	1.7	0.0
49.2	..	37.1	75.2	65.0	2.1	1.9	..
30.6	31.8	13.6	32.3	75.0	2.1	2.0	..
..	..	..	..	..	..	..	..
..	..	..	..	..	1.9	1.7	0.0
..	..	..	..	..	2.8	2.6	..
..	..	..	..	..	2.4	2.6	..
26.1	0.0	22.8	26.6	41.4	3.3	3.1	..
..	..	..	..	..	2.3	1.9	..
38.8	22.6	18.1	61.2	9.9	3.7	3.6	49.0
..	..	..	..	..	1.9	1.6	..
..	..	..	..	..	2.2	1.9	..
79.2	28.8	32.3	71.2	38.4	2.1	3.5	57.0
14.0	3.3	9.2	26.4	46.7	3.3	3.2	..
55.2	49.6	54.4	51.6	31.2	2.1	3.7	2.0
19.2	18.6	6.8	14.1	42.7	3.2	3.4	..
..	..	..	..	..	2.7	2.8	29.0
28.9	24.0	31.1	80.4	15.7	2.7	3.1	..
..	..	..	..	..	2.6	2.8	..
1.6	0.0	0.3	8.8	50.7	4.7	5.5	..
14.8	6.9	9.8	31.7	25.4	2.8	2.6	..
..	..	..	..	..	4.5	4.5	47.0
..	..	..	..	..	2.6	2.8	26.0
40.9	40.3	22.9	44.6	24.7	2.2	3.5	19.0
..	..	..	..	..	2.8	3.0	0.0
..	..	..	..	..	2.7	2.7	0.0
18.1	21.1	18.7	36.3	23.8	3.6	3.6	3.0
..	..	..	..	..	4.5	4.8	..
18.8	8.7	8.6	33.9	36.9	2.1	3.8	..
..	..	..	..	..	1.4	1.0	..
15.1	0.0	3.1	33.2	16.9	5.1	4.9	87.0
..	..	..	..	..	1.8	1.6	0.0
..	..	..	..	..	3.3	3.6	..
..	..	..	..	..	3.2	3.0	35.0
..	..	..	..	..	2.3	2.7	..
..	..	..	..	..	2.8	3.2	51.0
14.3	2.6	4.9	27.4	12.1	2.6	3.2	47.0
..	..	..	..	..	2.1	1.8	..
64.7	7.3	15.0	40.6	64.3	3.0	3.2	1.0
7.3	13.7	14.1	92.2	59.3	2.9	2.8	43.0
..	..	..	..	..	2.5	2.6	..
13.4	0.0	10.7	6.4	27.3	3.5	3.6	27.0
..	..	..	..	..	4.2	4.4	..

Table 12.5 Country Policy and Institutional Assessment ratings

	CPIA overall rating (IDA resource allocation index)[a]		Economic management							
			Average[b]		Macroeconomic management		Fiscal policy		Debt policy	
	2005	2008	2005	2008	2005	2008	2005	2008	2005	2008
SUB-SAHARAN AFRICA										
Angola	2.7	2.7	2.5	3.0	3.0	3.0	2.5	3.0	2.0	3.0
Benin	3.7	3.6	4.0	4.0	4.5	4.5	4.0	4.0	3.5	3.5
Botswana[c]	..	..	..	..	..	..	..	..	..	..
Burkina Faso	3.8	3.7	4.5	4.3	4.5	4.5	4.5	4.5	4.5	4.0
Burundi	3.0	3.0	3.3	3.3	3.5	3.5	3.5	3.5	3.0	3.0
Cameroon	3.3	3.2	3.3	3.7	4.0	4.0	3.5	4.0	2.5	3.0
Cape Verde	4.1	4.2	4.2	4.5	4.5	4.5	4.0	4.5	4.0	4.5
Central African Republic	2.4	2.5	2.5	2.8	3.0	3.5	3.0	3.0	1.5	2.0
Chad	2.9	2.5	3.3	2.7	4.0	2.5	3.0	2.5	3.0	3.0
Comoros	2.4	2.3	2.3	2.0	3.0	2.5	2.5	1.5	1.5	2.0
Congo, Dem. Rep.	2.8	2.7	3.2	3.2	3.5	3.5	3.5	3.5	2.5	2.5
Congo, Rep.	2.8	2.7	3.0	2.8	3.5	3.5	3.0	2.5	2.5	2.5
Côte d'Ivoire	2.5	2.7	2.0	2.5	2.5	3.0	2.0	2.5	1.5	2.0
Djibouti	3.1	3.1	3.2	3.0	3.5	3.5	3.0	3.0	3.0	2.5
Equatorial Guinea[c]	..	..	..	..	..	..	..	..	..	..
Eritrea	2.5	2.3	2.2	2.2	2.0	2.0	2.0	2.0	2.5	2.5
Ethiopia	3.4	3.4	3.7	3.3	3.5	2.5	4.0	4.0	3.5	3.5
Gabon[c]	..	..	..	..	..	..	..	..	..	..
Gambia, The	3.1	3.2	3.0	3.5	3.5	4.0	3.0	3.5	2.5	3.0
Ghana	3.9	3.9	4.2	3.7	4.0	3.5	4.5	3.5	4.0	4.0
Guinea	3.0	3.0	2.7	3.0	2.5	3.0	3.0	3.5	2.5	2.5
Guinea-Bissau	2.7	2.6	2.3	1.8	2.5	2.0	2.5	2.5	2.0	1.0
Kenya	3.6	3.6	4.2	4.0	4.5	4.0	4.0	4.0	4.0	4.0
Lesotho	3.5	3.5	4.0	4.0	4.0	4.0	4.0	4.0	4.0	4.0
Liberia[d]	..	2.7	..	2.7	..	3.0	..	3.0	..	2.0
Madagascar	3.5	3.7	3.3	3.8	3.5	4.0	3.0	3.5	3.5	4.0
Malawi	3.4	3.4	3.0	3.3	3.0	3.5	3.0	3.5	3.0	3.0
Mali	3.7	3.7	4.3	4.3	4.5	4.5	4.0	4.0	4.5	4.5
Mauritania	3.2	3.3	2.8	3.5	2.0	3.5	2.5	3.0	4.0	4.0
Mauritius[c]	..	..	..	..	..	..	..	..	..	..
Mozambique	3.5	3.7	4.2	4.3	4.0	4.5	4.0	4.0	4.5	4.5
Namibia[c]	..	..	..	..	..	..	..	..	..	..
Niger	3.3	3.3	3.3	3.7	3.5	4.0	3.0	3.5	3.5	3.5
Nigeria	3.1	3.4	3.8	4.3	4.0	4.0	4.0	4.5	3.5	4.5
Rwanda	3.5	3.7	3.5	3.8	4.0	4.0	3.5	4.0	3.0	3.5
São Tomé and Príncipe	3.0	3.0	2.8	2.8	3.0	3.0	3.0	3.0	2.5	2.5
Senegal	3.8	3.6	4.2	3.8	4.5	4.0	4.0	3.5	4.0	4.0
Seychelles[c]	..	2.9	..	1.8	..	2.0	..	2.0	..	1.5
Sierra Leone	3.1	3.1	3.7	3.7	4.0	4.0	3.5	3.5	3.5	3.5
Somalia[d]	..	..	..	..	..	..	..	..	..	..
South Africa[c]	..	..	..	..	..	..	..	..	..	..
Sudan	2.6	2.5	2.8	2.7	3.5	3.5	3.5	3.0	1.5	1.5
Swaziland[c]	..	..	..	..	..	..	..	..	..	..
Tanzania	3.9	3.8	4.5	4.3	5.0	4.5	4.5	4.5	4.0	4.0
Togo	2.5	2.7	2.0	2.7	2.5	3.0	2.0	3.0	1.5	2.0
Uganda	3.9	3.9	4.5	4.5	4.5	4.5	4.5	4.5	4.5	4.5
Zambia	3.3	3.5	3.3	3.7	3.5	4.0	3.5	3.5	3.0	3.5
Zimbabwe	1.8	1.4	1.0	1.0	1.0	1.0	1.0	1.0	1.0	1.0
NORTH AFRICA										
Algeria[c]	..	..	..	..	..	..	..	..	..	..
Egypt, Arab Rep.[c]	..	..	..	..	..	..	..	..	..	..
Libya[c]	..	..	..	..	..	..	..	..	..	..
Morocco[c]	..	..	..	..	..	..	..	..	..	..
Tunisia[c]	..	..	..	..	..	..	..	..	..	..

Structural policies							
Average[b]		Trade		Financial sector		Business regulatory environment	
2005	2008	2005	2008	2005	2008	2005	2008
2.8	2.8	4.0	4.0	2.5	2.5	2.0	2.0
4.0	3.7	4.5	4.0	3.5	3.5	4.0	3.5
..	..	..	..	..	..	..	..
3.3	3.5	4.0	4.0	3.0	3.0	3.0	3.5
2.8	2.8	3.0	3.5	3.0	2.5	2.5	2.5
3.3	3.2	3.5	3.5	3.0	3.0	3.5	3.0
4.0	3.8	4.0	4.0	4.0	4.0	4.0	3.5
2.7	2.7	3.5	3.5	2.5	2.5	2.0	2.0
3.0	2.8	3.0	3.0	3.0	3.0	3.0	2.5
2.3	2.7	2.0	3.0	2.5	2.5	2.5	2.5
3.0	2.7	4.0	4.0	2.0	2.0	3.0	2.0
2.7	2.8	3.0	3.5	2.5	2.5	2.5	2.5
3.2	3.3	3.5	4.0	3.0	3.0	3.0	3.0
3.5	3.7	4.0	4.0	3.5	3.5	3.0	3.5
..	..	..	..	..	..	..	..
1.8	1.5	1.5	1.5	2.0	1.0	2.0	2.0
3.2	3.2	3.0	3.0	3.0	3.0	3.5	3.5
..	..	..	..	..	..	..	..
3.3	3.3	4.0	3.5	3.0	3.0	3.0	3.5
3.8	4.0	4.0	4.0	3.5	4.0	4.0	4.0
3.5	3.3	4.5	4.0	3.0	3.0	3.0	3.0
3.0	3.2	3.5	4.0	2.5	3.0	3.0	2.5
3.8	3.8	4.0	4.0	3.5	3.5	4.0	4.0
3.3	3.3	3.5	3.5	3.5	3.5	3.0	3.0
..	2.8	..	3.0	..	2.5	..	3.0
3.8	3.5	4.0	4.0	3.5	3.0	4.0	3.5
3.5	3.5	4.0	4.0	3.0	3.0	3.5	3.5
3.5	3.5	4.0	4.0	3.0	3.0	3.5	3.5
3.5	3.3	4.5	4.0	2.5	2.5	3.5	3.5
..	..	..	..	..	..	..	..
3.2	3.7	4.0	4.5	2.5	3.5	3.0	3.0
..	..	..	..	..	..	..	..
3.5	3.3	4.0	4.0	3.0	3.0	3.5	3.0
2.8	3.3	2.5	3.5	3.0	3.5	3.0	3.0
3.5	3.5	3.5	3.5	3.5	3.5	3.5	3.5
3.2	3.2	4.0	4.0	2.5	2.5	3.0	3.0
3.8	3.8	4.5	4.0	3.5	3.5	3.5	4.0
..	2.7	..	3.0	..	2.0	..	3.0
3.0	3.2	3.5	3.5	3.0	3.0	2.5	3.0
..	..	..	..	..	..	..	..
..	..	..	..	..	..	..	..
2.8	2.7	3.0	2.5	2.5	2.5	3.0	3.0
..	..	..	..	..	..	..	..
3.7	3.8	4.0	4.0	3.5	4.0	3.5	3.5
3.2	3.2	4.0	4.0	2.5	2.5	3.0	3.0
3.8	3.8	4.0	4.0	3.5	3.5	4.0	4.0
3.3	3.7	4.0	4.0	3.0	3.5	3.0	3.5
2.2	1.5	2.0	2.0	2.5	1.0	2.0	1.5
..	..	..	..	..	..	..	..
..	..	..	..	..	..	..	..
..	..	..	..	..	..	..	..
..	..	..	..	..	..	..	..
..	..	..	..	..	..	..	..

(continued)

Table 12.5 Country Policy and Institutional Assessment ratings (continued)

	Policies for social inclusion and equity											
	Average[b]		Gender equality		Equity of public resource use		Building human resources		Social protection and labor		Policies and institutions for environmental sustainability	
	2005	2008	2005	2008	2005	2008	2005	2008	2005	2008	2005	2008
SUB-SAHARAN AFRICA												
Angola	2.6	2.7	3.0	3.0	2.5	2.5	2.5	2.5	2.5	2.5	2.5	3.0
Benin	3.2	3.3	3.0	3.5	3.0	3.0	3.5	3.5	3.0	3.0	3.5	3.5
Botswana[c]	..	..	..	..	..	..	..	..	..	..	..	..
Burkina Faso	3.6	3.6	3.5	3.5	4.0	4.0	3.5	3.5	3.5	3.5	3.5	3.5
Burundi	3.0	3.3	3.5	4.0	3.0	3.5	3.0	3.0	3.0	3.0	2.5	3.0
Cameroon	3.4	3.1	3.5	3.0	3.0	3.0	3.5	3.5	3.0	3.0	4.0	3.0
Cape Verde	4.3	4.3	4.5	4.5	4.5	4.5	4.0	4.5	4.5	4.5	4.0	3.5
Central African Republic	2.2	2.2	2.5	2.5	2.0	2.0	2.0	2.0	2.0	2.0	2.5	2.5
Chad	2.8	2.4	2.5	2.5	3.0	2.5	3.0	2.5	3.0	2.5	2.5	2.0
Comoros	2.7	2.5	3.0	3.0	3.0	2.5	3.0	2.5	2.5	2.5	2.0	2.0
Congo, Dem. Rep.	2.9	2.9	3.0	3.0	3.0	3.0	3.0	3.0	3.0	3.0	2.5	2.5
Congo, Rep.	2.9	2.7	3.0	3.0	3.0	2.5	3.0	3.0	2.5	2.5	3.0	2.5
Côte d'Ivoire	2.3	2.3	2.5	2.5	1.5	1.5	2.0	2.5	2.5	2.5	3.0	2.5
Djibouti	3.1	3.0	3.0	2.5	3.0	3.0	3.5	3.5	3.0	3.0	3.0	3.0
Equatorial Guinea[c]	..	..	..	..	..	..	..	..	..	..	..	..
Eritrea	3.2	3.0	3.5	3.5	3.0	3.0	3.5	3.5	3.0	3.0	3.0	2.0
Ethiopia	3.6	3.6	3.0	3.0	4.5	4.5	3.5	4.0	3.5	3.5	3.5	3.0
Gabon[c]	..	..	..	..	..	..	..	..	..	..	..	..
Gambia, The	3.1	3.2	3.5	3.5	3.0	3.0	3.5	3.5	2.5	2.5	3.0	3.5
Ghana	3.7	4.0	4.0	4.0	4.0	4.0	3.5	4.5	3.5	4.0	3.5	3.5
Guinea	3.2	3.0	4.0	3.5	3.0	3.0	3.0	3.0	3.5	3.0	2.5	2.5
Guinea-Bissau	2.8	2.6	3.0	2.5	3.0	3.0	2.5	2.5	2.5	2.5	3.0	2.5
Kenya	3.1	3.2	3.0	3.0	3.0	3.0	3.5	3.5	3.0	3.0	3.0	3.5
Lesotho	3.3	3.3	4.0	4.0	3.0	3.0	3.5	3.5	3.0	3.0	3.0	3.0
Liberia[d]	..	2.4	..	2.5	..	3.0	..	2.0	..	2.5	..	2.0
Madagascar	3.6	3.7	3.5	3.5	3.5	4.0	3.5	3.5	3.5	3.5	4.0	4.0
Malawi	3.5	3.4	3.5	3.5	3.5	3.5	3.5	3.0	3.5	3.5	3.5	3.5
Mali	3.4	3.4	3.5	3.5	3.5	3.5	3.5	3.5	3.5	3.5	3.0	3.0
Mauritania	3.4	3.5	3.5	4.0	3.0	3.5	3.5	3.5	3.5	3.0	3.5	3.5
Mauritius[c]	..	..	..	..	..	..	..	..	..	..	..	..
Mozambique	3.3	3.4	3.5	3.5	3.5	3.5	3.5	4.0	3.0	3.0	3.0	3.0
Namibia[c]	..	..	..	..	..	..	..	..	..	..	..	..
Niger	3.0	3.0	2.5	2.5	3.5	3.5	3.0	3.0	3.0	3.0	3.0	3.0
Nigeria	3.1	3.2	3.0	3.0	3.5	3.5	3.0	3.0	3.0	3.5	3.0	3.0
Rwanda	3.6	3.9	3.5	3.5	4.0	4.5	4.0	4.5	3.5	3.5	3.0	3.5
São Tomé and Príncipe	2.8	2.8	3.0	3.0	3.5	3.0	2.5	3.0	2.5	2.5	2.5	2.5
Senegal	3.4	3.4	3.5	3.5	3.5	3.5	3.5	3.5	3.0	3.0	3.5	3.5
Seychelles[c]	..	3.6	..	3.5	..	3.0	..	4.0	..	3.5	..	4.0
Sierra Leone	2.9	2.9	3.0	3.0	3.0	3.0	3.0	3.5	3.0	3.0	2.5	2.0
Somalia[d]	..	..	..	..	..	..	..	..	..	..	..	..
South Africa[c]	..	..	..	..	..	..	..	..	..	..	..	..
Sudan	2.3	2.3	2.0	2.0	2.5	2.5	2.5	2.5	2.0	2.5	2.5	2.0
Swaziland[c]	..	..	..	..	..	..	..	..	..	..	..	..
Tanzania	3.8	3.7	4.0	3.5	4.0	4.0	4.0	4.0	3.5	3.5	3.5	3.5
Togo	2.6	2.7	3.0	3.0	2.0	2.0	3.0	3.0	2.5	3.0	2.5	2.5
Uganda	3.9	3.8	3.5	3.5	4.5	4.0	4.0	4.0	3.5	3.5	4.0	4.0
Zambia	3.4	3.5	3.5	3.5	3.5	3.5	3.5	4.0	3.0	3.0	3.5	3.5
Zimbabwe	2.0	1.5	2.5	2.5	1.5	1.0	2.0	1.0	1.5	1.0	2.5	2.0
NORTH AFRICA												
Algeria[c]	..	..	..	..	..	..	..	..	..	..	..	..
Egypt, Arab Rep.[c]	..	..	..	..	..	..	..	..	..	..	..	..
Libya[c]	..	..	..	..	..	..	..	..	..	..	..	..
Morocco[c]	..	..	..	..	..	..	..	..	..	..	..	..
Tunisia[c]	..	..	..	..	..	..	..	..	..	..	..	..

Note: The rating scale for each indicator ranges from 1 (low) to 6 (high). The most recent external review of the CPIA ratings and methodology was in 2004.

a. Calculated as the average of the average ratings of each cluster.

b. All criteria are weighted equally.

c. Not an International Development Association (IDA) member.

d. Not rated in the IDA resource allocation index.

Public sector management and institutions											
Average[b]		Property rights and rule-based governance		Quality of budgetary and financial management		Efficiency of revenue mobilization		Quality of public administration		Transparency, accountability, and corruption in public sector	
2005	2008	2005	2008	2005	2008	2005	2008	2005	2008	2005	2008
2.4	2.4	2.0	2.0	2.5	2.5	2.5	2.5	2.5	2.5	2.5	2.5
3.4	3.3	3.0	3.0	4.0	3.5	3.5	3.5	3.0	3.0	3.5	3.5
..	..	..	..	..	..	..	..	..	..	..	..
3.6	3.5	3.5	3.5	4.0	4.0	3.5	3.5	3.5	3.5	3.5	3.0
2.7	2.6	2.5	2.5	2.5	3.0	3.0	3.0	2.5	2.5	3.0	2.0
3.1	2.9	2.5	2.5	3.5	3.0	4.0	3.5	3.0	3.0	2.5	2.5
3.9	4.0	4.0	4.0	3.5	4.0	3.5	3.5	4.0	4.0	4.5	4.5
2.2	2.3	2.0	2.0	2.0	2.0	2.5	2.5	2.0	2.5	2.5	2.5
2.4	2.2	2.0	2.0	3.0	2.0	2.5	2.5	2.5	2.5	2.0	2.0
2.3	2.2	2.5	2.5	2.0	1.5	2.5	2.5	2.0	2.0	2.5	2.5
2.3	2.2	2.0	2.0	2.5	2.5	2.5	2.5	2.5	2.0	2.0	2.0
2.6	2.6	2.0	2.5	3.0	2.5	3.0	3.0	2.5	2.5	2.5	2.5
2.5	2.5	2.0	2.0	2.5	2.0	4.0	4.0	2.0	2.0	2.0	2.5
2.8	2.8	2.5	2.5	3.0	3.0	3.5	3.5	2.5	2.5	2.5	2.5
..	..	..	..	..	..	..	..	..	..	..	..
2.8	2.7	2.5	2.5	2.5	2.5	3.5	3.5	3.0	3.0	2.5	2.0
3.1	3.3	2.5	3.0	3.5	4.0	4.0	4.0	3.0	3.0	2.5	2.5
..	..	..	..	..	..	..	..	..	..	..	..
2.9	2.9	3.5	3.0	2.5	3.0	3.5	3.5	3.0	3.0	2.0	2.0
3.7	3.9	3.5	3.5	3.5	4.0	4.5	4.5	3.5	3.5	3.5	4.0
2.7	2.6	2.0	2.0	3.0	3.0	3.0	3.0	3.0	3.0	2.5	2.0
2.6	2.6	2.5	2.5	2.5	2.5	3.0	3.0	2.5	2.5	2.5	2.5
3.3	3.3	3.0	2.5	3.5	3.5	4.0	4.0	3.0	3.5	3.0	3.0
3.4	3.4	3.5	3.5	3.0	3.0	4.0	4.0	3.0	3.0	3.5	3.5
..	2.7	..	2.5	..	2.5	..	3.0	..	2.5	..	3.0
3.4	3.6	3.5	3.5	3.0	3.5	3.5	4.0	3.5	3.5	3.5	3.5
3.4	3.4	3.5	3.5	3.0	3.0	4.0	4.0	3.5	3.5	3.0	3.0
3.6	3.4	3.5	3.5	4.0	3.5	4.0	3.5	3.0	3.0	3.5	3.5
2.9	3.0	3.0	3.0	2.0	3.0	4.0	3.5	3.0	3.0	2.5	2.5
..	..	..	..	..	..	..	..	..	..	..	..
3.2	3.3	3.0	3.0	3.5	3.5	3.5	4.0	3.0	3.0	3.0	3.0
..	..	..	..	..	..	..	..	..	..	..	..
3.2	3.2	3.0	3.0	3.5	3.5	3.5	3.5	3.0	3.0	3.0	3.0
2.8	2.9	2.5	2.5	3.0	3.0	3.0	3.0	2.5	3.0	3.0	3.0
3.3	3.5	3.0	3.0	3.5	4.0	3.5	3.5	3.5	3.5	3.0	3.5
3.1	3.1	2.5	2.5	3.0	3.0	3.5	3.5	3.0	3.0	3.5	3.5
3.6	3.4	3.5	3.5	3.5	3.0	4.5	4.0	3.5	3.5	3.0	3.0
..	3.4	..	3.5	..	3.0	..	3.5	..	3.5	..	3.5
2.9	2.7	2.5	2.5	3.5	3.5	3.0	2.5	3.0	2.5	2.5	2.5
..	..	..	..	..	..	..	..	..	..	..	..
..	..	..	..	..	..	..	..	..	..	..	..
2.4	2.3	2.0	2.0	2.5	2.0	3.0	3.0	2.5	2.5	2.0	2.0
..	..	..	..	..	..	..	..	..	..	..	..
3.8	3.5	3.5	3.5	4.5	3.5	4.0	4.0	3.5	3.5	3.5	3.0
2.2	2.2	2.5	2.5	2.0	2.0	2.5	2.5	2.0	2.0	2.0	2.0
3.3	3.4	3.5	3.5	4.0	4.0	3.0	3.5	3.0	3.0	3.0	3.0
3.2	3.2	3.0	3.0	3.0	3.5	4.0	3.5	3.0	3.0	3.0	3.0
2.1	1.6	1.0	1.0	2.5	1.5	3.5	3.5	2.0	1.0	1.5	1.0
..	..	..	..	..	..	..	..	..	..	..	..
..	..	..	..	..	..	..	..	..	..	..	..
..	..	..	..	..	..	..	..	..	..	..	..
..	..	..	..	..	..	..	..	..	..	..	..
..	..	..	..	..	..	..	..	..	..	..	..

Table 12.6 Polity indicators

	Combined polity score (–10 strongly autocratic to 10 strongly democratic)			Institutionalized democracy (0 low to 10 high)			Institutionalized autocracy (0 low to 10 high)		
	1995	2000	2008	1995	2000	2008	1995	2000	2008
SUB-SAHARAN AFRICA									
Angola	–2.0	–3.0	–2.0	..	1.0	2.0	..	4.0	4.0
Benin	6.0	6.0	7.0	6.0	6.0	7.0	0.0	0.0	0.0
Botswana	7.0	8.0	8.0	7.0	8.0	8.0	0.0	0.0	0.0
Burkina Faso	–5.0	–3.0	0.0	0.0	0.0	2.0	5.0	3.0	2.0
Burundi	0.0	–1.0	6.0	..	1.0	7.0	..	2.0	1.0
Cameroon	–4.0	–4.0	–4.0	1.0	1.0	1.0	5.0	5.0	5.0
Cape Verde	..	..	..	..	..	..	..	..	..
Central African Republic	5.0	5.0	–1.0	5.0	5.0	1.0	0.0	0.0	2.0
Chad	–4.0	–2.0	–2.0	0.0	1.0	1.0	4.0	3.0	3.0
Comoros	0.0	–1.0	9.0	..	1.0	9.0	..	2.0	0.0
Congo, Dem. Rep.	0.0	0.0	5.0	..	..	6.0	..	..	1.0
Congo, Rep.	5.0	–6.0	–4.0	6.0	0.0	0.0	1.0	6.0	4.0
Côte d'Ivoire	–6.0	4.0	0.0	0.0	5.0	..	6.0	1.0	..
Djibouti	–7.0	2.0	2.0	0.0	3.0	3.0	7.0	1.0	1.0
Equatorial Guinea	–5.0	–5.0	–5.0	0.0	0.0	0.0	5.0	5.0	5.0
Eritrea	–6.0	–6.0	–7.0	0.0	0.0	0.0	6.0	6.0	7.0
Ethiopia	1.0	1.0	1.0	3.0	3.0	3.0	2.0	2.0	2.0
Gabon	–4.0	–4.0	–4.0	0.0	0.0	0.0	4.0	4.0	4.0
Gambia, The	–7.0	–5.0	–5.0	0.0	0.0	0.0	7.0	5.0	5.0
Ghana	–1.0	2.0	8.0	1.0	3.0	8.0	2.0	1.0	0.0
Guinea	–1.0	–1.0	–1.0	1.0	1.0	1.0	2.0	2.0	2.0
Guinea-Bissau	5.0	5.0	6.0	5.0	5.0	6.0	0.0	0.0	0.0
Kenya	–5.0	–2.0	7.0	0.0	2.0	7.0	5.0	4.0	0.0
Lesotho	8.0	4.0	8.0	8.0	..	8.0	0.0	..	0.0
Liberia	0.0	0.0	6.0	..	3.0	7.0	..	3.0	1.0
Madagascar	9.0	7.0	7.0	9.0	7.0	7.0	0.0	0.0	0.0
Malawi	6.0	6.0	6.0	6.0	6.0	6.0	0.0	0.0	0.0
Mali	7.0	6.0	7.0	7.0	6.0	7.0	0.0	0.0	0.0
Mauritania	–6.0	–6.0	–5.0	0.0	0.0	0.0	6.0	6.0	5.0
Mauritius	10.0	10.0	10.0	10.0	10.0	10.0	0.0	0.0	0.0
Mozambique	6.0	6.0	6.0	6.0	6.0	6.0	0.0	0.0	0.0
Namibia	6.0	6.0	6.0	6.0	6.0	6.0	0.0	0.0	0.0
Niger	8.0	5.0	6.0	8.0	6.0	7.0	0.0	1.0	1.0
Nigeria	–6.0	4.0	4.0	0.0	4.0	4.0	6.0	0.0	0.0
Rwanda	–6.0	–4.0	–3.0	0.0	0.0	0.0	6.0	4.0	3.0
São Tomé and Principe	..	..	..	..	..	..	..	..	..
Senegal	–1.0	8.0	8.0	2.0	8.0	8.0	3.0	0.0	0.0
Seychelles	..	..	..	..	..	..	..	..	..
Sierra Leone	–7.0	0.0	7.0	0.0	..	8.0	7.0	..	1.0
Somalia	0.0	0.0	0.0	..	..	..	..	..	..
South Africa	9.0	9.0	9.0	9.0	9.0	9.0	0.0	0.0	0.0
Sudan	–7.0	–7.0	–4.0	0.0	0.0	0.0	7.0	7.0	4.0
Swaziland	–9.0	–9.0	–9.0	0.0	0.0	0.0	9.0	9.0	9.0
Tanzania	–1.0	–1.0	–1.0	2.0	2.0	2.0	3.0	3.0	3.0
Togo	–2.0	–2.0	–4.0	1.0	1.0	1.0	3.0	3.0	5.0
Uganda	–4.0	–4.0	–1.0	0.0	0.0	1.0	4.0	4.0	2.0
Zambia	6.0	1.0	7.0	6.0	3.0	7.0	0.0	2.0	0.0
Zimbabwe	–6.0	–3.0	–4.0	0.0	1.0	1.0	6.0	4.0	5.0
NORTH AFRICA									
Algeria	–3.0	–3.0	2.0	1.0	1.0	3.0	4.0	4.0	1.0
Egypt, Arab Rep.	–6.0	–6.0	–3.0	0.0	0.0	1.0	6.0	6.0	4.0
Libya	–7.0	–7.0	–7.0	0.0	0.0	0.0	7.0	7.0	7.0
Morocco	–7.0	–6.0	–6.0	0.0	0.0	0.0	7.0	6.0	6.0
Tunisia	–3.0	–3.0	–4.0	1.0	1.0	1.0	4.0	4.0	5.0

Technical notes

1. Basic indicators

TABLE 1.1. BASIC INDICATORS

Population is total population based on the de facto definition of population, which counts all residents regardless of legal status or citizenship, except for refugees not permanently settled in the country of asylum, who are generally considered part of the population of their country of origin. The values shown are midyear estimates.

Land area is the land surface area of a country, excluding inland waters, national claims to continental shelf, and exclusive economic zones.

Gross domestic product (GDP) per capita is gross domestic product divided by midyear population. GDP is the sum of gross value added by all resident producers in the economy plus any product taxes and minus any subsidies not included in the value of the products. It is calculated without making deductions for depreciation of fabricated assets or for depletion and degradation of natural resources. Growth rates are in real terms and have been calculated by the least-squares method using constant 2000 exchange rates (box 2).

Life expectancy at birth is the number of years a newborn infant would live if prevailing patterns of mortality at the time of its birth were to remain the same throughout its life.

Under-five mortality rate is the probability that a newborn baby will die before reaching age 5, if subject to current age-specific mortality rates. The probability is expressed as a rate per 1,000.

Gini index is the most commonly used measure of inequality. The coefficient ranges from 0, which reflects complete equality, to 100, which indicates complete inequality (one person has all the income or consumption, all others have none). Graphically, the Gini index can be easily represented by the area between the Lorenz curve and the line of equality.

Adult literacy rate is the percentage of adults ages 15 and older who can, with understanding, read and write a short, simple statement on their everyday life.

Net official development assistance per capita is calculated by dividing net disbursements of loans and grants from all official sources on concessional financial terms by midyear population. This indicator offers some indication of the importance of aid flows in sustaining per capita income and consumption levels, although exchange rate fluctuations, the actual rise of aid flows, and other factors vary across countries and over time.

Regional aggregates for GNI per capita, life expectancy at birth, and adult literacy rates are weighted by population.

Source: Data on population, land area, GDP per capita, life expectancy at birth, under-five mortality, Gini coefficient, and adult literacy are from the World Bank's World Development Indicators database. Data on aid flows are from the Organisation for Economic Co-operation and Development's Geographic Distribution of Aid Flows to Developing Countries database.

2. National and fiscal accounts

Africa Development Indicators uses the 1993 System of National Accounts (1993 SNA) to compile national accounts data. Botswana, Cameroon, Chad, the Democratic Republic of Congo, Ethiopia, Kenya, Lesotho, Namibia, Senegal, Sierra Leone, and South Africa report data using the 1993 SNA. Although more countries

Box 2 Growth rates

Growth rates are calculated as annual averages and represented as percentages. Except where noted, growth rates of values are computed from constant price series. Rates of change from one period to the next are calculated as proportional changes from the earlier period. Least-squares growth rates are used wherever there is a sufficiently long time series to permit a reliable calculation. No growth rate is calculated if more than half the observations in a period are missing. The least-squares growth rate, *r*, is estimated by fitting a linear regression trend line to the logarithmic annual values of the variable in the relevant period. The regression equation takes the form

$$\ln X_{t = a + bt}$$

which is equivalent to the logarithmic transformation of the compound growth equation,

$$X_t = X_o(1 + r)^2$$

where *X* is the variable, *t* is time, and $a = \ln X_o$ and $b = \ln(1 + r)$ are parameters to be estimated. If b^* is the least squares estimate of *b*, the average annual growth rate, *r*, is obtained as $[\exp(b^*) - 1]$ multiplied by 100. The calculated growth rate is an average rate that is representative of the available observations over the entire period. It does not necessarily match the actual growth rate between any two points.

are adopting the 1993 SNA, many still follow the 1968 SNA, and some low-income countries use concepts from the 1953 SNA.

Table 2.1. Gross domestic product, nominal

Gross domestic product (GDP), nominal, is the sum of gross value added by all resident producers in the economy plus any product taxes and minus any subsidies not included in the value of the products. It is calculated without making deductions for depreciation of fabricated assets or for depletion and degradation of natural resources. GDP figures are shown at market prices (also known as purchaser values) and converted from domestic currencies using single year official exchange rates. For a few countries where the official exchange rate does not reflect the rate effectively applied to actual foreign exchange transactions, an alternative conversion factor is used.

The sum of the components of GDP by industrial origin (presented here as value added) will not normally equal total GDP for several reasons. First, components of GDP by expenditure are individually rescaled and summed to provide a partially rebased series for total GDP. Second, total GDP is shown at purchaser value, while value added components are conventionally reported at producer prices. As explained above, purchaser values exclude net indirect taxes, while producer prices include indirect taxes. Third, certain items, such as imputed bank charges, are added in total GDP.

Source: World Bank and Organisation for Economic Co-operation and Development national accounts data.

Table 2.2. Gross domestic product, real

Gross domestic product (GDP), real, is obtained by converting national currency GDP series to U.S. dollars using constant (2000) exchange rates. For countries where the official exchange rate does not effectively reflect the rate applied to actual foreign exchange transactions, an alternative currency conversion factor has been used. Growth rates are in real terms and have been calculated by the least-squares method using constant 2000 exchange rates (see box 2).

Source: World Bank and Organisation for Economic Co-operation and Development national accounts data.

Table 2.3. Gross domestic product growth

Gross domestic product (GDP) growth is the average annual growth rate of real GDP (table 2.2) at market prices based on constant local currency. Aggregates are based on constant 2000 U.S. dollars.

Source: World Bank and Organisation for Economic Co-operation and Development national accounts data.

Table 2.4. Gross domestic product per capita, real

Gross domestic product (GDP) per capita, real, is calculated by dividing real GDP (table 2.2) by corresponding midyear population.

Source: World Bank and Organisation for Economic Co-operation and Development national accounts data.

Table 2.5. Gross domestic product per capita growth

Gross domestic product (GDP) per capita growth is the average annual growth rate of real GDP per capita (table 2.4).

Source: World Bank and Organisation for Economic Co-operation and Development national accounts data.

Table 2.6. Gross national income, nominal

Gross national income, nominal, is the sum of value added by all resident producers plus any product taxes (less subsidies) not included in the valuation of output plus net receipts of primary income (compensation of employees and property income) from abroad. Data are converted from national currency in current prices to U.S. dollars at official annual exchange rates.

Source: World Bank and Organisation for Economic Co-operation and Development (OECD) national accounts data.

Table 2.7 Gross national income, *Atlas* method

Gross national income (GNI), Atlas *method,* is the sum of value added by all resident producers plus any product taxes (less subsidies) not included in the valuation of output plus net receipts of primary income (compensation of employees and property income) from abroad. Data are converted from national currency in current prices to U.S. dollars using the *World Bank Atlas* method (see box 1). It is similar in concept to GNI in current prices, except that the use of three-year averages of exchange rates smoothes out sharp fluctuations from year to year. Growth rates have been calculated by the least-squares method (see box 2).

Source: World Bank and Organisation for Economic Co-operation and Development national accounts data.

Table 2.8. Gross national income per capita, *Atlas* method

Gross national income (GNI) per capita, Atlas *method,* is GNI, calculated using the *World Bank Atlas* method (see box 1), divided by midyear population. It is similar in concept to GNI per capita in current prices, except that the use of three-year averages of exchange rates smoothes out sharp fluctuations from year to year.

Source: World Bank and Organisation for Economic Co-operation and Development national accounts data.

Table 2.9. Gross domestic product deflator (local currency series)

Gross domestic product (GDP) deflator (local currency series) is nominal GDP in current local currency divided by real GDP in constant 2000 local currency, expressed as an index with base year 2000. GDP is the sum of gross domestic and foreign value added claimed by residents plus net factor income from abroad (the income residents receive from abroad for factor services including labor and capital) less similar payments made to nonresidents who contribute to the domestic economy, divided by midyear population. It is calculated by the *World Bank Atlas* method using constant 2000 exchange rates (see box 1).

Source: World Bank and Organisation for Economic Co-operation and Development national accounts data.

Table 2.10. Gross domestic product deflator (U.S. dollar series)

Gross domestic product (GDP) deflator (U.S. dollar series) is nominal GDP in current U.S. dollars (table 2.1) divided by real GDP in constant 2000 U.S. dollars (table 2.2), expressed as an index with base year 2000. The series shows the effects of domestic price changes and exchange rate variations.

Source: World Bank and Organisation for Economic Co-operation and Development national accounts data.

Table 2.11. Consumer price index

Consumer price index reflects changes in the cost to the average consumer of acquiring a basket of goods and services that may be fixed or changed at specified intervals, such as yearly. The Laspeyres formula is generally used.

Source: International Monetary Fund International Financial Statistics database and data files.

Table 2.12. Price indexes

Inflation, GDP deflator, is measured by the annual growth rate of the GDP implicit deflator and shows the rate of price change in the economy as a whole.

Consumer price index is a change in the cost to the average consumer of acquiring a basket of goods and services that may be fixed or changed at specified intervals, such as yearly. The Laspeyres formula is generally used.

Exports of goods and services price index is calculated by dividing the national accounts exports of goods and services in current U.S. dollars by exports of goods and services in constant 2000 U.S. dollars.

Imports of goods and services price index is calculated by dividing the national accounts imports of goods and services in current U.S. dollars by imports of goods and services in constant 2000 U.S. dollars.

Source: World Bank and Organisation for Economic Co-operation and Development national accounts data.

Table 2.13. Gross domestic savings

Gross domestic savings is calculated by deducting total consumption (table 2.17) from nominal gross domestic product (table 2.1).

Source: World Bank and Organisation for Economic Co-operation and Development national accounts data.

Table 2.14. Gross national savings

Gross national savings is the sum of gross domestic savings (table 2.13), net factor income from abroad, and net private transfers from abroad. The estimate here also includes net public transfers from abroad.

Source: World Bank and Organisation for Economic Co-operation and Development national accounts data.

Table 2.15. General government final consumption expenditure

General government final consumption expenditure is all current expenditure for purchases of goods and services by all levels of government, including capital expenditure on national defense and security. Other capital expenditure by government is included in capital formation.

Source: World Bank and Organisation for Economic Co-operation and Development national accounts data.

Table 2.16. Household final consumption expenditure

Household final consumption expenditure (formerly *private consumption*) is the market value of all goods and services, including durable products (such as cars, washing machines, and home computers), purchased by households. It excludes purchases of dwellings but includes imputed rent for owner-occupied dwellings. It also includes payments and fees to governments to obtain permits and licenses. Here, household consumption expenditure includes the expenditures of nonprofit institutions serving households, even when reported separately by the country.

Source: World Bank and Organisation for Economic Co-operation and Development national accounts data.

Table 2.17. Final consumption expenditure plus discrepancy

Final consumption expenditure plus discrepancy (formerly *total consumption*) is the sum of household final consumption expenditure (table 2.16) and general government final consumption expenditure (table 2.15) shown as a share of gross domestic product. This estimate includes any statistical discrepancy in the use of resources relative to the supply of resources. Private consumption, not separately shown here, is the value of all goods and services purchased or received as income in kind by households and nonprofit institutions. It excludes purchases of dwellings, but includes imputed rent for owner-occupied dwellings. In practice, it includes any statistical discrepancy in the use of resources.

Source: World Bank and Organisation for Economic Co-operation and Development national accounts data.

Table 2.18. Final consumption expenditure plus discrepancy per capita

Final consumption expenditure plus discrepancy per capita is final consumption expenditure plus discrepancy in current U.S. dollars (table 2.17) divided by midyear population.

Source: World Bank and Organisation for Economic Co-operation and Development national accounts data.

TABLE 2.19. GROSS FIXED CAPITAL FORMATION

Gross fixed capital formation consists of gross domestic fixed capital formation plus net changes in the level of inventories. Gross capital formation comprises outlays by the public sector (table 2.20) and the private sector (table 2.21). Examples include improvements in land, dwellings, machinery, and other equipment. For some countries the sum of gross private investment and gross public investment does not total gross domestic investment due to statistical discrepancies.

Source: World Bank and Organisation for Economic Co-operation and Development national accounts data.

TABLE 2.20. GROSS GENERAL GOVERNMENT FIXED CAPITAL FORMATION

Gross general government fixed capital formation is gross domestic fixed capital formation (see table 2.19) for the public sector.

Source: World Bank and Organisation for Economic Co-operation and Development national accounts data.

TABLE 2.21. PRIVATE SECTOR FIXED CAPITAL FORMATION

Private sector fixed capital formation is gross domestic fixed capital formation (see table 2.19) for the private sector.

Source: World Bank and Organisation for Economic Co-operation and Development national accounts data.

TABLE 2.22. EXTERNAL TRADE BALANCE (EXPORTS MINUS IMPORTS)

External trade balance is the difference between free on board exports (table 2.23) and cost, insurance, and freight imports (table 2.24) of goods and services (or the difference between gross domestic savings and gross capital formation). The resource balance is shown as a share of nominal gross domestic product (table 2.1).

Source: World Bank and Organisation for Economic Co-operation and Development national accounts data.

TABLE 2.23 . EXPORTS OF GOODS AND SERVICES, NOMINAL

Exports of goods and services, nominal, represent the value of all goods and other market services provided to the rest of the world. They include the value of merchandise, freight, insurance, transport, travel, royalties, license fees, and other services, such as communication, construction, financial, information, business, personal, and government services. They exclude labor and property income (formerly called factor services) as well as transfer payments, and expressed in current U.S dollars.

Source: World Bank and Organisation for Economic Co-operation and Development national accounts data.

TABLE 2.24. IMPORTS OF GOODS AND SERVICES, NOMINAL

Imports of goods and services, nominal, represent the value of all goods and other market services received from the rest of the world. They include the value of merchandise, freight, insurance, transport, travel, royalties, license fees, and other services, such as communication, construction, financial, information, business, personal, and government services. They exclude labor and property income (formerly called factor services) as well as transfer payments and expressed in current U.S dollars.

Source: World Bank and Organisation for Economic Co-operation and Development national accounts data.

TABLE 2.25. EXPORTS OF GOODS AND SERVICES AS A SHARE OF GDP

Exports of goods and services represent the value of all goods and other market services provided to the rest of the world. They include the value of merchandise, freight, insurance, transport, travel, royalties, license fees, and other services, such as communication, construction, financial, information, business, personal, and government services. They exclude labor and property income (formerly called factor services) as well as transfer payments, and expressed as a proportion of real GDP.

Source: World Bank and Organisation for Economic Co-operation and Development national accounts data.

Table 2.26. Imports of goods and services as a share of GDP

Imports of goods and services represent the value of all goods and other market services received from the rest of the world. They include the value of merchandise, freight, insurance, transport, travel, royalties, license fees, and other services, such as communication, construction, financial, information, business, personal, and government services. They exclude labor and property income (formerly called factor services) as well as transfer payments and expressed as a proportion of real GDP.

Source: World Bank and Organisation for Economic Co-operation and Development national accounts data.

Table 2.27. Balance of payments and current account

Exports of goods and services represent the value of all goods and other market services provided to the rest of the world. They include the value of merchandise, freight, insurance, transport, travel, royalties, license fees, and other services, such as communication, construction, financial, information, business, personal, and government services. They exclude labor and property income (formerly called factor services) as well as transfer payments, and expressed in current U.S. dollars and as a proportion of real GDP.

Imports of goods and services represent the value of all goods and other market services received from the rest of the world. They include the value of merchandise, freight, insurance, transport, travel, royalties, license fees, and other services, such as communication, construction, financial, information, business, personal, and government services. They exclude labor and property income (formerly called factor services) as well as transfer payments and expressed in current U.S. dollars and as a proportion of real GDP.

Total trade is the sum of exports and imports of goods and services.

Net income is the receipts and payments of employee compensation paid to nonresident workers and investment income (receipts and payments on direct investment, portfolio investment, other investments, and receipts on reserve assets).

Net current transfers are recorded in the balance of payments whenever an economy provides or receives goods, services, income, or financial items without a quid pro quo.

Current account balance is the sum of net exports of goods, services, net income, and net current transfers. All transfers not considered to be capital are current.

Total reserves including gold are the holdings of monetary gold, special drawing rights, reserves of International Monetary Fund (IMF) members held by the IMF, and holdings of foreign exchange under the control of monetary authorities.

Source: Data on exports and imports of goods and services are from World Bank and Organisation for Economic Co-operation and Development national accounts data. Data on net income, net current transfers, current account balance, and total reserves are from the International Monetary Fund International Financial Statistics database and data files.

Table 2.28. Exchange rates and purchasing power parity

Official exchange rate is the exchange rate determined by national authorities or to the rate determined in the legally sanctioned exchange market.

Purchasing power parity (PPP) conversion factor is the number of units of a country's currency required to buy the same amount of goods and services in the domestic market as a U.S. dollar would buy in the United States.

Ratio of PPP conversion factor to market exchange rate is the national price level, making it possible to compare the cost of the bundle of goods that make up gross domestic product across countries.

Real effective exchange rate is the nominal effective exchange rate (a measure of the value of a currency against a weighted average of several foreign currencies) divided by a price deflator or index of costs.

Gross domestic product (GDP), PPP, is gross domestic product converted to international dollars using purchasing power parity rates. An international dollar has the same purchasing power over GDP as the U.S. dollar has in the

United States. GDP is the sum of gross value added by all resident producers in the economy plus any product taxes and minus any subsidies not included in the value of the products. It is calculated without making deductions for depreciation of fabricated assets or for depletion and degradation of natural resources.

Gross domestic product (GDP) per capita, PPP, is GDP per capita based on purchasing power parity (PPP). PPP GDP is gross domestic product converted to international dollars using purchasing power parity rates. An international dollar has the same purchasing power over GDP as the U.S. dollar has in the United States. GDP at purchaser's prices is the sum of gross value added by all resident producers in the economy plus any product taxes and minus any subsidies not included in the value of the products. It is calculated without making deductions for depreciation of fabricated assets or for depletion and degradation of natural resources.

Source: International Monetary Fund International Financial Statistics database. Data on PPP are from the World Bank's International Comparison Program database.

Table 2.29. Agriculture value added

Agriculture value added is the gross output of forestry, hunting, and fishing, as well as cultivation of crops and livestock production (International Standard Industrial Classification [ISIC] revision 3 divisions 1–5) less the value of their intermediate inputs. It is calculated without making deductions for depreciation of fabricated assets or depletion and degradation of natural resources. For countries that report that report national accounts data at producer prices (Benin, the Republic of Congo, Côte d'Ivoire, Gabon, Ghana, Niger, Rwanda, Tanzania, Togo, and Tunisia), gross value added at market prices is used as the denominator. For countries that report national accounts data at basic prices (all other countries), gross value added at factor cost is used as the denominator.

Source: World Bank and Organisation for Economic Co-operation and Development national accounts data files.

Table 2.30. Industry value added

Industry value added is the gross output of mining, manufacturing, construction, electricity, water, and gas (ISIC revision 3 divisions 10–45) less the value of their intermediate inputs. It is calculated without making deductions for depreciation of fabricated assets or depletion and degradation of natural resources For countries that report that report national accounts data at producer prices (Benin, the Republic of Congo, Côte d'Ivoire, Gabon, Ghana, Niger, Rwanda, Tanzania, Togo, and Tunisia), gross value added at market prices is used as the denominator. For countries that report national accounts data at basic prices (all other countries), gross value added at factor cost is used as the denominator.

Source: World Bank and Organisation for Economic Co-operation and Development national accounts data files.

Table 2.31. Services plus discrepancy value added

Services plus discrepancy value added is the gross output of all other branches of economic activity, including wholesale and retail trade (including hotels and restaurants), transport, and government, financial, professional, and personal services such as education, health care, and real estate services (ISIC revision 3 divisions 50–99) less the value of their intermediate inputs. Also included are imputed bank service charges, import duties, and any statistical discrepancies noted by national compilers as well as discrepancies arising from rescaling. It is calculated without making deductions for depreciation of fabricated assets or depletion and degradation of natural resources. For countries that report that report national accounts data at producer prices (Benin, the Republic of Congo, Côte d'Ivoire, Gabon, Ghana, Niger, Rwanda, Tanzania, Togo, and Tunisia), gross value added at market prices is used as the denominator. For countries that report national accounts data at basic prices (all other countries), gross value added at factor cost is used as the denominator.

Source: World Bank and Organisation for Economic Co-operation and Development national accounts data files.

Table 2.32. Central government finances, expense, and revenue

Revenue, excluding grants, is cash receipts from taxes, social contributions, and other revenues such as fines, fees, rent, and income from property or sales. Grants are also considered as revenue but are excluded here.

Expense is cash payments for operating activities of the government in providing goods and services. It includes compensation of employees (such as wages and salaries), interest and subsidies, grants, social benefits, and other expenses such as rent and dividends.

Cash surplus or deficit is revenue (including grants) minus expense, minus net acquisition of nonfinancial assets. In the 1986 *Government Finance Statistics Manual* nonfinancial assets were included under revenue and expenditure in gross terms. This cash surplus or deficit is closest to the earlier overall budget balance (still missing is lending minus repayments, which are now a financing item under net acquisition of financial assets).

Net incurrence of liabilities is domestic financing (obtained from residents) and foreign financing (obtained from nonresidents) and, or the means by which a government provides financial resources to cover a budget deficit or allocates financial resources arising from a budget surplus. The net incurrence of liabilities should be offset by the net acquisition of financial assets (a third financing item). The difference between the cash surplus or deficit and the three financing items is the net change in the stock of cash.

Total debt is the entire stock of direct government fixed-term contractual obligations to others outstanding on a particular date. It includes domestic and foreign liabilities such as currency and money deposits, securities other than shares, and loans. It is the gross amount of government liabilities reduced by the amount of equity and financial derivatives held by the government. Because debt is a stock rather than a flow, it is measured as of a given date, usually the last day of the fiscal year.

Goods and services include all government payments in exchange for goods and services used for the production of market and nonmarket goods and services. Own-account capital formation is excluded.

Compensation of employees consists of all payments in cash, as well as in kind (such as food and housing), to employees in return for services rendered, and government contributions to social insurance schemes such as social security and pensions that provide benefits to employees.

Interest payments (expense) include interest payments on government debt—including long-term bonds, long-term loans, and other debt instruments—to domestic and foreign residents, expressed as a proportion of expense.

Subsidies and other transfers include all unrequited, nonrepayable transfers on current account to private and public enterprises; grants to foreign governments, international organizations, and other government units; and social security, social assistance benefits, and employer social benefits in cash and in kind.

Other expenses are spending on dividends, rent, and other miscellaneous expenses, including provision for consumption of fixed capital.

Interest payments (revenue) include interest payments on government debt—including long-term bonds, long-term loans, and other debt instruments—to domestic and foreign residents, expressed as a proportion of revenue.

Taxes on income, profits, and capital gains are levied on the actual or presumptive net income of individuals, on the profits of corporations and enterprises, and on capital gains, whether realized or not, on land, securities, and other assets. Intragovernmental payments are eliminated in consolidation.

Taxes on goods and services include general sales and turnover or value added taxes, selective excises on goods, selective taxes on services, taxes on the use of goods or property, taxes on extraction and production of minerals, and profits of fiscal monopolies.

Taxes on international trade include import duties, export duties, profits of export or import monopolies, exchange profits, and exchange taxes.

Other taxes include employer payroll or labor taxes, taxes on property, and taxes not allocable to other categories, such as penalties for late payment or nonpayment of taxes.

Social contributions include social security contributions by employees, employers, and self-employed individuals, and other contributions whose source cannot be determined. They also include actual or imputed contributions to social insurance schemes operated by governments.

Grants and other revenue include grants from other foreign governments, international organizations, and other government units; interest; dividends; rent; requited, nonrepayable receipts for public purposes (such as fines, administrative fees, and entrepreneurial income from government ownership of property); and voluntary, unrequited, nonrepayable receipts other than grants.

Source: International Monetary Fund, *Government Finance Statistics Yearbook* and data files, and World Bank and Organisation for Economic Co-operation and Development GDP estimates.

Table 2.33. Structure of demand

Household final consumption expenditure (formerly *private consumption*) is the market value of all goods and services, including durable products (such as cars, washing machines, and home computers), purchased by households.

General government final consumption expenditure (formerly *general government consumption*) is all government current expenditures for purchases of goods and services.

Gross fixed capital formation (formerly *gross domestic investment*) consists of outlays on additions to the fixed assets of the economy plus net changes in the level of inventories.

Exports of goods and services represent the value of all goods and other market services provided to the rest of the world. They include the value of merchandise, freight, insurance, transport, travel, royalties, license fees, and other services, such as communication, construction, financial, information, business, personal, and government services. They exclude labor and property income (formerly called factor services) as well as transfer payments, and expressed as a proportion of real GDP.

Imports of goods and services represent the value of all goods and other market services received from the rest of the world. They include the value of merchandise, freight, insurance, transport, travel, royalties, license fees, and other services, such as communication, construction, financial, information, business, personal, and government services. They exclude labor and property income (formerly called factor services) as well as transfer payments and expressed as a proportion of real GDP.

Gross national savings is the gross national income less total consumption, plus net transfers.

Source: World Bank and Organisation for Economic Co-operation and Development national accounts data files.

3. Millennium Development Goals

Table 3.1. Millennium Development Goal 1: eradicate extreme poverty and hunger

Share of population below PPP $1.25 a day is the percentage of the population living on less than $1.25 a day at 2005 international prices. As a result of revisions in purchasing power parity (PPP) exchange rates, poverty rates in this edition cannot be compared with those in editions before 2009.

Poverty gap ratio at PPP $1.25 a day is the mean shortfall from the poverty line (counting the nonpoor as having zero shortfall), expressed as a percentage of the poverty line. This measure reflects the depth of poverty as well as its incidence.

Share of population below PPP $2 a day is the percentage of the population living on less than $2.00 a day at 2005 international prices. As a result of revisions in PPP exchange rates, poverty rates in this edition cannot be compared with those in editions before 2009.

Poverty gap ratio at PPP $2 a day is the mean shortfall from the poverty line (counting the nonpoor as having zero shortfall), expressed as a percentage of the poverty line. This measure reflects the depth of poverty as well as its incidence.

Share of population below national poverty line (poverty headcount ratio) is the percentage of the population living below the national poverty line. National estimates are based on population-weighted subgroup estimates from household surveys.

Share of poorest quintile in national consumption or income is the share of consumption, or in some cases income, that accrues to the poorest 20 percent of the population.

Prevalence of child malnutrition, underweight, is the percentage of children under age 5 whose weight for age is more than two standard deviations below the median for the international reference population ages 0–59 months. The reference population, adopted by the World Health Organization in 1983, is based on children from the United States, who are assumed to be well nourished.

Population below minimum dietary energy consumption (also referred to as prevalence of undernourishment) is the population whose dietary energy consumption is continuously below a minimum dietary energy requirement for maintaining a healthy life and carrying out a light physical activity with an acceptable minimum bodyweight for attained height.

Source: Data on poverty measures are prepared by the World Bank's Development Research Group. The international poverty lines are based on nationally representative primary household surveys conducted by national statistical offices or by private agencies under the supervision of government or international agencies and obtained from government statistical offices and World Bank Group country departments. The national poverty lines are based on the World Bank's country poverty assessments. Data have been compiled by World Bank staff from primary and secondary sources. Efforts have been made to harmonize these data series with those published on the United Nations Millennium Development Goals website (www.un.org/millenniumgoals), but some differences in timing, sources, and definitions remain. Data on child malnutrition and population below minimum dietary energy consumption are from the Food and Agriculture Organization (www.fao.org/economic/ess/food-security-statistics/en/).

Table 3.2. Millennium Development Goal 2: achieve universal primary education

Primary education provides children with basic reading, writing, and mathematics skills along with an elementary understanding of such subjects as history, geography, natural science, social science, art, and music.

Net primary enrollment ratio is the ratio of children of official primary school age based on the International Standard Classification of Education 1997 who are enrolled in primary school to the population of the corresponding official primary school age.

Primary completion rate is the percentage of students completing the last year of primary school. It is calculated as the total number of students in the last grade of primary school minus the number of repeaters in that grade divided by the total number of children of official graduation age.

Share of cohort reaching grade 5 is the percentage of children enrolled in grade 1 of primary school who eventually reach grade 5. The estimate is based on the reconstructed cohort method.

Youth literacy rate is the percentage of people ages 15–24 who can, with understanding, both read and write a short, simple statement about their everyday life.

Source: Data are from the United Nations Educational, Scientific, and Cultural Organization Institute for Statistics. Efforts have been made to harmonize these data series with those published on the United Nations Millennium Development Goals website (www.un.org/millenniumgoals), but some differences in timing, sources, and definitions remain.

Table 3.3. Millennium Development Goal 3: promote gender equality and empower women

Ratio of girls to boys in primary and secondary school is the ratio of female to male gross enrollment rate in primary and secondary school.

Ratio of literate young women to men is the ratio of the female youth literacy rate to the male youth literacy rate.

Women in national parliament are the percentage of parliamentary seats in a single or lower chamber occupied by women.

Share of women employed in the nonagricultural sector is women wage employees in the nonagricultural sector as a share of total nonagricultural employment.

Source: Data on net enrollment and literacy are from the United Nations Educational, Scientific, and Cultural Organization Institute for Statistics. Data on women in national parliaments are from the Inter-Parliamentary Union. Data on women's employment are from the International Labour Organization's Key Indicators of the Labour Market, fourth edition.

Table 3.4. Millennium Development Goal 4: reduce child mortality

Under-five mortality rate is the probability that a newborn baby will die before reaching age 5, if subject to current age-specific mortality rates. The probability is expressed as a rate per 1,000.

Infant mortality rate is the number of infants dying before reaching one year of age, per 1,000 live births.

Child immunization rate, measles, is the percentage of children ages 12–23 months who received vaccinations for measles before 12 months or at any time before the survey. A child is considered adequately immunized against measles after receiving one dose of vaccine.

Source: Data on under-five and infant mortality are the harmonized estimates of the World Health Organization, United Nations Children's Fund (UNICEF), and the World Bank, based mainly on household surveys, censuses, and vital registration, supplemented by the World Bank's estimates based on household surveys and vital registration. Other estimates are compiled and produced by the World Bank's Human Development Network and Development Data Group in consultation with its operational staff and country offices. Data on child immunization are from the World Health Organization and UNICEF.

Table 3.5. Millennium Development Goal 5: improve maternal health

Maternal mortality ratio, modeled estimate, is the number of women who die from pregnancy-related causes during pregnancy and childbirth, per 100,000 live births. Data are estimated by a regression model using information on fertility, birth attendants, and HIV prevalence.

Maternal mortality ratio, national estimate, is the number of women who die during pregnancy and childbirth, per 100,000 live births.

Births attended by skilled health staff are the percentage of deliveries attended by personnel who are trained to give the necessary supervision, care, and advice to women during pregnancy, labor, and the postpartum period; to conduct deliveries on their own; and to care for newborns.

Source: Data on maternal mortality are from AbouZahr and Wardlaw (2003). Data on births attended by skilled health staff are from the United Nations Children's Fund's *State of the World's Children* and Childinfo, and Demographic and Health Surveys by Macro International.

Table 3.6. Millennium Development Goal 6: combat HIV/AIDS, malaria, and other diseases

Prevalence of HIV is the percentage of people ages 15–49 who are infected with HIV.

Contraceptive use, any method, is the percentage of women ages 15–49, married or in union, who are practicing, or whose sexual partners are practicing, any form of contraception.

Children sleeping under insecticide-treated nets are the percentage of children under age 5 with access to an insecticide-treated net to prevent malaria.

Incidence of tuberculosis is the estimated number of new tuberculosis cases (pulmonary, smear positive, and extrapulmonary), per 100,000 people.

Tuberculosis cases detected under DOTS are the percentage of estimated new infectious tuberculosis cases detected under DOTS, the internationally recommended tuberculosis control strategy.

Source: Data on HIV prevalence are from the Joint United Nations Programme on HIV/AIDS and the World Health Organization's (WHO) *Report on the Global AIDS Epidemic.* Data on contraceptive use are from household surveys, including Demographic and Health Surveys by Macro International and Multiple Indicator Cluster Surveys by the United Nations Children's Fund (UNICEF). Data on insecticide-treated net use are from UNICEF's *State of the World's Children* and Childinfo, and Demographic and Health Surveys by Macro International. Data on tuberculosis are from the WHO's *Global Tuberculosis Control Report 2006.*

Table 3.7. Millennium Development Goal 7: ensure environment sustainability

Forest area is land under natural or planted stands of trees, whether productive or not.

Nationally protected areas are totally or partially protected areas of at least 1,000 hectares that are designated as scientific reserves with limited public access, national parks, natural monuments, nature reserves or wildlife sanctuaries, and protected landscapes. Marine areas, unclassified areas, and littoral (intertidal) areas are not included. The data also do not include sites protected under local or provincial law.

Gross domestic product (GDP) per unit of energy use is the GDP in purchasing power parity (PPP) U.S. dollars per kilogram of oil equivalent of energy use. PPP GDP is gross domestic product converted to 2000 constant international dollars using purchasing power parity rates. An international dollar has the same purchasing power over GDP as a U.S. dollar has in the United States.

Carbon dioxide emissions per capita are those stemming from the burning of fossil fuels and the manufacture of cement divided by midyear population. They include carbon dioxide produced during consumption of solid, liquid and gas fuels, and gas flaring.

Population with sustainable access to an improved water source is the percentage of the population with reasonable access to an adequate amount of water from an improved source, such as a household connection, public standpipe, borehole, protected well or spring, or rainwater collection. Unimproved sources include vendors, tanker trucks, and unprotected wells and springs. Reasonable access is defined as the availability of at least 20 liters a person a day from a source within one kilometer of the dwelling.

Population with sustainable access to improved sanitation is the percentage of the population with at least adequate access to excreta disposal facilities that can effectively prevent human, animal, and insect contact with excreta. Improved facilities range from simple but protected pit latrines to flush toilets with a sewerage connection. The excreta disposal system is considered adequate if it is private or shared (but not public) and if it hygienically separates human excreta from human contact. To be effective, facilities must be correctly constructed and properly maintained.

Source: Data on forest area are from the Food and Agricultural Organization's Global Forest Resources Assessment. Data on nationally protected areas are from the United Nations Environment Programme and the World Conservation Monitoring Centre. Data on energy use are from electronic files of the International Energy Agency. Data on carbon dioxide emissions are from the Carbon Dioxide Information Analysis Center, Environmental Sciences Division, Oak Ridge National Laboratory, in the U.S. state of Tennessee. Data on access to water and sanitation are from the World Health Organization and United Nations Children's Fund's *Progress on Drinking Water and Sanitation* (2008).

Table 3.8. Millennium Development Goal 8: develop a global partnership for development

Heavily Indebted Poor Countries (HIPC) Debt Initiative decision point is the date at which a HIPC with an established track record of good performance under adjustment programs supported by the International Monetary Fund (IMF) and the World Bank commits to undertake additional reforms and to develop and implement a poverty reduction strategy.

HIPC completion point is the date at which the country successfully completes the key structural reforms agreed on at the decision point, including developing and implementing its poverty reduction strategy. The country then receives the bulk of debt relief under the HIPC Initiative without further policy conditions.

Debt service relief committed is the amount of debt service relief, calculated at the *Enhanced HIPC Initiative* decision point that will allow the country to achieve debt sustainability at the completion point.

Public and publicly guaranteed debt service is the sum of principal repayments and interest actually paid on total long-term debt (public and publicly guaranteed and private nonguaranteed), use of IMF credit, and interest on short-term debt.

Youth unemployment rate is the percentage of the labor force ages 15–24 without work but available for and seeking employment. Definitions of labor force and unemployment may differ by country.

Fixed-line and mobile telephone subscribers are subscribers to a fixed-line telephone service, which connects a customer's equipment to the public switched telephone network, or to a public mobile telephone service, which uses cellular technology.

Personal computers are self-contained computers designed for use by a single individual.

Internet users are people with access to the worldwide web.

Source: Data on HIPC countries are from the IMF's "HIPC Status Reports." Data on external debt are mainly from reports to the World Bank through its Debtor Reporting System from member countries that have received International Bank for Reconstruction and Development loans or International Development Association credits, as well as World Bank and IMF files. Data on youth unemployment are from the International Labour Organization's Key Indicators of the Labour Market, fourth edition. Data on phone subscribers, personal computers, and Internet users are from the International Telecommunication Union's (ITU) World Telecommunication Development Report database and World Bank estimates.

4. Private sector development

TABLE 4.1. DOING BUSINESS INDICATORS

Number of startup procedures to start a business is the number of procedures required to start a business, including interactions to obtain necessary permits and licenses and to complete all inscriptions, verifications, and notifications to start operations.

Time required for each procedure to start a business is the number of calendar days needed to complete each procedure to legally operate a business. If a procedure can be speeded up at additional cost, the fastest procedure, independent of cost, is chosen.

Cost to start a business is normalized by presenting it as a percentage of gross national income (GNI) per capita.

Minimum capital is the paid-in minimum capital requirement, which reflects the amount that the entrepreneur needs to deposit in a bank or with a notary before registration and up to three months following incorporation. It is reported as a percentage of the country's income per capita.

Number of procedures to register property is the number of procedures required for a business to secure rights to property.

Time required to register property is the number of calendar days needed for a business to secure rights to property.

Cost to register property is the official costs required by law to register a property, including fees, transfer taxes, stamp duties, and any other payment to the property registry, notaries, public agencies, and lawyers. Other taxes, such as capital gains tax or value added tax, are excluded from the cost measure. Both costs borne by the buyer and those borne by the seller are included. If cost estimates differ among sources, the median reported value is used. It is reported as a percentage of property value, which is assumed to be equivalent to 50 times income per capita.

Number of procedures to enforce a contract is the number of independent actions, mandated by law or courts that demand interaction between the parties of a contract or between them and the judge or court officer.

Time required to enforce a contract is the number of calendar days from the filing of the lawsuit in court until the final determination and, in appropriate cases, payment.

Cost to enforce a contract is court and attorney fees, where the use of attorneys is mandatory or common, or the cost of an administrative debt recovery procedure, expressed as a percentage of the debt value.

Number of procedures to deal with construction permits is the number of procedures required to obtain construction-related permits.

Time required to deal with construction permits is the average wait, in days, experienced to obtain construction-related permit from the day the establishment applied for it to the day it was granted.

Cost to deal with construction permits is all the fees associated with completing the procedures to legally build a warehouse, including those associated with obtaining land use approvals and preconstruction design clearances; receiving inspections before, during and after construction; getting utility connections; and registering the warehouse property. Nonrecurring taxes required for the completion of the warehouse project also are recorded. The building code, information from local experts and specific regulations and fee schedules are used as sources for costs. If several local partners provide different estimates, the median reported value is used. It is reported as a percentage of the country's income per capita.

Disclosure index measures the degree to which investors are protected through disclosure of ownership and financial information. Higher values indicate more disclosure.

Director liability index measures a plaintiff's ability to hold directors of firms liable for damages to the company. Higher values indicate greater liability.

Shareholder suits index measures shareholders' ability to sue officers and directors for misconduct. Higher values indicate greater power for shareholders to challenge transactions.

Investor protection index measures the degree to which investors are protected through disclosure of ownership and financial information regulations. It is the average of the disclosure, director liability, and shareholder suits indexes. Higher values indicate better protection.

Rigidity of hours index, a measure of employment regulation, is the average score in five areas: whether night work is unrestricted, whether weekend work is unrestricted, whether the work week can consist of 5.5 days, whether the workweek can extend to 50 hours or more (including overtime) for two months a year to respond to a seasonal increase in production, whether paid annual vacation is 21 working days or fewer. For each question the answer no is assigned a score of 1, and the answer yes a 0.

Difficulty of hiring index indicates the applicability and maximum duration of fixed-term contracts and minimum wage for trainee or first-time employee. It measures whether fixed-term contracts are prohibited for permanent tasks, the maximum cumulative duration of fixed-term contracts, and the ratio of the minimum wage for a trainee or first-time employee to the average value added per worker.

Difficulty of firing index indicates the extent of notification and approval requirements for termination of a redundant worker or a group of redundant workers, obligation to reassign or retrain, and priority rules for redundancy and reemployment. It has eight components: whether redundancy is disallowed as a basis for terminating workers, whether the employer needs to notify a third party (such as a government agency) to terminate 1 redundant worker, whether the employer needs to notify a third party to terminate a group of 25 redundant workers, whether the employer needs approval from a third party to terminate 1 redundant worker, whether the employer needs approval from a third party to terminate a group of 25 redundant workers, whether the law requires the employer to reassign or retrain a worker before making the worker redundant, whether priority rules apply for redundancies, and whether priority rules apply for reemployment. For the first question the answer yes is assigned a score of 10, and the rest of the questions do not apply. For the fourth question the answer yes is assigned a score of 2, and the answer no a 0. For every other question the answer yes is assigned score of 1, and the answer no a 0.

Firing cost indicates the notice requirements, severance, payments, and penalties due when terminating a redundant worker, expressed in weeks of salary.

Rigidity of employment index measures the regulation of employment, specifically the hiring and firing of workers and the rigidity of working hours. This index is the average of three subindexes: the rigidity of hours index, the difficulty of hiring index, and the difficulty of firing index.

Source: Data are from the World Bank's Doing Business project (http://rru.worldbank.org/DoingBusiness/).

TABLE 4.2. INVESTMENT CLIMATE

Private sector fixed capital formation is private sector fixed capital formation (table 2.21) divided by nominal gross domestic product (table 2.1).

Net foreign direct investment is investment by residents of the Organisation for Economic Co-operation and Development's (OECD) Development Assistance Committee (DAC) member countries to acquire a lasting management interest (at least 10 percent of voting stock) in an enterprise operating in the recipient country. The data reflect changes in the net worth of subsidiaries in recipient countries whose parent company is in the DAC source country.

Domestic credit to private sector is financial resources provided to the private sector, such as through loans, purchases of non-equity securities, and trade credits and other accounts receivable that establish a claim for repayment. For some countries these claims include credit to public enterprises.

Firms that believe the court system is fair, impartial, and uncorrupt are the percentage of firms that believe the court system is fair, impartial, and uncorrupted.

Corruption is the percentage of firms identifying corruption as a major constraint to current operation.

Crime, theft, and disorder are the percentage of firms identifying crime, theft, and disorder as a major constraint to current operation.

Tax rates are the percentage of firms identifying tax rates as a major constraint to current operation.

Finance is the percentage of firms identifying access to finance or cost of finance as a major constraint to current operation.

Electricity is the percentage of firms identifying electricity as a major constraint to current operation.

Labor regulations are the percentage of firms identifying labor regulations as a major constraint to current operation.

Labor skills are the percentage of firms identifying skills of available workers as a major constraint to current operation.

Transportation is the percentage of firms identifying transportation as a major constraint to current operation.

Customs and trade regulations are the percentage of firms identifying customs and trade regulations as a major constraint to current operation.

Number of tax payments is the number of taxes paid by businesses, including electronic filing. The tax is counted as paid once a year even if payments are more frequent.

Time to prepare, file, and pay taxes is the number of hours it takes to prepare, file, and pay (or withhold) three major types of taxes: the corporate income tax, the value added or sales tax, and labor taxes, including payroll taxes and social security contributions.

Total tax rate is the total amount of taxes payable by the business (except for labor taxes) after accounting for deductions and exemptions as a percentage of profit.

Highest marginal tax rate, corporate, is the highest rate shown on the schedule of tax rates applied to the taxable income of corporations.

Time dealing with officials is the average percentage of senior management's time that is spent in a typical week dealing with requirements imposed by government regulations (for example, taxes, customs, labor regulations, licensing, and registration), including dealings with officials, completing forms, and the like.

Average time to clear customs, direct exports, is the number of days to clear direct exports through customs.

Average time to clear customs, imports, is the average number of days to clear imports through customs.

Interest rate spread is the interest rate charged by banks on loans to prime customers minus the interest rate paid by commercial or similar banks for demand, time, or savings deposits.

Listed domestic companies are domestically incorporated companies listed on a country's stock exchanges at the end of the year. They exclude investment companies, mutual funds, and other collective investment vehicles.

Market capitalization of listed companies, also known as market value, is the share price of a listed domestic company's stock times the number of shares outstanding.

Turnover ratio for traded stocks is the total value of shares traded during the period divided by the average market capitalization for the period. Average market capitalization is calculated as the average of the end-of-period values for the current period and the previous period.

Source: Data on private sector fixed capital formation are from the World Bank's World Development Indicators database. Data on net foreign direct investment are from the World Bank's World Development Indicators database. Data on domestic credit to the private sector are from the International Monetary Fund's International Financial Statistics database and data files, World Bank and OECD gross domestic product (GDP) estimates, and the World Bank's World Development Indicators database. Data on investment climate constraints to firms are based on enterprise surveys conducted by the World Bank and its partners (http://rru.worldbank.org/EnterpriseSurveys). Data on regulation and tax administration and highest marginal corporate tax rates are from the World Bank's Doing Business project (http://

rru.worldbank.org/DoingBusiness). Data on time dealing with officials and average time to clear customs are from World Bank Enterprise Surveys (http://rru.worldbank.org/EnterpriseSurveys/). Data on interest rate spreads are from the IMF's International Financial Statistics database and data files and the World Bank's World Development Indicators database. Data on listed domestic companies and turnover ratios for traded stocks are from Standard & Poor's Emerging Stock Markets Factbook and supplemental data and the World Bank's World Development Indicators database. Data on market capitalization of listed companies are from Standard & Poor's Emerging Stock Markets Factbook and supplemental data, World Bank and OECD estimates of GDP, and the World Bank's World Development Indicators database.

Table 4.3. Financial sector infrastructure

Foreign currency sovereign ratings are long- and short-term foreign currency ratings that assess a sovereign's capacity and willingness to honor its existing and future obligations issued in foreign currencies in full and on time. Short-term ratings have a time horizon of less than 13 months for most obligations, or up to three years for U.S. public finance, in line with industry standards, to reflect unique risk characteristics of bond, tax, and revenue anticipation notes that are commonly issued with terms up to three years. Short-term ratings thus place greater emphasis on the liquidity necessary to meet financial commitments in a timely manner.

Gross national savings is the sum of gross domestic savings (table 2.13) and net factor income and net private transfers from abroad. The estimate here also includes net public transfers from abroad.

Money and quasi money (M2) are the sum of currency outside banks, demand deposits other than those of the central government, and the time, savings, and foreign currency deposits of resident sectors other than the central government. This definition of money supply is frequently called M2 and corresponds to lines 34 and 35 in the International Monetary Fund's (IMF) International Financial Statistics.

Real interest rate is the lending interest rate adjusted for inflation as measured by the gross domestic product (GDP) deflator.

Domestic credit to private sector is financial resources provided to the private sector, such as through loans, purchases of nonequity securities, and trade credits and other accounts receivable, that establish a claim for repayment. For some countries these claims include credit to public enterprises.

Interest rate spread is the interest rate charged by banks on loans to prime customers minus the interest rate paid by commercial or similar banks for demand, time, or savings deposits.

Ratio of bank nonperforming loans to total gross loans is the value of nonperforming loans divided by the total value of the loan portfolio (including nonperforming loans before the deduction of specific loan-loss provisions). The loan amount recorded as nonperforming should be the gross value of the loan as recorded on the balance sheet, not just the amount that is overdue.

Listed domestic companies are domestically incorporated companies listed on a country's stock exchanges at the end of the year. They exclude investment companies, mutual funds, and other collective investment vehicles.

Market capitalization of listed companies, also known as market value, is the share price of a listed domestic company's stock times the number of shares outstanding.

Turnover ratio for traded stocks is the total value of shares traded during the period divided by the average market capitalization for the period. Average market capitalization is calculated as the average of the end-of-period values for the current period and the previous period.

Source: Data on foreign currency sovereign ratings are from Fitch Ratings. Data on gross national savings are from World Bank country desks. Data on money and quasi money and domestic credit to the private sector are from the IMF's International Financial Statistics database and data files, World Bank and OECD estimates of GDP, and the World Bank's World Development Indicators database. Data on real interest rates are from the IMF's International Financial Statistics database and data files using World Bank data on the GDP deflator and the World Bank's World Development Indicators database. Data on interest rate spreads are from the IMF's International Financial Statistics database and data files and the World Bank's World Development Indicators database. Data on ratios of bank nonperforming loans to total are from the IMF's Global Financial Stability Report and the World Bank's World Development Indicators database. Data on bank branches are from surveys of banking and regulatory institutions by the World Bank's Research Department and Financial Sector and Operations Policy Department and the World Development Indicators database. Data on listed domestic companies and turnover ratios for traded stocks are from Standard & Poor's Emerging Stock Markets Factbook and supplemental data and the World Bank's World Development Indicators database. Data on market capitalization of listed companies are from Standard & Poor's Emerging Stock Markets Factbook and supplemental data, World Bank and OECD estimates of GDP, and the World Bank's World Development Indicators database.

5. *Trade and regional integration*

See box 3 for a discussion of the challenges of measuring the impact of regional integration.

Table 5.1. International trade and tariff barriers

Total trade is the sum of exports and imports of goods and services measured as a share of gross domestic product.

Merchandise trade is the sum of imports and exports of merchandise divided by nominal gross domestic product.

Services trade is the sum of imports and exports of wholesale and retail trade (including hotels and restaurants), transport, and government, financial, professional, and personal services such as education, health care, and real estate services (International Standard Industrial Classification revision 3 divisions 50–99) less the value of their intermediate inputs. Also included are imputed bank service charges, import duties, and any statistical discrepancies noted by national compilers as well as discrepancies arising from rescaling. It is calculated without making deductions for depreciation of fabricated assets or depletion and degradation of natural resources. For countries that report that report national accounts data at producer prices (Benin, the Republic of Congo, Côte d'Ivoire, Gabon, Ghana, Niger, Rwanda, Tanzania, Togo, and Tunisia), gross value added at market prices is used as the denominator. For countries that report national accounts data at basic prices (all other countries), gross value added at factor cost is used as the denominator.

Exports of goods and services represent the value of all goods and other market services provided to the rest of the world. They include the value of merchandise, freight, insurance, transport, travel, royalties, license fees, and other services, such as communication, construction, financial, information, business, personal, and government services. They exclude labor and property income (formerly called factor services) as well as transfer payments, and expressed in current U.S. dollars and as a proportion of nominal GDP.

Imports of goods and services represent the value of all goods and other market services received from the rest of the world. They include the value of merchandise, freight, insurance, transport, travel, royalties, license fees, and other services, such as communication, construction, financial, information, business, personal, and government services. They exclude labor and property income (formerly called factor services) as well as transfer payments and expressed in current U.S. dollars and as a proportion of nominal GDP.

Annual growth of exports and *imports* is calculated using real imports and exports.

Terms of trade index measures the relative movement of export and import prices. This series is calculated as the ratio of a country's export unit values or prices to its import unit values or prices shows changes over a base year (2000) in the level of export unit values as a percentage of import unit values.

Structure of merchandise exports and *imports* components may not sum to 100 percent because of unclassified trade.

Food comprises the commodities in Standard International Trade Classification (SITC) sections 0 (food and live animals), 1 (beverages and tobacco), and 4 (animal and vegetable oils and fats) and SITC division 22 (oil seeds, oil nuts, and oil kernels).

Box 3 **Measuring the impact of regional integration**

The simplest measure of regional integration is the share of imports from regional partners in the total imports of a regional group. Successful regional agreements may increase trade between partners relative to their trade with the rest of the world, with four caveats. First, preferential trade agreements are an example of a second-best economic policy, whereby the removal of one economic distortion (tariffs on imports from partners) is accompanied by a new distortion (discrimination against nonmembers that still have to pay the tariff). A regional trade agreement that increases trade among members by diverting trade away from nonmembers may not be economically beneficial. Only when an agreement creates new trade among partners will economic welfare increase. Second, successful regional integration is typically accompanied by reductions in most favored nation tariffs on imports from nonmembers, so the share of regional trade may not rise even though the volume of regional trade is increasing. Third, regional trade agreements may reduce trade costs other than those associated with formal trade policies, such as improved customs procedures, which are likely to stimulate trade with all countries. Fourth, regional agreements may cover issues not directly related to trade, such as movement of capital and labor, that may have important benefits in terms of growth and incomes. For these reasons another useful measure of regional integration is the share of extra- and intra-regional trade in regional GDP. A declining share of extra-regional trade in total trade will be less significant if the total value of trade is increasing.

Positive outcomes from regional integration depend on design and implementation, so when assessing the impact of a regional agreement, the nature and extent to which trade policy obligations under the agreement are actually being applied must be checked. Agreements that devote considerable resources to negotiating a large range of product exclusions from liberalization and complex and restrictive rules of origin tend to limit the scope for gains. Within the regional groupings in Africa not all members have made or implemented tariff commitments. For example, Angola has signed the Southern African Development Community Trade Protocol but has not submitted a market access schedule. Similarly, for the Common Market for Eastern and Southern COMESA, the Democratic Republic of Congo and Ethiopia are not party to the free trade agreement.

It is important to go beyond simple trade shares to identify the economic impact of regional trade agreements. For agreements in Africa, where combined markets remain very small relative to the global market, it is equally important to ask how the agreement can be used as part of a broad approach to openness and especially whether the agreement can provide a springboard to global markets for local exporters.

Regional agreements in Africa are typically associated with low shares of intraregional trade in total trade compared with groups in other regions. It is often suggested that this reflects the lack of complementarity between the production structures of Africa countries with total exports being dominated by primary products that are not consumed locally. Export diversification is therefore a key priority for most Africa countries. Nevertheless, African countries trade much more with each other than is reflected in official statistics. A range of surveys confirm that informal cross-border trade in a range of goods, such as processed and primary agricultural products and simple manufactures, and services amounts to a significant proportion of recorded trade. This indicates that the potential for growth of intraregional trade in Africa could be much larger than official figures would suggest.

In other regions, such as Southeast Asia, inward foreign direct investment and the increasing importance of regional production networks have been key drivers of the expansion of cross-border trade in parts and components. Such trade is very sensitive to trade costs, and a key reason for the lack of regional trade in Africa is continued high trade costs. These encapsulate not only the high costs of transportation (reflecting weak infrastructure) but also substantial policy related barriers to trade, including inefficient customs procedures, nontariff barriers and corruption as well as ineffective government responses to key market failures that limit exports, such as lack of information on overseas market opportunities and requirements. In Africa reducing trade costs is a prerequisite for export diversification, increasing regional integration and global competitiveness.

Source: World Bank 2005.

Agricultural raw materials comprise the commodities in SITC section 2 (crude materials except fuels), excluding divisions 22, 27 (crude fertilizers and minerals excluding coal, petroleum, and precious stones), and 28 (metalliferous ores and scrap).

Fuel comprises SITC section 3 (mineral fuels).

Ores and metals comprise the commodities in SITC sections 27, 28, and 68 (nonferrous metals).

Manufactures comprise the commodities in SITC sections 5 (chemicals), 6 (basic manufactures), 7 (machinery and transport equipment), and 8 (miscellaneous manufactured goods), excluding division 68.

Export diversification index measures the extent to which exports are diversified. It is constructed as the inverse of a Herfindahl index, using disaggregated exports at four digits (following the SITC3). A higher index indicates more export diversification.

Export concentration index, part of the Herfindahl-Hirschmann index, is calculated as

$$H_{ij} = 100 \times \left[\frac{\sqrt{\sum_i \left(\frac{X_{ij}}{X_j} \right)^2} - \sqrt{\frac{1}{n}}}{1 - \sqrt{\frac{1}{n}}} \right]$$

where X_{ij} is country *j*'s exports of product *i* (at the SITC 3-digit level, where the number of products imported and exported includes only products whose value exceeds \$100,000 or 0.3 percent of the country's total imports and exports, whichever is smaller; the maximum number of 3-digit products that could be imported and exported is 261), X_j is country *j*'s total exports, and *n* is the total number of 3-digit products. This type of concentration indicator is vulnerable to cyclical fluctuations in relative prices, with commodity price rises making commodity exporters look more concentrated.

Export destination index, part of the Herfindahl-Hirschmann index, is calculated as

$$H_{ij} = 100 \times \sqrt{\sum_j \left(\frac{X_{ij}}{X_j} \right)^2}$$

where X_{ij} is country *i*'s exports to country *j* (at the SITC 3-digit level) and X_i is country *i*'s total exports to all trading partners. This type of concentration indicator tends is vulnerable to cyclical fluctuations in relative prices, with commodity price rises making commodity exporters look more concentrated.

Competitiveness indicator has two aspects: *sectoral effect* and *global effect*. To calculate both indicators, growth of exports is decomposed into three components: the growth rate of total international trade over the reference period (2003–07); the sectoral effect, which measures the contribution to a country's export growth of the dynamics of the sectoral markets where the country sells its products, assuming that sectoral market shares are constant; and the competitiveness effect, which measures the contribution of changes in sectoral market shares to a country's export growth.

Tariff barriers are a form of duty based on the value of the import.

Binding coverage is the percentage of product lines with an agreed bound rate.

Simple mean bound rate is the unweighted average of all the lines in the tariff schedule in which bound rates have been set.

Simple mean tariff is the unweighted average of effectively applied rates or most favored nation rates for all products subject to tariffs calculated for all traded goods.

Dispersion around the mean is calculated as the coefficient of variation of the applied tariff rates, including preferential rates that a country applies to its trading partners available at the six-digit product level of the Harmonized System in a country's customs schedule.

Weighted mean tariff is the average of effectively applied rates or most favored nation rates weighted by the product import shares corresponding to each partner country.

Share of lines with international peaks is the share of lines in the tariff schedule with tariff rates that exceed 15 percent.

Share of lines with domestic peaks is the share of lines in the tariff schedule with tariff rates that are more than three times the simple average tariff.

Share of lines that are bound is the share of lines in the country's tariff schedule bound subject to World Trade Organization negotiation agreements.

Share of lines with specific rates is the share of lines in the tariff schedule that are set on a per unit basis or that combine ad valorem and per unit rates.

Primary products are commodities classified in SITC revision 2 sections 0–4 plus division 68.

Manufactured products are commodities classified in SITC revision 2 sections 5–8 excluding division 68.

GATS commitments index measures the extent of General Agreement on Trade in Services (GATS) commitments for all 155 services subsectors as classified by the GATS and in the four modes of the GATS. Each entry in the country's schedule is assigned scores based on its relative restrictiveness, using Bernard Hoekman's methodology. That resulted in 1,240 scores, ranging from 0 (unbound or no commitments) to 100 (completely liberalized), with an intermediate value of 50 for partial commitments. A simple average of the subsectoral scores were used to generate aggregate subsectoral scores (for the 12 main services sectors as classified by the GATS), modes scores, and market access and national treatment scores. The overall 12 GATS commitment index is a simple average of the subsectoral indexes.

Average cost to ship 20 ft container from port to destination is the cost of all operations associated with moving a container from onboard a ship to the considered economic center, weighted based on container traffic for each corridor.

Average time to clear customs, direct exports, is the number of days to clear direct exports through customs.

Average time to clear customs, imports, is the average number of days to clear imports through customs.

Source: Data on trade and services are from World Bank and Organisation for Economic Co-operation and Development national accounts data. Data on merchandise trade are from the World Trade Organization and World Bank GDP estimates. All indicators in the table were calculated by World Bank staff using the World Integrated Trade Solution system. Data on the export diversification index and the competitiveness indicator are from the Organisation for Economic Co-operation and Development. Data on the export concentration index and destination index data are from the United Nations Conference on Trade and Development Statistical Office and *Handbook of Statistics*, various issues. Data on tariffs are from the United Nations Conference on Trade and Development and the World Trade Organization. Data on global imports are from the United Nations Statistics Division's COMTRADE database. Data on merchandise exports and imports are from World Bank country desks. Data on shipping costs are from the World Bank's Sub-Saharan Africa Transport Policy Program. Data on GATS commitments are from the World Trade Organization, as scored by the World Bank Institute's *World Trade Indicators 2008* team. Scoring and subsectoral weights follow Hoekman (1995). Data on average time to clear customs are from World Bank Enterprise Surveys (http://rru.worldbank.org/EnterpriseSurveys/).

Table 5.2 Top three exports and share in total exports, 2007

Top exports and *share of total exports* are based on exports disaggregated at the four-digit level (following the Standard International Trade Classification revision 3).

Number of exports accounting for 75 percent of total exports is the number of exports in a country that account for 75 percent of the country's exports.

Source: Organisation for Economic Co-operation and Development data.

Table 5.3 Regional integration, trade blocs

Type of most recent agreement includes customs union, under which members substantially eliminate all tariff and nontariff barriers among themselves and establish a common external tariff for nonmembers; economic integration agreement, which liberalizes trade in services among members and covers a substantial number of sectors, affects a sufficient volume of trade, includes substantial modes of supply, and is nondiscriminatory (in the sense that similarly situated service suppliers are treated the same); free trade agreement, under which members substantially eliminate all tariff and nontariff barriers but set tariffs on imports from nonmembers; partial scope agreement, which is a preferential trade agreement notified to the World Trade Organization (WTO) that is not a free trade agreement, a custom union, or an economic integration; and not notified agreement, which is a preferential trade arrangement established among member countries that is not notified to the WTO (the agreement may be functionally equivalent to any of the other agreements).

Merchandise exports within bloc are the sum of merchandise exports by members of a trade bloc to other members of the bloc. They are shown both in U.S. dollars and as a percentage of total merchandise exports by the bloc.

Merchandise exports by bloc are the sum of merchandise exports within bloc and to the rest of the world as a share of total merchandise exports by all economies in the world.

Source: Data on merchandise trade flows are published in the International Monetary Fund's (IMF) Direction of Trade Statistics Yearbook and Direction of Trade Statistics Quarterly. The data in the table were calculated using the IMF's Direction of Trade database. The United Nations Conference on

Trade and Development publishes data on intraregional trade in its Handbook of International Trade and Development Statistics. The information on trade bloc membership is from the World Bank.

6. Infrastructure

TABLE 6.1. WATER AND SANITATION
Internal fresh water resources per capita are the sum of total renewable resources, which include internal flows of rivers and groundwater from rainfall in the country, and river flows from other countries.

Population with sustainable access to an improved water source is the percentage of population with reasonable access to an adequate amount of water from an improved source, such as a household connection, public standpipe, borehole, protected well or spring, or rainwater collection. Unimproved sources include vendors, tanker trucks, and unprotected wells and springs. Reasonable access is defined as the availability of at least 20 liters a person a day from a source within one kilometer of the user's dwelling.

Population with sustainable access to improved sanitation is the percentage of the population with at least adequate access to excreta disposal facilities that can effectively prevent human, animal, and insect contact with excreta. Improved facilities range from simple but protected pit latrines to flush toilets with a sewerage connection. The excreta disposal system is considered adequate if it is private or shared (but not public) and if it hygienically separates human excreta from human contact. To be effective, facilities must be correctly constructed and properly maintained.

Water supply failure for firms receiving water is the average number of days per year that firms experienced insufficient water supply for production.

Committed nominal investment in water projects with private participation is annual committed investment in water projects with private investment, including projects for potable water generation and distribution and sewerage collection and treatment projects.

Official development assistance (ODA) gross disbursements for water supply and sanitation sector are disbursements for water supply and sanitation by bilateral, multilateral, and other donors. The release of funds to, or the purchase of goods or services for a recipient; by extension, the amount thus spent. Disbursements record the actual international transfer of financial resources, or of goods or services valued at the cost of the donor.

Source: Data on fresh water resources are from the World Bank's World Development Indicators database. Data on access to water and sanitation are from the World Health Organization and United Nations Children's Fund's Meeting the MDG Drinking Water and Sanitation Target (www.unicef.org/wes/mdgreport). Data on water supply failure are from World Bank Enterprise Surveys (http://rru.worldbank.org/EnterpriseSurveys/). Data on committed nominal investment in potable water projects with private participation are from the World Bank's Private Participation in Infrastructure database. Data on ODA disbursements are from the Organisation for Economic Co-operation and Development.

TABLE 6.2. TRANSPORTATION
Road network is the length of motorways, highways, main or national roads, secondary or regional roads, and other roads.

Rail lines are the length of railway route available for train service, irrespective of the number of parallel tracks.

Road density, ratio to arable land, is the total length of national road network per 1,000 square kilometers of arable land area. The use of arable land area in the denominator focuses on inhabited sectors of total land area by excluding wilderness areas.

Road density, ratio to total land, is the total length of national road network per 1,000 square kilometers of total land area.

Rural access is the percentage of the rural population who live within 2 kilometers of an all-season passable road as a share of the total rural population.

Vehicle fleet is the number of motor vehicles, including cars, buses, and freight vehicles but not two-wheelers.

Commercial vehicles are the number of commercial vehicles that use at least 24 liters of diesel fuel per 100 kilometers.

Passenger vehicles are road motor vehicles, other than two-wheelers, intended for the carriage of passengers and designed to seat no more than nine people (including the driver).

Road network in good or fair condition is the length of the national road network, including the interurban classified network without the urban and rural network, that is in good or fair condition, as defined by each country's road agency.

Ratio of paved to total roads is the length of paved roads—which are those surfaced with crushed stone (macadam) and hydrocarbon binder or bituminized agents, with concrete, or with cobblestones—as a percentage of all the country's roads.

Price of diesel fuel and *gasoline* is the price as posted at filling stations in a country's capital city. When several fuel prices for major cities were available, the unweighted average is used. Since super gasoline (95 octane/A95/premium) is not available everywhere, it is sometime replaced by regular gasoline (92 octane/A92), premium plus gasoline (98 octane/A98), or an average of the two.

Committed nominal investment in transport projects with private participation is annual committed investment in transport projects with private investment, including projects for airport runways and terminals, railways (including fixed assets, freight, intercity passenger, and local passenger), toll roads, bridges, and tunnels.

Official development assistance (ODA) gross disbursements for transportation and storage are disbursements for transportation and storage by bilateral, multilateral, and other donors. Disbursements record the actual international transfer of financial resources or of goods or services valued at the cost of the donor.

Source: Data on length of road network and size of vehicle fleet are from the International Road Federation's World Road Statistics. Data on rail lines and ratio of paved to total roads are from the World Bank's World Development Indicators database. Data on road density and rural access to roads are from the World Bank's Sub-Saharan Africa Transport Policy Program (SSATP) and World Development Indicators database. Data on length of national network in good or fair condition and average time and costs are from the World Bank's SSATP. Data on fuel and gasoline prices are from the German Agency for Technical Cooperation (GTZ). Data on committed nominal investment in transport projects with private participation are from the World Bank's Private Participation in Infrastructure database. Data on ODA disbursements are from the Organisation for Economic Co-operation and Development.

Table 6.3. Information and communication technology

Telephone subscribers are subscribers to a main telephone line service, which connects a customer's equipment to the public switched telephone network, or to a cellular telephone service, which uses cellular technology.

Unmet demand is the number of applications for connection to the public switched telephone network that have been held back because of a lack of technical facilities (equipment, lines, and the like) divided by the number of main telephone lines.

Households with own telephone are the percentage of households possessing a telephone.

Average delay for firm in obtaining a mainline phone connection is the average actual delay in days that firms experience when obtaining a telephone connection, measured from the day the establishment applied to the day it received the service or approval.

Internet users are people with access to the worldwide network.

Telephone faults are the total number of reported faults for the year divided by the total number of mainlines in operation multiplied by 100. The definition of fault can vary. Some countries include faulty customer equipment; others distinguish between reported and actual found faults. There is also sometimes a distinction between residential and business lines. Another consideration is the time period: some countries report this indicator on a monthly basis; in these cases data are converted to yearly estimates.

Telephone faults cleared by next working day are the percentage of faults in the public switched telephone network that have been corrected by the end of the next working day.

Price basket for Internet is calculated based on the cheapest available tariff for accessing the Internet 20 hours a month (10 hours peak and 10 hours off-peak). The basket does not include telephone line rental but does include telephone usage charges if applicable. Data are compiled in the national currency and converted to U.S. dollars using the annual average exchange rate.

Cost of 3 minute fixed telephone local phone call during peak hours is the cost of a three-minute local call during peak hours. Local call refers to a call within the same exchange area using the subscriber's own terminal (that is, not from a public telephone).

Cost of 3 minute cellular local call during peak hours is the cost of a three-minute cellular local call during peak hours.

Cost of 3 minute phone call to the United States (US) during peak hours is the cost of a three-minute call to the United States during peak hours.

Residential telephone connection charge is the initial, one-time charge involved in applying for basic telephone service for business purposes. Where charges differ by exchange areas, the charge reported is for the largest urban area.

Business telephone connection charge is the one-off charge involved in applying for business basic telephone service. Where charges differ by exchange area, the charge reported is for the largest urban area.

Mobile cellular connection charge is the initial, one-time charge for a new subscription to a cellular phone service. It includes the price of the subscriber identity module (SIM) card but excludes refundable deposits. It also includes taxes.

Annual investment in fixed telephone service is the annual investment in equipment for fixed telephone service.

Annual investment in mobile communication is the capital investment on equipment for mobile communication networks.

Annual investment in telecommunications is the expenditure associated with acquiring the ownership of telecommunication equipment infrastructure (including supporting land and buildings and intellectual and non-tangible property such as computer software). It includes expenditure on initial installations and on additions to existing installations.

Committed nominal investment in telecommunication projects with private participation is annual committed investment in telecommunication projects with private investment, including projects for fixed or mobile local telephony, domestic long-distance telephony, and international long-distance telephony.

Official development assistance (ODA) gross disbursements for communication are disbursements for communication by bilateral, multilateral, and other donors. Disbursements record the actual international transfer of financial resources or of goods or services valued at the cost of the donor.

Source: Data on telephone subscribers, unmet demand, reported phone faults, and cost of local and cellular calls are from the International Telecommunications Union. Data on households with own telephone are from Demographic and Health Surveys. Data on delays for firms in obtaining a telephone connection are from World Bank Enterprise Surveys (http://rru.worldbank.org/EnterpriseSurveys/). Data on Internet users and pricing, telephone connection charges, and annual investment on telecommunications are from the International Telecommunication Union, World Telecommunication Development Report and database, and World Bank estimates. Data on cost of a call to the United States are from the World Bank's Global Development Finance and World Development Indicator databases. Data on committed nominal investment are from the World Bank's Private Participation in Infrastructure database. Data on ODA disbursements are from the Organisation for Economic Co-operation and Development.

Table 6.4. Energy

Electricity production is measured at the terminals of all alternator sets in a station. In addition to hydropower, coal, oil, gas, and nuclear power generation, it covers generation by geothermal, solar, wind, and tide and wave energy, as well as that from combustible renewables and waste. Production includes the output of electricity plants that are designed to produce electricity only as well as that of combined heat and power plants.

Hydroelectric refers to electricity produced by hydroelectric power plants.

Coal refers to all coal and brown coal, both primary (including hard coal and lignite-brown coal) and derived fuels (including patent fuel, coke oven coke, gas coke, coke oven gas, and blast furnace gas). Peat is also included.

Natural gas refers to natural gas but excludes natural gas liquids.

Nuclear refers to electricity produced by nuclear power plants.

Oil refers to crude oil and petroleum products.

Electric power consumption is the production of power plants and combined heat and power plants, less distribution losses and own use by heat and power plants.

GDP per unit of energy use is nominal GDP in purchasing power parity (PPP) U.S. dollars divided by apparent consumption, which is equal to indigenous production plus imports and stock changes minus exports and fuels supplied to ships and aircraft engaged in international transport.

Solid fuels use is the percentage of the population using solid fuels as opposed to modern fuels. Solid fuels include fuel wood, straw, dung, coal, and charcoal. Modern fuels include electricity, liquefied petroleum gas, natural gas, kerosene, and gasoline. The indicator is based on the main type of fuel used for cooking because cooking occupies the largest share of overall household energy needs. However, many households use more than one type of fuel for cooking and, depending on climatic and geographical conditions, heating with solid fuels can also contribute to indoor air pollution.

Firms identifying electricity as major or very severe obstacle to business operation and growth are the percentage of firms that responded "major" or "very severe" obstacle to the following question: "Please tell us if any of the following issues are a problem for the operation and growth of your business. If an issue (infrastructure, regulation, and permits) poses a problem, please judge its severity as an obstacle on a five-point scale that ranges from 0 = no obstacle to 5 = very severe obstacle."

Average delay for firm in obtaining electrical connection is the average actual delay in days that firms experience when obtaining an electrical connection, measured from the day the establishment applied to the day it received the service or approval.

Electric power transmission and distribution losses are technical and nontechnical losses, including electricity losses due to operation of the system and the delivery of electricity as well as those caused by unmetered supply. This comprises all losses due to transport and distribution of electrical energy and heat.

Electrical outages of firms are the average number of days per year that establishments experienced power outages or surges from the public grid.

Firms that share or own their own generator are the percentage of firms that responded "Yes" to the following question: "Does your establishment own or share a generator?"

Firms using electricity from generator are the percentage of firms using electricity supplied from a generator or generators that the firm owns or shares.

Committed nominal investment in energy projects with private participation is annual committed investment in energy projects with private investment, including projects for electricity generation, transmission, and distribution as well as natural gas transmission and distribution.

Official development assistance (ODA) gross disbursements for energy are disbursements for energy by bilateral, multilateral, and other donors. Disbursements record the actual international transfer of financial resources or of goods or services valued at the cost of the donor.

Source: Data on electricity production are from the International Energy Agency's *Energy Statistics of Non-OECD Countries, Energy Balances of Non-OECD Countries, Energy Statistics of OECD Countries,* and *Energy Balances of OECD Countries.* Data on electric power consumption and PPP GDP per unit of energy use are from the World Bank's World Development Indicators database. Data on solid fuels use are from household survey data, supplemented by World Bank Project Appraisal Documents. Data on firms identifying electricity as a major or very severe obstacle to business operation and growth, delays for firms in obtaining an electrical connection, electrical outages of firms, firms that share or own their own generator, and firms using electricity from generator are from World Bank Enterprise Surveys (http://rru.worldbank.org/EnterpriseSurveys/). Data on transmission and distribution losses are from the World Bank's World Development Indicators database, supplemented by World Bank Project Appraisal Documents. Data on committed nominal investment are from the World Bank's Private Participation in Infrastructure database. Data on ODA disbursements are from the Organisation for Economic Co-operation and Development.

7. Human development

Table 7.1. Education

Youth literacy rate is the percentage of people ages 15–24 who can, with understanding, both read and write a short, simple statement about their everyday life.

Adult literacy rate is the proportion of adults ages 15 and older who can, with understanding, read and write a short, simple statement on their everyday life.

Primary education provides children with basic reading, writing, and mathematics skills along with an elementary understanding of such subjects as history, geography, natural science, social science, art, and music.

Secondary education completes the provision of basic education that began at the primary level and aims to lay the foundations for lifelong learning and human development by offering more subject- or skill-oriented instruction using more specialized teachers.

Tertiary education, whether or not at an advanced research qualification, normally requires, as a minimum condition of admission, the successful completion of education at the secondary level.

Gross enrollment ratio is the ratio of total enrollment, regardless of age, to the population of the age group that officially corresponds to the level of education shown.

Net enrollment ratio is the ratio of children of official school age based on the International Standard Classification of Education 1997 who are enrolled in school to the population of the corresponding official school age.

Student-teacher ratio is the number of students enrolled in school divided by the number of teachers, regardless of their teaching assignment.

Public spending on education is current and capital public expenditure on education plus subsidies to private education at the primary, secondary, and tertiary levels by local, regional, and national government, including municipalities. It excludes household contributions.

Source: United Nations Educational, Scientific, and Cultural Organization Institute for Statistics.

Table 7.2. Health

Life expectancy at birth is the number of years a newborn infant would live if prevailing patterns of mortality at the time of its birth were to remain the same throughout its life. Data are World Bank estimates based on data from the United Nations Population Division, the United Nations Statistics Division, and national statistical offices.

Under-five mortality rate is the probability that a newborn baby will die before reaching age 5, if subject to current age-specific mortality rates. The probability is expressed as a rate per 1,000.

Infant mortality rate is the number of infants dying before reaching one year of age, per 1,000 live births.

Maternal mortality ratio, modeled estimate, is the number of women who die from pregnancy- related causes during pregnancy and childbirth, per 100,000 live births. The data are estimated by a regression model using information on fertility, birth attendants, and HIV prevalence.

Prevalence of HIV is the percentage of people ages 15–49 who are infected with HIV.

Incidence of tuberculosis is the number of tuberculosis cases (pulmonary, smear positive, and extrapulmonary) in a population at a given point in time, per 100,000 people. This indicator is sometimes referred to as "point prevalence." Estimates include cases of tuberculosis among people with HIV.

Clinical malaria cases reported are the sum of cases confirmed by slide examination or rapid diagnostic test and probable and unconfirmed cases (cases that were not tested but treated as malaria). National malaria control programs often collect data on the number of suspected cases, those tested, and those confirmed. Probable or unconfirmed cases are calculated by subtracting the number tested from the number suspected. Not all cases reported as malaria are true malaria cases; most health facilities lack appropriate diagnostic services. The misdiagnosis may have led to under- or overreporting malaria cases and missing diagnosis of other treatable diseases.

Reported malaria deaths are all deaths in health facilities that are attributed to malaria, whether or not confirmed by microscopy or by rapid diagnostic test.

Child immunization rate is the percentage of children ages 12–23 months who received vaccinations before 12 months or at any time before the survey for four diseases—measles and diphtheria, pertussis (whooping cough), and tetanus (DPT). A child is considered adequately immunized against measles after receiving one dose of vaccine and against DPT after receiving three doses.

Stunting is the percentage of children under age 5 whose height for age is more than two standard deviations below the median for the international reference population ages 0–59 months. For children up to age 2 height is measured by recumbent length. For older children height is measured by stature while standing. The reference population adopted by the World Health Organization (WHO) in 1983 is based on children from the United States, who are assumed to be well nourished.

Underweight is the percentage of children under age 5 whose weight for age is more than two standard deviations below the median reference standard for their age as established by the WHO, the U.S. Centers for Disease Control and Prevention, and the U.S. National Center for Health Statistics. Data are based on children under age 3, 4, and 5, depending on the country.

Births attended by skilled health staff are the percentage of deliveries attended by personnel trained to give the necessary supervision, care, and advice to women during pregnancy, labor, and the postpartum period; to conduct deliveries on their own; and to care for newborns.

Contraceptive use is the percentage of women ages 15–49, married or in union, who are practicing, or whose sexual partners are practicing, any form of contraception. Modern methods of contraception include female and male sterilization, oral hormonal pills, the intrauterine device, the male condom, injectables, the implant (including Norplant), vaginal barrier methods, the female condom, and emergency contraception.

Children sleeping under insecticide-treated nets are the percentage of the children under age 5 with access to an insecticide-treated net to prevent malaria.

Tuberculosis cases detected under DOTS are the percentage of estimated new infectious tuberculosis cases detected under DOTS, the internationally recommended tuberculosis control strategy.

Tuberculosis treatment success rate is the percentage of new smear-positive tuberculosis cases registered under DOTS in a given year that successfully completed treatment, whether with bacteriologic evidence of success ("cured") or without ("treatment completed").

Children with fever receiving any antimalarial treatment same or next day are the percentage of children under age 5 in malaria-risk areas with fever being treated with any antimalarial drugs.

Population with sustainable access to an improved water source is the percentage of the population with reasonable access to an adequate amount of water from an improved source, such as a household connection, public standpipe, borehole, protected well or spring, or rainwater collection. Unimproved sources include vendors, tanker trucks, and unprotected wells and springs. Reasonable access is defined as the availability of at least 20 liters a person a day from a source within one kilometer of the dwelling.

Population with sustainable access to improved sanitation is the percentage of the population with at least adequate access to excreta disposal facilities that can effectively prevent human, animal, and insect contact with excreta. Improved facilities range from simple but protected pit latrines to flush toilets with a sewerage connection. The excreta disposal system is considered adequate if it is private or shared (but not public) and if it hygienically separates human excreta from human contact. To be effective, facilities must be correctly constructed and properly maintained.

Physicians are the number of physicians, including generalists and specialists.

Nurses and midwives are professional nurses, auxiliary nurses, enrolled nurses, and other nurses, such as dental nurses and primary care nurses, and professional midwives, auxiliary midwives, and enrolled midwives.

Community workers include various types of community health aides, many with country-specific occupational titles such as community health officers, community health-education workers, family health workers, lady health visitors, and health extension package workers.

Total health expenditure is the sum of public and private health expenditure. It covers the provision of health services (preventive and curative), family planning activities, nutrition activities, and emergency aid designated for health but does not include provision of water and sanitation.

Public health expenditure consists of recurrent and capital spending from government (central and local) budgets, external borrowings and grants (including donations from international agencies and nongovernmental organizations), and social (or compulsory) health insurance funds.

Private health expenditure includes direct household (out-of-pocket) spending, private insurance, charitable donations, and direct service payments by private corporations.

External resources for health are funds or services in kind that are provided by entities not part of the country in question. The resources may come from international organizations, other countries through bilateral arrangements, or foreign nongovernmental organizations. These resources are part of total health expenditure.

Out-of-pocket expenditure is any direct outlay by households, including gratuities and in-kind payments, to health practitioners and suppliers of pharmaceuticals, therapeutic appliances, and other goods and services whose primary intent is to contribute to the restoration or enhancement of the health status of individuals or population groups. It is a part of private health expenditure.

Private prepaid plans are expenditure on health by private insurance institutions. Private insurance enrolment may be contractual or voluntary, and conditions and benefits or basket of benefits are agreed on a voluntary basis between the insurance agent and the beneficiaries. They are thus not controlled by government units for the purpose of providing social benefits to members.

Health expenditure per capita is the total health expenditure. It is the sum of public and private health expenditures as a ratio of total population. It covers the provision of health services (preventive and curative), family planning activities, nutrition activities, and emergency aid designated for health but does not include provision of water and sanitation. Data are in current U.S. dollars.

Source: Data on life expectancy at birth, under-five mortality, infant mortality, maternal mortality, prevalence of HIV, incidence of tuberculosis, child immunization, malnutrition, births attended by skilled health staff, contraceptive use, children sleeping under insecticide-treated nets, tuberculosis cases detected under DOTS, tuberculosis treatment success rate, and children receiving antimalarial drugs are from World Bank staff estimates based on various sources, including census reports, the United Nations Population Division's *World Population Prospects,* national statistical offices, household surveys conducted by national agencies and Macro International, the World Health Organization (WHO), and the United Nations Children's Fund. Data on clinical malaria cases reported and reported malaria deaths are from WHO's *World Malaria Report 2009.* Data on physicians, nurses, and community health workers are from the WHO, Organisation for Economic Co-operation and Development, and TransMONEE, supplemented by country data. Data on access to water and sanitation are from the WHO and United Nations Children's Fund, *Progress on Drinking Water and Sanitation* (2008). Data on health expenditure are from the WHO's *World Health Report* and updates and from the Organisation for Economic Co-operation and Development for its member countries, supplemented by World Bank poverty assessments and country and sector studies, and household surveys conducted by governments or by statistical or international organizations.

8. Agriculture, rural development, and environment

Table 8.1. Rural development

Rural population is the difference between the total population and the urban population.

Rural population density is the rural population divided by the arable land area. Arable land includes land defined by the Food and Agriculture Organization (FAO) as land under temporary crops (double-cropped areas are counted once), temporary meadows for mowing or for pasture, land under market or kitchen gardens, and land temporarily fallow. Land abandoned as a result of shifting cultivation is excluded.

Share of rural population below the national poverty line is the percentage of the rural population living below the national poverty line.

Rural population poverty gap is the mean shortfall from the poverty line (counting the nonpoor as having zero shortfall), expressed as a percentage of the poverty line. This measure reflects the depth of poverty as well as its incidence.

Share of rural population with sustainable access to an improved water source is the percentage of the rural population with reasonable access to an adequate amount of water from an improved source, such as a household connection, public standpipe, borehole, protected well or spring, or rainwater collection. Unimproved sources include vendors, tanker trucks, and unprotected wells and springs. Reasonable access is defined as the availability of at least 20 liters a person a day from a source within one kilometer of the dwelling.

Share of rural population with sustainable access to improved sanitation facilities is the percentage of the rural population with at least adequate access to excreta disposal facilities that can effectively prevent human, animal, and insect contact with excreta. Improved facilities range from simple but protected pit latrines to flush toilets with a sewerage connection. The excreta disposal system is considered adequate if it is private or shared (but not public) and if it hygienically separates human excreta from human contact. To be effective, facilities must be correctly constructed and properly maintained.

Share of rural population with access to transportation is the percentage of the rural population who live within two kilometers of an all-season passable road as a share of the total rural population.

Source: Data on rural population are calculated from urban population shares from the United Nations Population Division's World Urbanization Prospects and from total population figures from the World Bank. Data on rural population density are from the FAO and World Bank population estimates. Data on rural population below the poverty line and rural population poverty gap are national estimates based on population-weighted subgroup estimates from household surveys. Data on access to water and sanitation are from the World Health Organization and United Nations Children's Fund's *Progress on Water and Sanitation* (2008). Data on rural population with access to transport are from the World Bank's Sub -Saharan Africa Transport Policy Program.

Table 8.2. Agriculture

Agriculture value added is the gross output of forestry, hunting, and fishing, as well as cultivation of crops and livestock production (International Standard Industrial Classification [ISIC] revision 3 divisions 1–5) less the value of their intermediate inputs. It is calculated without making deductions for depreciation of fabricated assets or depletion and degradation of natural resources. For countries that report that report national accounts data at producer prices (Benin, the Republic of Congo, Côte d'Ivoire, Gabon, Ghana, Niger, Rwanda, Tanzania, Togo, and Tunisia), gross value added at market prices is used as the denominator. For countries that report national accounts data at basic prices (all other countries), gross value added at factor cost is used as the denominator.

Total agriculture gross production index is total agricultural production relative to the base period 1999–2001.

Crop gross production index is agricultural crop production relative to the base period 1999–2001. It includes all crops except fodder crops.

Livestock gross production index covers meat and milk from all sources, dairy products such as cheese, and eggs, honey, raw silk, wool, and hides and skins.

Food gross production index covers food crops that are considered edible and that contain nutrients. Coffee and tea are excluded because, although edible, they have no nutritive value.

Cereal gross production index covers cereals that are considered edible and that contain nutrients.

Cereal production is crops harvested for dry grain only. Cereal crops harvested for hay or harvested green for food, feed, or silage and those used for grazing are excluded.

Cereal includes wheat, rice, maize, barley, oats, rye, millet, sorghum, buckwheat, and mixed grains.

Agricultural exports and *imports* are expressed in current U.S. dollars at free on board prices. The term agriculture in trade refers to both food and agriculture and does not include forestry and fishery products.

Food exports and *imports* are expressed in current U.S. dollars at free on board prices for exports and cost, insurance, and freight prices for imports.

Permanent cropland is land cultivated with crops that occupy the land for long periods and need not be replanted after each harvest, such as cocoa, coffee, and rubber. It includes land under flowering shrubs, fruit trees, nut trees, and vines, but excludes land under trees grown for wood or timber.

Cereal cropland refers to harvested area, although some countries report only sown or cultivated area.

Irrigated land is areas equipped to provide water to the crops, including areas equipped for full and partial control irrigation, spate irrigation areas, and equipped wetland or inland valley bottoms.

Fertilizer consumption is the aggregate of nitrogenous, phosphate, and potash fertilizers.

Agricultural machinery refers to the number of wheel and crawler tractors (excluding garden tractors) in use in agriculture at the end of the calendar year specified or during the first quarter of the following year. Arable land includes land defined by the Food and Agriculture Organization (FAO) as land under temporary crops (double-cropped areas are counted once), temporary meadows for mowing or for pasture, land under market or kitchen gardens, and land temporarily fallow. Land abandoned as a result of shifting cultivation is excluded.

Agricultural employment includes people who work for a public or private employer and who receive remuneration in wages, salary, commission, tips, piece rates, or pay in kind. Agriculture corresponds to division 1 (International Standard Industrial Classification, ISIC, revision 2) or tabulation categories A and B (ISIC revision 3) and includes hunting, forestry, and fishing.

Agriculture value added per worker is the output of the agricultural sector (ISIC divisions 1–5) less the value of intermediate inputs. Agriculture comprises value added from forestry, hunting, and fishing as well as cultivation of crops and livestock production. Data are in constant 2000 U.S. dollars.

Cereal yield is dry grain only and includes wheat, rice, maize, barley, oats, rye, millet, sorghum, buckwheat, and mixed grains. Production data on cereals relate to crops harvested for dry grain only. Cereal crops harvested for hay or harvested green for food, feed, or silage and those used for grazing are excluded.

Source: Data on agriculture value added are from World Bank country desks. Data on crop, livestock, food, and cereal production, cereal exports and imports, agricultural exports and imports, permanent cropland, cereal cropland, and agricultural machinery are from the FAO. Data on irrigated land are from the FAO's Production Yearbook and data files. Data on fertilizer consumption are from the FAO database for the Fertilizer Yearbook. Data on agricultural employment are from the International Labour Organization. Data on agriculture value added per worker are from World Bank national accounts files and the FAO's Production Yearbook and data files.

Table 8.3. Environment

Forest area is land under natural or planted stands of trees, whether productive or not.

Renewable internal fresh water resources refer to internal renewable resources (internal river flows and groundwater from rainfall) in the country.

Annual fresh water withdrawals refer to total water withdrawals, not counting evaporation losses from storage basins. Withdrawals also include water from desalination plants in countries where they are a significant source. Withdrawals can exceed 100 percent of total renewable resources where extraction from nonrenewable aquifers or desalination plants is considerable or where there is significant water reuse. Withdrawals for agriculture and industry are total withdrawals for irrigation and livestock production and for direct industrial use (including withdrawals for cooling thermoelectric plants). Withdrawals for domestic uses include drinking water, municipal use or supply, and use for public services, commercial establishments, and homes.

Water productivity is calculated as gross domestic product in constant prices divided by annual total water withdrawal. Sectoral water productivity is calculated as annual value added in agriculture or industry divided by water withdrawal in each sector.

Emissions of organic water pollutants are measured in terms of biochemical oxygen demand, which refers to the amount of oxygen that bacteria in water will consume in breaking down waste. This is a standard water-treatment test for the presence of organic pollutants.

Energy production refers to forms of primary energy—petroleum (crude oil, natural gas liquids, and oil from nonconventional sources), natural gas, solid fuels (coal, lignite, and other derived fuels), and combustible renewables and waste—and primary electricity, all converted into oil equivalents.

Energy use refers to use of primary energy before transformation to other end-use fuels, which is equal to indigenous production plus imports and stock changes, minus exports and fuels supplied to ships and aircraft engaged in international transport.

Combustible renewables and waste comprise solid biomass, liquid biomass, biogas, industrial waste, and municipal waste, measured as a percentage of total energy use.

Carbon dioxide emissions are those stemming from the burning of fossil fuels and the manufacture of cement. They include carbon dioxide produced during consumption of solid, liquid, and gas fuels and gas flaring.

Methane emissions, total, are those from human activities such as agriculture and from industrial methane production.

Methane emissions, agricultural, are those from animals, animal waste, rice production, agricultural waste burning (nonenergy, onsite), and savannah burning.

Methane emissions, industrial, are those from the handling, transmission, and combustion of fossil fuels and biofuels.

Nitrous oxide emissions, total, are those from agricultural biomass burning, industrial activities, and livestock management

Nitrous oxide emissions, agricultural, are those produced through fertilizer use (synthetic and animal manure), animal waste management, agricultural waste burning (nonenergy, on-site), and savannah burning.

Nitrous oxide emissions, industrial, are those produced during the manufacturing of adipic acid and nitric acid.

Other greenhouse gas emissions are by-product emissions of hydrofluorocarbons, perfluorocarbons, and sulfur hexafluoride.

Official development assistance (ODA) gross disbursements for forestry are disbursements for forestry by bilateral, multilateral, and other donors. Disbursements record the actual international transfer of financial resources or of goods or services valued at the cost of the donor.

Official development assistance (ODA) gross disbursements for general environment protection are disbursements for general environment protection by bilateral, multilateral, and other donors. Disbursements record the actual international transfer of financial resources or of goods or services valued at the cost of the donor.

Source: Data on forest area and deforestation are from the Food and Agriculture Organization's (FAO) *Global Forest Resources Assessment*. Data on freshwater resources and withdrawals are from the World Resources Institute, supplemented by the FAO's AQUASTAT data. Data on emissions of organic water pollutants are from the World Bank. Data on energy production and use and combustible renewables and waste are from the International Energy Agency. Data on carbon dioxide emissions are from Carbon Dioxide Information Analysis Center, Environmental Sciences Division, Oak Ridge National Laboratory, in the U.S. state of Tennessee. Data on methane emissions, nitrous oxide emissions, and other greenhouse gas emissions are from the International Energy Agency. Data on official development assistance disbursements are from the Organisation for Economic Co-operation and Development.

Table 8.4. Fossil fuel emissions

Carbon dioxide emissions are those stemming from the burning of fossil fuels and the manufacture of cement. They include carbon dioxide produced during consumption of solid, liquid, and gas fuels and gas flaring.

Carbon dioxide emissions per capita are carbon dioxide emissions divided by midyear population.

Fossil fuel is any hydrocarbon deposit that can be burned for heat or power, such as petroleum, coal, and natural gas.

Total carbon dioxide emissions from fossil fuels is the sum of all fossil fuel emissions (solid fuel consumption, liquid fuel consumption, gas fuel consumption, gas flaring, and cement production).

Carbon dioxide emissions from solid fuel consumption refer mainly to emissions from use of coal as an energy source and from secondary fuels derived from hard and soft coal (such as coke-oven coke).

Carbon dioxide emissions from liquid fuel consumption refer to emissions from use of crude petroleum and natural gas liquids as an energy source, and secondary fuels derived from oil (such as jet fuel).

Carbon dioxide emissions from gas fuel consumption refer mainly to emissions from use of natural gas as an energy source and from secondary fuels derived from natural gas (such as blast furnace gas).

Carbon dioxide emissions from gas flaring refer mainly to emissions from gas flaring activities.

Carbon dioxide emissions from cement production refer mainly to emissions during cement production. Cement production is a multistep process, and carbon dioxide is actually released from klinker production during the cement production process.

Source: Data on carbon dioxide emissions are from Carbon Dioxide Information Analysis Center, Environmental Sciences Division, Oak Ridge National Laboratory, in the U.S. state of Tennessee.

9. Labor, migration, and population

TABLE 9.1. LABOR FORCE PARTICIPATION

Labor force is people ages 15 and older who meet the International Labour Organization (ILO) definition of the economically active population. It includes both the employed and the unemployed. While national practices vary in the treatment of such groups as the armed forces and seasonal or part-time workers, the labor force generally includes the armed forces, the unemployed, and first-time job seekers, but excludes homemakers and other unpaid caregivers and workers in the informal sector.

Participation rate is the percentage of the population of the specified age group that is economically active, that is, all people who supply labor for the production of goods and services during a specified period.

Source: ILO's Estimates and Projections of the Economically Active Population database..

TABLE 9.2. LABOR FORCE COMPOSITION

Agriculture corresponds to division 1 (International Standard Industrial Classification, ISIC, revision 2) or tabulation categories A and B (ISIC revision 3) and includes hunting, forestry, and fishing.

Industry corresponds to divisions 2–5 (ISIC revision 2) or tabulation categories C–F (ISIC revision 3) and includes mining and quarrying (including oil production), manufacturing, construction, and public utilities (electricity, gas, and water).

Services correspond to divisions 6–9 (ISIC revision 2) or tabulation categories G–P (ISIC revision 3) and include wholesale and retail trade and restaurants and hotels; transport, storage, and communications; financing, insurance, real estate, and business services; and community, social, and personal services.

Wage and salaried workers are workers who hold the type of jobs defined as paid employment jobs, where incumbents hold explicit (written or oral) or implicit employment contracts that give them a basic remuneration that is not directly dependent on the revenue of the unit for which they work.

Self-employed workers are self-employed workers with employees (employers), self-employed workers with without employees (own-account workers), and members of producer cooperatives. Although the contributing family workers category is technically part of the self-employed according to the classification used by the International Labour Organization (ILO), and could therefore be combined with the other self-employed categories to derive the total self-employed, they are reported here as a separate category in order to emphasize the difference between the two statuses, since the socioeconomic implications associated with each status can be significantly varied. This practice follows that of the ILO's Key Indicators of the Labour Market.

Contributing family workers (unpaid workers) are workers who hold self-employment jobs as own-account workers in a market-oriented establishment operated by a related person living in the same household.

Source: International Labour Organization, Key Indicators of the Labour Market database.

TABLE 9.3. UNEMPLOYMENT

Unemployment is the share of the labor force of the specified subgroup without work but available for and seeking employment.

Primary education provides children with basic reading, writing, and mathematics skills along with an elementary understanding of such subjects as history, geography, natural science, social science, art, and music.

Secondary education completes the provision of basic education that began at the primary level and aims to lay the foundations for lifelong learning and human development by offering more subject- or skill-oriented instruction using more specialized teachers.

Tertiary education, whether or not at an advanced research qualification, normally requires, as a minimum condition of admission, the successful completion of education at the secondary level.

Source: International Labour Organization, Key Indicators of the Labour Market database.

Table 9.4. Migration and population

Migrant stock is the number of people born in a country other than that in which they live. It includes refugees.

Net migration is the net average annual number of migrants during the period, that is, the annual number of immigrants less the annual number of emigrants, including both citizens and noncitizens. Data are five-year estimates.

Workers remittances, received, comprise current transfers by migrant workers and wages and salaries by nonresident workers.

Migrant remittance flows are the sum of worker's remittances, compensation of employees, and migrants' transfers, as recorded in the International Monetary Fund's *Balance of Payments.*

Population is total population based on the de facto definition of population, which counts all residents regardless of legal status or citizenship, except for refugees not permanently settled in the country of asylum, who are generally considered part of the population of their country of origin. The values shown are midyear estimates.

Fertility rate is the number of children that would be born to a woman if she were to live to the end of her childbearing years and bear children in accordance with current age-specific fertility rates.

Age composition refers to the percentage of the total population that is in specific age groups.

Dependency ratio is the ratio of dependents—people younger than 15 or older than 64—to the working-age population—those ages 15–64.

Rural population is calculated as the difference between the total population and the urban population.

Urban population is midyear population of areas defined as urban in each country.

Source: Data on migration and population are from the World Bank's World Development Indicators database. Data on workers remittances and migrant remittance flows are from World Bank staff estimates based on the International Monetary Fund's *Balance of Payments Statistics Yearbook 2008.*

10. HIV/AIDS

Table 10.1. HIV/AIDS

Estimated number of people living with HIV/AIDS is the number of people in the relevant age group living with HIV.

Estimated HIV prevalence rate is the percentage of the population of the relevant age subgroup who are infected with HIV. Depending on the reliability of the data available, there may be more or less uncertainty surrounding each estimate. Therefore, plausible bounds have been presented for each subgroup rate (low and high estimate).

Deaths of adults and children due to HIV/AIDS are the estimated number of adults and children that have died in a specific year based on the modeling of HIV surveillance data using standard and appropriate tools.

AIDS orphans are the estimated number of children who have lost their mother or both parents to AIDS before age 17 since the epidemic began in 1990. Some of the orphaned children included in this cumulative total are no longer alive; others are no longer under age 17.

HIV-positive pregnant women receiving antiretrovirals to reduce the risk of mother-to-child transmission are the number of pregnant women infected with HIV who received antiretrovirals during the last 12 months to reduce the risk of mother-to-child transmission.

Share of HIV-positive pregnant women receiving antiretrovirals, World Health Organization/Joint United Nations Programme on HIV/AIDS (WHO/UNAIDS) methodology, is the percentage of pregnant women infected with HIV who received antiretrovirals to reduce the risk of mother-to-child transmission divided by the total number of infected pregnant women infected with HIV in the last 12 months. The WHO/UNAIDS methodology may differ from country methodologies.

Official development assistance (ODA) gross disbursements for social mitigation of HIV/AIDS are spending on special programs to address the consequences of HIV/AIDS, such as social, legal, and economic assistance to people living with HIV/AIDS (including food security and employment); spending on support to vulnerable groups and children orphaned by HIV/AIDS; and spending on human rights advocacy for people affected by HIV/AIDS.

Official development assistance (ODA) gross disbursements for sexually transmitted diseases (STDs) control, including HIV/AIDS, are spending on all activities related to STDs and HIV/AIDS control, such as information, education, and communication; testing; prevention; and treatment care.

Source: Data on number of people living with HIV/AIDS, HIV prevalence rate, deaths due to HIV/AIDS, AIDS orphans, and HIV-positive pregnant women receiving antiretrovirals are from UNAIDS and WHO's *Report on the Global AIDS Epidemic.* A more detailed explanation of methods and assumptions can be found on the UNAIDS reference group on estimates, modeling, and projections website (www.unaids.org/en/KnowledgeCentre/HIVData/Epidemiology/) and in a series of papers published in *Sexually Transmitted Infections,* "Improved Methods and Tools for HIV/AIDS Estimates and Projections," 2008, 84(Suppl I), 2006, 82(Suppl III), and 2004, 80(Suppl I). Data on official development assistance disbursements are from the Organisation for Economic Co-operation and Development.

11. Malaria

Table 11.1. Malaria

Population is total population based on the de facto definition of population, which counts all residents regardless of legal status or citizenship, except for refugees not permanently settled in the country of asylum, who are generally considered part of the population of their country of origin. The values shown are midyear estimates.

Clinical malaria cases reported are the sum of cases confirmed by slide examination or rapid diagnostic test and probable and unconfirmed cases (cases that were not tested but treated as malaria). National malaria control programs often collect data on the number of suspected cases, those tested, and those confirmed. Probable or unconfirmed cases are calculated by subtracting the number tested from the number suspected. Not all cases reported as malaria are true malaria cases; most health facilities lack appropriate diagnostic services. The misdiagnosis may have led to under- or overreporting malaria cases and missing diagnosis of other treatable diseases.

Reported malaria deaths are all deaths in health facilities that are attributed to malaria, whether or not confirmed by microscopy or by rapid diagnostic test.

Under-five mortality rate is the probability that a newborn baby will die before reaching age 5, if subject to current age-specific mortality rates. The probability is expressed as a rate per 1,000.

Children sleeping under insecticide-treated nets is the percentage of children under age 5 with access to an insecticide-treated net to prevent malaria.

Children with fever receiving any antimalarial treatment same or next day are the percentage of children under age 5 in malaria-risk areas with fever being treated with any antimalarial drugs.

Children with fever receiving any antimalarial treatment any time are the percentage of children under age 5 in malaria-risk areas with fever being treated with any antimalarial drugs.

Pregnant women receiving two doses of intermittent preventive treatment are the number of pregnant women who receive at least two preventive treatment doses of an effective antimalarial drug during routine antenatal clinic visits. This approach has been shown to be safe, inexpensive, and effective.

Source: Data on population are from the World Bank's World Development Indicators database. Data on clinical cases of malaria reported and reported malaria deaths are from the World Health Organization's (WHO) *World Malaria Report 2009.* Data on children with fever receiving antimalarial drugs, and pregnant women receiving two doses of intermittent preventive treatment are from Demographic Health Surveys,

Multiple Indicator Cluster Surveys, and national statistical offices. Data on deaths due to malaria are from the United Nations Statistics Division based on WHO estimates. Data on under-five mortality are harmonized estimates of the WHO, United Nations Children's Fund, and the World Bank, based mainly on household surveys, censuses, and vital registration, supplemented by World Bank estimates based on household surveys and vital registration. Data on insecticide-treated bednet use are from Demographic and Health Surveys and Multiple Indicator Cluster Surveys.

12. Capable states and partnership

TABLE 12.1. AID AND DEBT RELIEF

Official development assistance is flows to developing countries and multilateral institutions provided by official agencies, including state and local governments, or by their executive agencies, that are administered with the promotion of the economic development and welfare of developing countries as their main objective and that are concessional in character and convey a grant element of at least 25 percent.

Net official development assistance (ODA) from all donors is net ODA from the Organisation for Economic Co-operation and Development's (OECD), Development Assistance Committee (DAC), non-DAC bilateral (Organization of Petroleum Exporting Countries [OPEC], the former Council for Mutual Economic Assistance [CMEA] countries, and China [OECD data]), and multilateral donors. OPEC countries are Algeria, Iran, Iraq, Kuwait, Libya, Nigeria, Qatar, Saudi Arabia, the United Arab Emirates, and Venezuela. The former CMEA countries are Bulgaria, Czechoslovakia, the former German Democratic Republic, Hungary, Poland, Romania, and the former Soviet Union).

Net official development assistance (ODA) from DAC donors is net ODA from OECD's DAC donors, which include Australia, Austria, Belgium, Canada, Denmark, Finland, France, Germany, Greece, Ireland, Italy, Japan, Luxembourg, the Netherlands, New Zealand, Norway, Portugal, Spain, Sweden, Switzerland, the United Kingdom, and the United States.

Net official development assistance (ODA) from non-DAC donors is net ODA from OECD's non-DAC donors, which include the Czech Republic, Hungary, Iceland, Israel, the Republic of Korea, Kuwait, Poland, Saudi Arabia, the Slovak Republic, Taiwan (China), Thailand, Turkey, the United Arab Emirates, and other donors.

Net official development assistance (ODA) from multilateral donors is net ODA from multilateral sources, such as the African Development Fund, the European Development Fund for the Commission of the European Communities, the International Development Association, the International Fund for Agricultural Development, Arab and OPEC financed multilateral agencies, and UN programs and agencies. Aid flows from the International Monetary Fund's (IMF) Trust Fund and Structural Adjustment Facility are also included. UN programs and agencies include the United Nations Technical Assistance Programme, the United Nations Development Programme, the United Nations Office of the High Commissioner for Refugees, the United Nations Children's Fund, and the World Food Programme. Arab and OPEC financed multilateral agencies include the Arab Bank for Economic Development in Africa, the Arab Fund for Economic and Social Development, the Islamic Development Bank, the OPEC Fund for International Development, the Arab Authority for Agricultural Investment and Development, the Arab Fund for Technical Assistance to African and Arab Countries, and the Islamic Solidarity Fund.

Net private official development assistance (ODA) is private ODA transactions broken, which comprise direct investment, portfolio investment, and export credits (net). Private transactions are undertaken by firms and individuals resident in the reporting country. Portfolio investment corresponds to bonds and equities. Inflows into emerging countries' stocks markets, are, however, heavily understated. Accordingly, the coverage of portfolio investment differs in these regards from the coverage of bank claims, which include export credit lending by banks. The bank claims data represent the net change in bank claims after adjusting for exchange rate changes and are therefore a proxy for net flow data but are not themselves a net flow figure. They differ in two further regards from other OECD data. First, they relate to loans by banks resident in countries that report quarterly to the

Bank for International Settlements. Second, no adjustment has been made to exclude short-term claims.

Net official development assistance (ODA) as a share of gross domestic product (GDP) is calculated by dividing the nominal total net ODA from all donors by nominal GDP. For a given level of aid flows, devaluation of a recipient's currency may inflate the ratios shown in the table. Thus, trends for a given country and comparisons across countries that have implemented different exchange rate policies should be interpreted carefully.

Net official development assistance (ODA) per capita is calculated by dividing the nominal total net ODA (net disbursements of loans and grants from all official sources on concessional financial terms) by midyear population. These ratios offer some indication of the importance of aid flows in sustaining per capita income and consumption levels, although exchange rate fluctuations, the actual rise of aid flows, and other factors vary across countries and over time.

Net official development assistance (ODA) as a share of gross capital formation is calculated by dividing the nominal total net ODA by gross capital formation. These data highlight the relative importance of the indicated aid flows in maintaining and increasing investment in these economies. The same caveats mentioned above apply to their interpretation. Furthermore, aid flows do not exclusively finance investment (for example, food aid finances consumption), and the share of aid going to investment varies across countries.

Net official development assistance (ODA) as a share of imports of goods and services is calculated by dividing nominal total net ODA by imports of goods and services.

Net official development assistance (ODA) as a share of central government expenditure is calculated by dividing nominal total net ODA by central government expenditure.

Cereal food aid shipments are transfers of food commodities (food aid received) from donor to recipient countries on a total-grant basis or on highly concessional terms. Processed and blended cereals are converted into their grain equivalent by applying the conversion factors included in the Rule of Procedures under the 1999 Food Aid Convention to facilitate comparisons between deliveries of different commodities. Deliveries of food aid refer to quantities of commodities that actually reached the recipient country during a given period. For cereals the period refers to July–June, beginning in the year shown.

Heavily Indebted Poor Countries (HIPC) Debt Initiative decision point is the date at which a HIPC with an established track record of good performance under adjustment programs supported by the International Monetary Fund and the World Bank commits to undertake additional reforms and to develop and implement a poverty reduction strategy.

HIPC Debt Initiative completion point is the date at which the country successfully completes the key structural reforms agreed on at the decision point, including developing and implementing its poverty reduction strategy. The country then receives the bulk of debt relief under the HIPC Initiative without further policy conditions.

Debt service relief committed is the amount of debt service relief, calculated at the decision point, that will allow the country to achieve debt sustainability at the completion point.

Source: Data on net official development assistance are from the Organisation for Economic Co-operation and Development. Data on food aid shipments are based on data compiled by from the Food and Agriculture Organization based on information from the World Food Programme.

Table 12.2. Status of Paris Declaration indicators

The Paris Declaration is the outcome of the 2005 Paris High-Level Forum on Aid Effectiveness, where 60 partner countries, 30 donor countries, and 30 development agencies committed to specific actions to further country ownership, harmonization, alignment, managing for development results, and mutual accountability for the use of aid. Participants agreed on 12 indicators. These indicators include good national development strategies, reliable country systems for procurement and public financial management, the development and use of results frameworks, and mutual assessment of progress. Qualitative desk reviews by the Organisation for Economic Co-operation and Development's Development Assistance Committee and the World Bank and a survey questionnaire for governments and donors are used to calculate the indicators.

PDI-1 Operational national development strategies are the extent to which a country has an operational development strategy to guide its aid coordination effort and overall development. The score is based on the World Bank's 2005 Comprehensive Development Framework Progress Report. An operational strategy calls for a coherent long-term strategy derived from it; specific targets serving a holistic, balanced, and well sequenced development strategy; and capacity and resources for its implementation.

PDI-2a Reliable public financial management is the World Bank's annual Country Policy and Institutional Assessment rating for the quality of public financial management. Measured on a scale of 1 (worst) to 5 (best), its focus is on how much existing systems adhere to broadly accepted good practices and whether a reform program is in place to promote improved practices.

PDI-2b Reliable country procurement systems measure developing countries' procurement systems. Donors use national procurement procedures when the funds they provide for the implementation of projects and programs are managed according to the national procurement procedures as they were established in the general legislation and implemented by government. The use of national procurement procedures means that donors do not make additional, or special, requirements on governments for the procurement of works, goods, and services. (Where weaknesses in national procurement systems have been identified, donors may work with partner countries to improve the efficiency, economy, and transparency of their implementation). The objective of this indicator is to measure and encourage improvements in developing countries' procurement systems.

PDI-3 Government budget estimates comprehensive and realistic are the percentage of aid that is accurately recorded in the national budget, thereby allowing scrutiny by parliaments.

PDI-4 Technical assistance aligned and coordinated with country programs is the percentage of technical cooperation that is free standing and embedded and that respects ownership (partner countries exercise effective leadership over their capacity development programs), alignment (technical cooperation in support of capacity development aligns with countries' development objectives and strategies), and harmonization (when more than one donor is involved in supporting partner-led capacity development, donors coordinate their activities and contributions).

PDI-5a and *5b Aid for government sectors uses country public financial management* and *procurement systems* is the percentage of donors that use country, rather than donor, systems for managing aid disbursement.

PDI-6 Project implementation units parallel to country structures is the number of parallel project implementation units, which refers to units created outside existing country institutional structures. The survey guidance distinguishes between project implementation units and executing agencies and describes three typical features of parallel project implementation units: they are accountable to external funding agencies rather than to country implementing agencies (ministries, departments, agencies, and the like), most of the professional staff is appointed by the donor, and the personnel salaries often exceed those of civil service personnel. Interpretation of the Paris Declaration survey question on this subject was controversial in a number of countries. It is unclear whether within countries all donors applied the same criteria with the same degree of rigor or that across countries the same standards were used. In several cases the descriptive part of the survey results indicates that some donors applied a legalistic criterion of accountability to the formal executing agency, whereas the national coordinator and other donors would have preferred greater recognition of the substantive reality of accountability to the donor. Some respondents may have confused the definitional question (Is the unit "parallel"?) with the aid management question (Is the parallelism justified in terms of the developmental benefits and costs?).

PDI-7 Aid disbursements on schedule and recorded by government are the percentage of funds that are disbursed within the year they are scheduled and accurately recorded by partner authorities.

PDI-8 Bilateral aid that is untied is the percentage of aid that is untied. Tied aid is aid provided on the condition that the recipient uses it to purchase goods and services from suppliers based in the donor country.

PDI-9 Aid provided in the framework of program-based approaches is the percentage of development cooperation that is based on the principles of coordinated support for a locally owned program of development, such as a national development strategy, a sector program, a thematic program or a program of a specific organization. Program-based approaches share the following features: leadership by the host country or organization, a single comprehensive program and budget framework, a formalized process for donor coordination and harmonization of donor procedures for reporting, budgeting, financial management, and procurement, and efforts to increase the use of local systems for program design and implementation, financial management, monitoring, and evaluation.

PDI-10a Donor missions coordinated are the percentage of missions undertaken jointly by two or more donors and missions undertaken by one donor on behalf of another (delegated cooperation).

PDI-10b Country analysis coordinated is the percentage of country analytic work that is undertaken by one or more donors jointly, undertaken by one donor on behalf of another donor (including work undertaken by one and used by another when it is co-financed and formally acknowledged in official documentation, and undertaken with substantive involvement from government.

PDI-11 Existence of a monitorable performance assessment framework measures the extent to which the country has realized its commitment to establishing performance frameworks. The indicator relies on the scorings of the 2005 Comprehensive Development Framework Progress Report and considers three criteria: the quality of development information, stakeholder access to development information, and coordinated country-level monitoring and evaluation. The assessments therefore reflect both the extent to which sound data on development outputs, outcomes and impacts are collected, and various aspects of the way information is used, disseminated among stakeholders, and fed back into policy.

PDI-12 Existence of a mutual accountability review indicates whether there is a mechanism for mutual review of progress on aid effectiveness commitments. This is an important innovation of the Paris Declaration because it develops the idea that aid is more effective when both donors and partner governments are accountable to their constituents for the use of resources to achieve development results and when they are accountable to each other. The specific focus is mutual accountability for the implementation of the partnership commitments included in the Paris Declaration and any local agreements on enhancing aid effectiveness.

Source: 2008 Survey on Monitoring the Paris Declaration: Making Aid More Effective by 2010.

TABLE 12.3. CAPABLE STATES

Firms that believe the court system is fair, impartial, and uncorrupt are the percentage of firms that believe the court system is fair, impartial, and uncorrupted.

Corruption is the percentage of firms identifying corruption as a major constraint.

Crime, theft, and disorder are the percentage of firms identifying crime, theft, and disorder as a major constraint to current operation.

Number of procedures to enforce a contract is the number of independent actions, mandated by law or courts, that demand interaction between the parties of a contract or between them and the judge or court officer.

Time required to enforce a contract is the number of calendar days from the filing of the lawsuit in court until the final determination and, in appropriate cases, payment.

Cost to enforce a contract is court and attorney fees, where the use of attorneys is mandatory or common, or the cost of an administrative debt recovery procedure, expressed as a percentage of the debt value.

Protecting investors disclosure index measures the degree to which investors are protected through disclosure of ownership and financial information. Higher values indicate more disclosure.

Director liability index measures a plaintiff's ability to hold directors of firms liable for damages to the company. Higher values indicate greater liability.

Shareholder suits index measures shareholders' ability to sue officers and directors for misconduct. Higher values indicate greater power for shareholders to challenge transactions.

Investor protection index measures the degree to which investors are protected through disclosure of ownership and financial information regulations. Higher values indicate better protection.

Number of tax payments is the number of taxes paid by businesses, including electronic filing. The tax is counted as paid once a year even if payments are more frequent.

Time required to prepare, file, and pay taxes is the number of hours it takes to prepare, file, and pay (or withhold) three major types of taxes: the corporate income tax, the value added or sales tax, and labor taxes, including payroll taxes and social security contributions.

Total tax rate is the total amount of taxes payable by the business (except for labor taxes) after accounting for deductions and exemptions as a percentage of gross profit. For further details on the method used for assessing the total tax payable, see the World Bank's Doing Business 2006.

Extractive Industries Transparency Initiative (EITI) status refers to a country's implementation status for the EITI, a multistakeholder approach to increasing governance and transparency in extractive industries. It includes civil society, the private sector, and government and requires a work plan with timeline and budget to ensure sustainability, independent audit of payments and disclosure of revenues, publication of results in a publicly accessible manner, and an approach that covers all companies and government agencies. The EITI supports improved governance in resource-rich countries through the verification and full publication of company payments and government revenues from oil, gas, and mining. *Intent to implement* indicates that a country intends to implement the EITI but have not yet met the four initial requirements to join: an unequivocal public statement of its intention to implement the EITI, a commitment to work with civil society and companies on EITI implementation, a senior official appointed to lead EITI implementation, and a widely distributed, fully costed work plan with measurable targets, a timetable for implementation, and an assessment of government, private sector, and civil society capacity constraints. *Candidate* indicates that a country has met the four initial requirements to join the EITI and has begun a range of activities to strengthen revenue transparency, as documented in the country's workplan. Once a country has become a EITI candidate, it has two years to be validated as compliant. *Compliant* indicates that a country has successfully undergone validation, an independent assessment of a country's progress toward the EITI goals by the EITI International Board. Validation is based on the country's work plan, the EITI validation grid and indicator assessment tools, and company forms that detail private companies' extractive industry activities; it provides guidance for countries' future activity related to EITI compliance. Countries must undergo validation every five years or at the request of the EITI International Board.

Source: Data on investment climate constraints to firms are based on enterprise surveys conducted by the World Bank and its partners during 2001–05 (http://rru.worldbank.org/EnterpriseSurveys). Data on enforcing contracts, protecting investors, and regulation and tax administration are from the World Bank's Doing Business project (http://rru.worldbank.org/DoingBusiness/). Data on corruption perceptions index are from Transparency International (www.transparency.org/policy_research/surveys_indices/cpi). Data on the EITI are from the EITI website, www.eitransparency.org.

Table 12.4. Governance and anti-corruption indicators

Voice and accountability measure the extent to which a country's citizens are able to participate in selecting their government and to enjoy freedom of expression, freedom of association, and a free media.

Political stability and absence of violence measure the perceptions of the likelihood that the government will be destabilized or overthrown by unconstitutional or violent means, including domestic violence or terrorism.

Government effectiveness measures the quality of public services, the quality and degree of independence from political pressures of the civil service, the quality of policy formulation and implementation, and the credibility of the government's commitment to such policies.

Regulatory quality measures the ability of the government to formulate and implement sound policies and regulations that permit and promote private sector development.

Rule of law measures the extent to which agents have confidence in and abide by the rules of society, in particular the quality of contract enforcement, the police, and the courts, as well as the likelihood of crime and violence.

Control of corruption measures the extent to which public power is exercised for private gain, including petty and grand forms of corruption, as well as "capture" of the state by elites and private interests.

Expected to pay informal payment to public officials to get things done is the percentage of firms that expected to make informal payments or give gifts to public officials to "get things done" with regard to customs, taxes, licenses, regulations, services, and the like.

Expected to give gifts to obtain an operating license is the percentage of firms that expected to give gifts or an informal payment to get an operating license.

Expected to give gifts in meetings with tax officials is the percentage of firms that answered yes to the question "Was a gift or informal payment expected or requested during a meeting with tax officials?"

Expected to give gifts to secure a government contract is the percentage of firms that expected to make informal payments or give gifts to public officials to secure a government contract.

Share of firms identifying control of corruption as a major constraint measures the extent to which public power is exercised for private gain, including petty and grand forms of corruption, as well as "capture" of the state by elites and private interests.

Mean corruption perceptions index score is the country's score in Transparency International's annual corruption perceptions index, which ranks more than 150 countries in terms of perceived levels of corruption, as determined by expert assessments and opinion surveys.

Open budget index overall score is the country's score on a subset of 91 questions from the open budget survey. The questions focus on the public availability of eight key budget documents (with a particular emphasis on the executive's budget proposal) and the information they contain. The open budget index is calculated based on detailed questionnaires completed by local experts in 59 participating countries from every continent. In 2008, based on inputs received from researchers and extensive in-house reviews, the International Budget Partnership made three changes in its methodology. The first change concerns the timing of the release of the eight key budget documents assessed by the survey. The second is the inclusion of the enacted budget in calculating country scores for the index. The third is revisions to the answers of a few questions used to assess Brazil and Nigeria.

Source: Data on governance indicators are from the World Bank Institute's Worldwide Governance Indicators database, which relies on 33 sources, including surveys of enterprises and citizens, and expert polls, gathered from 30 organizations around the world. Data on corruption perceptions index scores are from Transparency International (http://www.transparency.org/policy_research/surveys_indices/cpi/2009). Data on the open budget index are from www.openbudgetindex.org.

TABLE 12.5. COUNTRY POLICY AND INSTITUTIONAL ASSESSMENT RATINGS

The Country Policy and Institutional Assessment (CPIA) assesses the quality of a country's present policy and institutional framework. "Quality" means how conducive that framework is to fostering sustainable, poverty-reducing growth and the effective use of development assistance. The CPIA is conducted annually for all International Bank for Reconstruction and Development and International Development Association borrowers and has evolved into a set of criteria grouped into four clusters with 16 criteria that reflect a balance between ensuring that all key factors that foster pro-poor growth and poverty alleviation are captured, without overly burdening the evaluation process.

- Economic management
    - *Macroeconomic management* assesses the quality of the monetary, exchange rate, and aggregate demand policy framework.
    - *Fiscal policy* assesses the short- and medium-term sustainability of fiscal policy (taking into account monetary and exchange rate policy and the sustainability of the public debt) and its impact on growth.

- *Debt policy* assesses whether the debt management strategy is conducive to minimize budgetary risks and ensure long-term debt sustainability.
- Structural policies
  - *Trade* assesses how the policy framework fosters trade in goods. It covers two areas: trade regime restrictiveness—which focuses on the height of tariffs barriers, the extent to which nontariff barriers are used, the transparency and predictability of the trade regime, and customs and trade facilitation—which includes the extent to which the customs service is free of corruption, relies on risk management, processes duty collections and refunds promptly, and operates transparently.
  - *Financial sector* assesses the structure of the financial sector and the policies and regulations that affect it. It covers three dimensions: financial stability; the sector's efficiency, depth, and resource mobilization strength; and access to financial services.
  - *Business regulatory environment* assesses the extent to which the legal, regulatory, and policy environment helps or hinders private business in investing, creating jobs, and becoming more productive. The emphasis is on direct regulations of business activity and regulation of goods and factor markets. It measures three subcomponents: regulations affecting entry, exit, and competition; regulations of ongoing business operations; and regulations of factor markets (labor and land).
- Policies for social inclusion and equity
  - *Gender equality* assesses the extent to which the country has enacted and put in place institutions and programs to enforce laws and policies that promote equal access for men and women to human capital development, and to productive and economic resources and that give men and women equal status and protection under the law.
  - *Equity of public resource use* assesses the extent to which the pattern of public expenditures and revenue collection affects the poor and is consistent with national poverty reduction priorities. The assessment of the consistency of government spending with the poverty reduction priorities takes into account the extent to which individuals, groups, or localities that are poor, vulnerable, or have unequal access to services and opportunities are identified; a national development strategy with explicit interventions to assist those individuals, groups, and localities has been adopted; and the composition and incidence of public expenditures are tracked systematically and their results fed back into subsequent resource allocation decisions. The assessment of the revenue collection dimension takes into account the incidence of major taxes—for example, whether they are progressive or regressive—and their alignment with the poverty reduction priorities. When relevant, expenditure and revenue collection trends at the national and sub-national levels should be considered. The expenditure component receives two-thirds of the weight in computing the overall rating.
  - *Building human resources* assesses the national policies and public and private sector service delivery that affect access to and quality of health and nutrition services, including: population and reproductive health; education, early childhood development, and training and literacy programs; and prevention and treatment of HIV/AIDS, tuberculosis, and malaria.
  - *Social protection and labor* assess government policies in the area of social protection and labor market regulation, which reduce the risk of becoming poor, assist those who are poor to better manage further risks, and ensure a minimal level of welfare to all people. Interventions

include social safety net programs, pension and old age savings programs, protection of basic labor standards, regulations to reduce segmentation and inequity in labor markets, active labor market programs (such as public works or job training), and community driven initiatives. In interpreting the guidelines it is important to take into account the size of the economy and its level of development.

  - *Policies and institutions for environmental sustainability* assess the extent to which environmental policies foster the protection and sustainable use of natural resources and the management of pollution. Assessment of environmental sustainability requires multidimensional criteria (that is, for air, water, waste, conservation management, coastal zones management, and natural resources management).

- Public sector management and institutions
  - *Property rights and rule-based governance* assess the extent to which private economic activity is facilitated by an effective legal system and rule-based governance structure in which property and contract rights are reliably respected and enforced. Three dimensions are rated separately: legal basis for secure property and contract rights; predictability, transparency, and impartiality of laws and regulations affecting economic activity, and their enforcement by the legal and judicial system; and crime and violence as an impediment to economic activity.
  - *Quality of budgetary and financial management* assesses the extent to which there is a comprehensive and credible budget, linked to policy priorities; effective financial management systems to ensure that the budget is implemented as intended in a controlled and predictable way; and timely and accurate accounting and fiscal reporting, including timely and audited public accounts and effective arrangements for follow-up.
  - *Efficiency of revenue mobilization* assesses the overall pattern of revenue mobilization—not only the tax structure as it exists on paper, but revenue from all sources as they are actually collected.
  - *Quality of public administration* assesses the extent to which civilian central government staffs (including teachers, health workers, and police) are structured to design and implement government policy and deliver services effectively. Civilian central government staffs include the central executive together with all other ministries and administrative departments, including autonomous agencies. It excludes the armed forces, state-owned enterprises, and subnational government.
  - *Transparency, accountability, and corruption in public sector* assess the extent to which the executive branch can be held accountable for its use of funds and the results of its actions by the electorate and by the legislature and judiciary, and the extent to which public employees within the executive are required to account for the use of resources, administrative decisions, and results obtained. Both levels of accountability are enhanced by transparency in decision-making, public audit institutions, access to relevant and timely information, and public and media scrutiny.

Source: World Bank Group's CPIA database (www.worldbank.org/ida).

Table 12.6. Polity Indicators

Combined polity score is computed by subtracting the institutionalized autocracy score from the institutionalized democracy score; the resulting unified polity scale ranges from +10 (strongly democratic) to −10 (strongly autocratic).

Institutionalized democracy is conceived as three essential, interdependent elements. One is the presence of institutions and procedures through which citizens can express effective preferences about alternative policies and leaders. Second is the existence of institutionalized constraints on the exercise of power by the executive. Third is the guarantee of civil liberties to all citizens in their daily lives and in acts of political participation. Other aspects of plural democracy, such as the rule of law, systems of checks and balances, freedom of the press, and so on are means to, or specific manifestations of, these general principles. Coded data on civil liberties are not included. This is an additive eleven-point scale (0–10). The operational indicator of democracy is derived from codings of the competitiveness of political participation using some weights.

Institutionalized autocracy is a pejorative term for some very diverse kinds of political systems whose common properties are a lack of regularized political competition and concern for political freedoms. The term *autocracy* is used and defined operationally in terms of the presence of a distinctive set of political characteristics. In mature form autocracies sharply restrict or suppress competitive political participation. Their chief executives are chosen in a regularized process of selection within the political elite, and once in office they exercise power with few institutional constraints. Most modern autocracies also exercise a high degree of directiveness over social and economic activity, but this is regarded here as a function of political ideology and choice, not a defining property of autocracy. Social democracies also exercise relatively high degrees of directiveness.

Source: Data are from the Center for Systemic Peace's Polity IV Project Political Regime Characteristics and Transitions, 1800–2008 (http://www.systemicpeace.org/inscr/inscr.htm).

Technical notes references

AbouZahr, Carla, and Tessa Wardlaw. 2003. "Maternal Mortality in 2000. Estimates Developed by WHO, UNICEF, and UNFPA." World Health Organization, Geneva.

Chen, Shaohua, and Martin Ravallion. 2008. "The Developing World Is Poorer Than We Thought, But No Less Successful in the Fight Against Poverty." Policy Research Working Paper 4703. World Bank, Washington, D.C.

Hoekman, Bernard. 2005. "Tentative First Steps: An Assessment of the Uruguay Round Agreement on Services." Paper presented at the World Bank Conference on the Uruguay Round and the Developing Economies, January 26–27, Washington, D.C.

ILO (International Labour Organization). Various years. *Key Indicators of the Labor Market.* Geneva: International Labour Organization.

WHO (World Health Organization). 2009. *World Malaria Report 2009.* Geneva: World Health Organization.

World Bank. 2005. *Global Economic Prospects 2005: Trade, Regionalism and Development.* Washington, D.C.: World Bank.

Map of Africa

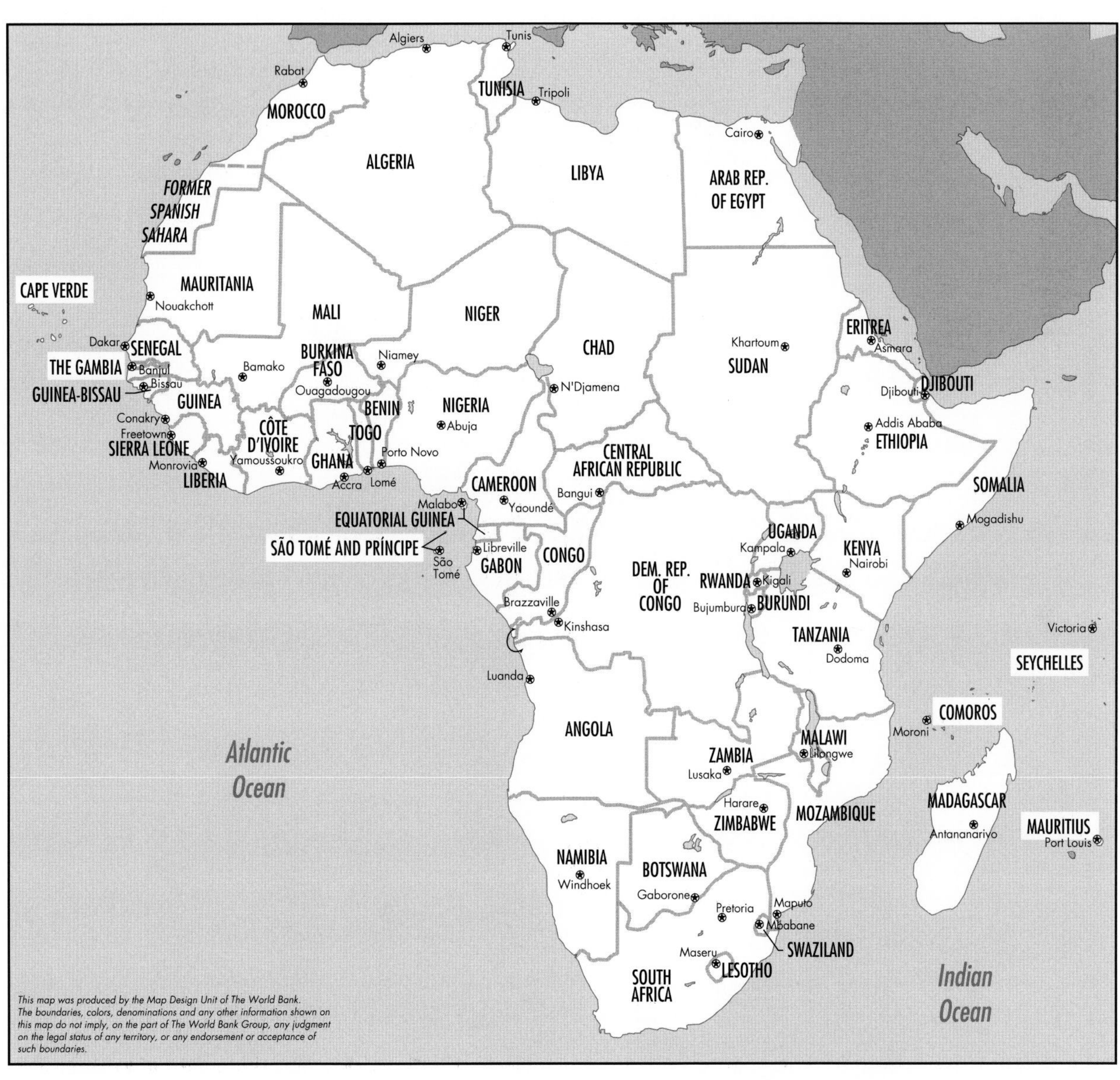

Users Guide

Africa Development Indicators 2010 CD-ROM

Introduction

This CD-ROM is part of the Africa Development Indicators suite of products. It was produced jointly by the Office of the Chief Economist and the Operational Quality and Knowledge Services Departments of the Africa Region in collaboration with the Development Data Group of the Development Economics Vice Presidency. It uses the latest version of the World Bank's DataPlatform version 3.0.

The CD-ROM contains about 1,600 macroeconomic, sectoral, and social indicators, covering 53 African countries. Time series include data from 1961 to 2008. A few macro indicators have provisional data for 2008, and other indicators have data for 2008–10.

The new DataPlatform version 3.0 has sophisticated features: enhanced mapping and charting, a choice of data selection techniques and versatile display options. We invite you to explore it.

A note about the data

Users should note that the data for the Africa Development Indicators suite of products are drawn from the same database. The general cutoff date for data is September 30, 2009, except for data on official development assistance, for which the cutoff date is December 8, 2009.

Help

This guide explains how to use the main functions of the CD-ROM. For details about additional features, click Help on the menu bar or the Help icon; or call one of the hotline numbers listed in the *Help* menu and on the copyright page of this booklet.

Installation

As is usual for Windows® products, you should make sure that other applications are closed while you install the CD-ROM.

To install the single-user version:

1. Insert the CD-ROM into your CD drive. The installation window should open automatically.
2. If the installation window does not open, click on *Start*, select *Run*. Type D:\run.bat and follow the instructions.
3. DataPlatform requires Microsoft® Internet Explorer 6.0 or higher. If you do not have Internet Explorer, it may be downloaded at no charge from www.microsoft.com. It does not need to be your default browser.

You can delete this program at any time by clicking on the *Remove ADI 2010* icon in the *WB Development Data* program folder.

Issues during installation

This section covers some of the issues that may occur during installation. It also provides all the troubleshooting steps you need to resolve the issue.

My Internet Explorer flickers when I try to launch the application on my desktop

You may experience this problem if you are using Microsoft Vista. This occurs because Internet Explorer 7 and higher versions block the application when there is an IP address in the URL for security reasons. *ADI 2010* is a secured application. Please follow these directions to resolve this issue:

1. Go to *Tools > Internet Options > Security Tab*
2. Select *Local Intranet*
3. Check the *Enabled Protected Mode* checkbox.

I am getting an Internet Explorer security warning message. Is this a security risk?

This is not a security risk. *ADI 2010* is a secure application. You can continue working if this message appears. To permanently disable this message, please follow these directions:

1. Go to *Tools > Internet Options > Security Tab*
2. Select *Local Intranet*
3. Check the *Enabled Protected Mode* checkbox.

I am getting the following message: "MSXML 5.0 from Microsoft Corporation. If you trust this website and the add-on and want to allow it to run, click here."

This message occurs the first time a web page attempts to execute a higher version of a plug-in in Internet Explorer. This is to alert the user the plug-in has been updated with a newer version and prompts this message for user approval. Please right click on the message and run the plug-in. To permanently disable this message, please follow these directions:

1. Go to *Tools > Internet Options > Security Tab*
2. Select *Local Intranet*
3. Check the *Enabled Protected Mode* checkbox.

This change requires Internet Explorer to restart. Please close the existing browser window and re-launch the application by clicking on the *ADI 2010* shortcut desktop icon.

NOTE: When *ADI 2010* launches after installation, the MS-DOS window remains on top of the browser. You should NOT close the window, but you can minimize the MS-DOS window.

Operation

To start the CD-ROM, click on the *ADI 2010* CD-ROM icon on your desktop. An ActiveX security pop-up warning may appear when clicking on a link. ActiveX is a framework for defining reusable controls that perform particular functions in Microsoft Windows. If you receive this security alert, please click "Yes" as the links are not a virus or security risk to your computer.

For detailed instructions, refer to the on-screen *Help* menu or tool tips (on-screen explanations of buttons that are displayed when the cursor rolls over them).

Features and instructions

ADI 2010 has two main screens—a text window featuring the contents of the *Africa Development Indicators 2010* book and other related tables, and a separate window featuring the ADI 2010 time series database.

Home

On the opening text screen you can access each element of the *ADI 2010* CD-ROM. Use the browser controls to link to the *Africa Development Indicators 2010* book, time series database, and other related information.

Database

Select variables

1. Click on each of the *Country, Series,* and *Year* tabs and make your selections on each screen. There are many ways to make a selection—see below, or use the *Help* menu. A *Search* option is also available.
2. Highlight the items you want.
3. Click on the *Select* button to move them into the *Selected* box.
4. Deselect items at any time by highlighting them and clicking on the *Remove* icon.
5. When selection is complete, click on *Next* to move to the next screen.

Making selections

- *Country:* You can select countries and group aggregates from an alphabetical list, group hierarchies, or by *Classification* (region, income group, or lending category). Aggregate data have been calculated only when there were adequate country data.
- *Series:* You can choose from an alphabetical list or by topic, or create your own custom indicators derived from indicators within the *ADI database*.
- *Year:* Select time periods from the list box. On all screens you can click *Notes* to view definition and source information for a highlighted item.

View results

On the *Report* tab, data are presented in a two-dimensional grid. Data for the third dimension are presented on separate screens. You can change the selection displayed by clicking on the third dimension list box. You can also change the scale (to millions, for example) and the number of digits after the decimal. Click on a column header to sort the results. Select *Show Notes* to view source notes and footnotes. To scale series individually click the *Series Level Settings* icon.

Please do not use the browser *Back* and/or *Forward* buttons on the *View Report* window. This will cause you to lose the report. You will not be able to retrieve data and will have to select the variables again.

Changing the orientation. You can view the result in six different orientations (countries down/periods across, series down/countries across, and so on). To change the orientation, click on *Customize* and drag and drop the dimensions to your desired orientation. *Customize* also has various formatting options for the report.

Saving. You can save the report or you can save the data in another format. You can also save your query selections for later use.

- Saving the report in Excel. Select the *Export Report as Excel File* icon on the toolbar. This will save the report in the same format.
- Saving the report in PDF. Select the *Export Report as PDF File* icon on the toolbar. This will save the report in the same format. Adobe Reader is required to view files downloaded in PDF format. If you do not have Adobe Reader, it can be downloaded from *www.Adobe.com.*
- Saving the data or notes in another format. Select the *Export Data and Notes as CSV File* icon on the toolbar. Saving data as a CSV file will allow you to export all countries, series, and years on to one file. The file will not retain the report format.
- Saving a query. Select the *Save Selections as Query* icon on the toolbar. Your query will be saved as "XXXYYY.dp." There is no need to open the file. If you wish to manually edit the query file, select *Notepad.*

Click on *Help* for more details.

Chart

On the *Chart* tab, data are displayed based on the report orientation setting. Click on *Customize* to change the chart type, add a title and to access various formatting options. You can set different chart types for each variable.

Adobe Flash Player 8 or higher is required to view the new features of the charts. It is a free and lightweight installation from www. Adobe.com. If you do not have the application already installed on your desktop, a message will appear asking you to download Adobe Flash Player. Please click "OK" when the message appears. It will take you directly to the Adobe website.

Printing and saving. Right-click on the chart image to print the chart. Click on the appropriate icon to save the chart or save the underlying data.

Map

On the *Map* tab, selected countries are colored according to their data values for the selected indicator and year. The country name and data value will appear as the cursor rolls over the map. The legend scale is based on the report scale and precision settings. To activate the zoom option for a closer look at the map, click directly on the desired location. Click the Reset link to zoom out.

Adobe Flash Player 8 or higher is required to view the new features of the maps. It is a free and lightweight installation from www. Adobe.com. If you do not have the application already installed on your desktop, a message will appear asking you to download Adobe Flash Player. Please click "OK" when the message appears. It will take you directly to the Adobe website.

Changing the map intervals and colors. The default interval range is an equal number of countries. Use the list boxes to set an equal interval range or to change the map color palette. You can also choose to map all countries or only your selected ones.

Printing and saving. Right-click on the map image to print the map. Click on the appropriate icon to save the map or save the underlying data.

License agreement

You must read and agree to the terms of this License Agreement prior to using this CDROM product. Use of the software and data contained on the CD-ROM is governed by the terms of this License Agreement. If you do not agree with these terms, you may return the product unused to the World Bank for a full refund of the purchase price.

1. **LICENSE.** In consideration of your payment of the required license fee, the WORLD BANK (the "Bank") hereby grants you a nonexclusive license to use the enclosed data and DataPlatform retrieval program (collectively the "program") subject to the terms and conditions set forth in this license agreement.

2. **OWNERSHIP.** As a licensee you own the physical media on which the program is originally or subsequently recorded. The Bank, however, retains title and ownership of the program recorded on the original CD-ROM and all subsequent copies of the program. This license is not a sale of the program or any copy thereof.

3. **COPY RESTRICTIONS.** The program and accompanying written materials are copyrighted. You may make one copy of the program solely for backup purposes. Unauthorized copying of the program or of the written materials is expressly forbidden and punishable by law.

4. **USE.** You may not modify, adapt, translate, reverse-engineer, decompile, or disassemble the program. You may not modify, adapt, translate, or create derivative works based on any written materials without the prior written consent of the Bank. If you have purchased the single-user version of this product, you may use the Program only on a single laptop/desktop computer used by one person and you may not distribute copies of the Program or accompanying written materials to others.

   If you have purchased the multiple-user version of this product, the license is valid for up to 15 authorized users. Should you need to make the program available for additional users through a network, including an intranet, please send a request, indicating the number of users you would like to add, to: World Bank Publications, Marketing and Rights, 1818 H Street NW, Washington DC 20433, fax 202 522 2422, e-mail pubrights@worldbank.org. The Bank will invoice you for an additional fee, depending on the number of users added to the license.

   This license does not entitle you to use the program on the internet. For libraries or institutions, we recommend an institutional subscription to the online version of the program. To subscribe, please contact World Bank Publications, Marketing and Rights, 1818 H Street NW, Washington DC 20433, fax 202 522 2422, e-mail pubrights@worldbank.org.

5. **TRANSFER RESTRICTIONS.** This program is licensed only to you, the licensee, and may not be transferred to anyone without prior written consent of the Bank.

6. **LIMITED WARRANTY AND LIMITATIONS OF REMEDIES.** The Bank warrants the CD-ROM on which the program is furnished to be free from defects in materials and workmanship under normal use for a period of ninety (90) days from the delivery to you as evidenced by a copy of your receipt. The Bank's entire liability and your exclusive remedy shall be the replacement of any CD-ROMs not meeting the Bank's limited warranty. Defective CD-ROMs should be returned within the warranty period, with a copy of your receipt, to the address specified in section 9 below.

   EXCEPT AS PROVIDED ABOVE, THE PRODUCT IS PROVIDED "AS IS" WITHOUT WARRANTY OF ANY KIND, EITHER EXPRESSED OR IMPLIED, INCLUDING, BUT NOT LIMITED TO, THE IMPLIED WARRANTIES OF MERCHANTABILITY AND FITNESS FOR A PARTICULAR PURPOSE. THE BANK DOES NOT WARRANT THAT THE FUNCTIONS CONTAINED IN THE PROGRAM WILL MEET YOUR REQUIREMENTS OR THAT THE OPERATION OF THE PROGRAM WILL BE UNINTERRUPTED OR ERROR-FREE.

   IN NO EVENT WILL THE BANK BE LIABLE TO YOU FOR ANY DAMAGES ARISING OUT OF THE USE OR INABILITY TO USE THE PROGRAM.

   THE ABOVE WARRANTY GIVES YOU SPECIFIC LEGAL RIGHTS IN THE UNITED STATES, WHICH MAY VARY FROM STATE TO STATE. SOME STATES DO NOT ALLOW THE EXCLUSION OF IMPLIED WARRANTIES OR LIMITATION OF EXCLUSION OF LIABILITY FOR INCIDENTAL OR CONSEQUENTIAL DAMAGES, SO PARTS OF THE ABOVE LIMITATIONS AND EXCLUSIONS MAY NOT APPLY TO YOU.

7. **TERMINATION.** This license is effective from the date you open the sealed package until terminated. You may terminate it by destroying the CD-ROM containing the program and its documentation and any backup copy thereof or by returning this material to the Bank. If any of the terms and conditions of this license are broken, the Bank reserves the right to terminate the license and demand that you return or destroy all copies of the program in your possession without refund to you.

8. **GOVERNING LAW.** This license shall be governed by the laws of the District of Columbia, in the United States of America, without reference to conflicts of law thereof.

9. **GENERAL.** If you have any questions concerning this product, you may contact the Bank by writing to CD-ROM Inquiries, The World Bank, 1818 H Street NW, Washington DC 20433, fax 202 522 1785, e-mail data@worldbank.org. All queries on rights and licenses should be addressed to World Bank Publications, Marketing and Rights, 1818 H Street NW, Washington DC 20433, fax 202 522 2422, e-mail pubrights@worldbank.org.